# Data Structures in Java™

# Data Structures in Java™

Thomas A. Standish

University of California, Irvine

## ADDISON-WESLEY

An imprint of Addison Wesley Longman, Inc.

Reading, Massachusetts • Harlow, England • Menlo Park, California
Berkeley, California • Don Mills, Ontario • Sydney • Bonn • Amsterdam
Tokyo • Mexico City

Java is a trademark of Sun Microsystems, Inc.

Many of the designations used by manufacturers and sellers to distinguish their products are claimed as trademarks. Where those designations appear in this book, and Addison-Wesley was aware of a trademark claim, the designations have been printed in caps or initial caps.

The programs and applications presented in this book have been included for their instructional value. They have been tested with care, but are not guaranteed for any particular purpose. The publisher does not offer any warranties or representations, nor does it accept any liabilities with respect to the programs or applications.

**Library of Congress Cataloging-in-Publication Data**

Standish, Thomas A., 1941–
    Data structures in Java/ Thomas A. Standish.
        p.   cm.
    Includes index.
    ISBN 0-201-30564-X
    1. Java (Computer program language)  2. Data structures (Computer science)
I. Title.
QA76.73.J38S78  1998
005.7'3—dc21                                                                          97-22058
                                                                                        CIP

*Reprinted with corrections, November 1997.*

5 6 7 8 9 10-DOC-010099

*T*o Elke

# Preface

This book covers material recommended for a second course in computer science—Computer Science 2 (or CS2, for short). Not only does it cover the CS2 material recommended by ACM's *Curriculum '78* (as revised in 1984[1]), it also covers the material recommended in the new *Computing Curricula 1991*, as set forth in the *Report of the Joint Curriculum Task Force*[2,3,4] of the ACM and the IEEE Computer Society. The Curricula 1991 material is presented in a format called *Knowledge Units* (KUs) in the Curricula 1991 Report. Accordingly, this book supports the KUs recommended for a second course in computing covering data structures.

---

[1] E. B. Koffman, D. Stemple, and C. E. Wardle, "Recommended Curriculum for CS2, 1984," *Communications of the ACM* 28:8 (August 1985), pp. 815–818.

[2] A. B. Tucker, B. H. Barnes, et al, *Computing Curricula 1991: Report of the ACM/IEEE-CS Joint Curriculum Task Force*. Association for Computing Machinery, New York, ACM Order Number 201910 (Dec. 17, 1990).

[3] A. Joe Turner, "Introduction to the Joint Task Force Report," *Communications of the ACM* 34:6 (June 1991), pp. 68–70.

[4] A. B. Tucker, "Computing Curricula 1991," *Communications of the ACM* 34:6 (June 1991), pp. 70–84.

In addition, Curricula '91 specifies a number of *recurring concepts* that it advocates covering. Recurring concepts are central ideas—such as *recursion, modularity, levels of abstraction, efficiency,* and *tradeoffs*—that occur throughout computer science. Such recurring concepts are used as *integrators* in this book in order to tie the material together conceptually and to help reveal its underlying unity and interrelationships.

The book is therefore appropriate to use either to support a traditional revised Curriculum '78 CS2 course or to use during the transition period from Curriculum '78 to the new Curricula '91, as we evolve our computer science courses to meet the challenges of the next millenium.

## Prerequisites for the Java™ Programming Language

We assume that students using this book for a CS2 course will have already taken a first course covering introductory programming using Java. Such students should be familiar with Java's statements (such as assignments, for-statements, if-statements, while loops, do-while loops, and switch statements) and with Java's block structure and control flow. Output using **System.out.print** and **System.out.println** should have been covered.

In addition, students should have been introduced to Java's primitive data types—ints, floats, doubles, chars, and booleans—as well as to Java's reference types—arrays and class instances. Basic familiarity with **Strings** and **StringBuffers** is also assumed.

Finally, the declaration and use of simple classes and methods should have been covered at an introductory level.

If these Java prerequisites are not met, it is still possible to use this book by first learning the simple core features of Java on which this book is based, in *Appendix A— A Review of Some Basic Java Features,* and by reading *Chapter 2—An Introduction to Object-Oriented Programming,* to gain an appreciation for the larger scale implications of programming in an object-oriented language. Students with a background in C or C++ should have little difficulty adjusting to the simple features of Java we employ to develop data structure concepts in this book.

## The Approach to Mathematical Foundations and Software Engineering

In this book, the coverage of mathematical foundations and software engineering has been reduced somewhat and has been placed partly in Appendices B and C. [By contrast, the earlier related books by the author, *Data Structures, Algorithms and Software Principles* (using Pascal), and *Data Structures, Algorithms and Software Principles in C* (both from Addison-Wesley), include treatments of mathematical foundations and software engineering topics as integrated chapters.] Because the scope of these earlier books (with these topics integrated in the main chapter sequence) proved too broad to cover in a single semester or quarter course, a shorter data structures book with a more focused scope was called for. Accordingly, the present book concentrates on core data structure concepts, with less emphasis placed on integrated discussion of mathematical foundations and software engineering.

With regard to software engineering topics, this book includes coverage of the advantages of object-oriented programming in Chapter 2, an introduction to modularity and data abstraction concepts in Chapter 5, and coverage of key software engineering concepts and skills related to programming-in-the-small in Appendix C. The coverage of mathematical foundations is based on the use of O-notation as the language for characterizing the efficiency of algorithms. Although this language of efficiency is introduced, in an intuitive, informal way in *Appendix B—The Language of Efficiency*, and is used throughout, the present book does not include the derivations and proofs of the author's two earlier books.

## Supplements

- *Instructor's Manual*

   An *Instructor's Manual* is available on-line in Adobe PDF (Portable Document Format). To receive it, please contact your local Addison-Wesley representative.

- *Lab Manual*

   A *Lab Manual* containing laboratory exercises to accompany the book is also available on-line in Adobe PDF (Portable Document Format). To receive it, please contact your local Addison-Wesley representative.

- *World Wide Web Access to Source Code*

   The sample Java 1.1 programs presented in this book are available on-line for your personal, noncommercial use. To download copies of these programs, please visit the World Wide Web site:

   http: / / www.awl.com/cseng/titles/0-201-30564-X

Please follow the instructions on the web page for file transfer to your computer. This web site also contains all of the programs in the book in Java 1.0 for the convenience of those who have not upgraded to Java 1.1 yet.

## Acknowledgments

The author is grateful to computer science editors at Addison-Wesley who persuaded him to write this book and who helped shape the book into its present form. Susan Hartman initiated the project, showed great editorial talent, and encouraged the author in numerous important ways. Lynne Doran Cote, editor-in-chief of computer science, supported the project enthusiastically. Julie Dunn, assistant to Susan Hartman, provided wonderful support and kept the project on schedule.

   The author is also grateful to many fine people at Addison-Wesley who participated with great excellence and professionalism in the design and production of this book. Patricia Unubun did a superb job as production editor. Molly Taylor helped significantly as a production assistant. Tom Ziolkowski contributed immensely with the marketing strategy. Lisa Ziccardi helped with the marketing materials. Jennifer Newburg did a fine job setting up the network server providing on-line access to the programs and instructional materials. Diana Coe designed the cover. In addition, Alwyn Velasquez did an outstanding job of book design. Jackie Davies did a fabulous job as compositor and helped the author to learn the intricacies of the production system we used. Adrienne Rebello was superb at copyediting and proofreading.

The author also wishes to express his thanks to faculty colleagues and students at UC Irvine who provided suggestions for improvement. In particular, Sandra Irani gave helpful feedback from the faculty's perspective. The following students and teaching assistants were of considerable help in finding errors and suggesting improvements: Shao Liu, Jolly Lin, David Otaguro, Matthew Smith, John King, and Craig Proctor. The author is particularly grateful to Dan Halem who helped translate the programs used in this book from Java 1.0 to Java 1.1 and then test-ran them in the JDK 1.1.1 environment to ensure they worked properly.

Finally, the author and Addison-Wesley are indebted to the following reviewers who contributed their experience and knowledge to improving this text throughout its development: N. Dwight Barnette, Virginia Tech; Daniel Berleant, University of Arkansas, Fayetteville; William Cohen, University of Alabama in Huntsville; Walter C. Daugherity, Texas A & M University; Stuart Reges, University of Arizona; Jan Stelovsky, University of Hawaii at Manoa; and Elaine Wenderholm, Syracuse University and Onondaga Community College.

The author is most of all indebted to his wife, Elke, for providing the devotion and encouragement without which this book could not have been written.

T.A.S.
Laguna Beach, California

# Contents

# Data Structures in Java™

# Preparing
# for the Journey

## 1.1 Where Are We Going?

Before beginning a journey, it's always a good idea to ask, "Where are we going?" and "Why are we going there?"

Computer science itself has been on a fast-paced journey of formulation and discovery since it got rolling in the early 1940s. It has introduced astonishing innovations, never before seen in human history, which have transformed our thought and our civilization in ways undreamed of a half-century ago. Learning about computer science is a journey filled with excitement and adventure.

This book covers material for a second course in computer science. Such a course is only the second leg of a longer journey—that of learning about computer science as a whole. The book makes the assumption that you have already covered the first leg of the journey by taking a first course in computer science.

This book focuses principally on *data structure concepts*—one of the areas of essential groundwork for making the rest of the journey of learning computer science. It also emphasizes fundamental questions of computer science, and explains significant accomplishments that all well-educated computer scientists should know about.

mathematics, science,
and engineering

An important goal is to help you develop competence in the field. By weaving together skills from mathematics, science, and engineering, you will be helped to develop competence in computer science that harmoniously integrates theory, experimentation, and design. Some of these skills are analytic and some are creative.

To help tie the material in the book together, attention is paid throughout to important *recurring concepts*. Some of these concepts relate to how computing systems or large software systems are structured, and they involve organizational principles, such as *layers*, *hierarchies*, *information-hiding*, *abstraction*, and *interfaces*. Others relate to important properties of algorithms and data structures, such as *efficiency*, *tradeoffs*, and *resource consumption* characteristics. Yet others relate to software engineering, and they involve aspects of the organization of human effort required to build large software systems so that they exhibit certain key properties such as *reliability*, *affordability*, *efficiency*, *correctness*, and *safety*.

## Plan for the Chapter

As a starting point, it's important to grasp why computer science, unlike other sciences, blends mathematics, science, and engineering. Section 1.2 discusses why you should develop competence in each of these three aspects of computer science.

Section 1.3 focuses on the process of searching for enduring principles in computer science. Even though hardware technology has been changing rapidly, other features of hardware and software systems have been much more stable over time. Section 1.4 discusses some of the enduring principles that have been discovered about the structure of software systems. Such systems involve the recurring concepts of *representation*, *abstraction*, *information-hiding*, and *interfaces*.

searching for
enduring principles

Section 1.5 discusses the recurring concepts of *efficiency* and *tradeoffs*. It is vital for computer science to discover the best ways of performing commonly occurring algorithmic tasks, used often as building blocks in the creation of larger systems. Insights into efficiency and tradeoffs can be gained sometimes by performing mathematical analyses of algorithms and sometimes by conducting experiments that measure the performance of algorithms and systems.

Software engineering principles, discussed in Section 1.6, are related to organizing and managing the human effort and resources needed to build software systems.

Section 1.7 comments on the approach to mathematics used in this book and Section 1.8 covers a few brief points about the style for indentation and line numbering of the Java programs used in the book.

Finally, Section 1.9 provides a brief description of what is covered in the remaining chapters.

## 1.2    Blending Mathematics, Science, and Engineering

Computer science is a bit different from other contemporary sciences, because it blends mathematics, science, and engineering activities more intimately than other sciences do. It's worth spending a few minutes discussing this topic in order to understand why computer science has this distinction.

how science, engineering, and mathematics differ

First, let's get clear in our minds how mathematics, science, and engineering are different. Science tries to discover fundamental laws and principles of nature. Engineering is the design and construction of artifacts to suit human purposes. It applies the sciences to build artifacts and systems. Mathematics attempts to discover significant facts and relationships that can be expressed precisely using symbolic or quantitative language.

For example, let's look at superconductivity, a phenomenon in which an electric current flows through an electrical conductor without resistance. A physicist might try to understand how and why superconductivity occurs while an engineer might try to build a magnetic levitating train or an efficient electrical power transmission system based on superconductivity. A mathematician might develop useful mathematical models that might help the physicists express their theories of superconductivity, or that might help engineers solve problems relating to how strong superconducting magnets need to be to support levitating trains.

Mathematics deals in the realm of pure thought, rather than in the realm of material artifacts. And yet, mathematics has a great deal to say about what is true and what is possible in this world of pure ideas. Furthermore, experience has shown that mathematics is vitally important for expressing the precise understanding that the sciences have achieved. Mathematics has been a key source of models and descriptions used by scientists in their fundamental quest to develop descriptive and predictive theories of nature.

In the contemporary academic world, physics, engineering, and mathematics are separate disciplines that are pursued in separate departments by separate groups of investigators. In computer science, however, there appears to be a blending of the mathematical, scientific, and engineering aspects of the investigation of computing into a single enterprise, typically housed in a single academic department. It is not entirely clear why computer science differs from the classical sciences, and from mathematics and engineering, in this regard—nor is it clear whether this difference will endure in the future.

Nevertheless, it is informative and interesting to try to make an educated guess as to why computer science has integrated mathematics, science, and engineering (see Fig. 1.1), while the other traditional fields have kept them separate. One such speculation goes like this: Computer science is a science that concerns artificial things—things made by human beings—instead of things that occur in nature that were not made by human beings. That is, rather than being a *natural science*, computer science is a *science of the artificial*.

Although an astronomer can study the phenomena of the stars and heavenly bodies, and can develop astronomical theories that are both descriptive and predictive (as in predicting when Halley's Comet will next appear), an astronomer cannot change the nature of the things astronomy studies. Likewise, the physicist Isaac Newton, studying the nature of light, developed astonishing theories describing its properties and behavior; but Newton did not have the option of changing the nature of light to make his theories easier to discover or formulate.

By contrast, a computer scientist studies phenomena—such as the behavior of operating systems or algorithms—that are exhibited by artifacts created by the human

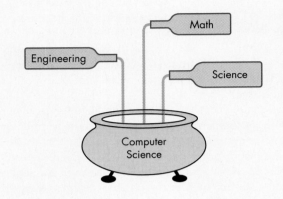

**Figure 1.1** Blending Mathematics, Science, and Engineering

imagination. Moreover, the objects of study can be changed by further creative acts of the human imagination. Thus computer science is a science in which it is possible to change the things you are studying and trying to understand.

Consequently, computer scientists can alter the objects they study to make them reveal better theories or yield better understanding. Because this opportunity is *open* in computer science, rather than being *shut* as it is in the traditional sciences, it is not surprising that computer scientists take advantage of it by interweaving activities of design and analysis: An episode of design produces something worthy of study because it exhibits interesting behavior. An episode of analysis follows, which reveals that if the design were changed, the behavior might be even more interesting and valuable to study. This is followed by more design activities, which in turn are followed by more analysis activities. The process ends when some important discoveries are made, providing key insights into how things work, or what is possible or impossible. Moreover, the process tends to lead to discoveries that reveal how to build things having useful applications—knowledge that answers the questions "How to?" as well as "What is?"

Suppose we accept as a matter of historical observation that design and analysis have tended to be interleaved during the past evolution of computer science. Let's now focus more concretely on the nature of these design and analysis activities. First, let's look at design. Design activities in computer science are sometimes very close in style to traditional engineering activities. You build a computer system or write a program to satisfy some requirements. (These requirements may have resulted from a requirements analysis process that is a traditional engineering practice.)

Sometimes, however, the design activities are very close in style to the process of formulation, definition, and conjecture that mathematicians perform when they are developing new mathematical theories. Formulating a new mathematical theory (consisting of definitions, theorems, and proofs) involves inventive acts of the human imagination. Unlike engineering activities that design new material artifacts and systems, the creative design of the mathematician is directed at discovering (or inventing) new systems of mathematical ideas that are found to exhibit interesting and profound properties.

*(margin note)* weaving design and analysis together

*(margin note)* development of theory

For example, one of the important problems faced in the early days of computer science was how to get a computer to translate and execute programs written in high-level programming languages. There was a critical need to develop some theories of parsing, translation, and compiling. To develop the theory of parsing (in which *parsing a program* is the process of grammatically analyzing how it is composed of its parts), computer scientists behaved like mathematicians. From linguistics, they borrowed definitions of grammars, called *context-free grammars*, useful for precisely describing the structure of programming languages. They formulated algorithms for parsing programs written in such programming languages, and they conjectured and then proved some powerful theorems characterizing exactly when such parsing algorithms would work and how efficiently they could be made to operate. The result was a body of discoveries that yielded deep understanding of what was possible in the realm of parsing, and which had important practical applications to the development of compilers.

Sometimes the analysis activities conducted by computer scientists resemble those in traditional experimental science. Experiments are conducted, observations are made, data are collected, and theories and laws are devised to account for the data. A successful theory is one that is both descriptive and predictive. Its laws describe the data and these laws can be used to predict the future behavior of computational systems. Scientific understanding has been achieved by this traditional scientific method when (1) the experiments can be repeated by independent observers under precisely understood experimental conditions, and (2) the results of these experiments agree with the predictions generated by the theory.

But the analysis activities undertaken by computer scientists sometimes also resemble those undertaken by pure mathematicians. An algorithm is an object expressed in a precise symbolic language with precise rules of operation. As such, it is a mathematical object. Mathematical reasoning can be applied to discover its properties and implications.

Sometimes the consequences of such mathematical reasoning can be very startling. For example, using a mathematical style of investigation, it has been discovered that (1) it is impossible to write a computer program $P_1$ that will look at another computer program $P_2$ and tell whether $P_2$ will halt or get into an endless loop when it is executed; (2) it is impossible to write a computer program that will take a look at a context-free grammar, G, and tell whether the language it describes is ambiguous or not (where an ambiguous sentence is one having two or more different grammatical structures, as in the sentences, "They are flying planes." or "He saw the man in the park with the telescope."); and (3) it is impossible to write a program that will simplify algebraic expressions in a general way (as in simplifying $x^2 - 2xy + y^2$ to become $(x - y)^2$). Historically, investigations conducted in the style of mathematical analysis have contributed important and deep results about what is possible and impossible in computer science.

One conclusion that we can draw from this discussion is that instead of investigating a part of nature that is already there and can't be changed, computer science is investigating a subject that is undergoing vigorous and rapid evolution. Fascinating new computing artifacts appear on the scene at a fantastic rate and tantalize the computer scientist to study and understand them. Consequently, computer science is a

experiments and the
scientific method

formulation and discovery

journey of *formulation* and *discovery*—formulation of interesting new artifacts and new systems of mathematical ideas and discovery of important fundamental principles of computation.

The creative acts of building computer systems or designing algorithms are essentially engineering activities (i.e., building things to suit purposes). Experimentation to collect data and study the behavior exhibited by the things created in this way is essentially a scientific activity. Moreover, the discovery and development of formal theories that express essential ideas underlying a class of computations are essentially mathematical activities. Historically, these three strands of activity—mathematics, science, and engineering—have been carried out by computer scientists in an interwoven fashion. And aspects of each activity have been essential to making progress in computer science.

The main implication of these observations for you as a student is that you should adopt the long-range goal of gaining competence in each of the three kinds of computer science activities—mathematics, science, and engineering—by (1) becoming skilled at conducting mathematical analyses and performing mathematical reasoning; (2) gaining understanding of the experimental scientific method and learning to conduct experiments, collect data, and discover meanings; and (3) learning how things work and developing creative capacities to design algorithms, choose appropriate data structures, and build software or computational systems to solve problems.

*implications for you*

This book is written with an eye toward supporting initial steps toward learning these three kinds of skills. First, there are many opportunities to design algorithms and data structures to solve both small and large programming problems, leading to opportunities to develop skills in software engineering. Second, by learning the meaning of the language of efficiency (O-notation) and by using it to become familiar with the comparative efficiencies of algorithms, you will have taken a significant first step toward gaining the benefits of mathematical analysis of algorithms and you will be motivated to learn how to perform basic mathematical analyses of algorithms in your later computer science courses. Third, experiments are described in the text in which data are collected and analyzed, illustrating the application of the scientific method. Some of the exercises invite you to conduct your own experiments.

## 1.3  The Search for Enduring Principles in Computer Science

Computer science is intimately involved with the search for enduring fundamental principles that help us understand the nature of computation and help us create useful new computing applications. In our computer science courses we certainly hope to present topics that have lasting value, rather than short-lived topics that will turn out to be useless a short while later. But it is often difficult to have the foresight to know ahead of time which discoveries will have lasting value and which will have only temporary value. On the other hand, by looking backward and observing which things lasted and which things were short-lived, we can determine important clues that can help us to choose topics that are likely to have enduring value.

*searching for ideas that have lasting value*

An example of something that didn't last and has been in flux is the nature of computer hardware, which has changed four times since the 1940s. Computers were first built from electromechanical parts, such as relay circuits and mercury delay line memories. They were then built from vacuum tube circuits and magnetic drum memories. Following this, processors were built from transistors and the memories began to use magnetic cores. (You will still occasionally hear old-timers refer to primary memory as "core" even though memory isn't built from magnetic cores any more—which proves that some language habits can be more long-lasting than computer hardware.) Most recently, both processors and memories have been built from chips. VLSI chips (Very Large Scale Integrated circuit chips) contain hundreds of thousands of transistors in a space smaller than your thumbnail, and operate with astonishing speed and reliability.

At the moment, we don't know what the future holds with regard to hardware. Perhaps the next few decades will see the introduction of hardware based on optical devices—computing based on light valves or holograms. Or perhaps biologically engineered macromolecules will be used to store massive amounts of data in tiny spaces. Though it is likely that new kinds of hardware will be faster, cheaper, and more reliable than today's hardware (otherwise why bother changing things), we really can't foresee which new ideas will be successful.

Nevertheless, it doesn't matter. Although computer hardware has changed four times in the past half-century and is likely to continue changing in the future, the essential nature of basic computer instructions and the basic building blocks of data (such as bits, bytes, and words) didn't change very much at all and probably won't change very much in the future. The basic machine-level instructions still perform arithmetic and logical operations on sequences of bits, they still perform branches in the execution of instruction sequences depending on the outcome of comparisons, and they still transfer information between processors and memory. Moreover, the underlying laws of arithmetic and logic didn't change at all—two plus two still equals four. And it is likely that none of them will change if we replace the current generation of computers with future optical or biological computers.

*basic machine organization principles survived hardware changes*

Since the fundamental arithmetic, logical, and data movement operations of computers stayed nearly the same, things built on top of them could survive the change from one generation of hardware to the next. In fact, many programming languages, such as COBOL, FORTRAN, LISP, C, and Pascal, survived hardware generation changes, as did many kinds of computer software written in these languages. The compilers for these programming languages turned out to be portable from one generation of hardware to the next, since not much needed to be changed in the way they were written. Their basic organizational principles—consisting of algorithms and data structures—stayed the same, even though the underlying machine instruction sets from which they were programmed changed slightly. They still used context-free grammars and parsers based on them to detect program structure. They still used tables in which to store and retrieve values. And the structure of these entities did not have to change at all, even though the hardware device technology was rapidly changing underneath in a fundamental way.

Let's focus now on the meaning of the word *abstraction*. When you form an abstraction from a set of instances, you ignore inessential differences, and identify common features that are important. For example, when building a radar air traffic control system, the only features of an airplane that are useful to display on a radar screen are the airplane's *position*, *velocity*, *altitude*, *aircraft type*, and *identification*. All other features, such as the aircraft's food service caterer and color, are inessential (and would hopelessly clutter the radar scope, if we foolishly attempted to display them). In this case, we could say that we had *abstracted* from the set of instances of airplanes under air traffic control just five essential features to display on controllers' radar scopes.

*the concept of abstraction*

Returning now to our discussion of what did and did not survive the changes in hardware generations, we can observe (with the benefit of hindsight) that the right kind of *abstractions* survived changes in the underpinnings. Because these abstractions turned out to have lasting value and utility, we are entitled to believe that they are fundamental, and that the principles by which they are organized and which describe how they operate are fundamental principles. And that's what computer science is partly about—finding enduring fundamental principles that govern the nature of computation and that can be applied to build new software and systems.

## 1.4  Principles of Software System Structure

Let's push this line of exploration a bit further. What other fundamental principles can we discover by studying with hindsight the way software systems have come to be organized?

In such a discussion it is helpful to focus on a specific example—for instance, an airline reservation system, where customers can phone in to make reservations to fly to various destinations on various future dates. Figure 1.2 shows some of the data structures that might be used to implement such a system. At the top level, the system must be programmed to deal directly with the entities of direct concern to users— things like schedules, flights, dates, and reservations. These top-level entities are represented using intermediate-level data structures—things like files, tables, lists, records, and strings. For example, the overall schedule of available flights might be represented using a big table of some sort. Reservations for a flight on a future date might be stored as lists of records in a file associated with that flight. The records in this file might contain strings and numbers representing names, phone numbers, and some other coded data for each passenger who has made a future reservation. The intermediate level data structures are in turn ultimately represented using the primitive data structures available on the naked machine—things like bytes and linear sequences of machine words.

*representation—a main idea in computer science*

The process of writing programs to create computer applications involves the *representation* of objects, operations, and behaviors required in the application in terms of the primitives available in the computational medium. In this representational process, the surface behaviors displayed by solutions are synthesized from compositions of primitive behaviors available in the computational medium. From this

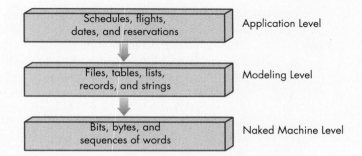

**Figure 1.2** Data Structures Used in an Airline Reservation System

point of view, we could see the computer as fundamentally being a *representation machine*.

We can construct a representation by organizing the data and processes of a given representational medium to exhibit the required properties and behaviors of some specified system of objects and operations being represented. Often two distinct conceptual levels are involved in the representational process, with each one using different levels of language and notation. One level describes the structures being modeled, and the other level describes the objects and operations in the underlying representational medium. In most large software systems more than two levels of representation are used, with intermediate layers serving both as representational media for higher layers and as specifications for underlying representations by lower layers.

Thus representations are often composed one or more times, using several layers of abstraction, spanning the gap from the machine domain to the application domain. In Fig. 1.2, the intermediate level of representation is called the "modeling level."

In building application systems, it is interesting to ask, Why do we use general-purpose, intermediate-level data structures, such as files, lists, trees, arrays, and strings? Why are they even needed? These entities do not actually exist in the naked machine. They are fictional entities that we create in our imaginations. They provide no essential capacity that cannot be implemented in terms of machine primitives by using assembly language directly.

The answers to these questions penetrate to the heart of the reason why the material in this book is of fundamental importance in computer science. The basic answers have to do with assisting the human mind in dealing with complexity and with software economics—the problem of how to build reliable, efficient systems as cheaply and rapidly as possible.

First, on purely economic grounds, it is more efficient to build systems out of intermediate-level components than it is to start from scratch. For example, to build a radio, you might want to start with intermediate-level components such as power supplies, voltage regulators, antennas, speakers, and potentiometers (i.e., dials). It would be costly for you to have to start with tin-foil and wax and wrap your own capacitors, or, worse, with iron ore that had to be smelted into iron to make magnets for the speakers. Likewise, to build software systems, it is often cheaper to use libraries of reusable software components than it is to start from scratch by using a programming

*why use intermediate-level data structures?*

*the software economics of reusable software components*

language to "roll your own." Much of the substance of several later chapters in this book covers the powerful basic ideas and concepts that are the foundation of such reusable software components. Equipped with a stock of such powerful ideas, you will find you have tremendously enhanced skill for crafting software representations and solutions. Java is an excellent programming language to use to describe software components and to assemble them into software systems.

Second, the human mind has limits to its capacity to deal with intellectual complexity. Psychologists have found evidence that human short-term memory can deal with only seven (plus-or-minus two) "chunks" of information at a given time. Constructing software representations often requires great mental precision, which cannot be attained if the things being thought about are too complex. Consequently, there is a premium on discovering ways to break the structure of a complex system into simpler parts. Ideally, such parts should consist of interacting subsystems that are simple, concise, and lucid, and that can be dealt with easily by the human mind.

*cognitive limits on dealing with complexity*

After much exploration and by virtue of much trial-and-error experience, it has been found that certain organizational principles greatly help the human mind to deal with the design and construction of software. (These organizational principles also help teams of programmers to build large software systems cooperatively.) Such principles include (1) using intermediate-level modeling structures to help break the overall representational mapping (of application-level entities into machine primitives) into simple steps that the human mind can deal with more easily one step at a time; and (2) packaging representational entities into *modules* and *layers* that hide the inner details of their operation from view and present clean, simple interfaces to their users, thus making them easier to handle. *Information-hiding* is the act of concealing the internal details from view, and *abstraction* is used to extract a few simple details to put into the interfaces for users to employ, while deciding which things to conceal from view to reduce complexity.

*modules, layers, information hiding, and abstraction*

Third, experience has shown that even though the intermediate-level data structures are figments of the human imagination, they have a high utility in solving programming problems. They present programmers with a stock of ideas to use for constructing representations in a remarkably broad range of application areas. In this sense, programming is analogous to mathematics. Mathematics abounds with imaginary objects that are creations of human thought—geometric figures, algebraic quantities, sets, differential equations, permutations, probabilities, and so forth. These mathematical entities are highly useful for constructing theories and models—especially because they are rich with important properties that have been extensively explored.

The situation is similar in computer science, although computer science is at a more primitive stage of development than mathematics. Computer science abounds with general purpose, intermediate-level data structures that are highly useful in constructing representations—things like lists, trees, arrays, strings, tables, stacks, queues, sets, and graphs. The notion of *abstract data types* (ADTs) refers to a way of packaging some intermediate-level data structures and their operations into a useful collection whose properties have been carefully studied. These ADTs have been organized to have clean, simple interfaces. They can be represented in many ways by lower-level

*abstract data types*

representations (such as sequential or linked representations)—but these ways have been hidden from view (through the use of information-hiding) so that they can be used simply by knowing only their abstract interface properties. Moreover, they have precisely defined behaviors, permitting clear reasoning about them to take place. Java classes, objects, and interfaces offer a clean way to package ADTs into a useful collection of software components suitable for building software systems.

Major parts of this book are devoted to presenting various kinds of ADTs in the form of Java classes and to developing their properties and uses, in order to enrich your knowledge of ideas and concepts useful for crafting practical representations and systems.

## 1.5 Efficiency and Tradeoffs

When we develop the properties of ADTs, we often focus on algorithms supporting the useful operations we can perform with them. In this connection, the recurring concept of *efficiency* is a major concern. It is useful to discover algorithms that work as efficiently as possible and to be able to characterize their efficiency with suitable mathematical formulas. Sometimes it is even possible to prove that certain algorithms work at maximum efficiency, and that it is impossible to do any better.

On other occasions, we shall be concerned with the recurring concept of *tradeoffs*. Among ADTs that have more than one representation, some representations take very little space, but the algorithms that implement their operations take substantial time. Other representations of the same ADT take more space but have algorithms using less time. In such a case, we say that space and time *trade off* against one another.

## 1.6 Software Engineering Principles

It is useful to distinguish two different levels at which software engineering principles apply: those concerning small programs and those concerning large software systems. The first is called *programming-in-the-small*. The second is called *programming-in-the-large*.

Programming-in-the-small concerns concepts that help us create small programs—those that vary in length from a few lines to a few pages. Sometimes the creation of small programs involves great subtlety of thought and requires great precision and ingenuity. It is important to be able to reason about small programs with clarity and mental precision and to be able to design them effectively. Appendix C addresses many of the issues and software engineering skills involved in programming-in-the-small.

We are also interested in ideas for program structuring that help make the flow of control during program execution mirror the textual structure of the program—called *structured programming*. By using good program structuring, our reasoning about programs is made easier and more effective, and programs are made easier to

programming-in-the-small

structured programming

understand. One technique that is useful for creating structured programs is called *top-down programming by stepwise refinement*, which is akin to starting with an outline of a program's major features and filling in the lower levels of detail, much as we might write a story starting from an outline of its plot.

In programming-in-the-large, we are concerned with principles that organize large, long-lived software systems, and we are concerned with processes for organizing the large-scale human effort needed to build such systems. *Large* software systems typically have over 100,000 lines of code. *Long-lived* software systems typically have useful service lifetimes of 25 years or longer. There are many topics to cover in learning about what software engineers have found to be useful for programming-in-the-large.

For instance, the *lifecycle* of a software system is the period of time that stretches from the system's initial conception to its eventual retirement from service. The human activities related to the lifecycle involve processes such as requirements analysis, design, coding, testing, verification, documentation, and maintenance.

During the *requirements analysis* process, software engineers develop precise definitions of the properties of the software system that they intend to build. The *design* process produces a detailed plan for building the system. The *coding* process translates the design into actual working computer programs. The *testing* process subjects both individual software components and the entire integrated software system to trial runs to see if they work properly. The *verification* process involves the construction of mathematical proofs (or the development of other kinds of convincing evidence) to help determine whether programs do what they are supposed to do. *Documentation* consists of producing written explanations of what the system does, how its parts work, and how the system is used. The *maintenance* process follows the release of the system into active service, and consists of correcting defects and upgrading the system to meet evolving conditions during its useful service lifetime.

Many fascinating questions arise in connection with lifecycle processes and methods. For instance, when is it useful to build a *prototype* of a system (or a part of a system) and to try it out? Automotive and aeronautical engineers frequently build and test prototypes to try out new design concepts. In the case of software engineering, a good answer is that using prototyping buys information to reduce risks that the system won't meet its goals or be finished on-time and within budget.

Software engineers also need to be concerned with the skills related to the organization and management of large software projects. Concepts such as schedules, budgets, resource management policies, risk assessment, and risk item resolution come into play.

Overall, software engineers try to build software systems on time and within budget, to exhibit the characteristics defined in the system requirements definition. Often such characteristics include general software system properties such as *reliability*, *affordability*, *efficiency*, *correctness*, and *safety*. Everyone wants to buy software that is cheap; that is reliable, safe, and efficient; and that does what it is supposed to do. (A *safe* system is defined as one whose operation causes no harm to persons or property.) Organizing human effort in large software projects is a demanding and subtle business,

programming-in-the-large

software lifecycle processes

fraught with risks. Software engineering is the art of organizing people and resources to achieve such aims with the highest quality possible.

Although the development of a full complement of software engineering skills for programming-in-the-large must await more advanced courses, Appendix C attempts to cover a number of software engineering concepts related to programming-in-the-small. Appendix C surveys some of the more important ideas, builds an appreciation for the issues, and gives you practice at solving problems that software professionals confront in areas such as object-oriented design (OOD), algorithm and data representation design, program verification, transforming and optimizing programs, testing, measurement and tuning, software reuse, program structuring, and documentation.

## 1.7 Our Approach to Mathematics

a language of
algorithm efficiency
for the practical
programmer

For the practical programmer, this book will demonstrate that simply by learning the meaning of O-notation, a language computer scientists use to characterize the efficiency of algorithms, you can go an amazingly long way toward being able to understand and compare the efficiency of the algorithms. Appendix B contains a gentle, easy introduction to O-*notation*. After reading this appendix, you will find that you will be able to grasp the *intuition* behind O-notation. Being able to do so is important for practical programmers, because it enables them to choose the best algorithms to solve the programming problems they face. This language is used in the rest of this book to describe the efficiency of algorithms and data structures.

In certain sciences, mathematics plays a central role in the development of the subject matter. For example, in college textbooks on physics or economics, you can expect to find mathematical formulas that describe important laws and relationships. Moreover, you can expect to find mathematical justifications, in which these formulas are derived from basic assumptions and in which their truth is demonstrated under carefully defined conditions. Computer science is one of the sciences in which mathematics plays a central role. Computer scientists have discovered many important laws and principles that are expressed in mathematical form. Oftentimes, to understand why such laws hold true, one needs to follow the steps of the mathematical argument that establishes their validity. However, while we use O-notation to describe algorithm efficiency, we have not incorporated any mathematical derivations or proofs that establish O-notation results rigorously. Instead, it is left to later courses in your computer science curriculum (such as CS7) to carry you beyond the basics. In this book we aspire only to take some easy preliminary steps and to whet your appetite to learn more later.

identifying the best
possible solutions

As we noted before, an important goal of computer science is knowing how to perform certain common algorithmic tasks as efficiently as possible. It could be said that the job of developing computer science fully isn't finished until we know absolutely the best ways of solving important algorithmic problems. Ideally, we would like to be able to exhibit the best algorithms and data structures that are possible, and to prove that it is not possible to do any better.

In practical terms, discovering efficient ways to solve algorithmic problems has important impact on the enterprise of building good hardware and software systems. For example, the performance of a software application, such as a spreadsheet or a word processor, may influence how well it sells. If it is blazing fast, when the competition's product is as slow as a snail, it may do much better in the marketplace.

There is a reason why computer scientists use mathematics to characterize the efficiency of algorithms and data structures. Every algorithm ultimately breaks the solution of a big problem into compositions of tiny steps (since that's the nature of computer programs). Consequently, the mathematics needed to describe the efficiency of an algorithm often mirrors an algorithm's decomposition of the overall problem into smaller subproblems. Sometimes, for example, the mathematics needed consists of summing up contributions that measure the work needed to solve the subproblems. As a result, skill in manipulating sums is quite valuable. Even knowing how to take sums of arithmetic and geometric progressions, something usually taught in high school, has tremendous payoffs.

Also, certain problems have a natural decomposition into subproblems that has a special mathematical pattern that can be expressed in the form of special types of equations called *recurrence relations*. Learning how to recognize these special mathematical patterns, and knowing how to characterize the overall result is often the key to knowing precisely how efficient an algorithm will be.

Although we explain and use O-notation to characterize the efficiency of algorithms and data structures in this book, it is left to later discrete mathematics courses and to later advanced algorithms and data structures courses (such as CS7) to explore how to use summations and recurrence relations to derive the O-notation for many of the key algorithmic efficiency results we cite and use.

## 1.8   Some Notes on Programming Notation

*using Java*

In this section, we cover a few brief points about the form in which Java programs are presented.

One convenient notational convention lies outside the domain of the Java language, which we need to introduce at this moment because it will be used frequently throughout the remainder of the book. This concerns the notation for an *integer range*

*integer ranges*

consisting of all the integers from $m$ to $n$, which is denoted by $m{:}n$. In symbols, $m{:}n = \{\, i \mid m \le i \le n \,\}$, meaning that "the integer range $m{:}n$ equals the set of all integers $i$ such that $i$ is greater than or equal to $m$ and $i$ is less than or equal to $n$." You can pronounce the quantity "$m{:}n$" by saying "*em to en*."

We will often use integer ranges to denote subarrays of an array or to denote the range of integer indexes for an entire array. For example, suppose we have a Java array A that consists of the 100 locations A[0], A[1], A[2], . . . , A[99]. We could describe these array locations using the expression A[0:99] in which the integer range 0:99 gives the set of integer indexes for the array A. Also, to designate, for example, the subarray of A consisting of locations A[10], A[11], A[12], . . . , A[20], we could write A[10:20].

In the Java language, the indexes of a declared array always start at 0 and increase in steps of 1 until reaching a number that is one less than the number of items in the array. For instance, suppose that, in Java, we were to write:

public final static int ARRAY_SIZE = 100;                // 100 is the array size

int[ ] A = new int[ARRAY_SIZE];                // A is an integer array with indexes
                                               // in the range 0:ARRAY_SIZE − 1

The first line declares **ARRAY_SIZE** to be a constant whose value is **100**. The next line declares **A** to be an array of integers indexed by the 100 integers in the range **0:99**.

*our format for Java programs*

To introduce the format in which we display Java programs in this book, let's state and solve a simple search problem.

*Problem:* Search an array of integers **A[0:99]** in increasing order of its array indexes to find the first negative integer. If one exists, return its index (i.e., its position) in the array. If **A** contains no negative integer, then return the index −1. To avoid doing useless work, the solution should exit as soon as the first negative integer is discovered.

In this book, we will pretend that our Java programs have been printed by an imaginary *listing program* that prints both line numbers and vertical bars to the left of each program to help the reader find parts of the program referenced in the discussion in the text. Program 1.3 illustrates the output from this imaginary listing program in which line numbers are explicitly given every five lines, in the margin to the left of a series of vertical bars.

*using line numbers to refer to parts of programs*

Throughout the book, line number ranges are used to identify parts of programs discussed in the running text. For example, in Program 1.3, the method **find(A)** is defined on lines 9:21. The method signature **int find(int[ ] A)** is given on line 9, and declares that **find** is a method that returns an integer value (**int**) and takes as a parameter (a reference to) an array of integer values, **A**. (Recall that, in Java, when an array is passed as an actual parameter to a method, a reference to the array is passed instead of passing a copy of the values in the entire array.)

Line 11 of Program 1.3 declares j to be an integer variable using the declaration **int j;**. Various lines of Program 1.3 have comments in color that are in the rightmost position on their lines. For example, the comment on line 11, to the right of the declaration **int j;** is **// j is an index variable used in the search**. Comments given in color at the rightmost end of a line *explain* how the statement or declaration to the left works, or else describe its *purpose*.

Another kind of comment is a *goal comment*, such as the one given on line 32, which states **// print test results**. Goal comments are given in black and they describe a goal that is achieved by executing the indented statements following them. Such goal comments are analogous to topic headers in an outline.

```
 1  | import java.applet.Applet;
    | import java.io.*;
    |
    | public class ProgramFormatExample extends Applet {
 5  |
    |     public final static int ARRAY_SIZE = 100;
    |
    |
    |     int find(int[ ] A) {                         // find operates on integer arrays, A
10  |
    |         int j;                                   // j is an index variable used in the search
    |
    |         for ( j = 0; j < ARRAY_SIZE; j++ ) {     // search upward starting
    |                                                  // at position 0
15  |             if (A[j] < 0) {                      // if A[j] is negative
    |                 return j;                        // return its index j as the result
    |             }
    |         }
    |
20  |         return −1;                               // return −1 if no negative integers were found
    |     }
    |
    |     public void init( ) {
    |
25  |         int[ ] A = new int[ARRAY_SIZE];    // declare A to be an integer array
    |         int i;                             // let i be an index variable used for intialization
    |
    |         // initialize array A to squares of integers. then make A[17] negative.
    |         for (i = 0; i < ARRAY_SIZE; i++) A[i] = i*i;
30  |         A[17] = −A[17];
    |
    |         // print test results
    |         System.out.println("First neg. integer in A is at index = " + find(A));
    |     }
35  |
    | }
```

**Program 1.3** Finding the First Negative Integer in an Integer Array

## 1.8 EXERCISES

*Note*: To solve Problems 1 and 2, refer again to the problem solved by Program 1.3. Also, if you are unfamiliar with Java, or your memory of Java is a bit rusty, you might want to read Appendix A first, in order to refresh yourself on some of Java's basic features.

1. One programmer suggested the following version of the method, find(A):

```
 1  | int find(int[ ] A) {
    |
    |     int i = 0;
    |
 5  |     while ((A[i] >= 0) && (i < ARRAY_SIZE)) {
    |         i++;
    |     }
    |
    |     return (i < ARRAY_SIZE) ? i : −1;
10  | }
```

Are there any flaws in the implementation of this program? [*Hint:* Recall that, in Java, any attempt to index an array outside its index bounds throws an ArrayIndexOutOfBoundsException. Suppose now that the array A contains no negative integers. What happens when you execute find(A)?] Suggest a way to fix this program by changing just one line.

2. Another programmer claims that the following version of the program for find(A) correctly solves the problem:

```
     |    int find( int[ ] A ) {
     |
     |         int i, result;
     |
  5  |         result = –1;
     |         for ( i = ARRAY_SIZE – 1; i >= 0; i–– ) if (A[i] < 0) result = i;
     |         return result;
     |    }
```

In what respect, if any, does this proposed solution fail to satisfy the statement of the problem?

3. Let A and B be two sets of integers each represented by an array of distinct integers. Write a Java program to compute the intersection of A and D. [*Hint:* Create a new array of integers C whose length is the lesser of the lengths of A and B. Consider C to be initially empty by defining its item count to be zero. For each integer A[i] in A, if A[i] is in B, insert A[i] after the end of the sequence of integers previously inserted in C and increase C's item count by one.]

## 1.9   Preview of Coming Attractions

Our discussion so far should have given you the big picture of what this book covers. But how are the individual chapters in the book organized to help you along your journey?

As mentioned previously, several chapters later in the book develop Java classes implementing various fundamental abstract data types (ADTs). These aim at developing the properties of important data types such as: stacks, queues, trees, and tables. Chapters 6 through 9 cover these individual ADTs and develop their properties. Before studying such individual ADTs, however, it is important to lay some fundamental groundwork. This is the purpose of Chapters 2, 3, 4, and 5.

*getting the big picture on object-oriented programming*

Chapter 2 gives the "big picture" on the importance of object-oriented programming (OOP). It also reviews how Java's class hierarchy works by presenting a case study of a graphics applet that lets you draw various colored filled and hollow shapes (such as ovals, rectangles, and rounded rectangles) by dragging your mouse. By reading this chapter, you'll know why OOP is important and you'll know what to look for in the rest of the book.

*linked data representations*

Chapter 3 develops the concepts of *linked data representations*, which are created by linking individual blocks of storage together using pointers. Some specific programming skills need to be covered regarding how to use Java's implicit object references in place of the explicit pointer data types used by other programming languages that are not usually covered thoroughly in CS1 courses, due to lack of time.

The notion of *representation* is one of the key recurring concepts that ties together the material in this book. Knowing about both linked representations and sequential representations is essential to the study of data abstraction that comes later. Oftentimes, a given ADT, such as the *list* ADT, will have both sequential and linked representations. Often these will exhibit tradeoffs. It is assumed that your previous CS1 course covered the use of basic sequential representations based on Java arrays.

recursion

Chapter 4 gives an introduction to recursion—a key recurring concept in computer science, and one that is used later in algorithms in the remaining chapters.

modularity and<br/>information-hiding

Chapter 5 covers modularity, information-hiding, and data abstraction. It uses Java classes and interfaces to focus on essential concepts of modularity, information hiding, and interfaces. After explaining how Java visibility modifiers work in Java classes, it presents examples of Java interfaces that define abstract data types, and that use information-hiding in Java classes to conceal whether linked or sequential representations have been used underneath. This helps reveal the benefits of data abstraction and information-hiding.

studying individual ADTs

At this point, the groundwork has been laid for studying individual ADTs. The next several chapters cover the important ADTs and develop their properties. Chapter 6 studies linear ADTs such as *stacks* and *queues*. Chapter 7 studies *lists* and *strings*. Chapter 8 studies *trees* and *graphs*. Chapter 9 studies the *table* ADT, and various important associated algorithms, such as hashing.

sorting

Chapter 10 studies important sorting algorithms. It is essential for well-educated computer scientists to know about a few of these algorithms, and to know a few of the main results of the mathematical analysis of their efficiencies. A few of the classical results are described and compared.

review of Java

Appendix A is a gentle introduction to some of the basic features of Java used in this book. It is useful as a review for those who have already have had some exposure to Java, either in their introductory CS1 course, or in some other format. Taken together, Chapter 2 and Appendix A cover all the features of Java needed to understand the critical algorithms and data structures in this book.

the language of<br/>efficiency for algorithms

Appendix B introduces the mathematical language of efficiency for algorithms. It starts by posing the question, "What do we use for a yardstick?"—meaning how can we compare algorithms meaningfully when the same algorithm will run at different speeds and will require different amounts of space when run on different computers or when implemented in different programming languages? This leads to an introduction to the important concept of *O-notation*. You will learn the intuitive meaning of O-notation and you'll learn how it is used to describe algorithm efficiency.

software engineering<br/>concepts

Appendix C introduces software engineering concepts related to programming-in-the-small that are important for practicing software professionals to know about. The exercises and problems provide an opportunity to "learn by doing," in topic areas such as object-oriented design, top-down development of programs by stepwise refinement, optimization by program transformation, proving programs correct, and other areas of software engineering skill.

## ■ Chapter Summary

Computer science blends skills from *science, engineering,* and *mathematics*. To become a competent computer scientist, it is important for you to master skills in these three areas, including skills in experimentation, design, and theory.

Computer scientists have tried to identify enduring concepts and principles that are useful for understanding the possibilities and limits of computing, and the useful forms of organization of software and hardware systems. Finding the right *abstractions* has been of value in this search. The right abstractions are of lasting value instead of being transitory.

*enduring concepts and principles*

The ideas of *abstraction* and *representation* help us organize and understand the structure of large software systems. Such software systems tend to be structured using several layers of representations. Using *abstraction* and *information-hiding*, such systems can be partitioned into subsystems having simple *interfaces*, making them easier to understand and use.

Computer scientists have discovered many kinds of useful data structures and algorithms that can be used as intermediate level representations in large software systems. These are best presented and studied as *abstract data types* (or ADTs). The ADTs studied in this book, such as lists, trees, queues, stacks, and tables, provide a useful stock of ideas for crafting new representations to use in new software applications. The properties of such ADTs have been extensively studied, including their useful algorithms and their alternative underlying representations.

*abstract data types*

*Efficiency* and *tradeoffs* are two additional recurring concepts that are important to study and master. It is an important goal of computer science to discover the most *efficient* algorithms possible. When studying different representations for a given ADT, we often find that space and time *trade off* against each other.

Software engineering methods and processes are also important to learn about. Many helpful things have been learned about how to organize people and resources in the enterprise of building software systems. The activities in the software lifecycle include many processes such as *requirements analysis, design, coding, testing, verification, documentation,* and *maintenance*. *Risk-based software process models* have recently been introduced incorporating new concepts such as the use of *prototyping* to buy information that reduces risk. Traditional topics such as *top-down structured programming by stepwise refinement* and *program verification* using *correctness proofs* are also important to know about. Appendix C provides opportunities to become acquainted with a number of software engineering concepts and skills, and provides you with problems and exercises to acquaint you with their meaning and use.

*software engineering*

Mathematics plays an important role in the development of computer science and has been used to discover many central results. Among the benefits of using mathematics to practical programmers are: being able to reason about why programs work, being able to determine the efficiency of algorithms, knowing what is possible and impossible in computing, being able to improve programs, and gaining the advantages of precision and structure that come from using precisely-defined mathematical models whose properties and implications have been carefully studied. Appendix B

*the role of mathematics*

gives you an easy-to-follow intuitive introduction to the language of O-notation, used to characterize the efficiency of algorithms. Once you have learned the intuitive meaning of O-notation you'll be able to understand and appreciate the comparative efficiency of the important data structure algorithms described in this book.

Java program format

We imagine that Java algorithms are printed by a *line-number listing program*, using line numbers and vertical bars in the left margin to the immediate left of each Java program text given. This aids the reader in following the discussion in the text since various parts of Java programs can be referenced directly by using the numbers of the lines on which such parts occur.

# Introduction to Object-Oriented Programming

Object-oriented programming (OOP) is a form of programming that has recently become widespread, although its origins stretch back many years. The proponents of object-oriented programming argue that it provides advantages for reducing the cost of software development and for improving software maintenance. New object-oriented programming languages, such as Java, provide capabilities for secure network programming, multi-threaded program execution, clean data-encapsulation, easy definition of graphical user interfaces, and flexible exception-handling. The purpose of this chapter is to give you "the big picture" on how OOP works and what it is good for. This will give you a framework in which to fit your understanding of the developments in the later chapters that cover specific object classes for various data structures of general utility. We start with the basic idea behind the concept of an object.

objects bundle data and behavior together

Basically, an *object* bundles together some *data* and some *behavior*. Think of an object's data as a collection of variables whose values give the object's internal state, and think of an object's behaviors as a set of operators that change its state. An object

21

is created during the running of a program as an *instance* of a "template" or "blueprint" specified by its *class*. The class definition that acts as an object's template furnishes descriptions of both the data and the behavioral components. The behavioral components are given in the form of function definitions called *methods*.

A collection of objects can act cooperatively to implement a software system by invoking one another's methods. A helpful analogy is to think of a collection of cooperating objects as resembling a collection of factories, each of which manufactures specialized products. A given factory can invoke the services of another factory as a subcontractor by sending it a purchase order for one of its products. When a factory receives a purchase order, it cranks up one of its local manufacturing methods that produces a manufactured product which is then returned to the factory that issued the original purchase order. When the original factory receives the resulting manufactured product it purchased, it may incorporate that product as a part in its own manufactured products. In this sense, some factories serve as subcontractors to make parts ordered by other factories that, in turn, manufacture products using parts supplied by its subcontractors.

message passing

When one object invokes another object's method, it is sometimes said that the object invoking the method is *the sender*, that the object whose method is invoked is *the receiver*, and that the sender *sends a message* to the receiver consisting of the method call. Dot notation is used to invoke a receiving object's method, as in **myObject.draw(20,50)**, which invokes the **draw** method of the receiver **myObject**, using the parameters **20** and **50**. The general format is

$$\text{receivingObject.methodCall}(\text{arg}_1, \text{arg}_2, ..., \text{arg}_n),$$

where **arg$_1$**, **arg$_2$**, ..., **arg$_n$** is a list of parameters (or *arguments*, as the parameters are sometimes called).

information-hiding and interfaces

In class definitions (i.e., the templates from which the actual objects are created as instances), it is possible to provide modifying descriptors to hide the internal details of an object, making such details inaccessible to outside users. This provides the basis for information-hiding and clean interfaces. Using the factory analogy, we can declare that a factory's internal state data and some of its methods are "industrial trade secrets," invisible to outside purchasers of the factory's products and services. The factory may choose to reveal to the public only those products and services that it wants to make publicly available to its customers. In fact, the modifier word **public** is used in Java class definitions to declare that an object's data fields or methods are accessible to such outside users.

subclasses and inheritance

Once a class definition is given in Java, it is possible to define *subclasses* that modify the meaning of the original class. A subclass definition *extends* a class definition by providing new data or new methods (or both). A subclass of a given class can also *inherit* all the data and methods of the given class—meaning that all the original class's data and methods are available for use by the new subclass. Returning to the factory analogy, a factory, $F_2$, corresponding to a subclass of another factory $F_1$, is an extension of $F_1$ that can access $F_1$'s internal data and methods, and that provides additional new internal data and manufacturing methods unique to $F_2$ itself. For example, a factory that makes a brand name product, like WESTINGHOUSE REFRIGERATORS, might build a factory extension to produce altered products, such as SEARS KENMORE REFRIGERATORS, for a large chain store like Sears that subcontracts with Westinghouse to manufacture a customized Sears product line. The Westinghouse factory extension that manufactures customized products for Sears can have access to all of the original Westinghouse factory's manufacturing methods and parts, if it needs to.

overriding

One of the ways that a subclass S can customize the behavior of the class C that it extends is to define a new method m having the same method name and the same types of parameters as the original method m in C. In this case, the redefined method m in S is said to *override* the method m in C—meaning that the new local version of the method m in S *replaces* the old inherited method m in C, whenever method m is invoked on an object of type S.

abstract classes and methods

Sometimes you define an *abstract class* having what are called *abstract methods*—meaning methods that act like blanks to be filled in later when customized subclasses are defined. Later you define actual subclasses of the original abstract class in which you provide actual specific methods that fill in the blanks named by the abstract methods. This mechanism can be used to provide for generalized software components that can be programmed by supplying the missing pieces (i.e., "filling in the blanks"). It can also be used to coordinate well-organized, case-by-case treatment of collections of slightly different subclasses expressing variations on a common theme. (We will see an example of this use of abstract classes later in this chapter when we use an abstract shape class having variations expressed by its subclasses that define separate hollow or filled shapes such as ovals, rectangles, and rounded rectangles.) Also, programming using such techniques saves effort because we need to express only the individual differences that define the variations, while expressing the common shared theme only once.

summary of advantages

Some of the notable advantages offered by object-oriented programming can be summarized as follows. Defining systems of objects using subclassing, inheritance, overriding, and various information-hiding properties, provides for a means of organizing software systems that can: (1) define modular software components that hide their internal details, present clean interfaces to their users, and allow for later modification and customization to suit the needs of software maintainers; (2) permit substitution of new data representations when needed for improving efficiency; and (3) allow prefabricated software subsystems to be built in which, by filling in blanks, working subsystems can be generated with minimal effort, thus vastly reducing the time and expense required to develop reliable software subsystems. In short, OOP helps us to gain economic advantage by building systems at low cost from reusable software components in a flexible, well-organized fashion.

## Plan for the Chapter

the importance of progressive examples

While the foregoing description gives "the big picture," it employs a few unfamiliar words that are likely to remain vague until their meaning is sharpened by reference to actual examples. Thus, in Sections 2.2 and 2.3, we give two progressive examples that illustrate, first with a simple Java applet, and then with a slightly more rich Java applet, some of the key ideas of object-oriented programming.

a rectangle
drawing example

Section 2.2 presents a **DrawRect** Java applet that allows you to draw rectangles on the screen by dragging your mouse. It shows how to create a subclass of the original class **Rectangle**, called a **DragRect**, which has a new method for ensuring that the (height and width) dimensions of the rectangle are positive. Unless a rectangle has such positive dimensions, it can't be drawn on the screen. (An attempt to use the Java graphics package to draw a rectangle with a negative **height** or **width** results in drawing nothing on the screen.) Such negative heights and widths can arise when dragging the mouse to create a rectangle because we use differences between the **(x,y)** coordinates where the mouse button first went down and the **(x,y)** coordinates of the mouse's current drag position to determine the **height** and **width** of the rectangle to be drawn.

the power of overriding

Also, we *override* (i.e., substitute our own special new meanings for) the **init( )** and **paint( )** methods and we provide implementations of some blank mouse event handlers in order to get our applet to take the appropriate drawing action. In short, we "fill in the blanks" in the general Java applet and event-handler templates with our own plug-in software components to create our applet. This illustrates a powerful technique for using prefabricated software components to build a system rapidly and cheaply. In fact, our rectangle drawing applet takes only 53 lines to express—proving that a lot of customized behavior can be specified quite quickly just by describing a few modifications (or customizations) of existing Java library classes and by assembling some available software parts.

a shape drawing example

Section 2.3 introduces a **DrawShapes** applet that is a bit more ambitious. It provides three pop-up menus in a graphical user interface (GUI) that allow the user to select a shape (oval, rectangle, or rounded rectangle), a color (red, yellow, or blue) and a fill choice (hollow or filled). When the user drags the mouse, a new shape is drawn having the characteristics selected from the pop-up menus. Each time the user drags the mouse, a new shape is added in the foreground of the picture (such that all of the shapes drawn earlier are retained in background layers in the back-to-front order they were drawn).

abstract classes and
type polymorphism

This **DrawShapes** applet introduces an abstract shape class having an abstract **draw()** method. Subclasses are then defined to create individual variations of shapes, consisting of hollow or filled ovals, rectangles, and rounded rectangles. This permits us to illustrate features of class hierarchies such as inheritance, overriding, subclassing, information-hiding, and the use of abstract classes to provide type polymorphism. We also use a prefabricated Java library class, called a **Vector**, to provide a growable list of shapes to be drawn. Moreover, we use the well-known computer graphics technique of drawing into an off-screen image buffer to eliminate the display flashing inherent in redrawing a list of shapes in back-to-front order each time we draw a new shape in the foreground.

using object-oriented
programming to
build systems

Section 2.4 draws conclusions from the **DrawRect** and **DrawShapes** examples studied in the previous sections. The **DrawShapes** example is rich enough to convey the flavor of what it is like to program in Java, using Java's class library. It is not a simple matter to learn to use such a class library effectively. The big lesson to be learned is that the knowledge of how to use the parts in a software component library does not lie in the parts themselves, but rather in the examples, strategies, and scripts that convey how the parts can be assembled to work cooperatively to achieve various desired effects. If you are trying to achieve a desired effect, you absolutely must know (or must discover) the strategy for assembling library components into a cooperating collection of objects that achieves the desired effect. You cannot learn such a strategy by reading the specs for the parts in a software parts catalog, because the knowledge isn't in the parts. The listing for the **DrawShapes** applet, given in Program 2.16, contains critical examples of the strategies (or scripts) for implementing expandable lists using Java **Vectors**, and for how to set up and use off-screen image buffers in Java. Because such strategies are not usually available in software component catalogs, you may need to learn to search for them in such program listings to learn how to assemble software components into useful combinations.

standard applet
method calls

Section 2.4 also comments on standard method invocations that the standard prefabricated Java applet executes. If you override these standard methods by substituting your own customized methods, you can expect your customized methods to be called at various predictable moments and under various predictable conditions during the standard applet's execution lifecycle.

If you are not familiar (or you are a bit rusty) with Java's basic expressions, operators, and control flow statements you should review Appendix A now before reading any further.

## 2.2  A Rectangle Drawing Applet

### LEARNING OBJECTIVES

1. To learn how to define a subclass by extending a given class.
2. To learn how to override applet and interface methods to create a customized new drawing applet.
3. To begin to understand how to develop programs starting with reusable software components.

creating a GUI

In this section we present an example of how to create a Java applet that has a simple *graphical user interface* (GUI). To create the interface, we use building blocks taken from Java's Abstract Window Tools (AWT) package, **java.awt**, and we extend the basic Java applet by overriding (i.e., providing plug-in substitutes for) some of its methods to produce the behavior we seek.

The applet we shall develop is called the **DrawRect** applet, because it allows the user to draw wire-frame rectangles by dragging the mouse. Figure 2.1 gives a picture of what the user sees after a rectangle has been drawn.

the Java applet
coordinate system

When you draw in a Java applet window, you use a coordinate system measured in units of pixel-widths, in which the points (x,y) are plotted in the following way. The point (0,0) is the origin of the coordinate system and is located in the upper-left corner of the drawing. As the value of the x-coordinate increases you move to the right in the horizontal direction. As the value of the y-coordinate increases you move down in the vertical direction. Thus, the point (41,23) has an x-coordinate with the value x = 41 that lies 41 pixel widths to the right of the left side of the drawing, and it has a y-coordinate with the value y = 23 that lies 23 pixel widths below the top of the

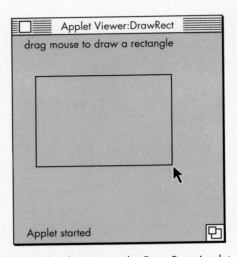

**Figure 2.1** A Rectangle Created by the User in the DrawRect Applet

drawing. (The word *pixel* is short for "picture element" and consists of a tiny colored or shaded gray dot that is the smallest unit from which a picture image is composed. A typical computer monitor resolution is **72** pixels per inch. At this resolution, each square inch contains $72 \times 72 = 5184$ pixels.)

A rectangle is specified in Java first by giving the coordinates of its top-left corner **(x,y)**, and then by giving its **width** and **height**. Figure 2.2 shows an example of a rectangle plotted in a Java applet drawing window.

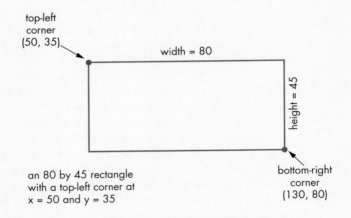

**Figure 2.2** An $80 \times 45$ Rectangle in a Java Drawing Window

prefabricated rectangles

Java provides a prefabricated **Rectangle** class in the **java.awt** package. (Here, the **java.awt** package is the Java Abstract Window Toolkit package which provides a set of easy-to-use standard GUI components.) There are four data fields in the **Rectangle** class:

```
// data fields of a Rectangle
public int x;              // the x-coordinate of the rectangle's top-left corner
public int y;              // the y-coordinate of the rectangle's top-left corner
public int width;          // the rectangle's width in pixels
public int height;         // the rectangle's height in pixels
```

public data fields

Because these data fields are declared to be **public**, they can be accessed by external users of **Rectangle** objects. For example, if **myRect** is a **Rectangle** object, we can refer to the values of its data fields using dot notation, such as **myRect.x**, **myRect.y**, **myRect.width**, and **myRect.height**. To create some instances of a **Rectangle**, we can use declarations having initializations, such as those shown in Fig. 2.3.

In Fig. 2.3, expressions such as **Rectangle()** and **Rectangle(50,35,80,45)** are called constructors. Constructors are methods that create objects that are instances of a class. The method name for a constructor is identical to the name of the class. The

no-arg constructors

constructor **Rectangle()** is called a no-argument constructor (or *no-arg constructor* for short), and is denoted by an empty pair of parentheses following the class name, **Rectangle**. This no-arg constructor creates an instance of a **Rectangle** having **(0,0)** as its top-left corner, and having both a zero width and a zero height. Another separate constructor takes four integer arguments and is of the form:

Rectangle(int x, int y, int width, int height);

In this constructor, you give the coordinates of the rectangle's top-left corner using the first two arguments, and you give its width and height using the last two arguments. The *signature* for a method consists of the method name together with the

more on Java constructors and signatures

number and types of its arguments. You can define several different constructors for a class by defining methods having different signatures, all of which share the class name as the constructor's method name. The two different constructors used in Fig. 2.3 have different signatures because one has no arguments whereas the other has four integer arguments (even though both constructors share the same method name, **Rectangle**). Java defines the no-arg constructor automatically for you whenever you don't define your own constructors. If you choose to define additional constructors,

```
Rectangle myRect = new Rectangle( );        // creates a Rectangle object
                                            // having a top-left corner at (0,0)
                                            // and having a height and width of zero

Rectangle anotherRect = new Rectangle(50,35,80,45);        // creates
                                            // an 80 by 45 Rectangle object
                                            // with its top-left corner at (50, 35)
                                            // identical to that shown in Fig. 2.2
```

**Figure 2.3** Java Declarations that Create Rectangle Objects

each new constructor must have a distinct new signature. If you define your own new constructors and you want to include the no-arg constructor, you must define it, since Java automatically provides the no-arg constructor only when you don't define any constructors yourself.

The prefabricated Java class **Rectangle** comes equipped with a number of predefined methods that you can use to perform useful operations on rectangle objects.

**prefabricated Java classes**

(Such methods, and all the other features of the prefabricated Java classes are described in the two volume series: *The Java™ Application Programming Interface*, *Volumes 1 and 2*, by James Gosling, Frank Yellin, and the Java Team, available from Addison-Wesley.) An example of such a predefined **Rectangle** method is the method

```
setBounds(int x, int y, int width, int height);
```

which applies to a given rectangle and sets its top-left corner to **(x,y)** and its width and height to **width** and **height**, respectively. For example, if **myRect** is a variable having a **Rectangle** object as its value, then executing the statement

```
myRect.setBounds(10,20,100,50);
```

changes the rectangle **myRect** to have its top-left corner at the point **(10,20)** and changes its **width** to **100** and its **height** to **50**.

A typical way to give a class definition is first to declare the data fields for the objects in the class, and then to follow the data fields by the definitions of the class's

**class definitions**

methods (usually starting with specialized constructors, if any are defined). Thus, we might imagine the class definition for Java's prefabricated **Rectangle** class to be something like that given in Program 2.4.

In the class definition in Program 2.4, the no-arg constructor is defined on lines 11:13. It would not have been necessary to define this no-arg constructor had no other constructors been defined, because Java defines the no-arg constructor for you automatically just when you define no other constructors of your own. However, since another constructor (with arguments) is defined on lines 15:20, it is necessary to define the no-arg constructor on lines 11:13 explicitly. In the constructor defined on lines 15:20, the formal parameters have the same names (**x, y, width, height**) as the **Rectangle** class's data fields (**x, y, width, height**). The formal parameters of a construc-

**the role of the special reserved word "this"**

tor or a method act like local variables (whose values are initialized with the values of the actual parameter expressions used when the constructor or method is invoked). Such local variables *hide* the identically named **Rectangle** data fields (that act like global variables, defined external to a method in the data field declarations of the class). To access or to assign values to these hidden class data variables, you need to precede them with "**this.**" The special reserved word "**this**" refers to the object on which a given method or constructor is invoked. When you execute an assignment such as **this.x = x;** given on line 28 of the **setBounds** method, which would occur, for example, if you were to execute a method call such as:

```
myRect.setBounds(30,40,100,50);
```

```
     |     public class Rectangle {
     |
     |       // data fields
     |           public int x;
  5  |           public int y;
     |           public int width;
     |           public int height;
     |
     |       // constructors
 10  |
     |           public Rectangle( ) {
     |               x = y = width = height = 0;              // set all data fields to zero
     |           }
     |
 15  |           public Rectangle(int x, int y, int width, int height) {
     |               this.x = x;                        // when the formal parameters of
     |               this.y = y;                        // the method have the same names as
     |               this.width = width;                // the Rectangle's data fields, they
     |               this.height = height;              // hide the Rectangle data fields.
 20  |           }                                      // Rectangle data field f must then
     |                                                  // be referenced as this.f
     |
     |           // and so forth. (only two of the six Rectangle constructors are shown)
     |
 25  |       // methods
     |
     |           public void setBounds(int x, int y, int width, int height) {
     |               this.x = x;                        // the Rectangle data fields
     |               this.y = y;                        // must be preceded by "this." in order to
 30  |               this.width = width;                // distinguish them from the identically
     |               this.height = height;              // named formal parameters
     |           }                                      // that hide them from view
     |
     |           public void translate(int dx, int dy) {        // move the Rectangle
 35  |               x += dx;                           // dx pixels to the right , and
     |               y += dy;                           // dy pixels down
     |           }
     |
     |           // and so forth. (only two of the sixteen Rectangle methods are shown)
 40  |
     |     }                                           // end of class definition
```

**Program 2.4** The Rectangle Class Definition

you designate that the value of the actual parameter **30** (passed as a value to the formal parameter **x** in the method call **setBounds(30,40,100,50);**) is assigned to be the new value of the data field **x** of the object **myRect**. This is because the reserved word **this** inside the **setBounds** method refers to the object that is the value of **myRect** on which the **setBounds** method is invoked. (Recall that each separate **Rectangle** *object* is an *instance* of the **Rectangle** *class*, and that each such separate **Rectangle** object has its own separate local copies of the **Rectangle** class's data fields.)

Now that we have explained how to give the class definition for a rectangle, it is time to consider how to create a new subclass of the **Rectangle** class, by *extending* its class definition. To illustrate how to do this, Program 2.5 defines a subclass **DragRect** that extends the **Rectangle** class to have a new method named **normalize**.

*inheritance*

When you define a new subclass **C2** to extend a given class **C1**, class **C2** *inherits* all of the data fields and methods of **C1**. More precisely, **C2** inherits only the data fields and methods of **C1** that are not marked as **private**. Any data fields of **C1** that are marked as **public** (i.e., accessible to outside users) or **protected** (meaning accessible to subclasses) or that are defined without using any of the three access modifiers (**private**, **public**, **protected**) and are in the same **package**, are inherited by **C2**. When line 1 of Program 2.5 declares "**class DragRect extends Rectangle**" it implies that each **DragRect** object has all the data fields and methods that a **Rectangle** does.

Lines 3:12 of Program 2.5 define the **normalize()** method of the **DragRect** class. This new method extends the set of methods inherited from the **Rectangle** class by providing a new method available to objects that are instances of the **DragRect** subclass. Now suppose that **myDragRect** is a variable having a **DragRect** object as its value. We can then write **myDragRect.normalize()** to invoke the **normalize** method on **myDragRect**. We can also invoke any of the methods that apply to a **Rectangle**, as in

*invoking methods and accessing data fields*

writing **myDragRect.translate(4,5)**, because all methods defined in the **Rectangle** class are inherited by objects in the **DragRect** subclass. In addition, we can access or assign the local data fields (**x, y, width, height**) of any **DragRect** object, as in writing **myDragRect.x++;** to increment the **x**-field of **myDragRect** by one, because all data fields defined in the **Rectangle** class are inherited by objects in the **DragRect** subclass. Finally, we can use **DragRect()** as the no-arg constructor for a new object of type **DragRect**, because the no-arg constructor is defined for us automatically by Java in the absence of our having defined any constructors of our own.

*what the normalize() method does*

In Program 2.5, the **normalize()** method takes a rectangle constructed with possibly negative widths or heights and redefines it to be a rectangle occupying the same position but having its (**x,y**) coordinates in the top-left corner and having a positive width and height. This will turn out to be useful in our **DrawRect** applet because we

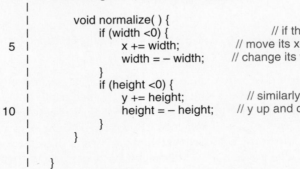

```
    |    class DragRect extends Rectangle {
    |
    |        void normalize( ) {
    |            if (width <0) {                    // if the rectangle's width is negative
  5 |                x += width;                    // move its x-coordinate to the left side and
    |                width = − width;               // change its width from negative to positive
    |            }
    |            if (height <0) {
    |                y += height;                   // similarly, if its height is negative, move
 10 |                height = − height;             // y up and change its height to be positive
    |            }
    |        }
    |
    |    }
```

**Program 2.5** The DragRect Class Definition

shall create rectangles using differences of successive coordinates taken from the action of dragging the mouse. It is possible for such rectangles to have negative widths or heights, and we need to normalize them before passing them on to the graphics drawing method that draws rectangles on the screen, because this graphics drawing method will not draw a rectangle having a negative width or height. For example, on lines 4:7 of Program 2.5, the if-statement says, in effect, if the width of this rectangle is negative (if (width < 0)), then move the x-coordinate of the rectangle from the right side to the left side (by adding the negative value of the rectangle's width to x's value, using the assignment x += width; which means the same as the assignment x = x + width;), and then replace the negative value of the width with a positive width value of the same magnitude (using the assignment width = − width;).

The DrawRect applet defines actions that cause a new rectangle to be drawn on the screen each time the user drags the mouse. When a mouse is *dragged* (along the surface of a desktop, for instance), it means that the mouse button is pressed at the beginning of the drag, and that the button is held down continuously as the mouse is moved to a new position. The dragging action terminates when the mouse button is released. There is a cursor (or pointer) on the computer screen that is under the control of the mouse and that is moved when the user moves the mouse. The cursor position can be designated by a point (x,y) giving the cursor's screen coordinates.

In what is called *event-based programming*, *events* are generated when the user takes certain actions (like pressing the mouse button, pressing a key on the keyboard, inserting a floppy disk, and so forth). Such events are handled by *event handler* code. Java makes it easy for you to write event handler code by allowing you to implement various event-handler methods supplied in prefabricated Java event-handler interfaces. All you have to do to implement a prefabricated event-handler method m is to supply a method definition for m in the definition of your own applet. (You set up the definition of your own applet to be a subclass of the prefabricated Java Applet, and you specify that your applet implements various event listener interfaces such as the MouseListener and MouseMotionListener interfaces. These interfaces are just collections of event-handler methods. When you implement a Java interface, it means that you supply your own actual method implementations for each different method call defined in the interface.)

*event-based programming in Java*

For example, to implement the mousePressed event handler method in your own applet, you might write

```
public void mousePressed(MouseEvent event) {
    anchorPoint.x = event.getX( );
    anchorPoint.y = event.getY( );
}
```

In this mousePressed method, you can expect Java to pass you the parameter (MouseEvent event), where event is a MouseEvent object having data fields describing things like the time the event occurred on the computer's clock, and giving the x and y coordinates of the cursor on the screen at the moment when the user pressed the mouse button. The values returned by the method calls event.getX() and event.getY() are the respective x and y coordinates of the "mouse-down" point.

The strategy we will use to translate a user's mouse drag action into a drawn rectangle has four parts. First, we capture the coordinates of the point at which the mouse button was first pressed as a fixed point, called the "anchor point." The (x,y) coordinates of the anchor point are stored as the x and y data fields of a Point object that is the value of the variable anchorPoint. The purpose of the mousePressed() method is simply to set the (x,y) coordinates of the anchorPoint to be the (x,y) coordinates of this mouse-down point. Second, we repeatedly capture the (x,y) coordinates of the cursor as the mouse is being dragged to different positions during the user's dragging action, and we set the bounds of a rectangle object, given as the value of the variable dragRect, such that its (x,y) coordinates are those of the anchorPoint, and such that its width and height are the respective differences between the current (x,y) coordinates of the mouse's drag point and the (x,y) coordinates of the anchorPoint.

the strategy for drawing<br>rectangles

Third, using the method call dragRect.normalize(), we normalize the dragRect to ensure that it will be drawable, because the originally constructed dragRect will have a negative width (or height) whenever the x (or y) coordinate of the current mouse drag point is to the left of (or above) the x (or y) coordinate of the anchorPoint. Fourth, and finally, we draw the normalized dragRect on the screen using the repaint() method call.

You can see from line 1 of Program 2.6 that the mouseDragged event-handler method is passed the current mouse-drag event as its actual parameter. The (x,y) coordinates of the current mouse drag position are stored as data fields of this event object and are accessed using the method calls event.getX() and event.getY(). On lines 2:4, the bounds of the dragRect object are set so that the (x,y) coordinates are identical to those of the anchorPoint, and so that the width and height are set to the differences of the respective x and y coordinates of the mouse-drag point and the anchorPoint. On line 5, the dragRect is normalized and on line 6, the repaint() method (of the applet we are defining) is called, causing the newly normalized dragRect to be drawn on the screen by a method we shall explain in a moment.

the mouseDragged()<br>method

Program 2.7 gives the entire code for the DrawRect applet. Lines 1:2 of this program import the Applet class from the java.applet package and import all the classes in the java.awt package. A package is just a collection of related classes. The star (*) in the statement import java.awt.*; is a wild-card character that causes all classes in the package java.awt to be imported. When you import a package or a class, you make the public classes in the package and each class's public data fields and methods available for use. In the java.awt package, the "awt" stands for Abstract Window Tools. This package provides useful building blocks for implementing graphical user interfaces (GUIs).

the DrawRect applet

```
 |       public void mouseDragged(MouseEvent event) {
 |           dragRect.setBounds(  anchorPoint.x, anchorPoint.y,
 |                                   event.getX( ) – anchorPoint.x,
 |                                   event.getY( ) – anchorPoint.y);
5|           dragRect.normalize( );
 |           repaint( );
 |       }
```

**Program 2.6** The mouseDragged Event-Handler Method

```
 1 | import java.applet.Applet;
   | import java.awt.*;
   |
   | public class DrawRect extends Applet
 5 |             implements MouseListener, MouseMotionListener  {
   |
   |     DragRect dragRect = new DragRect();        // define the applet's dragRect
   |     Point anchorPoint = new Point(0,0);           // and anchorPoint data fields
   |
10 |     public void init( )  {                     // during applet initialization, add the
   |         addMouseListener(this);                     // listeners that intercept mouse
   |         addMouseMotionListener(this);      // events and invoke their handlers
   |     }
   |
15 |     public void mousePressed(MouseEvent event) {             // to handle a
   |         anchorPoint.x = event.getX( );    // mousePressed event, set the (x,y)
   |         anchorPoint.y = event.getY( );       // coordinates of the anchorPoint
   |     }                                          // to those of the mouse-down point
   |
20 |     public void mouseDragged(MouseEvent event) {    // when mouse moves
   |         dragRect.setBounds( anchorPoint.x, anchorPoint.y, // during mouse
   |                             event.getX( ) – anchorPoint.x,      // dragging,
   |                             event.getY( ) – anchorPoint.y);       // set the
   |         dragRect.normalize( );                    // bounds of the dragRect. then
25 |         repaint( );                                // normalize it and draw it
   |     }
   |
   |     public void mouseMoved(MouseEvent event) {  }    // blank mouse event
   |     public void mouseReleased(MouseEvent event) {  } // handlers must be
30 |     public void mouseEntered(MouseEvent event) {  } // given to supply the
   |     public void mouseExited(MouseEvent event) {  }   // implementations of
   |     public void mouseClicked(MouseEvent event) {  } // all listener methods
   |                                                   // not used by the applet
   |     public void paint(Graphics g) {
35 |         g.drawString("drag mouse to draw a rectangle",30,10);
   |         g.drawRect( dragRect.x, dragRect.y,          // draw the dragRect
   |                     dragRect.width, dragRect.height);    // on the screen
   |     }
   |
40 | } // end applet
   |
   | class DragRect extends Rectangle {       // the DragRect class is a subclass
   |     void normalize( ) {                          // of the Rectangle class
   |         if (width <0) {                            // that introduces a
45 |             x += width;                             // new normalize( )
   |             width = – width;                            // method
   |         }
   |         if (height <0) {
   |             y += height;
50 |             height = – height;
   |         }
   |     }
   | }
```

**Program 2.7** The DrawRect Applet

Lines 4:5 of Program 2.7 state that the **DrawRect** class is a subclass of the Java **Applet** class that implements the **MouseListener** and **MouseMotionListener** interfaces (to enable the **DrawRect** applet to intercept and handle mouse events).

The init( ) method on lines 10:13 designates the **DrawRect** applet as a listener for mouse events generated when the user presses the mouse button or drags the mouse to draw a rectangle. This means that the **mousePressed** and **mouseDragged** event handlers will receive and process all mouse events generated when the user interacts with the applet during its execution.

We have already seen how to define the event-handler methods **mousePressed** (on lines 15:18) and **mouseDragged** (on lines 20:26). On lines 28:32 we have to complete the implementation of the **MouseListener** and **MouseMotionListener** interfaces by supplying blank method implementations for all methods in these interfaces that the applet doesn't use. Otherwise, the Java compiler will not compile the applet.

*Graphics objects and the paint() method*

We also override the **paint()** method (on lines 34:38). The **paint(Graphics g)** method takes a **Graphics** object **g** as its actual parameter. Such a graphics object **g** provides a prefabricated graphics drawing context defined in the **java.awt** package that comes equipped with many useful drawing methods. One of **g**'s methods is invoked by the method call **g.drawRect(x,y,width,height)** which draws a black, wire-framed rectangle on the screen. Thus, the **g.drawRect** method call on lines 36:37 causes the recently normalized **dragRect** to be drawn on the screen. The preceding statement on line 35 causes the string "drag mouse to draw a rectangle" to be drawn on the screen, starting at the position **x = 30** and **y = 10**.

*the repaint() method*

After you override the **paint()** method (by supplying a new definition such as that given on lines 34:38), you can cause the screen to be repainted using this new **paint()** method each time you call the **repaint()** method. Thus, line 25 of the **mouseDragged** event-handler causes the screen to be repainted just after a new **dragRect** has had its bounds set and has been normalized.

*the new DragRect subclass*

As we have seen earlier, lines 42:53 define the new **DragRect** subclass of the prefabricated **java.awt Rectangle** class by introducing a new **normalize()** method. The declaration **DragRect dragRect = new DragRect( );** on line 7 of Program 2.7 declares the variable **dragRect** to be a variable holding a reference to a **DragRect** object, and immediately initializes it to a newly created **DragRect** object, using the no-arg constructor **DragRect()**. This no-arg constructor was provided automatically by Java since Program 2.7 did not specify any new constructors for the **DragRect** class.

*constructing a new Point object*

Line 8 of Program 2.7 declares a new **Point** variable **anchorPoint** and immediately initializes it to be a new **Point** object using the predefined Java **Point** constructor **Point(0,0)**. Note here that the **java.awt** package does not provide a no-arg constructor for the **Point** class, so we have to use the two-argument constructor whose signature is **Point(int x, int y)** instead.

*executing the DrawRect applet*

Now let's summarize what happens when the **DrawRect** applet is executed. The **DrawRect** applet is started by a Java-aware applet viewer program that might, for example, reside in a web browser program of some sort. The **DrawRect** applet then comes alive in a portion of a web-page being visited by the browser. (Alternatively, your Java programming environment might furnish a Java applet viewer that makes your applet come alive in a special applet viewer window on your screen.)

When your **DrawRect** applet begins execution, it executes its **init()** method (which sets up the applet to receive and handle mouse events), and then it invokes its **paint()** method (which causes the string "drag mouse to draw a rectangle" to be drawn at the top of the window). The applet now waits for the user to cause events to which it can respond. The only events the **DrawRect** applet is programmed to respond to are **MouseEvent**s. When the user starts to drag the mouse by holding down the mouse button, a mouse event is generated and the **mousePressed()** method is invoked causing the coordinates of the mouse-down point to be captured as the **(x,y)** coordinates of the **anchorPoint**. When the user drags the mouse (by moving it with its button still held down) and the **(x,y)** position of the mouse changes, new mouse drag events are generated. When a **MouseEvent** is handled by the **mouseDragged** method, the **dragRect** is reshaped to be a new rectangle whose opposite corners are defined by the **anchorPoint** and the current mouse-drag point. After this newly reshaped **dragRect** is normalized to make sure its **(x,y)** coordinates are in its upper-left corner and that its **width** and **height** are positive, the **repaint()** method is invoked in order to draw the current **dragRect** on the screen. (If you're wondering why the previous **dragRect** was erased before the new **dragRect** was drawn, the answer is that the **repaint()** method calls the **paint()** method, which calls the **update()** method, which always repaints the screen to the background color before it paints the update image.) If the user starts a new, separate mouse dragging action, a new anchor point is established at the new mouse-down point, and a new drag rectangle is continuously displayed, whose opposite corners are defined by this new anchor point and the current mouse-drag point.

*a summary of the DrawRect applet's actions*

Let's draw some conclusions from the study of our **DrawRect** applet. We have actually seen a convincing example of the power of using object-oriented programming techniques to define an interactive graphics program. The program was assembled from reusable software components. The biggest prefabricated software component we used was the "blank" Java **Applet** class which we extended to create our own customized applet—the **DrawRect** applet. The process of extension consisted of implementing some mouse event-handler methods in some mouse event interfaces, and of overriding some **init()** and **paint()** methods in the "blank" prefabricated Java **Applet**. This overriding process was a bit like filling in some holes (originally containing blank event-handler and paint methods) with our own customized methods. In short, we programmed only by specifying the differences between our own applet and the inherited standard features of the prefabricated Java **Applet** and mouse event handler interfaces. Programming by expressing only what is different and assuming everything else stays the same is an economical way to build programs from reusable parts. We also used some standard graphics interface components by using Java's predefined **Point** and **Rectangle** classes. We used the **Point** class directly, without modification, to create a **Point** object to serve as the **anchorPoint** that saved the mouse-down point. However, we modified the **Rectangle** class by creating a new subclass, **DragRect**, having a new **normalize()** method. This **normalize()** method served as what the industry calls *glue code*. Glue code is code that is written to make some software parts "glue together"—meaning that it modifies inputs and outputs of standard prefabricated parts so that they are *plug-compatible*. Once the connectors for some parts have been modified to become plug-compatible, they can be plugged together to create a working application. The **normalize()**

*some conclusions*

method of the **DragRect** class was essentially some glue code we used to modify the rectangles created by the **mouseDragged** event handler to make them plug-compatible with the specifications of rectangles needed as inputs to the rectangle drawing method drawRect(x,y,width,height), given in Java's prefabricated **Graphics** object.

The essence of what we did to create this very small (53 line) **DrawRect** applet is very much typical of the flavor of object-oriented programming for building larger systems. Namely, we program by: (1) expressing differences, (2) filling in blanks in prefabricated parts, and (3) writing glue code to modify initially incompatible parts into plug-compatible parts and then by plugging the modified parts together. However, we have to surmount a barrier to gain the advantages of this software development method. Namely, we have to pay a high initial learning cost to learn what the prefabricated parts do and how to put them together to achieve intended effects.

*the essence of object-oriented programming*

It is not sufficient merely to read the parts catalog and learn about the specs for the parts, because the knowledge of how to put the parts together is not in the parts catalog. Think for a moment what you might do if somebody dumped a crate of parts on your desk and asked you to make a TV set. The parts might consist of a picture tube, a power supply, an antenna, some dials for volume and channel controls, and so forth. Having the parts in front of you does not give you the knowledge of how they are supposed to be assembled into a TV set. You can't get the knowledge by reading a TV parts catalog either. Instead, you have to identify a source of knowledge that explains some strategies (or gives hardware circuit diagrams) for putting the parts together and explains the *why* as well as the *how*.

*a critical knowledge barrier to surmount*

Building software systems from reusable software components is no different. You need to gain the knowledge of the strategies (or scripts or software patterns) for assembling software parts into systems, and you have to learn the *why* as well as the *how*.

## 2.2 REVIEW QUESTIONS

1. What is the difference between an object and a class in Java?
2. How do you define a subclass of a given class? Give an example.
3. What data fields and methods are inherited by a subclass **S** of a class **C**?
4. What is the signature of a method or a constructor? When do two methods have different signatures?
5. Let **S** be a subclass of a class **C**. What does it mean to say that a method **m** in **S** overrides a method **m** (having the same signature) in its superclass **C**?

## 2.2 EXERCISES

1. Write a new method **myRect.rotate()** that rotates a rectangle 90° around its center.

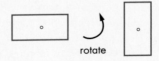

rotate

2. What happens if you delete the method invocation **dragRect.normalize();** on line 24 of Program 2.7? Can you still draw rectangles by dragging the mouse when the resulting applet is executed? If so, which kinds of rectangles can be drawn and which kinds cannot be drawn?

## **2.3** **The DrawShapes Applet**

### LEARNING OBJECTIVES

1. To learn how to use abstract classes and abstract methods.
2. To learn about inheritance and overriding in class hierarchies.
3. To learn how to use type polymorphism to advantage.
4. To learn how to draw into off-screen images to eliminate flashing.

*a slightly richer example*

This section presents a slightly richer example of OOP than the previous section—a **DrawShapes** applet that lets you draw a series of hollow or filled shapes, consisting of ovals, rectangles, or rounded rectangles. You can choose the characteristics of the drawn shapes using three popup menus and can create each actual shape by dragging the mouse. Each such drawn shape is inscribed inside a rectangle whose corners are the point where the mouse button was pressed when the mouse drag started and the point where the mouse button was released when the mouse drag ended. This example has been chosen to illustrate a few more features of OOP than the previous example, such as how class hierarchies and type polymorphism work in Java, and how to draw into an offscreen image to eliminate display flashing. Figure 2.8 illustrates some shapes created in the **DrawShapes** applet.

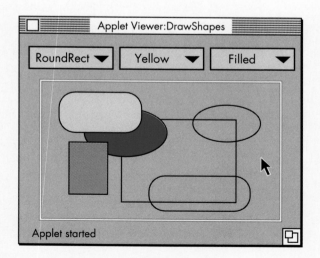

**Figure 2.8** Shapes Drawn with the DrawShapes Applet

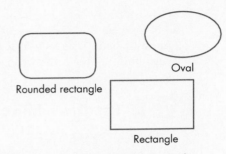

**Figure 2.9** Three Shapes Used by the DrawShapes Applet

We will be concerned with the three shapes shown in Fig. 2.9: rectangles, ovals, and rounded rectangles.

Let's begin the discussion of the technical details by looking at how these shapes fit inside rectangles. We define the **boundsBox** of a shape to be the smallest rectangle that encloses the shape. Figure 2.10 illustrates the bounds boxes of an oval and a rounded rectangle (although, for artistic reasons, the fit is not as tight as it is in the actual case where the bounds box **R** touches tangent points on the sides of the oval and shares line segments along the straight sides of the rounded rectangle).

We can invoke graphics drawing methods that belong to Java's **Graphics** object to draw either hollow or filled shapes that fit inside given bounds boxes. The filled shapes are drawn with interiors filled with the current foreground color taken from the current graphics context **g** in which the drawing methods are invoked. A Java graphics context object **g** supplies data that describe a current graphics drawing environment (such as the current foreground and background colors used when drawing). It also provides many useful drawing methods.

Thus, given a **Graphics** context object **g**, and given a **boundsBox**, if we make the method call

    g.fillOval(boundsBox.x, boundsBox.y, boundsBox.width, boundsBox.height);

it causes Java to paint the largest filled oval that fits inside the **boundsBox**, using **g**'s current foreground color as the fill color. Figure 2.11 shows what happens when this call is made.

If we make the method call

    g.drawRoundRect( boundsBox.x, boundsBox.y,
                     boundsBox.width, boundsBox.height, 20, 20);

*the boundsBox of a shape*

*using Java's Graphics drawing methods*

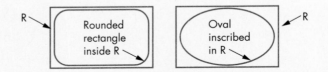

**Figure 2.10** Bounds Boxes for an Oval and a Rounded Rectangle

**Figure 2.11** A Filled Oval Inscribed in a Bounds Box Rectangle

it causes Java to draw the largest hollow (wire-framed) rounded rectangle that fits inside the **boundsBox**, having rounded corners that are quarter-circle arcs of a circle with a 20-pixel diameter.

We now define a class hierarchy consisting of a genealogical tree whose root is an abstract shape class called **Shape**. Figure 2.12 shows this class hierarchy. All the specific shapes in this hierarchy are *descendants* of this single abstract **Shape** class, and each specific shape, such as a filled oval, has the abstract **Shape** class as an *ancestor*. (We use the metaphors of family relationships when talking about such a class hierarchy, as in saying "the **HollowOval** class is the parent of the **FilledOval** class.")

*the Shape class hierarchy*

When we define the **Shape** class as an abstract class it means that no actual object is ever created to be an instance of the **Shape** class. Instead, we will define hollow ovals, rectangles, and rounded rectangles as subclasses of the **Shape** class, and then we will define filled ovals, rectangles, and rounded rectangles to be subclasses having their respective hollow shapes as parents. All specific shapes thus become descendants of the ancestral **Shape** class. The downward pointing arrows in Figure 2.12 illustrate the subclass relationships in this hierarchy.

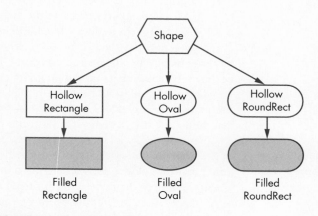

**Figure 2.12** The Shape Class Hierarchy

Each shape class in this class hierarchy has a distinct separate **draw()** method defined for it. When we have an object **shapeObject** that is an instance of one of the particular kinds of shapes in this hierarchy and we invoke its **draw()** method by writing

    shapeObject.draw();

it causes the particular object to be drawn using its own individual shape's drawing method. This means that if **shapeObject** is a hollow oval, then a hollow oval will be drawn, and if **shapeObject** is a filled rectangle, then a rectangle will be drawn that is filled with the current foreground color, and so forth.

Now comes the interesting part. If we have a list of shapes that are all objects that are instances of the various special shapes in the shape class hierarchy, and we invoke the **draw()** method on each shape in the list, each shape object gets drawn using its own individualized drawing method. The various shape objects on the list are not only instances of particular shapes in the shape hierarchy, they are also values of the general **Shape** type. For example, if you had declared a variable **myShape** to be of type **Shape**, as in the declaration

    Shape myShape;

you can later assign as the value of **myShape** one of the specialized shape objects that is an instance of any of the particular subclasses of shapes in the **Shape** hierarchy, as in the assignment

    myShape = new FilledOval();

Some time later (say, after the dimensions and color of this filled oval have been determined) you invoke the drawing method on **myShape**, as in

    myShape.draw();

sending the "draw
yourself" message to
a shape

Then what happens is that, in the metaphor of message passing, you send the message "draw yourself" to the object that is the current value of the variable **myShape**. This object, a filled oval object, receives the message, which tells it to invoke its own **draw()** method, and proceeds to draw a filled oval using its own individual drawing method.

If you then have an entire list containing instances of **Shape** objects, you can send the **draw()** message to each shape on this list, causing the entire list of shapes to be drawn (each using its own appropriate drawing method).

This is what we shall be doing in the **DrawShapes** applet. Each time the user drags the mouse, we'll create a new shape of the appropriate sort (having characteristics determined by the current settings in the popup menus). We'll add this shape to the end of a growing list of drawn shapes, and we'll send the **draw()** message to each shape in the list. This causes each shape in the list to be drawn in background-to-foreground order, as we go down the list sending **draw()** messages to the shapes in the order in which the shapes themselves were entered onto the end of the list. Also, we draw this list of shapes first into an offscreen image and then we transfer the completed image to the applet viewing window to avoid the *flashing effect* that occurs if we repeatedly draw the list of shapes over and over while the mouse is being dragged by the user.

```
 |   abstract class Shape {
 |
 |       protected Color color;
 |       protected DragRect boundsBox;        // the boundsBox is the smallest
5|                                            // rectangle enclosing the shape
 |
 |       abstract void draw(Graphics g);      // abstract placeholder method that
 |                                            // gets instantiated in subclasses
 |   }
```

**Program 2.13** The Definition of the Abstract Shape Class

*using a Java Vector to hold
an expandable shape list*

The data structure we use to hold the growing list of shapes to draw is a prefabricated entity taken from the java.util package called a **Vector**. In Java, a **Vector** is just an expandable array. It starts out as an array of objects of any kind whatsoever, and its initial capacity can be set by an appropriate constructor at the time it is first created. Each new shape is added to the end of the sequence of shapes already stored in this **Vector**. If the addition of a new shape exceeds the capacity of the **Vector**, a new **Vector** of greater capacity is allocated, the old **Vector**'s contents are transferred to the new **Vector**, and the new shape is appended to the end of the sequence in this new **Vector** of enlarged capacity. The name of the variable holding the **Vector** used in the **DrawShapes** applet is shapeList.

Before we examine the entire program for the **DrawShapes** applet, let's look at the way we define the class hierarchy of shapes in Java. Program 2.13 gives the definition of the abstract **Shape** class.

On lines 3 and 4 of Program 2.13, the data fields of an abstract **Shape** are defined. Namely, each **Shape** is defined to have a color that is a Java **Color** object, and a boundsBox that is a **DragRect** object. Here, the **DragRect** class is the same class we defined in Program 2.5 for the previous **DrawRect** applet. When we define subclasses of the abstract **Shape** class, each such subclass will inherit the color and boundsBox fields from its parent. Consequently, each individual specific shape object will have its own color field and boundsBox field. The modifier **protected**, used on lines 3 and 4 in Program 2.13, specifies a special access (or visibility) restriction for the color and boundsBox fields. Any data field that is marked as **protected** in a class **C** is visible only in subclasses that are descended from the ancestor class **C**, but is not visible to users outside the class hierarchy descending from **C**.

*protected data fields*

Let's now look at the definition of the **HollowOval** class that has the abstract **Shape** class as its immediate parent in the shape hierarchy, given in Program 2.14.

```
 |   class HollowOval extends Shape {
 |
 |       void draw(Graphics g) {
 |           g.setColor(Color.black);
5|           g.drawOval( boundsBox.x, boundsBox.y,
 |                           boundsBox.width, boundsBox.height);
 |       }
 |
 |   }
```

**Program 2.14** The Definition of the HollowOval Class

Line 1 of Program 2.14 says that the HollowOval class extends the Shape class. This is Java's way of saying that the HollowOval class is a subclass of the Shape class. The word **extends** is a good choice because subclasses always *extend* the meaning of their parents by adding new customized features. In particular, the HollowOval class extends the meaning of the abstract shape class by supplying its own version of the draw() method. In this case, we observe that the individualized **draw()** method of the HollowOval class *overrides* the abstract draw() method of the Shape class. You can now see that the word "override" means the same as "substitutes for" because the individual draw() method of a HollowOval substitutes for the abstract draw() method of the abstract Shape class whenever the draw() method of a HollowOval object is invoked. Note that each individual HollowOval object created during the running of a program will have two data fields, a color field and a boundsBox field, because these fields are *inherited* from the abstract Shape class by subclasses such as the HollowOval subclass.

The action of the HollowOval draw() method, given on lines 3:7 of Program 2.14, is first to set the foreground color of the graphics environment g to be black (using g.setColor(Color.black) given on line 4) and then to draw a hollow (wire-frame) oval, using the g.drawOval method call given on lines 5:6.

The FilledOval class definition is given in Program 2.15. Note that on line 1 of this program, the FilledOval class is defined to be a subclass of the HollowOval class. (We know this is so because the class FilledOval is defined so that it **extends** the HollowOval class definition.) All that the FilledOval class definition offers to extend its superclass HollowOval, is to define its own **draw()** method on lines 3:8, thus overriding the draw() method of its parent (which draws a black wire-frame oval). On line 4, the method call g.setColor(color); causes the foreground color of the current graphics environment g to be set to the value of the color field of the current object. This color field is inherited from the parent HollowOval class, which, in turn inherited it from the abstract Shape class. (We will see later that the color field of each shape will be set using the color designated by the current color popup menu setting at the time the shape object is created.) Lines 5:6 cause the FilledOval draw() method to draw an actual filled oval that is inscribed in the object's **boundsBox** using the current foreground color (that has just been set to the object's color immediately before).

After this occurs, we wish to draw a black wire-frame around the filled oval (an old-fashioned artist's photo retouching trick that gives it good graphic contrast when viewed in a scene containing a variety of other shapes). To do this, we want to call

```
    |    class FilledOval extends HollowOval {
    |
    |        void draw(Graphics g) {
    |            g.setColor(color);
    |            g.fillOval(boundsBox.x, boundsBox.y,
  5 |                    boundsBox.width, boundsBox.height);
    |            super.draw(g);              // call the parent class's draw
    |        }                              // method to draw a wire frame
    |                                       // around the filled oval
    |
    |    }
```

**Program 2.15** The Definition of the FilledOval Class

the **draw()** method of the parent class **HollowOval** from within the local **draw()** method for a **FilledOval** that overrides the parent's **draw()** method. The way to do this is to make the method call **super.draw();** given on line 7 of Program 2.15. Here, the word **super** refers to the *superclass* of the class containing the given method. The superclass of the **FilledOval** class is just the **HollowOval** class, so **super.draw()** refers to the drawing method of the **HollowOval** class. The effect of executing **super.draw()** within the **draw()** method of a **FilledOval** is to invoke its parent's **draw()** method—namely to draw a black wire-framed oval around the filled oval area. This produces exactly the artistic effect we want.

The definitions of the remaining classes for hollow and filled rectangles and rounded rectangles follow the same pattern as those for the hollow and filled oval classes. Lines 185:273 of Program 2.16 give the details.

Given this preparation, it's time to look at the listing of the **DrawShapes** applet in Program 2.16. We begin now a *rough explanation* of how it works—not a detailed explanation. The intent is to convey the *flavor* of how a Java applet is assembled with glue code using software components drawn from a software component library (namely, the **java.awt** and **java.util** packages plus the prefabricated Java **Applet** class with blanks to fill in).

Lines 1:3 of Program 2.16 import the Java **Applet** class from the **java.applet** package, and also import the **java.awt** and **java.util** packages. After the **import** statements, the classes in these packages are available for direct reference in the remainder of the program.

Lines 5:6 give the header for the definition of the **DrawShapes** applet which states that it **extends** (i.e., is a subclass of) the standard Java **Applet** and also **implements** the **MouseListener** and **MouseMotionListener** interfaces. We define the actions of our customized applet by supplying method definitions that override standard method definitions in the standard Java **Applet** and that supply implementations for all methods in the mouse listener interfaces. This is equivalent to saying that our specialized custom methods *fill in the blanks* in the standard **Applet** and standard mouse listener interfaces. In particular, when a Java applet is executed, the applet viewer or web browser that executes the applet passes messages to the applet to get it to invoke various of its standard methods. Specifically, the **init()** method of the applet is invoked exactly once at the beginning of each applet's execution. Also, each applet's **start()** and **stop()** methods are invoked by a web browser in order to stop and restart the execution of the applet (perhaps because user attention shifted somewhere else outside the applet during the web page browsing process). Finally, each applet's **destroy()** method gets executed exactly once at the end of an applet's life, giving it an opportunity to release resources it no longer needs. Only the **init()** method is overridden in the **DrawShapes** applet (on lines 28:57). This **init()** method takes the following four actions.

*executing the standard Java applet*

(1) On line 29 it creates a new **Vector** object with an initial capacity to hold ten shapes and assigns this **Vector** object to be the value of the variable **shapeList**. If more than ten shapes are created and stored in the **shapeList**, the method that adds new elements to the end of the list expands the **Vector** to accommodate the growth. The applet's **shapeList** data field is declared to be of type **Vector** on line 8. Note that each such applet data field acts like a global variable with respect to the text of the applet's method definitions. That is, you can use the variable **shapeList** within any method

*the actions of the DrawShapes init() method*

defined inside the DrawShapes applet class definition to access or assign the value of the applet's shapeList data field, just as if the shapeList variable had been declared global to the text of a procedure or function in an ordinary non-object-oriented programming language.

(2) On line 30, the anchorPoint data field (declared earlier on line 16) is set to a newly constructed Point object, using the constructor Point(0,0). As we mentioned before, the Point class in the java.awt package does not have a no-arg constructor of the form Point(). So we have to use the two-argument constructor Point(0,0) instead.

(3) Lines 32:52 create three popup menus for choices of shapes, colors, and fill and install these popup menus in the applet user interface, using method calls such as add(shapeChoice) found on line 36. In the absence of more specific instructions, a default Java *layout manager* places these popup menus in a row at the top of the applet's drawing area.

(4) Lines 54:55 set up the applet's mouse event handlers to intercept mouse events that are generated when the mouse button is pressed and when the mouse changes position as it is dragged. They do this by adding the applet as a mouse listener for mouse events and as a mouse motion listener for mouse drag events. The use of the Java reserved word this on lines 54:55 designates the current Applet object itself to be the event listener that will intercept and handle mouse events when they are generated by user actions during applet execution.

The DrawShapes applet next defines implementations for mouse event handlers such as the mousePressed and mouseDragged methods. The mousePressed method definition begins on line 60. Each time the mouse button is pressed by the user, a mouse event is generated and is passed as a parameter to its designated listener to be handled by the listener's mousePressed method. This mouse event parameter is a MouseEvent object that contains data fields giving the x and y coordinates of the "mouse down" point. Earlier on line 18, an applet data field variable s of type Shape was declared. This Shape variable will be initialized to an appropriate specific shape object in the Shape class hierarchy depending on the current settings of the popup menus. Lines 63:65 read the strings that are the current choices of the three popup menus and store them in string variables corresponding to each choice. Lines 67:83 create a new hollow or filled oval, rectangle, or rounded rectangle object, specified by the fillString and shapeString, and assign this specialized shape object to be the value of the Shape variable s. (Note how the variable s declared to be of the abstract type Shape can hold as a value any object created as an instance of one of the specialized shape subclasses in the shape hierarchy of Figure 2.12. This illustrates how variables declared to be of type C in Java can hold as values objects that are instances of any of the subclasses of class C.) Lines 85:92 set the color field of shape s according to the color currently selected on the colorChoice popup menu. Line 95 sets the boundsBox of shape s to be a new DragRect object. (The DragRect class is the same extension of the Rectangle class that we used earlier in the DrawRect applet in Section 2.2, having a normalize() method to ensure that the rectangle is drawable by Java. The DragRect class definition is repeated on lines 185:197 of Program 2.16.) Line 98 appends the new shape s to the end of the shapeList vector, using the addElement method of the Vector class. The complete method call is shapeList.addElement(s);.

*defining the mousePressed event-handler method*

```
1   import java.applet.Applet;
    import java.util.*;                                    // contains the Vector class
    import java.awt.*;                          // "awt" is short for "abstract windows tools"

5   public class DrawShapes extends Applet
                    implements MouseListener, MouseMotionListener  {

        Vector    shapeList:                     // maintains a list of the drawn shapes

10      Choice    shapeChoice;                    // a popup menu for shape choices

        Choice    colorChoice;                   // a popup menu for color choices

        Choice    fillChoice;                    // a popup menu for the choice of filled or
15                                               // hollow shapes
        Point     anchorPoint;                   // saves the coordinates of the
                                                 // mousePressed point
        Shape     s;                             // the shape s will be a filled or hollow oval,
                                                 // rectangle or rounded rectangle
20      Dimension offScreenDimension;            // the dimension of the offscreen
                                                 // drawing image
        Image     offScreenImage;                // offscreen image used to eliminate
                                                 // flashing
        Graphics offScreenGraphics;              // a graphics drawing context for
25                                               // the offscreen Image

        /** create the DrawShapes Graphical User Interface (GUI) */
        public void init( ) {
            shapeList = new Vector(10);       // let the shapeList's initial capacity be 10
30          anchorPoint = new Point(0,0);

            shapeChoice = new Choice();                  // create a popup menu of
            shapeChoice.addItem("Oval");                 // three shape choices:
            shapeChoice.addItem("Rectangle");            // Oval, Rectangle,
35          shapeChoice.addItem("RoundRect");            // and RoundRect
            add(shapeChoice);

            colorChoice = new Choice();          // create a popup menu of three color
            colorChoice.addItem("Red");          // choices: Red, Yellow, and Blue
40          colorChoice.addItem("Yellow");
            colorChoice.addItem("Blue");
            add(colorChoice);

            fillChoice = new Choice();           // create a popup menu of two fill
50          fillChoice.addItem("Filled");        // choices: Filled and Hollow
            fillChoice.addItem("Hollow");
            add(fillChoice);

            addMouseListener(this);              // to enable the applet to intercept
55          addMouseMotionListener(this);        // and handle mouse events

        } // end init( )
```

**Program 2.16** The DrawShapes Applet (*continued*)

Program 2.16 The DrawShapes Applet *(continued)*

```
      |    /** handle mouse events */
      |
60    |    public void mousePressed(MouseEvent event) {
      |
      |        // create a new shape of appropriate type
      |            String shapeString = shapeChoice.getSelectedItem();
      |            String colorString = colorChoice.getSelectedItem();
65    |            String fillString = fillChoice.getSelectedItem();
      |
      |            if (fillString.equals("Hollow")) {
      |                if (shapeString.equals("Oval")) {
      |                    s = new HollowOval();
70    |                } else if (shapeString.equals("Rectangle")){
      |                    s = new HollowRectangle();
      |                } else {
      |                    s = new HollowRoundRect();
      |                }
75    |            } else {                                        // create a filled shape
      |                if (shapeString.equals("Oval")) {
      |                    s = new FilledOval();
      |                } else if (shapeString.equals("Rectangle")){
      |                    s = new FilledRectangle();
80    |                } else {
      |                    s = new FilledRoundRect();
      |                }
      |            }
      |
85    |        // set the new shape's color
      |            if (colorString.equals("Red")) {
      |                s.color = Color.red;
      |            } else if (colorString.equals("Yellow")){
      |                s.color = Color.yellow;
90    |            } else {
      |                s.color = Color.blue;
      |            }
      |
      |        // let the shape's boundsBox be an empty DragRect
95    |            s.boundsBox = new DragRect( );
      |
      |        // append the new shape to end of the shapeList
      |            shapeList.addElement(s);
      |
100   |        // save the mouse down (x,y) coordinates as the anchorPoint
      |            anchorPoint.x = event.getX( );
      |            anchorPoint.y = event.getY( );
      |
      |    } // end mousePressed
105   |
      |    /** we must implement all unused mouse event methods using blank */
      |    /** methods in order to satisfy the compiler that we have implemented */
      |    /** the entire MouseListener and MouseMotionListener interfaces */
      |    public void MouseEntered(MouseEvent event) {   }
110   |    public void MouseExited(MouseEvent event) {   }
      |    public void MouseClicked(MouseEvent event) {   }
      |    public void MouseMoved(MouseEvent event) {   }
```

*(continued)*

Program 2.16 The DrawShapes Applet *(continued)*

```
        |    public void mouseDragged(MouseEvent event) {
        |
 115 |        // retrieve the boundsBox rectangle of Shape s
        |            DragRect dragRect = s.boundsBox;
        |            dragRect.setBounds(              // set the dragRect to a rectangle with
        |                    anchorPoint.x, anchorPoint.y,      // the mouse drag point
        |                    event.getX( ) – anchorPoint.x,     // and the anchorPoint
 120 |                    event.getY( ) – anchorPoint.y );    // at opposite corners
        |
        |            dragRect.normalize();                 // make sure the dragRect has (x,y)
        |                                                  // as its top-left corner, and has
        |                                                  // a positive width and height
 125 |
        |        // draw all the shapes in the applet window
        |            repaint();
        |
        |    } // end mouseDragged
 130 |
        |
        |
        |    public void mouseReleased(MouseEvent event) {
        |            repaint();
 135 |    }// end mouseReleased
        |
        |
        |
        |    public void paint(Graphics g) {
 140 |            update(g);
        |    }
        |
        |
        |    /** draw all the shapes. */
 145 |
        |    public void update(Graphics g) {
        |                                            // get the width and height dimensions
        |            Dimension d = getSize();                // of the applet's drawing area
        |
 150 |        // create an off-screen graphics drawing environment if none existed
        |        // or if the user resized the applet drawing area to a different size
        |            if ( (offScreenGraphics == null)
        |                || (d.width != offScreenDimension.width)
        |                || (d.height != offScreenDimension.height) ) {
 155 |                    offScreenDimension = d;
        |                    offScreenImage = createImage(d.width,d.height);
        |                    offScreenGraphics = offScreenImage.getGraphics();
        |            }
        |
 160 |        // erase the previous image
        |            offScreenGraphics.setColor(getBackground());
        |            offScreenGraphics.fillRect(0,0,d.width,d.height);
        |
        |        // paint a raised border around the drawing area
 165 |            offScreenGraphics.draw3DRect(5,30,d.width–11, d.height–31, true);
        |            offScreenGraphics.draw3DRect(8,33,d.width–17, d.height–37, false);
        |
```

*(continued)*

Program 2.16 The DrawShapes Applet (*continued*)

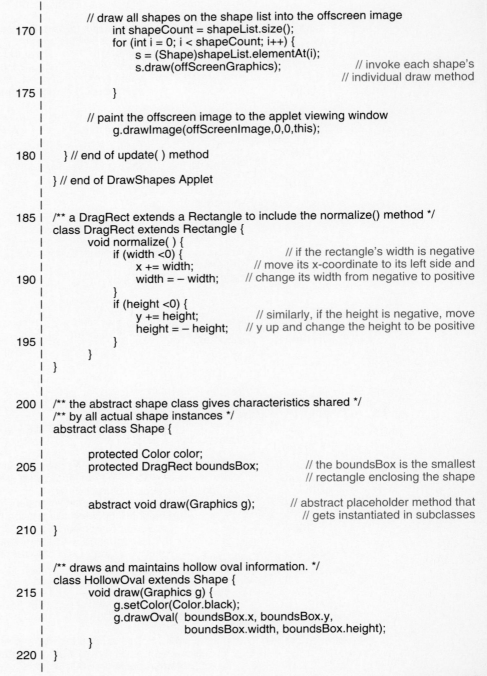

```
         // draw all shapes on the shape list into the offscreen image
170          int shapeCount = shapeList.size();
             for (int i = 0; i < shapeCount; i++) {
                 s = (Shape)shapeList.elementAt(i);
                 s.draw(offScreenGraphics);            // invoke each shape's
                                                       // individual draw method
175          }

         // paint the offscreen image to the applet viewing window
             g.drawImage(offScreenImage,0,0,this);

180    } // end of update( ) method

     } // end of DrawShapes Applet


185 /** a DragRect extends a Rectangle to include the normalize() method */
    class DragRect extends Rectangle {
         void normalize( ) {
             if (width <0) {                  // if the rectangle's width is negative
                 x += width;                  // move its x-coordinate to its left side and
190              width = − width;             // change its width from negative to positive
             }
             if (height <0) {
                 y += height;                 // similarly, if the height is negative, move
                 height = − height;           // y up and change the height to be positive
195          }
         }
    }


200 /** the abstract shape class gives characteristics shared */
    /** by all actual shape instances */
    abstract class Shape {

         protected Color color;
205      protected DragRect boundsBox;              // the boundsBox is the smallest
                                                    // rectangle enclosing the shape

         abstract void draw(Graphics g);            // abstract placeholder method that
                                                    // gets instantiated in subclasses
210 }


    /** draws and maintains hollow oval information. */
    class HollowOval extends Shape {
215      void draw(Graphics g) {
             g.setColor(Color.black);
             g.drawOval( boundsBox.x, boundsBox.y,
                         boundsBox.width, boundsBox.height);
         }
220 }
```

(*continued*)

Program 2.16 The DrawShapes Applet *(continued)*

```
     | /** draws and maintains hollow rectangle information. */
     | class HollowRectangle extends Shape{
225  |     void draw(Graphics g) {
     |         g.setColor(Color.black);
     |         g.drawRect(boundsBox.x, boundsBox.y,
     |                       boundsBox.width, boundsBox.height);
     |     }
230  | }
     |
     |
     | /** draws and maintains hollow rounded rectangle information. */
     | class HollowRoundRect extends Shape{
235  |     void draw(Graphics g) {
     |         g.setColor(Color.black);
     |         g.drawRoundRect(boundsBox.x, boundsBox.y,
     |                       boundsBox.width, boundsBox.height, 20,20);
     |     }
240  | }
     |
     |
     | /** draws and maintains filled oval information. */
     | class FilledOval extends HollowOval {
245  |     void draw(Graphics g) {
     |         g.setColor(color);
     |         g.fillOval(boundsBox.x, boundsBox.y,
     |                 boundsBox.width, boundsBox.height);
     |         super.draw(g);              // call the parent class's draw
250  |     }                              // method to draw a wire frame
     | }                                  // around the filled oval
     |
     |
     | /** draws and maintains filled rectangle information. */
255  | class FilledRectangle extends HollowRectangle{
     |     void draw(Graphics g) {
     |         g.setColor(color);
     |         g.fillRect(boundsBox.x, boundsBox.y,
     |                 boundsBox.width, boundsBox.height);
260  |         super.draw(g);
     |     }
     | }
     |
     |
265  | /** draws and maintains filled rounded rectangle information. */
     | class FilledRoundRect extends HollowRoundRect{
     |     void draw(Graphics g) {
     |         g.setColor(color);
     |         g.fillRoundRect(boundsBox.x, boundsBox.y,
270  |                         boundsBox.width, boundsBox.height, 20, 20);
     |         super.draw(g);
     |     }
     | }
     |
```

Then, on lines 101:102 the (x,y) coordinates of the mouse-down point are retrieved from the **event** object that stored them, using the method calls **event.getX( )** and **event.getY( )**, and are saved as the (x,y) coordinates of the **anchorPoint** data field (for later use during mouse dragging to construct the drag rectangle's dimensions).

Lines 109:112 supply blank mouse method handler definitions to implement all mouse event methods that the applet does not use. The Java compiler requires the applet to implement *all* methods in the **MouseListener** and **MouseMotionListener** interfaces because line 6, in effect, states a contractual promise that the applet will implement both of these listener interfaces. The Java compiler enforces this contract.

The **mouseDragged** method on lines 113:129 is invoked each time the mouse changes position when it is being dragged and receives, as its calling parameter, a **MouseEvent** object, **event**, whose method calls, **event.getX( )** and **event.getY( )**, give the respective **x** and **y** coordinates of the current mouse-drag position. Let's decode it step-by-step to see how it works.

The first step is to retrieve the bounds box rectangle that was stored in the **boundsBox** data field of shape **s** when **s** was created during the action of the **mousePressed** method. This is the purpose of line 116 where a reference to the rectangle **s.boundsBox** becomes the value of the new **DragRect** variable **dragRect**. Note how the **dragRect** variable is both declared (using "DragRect dragRect") and initialized (using "= s.boundsBox") in one convenient step recalling that Java allows declarations to be given anywhere in a block of statements. Now, by invoking the **setBounds()** method of a **dragRect** object, the **dragRect** has its data fields set on lines 117:120.

On line 118 the (x,y) fields of the **dragRect** are set to be the (x,y) coordinates of the mouse-down point, saved previously as the (x,y) coordinates of the **anchorPoint**. Then, on lines 119:120, the **width** and **height** of the rectangle are calculated to be the respective differences between the (x,y) coordinates of the current mouse-drag point and the (x,y) coordinates of the **anchorPoint**. Here, the **dragRect width** is set to **event.getX( ) – anchorPoint.x**, and the **dragRect height** is set to **event.getY( ) –**

*normalizing the dragRect*

**anchorPoint.y**. If the current mouse-drag point is above or to the left of the original mouse-down point, saved as the **anchorPoint**, then one or both of the **width** and **height** of the **dragRect** will have been set to a negative number, creating an improper rectangle that, when given to Java's drawing methods, will cause nothing to be drawn. As we saw before in the **DrawRect** applet of Section 2.2, we need to correct any such possible deficiency by applying the **normalize()** method of the **dragRect** class. This is performed on line 122.

```
|
|              dragRect.normalize();          // make sure the dragRect has (x,y)
|                                             // as its top-left corner, and has
|                                             // a positive width and height
```

Following the method call **dragRect.normalize()**, we can rest assured that the **dragRect** has a positive **width** and **height**, and that its (x,y) data fields refer to its top-left corner, thus constituting a **boundsBox** rectangle that will work properly in conjunction with the Java drawing methods for the particular type of shape this **boundsBox** contains.

*invoking repaint()*

Now comes the drawing action. On line 127, we invoke the repaint() method to draw all of the shapes in the current drawing window. The repaint() method, in turn, invokes the paint() method to paint an image. We will see in a moment how the paint() method works.

Lines 133:135 give a mouseReleased method that merely redraws the shapes on the shapeList. This method does not play a critical role in the DrawShapes applet, and could easily have been omitted. It is included to provide the opportunity to make the point that a mouseReleased method exists in Java that can sometimes be used to advantage. For example, on occasion, you want to drag a dimmed outline of a shape (or an icon, or an image) around the screen, and when you release the mouse at the end of the drag, you want to paint a full color image of the shape whose dimmed outline has just been dragged around. The mouse-released event occurs exactly when the mouse button comes up at the end of the dragging action, presenting the opportunity to implement the desired effect.

On lines 139:141, the paint() method is defined. It simply passes the responsibility for its action to the update() method. The paint() method calls the update() method when it wants to update those portions of the screen that have changed and need to be redrawn.

```
     |     public void paint(Graphics g) {
140 |         update(g);
     |     }
```

*what the update()*
*method does*

Finally, we come to the update() method that is responsible for doing the actual drawing of the shapes in the shapeList to the screen. Briefly, it draws the shapes into an offscreen image by sending the draw() message to each shape on the shapeList and then transfers the completed image of all drawn shapes from the offscreen image to the actual screen visible to the user. This way, it eliminates the flickering effect that would have occurred had it drawn the entire list of shapes in background-to-foreground order each time the mouse position was changed during mouse dragging.

First, on line 148, the update() method declares a Dimension variable d and initializes it to be the size of the current DrawShapes applet's on-screen graphics drawing area using

```
         Dimension d = getSize();
```

Note here that the Dimension object returned by the getSize() method is an object that has two data fields: a width and a height.

*creating the offscreen*
*drawing environment*

Then, on lines 152:158, the update() method creates a new offscreen graphics drawing environment under two circumstances: (1) no such offscreen graphics environment existed before (in which case, the object reference to it will have been null, and the test offScreenGraphics == null will return true), or (2) the user resized the applet's on-screen drawing window, giving it a different width or height, and a new offscreen image with a matching width and height needs to be created.

```
150 |         // create an off-screen graphics drawing environment if none existed
    |         // or if the user resized the applet drawing area to a different size
    |              if ( (offScreenGraphics == null)
    |                  | | (d.width != offScreenDimension.width)
    |                  | | (d.height != offScreenDimension.height) ) {
155 |                      offScreenDimension = d;
    |                      offScreenImage = createImage(d.width,d.height);
    |                      offScreenGraphics = offScreenImage.getGraphics();
    |              }
```

The next step is to erase the image previously drawn into the offscreen image. (Failure to do this results in a trajectory of superimposed partial images of the current shape whose bounds box is being dragged in the area not overlapped by the previously drawn shapes.) Line 161 invokes the **getBackground()** method to return the background color

**erasing the offscreen Image**

of the current applet's drawing environment, and it sets the color of the offscreen graphics environment to be this color. On line 162, the method invocation **fillRect(0,0,d.width,d.height)** fills the entire offscreen graphics image with the current background color. (The top-left point of the bounds box rectangle surrounding this off-screen image is at **(0,0)**, and its width and height are given by the **Dimension** object **d**.)

```
160 |         // erase the previous image
    |              offScreenGraphics.setColor(getBackground());
    |              offScreenGraphics.fillRect(0,0,d.width,d.height);
```

On lines 165:166, a raised border is painted around the user's drawing area again using the dimensions **d.width** and **d.height** to identify the borders of the drawing area, and allowing about 30 pixels of blank space on top of the drawing area to fit in the popup menus for the shape, color, and fill menu choices.

```
    |         // paint a raised border around the drawing area
    |              offScreenGraphics.draw3DRect(5,30,d.width–11, d.height–31, true);
    |              offScreenGraphics.draw3DRect(8,33,d.width–17, d.height–37, false);
```

Next, on lines 170:175, the entire list of shapes is drawn in background-to-foreground order by sending the **draw()** message to each shape on the **shapeList**. Line 170 initializes a new **shapeCount** variable to the number of shapes stored in the **shapeList**. Lines 171:175 loop through the **shapeList**, extracting the $i^{th}$ **shapeList** object with **shapeList.elementAt(i)**, typecasting it to be a **Shape** object by applying the **(Shape)** typecast operator, assigning the resulting shape to be the value of the **Shape** variable **s**, and finally sending it the message **s.draw(offScreenGraphics)**, which essentially tells each shape to "draw yourself into the offscreen graphics image." Note that when each individual shape object receives this **draw()** message, it invokes its own custom

**drawing the list of shapes**

**draw()** method (that overrides the abstract **draw()** method of the abstract **Shape** class). Here we see *type polymorphism* in action. A variable **s** declared to be of abstract type **Shape**, holds an actual object whose type is that of one of the customized subclasses in the **Shape** class hierarchy, and when the abstract **draw()** message is passed to the object **s**, it uses its own customized individual **draw()** method to do the actual drawing. Thus, if the value of **s** is of type **FilledOval**, a filled oval gets drawn, whereas if the type of s is HollowRectangle, a hollow rectangle gets drawn, and so forth. This is very powerful, and requires the use of awkward and time-consuming techniques to express in non-object-oriented languages.

```
        |       // draw all shapes on the shape list into the offscreen image
    170 |           int shapeCount = shapeList.size();
        |           for (int i = 0; i < shapeCount; i++) {
        |               s = (Shape)shapeList.elementAt(i);
        |               s.draw(offScreenGraphics);          // invoke each shape's
        |                                                   // individual draw method
    175 |           }
```

The final step in the update() method is to transfer the newly drawn offscreen image to the user's viewing screen. Line 178 does this.

```
        |       // paint the offscreen image to the applet viewing window
        |           g.drawImage(offScreenImage,0,0,this);
```

The update() method is the last of the custom methods given in the DrawShapes applet. The closing curly brace terminating the definition of the DrawShapes applet class is therefore given on line 182.

Lines 185:273 then define the remaining classes in Program 2.16. We have already seen these classes, which consist first of the DragRect class defined on lines 186:197, and then of the various classes in the Shape class hierarchy given on lines 200:273.

The structure of Program 2.16 is actually that of an *unnamed package*. It starts with the import statements on lines 1:3. It then gives a sequence of class definitions for the classes in the package. Each class in the package can refer to the data fields and methods of other classes in the package that are marked as public or that are unmarked (i.e., that have no access modifiers such as private, protected, or public). Outside the package, only the classes, methods, and data fields marked as public within the package are visible. We could have created a *named package* by giving a package declaration such as

*the textual structure of Java packages*

        package shapeDraw;

as the first statement in the file. You can create packages of classes you want to offer for use by others as software components. The java.awt and java.util packages are two packages of software components used by Program 2.16 offered by the creators of Java to provide convenient software components for building Java applets and applications.

## **2.3** REVIEW QUESTIONS

1. What are the access characteristics of a **protected** data field or method in a class?
2. How can you use abstract classes and methods to provide uniform treatment for a collection of objects that express variations on a common theme? Give an example.

3. What is a Java package? What is its textual structure? Give an example.
4. How can you eliminate flickering when drawing an image on the user's screen?

## 2.3 EXERCISE

1. Experiment with the artistic effects of drawing flickering images with smeared trajectories in the **DrawShapes applet** by deleting line 178 in Program 2.16 and by changing line 173 to be **s.draw(g);**.

## 2.4 Drawing Some Conclusions

### LEARNING OBJECTIVES

1. To understand the flavor of OOP that relies on heavy use of prefabricated software components.
2. To understand the role of standard applet method invocations.
3. To learn about the high cost of going up the OOP learning curve, and about the essential role of scripts and strategies.

Let's step back for a moment and reflect on some global issues that come to light from thinking about the **DrawShapes** applet given in Program 2.16. How did we create the **DrawShapes** applet? Did we start from scratch and write the code on a blank sheet of paper? Or did we assemble some prefabricated software components using some glue code? The answer is, of course, that we heavily used prefabricated software components. We took an expandable array, called a **Vector**, from the **java.util** package, and we used it to hold the **shapeList**, consisting of various shapes to be drawn. We defined a class hierarchy of such shapes by starting with an abstract **Shape** class at the root of a shape hierarchy tree, and by defining descendant subclasses having customized drawing methods, but each possessing a **color**, a **boundsBox**, and a common **draw()** method calling expression, in common with all other shapes.

*making heavy use of prefabricated software components*

From the **java.applet** package, we imported the blank prefabricated Java applet, **java.applet.Applet**, and we filled in the blanks in this standard Applet by overriding the **init()**, **paint()**, and **update()** methods. We also designated the applet to be a listener and event handler for mouse events and we supplied method definitions for the **mousePressed()**, **mouseDragged()**, and **mouseReleased()** methods. We depended on the Java applet execution system to make sure that method calls on our customized methods occurred at the proper times to cause our applet to perform correctly. That is, we expected the **init()** method to be invoked exactly once at the beginning of the applet's execution, we expected the mouse event methods to be invoked during mouse dragging actions, and we expected the **paint()** and **update()** methods to be invoked when the applet needed to draw changed images to the user's screen. This made event-driven programming, of the sort requiring thousands of lines of code in non-object-oriented languages, into a fairly brief exercise of only five pages in Java. We got by with such concise expression because we programmed only by specifying

*expecting the standard method invocations*

differences. Anything in the standard applet that we didn't need to change, we didn't need to mention. Instead, we mentioned only those customizations that made our applet different from the standard applet.

We also used software components in the java.awt package to draw the shapes in the shapeList into an offscreen image, to produce a flicker-free image seen by the user when the mouse was being dragged during drawing.

In addition, we implemented a special subclass of the predefined Rectangle class, called a DragRect, to supply a normalize() method, needed to convert rectangles from their possibly undrawable form into the proper drawable form. The normalize() method illustrated the concept of *glue code*, needed to convert prefabricated software components into *plug-compatible* form, given that they were not initially plug-compatible. To use an analogy, such glue code functions like one of those plug-adapters you can buy before you travel to a foreign country with a different electrical system, so that you can use the electrical appliances you take with you from home. To use your own appliances in the foreign country, you first must plug an adapter into the foreign wall socket to convert it into a socket into which you can plug your own appliances.

glue code and plug-compatible components

Even though our DrawShapes example illustrated impressive conciseness of expression, you should never underestimate the cost of going up the learning curve to use the software components in a collection of reusable software components. The knowledge of how to use such parts is not in the parts themselves. Rather, you have to learn how to use the parts by studying examples of how the parts are assembled into subsystems that achieve desired effects. For instance, you need to study the example of how to use Java parts to eliminate flickering by drawing into an offscreen image, before you can expect to be able to duplicate this feature in new Java programs you create. Even though offscreen image drawing is one of the well-known standard "tricks of the trade" in computer graphics (used commonly in simulators and in generating animations), you have to see how an actual example of it works in Java before you can hope to have the knowledge of how to use this technique in your own Java programs. It is sometimes said that such examples constitute *software scripts*, or *software patterns*. (Another way of expressing a software script or software pattern is to provide a slightly more general type of program illustrated by the *program strategies* in this book. Such program strategies have comments in them in places where you are later expected to fill in actual Java code. Thus, they act as top-level outlines for actual Java programs, much as a top-level outline can be used by a person writing a story. The comments for the parts allow for more general substitution in the program strategies, so that the strategies stand for a more general family of similar programs than a specific example entirely hard-coded in Java.)

the high cost of going up the OOP learning curve

When you learn the scripts and strategies for how Java parts can be assembled into programs that achieve desired effects, you are enlarging your repertoire of techniques for programming. A strong, but probably correct, statement would be that you cannot use collections of prefabricated software components effectively to reduce your software development time unless you understand the programming scripts and strategies required to assemble the components to achieve the effect you desire. A collection of parts buys you no leverage unless you have the *knowledge* of how to put them together to do significant things.

In conclusion, you can view one of the enduring benefits of a data structures course as being centrally connected to the concept of providing you with a repertoire of general-purpose strategies for assembling well-studied software parts of various sorts into subsystems that have interesting and useful effects. You should seek to gain such strategic knowledge from studying the particulars in a given data structures book. These central concepts will come through, whether the book is written in Java or in some other programming language, just as the central concepts of biology can come through in a biology book, whether it is written in English or in some foreign language.

*the nature of the enduring benefits*

## **2.4** REVIEW QUESTIONS

1. When is the init() method of a Java applet executed?
2. When are the mousePressed(), mouseDragged(), and mouseReleased() methods executed in a Java applet that implements the mouse listener interfaces?
3. Give an example of *glue code* that converts Java objects into plug-compatible form.
4. If you read about all the classes in the two-volume series entitled, *The Java Application Program Interface*, cited in the references at the end of this chapter, will you then become an experienced Java programmer capable of writing a broad range of Java applications? If so, why? If not, why not?

## **2.4** EXERCISES

1. Use one of the references cited in the reference section at the end of this chapter to find out what role the parameter this plays in the method invocation g.drawImage(offScreenImage,0,0,this); on line 178 of Program 2.16.
2. Explain the general strategy for implementing in Java the commonly known computer graphics technique of drawing into an off-screen image buffer to avoid generating flickering images on the user's screen.

---

 **Pitfalls**

- *Trying to Play the Tune Before You Know the Score*

    It is a nearly fatal mistake to assume that you know enough to build a large object-oriented programming system successfully just because you have read about the software components in a class library. In fact, you'll need the additional knowledge of the scripts and strategies for assembling these components into subsystems to produce the desired effects you seek. (For example, the DrawShapes listing given in Program 2.16 contains the scripts for how to use off-screen image buffers to eliminate display flashing and for how to use Java Vectors to implement expandable lists.) Also, remember the lessons learned from the early days of software engineering that the use of formatted debugging aids can cut system debugging times in half. And follow the words of the wise who have found good object browsers to be essential to their attempts to comprehend how complex object-oriented programs work.

## ▮ Tips and Techniques

- *Use OOP Techniques to Build Prototypes of User-Interfaces*
    User-interfaces tend to be risk-prone portions of a software system, because it is hard to anticipate whether users will find them convenient and suitable. To reduce the risk that a user-interface design will turn out to be inadequate, you can build a prototype rapidly, and then test it on actual users to try to identify its shortcomings, if any, and to collect suggestions for improvements. If you have graphics object editors and user-directed object assembly systems available for your use, you will likely find that it is easy and cheap to build a rapid prototype of your user-interface.

- *Use OOP Software Component Libraries to Build Key Subsystems*
    Object-oriented programming libraries often contain objects that can be customized to generate major subsystems of a system, such as the file or printing subsystems. You customize them by overriding abstract methods that give you blanks to fill in by supplying missing details from your program. (Filling in these empty slots specifies the necessary connections to your program.) Using this approach, the cost of building key subsystems can be greatly reduced, and the reliability and user-convenience of the result can be greatly increased, compared to a conventional systems programming approach starting from scratch with a clean sheet of paper.

- *Use OOP Techniques to Structure Your Software System for Ease of Modification*
    Software maintenance and modification activities occupy a major fraction of the lifecycle of a large software system, and typically constitute from 70% to 90% of the system's lifetime cost. By using OOP techniques to structure your software system, you can often provide for ease of future modification and upgrade, since you can then introduce new subclasses that inherit the behaviors you want to retain, while expressing new modifications of behaviors using new method definitions.

## ▮ References for Further Study

A good book for gaining a quick but thorough understanding of the Java programming language is:

basics of Java

Arnold, Ken and Gosling, James, *The Java™ Programming Language*. Addison-Wesley, Reading, MA (1996).

Some references on the Java class libraries are:

Java Class Libraries

Chan, Patrick, and Lee, Rosanna, *The Java™ Class Libraries: An Annotated Reference.* Addison-Wesley, Reading, MA (1997).

Gosling, James, Yellin, Frank, et al., *The Java™ Application Programming Interface, Vol. 1: Core Packages, and Vol. 2: Window Toolkit and Applets.* Addison-Wesley, Reading, MA (1996).

A good tutorial on object-oriented programming in Java is:

Campione, Mary, and Walrath, Kathy, The Java™ Tutorial: Object-Oriented Programming for the Internet. Addison-Wesley, Reading, MA (1996).

*a good tutorial*

## ■ Chapter Summary

As its name implies, object-oriented programming focuses on a style of programming involving various *classes* of *objects*. These classes can be arranged in hierarchies in which *subclasses* are descended from *superclasses*.

*objects and classes*

An object can be thought of as a composite data structure having data fields, that is extended to have local functions, called *methods*, attached to it, and which *inherits* (i.e., has copies of) the data fields and methods of the objects in its superclasses. The data fields and methods can be made selectively visible or invisible to subclasses and external users of the object.

*methods, data fields, and inheritance*

Suppose the class of objects of type **X** is defined to be a subclass of the class of objects of type **Y**. Then, not only does an **X** inherit all the visible data fields and methods of objects of type **Y**, but also, an **X** can have a local method **M** defined for it which has the same name as a method, named **M**, defined for **Y**. In this case, we can arrange for **X**'s local method, **M**, to *override* (i.e., replace) the inherited method **M** that would normally be conferred on **X** by virtue of its being a descendant of **Y**.

*overriding*

In a nutshell, then, we could say that *object-oriented programming* consists of manipulating classes of objects, each of which can have its own *data fields* and *methods*, and in which separate classes can be related to one another by *subclassing*, *inheritance*, and *overriding*.

*OOP in a nutshell*

In object-oriented programming, the metaphor of *message passing* between objects is used to designate the action in which one object invokes another object's method. Moreover, many different kinds of objects can each have their own versions of an identically-named method (such as the **draw()** method), and each can perform its own different individual action in response to the invocation of this identically-named method.

*the message passing metaphor*

If **Y** is a superclass of **X**, then a variable of type **Y** can hold values of type **X**, implying that Java's rules for variables and their permissible value types are more general than those for ordinary non-object-oriented programming languages. This added generality can be quite useful when applying shared method names to collections of objects having different subclass types all of which express variation on a common theme and share common method names having different locally defined effects in the various subclasses.

*the useful generality of Java's type system*

Object-oriented programming can be used to express the structure of a system of objects in a clean modular fashion, particularly at the level of individual objects, each of which is defined to have a clean interface and can have hidden internal details. Libraries of objects can provide reusable software components, such as objects that allow you to generate complete file and printing subsystems. To use these library objects, you define individual methods that override the blank methods in the library objects, to establish the necessary connections with the rest of your program.

*object libraries with reusable software components*

Successful use of such library objects allows you to take advantage of a great deal of prefabricated labor without having to master the details of building such subsystems for yourself.

Even though OOP class libraries often provide powerful collections of reusable software components for software system builders, usually a steep learning curve is associated with becoming proficient in the successful use of the software components. Not only do you have to understand how each individual part works, you must also acquire the knowledge of successful *strategies* for combining the parts into subsystems that achieve the effects you desire. Sometimes you need to learn how to write *glue code* that modifies the parts so that they become *plug-compatible* and can then be plugged together to form a subsystem. This strategic knowledge of how to assemble parts into subsystems that achieve desired effects is not usually found in the descriptions of software components in the class libraries. Instead, it is found in well-chosen examples accompanied by detailed explanations that reveal important strategies for system building. For instance, the listing of the **DrawShapes** applet given in Program 2.16 provides an example of a source from which you can learn how to assemble Java software components to implement the commonly known computer graphics techniques for drawing into an off-screen image buffer to eliminate display flashing, and for using Java **Vector**s to implement expandable lists.

the need to learn software strategies for using class libraries successfully

# Linked
# Data Representations

## Introduction and Motivation

Linked data representations, and the algorithms that use them, are a major topic of study in computer science. Sometimes, linked representations support efficient algorithms. Linked data representations are especially useful for applications in which it is difficult to predict the size and shape of the data structures needed.

For example, programs such as MATHEMATICA® and MAPLE® manipulate symbolic mathematical expressions that can expand, shrink, and change shape in unpredictable ways during program execution as problems are solved. The space needed to hold representations of individual symbolic expressions cannot be allocated in advance. Instead, the required space is allocated in response to the program's incremental demands for additional storage during mathematical problem solving.

*handling unpredictable space requirements*

To create linked representations, we link separate blocks of storage together using *pointers*. A pointer is just the memory address of a block of storage. If a given block contains a pointer to a second block, we can follow this pointer to access the second block. By following pointers one after another, we can travel along an access path

*pointers*

contained in a linked data representation. In diagrams of linked data structures, we will represent pointers by arrows.

Moreover, starting with a given linked data structure, we can add or delete a particular block of data by adding or deleting pointers that point to it. This means that linked representations can grow or shrink piece-by-piece—in small increments—enabling them to change shape a step at a time, using just a few pointer operations on each piece. This possibility opens up a very interesting class of growth and combining properties for linked representations that computer scientists have explored extensively.

The class of linked data representations that become possible using these techniques can have important advantages when compared to other data representation methods, such as sequential data representations that are allocated inside arrays.

Our journey in this chapter on linked representations, and later in Chapter 5 when we cover *modularity* and *information hiding*, will eventually reveal to us that certain high-level data structures, such as lists, stacks, sets, trees, and queues, can be represented in many ways by lower-level data representations. Two broad classes of such lower-level representations are *sequential representations* and *linked representations*. These observations will, in turn, lead us to introduce the idea of *levels of data abstractions*. This idea is fundamental to computer science and is another of the recurring concepts that unifies the explanations in this book.

Objects and operations at higher levels of data abstraction are represented by organizing objects and operations at lower levels. For example, at the highest level of abstraction, we find *abstract data types* (ADTs)—structures such as *lists*, *stacks*, *sets*, *trees*, and *queues*. Each of these ADTs can be represented in a variety of different ways by lower-level representations, including those in the two broad classes—*sequential representations* and *linked representations*. At still lower levels, the linked representations can be represented in a variety of different ways, such as using parallel arrays or Java objects that contain references to other Java objects in their data fields.

Later we will develop extensively the themes that surround the levels of data abstraction illustrated in Fig. 3.1. Introducing the key notion of linked representations in this chapter lays groundwork essential to the understanding of how alternative representations can support more abstract data types. Chapters 6 through 9 develop various ADTs and their different representations.

The marginal notes read:

growth and combining laws

levels of data abstraction

essential groundwork

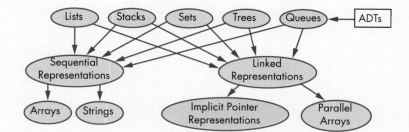

**Figure 3.1** Levels of Data Abstraction

For security reasons, Java does not provide explicit pointer values (in contrast to other programming languages such as C++ or Object Pascal). However, Java uses implicit pointers to access arrays and objects. In fact, Java divides its data values into two classes: *primitive data values* (such as integers, characters, boolean truth values, and floating point numbers) and *reference values* that are references to objects and arrays. Such Java reference values are just pointers to objects and arrays, even though Java does not provide any pointer following operators. Java reference values can be stored in data fields of objects, as items in arrays, or as values of variables. As we shall see, this provides a satisfactory basis for implementing linked data representations in Java.

*if Java has no pointers, how can it support linked representations?*

### Plan for the Chapter

We start with an intuitive discussion of pointers. Then we give two specific examples of linked representations in order to provide an intuitive feeling for how linked representations are used in important, real-world applications.

Next, we begin our study of the technical details of managing implicit references in Java by introducing a simple example of pointers—namely, pointers to **Rectangle** objects. We then introduce the diagramming language that will be used for pointers and linked representations in the remainder of this book. This pointer diagramming language is important because it provides a pictorial way to reason about linked representations that is programming language independent. That is, it works not only for Java, but for other programming languages as well.

*managing pointers in Java*

A topic of key importance—*linear linked lists*—is discussed next. We show how to declare the Java classes for list nodes and linked lists, how to create list node objects, and how to link them together. Following this, we study how to perform various important list operations such as insertion and deletion of nodes in lists. We also investigate how to search for a node on a linked list containing a given search key.

*linear linked lists*

The last section presents examples of linked representations that can be constructed from nodes having two links per node, such as two-way linked lists and linked binary trees. These illustrate that a given building block can be used to form a variety of different kinds of linked data representations, having differing shapes and organizational principles.

## 3.2   What are Pointers? The Basic Intuition

## LEARNING OBJECTIVES

1. To understand what pointers are and how they can be used.
2. To appreciate the importance of pointers in real-world systems.

Linked data representations can be supported by any addressable storage medium. The random-access memory (RAM) of a computer, the read-write memory on a floppy disk, and the read-only memory (ROM) on a CD-ROM, illustrate three different kinds of addressable storage media. In the case of the RAM in a computer's main memory, the units of addressable storage might be words or individual bytes.

*addressable storage media*

Floppy disks can be formatted for storage in many ways. One computer company formats its floppy disks as follows: the disk is formatted into 80 circular tracks, each

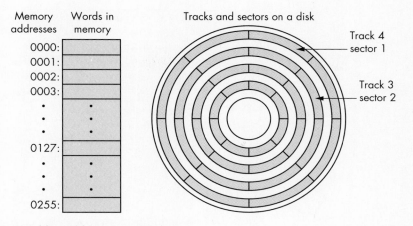

**Figure 3.2** Addressable Storage Media

track is divided into sectors, and each sector contains a block of 512 bytes of disk storage. Thus, an addressable unit of disk storage is a 512 byte block with a two-part address $(t,s)$ consisting of a track number $t$ and a sector number $s$. A CD-ROM can be formatted in much the same way, only it would have many more tracks and sectors per track than a floppy disk.[1] Even though the CD-ROM is a *read-only* device, it is still possible to use pointers in the data structures stored on it.

## Two Examples of Linked Representations

Using arrows to denote pointers, let's look at two practical uses of pointers to help develop intuition about what linked representations are good for.

### Example 1—Storing Files on Disks

First, let's look at a how a file can be stored on the floppy disk of Fig. 3.2. On many computers, a file is defined as a finite sequence of bytes. We can break this sequence of bytes into successive blocks of 512 bytes each and we can store each 512-byte block in an empty sector of the disk. We link the successive sectors together by storing in each sector, the address of another sector that contains the next 512-byte block of the file. Thus, each sector contains not only a 512-byte block of data, but also a *pointer* to the next block in sequence in the file.

It is also usual to save some of the empty sectors on the disk to contain a file directory. Imagine this as a table that contains one record for each file on the disk. Each record in the directory contains the characters spelling the file name, such as **MyProgram.java**, some file attributes, such as the length of the file in bytes, its date of creation, a code designating the type of the file, and finally a pointer to the first 512-byte block in the series of linked blocks containing the contents of the file. If the directory containing these individual file records fills more than one 512-byte sector,

---

[1] Some CD-ROMs contain a single spiral track up to three miles long, which can be formatted into addressable blocks of storage. CD is an abbreviation for compact disk.

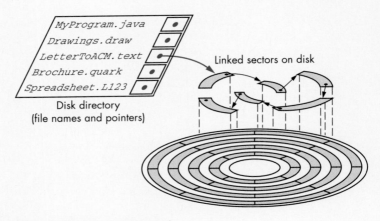

**Figure 3.3** Files and Directories on a Disk

additional sectors can be allocated and "linked on" to the end of the directory in order to extend it. Figure 3.3 presents a diagram of this situation.

## Example 2—Window Lists

Consider a window package for the user-interface of a desktop computer. The windows displayed on the screen can be layered on top of one another in an overlapping fashion, as shown in Fig. 3.4. Inside the main memory of the desktop computer, the operating system has to keep track of these windows. One way of doing this is with a *window list*, which keeps one record per window. Each window record in the window list contains a pointer to the record for the window immediately underneath it on the screen. Each window record also contains information such as the window's size, its position on the screen, and its visible region (which is the part of the window that can be seen because it is not overlapped with parts of other windows lying on top of it).

Suppose a user issues a command to bring one of the partially overlapped background windows, *W*, to the front of the screen. To carry out this command, the operating

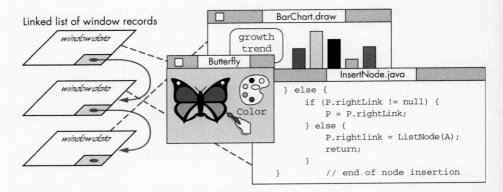

**Figure 3.4** A Stack of Windows and a Window List

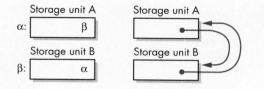

**Figure 3.5** Two Equivalent Notations for Pointers

system can execute a routine to remove the record for window *W* from its position somewhere in the middle of the window list and to insert it as the new first record on the window list (giving it a new status as the topmost window). It then goes down the window list drawing the contents of each window from top to bottom, making sure to clip the drawing of each window's contents so that it will occur only in its visible region.

### Pointers Defined

When we store the address α of a storage unit A inside another storage unit B, we say that B contains a *pointer* to A, and we say that α is a *pointer*. In Fig. 3.5, we can also say that B *links* to A, or that B contains a *reference* to A. Also, we can say that A is B's *referent*. When we follow a pointer to the unit of storage for which the pointer value is the address, we *dereference* the pointer.

> A **pointer** is a data value that references a unit of storage.

On the right side of Figure 3.5, the upward pointing arrow ( ●——➤ ) gives an alternative way to represent a pointer to the storage unit A. The tail of the arrow ( ●—— ) represents a stored copy of a data value equal to the address of the storage unit that the tip of the arrow ( ——➤ ) touches. Thus, the left and right sides of Fig. 3.5 depict identical situations.

## 3.3 Using Java's Implicit Pointers—The Rudiments

### LEARNING OBJECTIVES

1. To understand how Java's reference values can represent pointers and links.
2. To know how to allocate object memory dynamically and obtain references to it.
3. To be able to manipulate reference values in Java to create linked data representations.

*creating some rectangles*

Let's begin by constructing some **Rectangle** objects and assigning them to be the values of two variables declared to be of type **Rectangle**. For this purpose we return to take a closer look at what happens behind the scenes when we execute the declarations and initializations of Fig. 2.3 of Chapter 2, which is reproduced as Fig. 3.6.

```
Rectangle myRect = new Rectangle( );              // creates a Rectangle object
                                                  // having a top-left corner at (0,0)
                                                  // and having a height and width of zero
Rectangle anotherRect = new Rectangle(50,35,80,45);        // creates
                                                  // an 80 by 45 Rectangle object
                                                  // with its top-left corner at (50, 35)
```

**Figure 3.6** Java Declarations That Create Rectangle Objects

First, recall that a Java **Rectangle** object has four integer data fields **x, y, width**, and **height**. (Refer to the **Rectangle** class definition in Fig. 2.4 of Chapter 2 if you need to refresh your memory.) In the first declaration of Fig. 3.6, the no-arg constructor expression **new Rectangle()**; does three things: (1) it allocates memory for a new **Rectangle** object, (2) it initializes all of the object's data fields to zero (by setting **x = 0; y = 0; width = 0;** and **height = 0;**), and (3) it returns a *reference* to this newly constructed object as the value of the constructor expression. This reference value is stored in the **Rectangle** variable **myRect** by the assignment operator that initializes **myRect** in the initializing declaration **Rectangle myRect = new Rectangle( );**.

The second declaration in Fig. 3.6 performs a similar action. It constructs a new **Rectangle** object (this time with initial data field values **x = 50, y = 35, width = 80** and **height = 45**), and stores a reference to this object as the value of the newly declared variable **anotherRect**. Figure 3.7 illustrates the results of these actions.

In Java, each *variable* has a *name* and a *value*. Looking at the variable **myRect** in Fig. 3.7, we see that the variable name **myRect** is used as a label for a box that holds the variable's value. The label lies to the left of its value box and is followed by a colon (:). The value box holds the tail of an arrow denoting a Java reference value. This arrow points to the right to another box that denotes a **Rectangle** object. Each such **Rectangle** object is an instance of the **Rectangle** class, and is allocated a region of memory that holds the four data fields of a **Rectangle** (**x, y, width,** and **height**). The labels for these four data fields are placed on the top border of the **Rectangle** box, and the values contained in these data fields are denoted by the integers inside the four partitions of the rectangle box lying underneath the four border labels. Here, even though the data fields of an object are shown, the methods associated with an object are not shown. (The class browsers that accompany several of the advanced contemporary Java programming environments can display not only the data fields of an

*using boxes with labels to denote variables and objects*

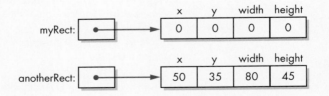

**Figure 3.7** Two Variables That Reference Two Rectangle Objects

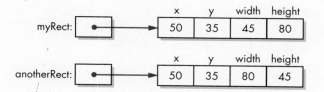

**Figure 3.8** Two Rectangles After Performing Some Assignments

object, but also the names and texts of its methods. For brevity and focus, we display here only the data fields of an object, and we rely on the context of the discussion to communicate facts about an object's class and methods when necessary.)

We can now use dot notation to refer to the values of the data fields of the two rectangle variables **myRect** and **anotherRect**, declared in Fig. 3.6 and pictured in Fig. 3.7. In particular, the expression **anotherRect.width** has the value **80**, and the assignments

```
myRect.x = 50;
myRect.y = 35;
myRect.width = anotherRect.height;
myRect.height = anotherRect.width;
```

assign the data fields of **myRect** to be those of a rectangle having the same top-left corner as **anotherRect**, but having a **width** and **height** that are the respective **height** and **width** of **anotherRect**. The situation that results from performing these assignments is shown in Fig. 3.8.

Note that the dot notation automatically dereferences pointers to access or assign values to data fields of objects in Java. In other words, when you write **myRect.x**, even though **myRect** is a variable that contains a reference (i.e., a pointer) to the storage for a **Rectangle** object, the expression **myRect.x** denotes the action of following the pointer to the storage allocated for the **Rectangle** object and then accessing the contents of its **x** data field. (For comparison, you would have to write **myRect–>x** in C++ to follow the reference value in **myRect** and then access the **x** data field of the storage to which this reference value points.)

*automatic dereferencing in Java*

Now comes the interesting part. Given the situation pictured in Fig. 3.8, what happens in Java when we perform the assignment

```
myRect = anotherRect;
```

Do the contents of all the data fields in **anotherRect** overwrite and replace the contents of the corresponding data fields in **myRect**, as shown in Fig. 3.9, or does the reference value in **myRect** get replaced with a copy of the reference value in **anotherRect**, as shown in Fig. 3.10? (Make a guess before reading on, if you don't know the answer already.)

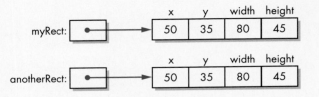

**Figure 3.9** One Rectangle Object's Data Fields Are Assigned Copies of the Other Rectangle Object's Data Fields

If you chose the picture in Fig. 3.10 as your answer, you chose correctly. The meaning of the assignment **myRect = anotherRect;** in Java is to create a copy of the reference value contained in the variable **anotherRect** and to store this copy as the new reference value of **myRect**. The old reference value in **myRect** is destroyed in the process.

Now we might ask, what happens to the storage for the previous **Rectangle** object that used to be the value of **myRect**? If no other reference to it exists from somewhere else in the Java system, does it not become inaccessible wasted storage? The answer is that if Java runs out of dynamic storage to allocate, it executes a *garbage collection* process that identifies inaccessible storage and *recycles* it into new dynamic storage to allocate. We'll learn how this works when we study dynamic memory allocation and garbage collection in Chapter 7. Unlike other contemporary languages such as C++ and Pascal, Java can recover and use inaccessible memory when it needs to. In Java, you do not need to call an explicit memory recycling method to ensure that inaccessible memory can be recovered and used later.

Given the situation that is pictured in Fig. 3.10, we can take advantage of shared references to the same **Rectangle** object. For example, if we change the **x**-coordinate of **myRect** to **20**, by executing the assignment

myRect.x = 20;

*shared memory references*

*inaccessible memory and garbage collection*

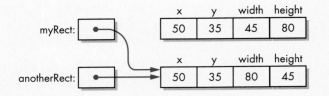

**Figure 3.10** One Rectangle Variable Is Assigned a Copy of the Other Rectangle Variable's Reference Value

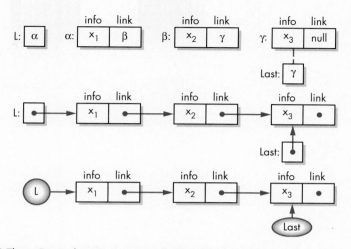

**Figure 3.12** Three Equivalent Diagrams in Pointer Diagramming Notation

There exists a special *null* address which, by convention, is not the address of any node. It is depicted by a solid dot (•), representing an arrow with no tip that points nowhere. In Java, the null pointer is represented by the special pointer value **null**. This special null address is used to show where a linked list ends, and it is used to represent an empty structure (such as a linked list having no nodes).

*the null address*

Finally, Fig. 3.12 shows some examples of the diagramming notation for the Java variables **L** and **Last**. In the following diagram, the two notations for **L** and **Last** are equivalent.

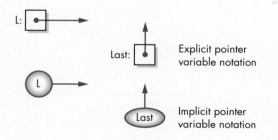

*pointer variable notation*

Pointer variables can be written two ways: either (1) *explicitly* as a box containing a pointer value labeled on the left side with the name of the variable followed by a colon, or (2) *implicitly* as an oval (or circle) containing the variable name and pointing to the node the pointer value references.

We can use a pointer to **null** to represent the null pointer in diagrams where we want to show explicitly how the null pointer is replaced by a non-null pointer value. For instance, Fig. 3.13 shows how we can insert a new second node into a linked list by changing the link of the first node to point to it, and by replacing its null link with

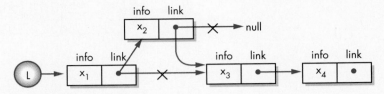

**Figure 3.13** Inserting a New Second Node into a Linked List

a pointer to the previous second node. The arrows that are "crossed out" represent pointer values that were replaced with new pointer values during the operation shown in the diagram.

using implicit pointer variable notation

We will use the implicit notation for pointer variables (as ovals containing variable names) in diagrams with many nodes in which we use pointer variables to contain pointers to point to places in the overall linked data structure (1) where change is about to occur or (2) to keep track of a location we will need to use in the future. The implicit notation tends to be a bit more compact and less cluttered than the explicit notation in such circumstances, but we should always remember that it is equivalent to the explicit notation in which the variable name, followed by a colon, is to the left of a box containing a pointer.

the language-independent nature of pointer diagramming notation

Pointer diagramming notation (PDN) is actually a language-independent pictorial notation that you can use to design algorithms at a strategic level that operate on linked data representations. You can then implement your strategies in many different contemporary programming languages such as C++, Ada, and Object Pascal by translating the basic actions in PDN into equivalent expressions in the target programming languages. Shortly, we will show how to perform such translations into Java. But first let's comment briefly on the connection between pointer diagramming notation and Java.

the correspondence between Java and pointer diagramming notation

The pointers (i.e., arrows) in PDN correspond to *reference values* in Java. Such Java reference values point to instances of allocated storage for Java objects and Java arrays. You can access objects and arrays in Java only by using such reference values. The nodes in PDN therefore represent allocated storage for objects and arrays. The data fields in such nodes represent the data fields in Java objects or the indexed item positions in Java arrays. Such data fields may contain other Java reference values, corresponding to pointers in PDN that point to other nodes (representing other Java objects and arrays). Variables that contain pointers in PDN (whether given in explicit or implicit pointer variable notation) represent declared Java variables that contain reference values. Such variables can be declared as the data field variables of a Java class, as the formal parameters of a Java method, or as local variables in a Java method. Java dot notation can be used to designate the contents of data fields. For example, in Fig. 3.13 L.info is a Java expression having the value $x_1$, and L.link.link.info is a Java expression having the value $x_3$. Exercises 3.4 give you practice in reading and writing expressions in Java dot notation corresponding to the action of following pointers and obtaining the values of designated data fields in PDN diagrams. In a short while, we will use this skill as a building block for writing algorithms on linked data structures.

## 3.4 REVIEW QUESTIONS

1. What is the null address?
2. How is the null address depicted in pointer diagramming notation?
3. What value represents the null address in Java?
4. How is the end of a linked list indicated in pointer diagramming notation?
5. What is an empty linked list, and what value is used to indicate it?
6. Explain the difference between explicit pointer variable notation and implicit pointer variable notation.

## 3.4 EXERCISES

For the exercises below assume the following picture specifies the values of the variables N and L:

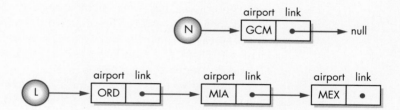

[*Note:* The three-letter codes ORD, MIA, GCM, and MEX are some codes that airlines use on baggage tags: ORD = Chicago's O'Hare airport; MIA = Miami, Florida; MEX = Mexico City, Mexico; and GCM = Grand Cayman in the Cayman Islands.]

1. In the diagram, if you assume L's referent is a node representing an object with an airport data field containing ORD, then you could write: L.airport == ORD. Similarly, you could conclude that L.link.airport == MIA. Using this line of reasoning, what are the values of the following four expressions: (a) N.link, (b) N.airport, (c) L.link.link.airport, and (d) L.link.link.link?
2. Write Java expressions possibly using: (i) the variables L and N, (ii) the object data field names airport and link, and (iii) the object field selection operator (.), having the following values: (a) the reference value for the node containing MIA, (b) the reference value for the node containing MEX, (c) the reference value for the node containing ORD, and (d) the airport code MIA.
3. Write two Java assignment statements that (when executed) will insert N's referent as the new third node of the list L. Before these assignments are executed, the airport codes of the nodes in the list referenced by L are ORD, MIA, MEX. After the assignments are executed, the airport codes should be in the sequence ORD, MIA, GCM, MEX.
4. Draw the picture of the result of executing the two assignment statements that solve problem 3, starting with the diagram for the values of L and N above.
5. Write a Java assignment statement that replaces the airport code ORD by JFK. Assume you can use Java string notation ("ORD" and "JFK") to specify airport codes.

6. Write some statements in Java that replace the node containing **MIA** with the node containing **GCM**. After execution, L should point to nodes with airport codes given in the sequence **ORD, GCM, MEX**.

## 3.5   Linear Linked Lists

### LEARNING OBJECTIVES

1. To understand how to represent and manipulate linked lists using Java objects and reference values.
2. To develop skill in designing and implementing linked list algorithms.
3. To learn a set of useful basic linked list operations.

*linear linked lists*

A *linear linked list* (or a *linked list*, for short) is a sequence of nodes in which each node, except the last, links to a successor node. The link field of the last node contains the null pointer value, **null**, which signifies the end of the list.

Figure 3.14 represents a linear linked list containing the three-letter airport codes for the stops on American Airlines flight number 89. This flight starts in Düsseldorf, Germany (**DUS**), stops at Chicago's O'Hare Airport (**ORD**), and continues on to its final destination, San Diego (**SAN**).

The pointer variable **L** contains a pointer to the first node on this list. We will sometimes say "L's value is the list (**DUS, ORD, SAN**)," imagining that the whole linked list is a single entity, and that this list is the value of the variable, **L**, even though **L** contains only a Java reference value pointing to the first node of the list.

### Inserting a New Second Node on a List

Suppose we want to add a new stop to the route of flight 89 represented by the list in Fig. 3.14 so that it stops in Brussels, Belgium (**BRU**) before flying to O'Hare. To represent this change, we need to insert a node for **BRU** as the new second node on the list.

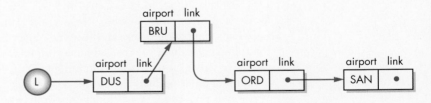

*program strategies*

A method for linking the new second node into the given list is shown in Program Strategy 3.15. Program strategies such as these specify high-level goals to accomplish.

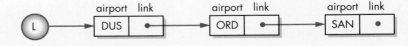

**Figure 3.14** A Linear Linked List

```
  |    void insertNewSecondNode(BRU) {                    // let the initial list L be given by
  |                                                        // L = (DUS, ORD, SAN)
  |
  |        (declare a pointer variable newNode, that can point to list nodes)
  |
5 |        (construct a new node and let the pointer variable newNode point to it)
  |        (set the airport field of the newNode to BRU)
  |        (change the link field of newNode to point to L's second node)
  |        (change the link of L's first node to point to the newNode)
  |    }
```

**Program Strategy 3.15** Inserting a Second Node for BRU in a List (DUS,ORD,SAN)

In this book, we use them as starting points for the development of Java programs. They are intended to help you grasp how algorithms work, by expressing concisely the essential plans, methods, and goals that lie at the heart of an algorithm's design. If the actual programming details are given too soon, they can often obscure what is really going on.

The goals in a program strategy can be achieved by supplying more specific programming details. The process of filling in such details in a series of specific steps is called *stepwise refinement*. The method of starting with a top-level design and expanding its details progressively until an actual program is developed is called *top-down programming*. Many of the algorithms in this book are developed by stepwise refinement to illustrate how to proceed clearly from the goals expressed in a program design to the actual working details.

**stepwise refinement and top-down programming**

We will now expand the goals in Program Strategy 3.15 into a specific Java program, in two separate steps. In the first, we use pointer diagramming notation to illustrate what is happening in addition to giving Java code. In the second step, we delete the diagrams and shorten the comments. What remains is a concise (but overly specific) Java program. In the next section, we will evolve this program into a more general Java method for inserting an arbitrary new airport code as the second item of a linked list.

```
  |    void insertNewSecondNode(BRU) {
  |
  |        // declare a pointer variable newNode, that can point to list nodes
  |            ListNode newNode;
  |
  |        // construct a new node and let the pointer variable newNode point to it
  |            newNode = new ListNode( );
```

```
  |        // set the airport field of the newNode to BRU
  |            newNode.airport = "BRU";
```

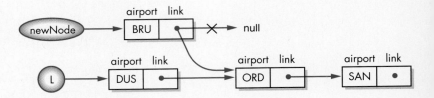

```
|        // change the link field of the newNode to point to L's second node
|           newNode.link = L.link;
```

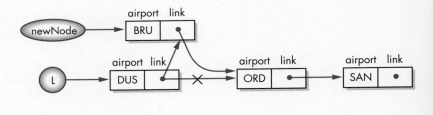

```
|        // change the link of L's first node to point to the newNode
|           L.link = newNode;
```

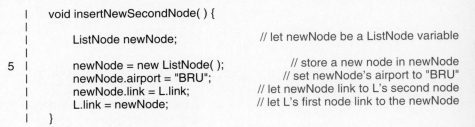

```
|    }
```

Next, we strip the pictures from this intermediate version of our method, and we shorten the original comments. The following (overly specific) Java method results.

```
|    void insertNewSecondNode( ) {
|
|        ListNode newNode;                      // let newNode be a ListNode variable
|
5 |      newNode = new ListNode( );                 // store a new node in newNode
|        newNode.airport = "BRU";              // set newNode's airport to "BRU"
|        newNode.link = L.link;             // let newNode link to L's second node
|        L.link = newNode;                  // let L's first node link to the newNode
|
|    }
```

In this program, note that in order to make the comments short, we have used language imprecisely. The shortened language makes it sound as if **newNode** were a variable containing a node, rather than being a variable containing a pointer to a node. Thus, instead of giving the untruthful comment, "**// store a new node in newNode**," we should have given the truthful comment, "**// construct a new node object and set the variable newNode to contain a reference value that points to it.**" Although we will not usually engage in this kind of falsifying brevity in this book, be aware that real-world programmers, in an attempt to achieve brevity and conciseness, sometimes use short comments that are slightly out-of-correspondence with the truth expressed by

*the problem of slightly untruthful comments*

the underlying code. This is not an unreasonable programming practice. Any competent programmer can infer from the underlying code exactly what is going on. Not only do the brief comments give valid descriptions of top-level goals being achieved by the code, they also help make the program concise and easy to read.

Another important thing to note about the method **insertNewSecondNode**, is that the variable, **newNode**, is a *local* variable. **newNode** exists only during the execution of the method, and contains a pointer to a newly constructed node only when it is in existence. **newNode**'s pointer value is placed in the **link** field of the first node of list **L** before the method terminates, causing the first node of list **L** to link to the newly constructed node. After the method terminates execution, the variable **newNode** and its contents vanish. However, the dynamically allocated storage for the new second node of list **L** created during this method's execution remains in place after the execution of the method has terminated:

*dynamically allocated storage remains in existence*

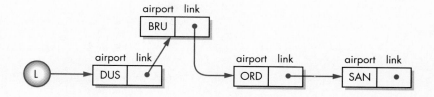

Actually, the process of stepwise refinement is not complete yet, since we haven't yet given any declarations for the Java classes needed to make this program work properly. We now turn to this task.

## Declaring Java Classes for Linked Lists

*node and pointer types*

We need to declare a system of nodes and pointers to serve as the foundation for manipulating linked lists. To do this, we give two class definitions. We first define a class for list nodes.

```
public class ListNode {
    String      airport;
    ListNode    link;
}
```

Objects that are instances of the **ListNode** class contain two data fields: (1) an **airport** data field containing a **String**, and (2) a **link** field containing a reference value pointing to another **ListNode** object. Note that the **ListNode** class has no methods defined for it. Its sole purpose is to bundle two data values (an **airport** and a **link**) together into a single unit that can occupy an allocated region of storage in the computer memory and can have a reference value that points to its memory region. (Classes in Java can play many specialized roles. One such role is merely to bundle several data values together into a single unit.) Note that when the **null** value occupies the **link** data field of the last node on a list, it denotes the end of the list, and when a **ListNode** variable has the value **null**, it signifies an *empty* linked list.

We can use the no-arg constructor **ListNode()** and appropriate dot notation expressions on the left side of assignment statements to construct linked sequences of nodes. Here's a short example using diagrams inserted at various stages of the construction.

```
| // declare M to be a ListNode variable initialized to a new ListNode
|     ListNode M = new ListNode();
```

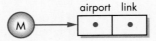

```
| // set the airport field of node M to "DUS" and set its link field to null
|     M.airport = "DUS";
|     M.link = null;
```

```
| // insert two new ListNodes for ORD and SAN on the end of the list
|     M.link = new ListNode();
|     M.link.airport = "ORD";
|     M.link.link = new ListNode();
|     M.link.link.airport = "SAN";
|     M.link.link.link = null;
```

In a moment, we will define examples of methods that operate on linked lists. For this purpose, we need to define the **LinkedList** class given in Program 3.16.

Each **LinkedList** object has a **length** data field whose value is an integer giving the number of items in the list, and has a **firstNode** data field containing a reference value that points to the first **ListNode** in the sequence of linked nodes containing the items in the list. (If the **length** field contains **0**, the **firstNode** field contains **null**, signifying the empty linked list that contains no items.)

Because no user-defined constructors are given in the **LinkedList** class, Java defines the no-arg constructor **LinkedList()** automatically. This constructor allocates an empty **LinkedList** object whose **length** field is initialized to **0** and whose **firstNode** field is initialized to **null**.

For example, we could construct an empty **LinkedList** object **L** and then assign its **length** to be **3** and its **firstNode** to be the sequence of linked nodes pointed to by **M** in the previous construction by executing the following statements:

```
 |    public class LinkedList {
 |
 |        // the two data fields of a LinkedList are:
 |
5|            int         length;            // the number of nodes in the list.
 |            ListNode    firstNode;         // contains a pointer to the first node
 |                                           // of its list of linked ListNodes
 |
 |        // definitions of methods that manipulate LinkedLists are given next.
10|        // for example, the size() method gives the number of items in the list
 |
 |            public int size( ) {           // returns the number of items in the list
 |                return length;
 |            }
15|
 |        // insert here the texts of the following LinkedList methods given in:
 |            // Program 3.17   insertNewSecondNode(airportCode)
 |            // Program 3.19   listSearch(airportCode)
 |            // Program 3.21   deleteLastNode( )
20|            // Program 3.22   insertNewLastNode(airportCode)
 |            // Program 3.23   print( )
 |    }
```

**Program 3.16** The LinkedList Class Definition

```
 |    // construct a new LinkedList L of length 3 having M's linked nodes
 |        LinkedList L = new LinkedList();
 |        L.firstNode = M;                   // where M points to the three linked
 |        L.length = 3;                      // linked nodes constructed earlier
```

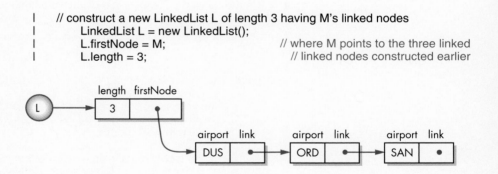

We now define some new methods for the **LinkedList** class (to be inserted in lines 17:21 in Program 3.16). To show what is visible inside the text of each such **LinkedList** method we will use diagrams that portray the **firstNode** data field of a **LinkedList** object as if it were a separate global variable pointing to the first node of a sequence of linked **ListNodes**. In effect, inside the text of a method applied to **LinkedList L** above, we would see:

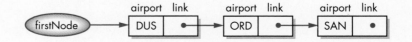

Program 3.17 generalizes the (overly specialized) insertNewSecondNode() method we sketched when we illustrated how to translate pointer diagramming notation into Java code. It takes an airport code as its input and inserts a new second node in the LinkedList object on which the method is invoked. Note how Program 3.17 maintains the length of the list (see lines 20:21), and how it performs no action (see lines 3:5) on an initially empty list for which the meaning of inserting a new second node is undefined.

We now proceed to give a few more examples of methods that act on linked lists, using pointer diagramming notation to help visualize the main concepts.

## Searching for an Item on a List

Suppose we are given the task of finding the node N on a list of airport codes L containing the airport code A. Assume that all types and variables have been declared using the class definitions just given. Suppose that the problem statement asks us to write a LinkedList method that, when invoked on a given LinkedList object L, returns a pointer to the node on list L containing the airport code A, if there is such a node. If no such node exists, we are to return the null pointer, null.

*strategy for list searching*

One strategy for solving this search problem is to let N be a ListNode variable and to let it point to each node of list L in succession, checking each node to see if it contains the airport code A. As soon as a node N containing airport code A is found, the pointer in node N is returned as the return value of the listSearch method, and the search terminates. If no node on the list contains the airport code A, the null pointer is returned as the return value of the method. The general idea is sketched in Program Strategy 3.18.

```
     |   public void insertNewSecondNode(String airportCode) {
     |
     |       // if the list has no first node, the result is undefined.
     |       // in this case, exit the method instead of trying to insert a second node
 5   |          if (length == 0) return;
     |
     |       // declare a pointer variable newNode that can point to ListNodes
     |       // and initialize it to an initially empty ListNode object
     |          ListNode newNode = new ListNode();
10   |
     |       // set the airport of the newNode to the method's airportCode argument
     |          newNode.airport = airportCode;
     |
     |       // change the link field of the newNode to point to the list's second node
15   |          newNode.link = firstNode.link;
     |
     |       // change the link field of the firstNode to point to the newNode
     |          firstNode.link = newNode;
     |
20   |       // increase the length of the list by one
     |          length++;
     |   }
```

**Program 3.17** General Method for Inserting a New Second Node

```
   |    public ListNode listSearch(String airportCode) {
   |
   |        (declare a variable N that can point to ListNodes)
   |
 5 |        (initially, set N to point to the first node of the list)
   |
   |        while (N points to a non-null node on the list) {
   |
   |            if (N's airport field contains the airportCode) {
10 |
   |                (exit the method and return the node pointer in N)
   |
   |            } else {
   |
15 |                (advance the pointer N to point to the next node on the list)
   |            }
   |        }
   |
   |        (return N's value, null, as the result of the list search)
20 |    }
   | }
```

**Program Strategy 3.18** Strategy for List Searching

Using the method of top-down programming by stepwise refinement, we proceed to fill in actual Java code that accomplishes the goals given in this program strategy. Program 3.19 is a refinement of the program strategy with specific Java code inserted.

```
   |    public ListNode listSearch(String airportCode) {
   |
   |        // declare a variable N that can point to ListNodes
   |            ListNode N;
 5 |
   |        // initially, set N to point to the first node of the list
   |            N = firstNode;
   |
   |        // while N points to a non-null node on the list
10 |        // examine N's airport field
   |            while (N != null) {
   |                if (airportCode.equals(N.airport)) {     // if node N contains the
   |                    return N;                            // airportCode, return the
   |                } else {                                 // node pointer in N; otherwise,
15 |                    N = N.link;                          // advance N to point to
   |                }                                        // the next node on the list
   |            }
   |
   |        // return null if no node's airport equals the airportCode
20 |            return N;
   |    }
```

**Program 3.19** List Searching Method

a worked example
with diagrams

To make sure that you understand how this program works, it is useful to go over a specific example that uses diagrams generously to help make the explanation clear. Suppose we are searching for the airport code A = "ORD" on the list L = (DUS, BRU, ORD, SAN). This search would be initiated if we made the method call, L.listSearch("ORD"). This method call assigns the actual parameter "ORD" to be the value of the method's formal parameter airportCode. On line 7 in the text of listSearch, we perform the assignment N = firstNode; which makes the node pointer variable N point to the first node on L's linked node list. This initializes the search, so that the pointer N is pointing to the node shown in the following diagram:

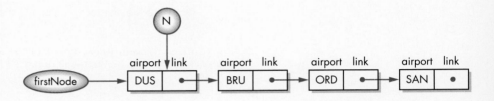

We are now set up to perform the while-loop on lines 11:17. Inside this while-loop we advance N along the list, so that it points to each node in sequence.

Each time N points to a new nonempty node, we check to see if that node's airport field contains a string equal to the airportCode string "ORD" using the string equality method call airportCode.equals(N.airport). If N points to a node having the airport code ORD, the search terminates successfully, by returning node N's pointer value on line 13. In the specific case shown in the following pointer diagram, when N advances to point to the third node of the list, we find that N is pointing to a node containing the airport code ORD, so the listSearch method will exit, returning N's value as the return value of the method.

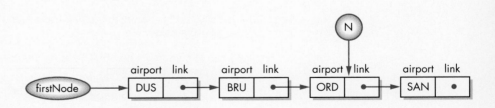

On the other hand, if the node to which N points does not contain the airport code we are searching for, we change the pointer in N to point to the next node in the list. To do this, we replace N's pointer with the pointer in the link field of the node that N is currently pointing to. The statement, N = N.link; on line 15, advances the pointer in N to the next node in this fashion.

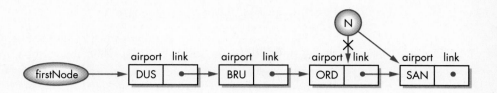

As we travel step-by-step down the list, with **N** pointing at each node in sequence, either we find a node with airport code **ORD**, or we come to the end of the list. This leads us to consider what happens in cases of unsuccessful search. If the list is empty to begin with (meaning that the **firstNode** data field of the **LinkedList** object **L** contains the value **null**), or the airport code **ORD** that we are searching for is not on the list, the pointer **N** eventually takes the value **null**.

*unsuccessful search*

In the case of a nonempty list not containing an airport code **ORD**, this happens as follows. As **N** is advanced to point to each node of the list in sequence, it eventually is made to point to the last node of the list.

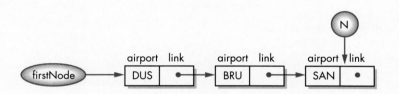

The last node of a list always has **null** as the value of its **link** field. When it is discovered that this last node doesn't contain airport code **ORD**, we attempt to advance the pointer to the next node by executing **N = N.link;** on line 15. But since there is no next node, the value **null** in the **link** field of the node that **N** points to becomes the next value of **N**.

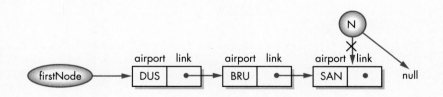

At this point, when we return to the beginning of the while-loop, on line 11, the condition **N != null** becomes **false**. Control exits the while-loop and passes down to the statement on line 20, which returns **N**'s value **null** as the value of the method, to signify that the result of the search was unsuccessful. (Recall that the problem statement required us to return a **null** pointer value in place of a pointer to an actual nonempty node in order to designate the result of an unsuccessful search.)

## Deleting the Last Node of a List

list termination

Now let's turn to a second fully-worked example. Suppose we are asked to write a method that deletes the last node when invoked on a LinkedList object L. Again assume we are using the Java class definitions for linked lists of airport codes. Since the last node of a linked list is designated by setting its link field to contain null, to delete the last node of a linked list, we must somehow find the next-to-last node so we can set its link field to contain null.

In the solution that follows, we will use two ListNode pointer variables called previousNode and currentNode. As we advance the currentNode pointer to point to each successive node on the list, we will advance the previousNode pointer to point to the node immediately before the one that currentNode points to. The two pointers therefore travel down the list as a *pointer pair*.

When currentNode gets to the last node of the list, previousNode will be pointing to the next-to-last node of the list. At this moment, we can set the link of this next-to-last node to be null, designating it as the new last node of the list.

handling two special
cases first

In order for our pointer-pair process to work properly, we need to use lists with at least two nodes on them. But since the empty list, L = null, and the list having only one node do not fit this requirement, we need to treat them as special cases at the beginning of the method. In the case of an empty list, we don't need to do anything, since there is no last node to delete. In the case of a list with one node, we need to set the firstNode data field of the LinkedList object L to the empty list. A summary of these considerations is given in Program Strategy 3.20.

A diagram of what needs to happen on line 22, when we advance the pointer pair to the next pair of nodes is given in the following diagram:

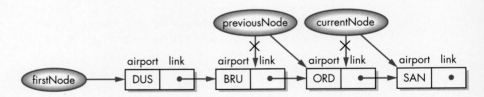

We now make a top-down, stepwise refinement of this program strategy so that it contains the actual working details in Java shown in Program 3.21 (on page 86).

The last two programs we have developed (Programs 3.19 and 3.21) share a common theme. They both use a while-loop to step down the successive nodes of a linked list until a specific condition is satisfied. The strategy for this theme is while (condition not satisfied) { (move to next node on list) }. This strategy can be used to solve the problem of inserting a new last node on a list.

## Inserting a New Last Node on a List

Another important building block to learn about is the method for inserting a new node on a list. Suppose we are given an airport code A, and a variable L whose ref-

```
 1 |  public void deleteLastNode() {            // a method that deletes the last node
   |                                            // of a LinkedList object
   |
   |     (let previousNode and currentNode contain pointers to ListNodes)
 5 |
   |     if (the list is not the empty list) {
   |
   |         if (the list has exactly one node) {
   |
10 |             (set the list to be empty)
   |             (and decrease its length by one)
   |
   |         } else {        // otherwise the list must have two or more nodes
   |
15 |             (initialize a pair of pointers, (previousNode, currentNode) )
   |             (to point to the first and second nodes)
   |
   |             (advance the pointer pair along the list until)
   |             (currentNode points to the last node)
20 |
   |             while (currentNode does not point to the last node) {
   |                 (advance the pair of pointers to the next pair of nodes)
   |             }
   |
25 |             (now previousNode points to the next-to-last node on the list)
   |             (and currentNode points to the last node on the list)
   |
   |             (finally, change the next-to-last node into the new last node)
   |             (and decrease the list length by one)
30 |         }
   |
   |     }
   |
   |  }
```

**Program Strategy 3.20** Strategy for Deleting the Last Node of a List

erence value is a **LinkedList** object. We want to insert a new node containing the airport code **A** at the end of this list. A **LinkedList** method that accomplishes this is given as Program 3.22 (on page 87). To invoke this method, we make the method call **L.insertNewLastNode(A)**; This passes the airport code **A** as the value of the method's formal parameter, **airportCode**.

On line 4, a new node is constructed. A pointer to it is placed in the pointer variable **N**, and its **airport** and **link** fields are set to contain **A** and **null**, respectively. Lines 9:11 handle the special case in which the list, **L**, was empty to begin with. In this case, we need to set **L**'s **firstNode** data field point to the new node **N** we have just constructed.

On the other hand, if the original list, **L**, was not empty, we can be assured that it contains one or more nodes. In this case, we need to search for the last node. We do

```
 1   public void deleteLastNode() {

         // let previousNode and currentNode contain pointers to ListNodes
            ListNode previousNode, currentNode;
 5
         if (firstNode != null) {                        // do nothing if the list was empty

            if (firstNode.link == null) {      // if the list had exactly one node, then

10              firstNode = null;                        // set the list to be empty, and
                length − −;                              // decrease its length by one

            } else {                    // otherwise the list must have two or more nodes

15              // initialize a pair of pointers (previousNode, currentNode)
                // to point to the first and second nodes
                previousNode = firstNode;
                currentNode = firstNode.link;

20              // advance the pointer pair along the list until
                // currentNode points to the last node on the list
                while (currentNode.link != null) {
                    previousNode = currentNode;
                    currentNode = currentNode.link;
25              }

                // now previousNode points to the next-to-last node on the list
                // and currentNode points to the last node on the list
                previousNode.link = null;       // set null link in new last node
30              length − −;                      // decrease list length by one

            }

         }
35
     }
```

**Program 3.21** Deleting the Last Node of a List

this on lines 16:19 using a pointer variable, P, which is made to step along the nodes of L until it comes to rest on L's last node.

Initially, P is made to point to L's first node, using the assignment statement, P = firstNode; on line 16. The while-loop on lines 17:19 is now executed to locate the last node of L. This while-loop is an instance of the strategy while (condition not satisfied) { (move to next node on list) } that shares the same theme as Programs 3.19 and 3.21.

```
|      public void insertNewLastNode(String airportCode) {
|
|          // construct a new node N with airport == airportCode and link == null
|              ListNode N = new ListNode();
5 |              N.airport = airportCode;
|              N.link = null;
|
|          // insert N as the new last node on the list
|              if (firstNode == null) {                              // if the list was empty
10 |
|                  firstNode = N;                              // let N become the new first node
|
|              } else {
|
15 |                  // locate the last node of the list, using the node pointer P
|                      ListNode P = firstNode;
|                      while (P.link != null){
|                          P = P.link;
|                      }
20 |
|                  // finally, link node N onto the end of the list
|                      P.link = N;
|
|              }
25 |
|          // increase the length of the list by one
|              length++;
|
|      }
```

**Program 3.22** Inserting a New Last Node on a List

Once **P** has been made to point to the last node of **L**, the new last node, **N**, can be linked to it. This is accomplished on line 22 by setting **P.link = N;**.

Finally, on line 27, the **length** data field of the **LinkedList** object **L** is incremented to reflect the fact that a new last node has just been inserted.

## How to Print a List

Before we can write a small program that meaningfully builds up an airport code list, changes it, and shows us the changes, we need to define the **LinkedList** printing method illustrated in Program 3.23.

The heart of this **print()** method is also a while-loop (given on lines 14:20) that steps down the list, visiting each successive node. In this case, the pointer variable **N** is made to point to each such node.

```
     |    public void print( ) {
     |
     |        ListNode N;                          // N points to successive nodes on the list
     |
 5   |        // first, print a left parenthesis
     |            System.out.print( "(" );
     |
     |        // let N start by pointing to the first node on the list
     |            N = firstNode;
10   |
     |        // provided N doesn't point to an empty node, print N's airport
     |        // and advance N to point to the next node on the list
     |
     |        while (N != null) {
15   |            System.out.print(N.airport);              // print airport code
     |            N = N.link;                               // make N point to next node
     |            if (N != null) {
     |                System.out.print(", ");       // print comma between list items
     |            }
20   |        }
     |
     |        // finally, print a closing right parenthesis
     |            System.out.println( ")" );
     |    }
```

**Program 3.23** Printing a List

Inside the while-loop, the airport code for each node, N, is printed (using the statement on line 15, System.out.print(N.airport); which does *not* advance to the next line). Following this, N is made to point to the next node on the list, by executing the statement N = N. link;. To print commas *between* the airport codes on the list but not *after* the last airport code, the statement, if (N != null) { System.out.print(","); } is executed. The reason this does not print a comma after the last node of the list is because the variable N is made to point to null immediately beforehand.

## Getting Our Act Together

At this point, we have developed a small library of building blocks useful for writing linked-list programs. Consequently, we are in a position to assemble some of the pieces together to make a complete Java program. Program 3.24 is an example of one such program (presented as the init( ) method of a Java applet in order to execute it).

When we run this program, it prints three lines:

```
( DUS , ORD , SAN )
( DUS , BRU , ORD , SAN )
( DUS , BRU , ORD )
```

```
 1  |   import java.io.*;
    |   import java.applet.Applet;
    |
    |
 5  |   public class LinkedListApplet extends Applet {
    |
    |       public void init( ) {
    |
    |           // let L be a new linked list
10  |               LinkedList L = new LinkedList( );
    |
    |           // first, construct the list L = (DUS, ORD, SAN)
    |               L.insertNewLastNode("DUS");
    |               L.insertNewLastNode("ORD");
15  |               L.insertNewLastNode("SAN");
    |
    |           // now, print the list to show what it looks like before changing it
    |               L.print( );
    |
20  |           // then, insert a new second node with the airport code BRU
    |               L.insertNewSecondNode("BRU");
    |
    |           // print the modified list
    |               L.print( );
25  |
    |           // delete the last node of the list
    |               L.deleteLastNode( );
    |
    |           // finally, print the shortened list
30  |               L.print( );
    |
    |       } // end init( )
    |
    |
35  |   } // end class LinkedListApplet
    |
    |   // to finish the program, insert the full texts for the class
    |   // definitions of ListNode and LinkedList here.
    |
```

**Program 3.24** An Example That Puts Some Pieces Together

## Where to Go From Here?

*building your skills*

We have now studied five examples that illustrate key foundations of linked list programming in Java. But if you have never programmed with linked lists before, you might need further development of your skills before you can attain an intermediate level of mastery. An excellent way to improve your skills is to write perhaps seven to twelve new linked list methods implementing basic linked list operations.

Exercises 3.5 ask you to write programs to do typical list operations such as: (1) inserting a node as the new first node on a list, (2) deleting the first node on a list, (3) making a copy of a list, (4) reversing the order of the nodes on a list, and (5) joining two lists together to make a single combined list.

## 3.5 REVIEW QUESTIONS

1. What is top-down programming using stepwise refinement?
2. Give three examples of methods defined in this section that use a while-loop with the theme while (condition not satisfied) { (move to next node on list) }.
3. What value in Java is automatically a reference value belonging to every reference type?

## 3.5 EXERCISES

For the following exercises, assume that the ListNode and LinkedList classes have been defined the same way they have been given in this section, and that the following variables have been declared:

    ListNode L, M, N;

1. Write a method, which is invoked by the method call L.insertNewFirstNode(A), that inserts a new ListNode object with an airport code A as the new first node of the LinkedList object L.
2. Write a method, L.deleteFirst(), that deletes the first node of a LinkedList object L.
3. Given a non-null pointer N to a ListNode of a list L, and a pointer M to a new ListNode to be inserted, write a Java method to insert the node that is M's referent *before* the node that is N's referent on list L. [*Hint*: Adjust pointers to insert M after N and then swap the airport codes in N and M.]
4. Write a method, L.clone(), which makes a copy of a LinkedList object L, and returns a pointer to the copy.
5. Write a method, L.reverse(), which reverses the order of the nodes on list L. For example, if L = (ZRH, GLA, YYZ) beforehand, then executing L.reverse() changes L to be the list L = (YYZ, GLA, ZRH).
6. What is wrong with the following search method for finding the node on list L containing the airport code A and returning a pointer to it?

```
  |    public ListNode findNode(String A) {
  |         ListNode N = firstNode;
  |         while ( ( !A.equals(N.airport) ) && ( N != null ) ) {
  |              N = N.Link;
5 |         }
  |         return N;
  |    }
```

7. Given two lists L1 and L2, write a method invoked by L1.concat(L2), to return a pointer to a list in which the nodes of L2 follow the nodes of L1. For example, if, beforehand, L1 = (ARN, BRU) and L2 = (JFK, SAN, HKG), then the node pointer returned by the method call L1.concat(L2) should point to the list (ARN, BRU, JFK, SAN, HKG).
8. What is wrong with the following method for finding the last node of a list L and

returning a pointer to it?

```
    |    public ListNode lastNode( ) {
    |        ListNode N = firstNode;
    |        if ( N != null ) {
    |            do {
 5  |                N = N.link;
    |            } while (N.link != null);
    |        }
    |        return N;
    |    }
```

## 3.6 Other Linked Data Structures

### LEARNING OBJECTIVES

1. To understand some possibilities for linked data representations other than simple, one-way linked lists.
2. To illustrate how nodes with two links can be linked into representations such as two-way linked lists, rings, and trees.

As you might expect, the simple linked lists we studied in the previous sections in this chapter are not the only kinds of linked data representations that are possible. For example, starting with nodes that contain airport codes and two separate link fields—a **leftLink** field and a **rightLink** field—we can build linked data structures using a variety of different organizational principles. We proceed to illustrate just three of the many possibilities.

First, we need to declare a new kind of **ListNode** class in Java to represent the nodes of these structures. We do this as follows.

```
    |    public class ListNode {
    |
    |        String        airport;
    |        ListNode      leftLink;
 5  |        ListNode      rightLink;
    |
    |    }
```

We assume that the strings used as airport codes are the same as those used in the previous examples of linked lists of airport codes. Note that each **ListNode** object contains *two* pointer fields, a **leftLink** field and a **rightLink** field, both of which contain reference values pointing to other **ListNode**s.

Figure 3.25 illustrates a typical node object used to construct various linked representations. One type of data structure that we can build by linking such nodes is called a *two-way linked list* (or, sometimes, a *symmetrically linked list*). Figure 3.26 gives an example of a two-way list of airport codes. If we were to replace the null links marking the left and right ends of the list in Fig. 3.26 with links to the respective opposite ends

**Figure 3.25** Typical ListNode with Two Links

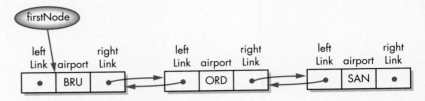

**Figure 3.26** Two-Way Linked List of Airport Codes

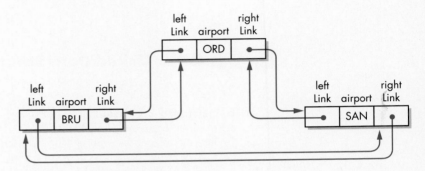

**Figure 3.27** Two-Way Ring of Airport Codes

of the list, we would get the two-way ring structure illustrated in Fig. 3.27.

Let's now take a look at another type of linked representation—a *linked binary tree*. Table 3.28 gives 15 airport codes in alphabetical order, and Fig. 3.29 shows the airport codes of Table 3.28 arranged in a linked binary tree, constructed from nodes of the type illustrated in Fig. 3.25. It is a common convention in computer science to picture such trees *upside-down*, with their branches growing downwards.

**linked binary trees**

**Table 3.28** Three-Letter Airport Codes

| | |
|---|---|
| ARN | Stockholm, Sweden |
| BRU | Brussels, Belgium |
| DUS | Düsseldorf, Germany |
| GCM | Grand Cayman, Cayman Islands |
| GLA | Glasgow, Scotland |
| HKG | Hong Kong |
| JFK | Kennedy Airport, New York |
| MEX | Mexico City, Mexico |
| MIA | Miami, Florida |
| NRT | Narita Airport, Tokyo, Japan |
| ORD | O'Hare, Chicago, Illinois |
| ORY | Orly Field, Paris, France |
| SAN | San Diego, California |
| YYZ | Toronto, Ontario |
| ZRH | Zürich, Switzerland |

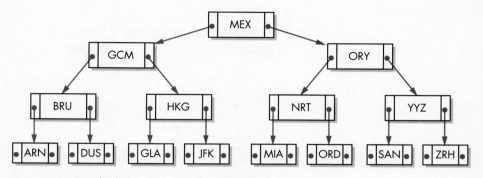

**Figure 3.29** A Linked Data Structure for a Binary Tree

We will have more to say about different kinds of linked list representations in Chapter 7, and about linked binary tree representations in Chapter 8. In Chapter 8 when we discuss the anatomy of trees, we will define terms such as the *root*, *leaves*, and *branches* of a tree.

## 3.6 REVIEW QUESTIONS

1. Name some linked data structures that can be constructed from nodes having two separate pointer fields.
2. What is a symmetrically linked list?

## 3.6 EXERCISE

1. Write a Java **LinkedList** method to delete the second node of a two-way linked list L pointed to by the pointer **firstNode.rightLink** in Fig. 3.26. Assume **firstNode** is a data field that contains a reference value of type **ListNode**, and that the nodes of Fig. 3.26 are two-way **ListNode** objects, as defined previously.

---

 **Pitfalls**

- *Dereferencing the null pointer*

    It is easy to run off the end of a path formed by successive links in a data structure, leading to an accidental attempt to dereference the null pointer, null. Another way this can happen easily is by forgetting to initialize a reference value variable to a suitable object or array reference and by later acting on the assumption that the variable contains a non-null reference.

- *Forgetting to mark the end of a list*

  By convention, the link field of the last node on a list should contain null to designate it as the end node of the list. If you forget to mark the last node in this fashion when constructing or altering a list and then use another algorithm that assumes the last node has a null link, the algorithm could fail to work properly.

- *Watch out for the boundary cases*

  When algorithms are being designed to operate on linked data structures, it is dangerous to forget to consider the *boundary cases* that often require special treatment. Boundary cases occur at the *boundaries* of the range of problem situations—such as the *empty list* on the one hand or the largest possible list to which the algorithm applies, on the other hand. For example, in Program 3.21, which deletes the last node of a linked list, both the empty list and the list with exactly one node need to be given special treatment. It is important to check the operation of an algorithm design carefully for proper operation on these boundary cases, since experience indicates this is where bugs are frequently found.

## Tips and Techniques

- *Using pointer diagrams during design*

  When designing an algorithm that processes linked representations, it helps to use pointer diagramming notation to draw pictures of typical situations that can arise. Pointer diagramming notation can be used in the pre-Java stage of program design when program strategies are being sketched. Later, Java classes can (usually) be defined to provide specific stepwise refinements of the linked data structures designed earlier using pointer diagramming notation.

- *Preserving access to nodes needed later on*

  There is a basic (usually unwritten) law to observe when programming with linked data structures, which might be called "The Law of Preservation of Access." Loosely stated, it says that access must be preserved to all nodes that will be needed later in the solution of a problem. Bugs can arise from failure to observe this law.

  For example, consider the following diagram of a linked list of three nodes P = (GLA, ORD, NRT) in which we intend to replace the node with airport code ORD in list P with the new node YYZ, which is given as the referent of pointer variable N. Also suppose that we want to save the ORD node that got replaced on a list called the savedNodeList.

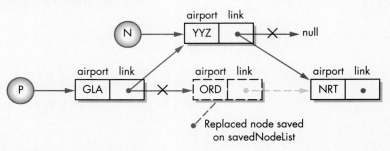

Replaced node saved
on savedNodeList

Suppose someone wrote the following method (defined as a method in the LinkedList class of Program 3.16) to attempt to accomplish this replacement:

```
     public void replace(ListNode N) {

         ListNode P = firstNode;

5        // link the YYZ node to the NRT node
             N.link = P.link.link;

         // link the GLA node to the YYZ node
             P.link = N;
10
         // save the replaced ORD node on the savedNodeList
             savedNodeList.insert(P.link);
     }
```

The problem here is that we lost access to the **ORD** node when we overwrote the only pointer referring to it, which was located in the link field of the **GLA** node. So when we tried to save the replaced **ORD** node on the **savedNodeList**, there was no pointer left to give us access to it. Instead, by accident, we inserted the **YYZ** node on the **savedNodeList**.

The cure is either to perform the operations in a correct order or to declare and use a new pointer variable that will retain access to a node to which later access is required. For example, the following method correctly solves the problem:

```
     public void replace2(ListNode N) {

         ListNode P = firstNode;

5        // link the YYZ node to the NRT node
             N.link = P.link.link;

         // save the ORD node on the savedNodeList
             savedNodeList.insert(P.link);
10
         // link the GLA node to the YYZ node
             P.link = N;
     }
```

The method in Program 3.21, for deleting the last node of a list, implicitly uses the law of preservation of access. The ultimate purpose of the **previousNode** pointer is to retain access to the next-to-last node. The **currentNode** pointer is used to locate the last node, by stepping it along the nodes of the list until it points to a node whose link field is **null**. At this moment, access to the next-to-last node is needed to mark it as the new end of the list by setting its link field to **null**.

**References for Further Study**

One of the great classic references in computer science for algorithms and data structures is the three-volume set by Knuth:

> Donald E. Knuth, *The Art of Computer Programming*. Addison-Wesley Publishing Company, Inc., Reading, MA.

The titles of the three volumes are:

a classic reference

- *Fundamental Algorithms*, Volume I, second edition, 1973
- *Seminumerical Algorithms*, Volume II, second edition, 1980
- *Sorting and Searching*, Volume III, 1973

Linked lists are covered in depth in Volume I, pp. 252–272.

## Chapter Summary

Linked data representations are a major topic of study in computer science. Sometimes they support efficient algorithms. They are also useful for applications requiring data structures of unpredictable size and shape. Because they can grow piece-by-piece, they can support elastic data representations that have important growth and combining properties. Consequently, they provide one of the principal ways for representing various important abstract data types.

linked representations are important in computer science

Linked representations are created by using pointers to link blocks of data storage together. Pointers are data values that represent the memory addresses of these data blocks.

Even though Java has neither explicit pointer data types nor pointer dereferencing operators, it accesses objects and arrays using implicit pointers called *reference values*. These reference values can be stored in data fields of objects, passed as actual parameters in method invocations, and stored as values of variables. This provides a satisfactory basis for implementing linked data representations in Java.

Java can support linked data representations

This chapter introduces a pointer diagramming language that is used for pointers and linked representations in the remainder of the book. This pointer diagramming language is handy to use in the initial stages of program design. It is also helpful to use it to reason precisely and pictorially about various linked data structures.

pointer diagramming notation is useful for algorithm design

Linear linked lists are of key importance. Several skills are important in relation to them: (1) knowing how to define classes supporting linked list objects in Java; (2) knowing how to create and delete list nodes, and how to link them together; and (3) knowing how to perform various important list operations such as insertion and deletion of nodes in lists, searching for items in lists, printing lists, and joining lists together.

Of course, linked representations come in many different shapes and patterns. For example, using nodes with two separate pointer fields, we can create linked representations for two-way lists and rings, and for linked binary trees, to name just three examples.

there are many different linked representations

# Introduction
# to Recursion

## 4.1 Introduction and Motivation

Recursion is an important recurring concept in computer science. It can some-times be used to formulate unusually simple and elegant solutions to problems that are hard to solve otherwise. It can sometimes be used to define things simply and concisely. Occasionally, recursion can help express algorithms in a form that makes their performance easy to analyze.

*recursion is a key recurring concept*

This chapter is an introduction that aims at covering the heart of the concept. It also gives you opportunities to build your skills for dealing with recursion. An impor-tant goal is for you to be able to implement algorithms that use recursion.

First, what is *recursion*? Let's answer this question by first talking about circular definitions. In elementary school, teachers usually instruct students to avoid circular definitions such as the following:

**mandiloquy.** (1) The conduct of mandiloquy between nations; (2) Skill in doing this.

Circular definitions are not helpful because they do not do what definitions are supposed to do—namely, tell you about something new by rendering its meaning in terms of what is already known. Instead, they exchange the unknown for more unknowns.

*recursive definitions are circular*

In this chapter, we will study a useful kind of circular definition called *recursion*. Recursive definitions are just circular definitions. When we define something recursively, we define it in terms of itself.

Initially, this sounds as if it might get us into the same unhelpful mess that ordinary circular definitions do. But what makes a recursive definition of an X work is that it shows how to define a big version of an X in terms of simpler versions of X. This enables us to solve a big problem by breaking it down into simpler subproblems of the same kind, until, at some point, we reach subproblems simple enough that we can give their solutions directly. Then subproblem solutions can be combined to get the solution to the original problem.

## Plan for the Chapter

Our approach is to discuss a graduated sequence of examples of recursive programs that aim at helping you learn to "think recursively." We begin by studying some simple programs to compute sums and products and to reverse several kinds of data structures. Studying simple examples first can help build intuition for how recursive programs work.

*learning to think recursively*

*we generalize*

*we cover a pitfall*

We then generalize briefly to try to capture the essence of what a recursive program is. At this point, you are invited to try your hand at solving some programming problems recursively. Next we pause to study a commonly occurring pitfall—a recursive program that keeps on calling itself forever, producing an infinite regress. We'll study some examples of infinite regresses in order to become aware of the danger. Then, as a small case study, the famous Towers of Hanoi problem is solved recursively, and we discover the number of steps it takes to achieve a solution (in Section 4.4). Finally, we give some useful tips and techniques for dealing with recursion.

## 4.2  Thinking Recursively

### LEARNING OBJECTIVES

1. To learn to think recursively.
2. To learn how strategies for recursion involve both base cases and recursion cases.
3. To learn how to search for different ways of decomposing a problem into subproblems.
4. To understand how to use call trees and traces to reason about how recursive programs work.

*a gradual introduction*

A good way to get a gradual introduction to the idea of recursion is to examine a sequence of solutions to simple problems. First, we study the simple problem of adding up the squares of some integers. Three different recursive solutions are presented to

```
    |   int sumSquares(int m, int n) {
    |
    |       int i, sum;
    |                                          // recall that the assignment
  5 |       sum = 0;                           // sum += i*i has the
    |       for (i = m; i <= n; i++) sum += i*i;   // same effect in Java as the
    |       return sum;                        // assignment sum = sum + i*i
    |   }
```

**Program 4.1** Iterative Sum of Squares

illustrate different ways of breaking problems into subproblems. We also discuss base cases and show how they are used to terminate the execution of recursive methods. Then we introduce call trees and traces and show how they can reveal the way recursive programs work.

After showing how the decomposition techniques explored in summing squares of integers can be applied to multiplying integers as well, we study a nonstandard way of computing the factorial function recursively.

We then broaden the range of examples of recursion to show how we can treat nonnumeric data such as linked lists and arrays. We study some recursive solutions for reversing linked lists and arrays to illustrate some possibilities. Then it's time to generalize. We look back on our examples and try to extract the essence of what recursion involves.

## How to Make Things Add Up Recursively

adding up squares

Our first example is a simple program to add up all the squares of the numbers from $m$ to $n$. That is, given two positive integers, $m$ and $n$, where $m \leq n$, we want to find sumSquares$(m,n) = m^2 + (m + 1)^2 + \ldots + n^2$. For example, sumSquares$(5,10) = 5^2 + 6^2 + 7^2 + 8^2 + 9^2 + 10^2 = 355$.[1]

the iterative way

An ordinary iterative program to compute sumSquares$(m,n)$ is shown in Program 4.1. The strategy for this program is familiar to beginners. The variable sum holds partial sums during the iteration, and, initially, sum is set to 0. On line 6, a for-statement lets its controlled variable, i, range over the successive values in the range m:n (where the range m:n consists of the integers i, such that $m \leq i \leq n$).

iteration builds up solutions stepwise

For each such integer i, the partial sum in the variable, sum, is increased by the square of i (by adding i*i to it). After the iteration is finished, sum holds the total of all the contributions of the squares i*i, for each i in the range m:n. The value of sum is finally returned as the value of the method on line 7.

---

[1] When implementing practical applications, professional programmers would be unlikely to write iterative or recursive programs to compute sumSquares$(m,n)$, since this sum can be computed more directly and efficiently by evaluating a simple algebraic formula involving $m$ and $n$, such as sumSquares$(m,n) = (n^3 - m^3)/3 + (n^2 + m^2)/2 + (n - m)/6$. But for the purpose of this chapter, the value of writing iterative and recursive programs to compute sumSquares$(m,n)$ lies not in their efficiency but rather in their value as a device for illustrating the principles of recursion.

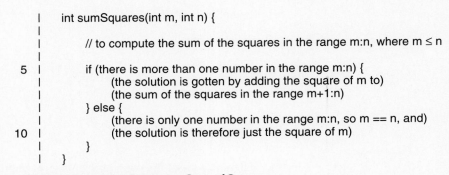

```
|     int sumSquares(int m, int n) {
|
|          // to compute the sum of the squares in the range m:n, where m ≤ n
|
5 |         if (there is more than one number in the range m:n) {
|                  (the solution is gotten by adding the square of m to)
|                  (the sum of the squares in the range m+1:n)
|          } else {
|                  (there is only one number in the range m:n, so m == n, and)
10 |                 (the solution is therefore just the square of m)
|          }
|     }
```

**Program Strategy 4.2** Recursive Sum of Squares

In an iterative solution such as this, a typical pattern is to build up the final solution in stages, using a repetitive process that enumerates contributions step-by-step and combines the contributions with a partial solution that, stepwise, gets closer and closer to the overall solution.

To compute sumSquares(m,n) recursively, a new way of thinking needs to be used. The idea is to find a way of solving the overall problem by breaking it into smaller subproblems, such that some of the smaller subproblems can be solved using the *same* method as that used to solve the overall problem. The solutions to the subproblems are then *combined* to get the solution to the overall problem.

Program Strategy 4.2 illustrates one such way of thinking about the solution. To refine this program strategy into an actual recursive solution, all we have to do is to replace the comments in parentheses with appropriate implementations in Java, as illustrated in Program 4.3.

Line 4 of Program 4.3 contains the *recursive call*, sumSquares(m+1,n). A recursive call is one in which a method calls itself *inside* itself. In effect, what line 4 says is that the solution to the overall problem can be gotten by adding (a) the solution to the smaller subproblem of summing the squares in the range m+1:n, and (b) the solution to the subproblem of finding the square of m. Moreover, the smaller subproblem (a) can be solved by the same method as the overall problem by making the recursive call, sumSquares(m+1,n), in which the method sumSquares calls itself *within* itself.

*recursion combines subproblem solutions*

*refining the strategy*

*recursive calls*

```
|     int sumSquares(int m, int n) {                              // assume m ≤ n
|
|          if (m < n) {
|                  return  m*m + sumSquares(m+1,n);               // the recursion
5 |         } else {
|                  return m*m;                                    // the base case
|          }
|     }
```

**Program 4.3** Recursive Sum of Squares

base cases

It is important to be aware that there is always a potential danger that a recursive method could attempt to go on endlessly splitting problems into subproblems and calling itself recursively to solve these subproblems, without ever stopping. Consequently, each properly designed recursive method should have a *base case* (or several base cases).

Line 6 of Program 4.3 contains the base case that occurs when the range m:n contains just one number, in which case m == n. The solution can then be computed directly by returning the square of m. This stops the recursion, since sumSquares is *not* called recursively on line 6.

the general pattern

Now let's generalize. The overall pattern of a recursive method is that it breaks the overall problem into smaller and smaller subproblems, which are solved by calling the method recursively, until the subproblems get small enough that they become base cases and can be solved by giving their solutions directly (without using any more recursive calls). At each stage, solutions to the subproblems are combined to yield a solution to the overall problem. Let's look at two more recursive solutions to sumSquares(m,n) that fit this overall general pattern.

reading what a program does

Program 4.4 gives a new solution that is only slightly different than the first solution given in Program 4.3. The process of reading what a program such as this does involves inferring the goals that the individual parts of the program achieve and describing how the program achieves these goals. Therefore one way of summarizing the results of reading what a program does is to replace the program by the program strategy that describes its goals and methods. (This can be thought of as the reverse of the process of refining a program strategy into a specific realization of the strategy—a process of *antirefinement*, so-to-speak, in which we infer the program strategy from the specific program text.) The result of this process is shown in Program Strategy 4.5. Comparing Program 4.4 with Program 4.3 reveals that the decomposition of the overall problem into subproblems is slightly different. Program 4.3 specifies that to get the sum of the squares in the range m:n, we add $m^2$ to the sum of the squares in the range m+1:n, whereas Program 4.4 gets the same sum by adding $n^2$ to the sum of the squares in the range m:n−1. The former could be called a *going-up recursion* since the successive subproblems called in the recursive calls "go upward," starting with the full range m:n, progressing next to subranges (m+1:n), (m+2:n), …, and finally stopping at the uppermost subrange containing the base case (n:n). Program 4.4 could be called a

going-up recursions

```
  |   int sumSquares(int m, int n) {                        // assume m ≤ n
  |
  |       if  (m < n) {
  |           return sumSquares(m, n − 1) + n*n;            // the recursion
5 |       } else {
  |           return n*n;                                   // the base case
  |       }
  |
  |   }
```

**Program 4.4** Going-Down Recursion

```
|    int sumSquares(int m, int n) {
|
|        // to compute the sum of the squares in the range m:n, where m ≤ n
|
5 |        if (there is more than one number in the range m:n) {
|            (the solution is gotten by adding the square of n to)
|            (the sum of the squares in the range m:n–1)
|        } else {
|            (there is only one number in the range m:n, so m == n, and)
10 |           (the solution is therefore just the square of n)
|        }
|
|    }
```

**Program Strategy 4.5** Strategy for Going-Down Recursion

going-down recursions

splitting a range in halves

*going-down recursion* since the successive subproblems called in the recursive calls "go downward," starting with the full range m:n, progressing next to subranges (m:n–1), (m:n–2), …, and finally stopping at the bottommost subrange containing the base case (m:m).

The final example for computing sumSquares(m,n) uses yet another decomposition principle to break the overall problem into subproblems—namely, splitting the overall problem into two *halves*.

In Program 4.6, if a range of numbers, m:n, contains just one number (i.e., if m == n), then the base case solution $m^2$ is given on line 6. Otherwise, the range m:n contains more than one number and is split into two half-ranges. Assuming that middle is a midpoint for the range m:n, then the left half-range, m:middle, goes from m up to and including the middle. The right half-range, middle+1:n, goes from the number just past the middle up to and including n.

The recursion case on line 9 simply says that the sum of the squares of the entire range of integers m:n can be obtained by adding the sum of the squares of the left half-range, m:middle, to the sum of the squares of the right half-range, middle +1:n.

```
|    int sumSquares(int m, int n) {                          // assume m ≤ n
|
|        int middle;
|
5 |        if (m == n) {
|            return m*m;                                      // the base case
|        } else {
|            middle = (m+n) / 2;
|            return sumSquares(m, middle) + sumSquares(middle +1, n) ;
10 |        }
|    }
```

**Program 4.6** Recursion Combining Two Half-Solutions

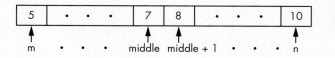

**Figure 4.7** Splitting a range m:n into two halves

Let's take a closer look at the method used on line 8 to compute the **middle**. An example, shown in Fig. 4.7, is splitting the range **5:10** into two half-ranges.

**computing the middle**

In this example, the range **5:10** is split into a left half-range, **5:7**, and a right half-range, **8:10**, using a **middle == 7**. To compute the middle of the range m:n, we divide **m + n** by 2, using *integer division* by 2, which keeps the quotient and throws away the remainder. The / operator in Java performs integer division on two integer operands.

In the case of the range **5:10**, we set **middle = (5 + 10) / 2**, on line 8 of Program 4.6, which gives **middle** the value 7, since (5 + 10) = 15, and 15 divided by 2 gives a quotient of 7 and a remainder of 1/2. This remainder is discarded in the integer division, **15 / 2**. (If the range m:n contains an odd number of integers, as in the example **10:20**, which contains 11 integers, then the middle value 15 divides the range into two half-ranges of unequal size. In this case, the left half-range, **10:15**, contains six integers, and the right half-range, **16:20**, contains only five integers.)

In summary, Program 4.6 presents a way of decomposing the overall problem into two subproblems different from that in Programs 4.3 and 4.4, because it uses two subproblems whose size is (roughly) half the size of the overall problem, and, whenever the range includes more than one number, it uses two recursive calls to compute the sum of the squares of the numbers in the two half-ranges.

## Call Trees and Traces

It is informative to look at the *call tree* of Program 4.6, when the method call **sumSquares(5,10)** is evaluated. This is illustrated in Fig. 4.8. The evaluation of the calling expression, **sumSquares(5,10)**, causes a method call on Program 4.6 generating two more recursive calls, **sumSquares(5,7)** and **sumSquares(8,10)**. These latter two calls are shown as the descendants of the topmost call, **sumSquares(5,10)**. In Fig. 4.8, we see that the calls of the form **sumSquares(m,m)** have no descendants beneath

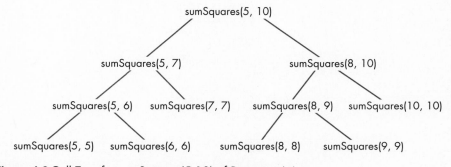

**Figure 4.8** Call Tree for sumSquares(5,10) of Program 4.6

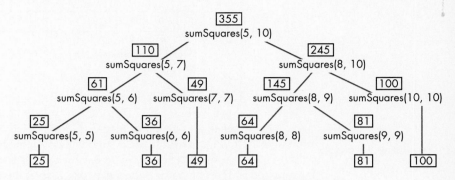

**Figure 4.9** Annotated Call Tree for sumSquares(5,10) of Program 4.6

them in the call tree since they do not generate any further recursive calls. This is because calls of the form sumSquares(m,m) result in base cases in Program 4.6, in which $m^2$ is returned as the direct result.

Suppose we annotate each calling expression in the call tree of Fig. 4.8 with the results returned by each recursive call. To do this, assume each call resulting in a base case has the value computed by the base case placed in a box directly beneath the calling expression, and also directly above the calling expression to indicate the value returned by the call. Then to compute the value returned by each calling expression, E, that does not result in a base case, we add the values in the annotation boxes above E's two immediate descendant calling expressions and place the sum in a new annotation box directly above E itself. For example, we can see how the topmost final value, 355, for the calling expression, sumSquares(5,10), is computed by adding the solutions, 110 and 245, returned by the recursive calls, sumSquares(5,7) and sumSquares(8,10). The entire annotated call tree is shown in Fig. 4.9. The call trees for Programs 4.3 and 4.4 are much simpler, consisting of the chains of calls, shown in Fig. 4.10.

*annotating call trees*

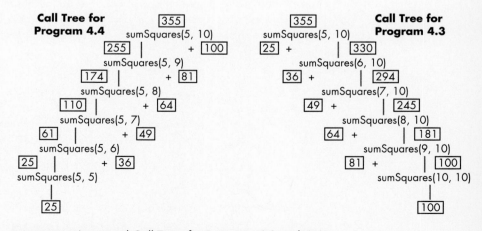

**Figure 4.10** Annotated Call Trees for Programs 4.3 and 4.4

call traces

Another way of conceptualizing what happens when we call sumSquares(5,10) recursively is to use a *call trace*. Some Java systems can print the trace of their method calls when appropriate debugging commands are given. Some traces of the call sumSquares(5,10) are shown next.

*Trace of "going-up" recursion from Program 4.3*

```
sumSquares(5,10) = (25 + sumSquares(6,10))
                 = (25 + (36 + sumSquares(7,10)))
                 = (25 + (36 + (49 + sumSquares(8,10))))
                 = (25 + (36 + (49 + (64 + sumSquares(9,10)))))
                 = (25 + (36 + (49 + (64 + (81 + sumSquares(10,10))))))
                 = (25 + (36 + (49 + (64 + (81 + 100))))))
                 = (25 + (36 + (49 + (64 + 181))))
                 = (25 + (36 + (49 + 245)))
                 = (25 + (36 + 294))
                 = (25 + 330)
                 = 355
```

*Trace of "going-down" recursion from Program 4.4*

```
sumSquares(5,10) = (sumSquares(5,9) + 100)
                 = ((sumSquares(5,8) + 81) + 100)
                 = (((sumSquares(5,7) + 64) + 81) + 100)
                 = ((((sumSquares(5,6) + 49) + 64) + 81) + 100)
                 = (((((sumSquares(5,5) + 36) + 49) + 64) + 81) + 100)
                 = (((((25 + 36) + 49) + 64) + 81) + 100)
                 = ((((61 + 49) + 64) + 81) + 100)
                 = (((110 + 64) + 81) + 100)
                 = ((174 + 81) + 100)
                 = (255 + 100)
                 = 355
```

*Trace of "division in halves" recursion from Program 4.6*

```
sumSquares(5,10) = (sumSquares(5,7) + sumSquares(8,10))
                 = (sumSquares(5,6) + sumSquares(7,7))
                     + (sumSquares(8,9) + sumSquares(10,10))
                 = ((sumSquares(5,5) + sumSquares(6,6))
                         + sumSquares(7,7))
                     + ((sumSquares(8,8) + sumSquares(9,9))
                         + sumSquares(10,10))
                 = ((25 + 36) + 49) + ((64 + 81) + 100)
                 = (61 + 49) + (145 + 100)
                 = (110 + 245)
                 = 355
```

```
 |     int factorial(int n) {
 |
 |         int i, f;
 |
5|         f = 1;                              // recall that f *= i has the
 |         for (i=2; i <= n; i++)  f *= i;     // same effect as f = f*i in Java
 |         return f;
 |     }
```

**Program 4.11** Iterative Factorial

## Multiplying Things Recursively

If we multiply together the integers from 1 to n, we get the *factorial of* n, which is denoted by n!. Thus n! = 1 * 2 * 3 * ... * n. It is easy to write an iterative program in Java to compute n!, as shown in Program 4.11. The program builds up the final product by repeatedly multiplying an initial partial product, f == 1, by each successive integer in the range 2:n.

The factorial of n can also be computed recursively. As usual, we need a base case and a recursive call that solves the overall problem by solving a smaller subproblem of the same kind. The base case is computed on line 4 of Program 4.12. It specifies that to multiply together the numbers in the range 1:1, we directly return 1 as the answer, without making any recursive calls. But if the range 1:n consists of more than one integer, we can multiply all the integers in 1:n together by multiplying the product of all the numbers in 1:n−1 by the multiplier n. This is the purpose of the recursive call on line 6. A trace of the call factorial(6) is as follows:

recursive factorial

*Trace of the call factorial(6)*

```
factorial(6)  = (6 * factorial(5))
              = (6 * (5 * factorial(4)))
              = (6 * (5 * (4 * factorial(3))))
              = (6 * (5 * (4 * (3 * factorial(2)))))
              = (6 * (5 * (4 * (3 * (2 * factorial(1))))))
              = (6 * (5 * (4 * (3 * (2 * 1)))))
              = (6 * (5 * (4 * (3 * 2))))
              = (6 * (5 * (4 * 6)))
              = (6 * (5 * 24))
              = (6 * 120)
              = 720
```

```
 |     int factorial(int n) {
 |
 |         if (n == 1) {
 |             return 1;                       // base case
5|         } else {
 |             return  n * factorial(n − 1);   // recursion
 |         }
 |     }
```

**Program 4.12** Recursive Factorial

```
 |    int product(int m, int n) {
 |
 |        // to compute the product of the integers from m to n
 |
 5  |        if (the range m:n has only one integer in it) {
 |            (return m as the solution, since m == n)          // the base case
 |        } else {
 |            (the range m:n must have more than one integer in it, so)
 |            (compute the midpoint of m:n as the value of the variable middle)
10  |            (and return the product of the integers in the range m:middle)
 |            (times the product of the integers in the range middle+1:n)
 |        }
 |
 |    }
```

**Program Strategy 4.13** Multiplying m:n Together Using Half-Ranges

several ways of computing
the factorial

Program 4.12 uses a "going-down" recursion in which the parameter n in the recursive calls of factorial(n) goes down by one on each successive recursive call. We can also multiply together the numbers in the range 1:n, using a "going-up" recursion or by dividing the range into halves, similar to the way we summed the squares in the range m:n earlier. To do this, we can first write an auxiliary method, product(m,n), which multiplies together the numbers in the range m:n, and then we can compute n! using factorial(n) = product(1,n).

auxiliary methods
can be helpful

Let's write the product method using recursive division of the range into halves, as shown in Program Strategy 4.13. A refinement of this program strategy is given in Program 4.14. Having defined this auxiliary method, it is now easy to compute factorial(n) by calling product(1,n). It is also easy to write product(m,n) so that it uses a going-up recursion (see Exercise 6 at the end of this section). Note, however, that it is hard to write a going-up recursion for factorial(n), in which the parameter m, for the lower end of the range of numbers to be multiplied, is absent. Sometimes, writing an auxiliary method first helps you get a handle on the solution of a problem to be solved recursively.

```
 |    int product(int m, int n) {                              // assume m ≤ n
 |
 |        int middle;
 |
 5  |        if (m == n) {
 |            return m;                                        // the base case
 |        } else {
 |            middle = (m+n) / 2;
 |            return product(m, middle) * product(middle+1, n);
10  |        }
 |
 |    }
```

**Program 4.14** Multiplying m:n Together Using Half-Ranges

```
|    class ListNode {                          // define linked list nodes
|        String        airport;                // holding airports as items
|        ListNode      link;
|    }
5 |
|    class LinkedList {                        // a linked list has a header node
|        int           length;                 // having an integer length field
|        ListNode:     firstNode;              // and a firstNode field that points
|                                              // to its linked ListNodes
10 |
|        void reverse( ) {                     // insert here the text of one of the
|            . . .                             // Programs 4.16 or 4.19 below giving
|        }                                     // a LinkedList's reverse( ) method
|    }
```

**Program 4.15** Classes Defining Linked Lists and ListNodes

## Reversing Lists and Arrays

Continuing with our graduated sequence of introductory examples, let's look at two reversal problems: (1) reversing the order of the items in a linked list, and (2) reversing the order of the items in an array. Assuming that LinkedLists and ListNodes are defined as shown in Program 4.15, an iterative solution to the list reversal problem is given in Program 4.16.

*recursive list reversal*

Let's rethink this solution to see if we can come up with a recursive way to solve the same problem. Consider a typical list, such as L = (SAN, ORD, BRU, DUS). We might imagine breaking this list into two lists called the head and the tail, where: head(L) = (SAN), and tail(L) = (ORD, BRU, DUS). That is, the head is a list containing the first node of L, and the tail of L is the remainder of the list, after the first node has been removed. In other words, the tail of L is the list consisting of L's second and succeeding nodes. (Let's also agree that if L = null, head(L) and tail(L) are not defined. But if L consists of just one node, as in L = (SAN), then head(L) = (SAN), and tail(L) = null.)

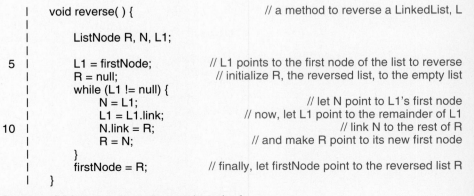

```
|    void reverse( ) {                         // a method to reverse a LinkedList, L
|
|        ListNode R, N, L1;
|
5 |      L1 = firstNode;                       // L1 points to the first node of the list to reverse
|        R = null;                             // initialize R, the reversed list, to the empty list
|        while (L1 != null) {
|            N = L1;                           // let N point to L1's first node
|            L1 = L1.link;                     // now, let L1 point to the remainder of L1
10 |           N.link = R;                      // link N to the rest of R
|            R = N;                            // and make R point to its new first node
|        }
|        firstNode = R;                        // finally, let firstNode point to the reversed list R
|    }
```

**Program 4.16** Iterative List Reversal Method

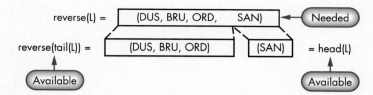

**Figure 4.17** A Possible Solution

*partitioning a list into its head and tail*

Now, supposing we had a way to partition a nonempty list **L** into its **head** and its **tail**, what strategy could we use to reverse the entire list? (Before peeking at the solution, try conceptualizing it yourself, starting with the hint that since **tail(L)** is a subproblem of smaller size, you might somehow be able to combine **reverse(tail(L))** into a solution to the overall problem.)

To go after the solution systematically, let's take our example list **L** and write out both **L** and its reversal, together with **L**'s **head** and **tail** and their reversals:

$$
\begin{aligned}
\text{L} &= \text{(SAN, ORD, BRU, DUS)} \\
\text{reverse(L)} &= \text{(DUS, BRU, ORD, SAN)} \\
\text{tail(L)} &= \text{(ORD, BRU, DUS)} \\
\text{reverse(tail(L))} &= \text{(DUS, BRU, ORD)} \\
\text{head(L)} &= \text{(SAN)} \\
\text{reverse(head(L))} &= \text{(SAN)}
\end{aligned}
$$

*we can concatenate to get a solution*

Now we can ask, "Which of the above pieces combine to yield the needed solution, **reverse(L)**?" One possible answer is indicated in Fig. 4.17. We see that (except for the base cases, which are not yet considered) a possible solution could result if we could concatenate (i.e., join together) the two lists **reverse(tail(L))** and **head(L)** into a single list. This partial solution is shown in Program Strategy 4.18.

```
    |   ListNode reverse( ) {
    |
    |       (let L point to the firstNode of the linked list of ListNodes to be reversed)
    |
  5 |       if (L is the empty list) {
    |           (the result is the reverse of the empty list)          // base case
    |       } else {                                        // otherwise, if L is nonempty
    |           (partition the list L into its head and tail.)
 10 |           (then, concatenate the reverse of the tail of L)       // recursion step
    |           (with the head of L and let firstNode point to)
    |           (the result of the concatenation.)
    |       }
    |
    |   }
```

**Program Strategy 4.18** For Reversing a List, **L**

To refine this strategy into a final working Java program, we need to solve three subproblems: (1) deciding how to reverse the empty list, (2) finding out how to partition a nonempty list into its **head** and its **tail**, and (3) writing a method to concatenate (or join together) two lists into a single list. It seems reasonable that the reverse of an empty list () is another empty list (), so let's put **reverse(null) = null**. The next problem is to partition **L** into a **head** and a **tail**. The solution to this is shown on lines 10:12 of Program 4.19.

The final subproblem to solve is that of joining two lists, **L1** and **L2**, together to make a single list in which the items on list **L2** follow the items on list **L1**. This process is called concatenation. The following recursive program returns a **ListNode** pointer to the result of concatenating the two lists pointed to by the **ListNode** pointers given in **L1** and **L2** respectively:

```
  | ListNode concat(ListNode L1, ListNode L2) {
  |     if (L1 == null) {
  |         return L2;                                     // base case
  |     } else {
5 |         L1.link = concat(L1.link, L2);                 // recursion step
  |         return L1;           // return the pointer to the concatenated lists
  |     }
  | }
```

Now that we have solved our three subproblems, we are ready to refine Program Strategy 4.18 into an actual Java program to reverse a list. This is given as Program 4.19. (To complete the class definition of **LinkedList**, the text of Program 4.19 could be inserted on lines 11:13 of Program 4.15.) Note that we used the process of top-down programming by stepwise refinement to create the method for **reverse(L)**. We started with a strategy providing the topmost goals we would need to achieve in order to accomplish list reversal in Program Strategy 4.18. This presented us with three subproblems to solve. After solving these, we combined the three solutions in the last step—creating a final refinement of Program Strategy 4.18 to yield Program 4.19.

```
   | void reverse() {                    // the reverse() method applies the auxiliary
   |     firstNode = reverse1(firstNode);       // method reverse1(L) below to the
   | }                                          // linked list L pointed to by the firstNode
   |                                            // field of the LinkedList header node
5  |
   | ListNode reverse1(ListNode L) {
   |     if (L == null) {
   |         return null;                                  // base case
   |     } else {
10 |         ListNode head = L;                // partition L into its head and tail
   |         ListNode tail = L.link;
   |         head.link = null;
   |         return concat(reverse1(tail), head);          // recursion step
   |     }
   | }
```

**Program 4.19** Refinement for **reverse(L)**

**identifying and solving the subproblems**

**concatenation**

**we used top-down programming**

In fact, according to good software engineering practice, we are not yet finished with our task. Having created Program 4.19 as a refinement, we really don't know that it works properly yet. We should test it, together with its components and auxiliary functions, and/or we should verify that it works by attempting to prove mathematically that it terminates and gives the correct outputs. Moreover, we should analyze it for its efficiency and see if it runs as well as might be expected. It turns out that Program 4.19 is an example of a recursive program with a clear design structure that, nonetheless, is not as efficient as it should be. Exercise 4.2.7 asks you to compare the efficiency of Program 4.19 with another recursive list reversal method that runs faster (but is, perhaps, more difficult to understand initially). This raises the issue that even though recursive programs are often easy to write, they sometimes conceal inefficiency behind their facade of simplicity and clarity. Rather than accepting the first recursive solution that comes to mind, it is good software engineering practice to examine recursive solutions carefully to see if alternative iterative or recursive solutions of greater efficiency exist.

*some software engineering considerations*

## Reversing Arrays

Let's take a moment to expand our repertoire of decomposition methods for splitting an overall problem into subproblems. In the case of linked-list reversal we decomposed a list L into its **head** and its **tail**. This is a natural decomposition for linked lists, since the **tail** can be accessed starting with a pointer to L, just by accessing the link of L's first node. Other decompositions of a linked-list into sublists, such as dividing the list into two half lists, are more cumbersome and expensive to implement.

*enlarging our bag of tricks*

However, if we have an array whose components can be accessed by integer indexes, the kinds of decompositions into subproblems that can be arranged conveniently increases. Let A be an array, and let A[m:n] denote the subarray of A consisting of the $m^{th}$ through the $n^{th}$ items of A. Three different types of decompositions we can use are:

*Decomposition 1.* First and Rest
   Split A[m:n] into its **first** item, A[m], and the **rest** of them, A[m+1:n]

*Decomposition 2.* Last and All but Last
   Split A[m:n] into its **last** item, A[n], and **allButLast** == A[m:n – 1]

*Decomposition 3.* Split into Halves
   Compute **middle** = (m + n) / 2, and then split A[m:n] into its **leftHalf** == A[m:middle] and **rightHalf** == A[middle+1:n]

We have actually seen these three different decompositions in slightly different dress before. For instance, when considering how to compute the sum of the squares of the numbers from m to n, the going-up recursion of Program 4.3 split m:n into "First and Rest." The going-down recursion of Program 4.4 split m:n into "Last and All but Last." Moreover, Program 4.6 split m:n into two halves. Also, the list reversal Program 4.19 split the list L into "First and Rest," where the "First" of a list L was its **head**, and the "Rest" was its **tail**.

*three familiar ways to decompose a range*

```
    |    void reverseArray(int [ ] A, int m, int n) {        // to reverse the items from
    |                                                         // m through n in an array A
    |        if (m < n) {
    |            int temp = A[m];                             // first, swap the edges
  5 |            A[m] = A[n];
    |            A[n] = temp;
    |            reverseArray(A, m + 1, n – 1);               // and then, reverse the center
    |        }
    |
    |    }
```

**Program 4.20** Reversing the Items  A[m:n] of Array A

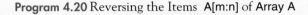

and a new one

Let's expand the set of ideas available for splitting problems into subproblems by considering a fourth decomposition method—splitting a range **m:n** into its "Edges and Center."

> *Decomposition 4.* Edges and Center
>     Split A[m:n] into its **edges**: (A[m], A[n]), and **center** == A[m +1:n – 1]

This decomposition can form the basis for a recursive array reversal algorithm, such as that given in Program 4.20. For example, when applied to an array of five integers of the form, **A** = {11, 22, 33, 44, 55}; the method call **reverseArray(A,0,4)** first swaps the first and last integers **11** and **55** (on lines 4:6) and then reverses the middle items of the array **22, 33, 44** (using the recursive call on line 7).

## The General Idea

Let's generalize from our experience with this series of graduated examples to reach some conclusions about how recursive programs work.

what are recursive programs?

Recursive programs are just programs that call themselves in order to obtain a solution to a problem. The reason that they call themselves is to compute the solution to a subproblem that has three general properties: (1) the subproblem is *smaller* than the overall problem to be solved (or is *simpler*, in the sense that it is closer to a final solution), (2) the subproblem can be solved either directly (as a base case) or recursively by making a recursive call, and (3) the subproblem's solution can be combined with solutions to other subproblems to obtain the solution to the overall problem.

divide and conquer

Inherent in this overall strategy is the implication that you can break a big problem into smaller subproblems of the same kind that can be solved by application of the same method, and that you can combine subproblem solutions back into the overall solution. This breakdown of a big problem into similar component problems is an instance of the *divide and conquer strategy*. We'll see more examples of this strategy later in the book.

how to think recursively

To *think recursively*, ask yourself a series of questions: first, "How can I break this big problem into smaller problems of the same kind that can be solved by the same method?" Second, "When the problems get small enough, how can they be solved directly, without breaking them down any further and making more recursive calls, so the process of recursion can stop?" Finally, "If I assume I've got the solutions to the subproblems, how can I combine these solutions to get the overall solution to the original problem?"

It sometimes helps to consider a typical example. From the example of the overall problem, you apply the problem decomposition method you have chosen, yielding examples of the subproblems. Then, you assume you have the solutions to the sub-problems (either as results of base cases or recursion cases) and you write out the examples of the subproblem solutions. Finally, you have a table of parts, consisting of the subproblems and their solutions, and you can gain insight into what method of combination is needed to compose the subproblem solutions into the overall solution. Sometimes, through trial and error, you may have to back up and try several different decomposition methods before discovering one that works.

*considering a typical example*

Perhaps you are ready to solve some recursive programming problems on your own now. Experience indicates that it is difficult to gain mastery of recursion just by reading about it. You should thus try solving, say, a dozen recursion problems. The wider the range of problems you solve, the better your recursive programming skills will become.

## **4.2** REVIEW QUESTIONS

1. What is the base case in a recursive program?
2. Give four different decomposition methods for splitting an integer interval, m:n, into parts that can be helpful in determining subproblems to solve in a recursive program.
3. What is a call tree?
4. What is the trace of a recursive method call?
5. What is a natural way to consider decomposing a linked list into substructures helpful for devising a recursive solution to a problem?

## **4.2** EXERCISES

1. Write a recursive method that computes $x^n$, called power($x,n$), where $x$ is a floating point number and $n$ is a nonnegative integer. [*Hint*: power($x,n$) can be defined by the following two equations: power($x,0$) = 1.0 and for $n \geq 1$, power($x,n$) = $x *$ power($x, n-1$).]
2. Write an improved recursive version of power($x,n$) that works by breaking $n$ down into halves (where half of $n = n / 2$), squaring power($x,n / 2$), and multiplying by $x$ again if $n$ was odd. For example, $x^{11} = (x^5)*(x^5)*x$, whereas $x^{10} = (x^5)*(x^5)$. Find a suitable base case to stop the recursion.
3. Write a recursive method, mult($m,n$), to multiply two positive integers, $m$ and $n$, using only repeated addition.
4. According to Euclid's algorithm for finding the greatest common divisor, gcd($m,n$), of two positive integers $m$ and $n$, one can take successive pairs of

remainders. When one of the remainders is zero, the other number in the pair is the gcd. Letting $(m,n)$ be the first remainder pair, we can write $m = q * n + r$, such that $0 \leq r < n$. Here, $q$ is the quotient of $m$ upon division by $n$ ($q = m / n$), and $r$ is the remainder of $m$ after division by $n$ ($r = m \% n$). Any divisor (including the gcd) that divides $m$ and $n$ must also divide $r$, since $r = m - q*n$. Consequently, the gcd of $m$ and $n$ must be the same as $\gcd(n,r)$. In Euclid's algorithm, one starts with the pair $(m,n)$ and computes the pair $(n,r)$. Then, if $r = 0$, the $\gcd(m,n) = \gcd(n,r) = n$. But if $r \neq 0$, the pair $(n,r)$ is replaced by the next successive remainder pair, which is guaranteed to have the same gcd. Write a recursive version of Euclid's algorithm to compute $\gcd(m,n)$.

5. In good software engineering practice, you gain an advantage if you can *verify* that your algorithm works by providing a *proof of program correctness*. This is called *program verification*. Prove that your solution to the previous exercise correctly computes the gcd. Divide your proof into two parts: (a) *termination*: a proof that your algorithm must terminate, and (b) *correctness*: a proof that after termination, the result is the gcd.

6. Write a "going-up" recursive version of **product(m,n)**, which gives the product of the integers in the range m:n.

7. The following recursive list reversal method works by a slightly different principle than the one given in Program 4.19. Compare its efficiency with that of Program 4.19. What results do you get? Can you explain why the efficiencies of these two recursive programs differ?

```
       | void reverse( ) {                              // applies the auxiliary method
       |     firstNode = reverse2(firstNode, null);        // reverse2 to reverse the
       | }                                               // list referenced by firstNode
       |
    5  | ListNode head(ListNode L) {                          // detaches the head of
       |     L.link = null;                                      // a nonempty list L
       |     return L;
       | }
       |
   10  | ListNode tail(ListNode L) {          // computes the tail of a nonempty list L
       |     return L.link;
       | }
       |
       | ListNode join(ListNode L, ListNode R) {          // joins a single node L
   15  |     L.link = R;                            // to the front of a linked list R
       |     return L;                     //  by inserting L as the new head of R
       | }
       |
       | ListNode reverse2(ListNode L, ListNode R) {
   20  |     if (L == null) {
       |         return R;                          // return R if first parameter is null
       |     } else {
       |         return reverse2(tail(L), join(head(L),R));
       |     }
       | }
```

8. Write a recursive method to find the length of a linked list, where the length of a linked list, L, is defined to be the number of nodes in the list referenced by the pointer in the firstNode field of the list's header node.

9. Write a recursive method min(A) to find the smallest integer in an integer array A[n]. [*Hint:* Define an auxiliary method min2(A,k,j) that finds the smallest integer in A[k:j], and let min(A) = min2(A, 0, n − 1).]

10. Ackermann's function, A($m,n$), is a two-argument function defined as follows:

$$A(0,n) = n + 1 \qquad \text{for } n \geq 0,$$
$$A(m,0) = A(m − 1, 1) \qquad \text{for } m > 0,$$
$$A(m,n) = A(m − 1, A(m, n − 1)) \quad \text{for } m,n > 0.$$

Write a recursive method that gives the value of Ackermann's function.

11. For what range of integer parameters, ($m,n$), does the output of your implementation of Ackermann's function, A($m,n$), *not* exceed the value of the maximum integer in your Java system?

12. Describe in words what the following method p(int n) does:

```
   |   void pDigit(int d) {        // auxiliary procedure used below in p to write the
   |                               // character corresponding to the digit d
   |       System.out.print( (char) ( (int)'0' + d ) );
   |   }
 5 |
   |   void p(int n) {                          // assume n is a nonnegative integer
   |
   |       if (n < 10) {
   |           pDigit(n);
10 |       } else {
   |           p(n / 10);
   |           pDigit(n % 10);
   |       }
   |   }
```

13. What does the following method do?

```
   |   void r(int n) {                          // where n is a nonnegative integer
   |
   |       // output the rightmost digit of n
   |       System.out.print(n%10);
 5 |
   |       if ((n / 10) != 0)  r(n / 10);
   |   }
```

14. Let $x$ be a positive real. To calculate the square root of $x$ by Newton's Method, so that the square of the solution differs from $x$ to within an accuracy of *epsilon*, we start with an initial approximation $a = x/2$. If $|a*a − x| \leq$ *epsilon*, we stop with the result $a$. Otherwise we replace $a$ with the next approximation, defined by $(a + x/a)/2$. Then, we test this next approximation to see if it is close enough and

we stop if it is. In general, we keep on computing and testing successive approximations until we find one close enough to stop. Write a recursive method, sqrt($x$), that computes the square root of $x$ by Newton's Method.

## 4.3 Common Pitfall—Infinite Regresses

### LEARNING OBJECTIVES

1. To learn about infinite regresses.
2. To understand the symptoms caused by the occurrence of infinite regresses.

We now pause briefly to explore a common pitfall with recursive programs—*infinite regresses*. An infinite regress in a recursive program is somewhat analogous to an endless loop in an iterative program. It occurs when a recursive program calls itself endlessly and never encounters a base case that forces it to stop its execution.

There are two reasons that a recursive program can call itself endlessly: (1) there is no base case to stop the recursion, or (2) a base case never gets called. The second possibility tends to happen more frequently, and sometimes it happens because the set of values used in a recursive call is bigger than the set of values that the recursive program was designed to handle. It may therefore not be the fault of the program designer, or even the fault of the user who made the call with a value lying outside the set for which the design works. Rather, the fault could lie in faulty or incomplete documentation about the set of values for which the given recursive program is designed to work.

For a specific example of this, reconsider the program for factorial(n) given earlier as Program 4.12. Let's ask two questions: (1) What happens if we call this method with n == 0, by making the call factorial(0)?, and (2) What happens if we make the method call factorial(− 1)?

*Warning:* Don't fire up your computer, type in Program 4.12, and try out the calls factorial(0) and factorial(− 1) without first knowing how to recover from program crashes and also how to stop the execution of a nonterminating infinite loop. Do you know how to perform the crash recovery procedure and do you know how to stop the execution of an infinite loop?

Why this warning? Let's try our method for writing out a call trace, starting with the call, factorial(0).

$$
\begin{aligned}
\text{factorial}(0) \quad &= \quad 0 * \text{factorial}(-1) \\
&= \quad 0 * (-1) * \text{factorial}(-2) \\
&= \quad 0 * (-1) * (-2) * \text{factorial}(-3) \\
&= \quad 0 * (-1) * (-2) * (-3) * \text{factorial}(-4) \\
&= \quad 0 * (-1) * (-2) * (-3) * (-4) * \text{factorial}(-5) \\
&= \quad \text{and so on, in an infinite regress.}
\end{aligned}
$$

*infinite regresses*

*prepare to crash or interrupt an infinite loop*

This happens because, when n == 0 or n is any negative integer, the condition n == 1, in the if-condition on line 3 of Program 4.12, evaluates to *false*, after which the else-part is evaluated, causing an evaluation of the expression n*factorial(n − 1). This results in a recursive call of factorial(n − 1) with a new argument one less than the previous argument, for which the base case will not be encountered. So yet another recursive call on factorial(n − 2) will occur—and so on, endlessly.

*a base case that never gets called*

To be truthful, the process can go on almost endlessly, except for the fact that the computer may run out of resources sooner or later. One thing that may happen is that the computer can run out of space in the region of memory where it stores separate structures containing information about each method call that has been initiated but which has not yet been completed. Each time a method is called in Java, some space for a *call frame* for the call is allocated in a call-frame region of memory where call frames are stored for all previous calls that have been made but have not yet been completed. (*As an aside*: This can happen on a stack allocated to the current execution thread in the Java Virtual Machine. If your Java program has been compiled into native code for your computer, perhaps by a Java JIT compiler, it could happen in a region of memory that handles the stack of current method calls. We will explain these mechanisms further in Chapter 6 in the discussion on stacks. For now it suffices to think of call frames as being allocated in a region of memory of an unspecified nature.) Since each such call frame uses up a finite amount of space, an unending sequence of recursive calls results in an unending sequence of call frame allocations. This may cause the program to request additional space for call frames, without limit.

*running out of resources*

In one of the Java programming environments we tried, executing the call factorial(−1) caused the error message error: java.lang.StackOverflowError:null to be displayed in the bottom of the Java applet viewer window, while the applet continued to execute in an infinite loop and printed an unending sequence of error messages in the standard error output message window, StdErr.

It is a common occurrence for programmers to encounter infinite regresses accidentally—especially during the phase when they are first learning about recursive programs. Rather than "flying blind" into a situation where you accidentally encounter infinite regresses, it might be best if you could first find out what your Java system is likely to do if a recursive method with an infinite regress is executed. By this means, you might become prepared to recognize the symptoms of an accidental encounter with an infinite regress, and you might be prepared with knowledge of the proper recovery procedure.

*a useful precaution*

A *word of caution*: It is especially irritating to lose the entire Java program text you have typed in when you encounter an accidental program crash (or you have to stop an infinite loop by exiting to the operating system). This can happen in some Java systems. A useful habit to acquire is that of saving the text of any program you have written in a program text file *before* you start trial executions for debugging or testing purposes. This way, if your program gets into an infinite regress that causes a system crash, the text of your program will already have been safely stored in an external storage medium, preventing it from vanishing in a crash or in an exit to the operating system that loses access to the Java program text in primary computer memory.

## 4.3 REVIEW QUESTIONS

1. What is an infinite regress?
2. What are two programming errors that cause infinite regresses?
3. Why can executing a recursive method that causes an infinite regress result in a Java run-time system's running out of space?
4. Why might Program 4.12 have returned 0 when factorial(0) was called (if , by good fortune, the program terminated and returned a result at all)?

## 4.3 EXERCISE

1. The following method, f(n), is intended to be defined for all nonnegative integers.

```
  |    int f(int n) {
  |
  |        if (n == 0) {
  |            return 1;
  |        } else if (n == 1) {
5 |            return 2;
  |        } else {
  |            return f(n − 1) * f(n − 3);
  |        }
  |    }
```

Is there any nonnegative value, n, for which f(n) does not terminate properly?

## 4.4  A Recursive Algorithm with Exponential Running Time

## LEARNING OBJECTIVES

1. To learn that some recursive algorithms have exponential running times.
2. To learn why it is impractical to use exponential algorithms to solve problems of large size.

In this section the famous Towers of Hanoi problem is solved recursively, and we determine the number of steps it takes to achieve a solution. We discover that it takes an exponential number of steps. Then the notion of exponential complexity classes is introduced, and the practical impact of trying to use exponential algorithms to solve problems is assessed. It is discovered that even though you can use exponential algorithms to solve problems of small size, it is often not practical to use them for problems of large size.

## Towers of Hanoi

when will the universe dissolve?

It is rumored that somewhere in Asia a group of spiritually advanced monks is hard at work transferring golden disks. When they are finished moving a tower of 64 of these golden disks from the first peg to the third peg of a sacred three-peg stand, then the next *Maha Pralaya* will begin, in which the universe will dissolve and revert to its unmanifested state. The 64 disks have different sizes, and the monks must obey two rules: (1) only one disk can be moved at a time, and (2) a bigger disk can never be placed on top of a smaller disk. If the monks work nonstop in shifts, 24 hours a day, moving one disk every second and never wasting any moves, how long after they started their task will the next *Maha Pralaya* begin?

This puzzle is popularly known as the Towers of Hanoi. The four-disk version of this puzzle is shown in Figure 4.21.

the solution is forced to work a certain way

Suppose the objective is to move the tower of four disks from peg 1 to peg 3. To solve this puzzle, we could reason as follows. In any solution, we must move the bottommost disk from peg 1 to peg 3. Since it is the biggest disk, there can be no smaller disk on peg 3 at the time we try to move it. Consequently, we must move the three disks on top of it from peg 1 to peg 2. Following this, we can move the bottom disk from peg 1 to peg 3. Finally, we need to move the three-disk tower from peg 2 to peg 3. To summarize:

*To Move 4 disks from Peg 1 to Peg 3:*

  *Move 3 disks from Peg 1 to Peg 2*

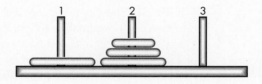

  *Move 1 disk from Peg 1 to Peg 3*

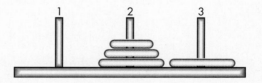

  *Move 3 disks from Peg 2 to Peg 3*

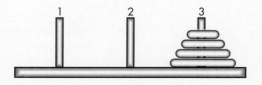

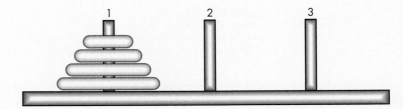

**Figure 4.21** Towers of Hanoi with Four Disks

```
|    void moveTowers(int n, int start, int finish, int spare) {
|
|        // to move a tower of n disks on the start-peg to the finish-peg
|        // using the spare-peg as an intermediary.
5  |
|        if (n == 1) {
|            (move one disk directly from start-peg to finish-peg)
|        } else {
|            (move a tower of n – 1 disks from start-peg to spare-peg)
10 |            (move one disk directly from start-peg to finish-peg)
|            (move a tower of n – 1 disks from spare-peg to finish-peg)
|        }
|    }
```

**Program Strategy 4.22** Recursive moveTowers Procedure

This breaks down the solution of the overall problem (moving four disks) into a composition of three smaller subproblems (two of which involve moving three disks). Thus we have discovered a basis for the recursive solution shown in Program Strategy 4.22. It's easy to see how to refine this strategy into a program that prints disk move instructions. All we need to do is to implement the base case of the recursion with a single print instruction, by letting (move one disk directly from start-peg to finish-peg) refine to System.out.println("move a disk from peg " + start + " to peg " + finish). The final program is shown in Program 4.23.

```
|    void moveTowers(int n, int start, int finish, int spare) {
|
|        // to move a tower of n disks on the start-peg to the finish-peg
|        // using the spare-peg as an intermediary.
5  |
|        if (n == 1) {
|            System.out.println("move a disk from peg "+ start +" to peg "+ finish);
|        } else {
|            moveTowers(n – 1, start, spare, finish);
10 |            System.out.println("move a disk from peg "+ start +" to peg "+ finish);
|            moveTowers(n – 1, spare, finish, start);
|        }
|    }
```

**Program 4.23** Recursive Towers of Hanoi Solution

If we call this program to move a tower of three disks from peg 1 to peg 3, the program prints the following list of instructions:

```
moveTowers(3 /*disks*/, /*from peg*/ 1, /*to peg*/ 3, /*using spare peg*/ 2) prints:
    move a disk from peg 1 to peg 3
    move a disk from peg 1 to peg 2
    move a disk from peg 3 to peg 2
    move a disk from peg 1 to peg 3
    move a disk from peg 2 to peg 1
    move a disk from peg 2 to peg 3
    move a disk from peg 1 to peg 3
```

Now the burning question remains, "When will the universe dissolve?" To answer this question, we must discover a formula that gives the length of the list of move instructions in terms of the number of disks in the tower to be moved. If $n$ is the number of disks in the tower to be moved, we could define $L(n)$ to be the length of the list of move instructions. Table 4.24 gives the values of $L(n)$ obtained from running Program 4.23 for various values of $n$ starting at $n = 1$ and ending at $n = 8$. Try comparing the values of $L(n)$ to the powers of two of the form $2^n$. Here, $2^1 = 2$, $2^2 = 4$, $2^3 = 8$, $2^4 = 16$, $2^5 = 32$, $2^6 = 64$, $2^7 = 128$, and $2^8 = 256$. By doing this, you can readily discover that $L(n) = 2^n - 1$, because each value for $L(n)$ in Table 4.24 is just one less than the corresponding power, $2^n$.

This means that the length of the instruction sequence needed for the monks to move a tower of 64 golden disks is just $L(64) = 2^{64}-1$. If the monks move one disk every second, then it will take $2^{64}-1$ seconds to move all 64 disks. Since there are $31,536,000 = 3.1536 * 10^7$ seconds in a year, the universe will dissolve in approximately $(2^{64}-1)/(3.1536 * 10^7) \cong 584,942,417,355$ years after the monks started moving disks. We need not worry that the universe will dissolve soon unless the monks started a long, long, time ago. In fact, if the sun lasts only another 5 to 10 billion years before it burns out, we might want to worry first about how to escape from the solar system before we worry about how to survive the dissolution of the universe.

The solution to the Towers of Hanoi puzzle is an *exponential running-time algorithm*, since it takes time proportional to $2^n$ to print the instructions required to move

*now for the important question*

*we learn when tragedy will strike*

| Number of Disks, $n$ | Number of Instructions, $L(n)$, Needed to Move the Tower |
|:---:|:---:|
| 1 | 1 |
| 2 | 3 |
| 3 | 7 |
| 4 | 15 |
| 5 | 31 |
| 6 | 63 |
| 7 | 127 |
| 8 | 255 |

**Table 4.24** Lengths of Instruction Sequences for Towers of Hanoi

a tower of size $n$. For this reason it is said to belong to the *exponential complexity class*. From the solution to Exercise 4.4.1, you can discover that you can't solve a Towers of Hanoi problem of very large size at one move per second, even if you have a year to solve it. Speeding up the rate at which you can move disks to a million disks per second permits you to solve a Towers of Hanoi problem with only 44 disks in a year's time. By studying further the examples in Table B.10 of Appendix B, you can conclude that exponential algorithms are useful for solving problems only of small size in actual practice. Generally, we try to avoid such exponential algorithms like the plague in computer science (but it is not always possible to do so).

## 4.4 REVIEW QUESTIONS

1. What is the name of the complexity class that characterizes the running time of the recursive solution to the Towers of Hanoi puzzle given in Program 4.23?
2. What is the principal disadvantage of solutions in the complexity class that is the answer to Question 1?

## 4.4 EXERCISE

1. Assume that the Towers of Hanoi puzzle must be solved completely in one year's time. If disks are moved at one disk per second and no wasteful moves are made, what is the largest number of disks, $n$, that can be used in the puzzle?

---

 **Pitfalls**

- *Infinite regresses*

    Infinite regresses can happen when you write a recursive program with no base case, or when you call a recursive program with a value for which no base case will ever be invoked in order to stop the recursion. Executing a recursive method that gets into an infinite regress could cause your Java system to halt with an error message indicating it is out of space for processing more method calls, or your system could get into an endless loop from which it might not be easy to recover.

- *Ranges that are not checked carefully*

    Be careful about the ranges of acceptable values to use as parameters when calling a recursive method—particularly for fast-growing methods with exponential growth properties. The range of acceptable input values can be surprisingly small in order not to exceed the allowable numerical precision, or the maximum size of the output, or the permissible maximum size of the Java run-time call-frame memory region.

## Tips and Techniques

- *Use auxiliary methods*

  Sometimes the definition of a recursive method can be simplified by introducing an auxiliary method with more parameters. The additional parameters can serve to transmit critical data across recursive calls that can be helpful in determining when the base case has been reached or to avoid solving the same subproblems over and over. For example, consider the problem of writing a "going-up" recursive method to compute the sum, $1 + 2 + 3 + \ldots + n$. We could write sum(n) = sum2(1,n), where sum2(m,n) is an auxiliary method that adds the numbers from m to n and which has the value:

  $$\text{sum2(m,n)} \; = \; ( \, m == n \; ? \; m \; : \; m + \text{sum2}(m + 1, n) \, )$$

- *Use call traces and call trees to help understand and debug recursive programs*

  Sometimes it is difficult to understand how a recursive program works. One technique that sometimes proves helpful is to choose a small problem size and to write out the call trace or the call tree of the recursive program to observe the pattern by which it splits its inputs into subproblems and solves them. Once the patterns for the base cases are understood, it can usually be readily seen how to combine the base case solutions into larger non–base-case solutions.

  Writing out the call trace of a recursive program you are trying to debug can sometimes provide the clues you need to discover your mistakes. Sometimes, Java programming systems permit traces to be generated when programs are executed. Using such a feature, if it is available in your Java system, can be helpful when testing or debugging your programs.

## References for Further Study

Jon Bentley, author of the "Programming Pearls" column in the *Communications of the ACM* offers many elegant recursive algorithms along with helpful programming tips.

> Jon Bentley, *Programming Pearls*. Addison-Wesley, Reading, MA (1986) and *More Programming Pearls: Confessions of a Coder*. Addison-Wesley, Reading, MA (1988).

Eric Roberts has written a helpful book on the subject of thinking recursively.

> Eric S. Roberts, *Thinking Recursively*. Wiley, New York (1986).

## Chapter Summary

Recursion is an important recurring concept in computer science. This chapter offers an introduction to this topic, and prepares you to understand the uses of recursion in the remainder of the book.

In a recursive solution to a problem, the overall problem is solved by combining solutions to smaller subproblems. These smaller subproblems either can be solved by applying the recursive method itself, or are base cases that can be solved directly without using recursion. Often, there are many ways to decompose the overall problem into smaller subproblems of the same nature. It is worthwhile to search for different kinds of decompositions in order to devise several different alternative recursive solutions whose characteristics can be compared and from which the best solution can be chosen.

Infinite regresses occur when recursive programs call themselves endlessly. A recursive program can get into an infinite regress if (a) it has no base cases, or (b) its base cases never get called.

Sometimes, there are problems that have recursive solutions that are simple, concise, and elegant, for which it is hard to devise iterative solutions having the same simplicity and clarity. For example, the recursive solution to the Towers of Hanoi problem is an example of a recursive solution to a problem for which it has been hard to find iterative versions that are as clear and simple.

Some recursive algorithms have exponential running times, even though they are simple to write. Such exponential algorithms are often impractical to use for solving problems of large size.

# 5

# Modularity and Data Abstraction

**Introduction and Motivation**

The goal of this chapter is to learn about *modularity*, *information hiding*, and *data abstraction*. Generally speaking, a *module* is a unit of organization of a software system that packages together a collection of entities (such as data and operations) and that carefully controls what external users of the module can see and use. Ordinarily, modules have ways of hiding things inside their boundaries to prevent external users from using them. In this way modules can protect their internal mechanisms from external interference. This is called *information hiding*, and it can be used to protect against software errors, to provide security, and as a basis for implementing *abstract data types*.

*modularity and information hiding*

Abstract data types (ADTs) are collections of objects and operations that present well-defined abstract properties to their users, meanwhile hiding the way they are represented in terms of lower-level data representations. When a module is used to implement an abstract data type, it provides an *interface* that makes the ADT's abstract operations available to outside users, meanwhile hiding the ADT's actual data representation inside the module's *private part*.

*abstract data types*

125

a useful analogy

To give a rough analogy for a *module*, consider a microwave oven. You can use a microwave by setting its dials or buttons, without knowing how it works internally (which relies on the miracles of magnetron tubes, computer chips, and microwave technology). To use a microwave, you need know only the available operations in the microwave's external user interface. You do not need to know any of its internal details.

separate compilation
modules

Many modern programming languages offer *modules* that have several important features: (1) they provide a way of grouping together collections of related data and operations; (2) they present clean, well-defined interfaces to users of their services; (3) they hide internal details of operation to prevent interference; and (4) they can be separately compiled.

using Java's
modularity features

In this book, we use Java's *classes*, *interfaces*, and *packages* as vehicles to express concepts of modularity, information hiding, and data abstraction. The access modifiers for data fields and methods in Java class definitions permit us to define whether such data fields and methods are **public** (and thus visible to and available for use by outside users of the class) or are **private** (and thus invisible to and unavailable for use by outside users). Generally speaking, we want to make **public** the features of a class that are in its external user-interface, and we want to make **private** the internal mechanisms that implement the class, sometimes including the particular data representation we used—such as a linked or a sequential representation.

Even though a Java class has an *interface*, consisting of its public methods and data fields, and even though we will use such class interfaces to implement ADTs, there is another technical meaning for the reserved word **interface** in Java. A Java **interface** is a definable entity that specifies a collection of abstract methods that can be implemented by a class. When several different classes implement a common **interface**, objects that are instances of those classes can be used wherever variables of

two kinds of Java interfaces

that **interface** are declared. This enables Java users to exploit another very powerful software composition technique, in which you can write very general ADT methods that use abstract components required only to obey the rules of a particular **interface**, and later you can substitute many different varieties of specialized components that implement the **interface**. What results is a general-purpose way to construct ADTs so that they can be written once and yet can utilize many different types of internal components.

For example, you might want to write a searching method that can search for many different kinds of keys. When given a particular search key, the general search method might try to find a matching key contained in a given collection of keys. We want to write the search method only once, but after it has been written, we want to be able to use it, no matter whether the search keys are integers, floating point numbers, or strings. The question is, how can we express a search method in a sufficiently general way so that we can change the types of keys it uses (from integers to strings, say), and it will still work without having to be rewritten. In most programming languages of an earlier generation, this problem is quite challenging to solve.

writing a general
search method

In Java, we can solve the problem elegantly by defining and using a Java **interface** to express the abstract properties that keys require to be usable inside a general search method. We merely define a Java **interface**, called say, a **ComparisonKey** interface, in which we require that comparison keys have a **compareTo** method, usable in a method call such as **k1.compareTo(k2)**, that compares the values of keys **k1** and **k2** and says whether they are equal (**k1 == k2**), whether **k1** is greater than **k2** (**k1 > k2**), or whether **k1** is less than **k2** (**k1 < k2**). This is called a *three-way comparison*, and usually we implement it by returning an integer value that is −1, 0, or +1 depending on whether **k1** is less than, equal to, or greater than **k2**, respectively.

Next, we write our general search method to use a search key of type **ComparisonKey** and to work on collections of **ComparisonKey**s. Then, to apply the general search method to use search keys of a particular type (such as integers, floating point numbers, or strings), we define an extension of a class containing an integer (or floating point number, or string) so that it **implements** the **compareTo** method of the **ComparisonKey interface**. We can then plug in our new search keys into the general search method, and—presto—the general method now works smoothly, using our special new brand of search keys substituted for its general abstract **ComparisonKey**s. The magic of this pays off when we realize we can write very general software components that can plug-and-play with many other types of software components in flexible combinations not foreseen in advance.

Thus far, we have seen that Java classes can be used to implement ADTs having hidden internal mechanisms and clean external user-interfaces, and that Java interfaces can be used to write general-purpose methods that can operate, without having to be rewritten, on many different component data types. A third and final Java

*the role of Java packages*

mechanism that helps to express modularity is the Java **package**. A **package** is a named collection of related classes and interfaces that can be separately compiled and can be imported for use in other packages or in Java applets and applications. You can think of a **package** as a way to bundle your useful software components into a library for use by others in building their own Java programs.

## Plan for the Chapter

In this chapter, we study how to implement a *priority queue* to illustrate how an ADT can be expressed in Java in a very general way. A priority queue *PQ* is a collection of prioritized items. We can *insert* new prioritized items into *PQ* in any order, but when

*priority queues*

we *remove* an item from *PQ*, we always get an item having the highest priority among all the items contained in *PQ*.

First we will define the interface of the priority queue ADT, which expresses the abstract operations every implementation of a priority queue must support. Then we show how to use priority queues in a simple sorting program that sorts an array of keys into increasing order using a priority queue *PQ*. We write and run this priority queue sorting method *before* we show how to implement priority queues to emphasize that all we need to know to use an ADT is *what* is in its public interface—not *how* it is implemented internally.

*changing underlying data representations*

We then show how to define two different Java classes that implement the priority queue ADT. One implementation uses sorted linked lists of priority items in which the items are arranged in decreasing order of priority in the successive nodes of a linked list. A second separate implementation uses unordered arrays of priority items. We have to search for and find the item of highest priority in such an unordered array before we can remove it. We show how to hide the internal details of operation of these two implementations (by making their internal mechanisms private) at the same time that we make public the methods that support the required operations in the priority queue ADT interface. In addition to showing how to express modularity and information-hiding in Java, these two priority queue implementations show how to accomplish *substitutability of data representations* without disturbing external users of an ADT. This accomplishes the important objective of showing how to structure software systems so that we can change underlying data representations for purposes of efficiency without having to change the way that the representation's users work.

Another important aspect of data abstraction is revealed by the way we implement Java classes for the priority queue ADT. Namely, we use a generalized **ComparisonKey** interface to express the abstract properties needed by prioritized items used inside priority queues. Having done this, we show how to substitute integers and strings interchangeably as the prioritized items used in priority queues. This demonstrates that we have implemented our priority queue ADTs in Java in a sufficiently general way that we can use an unlimited variety of new kinds of prioritized items without having to rewrite our priority queue implementations to adjust to the differences in treatment that different new prioritized items might require.

In the final section of the chapter, we review and summarize the benefits of modules and information hiding. Specifically, we state a philosophy of software system structuring, centering on concepts of modularity, that emphasizes the importance of clarity of program structure and ease of program modification.

*priority queues that use interchangeable components*

*the benefits of modular programming*

## ▋ 5.2 ▋ Priority Queues—An Abstract Data Type

## LEARNING OBJECTIVES

1. To learn what an abstract data type is by means of a simple example.
2. To understand how it is possible to replace the underlying representation for an abstract data type without changing the operations it presents to its external users through its interface.
3. To learn how to use information-hiding features of Java to hide the implementation details of an abstract data type's operations.

In this section, we study an example of an abstract data type called a *priority queue*. After defining priority queues, we present the interface of a priority queue ADT. This defines the services that external users can use. We then show how to use these services to perform sorting using priority queues. But while this is going on, we still don't know how priority queues are implemented. That's because the implementation of the ADT as a Java class hasn't been defined yet.

*the priority queue ADT*

In Section 5.3, we provide two implementations for the priority queue ADT, each implementating priority queues differently. This demonstrates that the data type that users of a Java class can access externally is *abstract*—because nothing in the way

*hidden representations*

its operations are expressed reveals the particular implementation details that were chosen for its hidden representation.

## A Priority Queue ADT Interface

*the definition of
priority queues*

You can think of a *priority queue* as a container that holds some prioritized items. It is assumed that these items can be compared to one another and that they can be ranked in their order of priority. One scale of priorities useful for ranking might simply be the items' magnitudes, with the item of largest magnitude having the highest priority. Another possible priority scale might be defined in terms of urgency for processing. Each item might be stamped with a specific processing time deadline. The highest priority item might be defined to be the most urgent item to process next. This, in turn, could be defined as the item having the earliest deadline for processing. No matter which way you define priorities, when you remove an item from a priority queue, you always get the item of highest priority.

*deadline-driven scheduling*

For example, you might decide to put all the bills you have to pay into a pile, and you might decide to pay them in the order defined by their payment deadlines, with the earliest payment deadline having the highest priority. If you remove and pay bills from your pile, one at a time, in earliest-to-latest order of their payment deadlines, you are using a priority queue. (In fact, priority queues are used in this fashion by deadline-driven scheduling algorithms in operating systems.)

To define an abstract data type we must define the operations that external users can use, without constraining how to represent its underlying data structures or how to program its operations in Java.

### Priority Queues

A *Priority Queue* (PQ) is a finite collection of items for which the following operations are defined:

1. *Construct* an initially empty priority queue, *PQ*.
2. Obtain the *size* of *PQ*, which gives the number of items *PQ* contains.
3. *Insert* a new item, *X*, into the priority queue, *PQ*.
4. If *PQ* is nonempty, *remove* from *PQ* an item, *X*, of highest priority in *PQ*, (where the highest priority item in *PQ* is defined as an item *X* in *PQ* such that $X \geq Y$ for all items *Y* in *PQ*).

You can see from these definitions that you can insert items into a priority queue *PQ* in any order of priority, but when you remove an item from *PQ*, you always get a highest priority item in *PQ*. (There may be more than one item of highest priority in *PQ* in the event that *PQ* contains several items of equal priority value all having a common priority higher than that of the other items in *PQ*. Thus, while the item you remove will have highest priority, it may not be the unique item of highest priority.)

If we define the interface of a Java **PriorityQueue** class to contain the operations on priority queues just defined, we can immediately begin using priority queues in our program designs. For example, Program 5.1 gives one possible list of public method calls that the interface of a **PriorityQueue** class might have. (*Note*: This is an informal

```
 |   /*
 |    *    The public interface for the PriorityQueue class contains
 |    *    the following method calls. Here, let PQ be a variable having
 |    *    a PriorityQueue object as its value, let X be a variable that
5|    *    contains a priority queue item, and let n be an integer variable.
 |    */
 |
 |   PQ = new PriorityQueue();        // creates an initially empty priority queue PQ
 |
10|   n = PQ.size();                              // returns the number of items in PQ and
 |                                               // stores it in the integer variable n
 |
 |   PQ.insert(X);                                              // puts X into PQ
 |
15|   X = PQ.remove( );              // removes the highest priority item from PQ and
 |                                         // assigns it to be the value of the variable X
 |
```

**Program 5.1** Informal Interface for a PriorityQueue Class

use of the word interface, in contrast to the formal Java **interface** that we'll define later for **ComparisonKey**s.)

To illustrate with a simple example, suppose we have defined an array, **A**, to hold ten suitable priority queue items. These items are declared to be of the general type **ComparisonKey**, which we will define in detail later. However, for the sake of something specific to aid our thinking process during the initial stage of our study, let's imagine that these **ComparisonKey**s are simple integer values, such that bigger integers have higher priority than smaller ones. It is now possible to employ the priority queue operations defined in Program 5.1 to define a simple sorting method that sorts the elements in array **A** into increasing order of priority.

*a simple sorting example*

The sorting method in Program 5.2 works by first taking the items in array **A** one-by-one and inserting them into a priority queue, **PQ**, and, second, by removing the items from **PQ** in order of highest-to-lowest priority while putting them back into array **A** in decreasing order of the index positions in **A**.

*how to sort using priority queues*

Assembling these pieces into a complete program, together with a test case, gives Program 5.3 (shown on page 132). The interesting thing about this program is that it successfully uses the abstract data type—priority queues—without knowing any of the details of its implementation. We have cleanly separated the *what* from the *how*.

This is our first illustration of the benefits of abstract data types. Program 5.1 gives the operations we are allowed to use to manipulate the ADT, called priority queues. The interface specifications in Program 5.1 give external users the calling forms to be used to invoke operations on priority queues. But this interface does not reveal the implementation details for priority queues. Consequently, we can write programs that use priority queues in a way that makes them independent of the way priority queues are represented using lower-level data representations. Having done so, we can later substitute a new lower-level data representation for priority queues to improve their efficiency without having to change any of the code that uses priority queues elsewhere.

*illustrating the benefits of abstract data types*

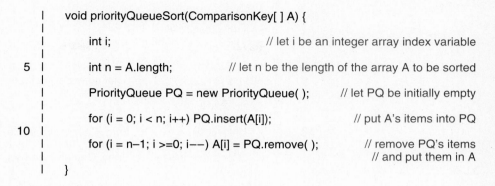

```
    |    void priorityQueueSort(ComparisonKey[ ] A) {
    |
    |        int i;                                 // let i be an integer array index variable
    |
  5 |        int n = A.length;              // let n be the length of the array A to be sorted
    |
    |        PriorityQueue PQ = new PriorityQueue( );         // let PQ be initially empty
    |
    |        for (i = 0; i < n; i++) PQ.insert(A[i]);              // put A's items into PQ
 10 |
    |        for (i = n−1; i >=0; i−−) A[i] = PQ.remove( );          // remove PQ's items
    |                                                                // and put them in A
    |
    |    }
```

**Program 5.2** A Priority Queue Sorting Method

We will later fill in some missing pieces to make Program 5.3 work. In particular, line 17 of Program 5.3 uses the constructor **PQItem(int p)** to convert an integer **p** into a **PQItem** object that can be stored in the i[th] position of array **A**.

A[i] = new PQItem( squareOf(3*i − 13) );

The array **A**, in turn, is declared on line 12 to hold items that are **ComparisonKey**s. We will later define the class **PQItem** to implement the **interface** for a **ComparisonKey**. This will make it legitimate to store **PQItem** objects in a **ComparisonKey** array, such as **A**. Then, after we define priority queues to hold any type of object that implements the **ComparisonKey** interface, the whole program will become plug-compatible and everything will work together in a very general way. For instance, we will be able to substitute other different types of **PQItem**s, such as strings, that are also defined to implement the **ComparisonKey** interface.

## 5.2 REVIEW QUESTIONS

1. What is a priority queue?
2. What operations can be performed on a priority queue, **PQ**?
3. In Program 5.3, what is known about the way **PQ** is implemented? Is it known whether **PQ** is implemented using a sorted linked list of **PQItem**s, or whether it is implemented using an unsorted array of **PQItem**s? Why?

## 5.2 EXERCISE

1. Write a boolean expression to determine if a priority queue **PQ** is empty. [*Hint:* If **PQ** is empty, what must be the value of **PQ.size()**?]

```
   |   import java.io.*;
   |   import java.lang.*;
   |   import java.applet.Applet;
   |
 5 |
   |   public class PriorityQueueApplet extends Applet {
   |
   |       public void init() {
   |
10 |           int n = 10;              // for this simple example, we sort only n = 10 integers
   |
   |           ComparisonKey[ ] A = new ComparisonKey[n];      // let A be an array of
   |                                                           // 10 items to sort
   |
15 |           // initialize the array A to ten integers to sort and print them
   |           for (int i = 0; i < n; i++) {
   |               A[i] = new PQItem( squareOf(3*i – 13) );
   |               System.out.print(A[i]+", ");
   |           }                                       // the unsorted integers printed are:
20 |           System.out.println( );                  // 169,100,49,16,1,4,25,64,121,196
   |
   |           // sort the array A using priorityQueueSorting
   |           priorityQueueSort(A);
   |
25 |           // print the values in the array A after sorting
   |           for (int i = 0; i < n; i++) {
   |               System.out.print(A[i]+", ");
   |           }                                       // the sorted integers printed are:
   |           System.out.println( );                  // 1,4,16,25,49,64,100,121,169,196
30 |
   |       } // end init()
   |
   |   /*--------------*/
   |
35 |       int squareOf(int x) { return x*x; }                     // compute the square of x
   |
   |   /*--------------*/
   |
   |       void priorityQueueSort(ComparisonKey[ ] A) {
40 |
   |           int i;                              // let i be an array index variable
   |           int n = A.length;                   // n is the length of the array to be sorted
   |
   |           PriorityQueue PQ = new PriorityQueue();             // let PQ be an empty
45 |                                                               // priority queue
   |           for (i = 0; i < n; i++) PQ.insert(A[i]);            // insert A's items into PQ
   |
   |           for (i = n –1; i >= 0; i––) A[i] = PQ.remove();     // put PQ's items into A
   |                                                               // in reverse index order
50 |       }
   |
   |   } // end class PriorityQueueApplet
```

**Program 5.3** Sorting Using a Priority Queue

# 5.3 Two Implementations for Priority Queues

## LEARNING OBJECTIVES

1. To understand how it is possible to replace the underlying representation for an abstract data type without changing the operations it presents to its external users through its interface.
2. To learn how to use information-hiding features of Java to hide the implementation details of an abstract data type's operations.
3. To learn how to change underlying data representations implementing an ADT without changing any of the code that uses the ADT.

*different ways to implement priority queues*

A moment's thought reveals that there is a variety of ways that we could implement priority queues. For example, we could let a priority queue, **PQ**, be represented by a linked list in which the succeeding nodes in the list contain items sorted in decreasing order of priority. Removing an item from **PQ** is easy, since all we have to do is remove the first node of the linked list, which is guaranteed to contain the item of highest priority. To insert a new item, we have to link-in a new node containing the item in the proper position in the linked list, immediately beyond the nodes containing items whose priority is higher than that of the item we are inserting.

Another possibility is to keep an unsorted array of items, **PQ**. In this case, inserting an item is easy, since all we have to do is add a new item to the end of the array **PQ**. But to remove an item, we have to search for the item of highest priority, then delete it, and finally move the last item into the hole created by the deletion. In this case, removal is expensive while insertion is cheap. In the previous case, removal was cheap, but insertion was expensive.

We will study another representation for priority queues in Chapter 8 (on trees) that has greater efficiency than the two representations just mentioned. This particular representation places items into nodes of a binary tree in a clever way, creating what is called a *heap*.

*using an ADT without knowing its representation*

At this point, we have successfully accomplished something important—we have laid the groundwork for understanding the importance of data abstraction in the rest of this book by successfully using an ADT without knowing its representation. We have shown that we need to know only *what* an ADT does, not *how* it does it, to use it successfully as a building block for doing something else. This is an extremely important principle for two reasons: (1) It is easier to use something if you don't need to know how it works in order to use it. This is a great help in making complex systems more intellectually manageable. (2) It is easier to change the internal mechanics that determine how something works (in order to improve it, for instance), if the description of how it works is concentrated all in one place, and you don't have to make changes everywhere it got used. Since the details of how the priority queue ADT works haven't been revealed yet, we did not make use of priority queue operations in Program 5.3 in a way that depended on the details of their implementation.

```
|    class ListNode {
|        ComparisonKey    item;
|        ListNode         link;
|    }
```

**Program 5.4** The ListNode Class Definition

**containers that hold interchangeable kinds of items**

To implement priority queues in the flexible, general-purpose way we have previously outlined, we will let priority queues act as containers for abstract items of type ComparisonKey. In effect, ComparisonKeys will act as *sockets* in which to *plug in* various different kinds of PQItems, such as integers and strings. In Section 5.4, we will show how to define the socket property of ComparisonKeys by defining the Java interface ComparisonKey. Then, we will define the plug-in PQItems that fit into these ComparisonKey sockets by showing how to define PQItem classes that implement the ComparisonKey interface.

As our next step, we will implement the general-purpose PriorityQueue class to function as containers that hold ComparisonKeys, which are assumed to have a compareTo method defined to compare the priority of any two keys.

## Implementing Priority Queues Using Sorted Linked Lists

The first implementation of priority queues we will examine uses a sorted, linked-list representation. The essence of the idea is that the hidden representation of a priority queue uses a linked list of ComparisonKeys kept in decreasing sorted order of priority.

**defining linked-list nodes**

To implement linked lists, we first need to define the structure of individual linked-list nodes. Program 5.4 gives the class definition for a ListNode that defines the linked-list nodes we will need. This program says that a ListNode is a unit of data having an item data field containing a ComparisonKey and a link data field containing a reference to another ListNode (or a null reference to indicate the last node of a linked list).

**the PriorityQueue class definition**

Now we are ready to examine the complete linked-list implementation of the class PriorityQueue given in Program 5.5. First, lines 3 and 5 define two private data

```
|    class PriorityQueue {
|
|        private int      count;          // the number of items in the priority queue
|
5   |        private ListNode itemList;                       // the linked list of items
|
|        /*--------------------------------------------*/
|
|            // Note that Java automatically defines the no-arg constructor
10  |            // PriorityQueue( ) that creates an initially empty PriorityQueue
|            // object having a count of zero and an empty itemList
|
```

**Program 5.5** The Sorted Linked-List Representation of the PriorityQueue Class
*(continued)*

Program 5.5 The Sorted Linked-List Representation of the PriorityQueue Class *(continued)*

```
/*-----------------*/

/** the size( ) method returns the count of the number of items */

public int size( ) {
    return count;
}

/*-----------------*/

/** the private sortedInsert( ) method is used by the Insert( ) method */

private ListNode sortedInsert(ComparisonKey newItem, ListNode P) {
    if ( ( (P == null) || ( newItem.compareTo(P.item) >= 0 ) ) {
        ListNode N = new ListNode( );        // if P points to an empty list or
        N.item = newItem;            // the newItem to insert is of higher priority
        N.link = P;                  // than P's item, insert a new ListNode N with
        return(N);                   // newItem as its item that links to P, and return N
    } else {
        P.link = sortedInsert(newItem, P.link);        // otherwise, insert the
        return(P);                   // newItem on the list referenced by P.link
    }
}

/*-----------------*/

/** the method insert(newItem) inserts newItem on the itemList */

public void insert(ComparisonKey newItem) {
    itemList = sortedInsert(newItem, itemList);        // insert the newItem on
    count++;                         // the itemList of the priority queue, and
                                     // increase the size of the priority queue by one
}

/*-----------------*/

/** the remove( ) method removes and returns the highest priority item */

public ComparisonKey remove() {
    if (count == 0) {                        // if the priority queue is empty,
        return null;                         // return the null Object
    } else {                                 // otherwise,
        ComparisonKey K = itemList.item;     // save item to return,
        itemList = itemList.link;            // link to second list node,
        count--;                             // reduce the count by one,
        return(K);                           // and return the first ListNode's item
    }
}

/*----------------------------------------------*/

} // end PriorityQueue class
```

fields of a PriorityQueue object—the count field that contains the number of items contained in the priority queue, and the itemList field that contains a pointer to the first node of the sorted linked list of items. Because these fields are private, they are accessible only to the methods defined in the PriorityQueue class. Thus, they function as hidden internal information fields. (This is a specific example of *information hiding* and *encapsulation*.)

The size() method is given on lines 17:19 of Program 5.5. If PQ is a priority queue variable that contains a reference to a PriorityQueue object, the method call PQ.size() returns an integer value giving the number of items contained in PQ. You can see that the size() method works by returning the value contained in PQ's count field. Even though this count field is private, its value can be obtained by calling the size() method. In effect, for external users of a priority queue PQ, the count field is a *read-only* field, because no external priority queue user can directly change the contents of PQ's private count field.

*the size() method*

Lines 23:45 of Program 5.5 show how to insert a new item, X, into the priority queue PQ in priority order. There are three cases to consider. First, if PQ's itemList is empty, then we need to replace it with a new list having a single node, N, with X as its item and null as its link (see lines 26:30). Second, if the new item, X, to insert has a priority greater than or equal to that of the first item on the itemList (again see lines 26:30), then we need to insert a new first node N on the itemList having X as its item. Finally, if X's priority is less than that of the item in the first node of the itemList, we need to insert X recursively in the *tail* of the itemList (where the *tail* is the linked list consisting of the second and succeeding nodes of the itemList). This is done on lines 31:34. The private sortedInsert() method that performs these insertions is used as an auxiliary subroutine by the actual insert() method given on lines 41:45. Because the sortedInsert() method is declared to be private, it cannot be used outside the PriorityQueue class by external users. (Thus, the sortedInsert() method is another example of information hiding and encapsulation, because it is a hidden internal mechanism of the PriorityQueue class that external users can neither see nor use.)

Removal of the highest priority item is simple. You just extract the item in the first node of the linked list representing PQ (see lines 51:60 in Program 5.5), reduce PQ's item count by one, set the itemList field to point to the tail of the previous itemList, and return the first node's item. (Note that the remove() method chooses to signal an erroneous attempt to remove an item from an empty priority queue by returning the null value. An alternative way to signal an erroneous operation is to throw a Java exception, such as EmptyPriorityQueueRemovalException. Java exceptions are not covered in this book because some of the Java environments we tried didn't compile them properly, and for those learning about data structures for the first time, it simplifies the presentation if the reader does not have to disentangle the data structure ideas from code laced with Java try-catch statements.)

*the remove() method*

## Implementing Priority Queues Using Unsorted Arrays

We now study a second implementation of priority queues that uses an unsorted array representation. The essence of the idea is that the hidden representation of a priority queue uses an array of ComparisonKey items kept in arbitrary order. Program 5.6 gives

```
      class PriorityQueue {

          private int    count;               // the number of items in the priority queue
          private int    capacity;            // the number of available array positions
 5        private int    capacityIncrement;   // the amount to increase the capacity
                                              // during array expansion
          private ComparisonKey[ ] itemArray; // the array that holds PQ items

          /*----------------*/

10        /** construct an initially empty PriorityQueue */

          public PriorityQueue() {            // we need to define a no-arg constructor.
              count = 0;                      // the empty priority queue has no items
15            capacity = 10;                  // but there is capacity for ten items
              capacityIncrement = 5;          // and the capacity will expand
              itemArray = new ComparisonKey[capacity];  // in increments of five
          }                                   // when necessary

20        /*----------------*/

          /** the size( ) method returns the count of the number of items */

          public int size() {
25            return count;
          }

          /*----------------*/

30        /** the insert( ) method inserts a new item into a priority queue */

          public void insert(ComparisonKey newItem) {

              // if the itemArray does not have enough capacity,
35            // expand the itemArray by the capacity increment
              if (count == capacity) {
                  capacity += capacityIncrement;
                  ComparisonKey[ ] tempArray = new ComparisonKey[capacity];
                  for (int i = 0; i < count; i++) {
40                    tempArray[i] = itemArray[i];
                  }
                  itemArray = tempArray;
              }

45            // insert the newItem at the end of the current sequence of items
              // and increase the priority queue's count by one
                  itemArray[count++] = newItem;
          }

50        /*----------------*/

          /** the remove( ) method removes the highest priority item */
```

**Program 5.6** The Unordered Array Representation of the PriorityQueue Class (*continued*)

Program 5.6 The Unordered Array Representation of the PriorityQueue Class (*continued*)

```
      |      public ComparisonKey remove() {
  55  |          if (count == 0) {                              // return null if the priority
      |              return null;                                     // queue is empty.
      |          } else {                                // otherwise, find the highest priority
      |              int maxPosition = 0;                              // item's position
      |              ComparisonKey maxItem = itemArray[0];
  60  |              for (int i = 1; i < count; i++) {
      |                  if ( itemArray[i].compareTo(maxItem) > 0 ) {
      |                      maxPosition = i;
      |                      maxItem = itemArray[i];
      |                  }                                      // then move the last item into
  65  |              }                                              // the hole created by
      |              itemArray[maxPosition] = itemArray[--count];       // removing the
      |              return maxItem;                               // highest priority item
      |          }                                     // and, return the highest priority item
      |      }
  70  |
      |      /*----------------*/
      |
      |  } // end PriorityQueue class
```

the details. In what follows, we let **PQ** be a **PriorityQueue** variable that holds a reference to a **PriorityQueue** object.

Looking first at the private data fields on lines 3:7, we see that each **PriorityQueue** object: (1) has a **count** field giving the number of items currently contained in the priority queue, (2) has a **capacity** field containing the length of the array that the **itemArray** field references, (3) has an increment in its **capacityIncrement** field that specifies the amount to expand the **itemArray**'s capacity when, and if, the insertion of new items would cause the **itemArray** to overflow, and (4) has an **itemArray** field whose value references an array of priority queue items.

*private data fields*

The **size()** method, given on lines 24:26, returns the number of items currently contained in the priority queue. For example, if **PQ** contained six items, the value returned by the method call expression **PQ.size()** would be **6**. This **size()** method works by returning the integer value stored in **PQ**'s **count** data field.

*the size() method*

Inserting a new item would be simple if we needed only to append it to the end of **PQ**'s **itemArray** and increase **PQ**'s **count** by one (see line 47). However, if the addition of a new item would cause the capacity of the **itemArray** to be exceeded, we need first to expand the capacity of the **itemArray** by allocating a new **itemArray** that is larger than the old one (by an amount equal to the **capacityIncrement**), after which we transfer the contents of the old **itemArray** into the new **itemArray** and set the pointer in **PQ**'s **itemArray** field to point to the new **itemArray** (see lines 36:43).

Removing an item of highest priority takes a bit more work because we have to scan **PQ**'s **itemArray** to find it first (see lines 58:65). When we have located its position, we remove it, and then move the last item in the array into the hole created by the deletion of the highest priority item. Finally, we decrement the count by one and return the largest item's value as the value of the **remove()** method (see lines 66:67).

## **5.3** REVIEW QUESTIONS

1. How do you hide the data fields of a PriorityQueue object so that external users of PriorityQueue objects cannot access them or change them?
2. How do you hide a method that is used only internally by other methods in the PriorityQueue class and is not intended for use by external users?
3. Name two different ways that a priority queue can be represented, and sketch the main idea of how each representation works.
4. Which of the two representations in your answer to Exercise 3 has a more efficient insertion operation? Why? Which one has a more efficient removal operation? Why?

## **5.3** EXERCISE

1. Implement another constructor of the form PriorityQueue(cap, inc); for the unsorted array representation of a PriorityQueue (given in Program 5.6). The meaning of

   PriorityQueue PQ = new PriorityQueue(20,15);

   is to construct a new initially empty PriorityQueue object PQ whose capacity is initially set to 20 and whose capacityIncrement is initially set to 15.

## **5.4**  **Plugging In New Kinds of Objects into Priority Queues**

## LEARNING OBJECTIVES

1. To understand how easy it is to replace integer items with String items in abstract priority queue sorting.
2. To know how to use Java interfaces to make such plug-compatible replacement work.
3. To understand the roles of Java interfaces and classes in implementing modular software.

In previous sections, we made the claim that we had implemented the priority queue sorting method in a general-purpose way that would allow us to switch the underlying types of priority queue items without changing any of the general-purpose code for the PriorityQueue class definition. In this section, we show how to exchange the underlying item types using the concept of a Java interface and showing how to define classes that implement such interfaces.

*making good on the claim of interchangeable items*

We begin by studying the ComparisonKey interface defined in Program 5.7. The only lines of Program 5.7 that aren't comments are lines 7 and 12. Line 7 defines the signature of an abstract compareTo method

*the ComparisonKey interface*

   int compareTo(ComparisonKey value);

that can be applied to compare the priorities of two keys k1 and k2 using a method call expression of the form k1.compareTo(k2). If the value of this expression is −1, it means k1 < k2, if the value is 0, it means k1 == k2, and if the value is +1, it means

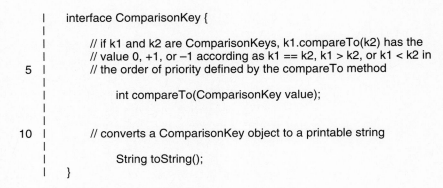

```
    |   interface ComparisonKey {
    |
    |       // if k1 and k2 are ComparisonKeys, k1.compareTo(k2) has the
    |       // value 0, +1, or –1 according as k1 == k2, k1 > k2, or k1 < k2 in
 5  |       // the order of priority defined by the compareTo method
    |
    |           int compareTo(ComparisonKey value);
    |
    |
10  |       // converts a ComparisonKey object to a printable string
    |
    |           String toString();
    |   }
```

**Program 5.7** The ComparisonKey Interface

k1 > k2. This is called a three-way comparison because there are three possible out-comes to the comparison test.

Line 12 gives the signature of a **String**-valued method, **toString()**. This method comes in handy when we want to print **ComparisonKey**s because when we use a general Java reference data type **X** in **System.out.print(X)**, Java's print method calls the **toString()** method of **X** to obtain a string to print. This guarantees that we will be able to write printing and debugging methods that print **ComparisonKey** values, should we need to.

The important fact to note about the **compareTo()** and **toString()** methods in the **ComparisonKey** interface is that they are *abstract methods*. This means that they function like blank slots that need to be filled in later with actual method implementations in order to give them actual meanings. When we give an actual class definition that **implements** an interface, we must supply actual method definitions that implement the interface's abstract methods.

When an actual Java class **C** implements a Java **interface D**, then objects constructed to be of type **C** can be used as values of variables and parameters declared to be of type **D**. Specifically, if the interface **D** = **ComparisonKey** and the actual class **C** = **PQItem**, then if we write some methods that use variables and parameters of type **ComparisonKey**, we can later apply them to actual values of type **PQItem**, and Java will accept the **PQItem** values as valid instances of **ComparisonKey** data types. This is exactly how we set up the **PriorityQueue** class definition. We used the data type **ComparisonKey** to declare variables and parameters inside the methods of the **PriorityQueue** class definition (see Programs 5.5 and 5.6) and we used only the abstract **compareTo()** method to compare the priorities of items stored in these priority queues (see line 26 of Program 5.5 and line 61 of Program 5.6).

But when we used the **PriorityQueue** class's methods to do actual priority queue sorting, we used actual integer keys that were converted into **PQItems** (see line 17 of Program 5.3). Java can accept such **PQItems** as valid instances of the general-purpose **ComparisonKey** type provided we first define the class **PQItem** to *implement* the **ComparisonKey** interface. This crucial step is given in Program 5.8.

*the toString() method*

*Java interfaces give abstract methods*

```
 1  | class PQItem implements ComparisonKey {
    |
    |      private int key;                 // the key data field contains an integer key
    |                                       // giving the priority of the item
 5  |
    |   /*-----------------*/
    |
    |      /** the single int argument constructor sets the key to its argument */
    |
10  |      PQItem(int value) {
    |          key = value;
    |      }
    |
    |   /*-----------------*/
15  |
    |      /** the toString() method converts an integer key into a String */
    |
    |      public String toString() {
    |          return Integer.toString(key);         // convert the int key to a String
20  |      }
    |
    |   /*-----------------*/
    |
    |      /** the k1.compareTo(k2) method is a three-way comparison of two */
25  |      /** keys, k1 and k2, that returns 0, 1, and −1 when k1 == k2, k1 > k2, */
    |      /** and k1 < k2, respectively */
    |
    |      public int compareTo(ComparisonKey value) {
    |          int a = this.key;
30  |          int b = ((PQItem)value).key;
    |          return ( (a == b) ? 0 : ( (a > b) ? 1 : −1) );
    |      }
    |
    |   /*-----------------*/
35  |
    | }
```

**Program 5.8** An Integer PQItem Class Implementing the ComparisonKey Interface

On lines 10:12 of Program 5.8, we define a constructor of the form **PQItem(V)** that takes an integer value **V** and converts it into an object that is an instance of the **PQItem** class. This constructor is applied to integer arguments on line 17 of Program 5.3 to convert integers of the form **squareOf(3\*i–13)** into **PQItems** that are stored in array position A[i] of the array A of **ComparisonKeys** (declared on line 12 of Program 5.3).

A[i] = new PQItem( squareOf(3\*i − 13) );

storing PQItems in ComparisonKey slots

This means that **PQItem** objects are being stored in array positions declared to hold values of the type **ComparisonKey**. Later, during priority queue sorting, these **PQItems** are removed from the array **A**, inserted in a priority queue **PQ**, and then removed in decreasing priority order from **PQ** and inserted back into **A**. The general-purpose methods that accomplish these insertions and removals were defined to work on **ComparisonKey** data types, but actually got applied to **PQItem** objects that were instances of a class defined to implement the abstract **ComparisonKey** interface's methods. By this means, we instructed Java to *plug-in* actual integer **PQItems** into the *sockets* defined by the **ComparisonKey** slots in the general-purpose **PriorityQueue** code.

We are now ready to define a different class of plug-in items to use in priority queue sorting. Suppose we want to sort a set of strings representing people's names into alphabetical order. To do this, we can first define a new plug-compatible **PQItem** class containing strings as keys that implements the **ComparisonKey** interface. Program 5.9 gives the details.

*sorting Strings instead of integers*

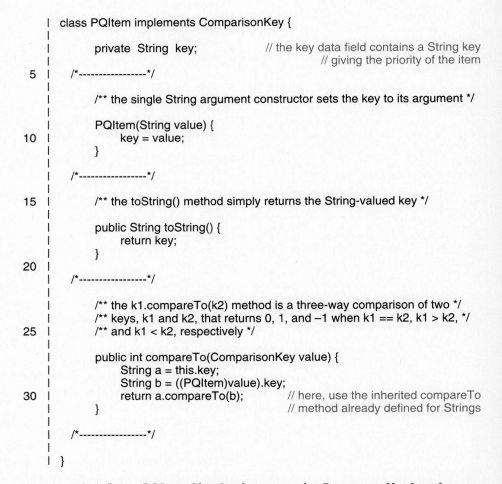

```
     | class PQItem implements ComparisonKey {
     |
     |         private  String  key;              // the key data field contains a String key
     |                                            // giving the priority of the item
   5 |     /*----------------*/
     |
     |         /** the single String argument constructor sets the key to its argument */
     |
     |         PQItem(String value) {
  10 |             key = value;
     |         }
     |
     |     /*----------------*/
     |
  15 |         /** the toString() method simply returns the String-valued key */
     |
     |         public String toString() {
     |             return key;
     |         }
  20 |
     |     /*----------------*/
     |
     |         /** the k1.compareTo(k2) method is a three-way comparison of two */
     |         /** keys, k1 and k2, that returns 0, 1, and −1 when k1 == k2, k1 > k2, */
  25 |         /** and k1 < k2, respectively */
     |
     |         public int compareTo(ComparisonKey value) {
     |             String a = this.key;
     |             String b = ((PQItem)value).key;
  30 |             return a.compareTo(b);          // here, use the inherited compareTo
     |         }                                   // method already defined for Strings
     |
     |     /*----------------*/
     |
     | }
```

**Program 5.9** A String PQItem Class Implementing the ComparisonKey Interface

Lines 9:11 of Program 5.9 define a single-argument constructor that converts its String argument into a PQItem object. Thus, the expression new PQItem("Amy") converts the String "Amy" into a PQItem having the String "Amy" stored in its hidden internal key data field.

Lines 17:19 implement the toString() method required in the ComparisonKey interface by simply returning the String item stored in a PQItem's key field.

Lines 27:31 of Program 5.9 implement the compareTo() method of a PQItem simply by using the inherited compareTo() method predefined for Java String objects.

After giving the PQItem class definition in Program 5.9 that implements String-valued ComparisonKeys, we can proceed immediately to perform priority queue sorting on strings without changing any of the previously defined class or interface definitions. The details are given in Program 5.10.

If you compare the texts of the method priorityQueueSort() on lines 39:50 of Program 5.3 (that sorts integers) and on lines 37:48 of Program 5.10 (that sorts strings), you'll conclude that both methods are identical and did not have to change at all when string sorting items replaced integer sorting items.

We have convincingly demonstrated the power of data abstraction in this chapter. Not only have we shown how to change the underlying hidden data representation of an ADT (from sorted linked lists to unsorted arrays) without having to change any code that uses the ADT, we have also shown how to implement the priority queue ADT in a general-purpose way that permits substitution of any kind of prioritized items so long as they supply a method for comparing two items to determine their relative priorities (using a three way comparison).

*Technical note*: In Java, you can actually define a new subclass S that **extends** a given class C and also simultaneously **implements** an interface J as in

```
class S extends C implements J {

    // insert S's data field and method definitions here

}
```

The new subclass S provides implementations for all of the methods specified in J's interface, and it also inherits all (**protected** or **public**) data fields and methods from C. This provides many of the benefits (and none of the drawbacks) of what is called *multiple inheritance* in some other object-oriented programming languages, even though Java is a single-inheritance language (in which subclasses can inherit from only one parent class).

*demonstrating the power of data abstraction*

## **5.4** REVIEW QUESTIONS

1. How is it possible in Java to implement ADTs for containers (such as sets, lists, or priority queues) that can hold different kinds of items that are plug-compatible and can be changed without having to change the implementation of the ADT?
2. How is it possible in Java to change the underlying hidden data representation of an ADT without having to change any of the code that uses the ADT?

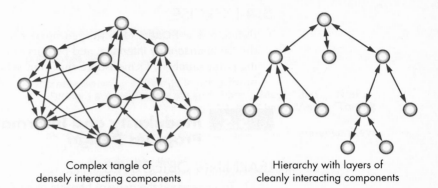

Complex tangle of
densely interacting components

Hierarchy with layers of
cleanly interacting components

**Figure 5.11** Alternative Software System Organizations

In your first computer science course, you may also have learned about beneficial techniques for creating and using locally declared variables and locally declared subprograms inside another outer procedure (Java, C, and C++ do not permit the latter, so possibly you may not have seen it). These local entities are visible only from inside the outer procedure, and cannot be seen or used outside of it. This is an instance of *information hiding* because the local entities are *hidden* from outside view. Such information hiding has two benefits: (1) the use of the local entities (e.g., variables and subprograms) does not interfere with identically named entities outside the procedure, and (2) the use of outside entities cannot interfere with the local entities. Object-oriented languages, such as Java, provide even more elaborate, fine-grained control over what is accessible and what is visible inside and outside classes, interfaces, methods, and packages. Consequently, Java is an even richer medium in which to express careful policies for information hiding.

*the benefits of
information hiding*

Information hiding builds a protective wall around the local entities that shields both them and the outside world from accidental (or even intentional) interference. Consequently, the region of text with which they can interact has been confined to a well-understood, local region of the overall program. This restricts and simplifies the possible interactions among program components. (In some programming languages, in which no local declarations are possible and every defined entity is visible everywhere throughout the program, the use of local name scoping is impossible, creating a disadvantage for the programmer.)

*encapsulation*

When we introduce devices into programming languages for building protective walls around collections of entities, we sometimes use the term *encapsulation*. The hidden local entities are said to be *encapsulated*, and we sometimes refer to the unit containing them as a *capsule*.

*modules, packages,
and units*

Procedures and functions are not the only kind of program component that can benefit from the notions of *information hiding* and *encapsulation*. Sometimes we need to gather together a somewhat larger collection of interacting entities that need to be packaged into a named unit of organization, and on which we need to confer the protective benefits of *information hiding*. *Modules*, *packages*, and *units* are three terms that are used in different contemporary programming languages for the notion of creating capsules containing collections of procedures, functions, variables, constants, and data type declarations, some of which are hidden internally, and others of which are made available for external use through the *interface* of the capsule.

In some modular programming languages, interface entities must be made visible explicitly by *exporting* them (i.e., by mentioning their names in explicit *export* declarations). Moreover, in some such languages, the clients wishing to use such exported services must explicitly declare which ones they intend to use by mentioning their names in explicit *import* declarations. Such declarations of intent serve further to make the exact nature of the interaction between modules more explicit and well-defined.

Finally, another type of use for the information-hiding capabilities of modules is to create separate *layers* of data representations. As we have seen, it is possible to hide the details of data representations inside modules in such a way that the services available in their interfaces do not reveal what data representation has been chosen. The clients get to use only the *abstract data type* (or ADT) exported through the interface. The data representation used is then encapsulated entirely within the hidden part of the module. By using abstraction in this fashion to create *representation-independent modules*, clarity, simplicity, and ease of modification are again promoted in the overall program design. Specifically, the hidden internal data representations and algorithms can be changed without changing any text in client programs—thus promoting *ease of modification*. Moreover, when properly programmed, no notational dependencies exist between the nature of the data representations used inside the module and the data access notation used by the clients, forcing the clients to change their programs whenever changes in the internal data representations used inside the module force changes in the data access notation used by clients.

## 5.5 REVIEW QUESTIONS

1. What is procedural abstraction?
2. What is data abstraction?
3. What is encapsulation?
4. Summarize the benefits of using Java classes, packages, and interfaces properly.

## Pitfalls

- *Avoid Complex Tangles of Components*

    The structure of a software system tends to become more complex and harder to debug, test, and modify, the more it exhibits a complex tangle of many components having many interactions. The use of modularity and information hiding to divide the structure into a hierarchy of a few simple components or into layers having a few simple interactions (if possible) greatly simplifies the overall structure, and increases the chances of successfully debugging, testing, and modifying the system.

## ▮ Tips and Techniques

- *Use Representation-Independent Notation to Hide a Data Representation*

    If you are going to succeed in hiding a data representation, you need to present an interface to the users that offers a representation-independent notation. Generally, this can be done by using only Java's method invocation notation in the public interface of a class, meanwhile hiding any instances of particular data access and update notation (such as the notations for selecting object data fields, **Obj.field**, or indexing components of arrays, **A[index]**, both of which reveal choices of data representations to their users).

- *Use Classes, Packages, and Interfaces to Help Organize the Work Breakdown Structure of Your Software Project*

    A software project can often be broken into cleanly organized subprojects by defining modules with separate responsibilities that interact through clean, simple interfaces. The interfaces can be specified first, without having to specify the implementations. The overall interaction between the modules can be given in a shell program that calls upon and coordinates the actions of the modules. After this is done, separate teams can address the problems of implementing the project's separate modules.

    This organizational strategy can be repeated when designing the structure of the modules, yielding a hierarchical work breakdown structure. The debugging, testing, and integration strategies for completion of the project can benefit from this overall organization, too.

## ▮ References for Further Study

Two influential early papers on modularity in the design of software systems were written by David Parnas:

David L. Parnas, "On the Criteria for Decomposing Systems into Modules," *Communications of the ACM*, 15:12, pp. 1053–1058 (December 1972).

David L. Parnas, "Designing Software for Ease of Extension and Contraction," *IEEE Transactions on Software Engineering*, SE-5(2), pp. 128–138 (1979).

*two key papers on modularity*

## ▮ Chapter Summary

*modules, interfaces, and information hiding*

Generally speaking, a *module* is a unit of organization within a larger software system that bundles together some operations and some data and has a carefully defined *interface*. External users of the module can make use of the operations and data provided in the module interface. At the same time, the internal implementation of the module is concealed and is made inaccessible to external users. *Information hiding* is the act of concealing such internal implementation details and preventing their use by external users. A module is said to be *encapsulated* if it uses information hiding to conceal internal implementation details, thus rendering them inaccessible to outside users.

*abstract data types*

*Abstract data types* (ADTs) are a way of organizing the objects and operations that define a data type in such a way that the data type's *behaviors* are rigorously separated from the data type's *implementation*. When modular programming techniques are used to implement ADTs, the data type's behaviors are specified in the publicly accessible interface of the module, and information hiding techniques are used to conceal the implementation. Because external users of an ADT use only those features of the ADT revealed in its public interface, the ADT's hidden internal data representation can be completely replaced without affecting the ADT's external users. This is called *substitutability of data representations*, and it can often be used to improve the efficiency of a software system by replacing less efficient data representations with more efficient ones.

*Java classes, interfaces, and packages*

Java provides strong, general-purpose support for modular programming through its mechanisms of *classes*, *interfaces*, and *packages*. An ADT can be conveniently expressed as a Java class in which the ADT's externally accessible operations and data are given by the **public** methods and data fields declared in the class, and in which the ADT's hidden implementation details are represented by the class's **private** data fields and methods. Java **interface**s can be used to define ADTs that can incorporate general purpose replaceable data components. The **interface** defines the abstract behavioral characteristics that allowable components must implement. Any specific kinds of data components that implement the **interface** can then be used as plug-compatible components, suitable for plugging-in to the ADT. Java **package**s are named collections of related classes and interfaces that can be separately compiled for use in Java applets or applications. Typically, packages, such as the Java **util** (utilities) package or the Java **awt** (abstract window tools) package, bundle collections of useful software components into a software component library suitable for use by others in building their own Java programs.

*using Java classes to implement ADTs*

This chapter demonstrated how to use Java classes to implement the priority queue ADT. Speaking abstractly, priority queues are containers that hold prioritized items. Items can be inserted into a given priority queue, PQ, in any order, but when an item is removed from PQ, it is guaranteed to be an item of highest priority. After giving the public methods available to external users of the priority queue ADT, an abstract priority queue sorting algorithm was implemented. This sorting algorithm used only the public ADT priority queue methods, and did not depend in any fashion on the hidden internal priority queue implementation details. Consequently, it was later possible to provide two different exchangable priority queue implementations. One of these used linked lists of items sorted in decreasing order of priority and the other used unsorted item arrays. It was shown how either of these internal implementations could replace the other without affecting the validity of the priority queue sorting algorithm. This demonstrated how to achieve the important goal of substitutability of data representations in Java.

In this chapter, it was also shown how to use Java interfaces to provide for plug-compatible interchangeable priority queue data items. Specifically, it was shown how to replace integers with strings in the abstract priority queue sorting algorithm. This was accomplished by unplugging the integer-based PQItem class and plugging in a String-based PQItem class. Nothing had to change in the sorted linked-list PriorityQueue representation or in the unsorted array PriorityQueue representation. The key to success was using the ComparisonKey interface definition to establish plug-in sockets to accept interchangeable components, and afterward defining the plug-compatible interchangeable components by defining PQItem classes to implement the ComparisonKey interface.

general-purpose methods that use interchangeable components

In general, modular programming has numerous benefits. There is a philosophy of software system structuring, based on modular programming practices, that emphasizes the importance of clarity and simplicity of program structure and ease of program modification. Not only can modules be used to provide packages of services and to provide collections of software components, they can also be used to organize the structure of a large software system either into cleanly separated layers or into major components that have simple, well-defined interactions. Generally speaking, a software system can be given a clean organization if it can be structured using a few major components having only a few well-defined interactions. Conversely, a software system tends to exhibit a complex organization if it is a disorganized tangle of many components having a complicated pattern of interactions.

providing clean software system organization

Programs will tend to be easier to modify if the modifications can be confined to a few places within well-defined boundaries and within a small local region of the total program text. If each of the users of a module has to be changed when the module itself is modified, then the changes are said to be *distributed* rather than *local*. By using Java classes to implement ADTs, the hidden implementation details can be modified (or can even be totally replaced) within the local boundaries of the Java class definitions without having to make a single external change elsewhere in the program. Ease of modification is thus convincingly achieved.

providing for ease of modification

# Linear Data Structures— Stacks and Queues

## 6.1 Introduction and Motivation

*Linear data structures* are collections of components arranged in a straight line. When we add or remove components of linear data structures, they grow or shrink. If we obey certain restrictions on the places where we add or remove elements, we obtain two important special cases of linear data structures—*stacks* and *queues*.

stacks and queues

If we restrict the growth of a linear data structure so that new components can be added and removed only at one end, we have a *stack*. If new components can be added at one end but removal of components must take place at the opposite end, we have a *queue*.

Stacks and queues can be thought of as abstract data structures obeying certain well-defined growth and decay laws, which can be represented in several ways by lower-level representations. For example, stacks and queues can each have either linked or sequential representations.

In this chapter, we will introduce and define the abstract data types (ADTs) for stacks and queues. Then we will study a few of the ways they can be represented using linked or sequential data structures.

151

Stacks are useful for processing nested structures or for managing algorithms in which processes call subprocesses. A nested structure is one that can contain instances of itself embedded within itself. For example, algebraic expressions can be *nested* because a subexpression of an algebraic expression can be another algebraic expression. Other examples of nested structures are levels of outlines for a term paper, the use of Java repetition statements inside other repetition statements, and nested sets—sets containing other sets as elements. Stacks are used to implement method calls when a Java thread is executed on the Java Virtual Machine. Stacks are natural to use because method calls are nested inside one another during program execution whenever methods call other methods.

Within the realm of algorithms, stacks are used to implement *parsing, evaluation,* and *backtracking* algorithms. Parsing algorithms are used by compilers to detect the structure of computer programs being compiled. Because the structure of such programs often contains nested program parts (such as blocks within blocks, statements within statements, and subexpressions inside expressions), stacks are natural to use.

Stacks can be used to perform expression evaluation. Such evaluation is inherently nested because you need to obtain the values of subexpressions before combining the subexpression values with an operator. Finally, stacks can be used to implement backtracking algorithms. When searching for solutions, backtracking algorithms typically organize themselves to search several subspaces of possible solutions in some order. If a solution is found when searching the first subspace, it is reported. But if no solution is found, the backtracking algorithm backs up to a previous choice point in the search, where it branched into the most recent subspace, and then branches into another subspace to continue the search. Backtracking is the process of backing up to a previous branch point in order to search a different new subspace along a different branch.

If you are searching a maze, suppose you leave a thread on the floor behind you as you travel. When you hit a dead-end (or *cul-de-sac*) you can retrace your thread to the nearest intersection and try some unexplored directions. You would thus be using the method of *backtracking*.

Queues can be used for regulating the processing of tasks in a system so as to ensure "fair" treatment. A queue is sometimes also called a *waiting line*. If a system consists of clients and servers, sometimes clients must "line up" to await service from various servers. After successfully obtaining service from one server, a client may need to obtain service from another server. When clients are placed in queues to await service, a *first-come, first-served policy* is in effect.

Many operating systems use queues of tasks to regulate the work performed by a computer. In this case, task records (representing users' jobs) are placed in queues to await service by various components of the system, such as the printer, the CPU (central processing unit), or various storage devices (such as disk and tape drives).

Queuing disciplines are also used in simulation and modeling. For example, to simulate the behavior of an air traffic control system, task records representing airplanes in flight can be placed in queues representing various states they can be in, such as: (a) waiting to take off at a given airport, (b) approaching to land at a given airport, (c) flying a particular route segment between an origin and a destination, and so on. When the system simulates a flight taking off, it removes its task record from the queue of planes awaiting takeoff and places it in the queue of airplanes in enroute flight. The flight records for airplanes in various queues are periodically processed to update their status. As a simulated flight progresses, its task record migrates from one queue to the next along its route of flight, to simulate its changing position and flight status. As a simulated flight nears its arrival airport, its task record is placed in the queue of simulated arrivals for that airport.

predicting performance

Computer simulations can thus be useful for understanding how a proposed system will function under various loads and processing capacities. For instance, we can gain insight into how telephone systems or urban transportation systems will function under forecasted future demands for service.

By separating the design of stacks and queues into an abstract layer and several supporting underlying representation layers, we can organize our software design around the use of ADTs at the highest levels. The underlying representations can be hidden and can be implemented as interchangeable modules. Such techniques enable us to gain clarity and brevity of the top-level design, modularity and substitutability of the underlying representations, and enhanced conditions for establishing the correctness, reliability, and efficiency of a software system. In short, using ADTs can help achieve many important software engineering goals.

## Plan for the Chapter

In Section 6.2 our goal is to develop an intuition for stacks and to become acquainted informally with some of the important roles stacks play elsewhere in computer science.

In Section 6.3 we introduce the ADTs for stacks and queues. The interface specifications for Java stacks and queues are presented, and the meanings of the stack and queue operations are discussed. Then we relate this method for presenting ADTs to the discussion on modularity and information hiding in Chapter 5.

Sections 6.4 and 6.5 present two applications of the stack ADT. The idea is to show how we can develop applications using only the operations in the stack ADT interface *before* giving low-level implementations of stacks. This way, we can be assured that the applications using stacks don't use any low-level representational features, and that they use only abstract stack operations available in the stack ADT interface. Section 6.4 studies a use of stacks to check for properly balanced parentheses in algebraic expressions. Section 6.5 presents a way to evaluate postfix expressions using stacks. Section 6.6 presents both sequential and linked representations for stacks. Section 6.7 studies an additional application of stacks by discussing how stacks are used to implement recursion in Java. This helps develop understanding for what happens when Java encounters infinite regresses (i.e., chains of recursive calls that are never stopped by base cases). It also helps explain how recursion can be implemented in programming languages.

Section 6.8 introduces both sequential and linked representations for the queue ADT. We discover that queues are more representationally demanding than stacks. Linked queue representations need either special header nodes or circular two-way linking to make them work well. Sequential queue representations can be made circular to confine their travel to a bounded region of memory.

Section 6.9 discusses several different applications of queues. We first look at operating systems and how queues are used in print buffers and printer spoolers as well as in regulating task processing in time-shared operating systems. We then discuss how queues are used in simulation and modeling.

## 6.2    Some Background on Stacks

### LEARNING OBJECTIVES

1. To learn some of the common terminology.
2. To become informally acquainted with a significant use of stacks in handling recursion, in the theory of push-down automata, and in the theory of parsing, translation, and compiling.

If you have a pile of objects of any kind, such as a pile of books or a pile of coins, and you add and remove objects only at the top of the pile, you have a *stack* (see Fig. 6.1).

Stacks are sometimes referred to as *push-down stacks*. Adding a new object to the top of such a push-down stack is called *pushing* a new object onto the stack, and removing an object from the top of the push-down stack is called *popping* the object from the stack. Pushing and popping are *inverse* operations: If you push an object onto a stack and then pop it off immediately afterward, you leave the original stack unchanged.

Perhaps you have seen spring-loaded piles of trays in a cafeteria. As you add new trays to a spring-loaded pile of trays, the increased weight of the pile causes the sup-

*pushing and popping*

*spring-loaded piles in a cafeteria*

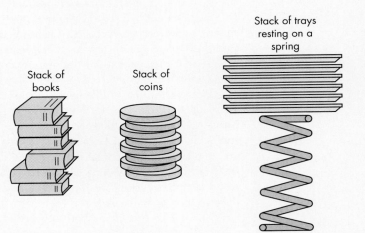

**Figure 6.1** Various Kinds of Stacks

porting spring underneath to compress, and the top of the pile remains in a fixed position. Conversely, when you remove trays from the top, the weight of the pile decreases, the underlying spring decompresses, and the pile rises so that its top remains in a fixed position.

The image of a push-down stack with its top remaining in a fixed position, and with the whole stack being pushed down under addition of a new item, and rising up under removal of an item, is an image associated with an idealized machine, called a *push-down automaton* (or PDA, for short). As illustrated in Fig. 6.2, a push-down automaton has a *read head* that reads symbols on an input tape. It also uses a push-down stack for an internal memory. A read-write head sits next to the top symbol of the PDA's push-down stack, and it is able to push and pop symbols on this stack as well as being able to read the topmost symbol on the stack. The PDA's control unit is a "finite state control unit." This means it has a finite number of different *states* it can be in. In a given state, when the PDA is looking at a particular input symbol $i_k$ on its input tape, and sees a particular symbol $s_j$ on top of its push-down stack, it can specify an action to perform that involves (a) entering a new state, (b) reading the next symbol on its input tape, and (c) pushing or popping a symbol from its push-down stack.

**push-down automata**

Push-down automata play a key role in the theory of formal languages and in the theory of parsing, translation, and compiling used in programming language translators (i.e., compilers). In formal language theory, a *language* is just a set of strings spelled from the letters in a given alphabet. The languages that PDA's can recognize are exactly those that are described by a commonly occurring kind of programming language grammar called a *context-free grammar*. Context-free grammars are often used to give formal definitions of the syntax of programming languages. You may have seen such grammars used in various textbooks to define the syntax of Java or of other programming languages.

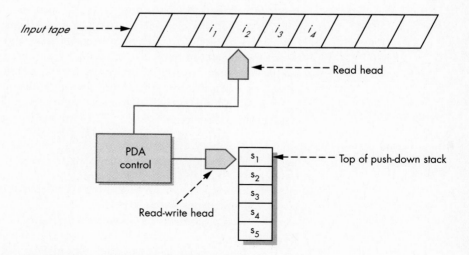

**Figure 6.2** Schematic Diagram of a Push-Down Automaton

To summarize, stacks are used as the memory-structure in push-down automata that play a key role in formal language theory as the automata that serve as the recognizers for context-free languages (which are the languages generated by context-free grammars). As a consequence, syntax analyzers for programming languages often employ push-down stacks to accomplish recognition of the structure of computer programs during compilation.

Of course, even though we imagine that the entire stack moves *down* when a new item is pushed onto it, or *up* when the topmost item is popped, the underlying data representations we use for stacks do not behave this way. For instance, if we use arrays to hold stack items, the growth end of the stack travels through memory, and the items in the stack remain fixed in place—rather than having the growth end remaining fixed and moving all items in the stack.

**stack representations**

Stacks are often used in ingenious ways in various algorithms to hold information about postponed obligations for further processing. We use a stack of *activation records* to keep track of a sequence of method calls during program execution. Each time a method call is made, an activation record for the call is pushed on a stack. This activation record contains space for information needed during the time the method call is being processed, and it contains information for how to resume the execution of its caller after its own execution is finished. The stack is the perfect data structure to use for this purpose, since method calls are always dynamically nested—that is, at program execution time, when one method calls another, the caller's activity is suspended while the callee is executed. The time span for the callee's execution is therefore nested inside the time span for its caller.

**using stacks to hold postponed obligations**

Sometimes the space for stack items can be found in unused fields of nodes in a larger data structure. For example, some algorithms for traversing the nodes of trees in a linked tree representation (such as that shown in Fig. 3.29 of Chapter 3) make use of empty pointer fields in the tree to encode the information for a stack of postponed obligations for further traversal of the tree. This leads to algorithms that do not need external auxiliary stacks to traverse trees. Such algorithms can become quite important to use for garbage collection (i.e., storage reclamation) in list structure memory, since garbage collection tends to occur at the very moment that there is no more space to allocate. In particular, it occurs when there is no space for allocating a stack to use to enable traversal of list structures that need to be marked as being in use, so that they will not be swept up during garbage collection.

**LIFO versus FIFO**

Stacks are sometimes called LIFO lists, where LIFO stands for "last-in, first-out," and queues are sometimes called FIFO (first-in, first-out) lists.

## 6.2 REVIEW QUESTIONS

1. Why are stacks useful for processing nested structures?
2. Give four examples of nested structures.
3. What can push-down automata accomplish according to the theory of formal languages?
4. Can stacks be used to process method calls?

## **6.2** EXERCISES

1. According to a law of physics known as Hookes' Law, the displacement, $d$, in a spring due to compression when an additional load, $L$, is added, is directly proportional to $L$, $d = \alpha L$. Given a stack of trays (where each tray is of weight $L$ and thickness $d$) riding on a compressed spring, having a "spring constant" $\alpha$, and obeying Hookes' Law, $d = \alpha L$, show that the top of the stack stays in a fixed position as trays are pushed or popped from the stack.

2. If you have two stacks, $S_1$ and $S_2$, and a single array A[0:n−1] to use for holding the stack items for both stacks, how should you arrange to represent $S_1$ and $S_2$ so that they each have the greatest possible room for growth before no more space remains inside A[0:n−1]?

## **6.3**  **ADTs for Stacks and Queues**

### LEARNING OBJECTIVES

1. To learn about data structuring methods and about how they differ from ADTs.
2. To learn about abstract sequences as a data structuring method.
3. To understand the view of ADTs as data structures + operations.
4. To learn about the abstract operations and interfaces for stack and queue ADTs.

An *abstract data type* (ADT) consists of a collection of data structures together with a set of operations defined on those data structures. The data structures are usually *composite* data structures obtained by applying a *structuring method* to a collection of *components*.

*structuring methods*

You are, no doubt, already familiar with several structuring methods from studying Java in your first course in computer science. The formation of arrays, objects with data fields, and strings using various types of components illustrate three structuring methods used in Java. In addition, using references to designate components and embedding such references inside other structures (such as objects or arrays) enables us to create linked data structures—a fourth structuring method that Java offers.

*sequences*

Speaking abstractly, the formation of linear *sequences* of components is a structuring method that many data structures share in common. For example, strings, arrays, lists, stacks, and queues each consist of linear sequences of components. Each of these sequential data structures has a different set of operations defined on it. Differences in the allowable operations and in the types of components distinguish these different data structures from one another.

Although the sequences generally used in mathematics can be infinite in length, we usually use finite length sequences in computer science. A finite length sequence $S = (s_1, s_2, s_3, \ldots, s_n)$ is just an ordered arrangement of finitely many components, $s_i$, $(1 \leq i \leq n)$. We sometimes include the empty sequence, symbolized by the Greek letter, $\Lambda$, in our considerations. We say that the *length* of a sequence S is the number of components in it. The length of the empty sequence is 0.

Having defined sequences in this manner, we could say that we had applied the structuring method of forming sequences to the set of elements {1,2,3,4,5} to create a sequence such as S = (5, 3, 4, 3, 1, 2). [Note: in a *set*, the elements are considered to be unordered and have no repetitions, whereas in a *sequence*, the elements appear in a specific order and occurrences of elements may be repeated.]

To define an ADT, in addition to defining a set of data structures, we need to define *operations* on those structures. Thus, starting with *sequences* as the basic data structure, we can define *Stacks* and *Queues* by defining two separate sets of operations on sequences. This is done as follows:

ADTs = sequences + operations

## Stacks

A *Stack*, S, is a sequence of items on which the following operations are defined:

1. *Construct* an initially empty stack, S.
2. Determine whether or not the stack, S, is *empty*.
3. *Push* a new item onto the top of the stack, S.
4. If S is nonempty, *pop* an item from the top of stack, S.
5. If S is nonempty, *peek* at the top of stack S by reading a copy of the top item of S without removing it.

## Queues

A *Queue*, Q, is a sequence of items on which the following operations are defined:

1. *Construct* an initially empty queue, Q.
2. Determine whether or not the queue, Q, is *empty*.
3. *Insert* a new item onto the rear of the queue, Q.
4. Provided Q is nonempty, *remove* an item from the front of Q.

As you can see, the differences between the Stacks and Queues consist only of differences in the operations that are defined on them—*not* in differences between the structuring method that is applied to their components to bundle the components into an aggregate structure.

differences in the operations sometimes define the distinction between ADTs

A similar situation occurs in mathematics. For instance, points in the two-dimensional plane can be specified using either Cartesian or polar coordinates. In either system, pairs of real numbers are used for the coordinates. But you can't tell just by looking at a pair of real numbers, such as (1.6, 2.5), whether it represents a point in polar or Cartesian coordinates. What distinguishes Cartesian and polar coordinates is the set of operations we apply to them to determine various known results. For instance, the distance from the origin of the coordinate system of a point $(r,\theta)$ in polar coordinates is given by $r$, whereas if the point $(x,y)$ is given in Cartesian coordinates, this distance is given by

$$\sqrt{x^2 + y^2}.$$

The definitions of the Stack and Queue ADTs deliberately do not mention any required underlying data representation that must be used. As we shall see presently, either linked data representations or sequential data representations can be used. In forming the linked representations, we can use nodes to hold the individual items and we can link these nodes to one another in a linear linked list, using node references in the usual fashion. It may seem strange to talk about using low-level sequential data representations to represent abstract sequences at a higher level, but this is exactly what we do when we use an array as the underlying representation for an abstract stack or queue.

In short, data structures that are viewed abstractly as *sequences* at the level of ADTs can be represented in an underlying memory medium using either *linked representations* or *sequential representations*. (In fact, these are not the only two possibilities. For instance, if we had a language that offered a general-purpose set representation, we could even represent abstract stacks and queues using sets of ordered pairs constructed in an appropriate fashion. We choose to study only some of the frequently used common representations in this book, however.)

underlying representations
for abstract sequences

## Interfaces for Stack and Queue Classes

The ADTs for stacks and queues can be represented conveniently in Java by defining a **Stack** class and a **Queue** class having the public method calls given in Figs. 6.3 and 6.4. These public method calls give the external interfaces of stacks and queues (without revealing the hidden internal stack and queue representations).

We deliberately postpone giving implementations for the stack and queue operations in Figs. 6.3 and 6.4 until after we have given some examples of applications. This way, when we write application programs, we are guaranteed that we will use

```
      |    /*
      |     *    The public interface for the Stack class contains
      |     *    the following method calls. Here, let S be a variable having
      |     *    a Stack object as its value, and let X be a variable that
   5  |     *    contains a stack item.
      |     */
      |
      |         S = new Stack();              // creates an initially empty Stack S
      |
  10  |         S.empty( );                   // a boolean expression that is true if and
      |                                       // only if Stack S contains no items
      |
      |         S.push(X);                    // pushes an item X onto the top of Stack S
      |
  15  |         X = S.pop( );                 // removes the top item of S and puts it in X
      |
      |         X = S.peek( );                // puts a copy of the top item of S in X
      |                                       // without removing it from S
      |
```

**Figure 6.3** Informal Method Calls in a Stack ADT Interface

```
 1   |   /*
     |   *    The public interface for the Queue class contains
     |   *    the following method calls. Here, let Q be a variable having
     |   *    a Queue object as its value, and let X be a variable that
 5   |   *    contains a queue item.
     |   */
     |
     |       Q = new Queue( );              // creates an initially empty Queue Q
     |
10   |       Q.empty( );                    // a boolean expression that is true if and
     |                                      // only if the Queue Q contains no items
     |
     |       Q.insert(X);                   // inserts an item X onto the rear of Queue Q
     |
15   |       X = Q.remove( );               // removes an item from the front of Q
     |                                      // and puts it in X
```

**Figure 6.4** Informal Method Calls for a Queue ADT Interface

only the features of stack and queue ADTs revealed in the interface, and that we cannot build in any features that depend on hidden details of a particular low-level representation or implementation.

Later, we will define Java classes that give both linked and sequential representations for stacks and queues that implement the interfaces given in Figs. 6.3 and 6.4. This way, we will again demonstrate (a) substitutability of different underlying data representations, and (b) proper modular programming discipline by separating cleanly the representational details of abstract data types from their uses.

## 6.3 REVIEW QUESTIONS

1. Java supplies users with several structuring methods for forming composite data structures from components. Name some of Java's structuring methods.
2. What is a convenient way to express the objects and operations of an ADT in Java?
3. How can you be sure that you have used proper modular programming practices when defining and using an ADT?

## 6.3 EXERCISES

1. Suppose you have a programming language that permits you to define unordered sets of items of any type. How could you represent a sequence of real numbers using sets of ordered pairs as the underlying representation?
2. Would the representation you devised as your answer to Exercise 1 be efficient to use if you wanted to add or delete a new last item in your sequence? Would it be efficient if you wanted both to add a new last item and remove the first item? Would it therefore be a good representation to use for stacks or queues, or both?

**Using the Stack ADT to Check for Balanced Parentheses**

## LEARNING OBJECTIVES

1. To see how the Stack ADT can be used to support an application even though we don't know the Stack's implementation yet.
2. To lay the groundwork for defining two substitutable representations of the Stack ADT later.

The first application of the Stack ADT that we will study involves a small program to determine whether parentheses and brackets are balanced properly in algebraic expressions.

In mathematics, we sometimes use parentheses, brackets, and braces of various sizes to indicate the boundaries of subexpressions. In properly formed algebraic expressions, the various types of parentheses must occur in properly matching balanced pairs.

For example, consider the algebraic expression:

$$\{a^2 - [(b + c)^2 - (d + e)^2] * [\sin(x - y)]\} - \cos(x + y)$$

This incorporates parentheses ( ), square brackets [ ], and braces { }, in balanced pairs according to the pattern { [ ( ) ( ) ] [ ( ) ] } ( ).

We can use stacks to check whether such algebraic expressions have properly balanced parentheses or not. To do this, we start with an empty stack and scan a string representing the algebraic expression from left to right. Whenever we encounter a left parenthesis (, a left square bracket [, or a left brace {, we push it onto the stack. Whenever we encounter a right parenthesis ), a right square bracket ], or a right brace }, we pop the top item off the stack and check to see whether its type matches the type of the right parenthesis, bracket, or brace encountered.

*pushing and popping to keep track of matching pairs*

If the stack is empty by the time we get to the end of the expression string and if all pairs of matched parentheses were of the same type, the expression has properly balanced parentheses. Otherwise, the parentheses are not balanced properly.

Figure 6.5 shows the result of entering a parenthesized expression into an input window and pressing the Enter key in a parenthesis matching applet.

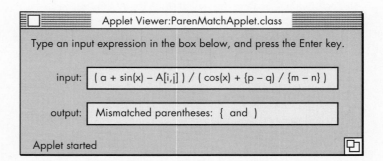

**Figure 6.5** Results of Checking for Balanced Parentheses

Program 6.6 gives the Java applet that interacts with the user using the graphical user interface shown in Fig. 6.5. It asks the user to type an expression in the input box. When the user presses the Enter key, it conducts a parenthesis matching analysis of the input expression and displays the results of its analysis in the output box.

```
     /*
      * This applet accepts a string typed by the user that contains parentheses
      * in the set '{','(','[','}',')',']' and checks it for parenthesis balance
      */
 5
     import java.applet.*;
     import java.awt.*;

     public class ParenMatchApplet extends Applet implements ActionListener  {
10
     // declare the data fields as follows:

     Label
         instructionLabel,                 // gives the instructions for user input
15       inputLabel,                       // labels the input text box
         outputLabel;                      // labels the output text box

     TextField
         inputField,                              // the input text box
20       outputField;                             // the output text box

     ParenMatcher PM;                    // the object that computes results


25   // the applet's methods follow

     /*--------------------------------------*/

     public void init() {
30
         instructionLabel = new Label(
             "Type an input expression in the box below, and press the Enter key.",
             Label.CENTER );

35       add(instructionLabel);                    // add the instruction label to
                                                   // top of applet layout
         inputLabel = new Label(" input:");

         add(inputLabel);                          // then, add the input label
40
         inputField = new TextField(40);           // create a 40-column-wide
                                                   // input field and add it to
         add(inputField);                          // the applet's layout

45       inputField.addActionListener(this);       // add the event handler
```

**Program 6.6** Applet that Checks for Balanced Parentheses (*continued*)

Program 6.6 Applet that Checks for Balanced Parentheses *(continued)*

```
          outputLabel = new Label("output:");              // add the output label

          add(outputLabel);
50
          outputField = new TextField(40);                 // create a 40-column-wide
                                                           // output field and add it to
          add(outputField);                               // the applet's layout

55        inputField.requestFocus();                       // put the blinking vertical text
                                                           // insertion cursor in the input box
          PM = new ParenMatcher();                        // create a new
                                                           // parenthesis matcher object
      } // end init
60
      /*--------------------------------------*/

      public void actionPerformed(ActionEvent e)  {

65        PM.setInput(e.getActionCommand());               // send the input string to the
                                                           // parenthsis matcher object, PM.
          PM.parenMatch();                                // analyze parenthesis balance

          outputField.setText(PM.getOutput());            // put result in output field
70
      } // end actionPerformed

      /*--------------------------------------*/

75    }// end applet

      /* insert the text for the class ParenMatcher from Program 6.7 here */
```

The init() method, given on lines 29:59 of Program 6.6, creates the graphical user interface shown in Fig. 6.5 by placing a centered instruction label at the top of the applet (see lines 31:35), and then by placing labeled input and output text boxes directly under the instruction label. Line 45 designates the applet as the event-handler that receives text input events that occur when the user types an input string and then presses the Enter key. These text input events are handled by the actionPerformed event handler defined on lines 63:71. Line 55 requests the focus of attention to be placed in the input text box. As a result, a blinking vertical bar cursor is made active in the input text box to designate that the input box is the focus of attention for receiving characters typed by the user.

The last action of the init() method is to create a parenthesis matcher object, PM, that is an instance of the ParenMatcher class defined in Program 6.7. You can think of the ParenMatcher object PM as a factory. This factory receives input strings to analyze

```
class ParenMatcher {

    private String inputString, outputString;

5   /*-------------------------------------*/

    private boolean match (char c, char d) {        // this boolean method
                                                     // returns true if and
        switch (c) {                                 // only if c and d are
10          case '(' : return (d == ')');            // matching pairs
            case '[' : return (d == ']');            // of parentheses ( ),
            case '{' : return (d == '}');            // square brackets [ ],
            default : return false;                  // or braces { }
        }
15
    }//end match

    /*-------------------------------------*/

20  public void parenMatch() {

        Stack parenStack = new Stack();         // the parenStack holds left parens
                                                 // and is popped when right
        int n = inputString.length();            // parens are encountered
25
        int i = 0;                        // i is the index of the ith input string character

        char c,d;                         // c and d hold characters to match

30      while (i < n) {

            d = inputString.charAt(i);             // d is assigned the ith character

            if (d == '(' || d == '[' || d == '{') {    // push each of the three types
35                                                      // of left parentheses
                parenStack.push(new Character(d));

            } else if (d == ')' || d == ']' || d == '}') {    // match each of the three
                                                               // types of right parentheses
40              if (parenStack.empty()) {

                    output("More right parentheses than left parentheses");
                    return;

45              } else {

                    c = ((Character)parenStack.pop()).charValue();

                    if (!match(c,d)) {    // if c doesn't match the right parenthesis
50
                        output("Mismatched parentheses: "+ c +" and " + d);
                        return;

                    }//end if
```

**Program 6.7** Checking for Balanced Parentheses *(continued)*

Program 6.7 Checking for Balanced Parentheses *(continued)*

```
 55 |
    |                          }//end if
    |
    |                     }//end if
    |
 60 |                     ++i;                              // increase index i to scan next input char
    |
    |                }//end while
    |
    |
 65 |                if (parenStack.empty()) {
    |
    |                     output("Parentheses are balanced properly");
    |
    |                } else {
 70 |
    |                     output("More left parentheses than right parentheses");
    |
    |                }//end if
    |
 75 |           }//end parenMatch
    |
    |      /*-------------------------------------*/
    |
    |      private void output(String s) {
 80 |
    |           outputString = s;
    |
    |      }//end output
    |
 85 |      /*-------------------------------------*/
    |
    |      public void setInput(String input) {
    |
    |           inputString = input;
 90 |
    |      }//end setInput
    |
    |      /*-------------------------------------*/
    |
 95 |      public String getOutput() {
    |
    |           return outputString;
    |
    |      }//end getOutput
100 |
    |      /*-------------------------------------*/
    |
    | }//end class ParenMatcher
105 |
    |      /* insert here the text of the Stack class from either Program 6.11 or 6.12 */
    |
```

for parenthesis balance, processes orders that you send to it to conduct the analysis, and reports the results of its analysis back to you as its output. You use method calls to send messages to the factory to request it to perform its various functions.

The event handler method actionPerformed(ActionEvent e), defined on lines 63:71, makes the method calls that send messages to the PM factory. This actionPerformed() method is invoked when the user finishes typing an expression into the input text box and presses the Enter key. The input text typed by the user is transmitted to the actionPerformed() method in a data field of the ActionEvent parameter e. On line 65, the method call PM.setInput(e.getActionCommand()); causes this user input string to be transmitted to the PM object, using the PM object's setInput() method. (The setInput() method of the PM object, in turn, places the string value of this input text in its own private internal inputString data field in preparation for its analysis of parenthesis balance.)

On line 67, the actionPerformed() method directs PM to do a parenthesis matching analysis, using the method call PM.parenMatch();, and on line 69, the actionPerformed() method retrieves the results of PM's analysis and displays it in the output text field, using the method call outputField.setText(PM.getOutput());.

Turning now to Program 6.7, the statement Stack parenStack = new Stack(); given on line 22, declares a new Stack valued variable parenStack, and initializes it to a newly constructed empty Stack. The Stack class that is instantiated to create this new parenStack object is defined by a class definition to be inserted later on line 106. In fact, we can interchangeably substitute the sequential stack representation of the Stack class defined in Program 6.11 or the linked stack representation of the Stack class defined in Program 6.12, and Program 6.7 will work without having to change anything. This is because Program 6.7 uses only the Stack method calls in the public interface of the Stack class (given in Fig. 6.3). Both the sequential and linked stack class definitions of Programs 6.11 and 6.12 implement these public Stack ADT method calls with identical meanings (even though they use different hidden internal representation techniques to do so).

For example, line 40 of Program 6.7 checks to see whether the parenStack is empty, using the boolean expression parenStack.empty(). When the empty() method of the sequential stack representation is called, it checks to see whether an internal hidden count of the number of items in the stack is zero, but when the empty() method of the linked stack representation is called, it checks to see whether a hidden internal topNode data field points to a null top node for its hidden internal linked list of stack nodes.

We now trace through an example of how the parenMatch method, given on lines 20:75 in Program 6.7, processes an input expression such as, {a^2 − [ (c − d)^2 + (e − f)^2] } * sin(x − y), which has a parenthesis structure of the form { [ ( ) ( ) ] } ( ). Given this input, parenMatch first pushes the left parentheses { [ ( onto the parenStack, yielding a parenStack with ( on its top, of the following form:

$$\text{parenStack} = \begin{array}{|c|} ( \\ [ \\ \{ \end{array} .$$

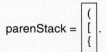

When **parenMatch** then encounters the first instance of a right parenthesis ), it pops the left parenthesis ( from the top of the stack and matches it against the right parenthesis, leaving a **parenStack** of the form:

$$\text{parenStack} = \begin{bmatrix} [ \\ \{ \end{bmatrix}.$$

**parenMatch** then processes the next parenthesis pair ( ), by pushing ( on the stack and immediately popping it off again to match the right parenthesis ). Upon encountering ] and }, **parenMatch** pops [ and { off the **parenStack** to match them. Finally, **parenMatch** pushes ( on the stack and then pops it to match the final ). At the end, the **parenStack** is empty.

## **6.4** REVIEW QUESTIONS

1. Is the "last-in, first-out" property of stacks crucial for detecting matching pairs of parentheses? Would it be possible to use a queue, having a "first-in, first-out" property to replace the role played by the stack in Program 6.7?
2. What property of Program 6.7 guarantees that separately defined linked and sequential representations of the Stack ADT can be used interchangeably, and thus that the property of "substitutability of representations" will be achievable?

## **6.4** EXERCISES

1. Run Program 6.6 on the following expressions having both balanced and unbalanced parentheses. Check the results for correctness.

   | | |
   |---|---|
   | { a^2 − [ (b+c)^2 − (d+e)^2]* [sin(x−y)] } − cos(x+y) | — balanced |
   | { a− [ (b+c))) − (d+e) ] } | — too many right parens |
   | { a− [ [ [(b+c) − (d+e) ] } | — too many left parens |
   | { a− [ (b+c) − (d+e) } ] | — unmatched paren types |

2. Alan Aardvark decides he doesn't need to use a stack to check for properly balanced parentheses. Instead, he decides to keep three integers called **parenCount**, **bracketCount**, and **braceCount**. Each of these counts is set initially to zero. When scanning an input expression, if he encounters (, [, or {, he increments the respective **parenCount**, **bracketCount**, or **braceCount** by one. If he encounters ), ], or }, he decrements the respective **parenCount**, **bracketCount**, or **braceCount** by one. At the end of the input expression, if the three counts are zero, he decides all types of parentheses are balanced properly. Will his method work? If so, why? If not, say why not and give a counterexample.

<table>
<tr><td>6.5</td><td>

## Using the Stack ADT to Evaluate Postfix Expressions
</td></tr>
</table>

## LEARNING OBJECTIVES

1. To learn how stacks can be used to evaluate postfix expressions.
2. To see another example of modular programming techniques illustrating postponed choice of the underlying data representation for stacks.

Ordinarily, for human use, algebraic expressions are given in *infix notation* in which a binary operator $\beta$ is placed between its left and right operands, L and R, as in the expression (L $\beta$ R). Parentheses are used to specify the order of operations.

*Postfix expressions* can be used to specify algebraic operations using a parenthesis-free notation. The postfix expression, L R $\beta$, corresponds to the infix expression (L $\beta$ R). To translate an infix expression, (L $\beta$ R), into postfix, you write the postfix expression for L, followed by the postfix expression for R, followed by the operator $\beta$. Table 6.8 gives examples of infix expressions and their corresponding translations into postfix. Note that the caret operator ($\wedge$) is used in postfix expressions in Table 6.8 to denote exponentiation, so that the square of $a$, denoted $a^2$ in infix, is translated as $a\ 2\wedge$ in postfix.

Figure 6.9 shows the result of entering a postfix expression in an input box of a postfix evaluator applet and then pressing the Enter key. The value of the input expression is shown in the output box.

It is convenient to use stacks to evaluate postfix expressions. To evaluate a postfix expression, $P$, you scan $P$ from left-to-right. When you encounter an operand, $X$, while scanning $P$, you push it onto an evaluation stack, $S$. When you encounter an operator, $\beta$, while scanning $P$, you pop the topmost operand stacked on $S$ into a variable $R$ (which denotes the right operand), then you pop another topmost operand stacked on $S$ into a variable $L$ (which denotes the left operand). Finally, you perform the operation $\beta$ on $L$ and $R$, getting the value of the expression (L $\beta$ R), and you push this value back onto the stack, $S$. When you are finished scanning $P$, the value of $P$ is the only item remaining on the stack $S$.

Some early computers and some recent pocket calculators use postfix instructions for evaluating arithmetic expressions. In fact, the Java Virtual Machine (JVM) uses postfix instructions and evaluation stacks to perform arithmetic operations on

*the evaluation method in a nutshell*

| Infix Expression | Postfix Expression |
|---|---|
| (a + b) | a b + |
| (x − y − z) | x y − z − |
| (x − y − z)/(u + v) | x y − z − u v + / |
| $(a^2 + b^2)*(m − n)$ | a 2 ^ b 2 ^ + m n − * |

**Table 6.8** Translations of Infix Expressions into Corresponding Postfix Expressions

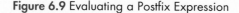

```
┌──────────────────────────────────────────────────────┐
│ ☐ ═══════ Applet Viewer:PostfixInterpApplet.class ═══ │
├──────────────────────────────────────────────────────┤
│ Type an input expression in the box below, and press the Enter key. │
│                                                        │
│   input: │ 1.3 7.5 + 1.1 / 12 10 − *                 │ │
│                                                        │
│  output: │ Value of postfix expression  = 16          │ │
│                                                        │
│ Applet started                                      ⊡ │
└──────────────────────────────────────────────────────┘
```

**Figure 6.9** Evaluating a Postfix Expression

operands. For example, the JVM instruction *iadd* pops the top two integer operands from its eval stack, adds them, and pushes the sum back onto the eval stack.

Program 6.10 presents an evaluator for postfix expressions. It assumes that a postfix expression is given as input using numerical operands, and using any of the binary operators (+) for addition, (−) for subtraction, (*) for multiplication, (/) for division, and (^) for exponentiation. The numerical operands must be separated from one another either by operators or by spaces as shown in the example in Fig. 6.9.

The class **PostfixInterpreter** in Program 6.10 is designed to share the same user interface that the parenthesis matching applet uses (given earlier in Program 6.6). In software engineering, this is called *software reuse*. It is held to be a virtue because reusing previously written software components accelerates software development and usually improves reliability.

To change Program 6.6 from a parenthesis matching applet into a postfix expression evaluator, all you need to do is (1) replace the class name **ParenMatcher** on lines 22 and 57 with the class name **PostfixInterpreter**, (2) replace the method call **parenMatch()** on line 67 with the method call **interpretPostfix()**, and (3) substitute the text of Program 6.10 for that of Program 6.7 on line 77 (at the end of Program 6.6).

Let's trace through a simple example of the operation of Program 6.10. Suppose a postfix string "6 7 * 2 −" is given as the value of the variable, **postfixString**. Line 25 constructs and initializes an **evalStack** to be used during evaluation. On line 31, a **StringTokenizer** object is created that breaks the **postfixString** into separate token strings consisting of numbers, operators, and spaces. The while-statement on lines 33:71 is used to scan through the tokens of the **postfixString** from left to right. First, **6** is scanned and becomes the **String** value of the variable **token**. (The char variable **c** is used to hold the first character of the **token** string currently scanned.)

tracing through an example

On line 39, a determination is made whether or not the current token is an operator. Because the string "6" is not an operator, control passes to line 61 where it is determined that "6" is not a space token. (All space tokens are ignored.) Then control passes to line 67 where the token string "6" is converted to a double-precision floating point number that is pushed onto the **evalStack**. The **evalStack** now has the left operand 6 pushed onto it and appears as follows:

evalStack = │ 6.0 │ .

```
class PostfixInterpreter {

        private String postfixString, outputString;

5    /*----------------------------------------*/

     private boolean isOperator(char c) {

         return (c == '+' || c == '−' || c == '*' || c == '/' || c == '^');

10    }//end isOperator

     /*----------------------------------------*/

15    private boolean isSpace(char c) {

         return (c == ' ');

     }//end isSpace

20    /*----------------------------------------*/

     public void interpretPostfix() {

25        Stack evalStack = new Stack();

          double leftOperand, rightOperand;

          char c;

30        StringTokenizer parser = new StringTokenizer(postfixString,"+−*/^ ",true);

          while (parser.hasMoreTokens()) {          // provided there are more
                                                    // tokens in the postfixString
35            String token = parser.nextToken();              // get the next token
                                                            // and let c be
              c = token.charAt(0);                // the first character of this token

              if ( (token.length() == 1) && isOperator(c) ) { // if token is an operator
40
                  rightOperand = ((Double)evalStack.pop()).doubleValue();
                  leftOperand = ((Double)evalStack.pop()).doubleValue();

                  switch (c) {                              // perform the operation
45
                  case '+': evalStack.push(new Double(leftOperand+rightOperand));
                              break;
                  case '−': evalStack.push(new Double(leftOperand−rightOperand));
                              break;
50                case '*': evalStack.push(new Double(leftOperand*rightOperand));
                              break;
                  case '/': evalStack.push(new Double(leftOperand/rightOperand));
                              break;
```

**Program 6.10** The PostfixInterpreter Class That Evaluates a Postfix String (*continued*)

Program 6.10 The PostfixInterpreter Class That Evaluates a Postfix String *(continued)*

```
55              case '^': evalStack.push(new Double(Math.exp(
                                      Math.log(leftOperand)*rightOperand) ) );
                           break;
                default:
                           break;
                }//end switch

60
                } else if ( (token.length() == 1) && isSpace(c) ) {        // else if token
                                                                          // was a space
                    ;                                                     // ignore it

65              } else {                                  // otherwise, push the numerical value
                                                          // of the token
                        evalStack.push(Double.valueOf(token));           // on the stack

                }//end if
70
            }//end while

            // remove final result from stack and output it

75          output("Value of postfix expression = " + evalStack.pop() );

        }//end interpretPostfix

        /*--------------------------------------*/
80
        private void output(String s) {

            outputString = s;

85      }//end output

        /*--------------------------------------*/

        public void setInput(String input) {
90
            postfixString = input;

        }//end setInput

95      /*--------------------------------------*/

        public String getOutput() {

            return outputString;
100
        }//end getOutput

        /*--------------------------------------*/

105 }//end class PostfixInterpreter

        /* insert here the Stack class given either in Program 6.11 or 6.12 */
```

(Note that the operand on the evalStack has been pictured as 6.0 to denote the fact that it is stored as a Java double number.)

Control now returns to the while-statement, where the next token in the postfix string is scanned. This is a space token that is ignored. Then the next token, 7, is scanned. By a process identical to that just explained, the value of this string token, "7" is obtained, converted to a double, and then stacked on top of the evalStack as the new value 7.0:

$$\text{evalStack} = \boxed{\begin{array}{c} 7.0 \\ 6.0 \end{array}}.$$

The next token in the postfix string is the multiplication operator "*". The character variable c is set to the first character of the string "*" on line 37. The value of c is tested in the if-clause on line 39 to see if it is an operator in the set of operators: {'+','−','*','/','^'} . Because this test succeeds, statements 41:59 are performed. First the topmost item on the evalStack is popped and becomes the value of the variable rightOperand, using the pop() method on line 41. Following this, the evalStack is popped again, and its topmost item becomes the value of the variable, leftOperand. The evalStack is now empty, and the left and right operands to be used have been transferred into the values of the variables leftOperand and rightOperand, respectively. (Note that since the evalStack contains items of type Object, the item popped off the stack has to be typecast to a Double object before the method doubleValue() can be applied to it to extract the primitive data type double that is its numerical value.) The switch-statement now performs the multiplication operation on the operands, and pushes the product back onto the evalStack, using the push() method call on line 50. The resulting evalStack now has the following appearance:

$$\text{evalStack} = \boxed{42.0}.$$

As the scan of the postfix input string continues, the token "2" is scanned and its value is pushed on the evalStack:

$$\text{evalStack} = \boxed{\begin{array}{c} 2.0 \\ 42.0 \end{array}}.$$

Following this, the final operator in the postfix input string ("−") is scanned, and its operation is performed on the top two operands on the evalStack. The resulting difference (42.0 − 2.0) is pushed back onto the evalStack:

$$\text{evalStack} = \boxed{40.0}.$$

Finally, the result, 40.0, is popped from the evalStack, and becomes the output, using the statements on line 75. (The output method saves the string for the result as the value of the outputString data field, which, in turn, is read by the applet that displays it in its output text box.)

## 6.5 REVIEW QUESTIONS

1. Translate the following infix expression into postfix: $( ( a * b - c ) / 5 )^{1/3}$
2. Translate the following postfix expression into infix: $x\ y\ z + - a\ b * / 2\ \wedge$
3. Why are parentheses needed to specify the order of operations in infix, but not in postfix?
4. Why is a stack useful for evaluating postfix expressions? Would a queue work just as well?

## 6.5 EXERCISES

1. What does Program 6.10 print if the postfix input string is: **6 7 * 2 − 5 / 1 3 / ^** ?
2. Program 6.10 could fail if an attempt is made to divide by zero, or if a malformed postfix expression is encountered that causes an empty **evalStack** to be popped (as in evaluating the postfix expression: **8 9 * \*** ). Extend Program 6.10 to handle these error conditions.

## 6.6 Implementing the Stack ADT

### LEARNING OBJECTIVES

1. To understand how to implement stacks in two different but substitutable ways.
2. To finish learning how to separate implementation details from abstract operations in an ADT interface.
3. To understand features of sequential and linked representations.

Our goal in this section is to show how to implement the Stack ADT in two different but behaviorally equivalent ways. These representations can be used interchangeably to implement the applications given in Programs 6.7 and 6.10. One of the implementations uses a sequential representation and the other uses a linked representation.

After accomplishing this, we can then use either representation to implement the applications of the Stack ADT used in Sections 6.4 and 6.5. This accomplishes, finally, (a) substitutability of representations and (b) clean separation of the implementation details from Stack ADT usage notation.

### The Sequential Stack Representation

Stacks can be represented by expandable arrays of items. The stack implementation given in Program 6.11 uses such expandable arrays. Lines 13:18 give a no-arg constructor that creates an empty **Stack** object. First, on line 14, the **count** is set to zero, indicating that the stack contains no items. Then, on lines 15:16, the **capacity** and the **capacityIncrement** are initialized. Finally, an empty array is constructed whose length is equal to the capacity, and the **itemArray** field is set to point to this array.

```
class Stack {

        private int    count;              // the number of items in the stack
        private int    capacity;           // the number of available array positions
5       private int    capacityIncrement;  // the amount to increase the
                                           // capacity during array expansion
        private Object[ ] itemArray;       // the array that holds stack items

    /*-----------------*/
10
        // the following defines a no-arg constructor for Stack objects

        public Stack( ) {
            count = 0;
15          capacity = 10;
            capacityIncrement = 5;
            itemArray = new Object[capacity];
        }

20  /*-----------------*/

        public boolean empty( ) {          // the stack is empty if and only if
            return (count == 0);           // its item count is zero
        }
25
    /*-----------------*/

        public void push(Object X) {

30          // if the itemArray does not have enough capacity,
            // expand the itemArray by the capacity increment
                if (count == capacity) {
                    capacity += capacityIncrement;
                    Object[ ] tempArray = new Object[capacity];
35                  for (int i = 0; i < count; i++) {
                        tempArray[i] = itemArray[i];
                    }
                    itemArray = tempArray;
                }
40
            // insert the new item X at the end of the current item sequence
            // and increase the stack's count by one
                itemArray[count++] = X;

45      }

    /*-----------------*/
```

**Program 6.11** Sequential Stack Implementation (*continued*)

Program 6.11 Sequential Stack Implementation *(continued)*

```
50        public Object pop() {

              if (count == 0) {                    // if the stack is empty,
                  return null;                     // return the null object.
              } else {                             // otherwise, remove and
                  return itemArray[--count];       // return the top object
55            }

          } // end pop()

          /*----------------*/
60
          public Object peek() {

              if (count == 0) {                    // if the stack is empty,
                  return null;                     // return the null object.
65            } else {                             // otherwise, return a reference
                  return itemArray[count-1];       // to the top object
              }                                    // without removing it

          } // end peek()
70
          /*----------------*/

      } // end Stack class
```

The stack items held in the **itemArray** are of Java type **Object**, implying that any type of stack item can be held in a **Stack**. (However, when an item is popped from the stack, it must first be typecast to its own type before any of its own methods can be invoked.) By this means, the stacks we have defined are made general enough to hold items of arbitrary type.

The **push()** method defined on lines 28:45 first checks to determine if there is unused capacity in which to store an additional stack item. If all of the stack's capacity has been used previously, the stack is expanded by constructing a new **itemArray** of larger capacity (see lines 30:39). Finally, the new item is inserted at the end of the current item sequence, and the **count** is increased by one (see line 43).

The **pop()** method (on lines 49:57) returns **null** if the stack is empty. Otherwise, it removes and returns the item from the end of the current item sequence and decreases the stack's item **count** by one. The **peek()** method (on lines 61:69) is similar, except that it doesn't decrease the stack's **count**.

## The Linked Stack Representation

A stack can be represented by a linked list of stack nodes in which each node contains a stack item. The **Stack** class, given in Program 6.12, implements the stack ADT method calls of Fig. 6.3. A **Stack** object contains a **topNode** data field (declared on

```
     /*------------------------------------------*/

     class StackNode {
          Object          item;
5         StackNode     link;
     }

     /*------------------------------------------*/

10   class Stack {

          private StackNode topNode;

          /*------*/
15
               // note: Java's default no-arg constructor, new Stack(),
               // works fine for the linked stack representation
               // so there is no need to define one here

20        /*------*/

               public boolean empty() {
                    return (topNode == null);
               }
25
          /*------*/

               public void push(Object X) {
                    StackNode newNode = new StackNode();
30                  newNode.item = X;
                    newNode.link = topNode;
                    topNode = newNode;
               }

35        /*------*/

               public Object pop() {
                    if (topNode == null) {
                         return null;
40                  } else {
                         StackNode tempNode = topNode;
                         topNode = topNode.link;
                         return tempNode.item;
                    }
45        }

          /*------*/
```

**Program 6.12** The Linked Stack Class (*continued*)

Program 6.12 The Linked Stack Class *(continued)*

```
    |            public Object peek() {
50  |                if (topNode == null) {
    |                    return null;
    |                } else {
    |                    return topNode.item;
    |                }
55  |            }
    |
    |        /*------*/
    |
    |    } // end class Stack
60  |
    |
```

line 12 of Program 6.12) that holds a reference to the topmost node of the linked list of stack nodes. The structure of a linked stack node is declared in the class **StackNode** on lines 3:6.

To determine whether a **Stack** object is empty, the **empty()** method (on lines 22:24) checks to see whether the **topNode** data field contains the **null** reference or points to a nonnull **StackNode** object. To push an object **X** onto a **Stack**, the **push()** method (on lines 28:33) constructs a new **StackNode**, sets its **item** field to **X**, sets its **link** field to reference the current top node, and resets the **topNode** field to point to the new node being pushed onto the top of the stack.

To pop an item from a **Stack** (see lines 37:45) if the stack is empty, the **null** value is returned; but if a nonnull top node exists, the contents of its **item** field are returned and the **topNode** field is reset to contain the reference in the **link** field of the current top node (which implies that the new top node is the successor of the previous top node on the linked item list). The **peek()** method (on lines 49:55) is similar, except that it does not remove the top stack item.

Both the sequential stack representation of Program 6.11 and the linked stack representation of Program 6.12 can be used interchangeably to implement either or both of the parenthesis matching applet of Program 6.7 and the postfix expression evaluator applet of Program 6.10. (Exercise 6.6.1 asks you to verify this fact by running both applets using both stack representations.) You can also omit the **Stack** class definitions of Programs 6.11 and 6.12 and use Java's predefined **Stack** class instead. To do this, insert the statement **import java.util.Stack;** as the third **import** statement after line 7 of Program 6.6. Java's predefined **Stack** class is based on an extension of Java's expandable array class, **Vector**.

## **6.6** REVIEW QUESTIONS

1. What is meant by substitutability of representations of an ADT?
2. What is meant by saying that a stack ADT has a representation-independent notation for use of its operations?

3. Discuss the aspects of modular programming exhibited by Programs 6.7, 6.10, 6.11, and 6.12.

## 6.6 EXERCISES

1. Try substituting both the sequential and linked representations given in Programs 6.11 and 6.12 into the postfix interpreter in Program 6.10 and the balanced parenthesis checker in Program 6.7. Verify that the latter programs work identically when the underlying stack representations are switched.

2. Instead of using either of the Stack classes defined in Programs 6.11 and 6.12, try using Java's predefined Stack class by adding the statement import java.util.Stack; at the beginning of the applet text in Program 6.6. Verify that the applet program runs identically after this replacement is made.

## 6.7    How Java Implements Recursive Method Calls Using Stacks

### LEARNING OBJECTIVES

1. To understand how Java can use stacks to execute recursive method calls.
2. To learn a bit of terminology concerning stack frames (or activation records).
3. To learn key background information.

The Java Virtual Machine (JVM) uses a separate run-time stack to execute the Java bytecode instructions associated with each active execution thread in a running Java program. In this section, we look at an example of how a typical run-time stack can be used to evaluate a recursive method call. The example is deliberately simple, and is intended to be illustrative of how stack evaluation can work in principle, rather than being definitive. There are many different ways to compile Java bytecodes to execute recursive method calls on the JVM—just as there are many different ways to compile machine instructions for a given chip, such as the Pentium or the PowerPC, to execute recursive procedure calls in other programming languages such as Ada, Modula, Pascal, C, or C++. The goal is basic understanding.

*an illustrative example*

When executing a method call $f(a_1, a_2, \ldots, a_n)$ with actual parameters $a_i$ (for $1 \leq i \leq n$), Java uses a run-time stack. A collection of information, sometimes called a *stack frame* (or a *call frame* or an *activation record*), is prepared to correspond to the call $f(a_1, a_2, \ldots, a_n)$, and is placed on top of a stack of other previously generated *stack frames*.

*using run-time stacks*

The information in a stack frame consists of: (1) space to hold the value, $v$, returned by the method; (2) a pointer to the base of the previous stack frame in the stack; (3) a return address, which is the address of a Java bytecode to execute in order to resume execution of $f$'s caller after the execution of $f$ has terminated; (4) parameter storage sufficient to hold the actual parameter values, $a_1, a_2, \ldots, a_n$, used in the call

*what's in a stack frame*

```
|    double factorial( int n) {
|
|        if (n <= 1) {
|            return 1.0;
5 |        } else {
|            return n * factorial( n – 1 );
|        }
|    }
```

**Program 6.13** A Recursive Factorial Method

of $f$; and (5) a set of storage locations sufficient to hold the values of variables declared locally within $f$. (When considering a void method call $p(a_1, a_2, \ldots, a_n)$ that does not return a value, the undefined or void value returned by the method is ignored and is discarded from the stack when the method's stack frame is popped from the stack.)

Let's consider a simple model of what might happen when we execute the assignment, x = factorial(3), given that a recursive factorial method has been declared as shown in Program 6.13. We first calculate and place $\psi$ = (the address of x) on the stack. On top of that we place a stack frame for the call **factorial(3)**, as shown in Fig. 6.14. Note that the space for locally declared variables is not used in the method **factorial(n)**, since no local variables are declared. But if local variables had been declared in **factorial(n)**, space for them would have been reserved in the space marked *empty* in Figure 6.14.

The computation of **factorial(3)**, in Figure 6.14, is free to use more stack space on top of the stack frame for the call of **factorial(3)**. It can use this stack space for temporary storage of intermediate values that have been computed and that await later use. It can also interrupt its execution of the call of **factorial(3)** and place a new stack frame on the stack to make a recursive call. This is exactly what happens next, since the compu-

*a simple model*

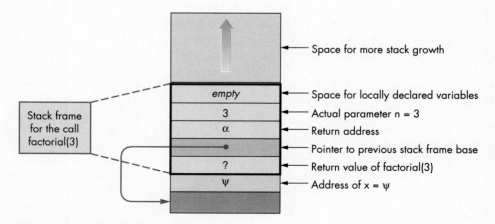

**Figure 6.14** Stack Frame for Factorial(3)

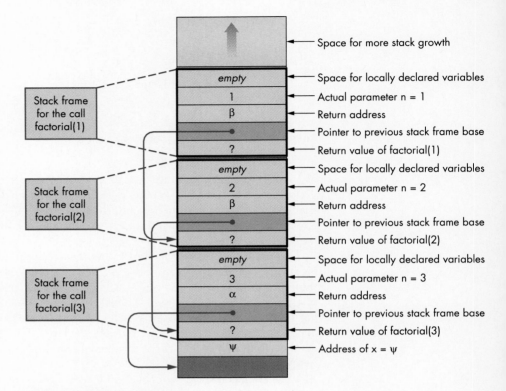

**Figure 6.15** Stack Frames for Factorials of 3, 2, and 1

tation in factorial(3) results in making a call on factorial(2). In turn, the call on factorial(2) results in making a further recursive call on factorial(1). So two more stack frames get added to the top of Fig. 6.14's stack, as shown in Fig. 6.15.

Since no values have yet been returned by any of the nest of recursive calls on factorial(n), the return value positions in these stack frames are shown as having the value "?" indicating that nothing has yet been assigned to them.

However, when the computation in the call factorial(1) takes place, it determines that the condition (n <= 1) on line 3 of Program 6.13 is true, so the return statement on line 4 of Program 6.13 is executed. The value 1.0 is returned by this statement causing the floating point value 1.0 to be placed in the space for the return value of the stack frame for the call factorial(1). Following this, the call of factorial(1) terminates by (a) resetting the current stack frame pointer to point to the base of the previous frame, using the pointer saved in the stack frame for factorial(1) and (b) resuming execution at the address β in the code for the factorial method, this being the place immediately after the call of factorial(1), which is about to use the value returned by the call of factorial(1). Figure 6.16 illustrates what happens immediately after the return from factorial(1) and immediately upon resuming the computation in factorial(2).

Now the code beginning at address β is executed and consumes the return value for factorial(1), which it finds sitting on the stack immediately above its own stack

*unknown return values*

*unwinding the stack of calls*

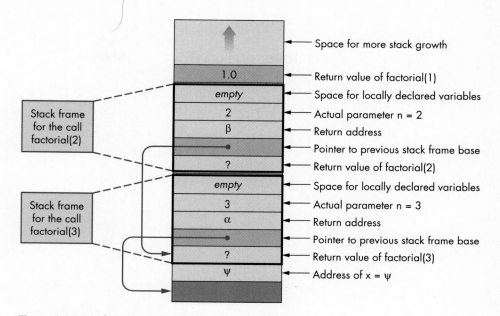

**Figure 6.16** Stack Frames after Return from factorial(1)

frame. It multiplies this value for **factorial(1)**, which is **1.0**, by the value of its own actual parameter, which is **2**, to compute the value of the expression, n \* **factorial(n – 1)**, on line 6 of Program 6.13, and it places the result, which is **2.0**, in the space for the return value in its own stack frame. It then returns from its own call by resetting the stack frame pointer to the previous frame and resuming execution again at address β. This produces Fig. 6.17.

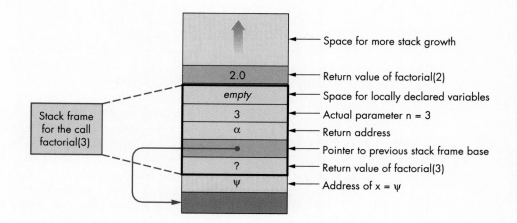

**Figure 6.17** Stack Frames after Return from factorial(2)

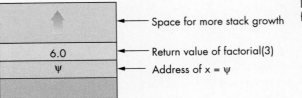

**Figure 6.18** Stack after Return from the Call factorial(3)

Space for more stack growth

Return value of factorial(3)

Address of x = ψ

In the same fashion, the computation of **factorial(3)** resumes. It consumes the result left by **factorial(2)** on the stack, which is **2.0**, by multiplying it by its own copy of the actual parameter **n == 3**, getting **6.0**, and it places this result in the space for the return value in its own stack frame. Finally, it returns from its own call by resetting the stack pointer to the saved pointer for the previous stack base, and by resuming execution at address $\alpha$, which is the place in the bytecode where execution needs to resume in order to finish the interrupted computation of the assignment statement, **x = factorial(3)**. The resulting diagram after returning from the call of **factorial(3)** is shown in Fig. 6.18.

*finishing the job*

The code to complete this assignment can now take the value **6.0** from the stack, just where it expected to find it upon return from the call of **factorial(3)**, and can place this value into the address $\psi$, which was the address for **x** saved on the stack previous to the call of **factorial(3)**.

A *word of caution*: There are many ways to implement recursive method calls using stacks. Different Java compilers might compile different bytecodes for the JVM, and languages other than Java may still use other arrangements. The scenario we have just sketched is only one possibility. Courses in the theory and construction of com-

*some subtleties have not been covered*

pilers cover such subtleties, and they constitute the proper place to learn about the many important remaining details. Our purpose here was to give a rough sketch of some of the basic ideas, so we could help you imagine a possible mechanical basis for how the Java Virtual Machine could be used to implement recursive method calls. By providing one example of a model, the process is demystified, and you are prepared to understand explanations such as those dealing with why infinite regresses can cause the JVM to exceed its "stack space," or to run out of heap space in case JVM stack frames are allocated using heap space.

*stacks + iteration = recursion*

Even though the example just considered was specific and lacking in additional detailed considerations, the stage is now set for being able to reach some important general conclusions. The main general conclusion is that *stacks + iteration* can implement *recursion*.

As mentioned in the chapter introduction, stacks can be used to process any kind of *nested structure*, in which things are contained in themselves in a nested fashion. When processing nested structures, we can start processing the outermost level of the structure, and if we encounter a nested substructure, we can interrupt the processing of the outer layer to begin processing an inner layer by putting an object that records the interrupted status of the outer layer's processing on top of a stack. Later, when we have finished processing the inner layer and have returned with the results, we can resume processing the outer layer after the point of interruption, using the information saved on the stack. The stack therefore contains *postponed obligations* to resume and complete the processing of interrupted outer layers containing the current level at which we are working at any given moment. An important generalization we can reach is that stacks of objects that record postponed obligations can help process nested structures to any depth of nesting.

Since calls on recursive methods are nested inside one another, and since processing the callee interrupts the processing of the caller, it is natural that stacks of recursive method stack frames can handle nested processing of recursive calls.

## 6.7 REVIEW QUESTION

1. Why will a nonterminating recursive Java method cause the JVM to run out of stack space at program execution time?

## 6.7 EXERCISE

1. Explain how the JVM run-time stack model discussed in this section can stack the value returned by a method call in the same fashion that it can stack the value resulting from evaluation of a subexpression of a larger expression.

## 6.8 Implementations of the Queue ADT

### LEARNING OBJECTIVES

1. To learn how to confine the travel of a sequentially represented queue to a circular track.
2. To understand some ways to represent queues using linked representations.
3. To learn how to implement the Queue ADT.

Not surprisingly, queues can have either sequential or linked representations. However, it turns out that queue representations involve a bit more subtlety than stack representations. We consider sequential representations of queues first.

### Sequential Queue Representations

Suppose we place several queue items next to one another in an array. We insert new queue items at the rear and remove items from the front. As these insertions and removals take place, the queue travels through the array in the rearward direction (see Fig. 6.19). Eventually it bumps up against the size limit of the array, after which it can travel no farther.

Queue representations that march through memory in a single direction, overwriting what is underneath as they go, are not very handy. Instead, it makes sense to confine the motion of a queue to a bounded region of memory. We can do this if we put a sequential queue representation on a circular track, and let it wind around and around as it moves rearward, as illustrated in Fig. 6.20.

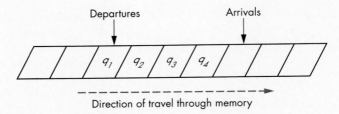

**Figure 6.19** Rearward Marching Queue

It is easy to simulate the effect of a circular track in a linear array, using modular arithmetic. Modular arithmetic uses expressions of the form $(x \% n)$ to keep the values of x in the range 0:n −1. The expression $(x \% n)$ has this effect, since it computes the remainder of x after division by n, and this remainder is always less than n. Thus, as we add new items to a circular queue, we place them in the location given by the queue index, rear, and then we let the rear of the queue grow by incrementing rear, as shown in Fig. 6.20. But whenever rear is incremented so that its value becomes equal to the capacity of the queue, n, we set it to be zero—which has the effect of causing it to "wrap around" after it falls off the high end of the array so that it points to the first position at the opposite end of the array.

A similar consideration holds when we remove items from the front of a queue. A queue index, front, is used to designate the item that can next be removed at the front of the queue. After we remove an item, we increment the front index so that it designates the next position. But if this index falls off the high end of the array (by becoming equal to n), we wrap it around, by setting it equal to zero.

To summarize, given an array, itemArray[n], consisting of n item positions numbered from 0 to n −1, and given two indexes, front and rear, that can designate positions in the itemArray, we can use the assignments shown in Fig. 6.21 to increment the pointers so that they always wrap around after falling off the high end of the array.

In the sequential queue implementation given in Program 6.22, a queue is represented by an object that has: (1) a counter, count, that keeps track of the number of

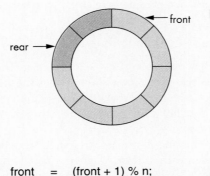

**Figure 6.20** Queue on a Circular Track

```
front  =  (front + 1) % n;
rear   =  (rear + 1) % n;
```

**Figure 6.21** Incrementing Indexes Using Modular Arithmetic

```
1  | class Queue {
   |
   |     private int     front;              // the array index of the front item of the queue
   |     private int     rear;               // the array index for the next item to insert
5  |     private int     count;              // the number of items in the queue
   |     private int     capacity;           // the number of available array positions
   |     private int     capacityIncrement;  // the amount to increase the capacity
   |                                         // during array expansion
   |     private Object[ ] itemArray;        // the array that holds queue items
10 |
   |     /*----------------*/
   |
   |     // here, we need the no-arg constructor
   |
15 |     public Queue() {
   |         front          =   0;
   |         rear           =   0;
   |         count          =   0;
   |         capacity       =  10;
20 |         capacityIncrement = 5;
   |         itemArray = new Object[capacity];
   |     }
   |
   |     /*----------------*/
25 |
   |     public boolean empty() {
   |         return (count == 0);
   |     }
   |
30 |     /*----------------*/
   |
   |     public void insert(Object newItem) {
   |
   |         // if the itemArray does not have enough capacity,
35 |         // expand the itemArray by the capacity increment
   |         if (count == capacity) {
   |             capacity += capacityIncrement;
   |             Object[ ] tempArray = new Object[capacity];
   |             if (front < rear) {            // if the items are in itemArray[front:rear−1]
40 |                 for (int i = front; i < rear; i++) {
   |                     tempArray[i] = itemArray[i];
   |                 }
   |             } else {          // otherwise, move the items in two separate sections
   |                 for (int i = 0; i < rear; i++) {              // section one:
45 |                     tempArray[i] = itemArray[i];              // itemArray[0:rear−1]
   |                 }
   |                 for (int i = front; i < count; i++) {         // and section two:
   |                                                               // itemArray[front:count−1]
   |                     tempArray[i+capacityIncrement] = itemArray[i];
50 |                 }
   |                 front += capacityIncrement;       // then change front to point to
   |                                                   // its new position
   |             }
   |             itemArray = tempArray;
55 |         }
```

**Program 6.22** Circular Queue Representation *(continued)*

Program 6.22 Circular Queue Representation (*continued*)

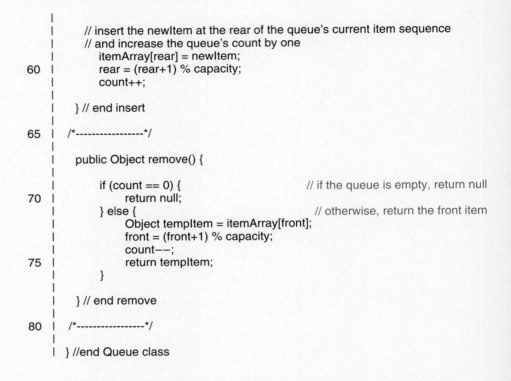

```
              // insert the newItem at the rear of the queue's current item sequence
              // and increase the queue's count by one
                itemArray[rear] = newItem;
60              rear = (rear+1) % capacity;
                count++;

         } // end insert

65   /*----------------*/

         public Object remove() {

             if (count == 0) {                          // if the queue is empty, return null
70              return null;
             } else {                                   // otherwise, return the front item
                 Object tempItem = itemArray[front];
                 front = (front+1) % capacity;
                 count--;
75               return tempItem;
             }

         } // end remove

80   /*----------------*/

     } //end Queue class
```

items in the queue, (2) an array index, **front**, that keeps track of the index of the item that can next be removed from the queue, (3) an array index, **rear**, that designates the place to insert the next queue item, (4) an array of queue items **itemArray** used to hold the contents of the queue, (5) a **capacity** that gives the number of index positions in the current **itemArray**, and (6) a **capacityIncrement** used when expanding the **itemArray** to have a larger capacity.

## Linked Queue Representations

Linked Queue representations come in many varieties. We present only one possibility here, and mention a few of the others in the exercises. The version presented here represents a queue using an object containing two pointers that point to the *front* and *rear* of a linked list of nodes. Each node in the linked list contains a queue item in its **item** field, and links to the next node in the list, using a pointer in its **link** field. The linked implementations of the Queue ADT operations are given in Program 6.23.

In the linked queue representation given in Program 6.23, a queue is an object with pointers to the **front** and **rear** of a linear linked list of item nodes. The **front** pointer points to the first item node in the linked list, and the **rear** pointer points to

```
/*-------------------------------------------------------------*/

class QueueNode {
    Object       item;
5   QueueNode  link;
}

/*-------------------------------------------------------------*/

10  class Queue {

    private QueueNode front;          // front contains a reference to the
                                      // front item of the queue
    private QueueNode rear;           // rear contains a reference to the
15                                    // rear item of the queue
    private int count;                // the number of items in the queue

    /*-----------------*/

20      // Java's automatically defined no-arg constructor suffices

    /*-----------------*/

    public boolean empty() {
25          return (count == 0);
    }

    /*-----------------*/

30      public void insert(Object newItem) {

            QueueNode temp = new QueueNode();

            temp.item = newItem;
35          temp.link = null;
            if (rear == null) {
                front = rear = temp;
            } else {
                rear.link = temp;
40              rear = temp;
            }
            count++;

        } //end insert
45
    /*-----------------*/

```

**Program 6.23** Linked Queue Representation (*continued*)

Program 6.23 Linked Queue Representation (*continued*)

```
50
                    public Object remove( ) {

                        if (count == 0) {                        // if the queue is empty, return null
                            return null;
                        } else {                                 // otherwise, return the front item
                            Object tempItem = front.item;
55                          front = front.link;
                            if (front == null) {
                                rear = null;
                            }
                            count--;
60                          return tempItem;
                        }

                    } //end remove

65          /*-----------------*/

            } //end Queue class
```

the last item node in the list. There is also a **count** field that contains the number of items in the queue, as illustrated in Fig. 6.24.

The empty queue is a special case, and is represented by a queue object whose **front** and **rear** pointers are each **null** (see Fig. 6.25). To insert a new item, r, at the rear of a linked queue, you allocate a new **QueueNode**, set its **item** field to contain r, and link it as the new last node of the linked list of item nodes. Finally, you adjust the **rear** pointer to point to this new last node and increment the **count** by one.

To remove an item, f, at the front of the queue, you extract the item from the **item** field of the first node in the linked list, and then delete the first node of the list. The **front** pointer in the queue object has to be adjusted to point to the second node in the list of item nodes, which then becomes the new first node. Care must be taken to handle the empty queue as a special case.

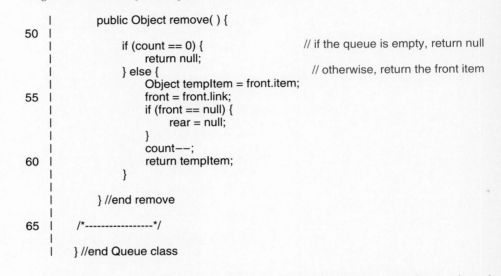

**Figure 6.24** Linked Representation of Nonempty Queue

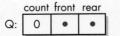

**Figure 6.25** Linked Representation of Empty Queue

## Comparing Linked and Sequential Queue Representations

Sometimes, in advance of the running of a program, it can be foreknown how big queues can get. To set the stage for our comparison, we sketch a brief portrait of the use of some queues in a *time-shared operating system*.

task records in time-shared operating systems

In a time-shared operating system, various jobs being processed have associated job status records called *task records*. These task records are placed in various queues to await processing. For instance, there may be an *I/O Wait Queue* that contains records of tasks waiting to perform output (say on a printer or a screen), or to receive input from a user (perhaps from the user's keyboard). There may also be a *High-Priority Run Queue* and a *Low-Priority Run Queue*. When a task comes out of the I/O Wait Queue, it is put into the High-Priority Run Queue. When tasks advance to the front of either of the run queues, they are executed for a period of time called a *time-slice*. A time-slice in a typical operating system might be a $60^{th}$ of a second. A task may not be able to run to completion in only one time slice. If its time-slice is exhausted and the task still needs to run some more, it is placed in the Low-Priority Run Queue. But if a task runs to completion, it is placed into the I/O Wait Queue to output its results.

The reason there is a High-Priority Run Queue is to allow the operating system to exhibit a key property of good interactive computing systems—namely, *fast response to trivial requests for computation*. If you ask an interactive, time-shared system to evaluate and print "2 + 2," you would like to see the answer "4" instantly. If you type "2 + 2" and press the Return key on the keyboard, your task, which has been sitting in the I/O Wait Queue waiting for a completed line of input from your keyboard, is taken out of the I/O Wait Queue and is placed in the High-Priority Run Queue. Every task in the High-Priority Run Queue gets to execute for up to one time-slice before any tasks in the Low-Priority Run Queue are executed for their respective time-slices.

ensuring rapid response to trivial requests

What happens, then, is that your task coming out of I/O Wait gets an immediate small amount of execution time. If it can compute a result and get ready to print it within one time-slice, the task migrates back into the I/O Wait Queue, where it prints the result "4" on your terminal. It then seems to you as if you have gotten immediate service.

In a time-shared system with only one run-queue, when your task comes out of *I/O Wait* and joins the rear of the run-queue, it may have to wait until every task ahead of it in the run queue has received a time-slice of service before it gets to run (even though its demand for computation is negligible). If this happens, you may experience sluggish response at your terminal when you present trivial requests for computation (like: "tell me the date," or "show me my file directory," or "compute 2 + 2," or whatever).

Experience suggests that users get annoyed if they have to wait a variable amount of time for responses to trivial requests. For example, you will get frustrated if you don't know whether you might get an instant reply or a delayed reply. Consequently, you are left hanging—do you have time just for a sip of coffee or should you go off and read a book for a while? Experience has shown that fast responses to trivial requests are psychologically important for users.

*limiting the maximum number of jobs*

Many time-shared operating systems are designed to handle only a certain maximum number of jobs simultaneously. This maximum number is set so as not to risk overloading the system and making computation proceed slowly for all users. Consequently, the number of jobs is bounded (i.e., it can't exceed a certain maximum number). Under these circumstances, the queues used by the system to regulate the processing of tasks can't get bigger than the known maximum, since each task record (representing a job) can be in only one of the queues at any one time. In this case it makes sense to use the sequential representation of queues because queue sizes are bounded. This representation is efficient, so long as queue overflow is impossible.

*applications in which linked queue representations work best*

By contrast, in some queue applications, it is hard to predict how long queues will become. For example, some systems handle transactions (such as phone calls, or electronic funds transfers). If the rate of incoming transactions temporarily exceeds the capacity of the system to service them, transactions are often placed in a queue (or waiting line) to await service. Such a waiting line could grow without limit in periods where the arrival rate of transactions exceeds the service rate of the system. Under such circumstances, it makes sense to use a linked representation for queues, since the queue can grow in length so long as there is any memory in the system to use to allocate new nodes for queue items. At least the system won't come to a grinding halt with a queue overflow when an insufficiently large predeclared queue-size limit gets exceeded accidentally, as can happen with a sequential representation of queues that uses preallocated, fixed-size arrays instead of the expandable arrays used in Program 6.22.

## 6.8 REVIEW QUESTIONS

1. What would be the disadvantage of having a linked queue representation in which there is only one pointer that points to the front of the queue?
2. Is it possible to have a queue representation using a one-way linked list of queue item nodes and having only a pointer to the rear of the queue? If it is impossible, say why. If it is possible, is it efficient? If it isn't efficient, what abstract queue operation(s) would be expected to take too much time?

## 6.8 EXERCISES

1. The fields, **count**, **front**, and **rear**, of the circular queue representation contain redundant information, since the relationship:

   rear = (front + count) % capacity

   is always true. Show how to implement circular queues by modifying Program 6.22 so that the field **rear** is eliminated, and the value for **rear** is computed whenever it is needed. What kind of a trade-off does this modification make in comparison to the original Program 6.22?

2. If we agree to give up one location in a circular queue representation and not to use it to store any queue items, so that a queue of n item locations is said to be *full* when it contains n − 1 items, then we need to use only the front and rear fields, and the condition front == rear can be used to determine whether the queue is *full* or *empty*. Show how this can be done. [*Hint:* Establish conventions for setting up the front and rear fields so that, when we attempt to insert an item, we do: rear = ++rear % n, and if now front == rear, then the queue has overflowed, but when we attempt to remove an item, if front == rear, then the queue has underflowed.]

3. Let Q be a nonempty Queue, and let S be an empty Stack. Using only the abstract operations for the Queue and Stack ADTs, write a program to reverse the order of the items in the queue, Q.

4. An alternative linked queue representation uses a circular list of item nodes together with a single pointer to the rear node of the queue (somewhere in the linked circular list of item nodes). Explain how this can work. How would you represent the empty queue in this method? Write a program to implement the Queue ADT operations using this circular linked representation.

5. Write an implementation of the abstract Queue ADT operations using two-way linked lists as a representation.

6. From an efficiency standpoint, what is wrong with a sequential queue representation that implements the operation F = Q.remove() by moving the item in itemArray[0] into F, and then shifting each of itemArray[1:rear] down one space into the locations itemArray[0: rear−1] ?

## 6.9 More Queue Applications

### LEARNING OBJECTIVES

1. To learn practical background information on how queues are used.
2. To learn about print buffers and printer spoolers.
3. To learn about synchronization problems using print buffers.
4. To learn about uses of queues in simulation and modeling.

In the last section we discussed how queues were used in operating systems to regulate the processing of tasks. We will now discuss more queue applications in operating systems, networks, simulation, and modeling.

### Queues in Operating Systems

Queues can be used in operating systems to act as *buffers* that help synchronize the interaction between two processes that run at different speeds. For example, a queue may be used as a *print buffer* that sits between a central processing unit (CPU) and a printer. A computation running in the CPU may produce output to be printed much faster than the printer can print it. The printer gets lines to print, one at a time, from the front of a queue of lines to be printed, which are stored in the print buffer. The CPU adds new lines to be printed to the rear of the queue in the print buffer, provided the print buffer queue is not full. If the print buffer is full and the CPU needs to add more lines to the print buffer, the CPU must wait until the print buffer has room for more lines (i.e., it must wait until the printer empties the print buffer a bit by printing some lines, rendering the print buffer *not full*). The two tasks acting on the print buffer are illustrated in Program 6.26.

Generally, the CPU and the Printer execute the two tasks in Program 6.26 concurrently (i.e., at the same time). If they both try to access the print buffer simultaneously there is a possibility of interfering with each other. Consequently, there needs to be a mechanism for each to use to seize control of the print buffer and to lock it out from access by the other for the duration of its access. After the print buffer access is completed, the print buffer needs to be unlocked so the next task needing to access it can gain control of it. This basic problem is called "the problem of synchronizing concurrent tasks," and the particular form of it mentioned here is sometimes called "the readers and writers problem."

*the readers and writers problem*

Two more uses of queues in connection with printing occur in operating systems and networks. A *printer spooler* is a queue that accepts a queue of lines to be printed and stores this queue as a *spooled-file*, while notifying the printer server that the spooled-file is ready to print. When the printer server is free, it starts to print the spooled-file by removing and printing lines from the front of the queue of lines in the spooled-file.

*printer spoolers*

As a second example, a network of computers may contain a shared printer server (such as a laser printer). The server associated with the printer may accept files to be printed. These files may be shipped to it by workstations or other computers on the network. When the files to be printed arrive at the printer server, they are placed in a queue on a first-come, first-served basis to await printing. Users sitting at workstations

```
     void writeLineToBePrinted() {                         // the CPU's task

         if ( (there is a line L to print) &&
 5           (the print buffer is neither full nor busy) )  {
                 printBufferQueue.insert(L);
         }
     }

10   void readLineToBePrinted() {                          // the Printer's task

         if (the print buffer is neither empty nor busy) {
             L = printBufferQueue.remove();
             (print line L on the Printer);
15       }
     }
```

**Program 6.26** Reading and Writing Print Buffer Lines

may be able to interrogate the status of the printer queue by executing an appropriate operating system command (such as the **interrogate printer queue** or **ipq** command available in some Unix network systems).

The advantage of printer spooling systems over the use of simple print buffers is that a task running on a CPU need not get blocked while waiting for a slow printer to print the lines in a full print buffer. For example, aircraft pilots have an aviation weather service called DUAT (which stands for Direct User Access Terminal). Using a desktop computer and a dial-in modem, a pilot using the DUAT service calls a central aviation weather computer. [A modem is a device that allows two computers to communicate over a phone line.] Pilots using DUAT service are allowed only fifteen minutes of on-line contact before their session is shut off automatically.

When getting a thorough preflight briefing, pilots sometimes need to access many screenfuls of information, such as current weather reports at various weather stations along the planned flight route, weather forecasts at various stations, winds aloft forecasts, significant weather alerts, and notices concerning unusual conditions (such as an area where parachute jumping is going on or an area where flight is prohibited because of a presidential visit, etc.).

It is convenient for pilots to print the key preflight briefing data on paper to take with them during the flight. If the DUAT access computer does not have a print spooler, but has only a print buffer, then the pilot may have to wait for the printer to print a full screen of data (usually 24 lines of 80 characters per line) before giving another command to the DUAT system to access the next screenful of information. If the printer is slow, it may be difficult for the pilot to print all the information needed before the 15 minute session cutoff occurs. On the other hand, if the system has a printer spooler, the screens of information to be printed can be placed in the printer spool queue to be printed later at the printer's pace, and the pilot can go ahead and enter more commands into the DUAT system to collect the rest of the preflight briefing information without having to wait for the printer to finish printing the current screen.

A similar increase in convenience is available to users of ordinary word processors, who would like to print one word processor document at the same time they continue to revise another word processor document on their workstations. Simultaneous printing and word processor operation are available on the latest generation of workstations with concurrent operating systems. A concurrent operating system is one that can process more than one job (or task) at the same time. Earlier types of simple home computers seldom had concurrent operating systems, forcing word processor users to wait until a print task ran to completion before resuming work on a word processor task. In such circumstances, the user could do nothing but wait for the printer to finish printing before resuming work in the word processor.

More generally, queues can be used as I/O buffers in operating systems between many different kinds of devices. For example, in a time-shared operating system having virtual memory, queues are used to regulate the flow of memory pages being swapped into and out of the main memory over a swapping channel connecting the main memory to a large secondary memory (which contains the extra memory pages implementing the virtual addresses in a task's virtual memory address space). Also,

*spoolers to make best use of limited access time*

*how pilots can beat the fifteen minute system cutoff time*

*added convenience for word processor users*

*using queues as memory buffers*

queues are used to regulate the processing of read/write requests serviced by large file storage devices, such as external disks or tapes.

## Using Queues in Simulation Experiments

Sometimes we need to study the behavior of models of a system we are trying to understand. Simulating such system behavior using a computer model is often a good way to gain insight. Computer simulations are particularly useful when dealing with systems that are sufficiently complex that it is hard to construct accurate mathematical models, but for which computer models can maintain descriptive accuracy.

Many systems used in everyday life incorporate queues. In fact, in highly-populated urban areas, many people may spend more time in waiting-lines than they might prefer. It seems that waiting-lines are everywhere to be seen: (a) at supermarket checkout counters, (b) at bank teller windows, (c) at ticket windows in ski areas and sports arenas, (d) at gas station pumps and car washes, (e) at the library information desk, (f) at the entrance for rides in amusement parks, (g) waiting to take off at the local airport, (h) at freeway, beltway, or autobahn on-ramps, (i) at the drive-up windows of fast food outlets, and (j) even waiting to see Santa Claus in a department store in December.

Each of these systems shares common features. There are queues of *clients* waiting in a first-come, first-served order for service. There are *servers* who dispense the service. Clients arrive and queue up according to some arrival time discipline. The time a server needs to serve a client is called a *service-time interval*. These service-time intervals may be of fixed duration, or they may vary. If they vary, they may be described by a *service-time distribution*. Such a distribution may have an *average* value and a *variance* (where the variance is a measure of how broadly or narrowly the various likely service times are spread out around the average time).

Sometimes there are multiple queues and multiple servers. When a client has gone to the front of one queue and advances to a server and obtains service, the client may then join another queue to obtain another part of the total service needed. (Getting your driver's license renewed may involve a system of several queues—a queue to get your eyes examined, a queue to get your picture taken, a queue to get your exam questions graded, a queue to get your new license issued, and a queue to pay the renewal fee.)

When we use a queuing system simulation to model an actual system, we try to model each queue in the real-world system with a queue in the simulation model. We try to model the arrival rate of clients entering the system and queuing up for service. We try to model accurately the service times taken by clients obtaining service from the servers, and we try to collect statistics that measure how well the overall system performs. For example, we may be interested in measuring (a) the average waiting time to obtain service, (b) the variance in the waiting times (i.e., how dispersed or spread out the waiting times are), (c) the length of the queues, and (d) the *throughput* of the system (i.e., how many clients are served per hour). We might want to run simulation experiments under different conditions—for example, by adding or removing servers, while holding the arrival rate of clients constant—to see what happens to the measures of system performance.

*our world abounds in queues*

*clients and servers*

*important aspects of queuing and simulation models*

For example, some supermarkets are aware that their popularity among customers is influenced by the time customers spend waiting in lines at the checkout counters. If a supermarket wants to attract more customers, it might attempt to keep checkout lines short by having a policy of opening a new checkout counter anytime a checkout line has more than three customers waiting in it. If they advertise this feature on radio and television, they may attract new customers or retain customers who might otherwise go shop at a competing supermarket. On the other hand, since profit margins in the supermarket business are thin (sometimes under two percent), supermarket managers need to be conscious about cost control. If too many checkout counters are open at once, and if there is slight demand, then it may cost too much. Perhaps a supermarket chain could gain insight into how some proposed policies would work by performing a computer simulation. First it would be important to collect some real data on service times and arrival rates at the checkout counter lines. These data could then be used to set up a realistic simulation. Various alternative policies could be modeled and simulated, and results could be collected to compare their differing performances.

**simulating supermarket checkout lines**

Here are some examples of questions that might be settled by queuing system simulations in various settings:

1. Do you get better service at an airline ticket counter (or at bank teller or sports arena ticket windows) if all customers feed from a single queue, or from separate queues for each ticket agent (or bank teller)?
2. During a gasoline shortage, do drivers spend more time in line on the average if each driver can wait in line to get four gallons (16 liters) on any day, or if drivers with license plates ending in even digits (or the letters A:L) can get eight gallons (32 liters) on even numbered days, and drivers with license plates ending in odd digits (or the letters M:Z) can get eight gallons (32 liters) on odd numbered days?
3. How much does it help alleviate freeway (or autobahn, or beltway, or interstate) traffic congestion to install on-ramp metering systems that force drivers to queue-up to await a traffic signal that lets them enter the freeway?
4. In a time-shared operating system, how much does it improve response times for trivial requests if a high-priority run queue is used (according to the description at the end of the previous section), versus having a single run queue for all jobs?

**the origins of queuing theory**

In the 1940s, a branch of mathematics called *queuing theory* was developed at Bell Laboratories to help predict how to build the telephone system to accommodate expected increases in telephone traffic. The objective was to find out how much copper wire to lay, and in what places around the country, so that future demand for phone service could be accommodated. The Bell Labs mathematicians needed a system of mathematics that enabled them to predict the probability that a customer might try to make a phone call and would find all circuits busy, under different conditions of telephone system loading. Statistical models for arrival rates, service time intervals, and the growth of queues were developed. It is said that the resulting models were so successful that the telephone company was saved millions of dollars in wasted copper wire. There is a story, perhaps apocryphal, that says, "So great were the savings, that Bell Labs paid for its entire future operating costs by virtue of the results of applying this queuing theory."

The mathematics of closed queuing systems has had particularly beneficial effects in the development of the theory of operating systems. A closed queuing system is one in which a fixed number of clients migrate around the system joining various queues to wait for service from various servers. Jobs in an operating system follow this discipline. It is possible to use the theory of closed queuing systems to *balance* an operating system by ensuring that the various servers (such as printers, swapping channels, CPUs, and disks) have enough capacity to service a particular expected job mix without developing *bottlenecks* (which show up as long queues where jobs are taken out of action awaiting service from a server of inadequate capacity).

## **6.9** REVIEW QUESTIONS

1. Describe several uses of queues in time-shared operating systems and computer networks.
2. What kinds of systems can be modeled by queuing simulations, and what kinds of questions can be answered by the results?

## **6.9** EXERCISE

1. Develop a simulation program to investigate queuing policies for gasoline shortages, as described earlier in situation (2).

---

## ▉ Pitfalls

- *Not being careful about boundary conditions*

  When implementing linked or sequential representations for stacks and queues (and especially for queues) be careful to check that the special cases are handled properly. In particular, empty stacks and queues should be thoroughly checked to ensure they work properly amongst all prescribed ADT operations.

- *Not checking modular arithmetic for circular queues*

  Be cautious when implementing circular queues that remainders computed by modular arithmetic (using expressions such as x % n) or computed by conditional logic (using statements such as: if (++x == n) x = 0;) lie within the proper numeric ranges, and that the index ranges of arrays used to store items are matched properly to the numeric ranges of these remainders.

## ■ Tips and Techniques

- *Use ADTs to achieve clean modular program designs*

  The use of Stack and Queue ADTs promotes clean modular program designs. The many benefits, covered in Chapter 5, accrue to the system designer who follows this advice. Among other things, top-level applications will not be contaminated with details of low-level representation choices, and inefficient implementations can be eliminated by substituting behaviorally equivalent representations having improved efficiency.

- *Use simulation and modeling to explore the behavior of proposed new designs*

  It is often helpful to use simulation and modeling techniques to explore the behavior of alternative designs for a proposed new system. If realistic data on arrival times and service times can be collected, alternative designs of a proposed new system can be simulated, and data can be collected that yield insight into system performance and efficiency. Such results can be helpful in choosing which design to implement.

- *Use queues to regulate tasks and to synchronize processes*

  Queues are useful for regulating the flow of tasks among servers in a system having multiple servers, and in which it is desirable to guarantee "first-come, first-served" service disciplines. Queues are also useful to synchronize the interaction of two concurrent processes running at different speeds that must exchange data.

- *Use stacks to process nested structures and to evaluate expressions*

  Stacks are ideal to use to process data structures that are inherently nested to any arbitrary degree of depth. They are also useful for expression evaluation in interpreters and calculators.

## ■ References for Further Study

The following is a good tutorial that covers how to set up and use interactive Java user interface objects such as buttons, menus, text fields, scroll bars, and labels.

Java GUI objects

Campione, Mary, and Walrath, Kathy, *The Java™ Tutorial, Object-Oriented Programming for the Internet*. Addison-Wesley, Reading, MA (1996).

## ■ Chapter Summary

An abstract model for a linear data structure is the *sequence*—a finite, ordered arrangement of data items. A sequence can be thought of as one of the possible structuring methods for arranging data structure components into aggregates. Other data structuring methods include the formation of arrays, objects, sets, and linked structures.

Abstract data types based on sequences can be defined by starting with sequences of items and adding sets of allowed operations. When we confine the growth of sequences to occur at their endpoints in certain designated ways, we get *stacks* and *queues*.

stacks

queues

uses for stacks

uses for queues

*Stacks* are sequences of items that are allowed to grow and shrink only at one end, called the *top*. Adding a new item, X, to the top of a stack, S, is called *pushing X onto S*. Removing an item, X, from the top of a stack is called *popping X from S*.

A *queue* is a sequence of items that grows at one end, called its *rear*, and shrinks at its other end, called its *front*.

Stacks are useful for processing nested structures of arbitrary depth, for evaluating arithmetic or algebraic expressions, and for parsing programs written in most programming languages. They can also be used for searching in search spaces using the method of backtracking. Stacks are used in the Java Virtual Machine to evaluate expressions and to execute method invocations associated with each concurrent execution thread.

Queues are useful for regulating the flow of tasks within a system, especially when tasks must be processed by several kinds of servers. Queues are commonly used in operating systems for this purpose. Additionally, queues are used to synchronize the exchange of data between two concurrent processes running at different speeds. Print buffers and printer spoolers offer two common examples of this use. Queues are also useful in setting up simulations and models of systems in which clients arrive and are given service.

Stacks and queues can have both sequential and linked representations. The sequential and linked representations of queues encompass a few subtleties that must be carefully considered, especially when considering the representations of full and empty queues.

The use of Stack and Queue ADTs is recommended as a good programming practice giving access to the benefits of modular programming. Low-level representation details can be hidden from use in the high-level system design, representations are made substitutable, and program clarity, simplicity, and reliability can be enhanced.

# 7

# Lists, Strings, and Dynamic Memory Allocation

## 7.1 Introduction and Motivation

In Chapter 6, we studied two special cases of linear data structures. We started by applying a structuring method to collections of items—namely, we formed *sequences* of items. Sequences were just finite, linear, ordered arrangements of items. Then we added operations. When we allowed items to be removed and inserted at only one end of a sequence, we got *stacks*. When we allowed items to be removed at one end of a sequence and inserted at the opposite end, we got *queues*.

We are now ready to investigate two more linear data structures based on sequences of items—namely, *lists* and *strings*. Moreover, in this chapter, we will also cover dynamic memory allocation techniques and generalized lists, which are simply lists whose individual items are permitted to be sublists of items.

lists, strings, and generalized lists

However, our emphasis in this chapter is less on packaging lists and strings into abstract data types (ADTs) and more on exploring various significant underlying representations. By now, the advantages of modular programming and the use of data

199

abstraction should be clear, and the techniques for achieving such advantages should be well-understood. Consequently, we do not place more than minor emphasis on how lists and strings can be presented as ADTs and how applications can be built from these ADTs. Instead, we emphasize the exploration of alternative data representations, and the crafting of these representations to yield various advantages from the perspectives of *efficiency* and *tradeoffs*.

In this context, several alternative representations of lists are explored—such as circular lists, doubly linked lists, and lists accessed via special header nodes.

For strings, we look at Java's read-only **String** objects and at Java **StringBuffers**, which contain character sequences that can be altered. We also look at how strings are represented in text files and in word processors.

**dynamic memory allocation**

With respect to dynamic memory allocation, we cover pointers and handles, allocation strategies for blocks of memory in heaps (such as the first-fit and best-fit strategies), and the concepts of fragmentation, coalescing, and compacting. We also explore garbage collection, marking algorithms, and the use of reference counts in incremental storage reclamation techniques.

## Plan for the Chapter

**list representations**

In Section 7.2, we begin by exploring list representations. We first discover that ordinary sequential representations, such as those that pack list items contiguously in arrays, have disadvantages when trying to represent certain kinds of list operations, such as insertion or deletion of items in arbitrary positions. We then explore several alternative linked list representations that overcome the disadvantages of the sequential representations.

**generalized lists**

In Section 7.3, we explore generalized lists—that is, lists having sublists. We differentiate between generalized lists having shared sublists and those having separate copies of sublists, and we give an algorithm for printing generalized lists. A short discussion of applications of generalized lists follows in Section 7.4.

**strings**

Section 7.5 studies both the Java **String** class and the Java **StringBuffer** class. A partial implementation is given that illustrates how the hidden internal mechanics of the **StringBuffer** work. We also comment on the kinds of string representations used in contemporary word processors and in text files containing sequences of characters.

**dynamic memory allocation techniques**

In Section 7.6, we investigate the underlying memory allocation problems that need to be solved to support linked data structures and data structures formed from applying structuring methods to blocks of memory of differing size. We cover the difference between pointers and handles when used to reference variable size blocks of memory in heaps, and we study heap compaction algorithms. We compare two different dynamic storage allocation strategies—first-fit and best-fit. Because Java is a garbage-collected language, we also study garbage collection policies, including the marking and gathering method and the reference-count method.

## 7.2 Lists

## LEARNING OBJECTIVES

1. To understand the advantages and disadvantages of sequential and linked representations of lists.
2. To become acquainted with one-way, two-way, and circular list representations.
3. To understand the role of list header nodes.
4. To understand that many varieties of list representations are possible.

A list is simply a sequence of items. The usual operations permitted on lists are insertions and deletions of items in arbitrary places, finding the length of a list, and determining whether or not a list is empty. (The *empty list* is a list having no items in it.)

### A List ADT

An ADT for lists might be defined by specifying an appropriate set of list operations. One possible List ADT uses the list operations given in Fig. 7.1.

When we can insert and delete list items in arbitrary places, we get a class of sequential structures with more general growth and combining laws than those for stacks and queues. Lists are therefore more elastic general containers for items than either stacks or queues. They tend to be used in applications where this added generality is needed.

### Sequential List Representations

the contiguous, sequential list representation

fast access to the $i^{th}$ item

One way to represent lists is to pack the list items next to one another in a sequential structure such as an array. When list items are stored next to one another (with no gaps in between), we say they are stored *contiguously*. Figure 7.2 illustrates the use of an array A[0:capacity − 1] to hold a sequential, contiguous representation of the items of the abstract list $L == (x_1, x_2, x_3, x_4)$. To complete the sequential representation of

A *List* (L) of items is a sequence of items on which the following operations are defined:

1. *Construct* an initially empty list, L.
2. Determine whether or not the list L is *empty*.
3. Find the *length* of a list L (where the *length* of L is the number of items in L, and the *length* of the *empty list* is zero).
4. *Select* the $i^{th}$ item of a list L, where $1 \le i \le length(L)$.
5. *Replace* the $i^{th}$ item, X, of a list, L, with a new item, Y, where $1 \le i \le length(L)$.
6. *Delete* any item, X, from a nonempty list, L.
7. *Insert* a new item, X, into a list, L, in any arbitrary position (such as *before* the first item of L, *after* the last item of L, or *between* any two items of L).

**Figure 7.1** List Operations Defining a List ADT

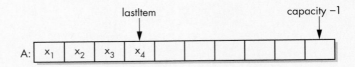

**Figure 7.2** An Array Holding List Items Sequentially

lists using arrays, we also need to save the length of the list (or, perhaps instead, the array index of the last item). This aspect of the sequential representation of lists using arrays is illustrated by the index, lastItem, in Fig. 7.2. The sequential representation in this figure permits fast access to the $i^{th}$ item of a list, since we can use the underlying array indexing capability to select or replace the $i^{th}$ array item.

However, to insert a new item or to delete some item, we may need to shift all the items beyond the point of insertion or deletion to maintain the contiguous sequential arrangement of items in the underlying array. This is inherently inefficient and on the average requires $O(n)$ time, where $n$ is the length of the list. (See Exercises 7.2.1 and 7.2.2, and see Appendix B for the meaning of $O(n)$.)

slow insertion and deletion of all items except the last item

Another potential difficulty is that the capacity of an array in Java is determined at the time the array is allocated (i.e., constructed). If an array, A[0:n–1], is used to represent a list $L == (x_1, x_2, \ldots, x_n)$, then the array is *full*, and we cannot insert another item in it without having the array *overflow*. In Java we typically expand an array to hold overflow items by allocating a new larger array, transferring the contents of the old overflowed array into the new array, adding the new overflow item to the new array, and throwing the old overflowed array away. This can waste time and causes a memory resource leak. Yet, lists are often used in circumstances where we want to handle unpredictable amounts of growth in our data, and it is inconvenient if they overflow. Rather, we need a representation of lists that can expand efficiently to handle unforecast growth that might occur during the running of a program.

the risk of overflow

Note that there is no operation among the List ADT operations in Fig. 7.1 that determines when a list is *full*, nor is there a restriction on the insertion operation to apply to nonfull lists only. If we preallocate arrays that are too small, the chances of having to perform wasteful expansions upon overflow are increased. If we preallocate arrays that are too big, we are in danger of wasting unused space. Thus, sequential list representations have several disadvantages.

Some of these disadvantages can be overcome by using the linked representations that we recall in the next section. However, these linked representations have disadvantages of their own, such as inefficient access to the $i^{th}$ list item, and storage penalties for the space needed to store the links.

## The One-Way Linked List Representation

In Chapter 3, we introduced simple one-way, linked list representations using chains of linked nodes. According to this technique, the way to represent the list $L == (x_1, x_2, x_3, x_4)$ is shown in Fig. 7.3. Recall that the empty list is represented by a list header node whose firstNode field contains the null pointer, null.

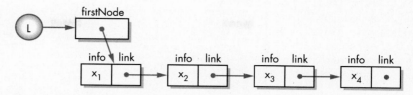

**Figure 7.3** One-Way Linked List with a List Header Node

To access the $i^{th}$ item of a linked list, L, we start with the reference value in L and follow it to the list header node that, in turn, references the first node of the linked list. We then repeatedly follow the pointers in the **link** fields of nodes, as necessary, in order to access the $i^{th}$ node. Finally, we can access the **item** field of the $i^{th}$ node. For example, to print the value of the $i^{th}$ item of a linked list, L, we can use a method such as the one given in Program 7.4. Starting with a reference to L's first node, the method call L.printItem(i) follows exactly $i$ pointers to access the $i^{th}$ item of the list L.

Suppose that list L has exactly $n$ items. If it is equally likely that each of these $n$ items can be printed, then, starting with the pointer to L's first node, the average number of pointers followed to access the $i^{th}$ item can be calculated by applying the familiar formula for the sum of an arithmetic progression:

$$\text{Average} = (1+2+\ldots+n)/n = \frac{n(n+1)}{2}/n = \frac{n}{2}+\frac{1}{2}.$$

*accessing the $i^{th}$ item is expensive in linked lists*

Consequently, the average time to access the $i^{th}$ item is $O(n)$. By contrast, the average time needed to access the $i^{th}$ item in a sequential array representation of a list L (as illustrated in Fig. 7.2) is $O(1)$, since it takes only a constant amount of time to access an array item $A[i]$, starting with the array index, $i$.

```
      |    void printItem(int i) {
      |
      |        ListNode N = firstNode;                    // let N point to L's first node
      |        int j = i;                                 // save i's value in j for later use
    5 |
      |        while ( ( i > 1 ) && ( N != null) ) {      // advance the pointer N to point to
      |            N = N.link;                            // the ith item of the list
      |            i--;
      |        }
   10 |
      |        if ( ( i == 1) && (N != null ) ) {
      |            System.out.println(N.item);            // print the ith item provided it exists
      |        } else {
      |            System.out.println("list has no item at index = " + j);
   15 |        }
      |    }
```

**Program 7.4** Printing the $i^{th}$ Item of a Linked List

| List Operation | Sequential Representation | Linked Representation |
|---|---|---|
| Finding the length of $L$ | $O(1)$ | $O(n)$ |
| Inserting a new first item | $O(n)$ | $O(1)$ |
| Deleting the last item | $O(1)$ | $O(n)$ |
| Replacing the $i^{th}$ item | $O(1)$ | $O(n)$ |
| Deleting the $i^{th}$ item | $O(n)$ | $O(n)$ |

We can generalize slightly by observing that any process that needs to access the $i^{th}$ node of a one-way linked list, $L$, of length $n$, starting with a pointer to the first node of the list, takes $O(n)$ time, whenever each of the nodes of $L$ is equally likely to be accessed. For example, processes such as accessing, deleting, or replacing the $i^{th}$ node, or inserting a new node before or after the $i^{th}$ node, each take time $O(n)$.

## Comparing Sequential and Linked List Representations

Let $L == (x_1, x_2, \ldots, x_n)$ be an abstract list of length $n$. Let's compare the average running times for doing several kinds of operations on the sequential array representation of $L$ (as illustrated in Fig. 7.2) and the simple, one-way linked representation of $L$ (as illustrated in Fig. 7.3). Table 7.5 gives the comparison.

Running time is not the only dimension on which we might wish to compare the efficiency of list representations. Space can also be an important resource to consider in some applications. The one-way, linked representation of a list requires space for comparing space costs one link in each node of the linked list representation. By contrast, the sequential array representation of a list requires no space for links, but it may waste unused space for items inside an array of preallocated size.

For a simple comparison, suppose that the space required by list items and the space required for pointers is identical. For example, the items might be floating point numbers each requiring 4 bytes of storage, and pointers might also take 4 bytes of storage each. Consider a list, $L$, of length $n$. The linked representation of $L$ requires $n$ nodes each requiring 8 bytes of storage, for a total of $8n$ bytes, to represent the entire list $L$. If we use an array $A[0:capacity - 1]$ to hold the items of $L$ sequentially, it takes $4n$ bytes to hold the $n$ items of $L$ inside $A$, but there is wasted space in the subarray $A[n:capacity - 1]$, since this space is unused to hold items of $L$. The total space required for the sequential representation of $L$ is equal to $4n + 4(capacity - n)$, which simplifies to $4 * capacity$.

We can find the tradeoff point for storage utilization efficiency between the finding the tradeoff point sequential and linked list representations by setting the storage used by the linked representation, $8n$, equal to the storage used by the sequential representation, which is $4 * capacity$, and by solving for $n$. Solving for $n$ in $8n = 4 * capacity$ yields the solution:

$$n = \frac{capacity}{2}.$$

In other words, assuming that list items and pointers each take the same number of bytes of storage, the sequential representation is more space-efficient whenever the average list is longer than half the size of the arrays used to store items in the sequential list representation. The tradeoff point shifts if list items and links take differing amounts of storage. For instance, if pointers require $p$ bytes of storage and items require $q$ bytes of storage, then the tradeoff point is given by:

$$n = \frac{q}{(p+q)} * capacity. \tag{7.1}$$

In particular, the cost in space of using linked list representations is low when list item representations take a large amount of storage in comparison to the storage required for pointers. For example, suppose we want to represent a list of employee records (each containing an employee's name, address, employee number, and department). Suppose each employee record takes 256 bytes, and each pointer takes 4 bytes. Then the storage efficiency tradeoff point according to Eq. 7.1 is $n = 256/260 * capacity$, which is the same as $n = 0.9846 * capacity$. In other words, you would have to operate sequential array-based list representations at better than 98 percent of capacity to gain a space efficiency advantage over the linked list representation. But attempting to operate at over 98 percent of capacity runs the risk of list overflow in the array-based representation, causing a memory resource leak if the array expands.

when efficiency in time outweighs efficiency in space

Consequently, if space efficiency is not the principal design constraint that needs to be met, and the efficiency of operations is instead of equal or greater importance, then one might choose to use either the linked or sequential list representation based on the average *time* consumed to perform an average mix of list operations (where the average mix could be measured by sampling the actual running application). The results in Table 7.5 show that the sequential representation will perform better if there is a preponderance of random accesses to list items (as in updating employee records when the positions of the records are known in advance). On the other hand, if we often insert new employee records as the new first item on a list, and we occasionally print a report enumerating the whole list, then the linked list representation is preferable (from the perspective of *time* efficiency not *space* efficiency).

other representations that give better solutions

(Actually, lists are not the most efficient way to store collections of employee records in a database that we intend to use for querying, updating, and occasional report printing. Instead, structures such as trees, hash tables, and large external file organizations give us much better solutions for many important mixes of different operations and many ranges of database sizes used in practice. We will explore the story of how different data structures have significant different advantages and drawbacks in the remaining chapters of this book. The remarks comparing linked and sequential list representations given in this subsection are just the beginning of a more extensive and thorough exploration of the possibilities.)

## Other Linked List Representations

Linked list representations come in almost limitless varieties. Eventually, you may want to craft your own special linked list representation for a particular purpose. In

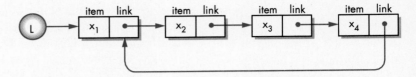

**Figure 7.6** A Circular Linked List

this subsection, we cover just three of the more common varieties of linked list representations above and beyond simple one-way, linked lists. These are (a) circular lists, (b) two-way linked lists, and (c) linked lists with header nodes.

## Circular Linked Lists

A circular linked list is formed by having the link in the last node of a one-way linked list point back to the first node. Figure 7.6 shows an example of a circular linked list. A circular linked list has the advantage that any node on it is accessible from any other node. That is, given a pointer to an arbitrary node, N, on a circular linked list L, we can follow links from node N to access any other node, M, on list L.

Exercise 7.2.3 explores the proper way to use a circular linked list to represent a queue.

## Two-Way Linked Lists

Two-way linked lists are formed from nodes that have pointers to both their left and right neighbors in the list. Figure 7.7 gives an example of such a list. In this figure llink is the title of a field holding a *left link* pointing to the left neighbor node of the given node, and rlink is the title of a field holding a *right link* pointing to the right neighbor of the given node. Sometimes a two-way linked list is called a *symmetrically linked list*.

Given a pointer to any node, N, in a two-way list, L, you can follow links in either direction to access other nodes. Moreover, you can delete node N, and you can insert a new node, M, either before or after N, starting only with the information given by the pointer in N. It is not possible to perform these same operations starting with a pointer N to a node in a one-way linked list.

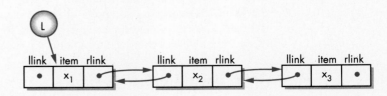

**Figure 7.7** A Two-Way Linked List

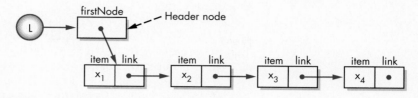

**Figure 7.8** A Linked List with a Header Node

## Linked Lists with Header Nodes

We have seen previously that in object-oriented programming it is convenient to have a special *header node* that points to the first node in a linked list of item nodes (see Fig. 7.8). The use of a header node can be combined with the use of circular or two-way lists. Header nodes can also be set up to contain additional information about the list, such as the number of nodes in the list, or a reference count (used in garbage collection and explained later in Section 7.6). In OOP, the object for a header node with a null **firstNode** pointer can represent the empty list and can allow methods (such as **insertItem**) to be applied to the empty list object. If the empty list is represented by the value **null**, it cannot have methods applied to it (because the value **null** is not an object that has methods).

Some examples of the use of header nodes from the published literature include the following:

1. To provide a stopping place on circular lists, or to provide a unique starting place.
2. To point to both ends of a two-way list (for fast insertion of all the list's items between two items in another two-way list, or for fast storage deallocation of the nodes in the list).
3. To permit ease of deletion of the first node on a list when the list is referenced by more than one external pointer.
4. To represent the empty list by a nonnull object in object-oriented programming, so that methods can be invoked on the empty-list object in order to perform operations such as insertion of a new list item into an empty list or printing the empty list.

## **7.2** REVIEW QUESTIONS

1. What is a list?
2. What are some disadvantages of using arrays of list items to represent lists sequentially?
3. When would it be advantageous to use a sequential array list representation instead of a linked list representation?
4. When would it pay to use a circular linked list instead of a one-way linked list?

## 7.2 EXERCISES

1. Let A[0:*capacity* – 1] be an array holding items in the list $L == (x_1, x_2, \ldots, x_n)$, where $n < capacity$. In this representation, we store list item $x_i$ in position $A[i – 1]$, for $(1 \leq i \leq n)$. Suppose that we want to delete an arbitrary list item, $x_i$. What is the average time needed to move all the items $x_j$, $(i + 1 \leq j \leq n)$ down one position, using $A[j – 1] = A[j]$ for each $j$ in $(i \leq j < n)$, assuming it is equally likely that any possible item $x_i$ in list $L$ is chosen to be deleted? Give the O-notation for this average deletion time.

2. What is the O-notation for the average time to insert a new item in the $i^{th}$ position of a list $L$ using the array representation in Exercise 1? Assume that insertions in any possible position are equally likely.

3. Mr. Alf Witt decides to use circular linked lists to represent queues. He lets a pointer variable **Q** point to the node on the circular list, **L**, containing the item at the front of the queue. Ms. Daisee Chayne thinks that a better design would be to have **Q** point to the node on the circular linked list **L** containing the rear item in the queue. Which queue representation is better, Alf's or Daisee's? Why?

4. Write a Java class definition implementing all of the operations given in Fig. 7.1 on circular, one-way linked lists having a special header node that points to the first node containing a list item. Let the empty circular linked list be represented by a header node whose **firstNode** data field contains **null**. Be especially careful to handle the special cases involving this empty list representation.

## 7.3   Generalized Lists

### LEARNING OBJECTIVES

1. To learn how generalized lists differ from simple linear lists.
2. To understand how to represent and manipulate generalized lists.
3. To understand the difference between shared and copied sublists.

*What are generalized lists?*

A *generalized list* is a list in which the individual list items are permitted to be sublists. (Sometimes a generalized list is called a *list structure*.) For example, consider the generalized list $L == (a_1, a_2, (b_1, (c_1, c_2), b_3), a_4, (d_1, d_2), a_6)$. The first two items on $L$ are $a_1$ and $a_2$, but the third item is the sublist $(b_1, (c_1, c_2), b_3)$. This sublist has another sublist $(c_1, c_2)$ as its second item. If a list item is not a sublist, it is said to be an *atomic* item (or, more simply, it is said to be an *atom*).

*linked representations*

In Java it is easy to construct the linked representation of generalized lists whose items are Java objects of any kind. Lines 3:6 of Program 7.9 define a class **ListNode** whose **item** field contains any Java **Object**. Lines 10:40 of Program 7.9 define a **GenList** class. Each **GenList** object has a private **firstNode** data field containing a reference to the first **ListNode** on its linked item list (or containing **null** if its item list is empty). A sublist in a **GenList** is represented by an **item** that is another **GenList** object.

*shared sublists*

Figure 7.10 illustrates a generalized list that is constructed and printed by the applet given in Program 7.11 (both are shown on page 210). Note that the sublist (**classOf**, **1998**) is shared by two separate items in other sublists of the main generalized list **L**.

```
/* ------------------------ */

class ListNode {
    Object      item;              // any Java Object can be an item in
    ListNode    link;              // a generalized list
}

/* ------------------------ */

class GenList {

    private ListNode  firstNode;          // the firstNode data field contains a
                                          // reference to the linked list's first ListNode
    /* ------------- */

    void insertItem(Object newItem) {          // this method inserts a new
        ListNode N = new ListNode( );          // ListNode on the front of the
        N.item = newItem;                      // generalized list and sets its item
        N.link = firstNode;                    // field to contain the newItem
        firstNode = N;
    }

    /* ------------- */

    void print( ) {                        // to print a generalized list, first print
        System.out.print( '(' );           // an opening left parenthesis
        ListNode N = firstNode;            // let N point to successive
        while (N != null) {                // nodes on the list
            if (N.item instanceof GenList) {
                ( (GenList)N.item).print( );       // print sublists recursively
            } else {
                System.out.print(N.item);
            }
            if ( (N = N.link) != null ) {      // advance N to point to next node
                System.out.print(",   ");      // print comma between items
            }
        }
        System.out.print( ')' );               // print a closing right parenthesis
    }
}

/* ------------------------ */
```

**Program 7.9** The ListNode Class and the Generalized List Class, GenList

The print( ) method given on lines 25:39 of Program 7.9 is designed to print generalized lists, no matter whether they have shared sublists or not. It uses a recursive call on line 30 to print items that are sublists. It is assumed that there is no path in the structure that forms a cycle of pointers. (A cycle is a path formed from pointers that starts at a given node and returns to itself.) If a linked representation, L, has a cycle of pointers in it, the print( ) method of Program 7.9 will not terminate when it tries to print L.

printing generalized lists

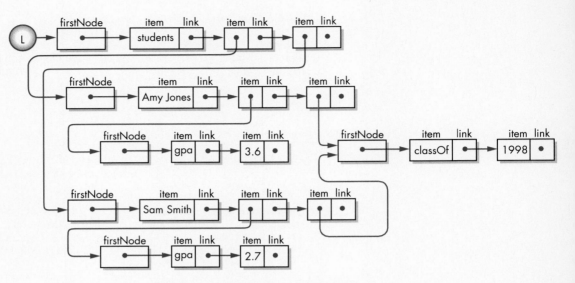

**Figure 7.10** Generalized List with a Shared Sublist

a property of
shared sublists

Whenever a generalized list contains two or more pointers to a shared sublist, the information accessed by all pointers sharing the sublist is updated whenever the information in the shared sublist changes.

This property of shared sublists can be either a useful feature or an annoying bug. In many applications, it is convenient to keep one shared copy of a record, **R**, that will be updated periodically, and to keep references to **R** in every structure that needs access to the latest updated version of **R**. In some contemporary operating systems,

```
 1 |   import java.io.*;
   |   import java.applet.Applet;
   |
   |   public class GenListApplet extends Applet {
 5 |
   |      public void init( ) {
   |
   |         /* -----
   |            When executed, this init( ) method prints:
10 |               (students, (Amy Jones, (gpa, 3.6), (classOf, 1998) ),
   |                          (Sam Smith, (gpa, 2.7), (classOf, 1998) )  )
   |         ----- */
   |
   |         // Create a generalized list S of the form (gpa, 3.6)
15 |            GenList S = new GenList( );
   |            S.insertItem(new Double(3.6));
   |            S.insertItem( "gpa" );
   |
```

**Program 7.11** Constructing and Printing a Generalized List *(continued)*

Program 7.11  Constructing and Printing a Generalized List *(continued)*

```
20 |              // Create a generalized list G of the form (classOf, 1998)
   |                  GenList G = new GenList( );
   |                  G.insertItem(new Integer(1998));
   |                  G.insertItem("classOf");
   |
   |              // Create a list H of the form (Amy Jones, (gpa, 3.6), (classOf, 1998) )
25 |                  GenList H = new GenList( );
   |                  H.insertItem(G);
   |                  H.insertItem(S);
   |                  H.insertItem( "Amy Jones" );
   |
30 |              // Create a list K of the form (gpa, 2.7)
   |                  GenList K = new GenList( );
   |                  K.insertItem(new Double(2.7));
   |                  K.insertItem( "gpa" );
   |
35 |              // Create a list M of the form (Sam Smith, (gpa, 2.7), (classOf, 1998) )
   |                  GenList M = new GenList( );
   |                  M.insertItem(G);          // G is a sublist shared by lists H and M
   |                  M.insertItem(K);          // K and S are separate "gpa" sublists
   |                  M.insertItem( "Sam Smith" );
40 |
   |              // Create the master student list L
   |                  GenList L = new GenList( );
   |                  L.insertItem(M);
   |                  L.insertItem(H);
45 |                  L.insertItem( "students" );
   |
   |              // Print the GenList L
   |                  L.print( );
   |                  System.out.println( );
50 |
   |          }//end init( )
   |
   |      }//end class GenListApplet
   |
   |  /* -- < To complete the applet, insert the text of Program 7.9 here > -- */
```

one application can furnish a "hot link" to some information, such as a spreadsheet, a drawing, or a paragraph of text that can be incorporated into another application's data. When the original application updates the information in the data to which hot links refer, the users of the hot links are notified and can substitute the newly updated versions.

On the other hand, it can be a pesky source of errors if you need to maintain your own separate copy of some information, but instead you unintentionally use a reference to shared information that gets updated by somebody else. It is important in designing generalized lists, therefore, to pay close attention to whether you want sublists to be shared, or to act as separate copies.

## 7.3 REVIEW QUESTIONS

1. How is a generalized list distinguished from an ordinary list?
2. How can you use Java class definitions to describe nodes for constructing generalized lists?
3. What condition in the pointers of a linked generalized list, L, would cause the print( ) method of Program 7.9 to get into an endless loop when it tried to print L using the method call L.print( )?

## 7.3 EXERCISES

1. Change Program 7.11 so that it replaces the year **1998** in the sublist **G** with the year **2003** and afterward prints the list **L**. What is printed? How does this demonstrate that the sublist **G** is a shared sublist?
2. Write a program to reverse a generalized list and all of its sublists. Make sure your program works whether or not the sublists are shared. (*Note:* You may need to add a new field to the **GenList** class to designate whether a given **GenList** object's item list has been reversed already.)
3. Write a program to "flatten" a generalized list by creating a single linear list consisting of all the items that would be printed in sequence when printing the generalized list with Program 7.9, but having no sublists. For example, (1, 2, 3, 4, 5, 6, 7) is the flattened version of the list (1, (2, 3), 4, (5, (6, 7))).

## 7.4   Applications of Generalized Lists

### LEARNING OBJECTIVES

1. To gain some practical background knowledge about list processing.
2. To learn about one of the early list processing languages, LISP.
3. To understand how garbage collection and available space lists work in list processing systems.

*early list processing languages*

The use of generalized lists in computer science has been especially important in connection with artificial intelligence applications (among others). Some early programming languages, such as LISP and IPL IV (among many others), introduced list processing at the programming language level. These languages permitted users to write programs to construct and manipulate generalized lists.

*supporting highly flexible data structures*

Generalized lists provide applications with a highly flexible data structure that can come in many possible shapes and sizes and can contain atomic data of many sorts. Procedures and functions can be written to give these general lists highly useful combining and growth laws. The result is a programming medium of considerable flexibility and generality that can meet the difficult requirements of applications having highly unpredictable demands for supporting information structures.

In artificial intelligence applications in particular, it is often required to support data representations whose size and shape cannot easily be forecast before the running of a program. For example, a chess playing program might need to explore many sequences of possible moves and replies. Each move and reply might have to be evaluated for its strategic significance. This can produce a highly branching network of possible imaginary situations.

*examples from artificial intelligence*

Again, in a natural language processing program, the parsing of input sentences and the assignment of meaning to them, can require structural descriptors and attached data representing analyzed meaning that can grow unpredictably large and can grow into arbitrary shapes.

*intermediate expression swell*

Finally, in symbolic mathematics systems, certain tasks often produce long chains of intermediate results, using expressions that can swell to unpredictably large sizes. A phenomenon called *intermediate expression swell* is often encountered in algebraic manipulation systems. For instance, suppose we are trying to multiply two polynomials $(x - 1)$ and $(x^2 + x + 1)$. We desire to have a result in simplified form.

A typical algebraic manipulation system might first try to multiply out all the terms, obtaining:

$$(x - 1) * (x^2 + x + 1) = (x^3 + x^2 + x - x^2 - x - 1),$$

after which, it collects terms of like degree, getting:

$$(1\ x^3 + (1 - 1)\ x^2 + (1 - 1)\ x - 1).$$

Following this, it needs to perform arithmetic where possible, enabling it to substitute zero for the two occurrences of the expression $(1 - 1)$, getting:

$$(1\ x^3 + (0)\ x^2 + (0)\ x - 1).$$

It then applies once the simplification law, $1 * y \Rightarrow y$, and it applies twice the simplification law, $0 * y \Rightarrow 0$, getting:

$$(x^3 + 0 + 0 - 1).$$

Finally, it performs arithmetic on constants again, simplifying $(0 + 0 - 1)$ to $-1$, getting the final result:

$$(x^3 - 1).$$

In this small derivation, you can see how the intermediate expressions used swelled up to a large size before simplification laws were applied to reduce them back down to a smaller final size.

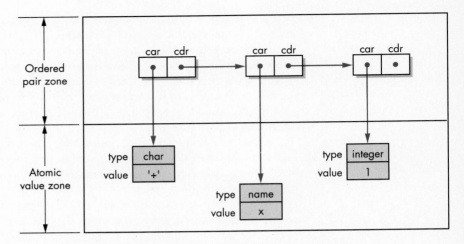

**Figure 7.12** List Representation Used in Some Early LISP Systems

In contrast to the postfix expressions used for stack evaluators in the previous chapter, symbolic algebraic manipulation systems often use prefix operator expressions inside generalized lists. For example, the expression $(x - 1)$ would be represented by the list $(-, x, 1)$ whose first item is the minus operator, and whose second and third items are the left and right operands to be subtracted. Similarly, the polynomial $(x^2 + x + 1)$ might be represented by $(+, (\wedge, x, 2), x, 1)$. Here, the addition operator $(+)$ can take arbitrarily many operands to be added together in the list that follows.

*using prefix operator expression lists*

In some early implementations of the LISP programming language, memory was divided into two zones. One zone contained representations of atoms, to be used as list items, and the other zone contained ordered pairs of pointers. The left pointer in a pointer pair was stored in a field named the **car** field, and the right pointer was stored in the **cdr** field, as shown in Fig. 7.12. This figure contains the representation of the prefix expression list $(+, x, 1)$ representing the infix algebraic expression $(x + 1)$.

*background on how LISP works*

You can see that in the *atomic value zone* in Fig. 7.12, each atom is a node having a **type** field and a **value** field. The **type** field contains a tag specifying the type of the value in the value field. For instance, if the **type** is *char*, the value in the value field represents a character value, and if the **type** is *integer*, the value in the value field represents an integer. This system is called a *tagged type system*, since each value is *tagged* with its type. When we operate on tagged values during program execution, we need to read the tags to decide which operation to perform. For example, if we try to add a value tagged as the integer 1 to another value tagged as the floating point number 6.0, we have to select some code to execute that applies a floating point conversion to the integer 1, getting the floating point constant, 1.0, and then we have to perform floating point addition on 1.0 and 6.0, to get 7.0. Finally, we have to package the result 7.0 into another node with a tag "real" to denote that it is a floating point value, and we have to find space in which to store this result in the atomic value zone. This kind of mechanics is called doing "interpreted arithmetic at run time," because it is similar to what a language interpreter would do during program execution (such as an interpreter for the BASIC programming language).

The unused pointer pairs in the *ordered pair zone* in Fig. 7.12 can be linked together into a single one-way list, using links in their **cdr** fields. This list of unused pairs is called an *available space list*.

When new lists are being formed, new pointer pairs are detached from the front of the available space list for use in construction of the new list. If the available space list becomes empty, a process needs to be invoked to identify and collect any unused pointer pairs that may have become detached during other manipulations and are no longer in use. A marking process is used to trace all pointer pairs that are in use in the system. Following this marking process, a sweep is made to gather and link all pairs marked as unused into a new available space list. This marking and gathering process is called *garbage collection*. We will study more about garbage collection in Section 7.6.

The LISP programming language is still in widespread use at the moment and is especially popular for artificial intelligence applications. Many generations of ingenious computer scientists have developed the early LISP systems into their current highly evolved forms. To overcome the inefficiency of interpretive run-time execution and tagged-type systems, many LISP systems today offer optional hard-type declarations with fully efficient compilation and run-time execution. They also have

*the LISP language*

many ingenious storage management enhancements that overcome, to a considerable degree, the inefficiencies of linked representations and garbage collection methods. Some LISP systems can even shift automatically to sequential (nonlinked) list representations (using what is called *cdr-direction linearization*) when efficiency considerations reveal it to be advantageous. (There is much more to this story than can be sketched here, and interested readers are urged to pursue the literature, which contains a gold mine of ingenious techniques that can often be applied in other circumstances.)

Like LISP, Java is a garbage collected language. Moreover, because it is possible to determine the type of any object at run-time (using Java's **instanceof** operator), it is possible to use Java to implement generalized lists having the full generality and flexibility possible in typeless languages.

## 7.4 REVIEW QUESTIONS

1. Under what circumstances are generalized lists useful?
2. Name some applications in which generalized lists are used.
3. What price is paid for the generality of typeless list processing languages?
4. What is intermediate expression swell in an algebraic manipulation system?

## 7.4 EXERCISES

1. (Project) Write a Java applet that multiplies polynomials and reduces them to simplest form.
2. (Project) Write a Java applet to add, subtract, multiply, and divide symbolic fractions, and to reduce the results to a single cleared fraction with a single numerator and denominator. (Implement laws such as: $a/b + c/d = (ad + bc)/bd$, $(a/b)/(c/d) = (ad/bc)$, and $(a/1) = a$, etc.)

 **Strings**

## LEARNING OBJECTIVES

1. To gain additional understanding of string operations and string representations beyond what is offered in first courses in computer science.
2. To learn about Java's read-only String class and about the Java StringBuffer class, used to manipulate a string's characters.
3. To gain an initial impression of how strings can be represented in text files and word processors.

Strings are sequences of characters. To name just a few of their many applications, strings are used in word processors, in fields of records used in databases, and in electronic mail systems as the text of messages that are exchanged. Many different kinds of string operations are defined on strings in these various contexts. Moreover, many different representations of strings are used.

Java has two different kinds of string objects—those whose internal characters *cannot* be changed, and those whose internal characters *can* be changed. The Java class **String** consists of read-only strings. The **String** class has no methods that change the characters of which a **String** object is composed. By contrast, the Java class **StringBuffer** has methods that operate on and change the characters inside a **StringBuffer** object.

### Read-Only Strings in Java

If you declare a variable **S** to be of type **String** and initialize it, as in the declaration

        String S = "lieutenant";

the value of **S** becomes a reference value referring to a new **String** object containing the internal character sequence "lieutenant". The string literal "lieutenant" in this initializing declaration causes a new string object to be constructed. You can also construct new **String** objects by invoking the string constructor **new String(X)**, where **X** is a character array, a byte array, or another **String** object, in which case the characters inside **X** are used to construct the new **String**. After a string object **S** has been constructed, you can't change the characters inside it. You can read **S**'s characters, by invoking the method **S.charAt(i)**, where i is the index of any of the **S**'s characters, and i lies in the range $0 \le i \le S.length() - 1$. You can also create a new string by applying the string conversion method **String.valueOf(v)** to a data value v, where v is an **int** such as **3**, a **float** such as **4.5**, a **char** such as '%', or a **boolean** truth value such as **false**. In these cases, the respective strings "3", "4.5", "%", and "false" would be constructed.

methods for constructing
Java String objects

examples using
string operations

For example, suppose we had initialized the string variables **S** and **T** using the declarations String S = "lieutenant"; and String T = "ten"; Then, since **T** is a substring of **S**, **S.indexOf(T)** is the index 4 of the character 't' of the leftmost occurrence of the substring "ten" in "lieutenant". Also, **S.length()** has the value **10** because the string "lieutenant" contains ten characters.

Two Java **String** objects, **S** and **T**, can be concatenated using the "+" operator, as in the expression **S + T**, or using the **String** method **S.concat(T)**. The string concatenation operator joins the successive characters of its two operand strings together to form the new string that results. For example if **S** = "**Catch**" and **T** = "**22**" then **S + T** is the new string "**Catch22**". If one of the operands of the concatenation operator is a **String** and the other is not a **String**, a string conversion is applied to the non-string operand before concatentation (by invoking an object's **toString()** method or by converting a primitive data value to a **String**). Thus, one can produce string output using a method invocation such as **System.out.print("Catch" + 22)**; in which the primitive integer value **22** is converted to the string "**22**" before being concatenated with "**Catch**" to produce the string output "**Catch22**".

concatenating
two strings

The Java **String** class has many more useful methods than we have space to describe in this book. A reference such as Patrick Chan and Rosanna Lee's book, *The Java™ Class Libraries: An Annotated Reference*, gives the complete details. Suffice it to say that the **String** class contains methods not mentioned here for converting a given string to a new string having equivalent lower- or uppercase characters, comparing two strings for equality or alphabetical ordering, creating a new string with leading and trailing white space removed, determining whether a string starts with a given prefix or ends with a given suffix, and so forth.

### String Buffers in Java

examples of some
StringBuffer methods

In this subsection, we discuss some elementary uses for Java **StringBuffer** objects and we give a partial implementation of the **StringBuffer** class to explain how the hidden internal representation of classes such as the **StringBuffer** class might work. Program 7.13 illustrates uses of some of the Java **StringBuffer** methods, using our own class **StrngBuffer** defined in Program 7.14 (on pages 219 and 220, spelled without the "i" to avoid a name conflict with the built-in Java class **StringBuffer** in java.lang).

Line 9 of Program 7.13 uses the constructor **StrngBuffer(20)** to construct a new **StrngBuffer**, buf, with a capacity to hold **20** characters. Line 12 appends two strings to the end of this **StrngBuffer**, filling it with the characters of the string, "**\"Say the secret word, and win $100.\""** Lines 15:18 print some characteristics of the **StrngBuffer**, buf, as follows:

```
buffer length = 36
buffer capacity = 36
the buffer's 8th character = e
the string in the buffer = "Say the secret word, and win $100."
```

Line 21 creates a new **StrngBuffer**, newBuf, holding the string "**Groucho Marx said,** " and line 24 appends the string in **buf** to the end of **newBuf**. Line 25 prints the resulting string in **newBuf**

```
string in new buffer = Groucho Marx said, "Say the secret word, and win $100."
```

Line 28 invokes the **copyStrngBuffer** method defined on lines 35:41. This method makes a copy of **newBuf** in a new **StrngBuffer**, anotherBuf. Finally, lines 29:30 print

```
 1 | import java.io.*;
   | import java.applet.Applet;
   |
   | public class StringBufferApplet extends Applet {
 5 |
   |     public void init( ) {
   |
   |         // create new StrngBuffer with capacity = 20
   |             StrngBuffer buf = new StrngBuffer(20);
10 |
   |         // append two strings to the end of the StrngBuffer, buf
   |             buf.append("\"Say the secret word").append(", and win $100.\"");
   |
   |         // print a few intermediate results
15 |             System.out.println("buffer length = " + buf.length());
   |             System.out.println("buffer capacity = " + buf.capacity());
   |             System.out.println("the buffer's 8th character = " + buf.charAt(7));
   |             System.out.println("the string in the buffer = " + buf.toString());
   |
20 |         // create another StrngBuffer with an initial contents
   |             StrngBuffer newBuf = new StrngBuffer("Groucho Marx said, ");
   |
   |         // append the old buffer's contents to the end of the new buffer
   |             newBuf.append(buf.toString());
25 |             System.out.println("string in new buffer = " + newBuf.toString());
   |
   |         // try out the string buffer copy method
   |             StrngBuffer anotherBuf = copyStrngBuffer(newBuf);
   |             System.out.println("another buffer holds = " + anotherBuf.toString());
30 |             System.out.println("buffer length = " + anotherBuf.length());
   |
   |     }// end init( )
   |
   |     /* A method that creates a new StrngBuffer as a copy of another */
35 |     public StrngBuffer copyStrngBuffer(StrngBuffer oldBuf) {
   |             char[ ] charArray = new char[oldBuf.length( )];
   |             oldBuf.getChars(0, oldBuf.length( ), charArray, 0);
   |             StrngBuffer result = new StrngBuffer(oldBuf.length( ));
   |             result.append(String.valueOf(charArray));
40 |             return result;
   |     }
   |
   | }//end applet
   |
   |     /* --< insert here the text of the StrngBuffer class from Program 7.14 >-- */
```

**Program 7.13** Using StringBuffers in String Operations

the contents and length of anotherBuf:

```
another buffer holds = Groucho Marx said, "Say the secret word, and win $100."
buffer length = 55
```

```
class StrngBuffer {

   private int count;
   private int capacity;
   private int capacityIncrement;
   private char[ ] charArray;

 /* --------------------- */

   // three StrngBuffer constructors are given

   StrngBuffer( ) {                              // creates a new empty StrngBuffer
         count = 0;                              // with a default capacity of 16
         capacity = 16;
         capacityIncrement = 8;
         charArray = new char[capacity];
   }

   StrngBuffer(int capacity) {                   // creates a new empty StrngBuffer
         count = 0;                              // whose capacity is set by
         this.capacity = capacity;               // the input parameter
         capacityIncrement = 8;
         charArray = new char[capacity];
   }

   StrngBuffer(String str) {                     // creates a new StrngBuffer
         count = str.length( );                  // initialized to contain the
         capacity = count;                       // characters in the String str
         capacityIncrement = 8;
         charArray = str.toCharArray( );
   }

 /* --------------------- */

   // this section gives definitions of some StrngBuffer methods

   int capacity ( ) {
         return this.capacity;
   }

 /* ------- */

   void ensureCapacity(int minimumCapacity) {
         if (capacity < minimumCapacity) {
               char [ ] tempCharArray = new char[minimumCapacity];
               for (int i = 0; i < count; i++) {
                     tempCharArray[i] = charArray[i];
               }
               charArray = tempCharArray;
               capacity = minimumCapacity;
         }
   }
```

**Program 7.14** A StrngBuffer Class Implementation *(continued)*

Program 7.14  A StrngBuffer Class Implementation (*continued*)

```
     |    /* ------- */
     |
55   |    int length ( ) {                        // returns the length of the string in the string buffer,
     |        return count;                       // where the length of a  string is the number of
     |    }                                       // characters the string contains
     |
     |    /* ------- */
60   |
     |    int charAt(int index) {                 // returns the character in the string buffer
     |        return charArray[index];            // at the position given by the index
     |    }
     |
65   |    /* ------- */
     |
     |    StrngBuffer append(String str) {        // appends the String str to the end of the
     |        int len = str.length( );            // characters in the buffer, expanding the
     |        ensureCapacity(count+len);          // buffer as necessary, and
70   |        int j = 0;                          // returns a reference
     |        for (int i = count; i < count + len; i++) {     // to the buffer
     |            charArray[i] = str.charAt(j++);
     |        }
     |        count += len;
75   |        return this;
     |    }
     |
     |    /* ------- */
     |
80   |    void getChars(int srcOffset, int srcEnd, char[ ] dst, int dstOffset) {
     |        for (int i = srcOffset; i < srcEnd; i++) {      // copies characters from
     |            dst[dstOffset++] = charArray[i];            // srcOffset:srcEnd−1 into the
     |        }                                               // character array dst starting at
     |    }                                                   // index dstOffset
85   |
     |    /* ------- */
     |
     |    public String toString( ) {             // generates the string contained
     |        char [ ] data = new char[length( )];            // in the StrngBuffer
90   |        getChars(0,length( ), data, 0);
     |        return String.valueOf(data);
     |    }
     |
     |    /* ------- */
95   |
     |    }//end class StrngBuffer
```

Program 7.14 provides a definition of the **StrngBuffer** class used in Program 7.13.
A **StrngBuffer** object has four private data fields visible only to internally defined
**StrngBuffer** methods. The **count** field on line 3 holds the number of characters in the
string contained in the **charArray** field defined on line 6. The **capacity** and
**capacityIncrement** fields give the size of the current **charArray** and the increment by
which to expand it if it needs to be enlarged to hold more string characters.

There are three constructors for a StrngBuffer. The no-arg constructor on lines 12:17 creates an empty StrngBuffer object with default capacity 16. Lines 19:24 define a constructor whose integer parameter defines the initial capacity of an empty StrngBuffer, and lines 26:31 define a constructor that uses a String parameter to initialize the contents of a newly constructed StrngBuffer.

the StrngBuffer methods

The ensureCapacity method defined on lines 43:52 first checks to see whether the current StrngBuffer's capacity is less than the minimumCapacity requested, and, if so, creates a new character array whose length is the minimumCapacity, transfers the current StrngBuffer's characters into it, and replaces the current charArray with the newly constructed character array. The append method on lines 67:76 adds the characters in its parameter string to the end of the StrngBuffer, expanding the buffer as necessary to accommodate the required growth. The getChars method on lines 80:84 copies characters from the StrngBuffer in the range srcOffset:srcEnd−1 into a destination character array dst starting at the index dstOffset. The toString( ) method on lines 88:92 uses a temporary character array to extract the characters in the StrngBuffer and converts it into a String, using the conversion method String.valueOf defined in the String class. When a StrngBuffer object is used as a parameter of the System.out.print( ) method, or as an operand of the string concatenation operator ("+"), the toString( ) method is applied to it to convert its contents to a String. For example, a StrngBuffer, B, can be used in System.out.print(B) to print the string contained in B. The copyStrngBuffer method on lines 35:41 of Program 7.13 uses the methods of the StrngBuffer class to create a copy of a StrngBuffer object.

## String Representations in Text Files and Word Processors

In this subsection, we briefly sketch limited examples of how strings can be represented in text files and in word processors. These examples come from a system used by one computer vendor, whose operating system furnishes basic building blocks for operating on files of text. You can think of these files of text as long strings of characters broken into individual lines of text by the occurrence of end-of-line characters. When a text file is read into main memory, a special representation is set up to make it convenient to operate on the text line-by-line. Here's how it works.

a few practical examples

A text file stored on an external memory medium (such as a floppy disk, a hard disk, or a tape) has both a *logical structure* and a *physical structure*. The logical file structure specifies the *logical length*, $L$, of the text in characters and provides a file *position counter*, $P$. Given a text file, $T$, which is $L$ characters long, the position counter, $P$, can assume any value in the range $0:L$. When $P == 0$, the position counter is positioned *before* the first character of the file, and when $P$ assumes any value $n$ in the range $(1 \leq n \leq L)$, the position of $P$ is *after* the $n^{th}$ character in $T$ and *before* the $(n+1)^{st}$ character in $T$. Thus $P$ always designates a position that is *between* two characters (or *before* the first character or *after* the last character) in the file $T$.

physical file lengths

The *physical length*, $L_{phys}$, of the file $T$ is a separate length number giving the total number of available character positions in a linked list of blocks of file space that hold the actual text of the file. Different media (such as floppy disks, hard disks, or tapes) are divided up into different size blocks. For example, a floppy disk may be divided up

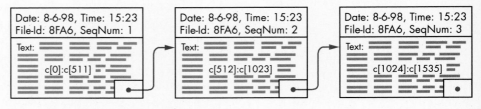

**Figure 7.15** Linked Character Blocks in a Text File

into storage blocks of 512 bytes each, and a hard disk may be divided up into blocks of 4096 bytes each.

Suppose that a text file $T$ has a logical length $L$ == 562 characters (meaning that its text is 562 characters long). On a floppy disk with 512-character blocks, one block is not long enough to hold the entire text, so two blocks would have to be used. The first block would contain the first 512 characters, and it would be linked to a second block containing the remaining 50 characters. In this case, the physical length of the text file would be $L_{phys}$ == 1024, since there are a total of 1024 physical character positions available in the two linked blocks holding the 562 characters in the logical file structure. The same 562 character text file would require only one 4096-character block on a hard disk, in which case $L_{phys}$ == 4096.

The physical structure of the file also contains some extra information hidden from the logical structure. Such information can be used to check on the accuracy of the storage media holding the file and to recover lost files. In addition to holding the text characters of the file, each block in the physical file representation is stamped with the date and time of its creation, a special unique file Id-number (different from the Id-numbers of all other files), and a block sequence number. Moreover, the first block of the file stores a "cyclical check sum," which is the sum of the integer values of all the characters in the file. In the event that the file directory on a given disk (or other storage medium) is lost or damaged, the information in the physical blocks can be used to help recover the lost files (by linking all blocks stamped with the same file Id-number into a linked list in the order given by their block sequence numbers).

*extra information in the physical text file structure*

Figure 7.15 shows some of the information in the physical representation of a text file that is stored in a medium (such as a floppy disk) using 512-byte blocks.

When a text file, $T$, is read into main memory to be operated on, another different text representation is created. This text representation has two parts: (a) a single large block, $B$, of text characters representing the text of the file, and (b) an array, $A$, of *line starts*. Each array entry, $A[i]$, gives the position of the beginning of the $i$th line of text in the text file (where lines are terminated by end-of-line characters, and where positions lie between two adjacent characters). Figure 7.16 illustrates the structure of a text file, $T$, in main memory.

*the representation of text in main memory*

The operating system supplies primitive operations enabling programmers to select the text between two positions, and to delete it or copy it, as well as permitting new text to be inserted at a given position. (This is how the text operations *Cut*, *Copy*, and *Paste*, are implemented.) The line start information in the array $A$ is useful for fast display and scrolling of lines of text inside a text window on the user's workstation.

```
         ┌──────────────────────────────────────────┐
         │  Line                                      │
         │  starts              Character text        │
         │ ┌──────┐ ┌──────────────────────────────┐ │
         │ │   0: │ │Forescore and seven           │ │
         │ │  21: │ │years ago our fathers         │ │
         │ │  43: │ │brought forth on this         │ │
         │ │  65: │ │continent, a new nation,      │ │
         │ │  90: │ │conceived in Liberty,         │ │
         │ │ 112: │ │and dedicated to the          │ │
         │ │ 133: │ │proposition that all          │ │
         │ │ 154: │ │men are created equal.        │ │
         │ │ 177: │ │   Now we are engaged in      │ │
         │ │ 201: │ │a great civil war,            │ │
         │ │ 220: │ │testing whether that          │ │
         │ │ 241: │ │nation or any nation so       │ │
         │ │ 265: │ │conceived and so              │ │
         │ │ 282: │ │dedicated, can long           │ │
         │ │ 302: │ │endure.                       │ │
         │ └──────┘ └──────────────────────────────┘ │
         └──────────────────────────────────────────┘
```

**Figure 7.16** A Text File in Main Memory

More advanced professional word processors need to use text representations that are even more complicated than the simple one described here. Some word processors permit users to designate whether they want to have the entire text file reside in main memory (assuming their computer has lots of main memory) or whether they want only a few pages of text to be in main memory at a time (in case their computer has only a limited amount of main memory). Depending on which option the user chooses, the word processor may attempt to read either the full file or only a few pages of it into main memory. Having the entire file in main memory reduces the time required to perform certain operations (such as searching for a keyword or doing spelling correction). But this advantage cannot be gained unless the user's computer has enough main memory.

*more advanced text representations*

Also, in advanced word processors, the raw characters of text in the text file are usually augmented with special invisible code characters that designate style and formatting features such as fonts, tabs, indents, paragraphing, and underlining. Finally, links can be planted in the text to link in pictures or special graphics. Moreover, new blocks of text to be inserted can be linked into a given block at an insertion point instead of being directly inserted in the sequential character sequence. These links can be eliminated when the text is transferred to an external file or is reorganized during operations such as repagination (in which an altered text is divided into pages).

## **7.5** REVIEW QUESTIONS

1. What is the difference between a Java **String** object and a Java **StringBuffer** object?
2. How could you reverse the characters in a string using Java?

allocation can then take place using blocks allocated from this region anytime during the running of a program. We refer to such a region of memory as a *heap*.

In addition to using stacks and heaps to support dynamic memory allocation, it is also possible to base dynamic memory allocation on the use of a list of available space—a form of dynamic allocation useful for lists formed by linking together nodes of identical size.

In the subsections that follow, we will discuss the kind of dynamic memory allocation that occurs when we organize a region of memory into an available space list and the techniques for dynamic memory allocation in heaps.

## Available Space Lists and Garbage Collection

In Fig. 7.12 we saw how to divide memory into two zones for use in list processing applications. One zone of memory held nodes containing pairs of pointers, and the second zone held representations of atomic values tagged with their types. In such a scheme, before execution of the main program begins, the zone of memory holding nodes for pairs of pointers is initialized by organizing it into a single one-way linked list called the *available space list*. The available space list is a pool of free memory containing nodes that can be allocated on demand whenever the need arises. Generalized lists can be constructed from building blocks removed from the front of this available space list. Thus the available space list turns memory into a flexible commodity that can be allocated on demand during the running of a program.

Now we consider two policies for recycling used list nodes. These are called *storage reclamation policies* since they reclaim space for nodes that are no longer in use. Policy 1 places deallocation of list nodes under direct programmer control. Policy 2 automatically collects deallocated nodes when they are needed.

- *Policy 1—Explicit Deallocation by the Programmer*

    In some list processing systems, when a list node is no longer needed, it is the direct responsibility of the programmer to return it to the available space list (by linking it back onto the available space list, either at the beginning or the end of the available space list). The early list processing language IPL IV used this policy for recycling unused list nodes for further use.

- *Policy 2—Automatic Storage Reclamation*

    In other list processing systems, while list nodes are removed from the front of the available space list when needed, the programmer is not responsible for returning unused nodes back to the available space list. When the available space list runs out of nodes to allocate (i.e., when it becomes empty), an automatic storage reclamation process, called *garbage collection*, is invoked. For example, the LISP programming language uses automatic storage reclamation policies.

Let's look for a moment at how the garbage collection process works. First of all, it is assumed that each list node has a special bit allocated in it, called the *mark bit*. This mark bit can be set to one of two values, *free* or *reserved* (where, for example, *free* is represented by the bit value "0" and *reserved* is represented by the bit value "1").

the available space list

explicit deallocation

automatic reclamation

how garbage
collection works

The process proceeds in three phases. In the first phase, called the *initialization phase*, a pass is made through the list memory region setting the mark bits on each node to *free*. In the second phase, called the *marking phase*, all list nodes currently in use are identified and are marked by having their mark bits set to *reserved*. The idea is to mark all the nodes in current use to prevent them from being collected during the final phase. In the third phase, called the *gathering phase*, another sweep is made through the list space, and all nodes marked *free* are linked together into a new available space list. The available space list now consists of all the inaccessible nodes that were not previously incorporated into structures in use. These inaccessible nodes are sometimes called *garbage*, and the process of identifying them and linking them together into a new available space list is called *garbage collection*.

Program Strategy 7.19 outlines the main steps in the "mark and gather" strategy for garbage collection. On line 8 of this program strategy, there is an **item** field in the **ListNode** class that contains an **Object** pointer. However, we assume that the **item** pointer in a list node containing a pointer pair can point either to another list node in the *ordered pair zone* or to an atomic value node in the *atomic value zone*. (See Fig. 7.12 for an illustration of these two zones in the case of a LISP-like list processing system.) An *address range discrimination* can be used at the assembly language level to distinguish whether a pointer points to an address inside the ordered pair zone or the atomic value zone. An assembly language test can thus distinguish which kind of operations to apply to a node, depending on whether the node resides in the ordered pair zone or the atomic value zone. (This is one way to implement the **instanceof** operator in a Java boolean expression such as (**L.item instanceof ListNode**) that is used in line 9 of Program Strategy 7.20 on p. 229.)

An unfinished method to implement in Program Strategy 7.19 is the marking method **markListNodesInUse**, which is called on line 31. Let's investigate how to organize a marking process. Program Strategy 7.20 provides a sketch. We assume that we start with a single **ListNode** pointer, as the value of the variable **L**, and our task is to trace out and mark all **ListNodes** accessible from **L** via any path of pointers starting with either the **item** field or the **link** field of **L**'s referent.

You can see that Program Strategy 7.20 makes two recursive calls (on lines 10 and 14). These recursive calls apply the node marking process to the nodes referenced by the **item** and **link** pointers of the node referenced by the pointer in **L**. When the function **markListNodesInUse** looks at the node referenced by the pointer in **L**, it immediately tests to see if the node is already marked as **RESERVED**. If a node is already marked as **RESERVED**, it has already been visited by the marking process along some other path of pointers, and it does not need to be considered further. However, if the node is not yet marked as **RESERVED**, its **markBit** field is immediately marked as **RESERVED**, and the marking process proceeds further to examine the nodes referenced by the **item** and **link** pointers. If the pointer in the **item** field points to a **ListNode**, then the marking process is applied to the node it references. In any event, the marking process is applied to the node referenced by the pointer in the **link** field. The process eventually terminates when every **ListNode** accessible via a path of pointers from the initial pointer in **L** is marked as **RESERVED**.

*using recursive calls to mark all accessible nodes*

```
   |    static final byte FREE = 0;
   |    static final byte RESERVED = 1;
   |
   |    /*  each ListNode has a markBit which is either FREE or RESERVED  */
 5 |
   |        class ListNode {
   |            byte            markBit;                        // FREE or RESERVED
   |            Object          item;
   |            ListNode        link;
10 |        }
   |
   |    /* assume further that all ListNodes are allocated inside a region of */
   |    /* memory as an array of nodes called the listNodeArray, as follows: */
   |
15 |        ListNode        listNodeArray[listNodeArraySize];
   |        ListNode        avail;              // avail will point to the available space list
   |
   |    void garbageCollection( ) {
   |
20 |        int i;                     // i is a local variable that indexes the listNodeArray
   |
   |        /* phase 1—Initialization Phase—mark all ListNodes FREE */
   |
   |            for ( i = 0; i < listNodeArraySize; i++ ) {
25 |                listNodeArray[i].markBit = FREE;
   |            }
   |
   |
   |        /* phase 2—Marking Phase—mark all ListNodes in use RESERVED */
30 |
   |            // use the method markListNodesInUse of Program Strategy 7.20
   |            // to mark all list nodes in use
   |
   |        /* phase 3—Gathering Phase—link all FREE ListNodes together */
35 |
   |            avail = null;
   |            for ( i = 0; i < listNodeArraySize; i++ ) {
   |                if ( listNodeArray[i].markBit == FREE ) {
   |                    listNodeArray[i].link = avail;
40 |                    avail = listNodeArray[i];
   |                }
   |            }                        // at the conclusion, avail is the new available space list
   |
   |    }
```

**Program Strategy 7.19** Garbage Collection by Marking and Gathering

## Heaps and Dynamic Memory Allocation

allocating blocks of
different sizes

To support dynamic memory allocation for Java objects of different sizes we cannot use the available space list technique discussed in the previous subsection. This is because the available space list contains linked blocks of *identical* sizes, whereas what we need to provide is a means for allocating blocks of memory of *differing* sizes.

```
1   void markListNodesInUse(ListNode L) {


        if ( ( L != null ) && ( L.markBit != RESERVED ) ) {
5           L.markBit = RESERVED;


            if (L.item instanceof ListNode) {
10              markListNodesInUse(L.item);
            }


            markListNodesInUse(L.link);
15      }

    }
```

**Program Strategy 7.20** Marking List Nodes in Use

The problem we face is this. Given a request size, $n$, for a block of memory of $n$ bytes, how can we allocate a block of size $n$? More generally, how can we organize a region of memory to allow us to allocate and free blocks of memory of various different sizes, given a sequence of requests to do so?

Figure 7.21 shows a region of memory called a *heap*. It contains blocks of memory of various sizes that have been reserved in response to allocation requests. The shaded region represents unallocated memory.

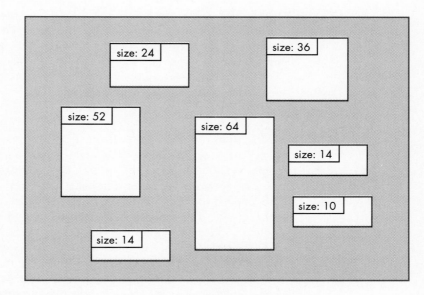

**Figure 7.21** A Heap Containing Reserved Blocks of Various Sizes

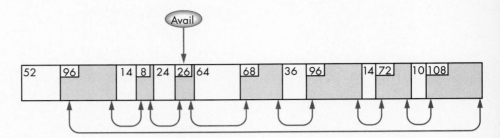

**Figure 7.22** The Two-Way Linked List of Free Blocks in a Heap

The question now arises: How can we organize the unallocated space sitting between the reserved blocks so that future allocation requests can be satisfied? Two of the allocation policies we shall examine use a circular, two-way linked list of unallocated blocks. Figure 7.22 gives us another picture of the heap shown in Fig. 7.21. It shows the heap as being arranged in one linear zone of memory (with memory addresses increasing, say, from left to right), with shaded blocks of free memory containing their sizes and arranged into a two-way linked list using double-headed arrows to symbolize the two-way links. Since this two-way list is circular, we will call it a *ring*, in what follows. (*Note:* Even though Fig. 7.22 shows the two-way linked list as linking the free blocks together in increasing order of their addresses, in general, this will not be the case in actual applications. Instead, the free blocks can be linked into a ring in any order.)

Suppose we are given a pointer, *Avail*, to one of the free blocks on the ring of free blocks. Starting from any block on the ring, we can move either left or right to neighboring blocks. We can also search the ring in either direction to find a block, *B*, of suitable size to satisfy a memory allocation request. We can also remove block *B* from the ring by linking *B*'s left and right neighbors to one another, and we can mark *B* as being reserved, to put it in service to satisfy a request.

Let's now take a look at two different policies for allocating a new block of memory, given a request for a block of size *n*.

## First-Fit

In the *first-fit* policy, we travel around the ring of free blocks starting at the block referenced by the pointer, *Avail*, until we find the first block *B* such that $Size(B) \geq n$, and we use *B* to satisfy the request. If $Size(B) > n$, then we break *B* into two blocks, $B_1$ of size *n* and $B_2$ of size $(Size(B) - n)$. We use $B_1$ to satisfy the request, and we link $B_2$ back into the ring of free blocks. If $Size(B) == n$, then we have what is called an *exact fit*, and we detach *B* from the ring of free blocks and use it directly to satisfy the request. In this second *exact fit* case, there exists no remaining unused block $B_2$ to link back into the ring of free blocks.

For example, in Fig. 7.22, suppose the request size is 72. We start at the block whose size is 26, which is referenced by the pointer *Avail*, and we compare the request size 72 with the block size 26. Since the block of size 26 is not big enough to satisfy

using circular two-way lists
of unallocated blocks

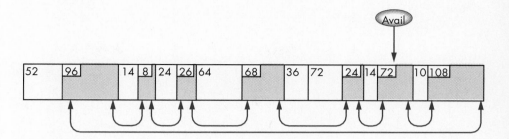

**Figure 7.23** First-Fit Allocation of a Block of Size 72

the request, we advance around the ring (moving, let us say, in the rightward direction), and we consider next the block of size 68. This block is not big enough either, so we again move to the right to the block of size 96. This time, the block of size 96 is big enough. So we divide it into a block of size 72 and a block of size 24. We use the block of size 72 to satisfy the request, and we link the remaining block of size 24 back onto the ring of free blocks. The result of doing this is shown in Fig. 7.23. Note that the *Avail* pointer has been reset to point to the block of size 72 to the right of the original block of size 96 that we split in order to satisfy the request.

### Best-Fit

Under the *best-fit policy*, we travel around the ring attempting to find a block that is the "best fit" for the request size $n$, as follows. Starting at the block, $B$, referenced by the pointer *Avail*, we compare $Size(B)$ to the request size $n$. If $Size(B) == n$, we have an *exact fit*, so we use block $B$ to satisfy the request immediately by detaching it from the ring of free blocks and marking it as reserved. But if $Size(B) \neq n$, then we continue to search around the ring. We stop whenever we find an exact fit. But if we travel all the way around the ring without having found an exact fit, we use the closest fit we discovered on our trip around the ring. The closest fit is the block $B$ on the ring having the property that $(Size(B) - n)$ is as small as possible. Again, we split the block $B$ into a block $B_1$ of size $n$ and a block $B_2$ of size $(Size(B) - n)$. We mark $B_1$ as reserved, and we link $B_2$ back into the ring of free blocks.

Figure 7.24 (on page 232) shows the result of using the best-fit policy to allocate a block of size 72, starting with the situation given in Fig. 7.22. Starting with the situation in Fig. 7.24, if we use the best-fit policy to satisfy a request to allocate a block of size 64, the block of size 68 would be selected (since it is the tightest fit, having the least excess storage of any of the blocks on the ring of sizes 108, 96, 68, and 96 that are large enough to satisfy a request of size 64).

### Fragmentation and Coalescing

fragmentation

If we operate a heap storage allocation system for a while, using either the first-fit policy or the best-fit policy, the ring of free blocks will tend to contain smaller and small-

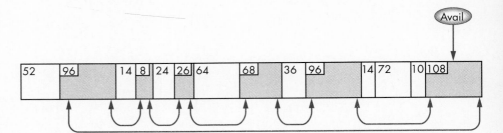

**Figure 7.24** Best-Fit Allocation of a Block of Size 72

er blocks. This happens because we keep splitting larger blocks to satisfy requests for more storage. This tendency is called *fragmentation*.

The problem with fragmentation is that if the free blocks on the ring keep getting divided up into smaller and smaller size blocks, there may come a time when we encounter a request to allocate a block of size *n* that cannot be satisfied because all the free blocks are too small. This is called *allocation failure*.

**allocation failure**

To reduce the chances of encountering allocation failure, we can perform what is called *coalescing*. When we *coalesce* two blocks that are sitting next to one another in memory, we join them into a single larger block. A good moment to try coalescing is when we free the storage for a block, *B*, and attempt to return it to the ring of free blocks. Instead of just linking *B* into the ring of free blocks, we can look at *B*'s immediate left and right neighbor blocks (in address order, not ring order) and if either of these neighbors is free, we can join it to *B* to make a larger coalesced block before putting this larger block back on the ring of free blocks.

**coalescing**

For example, if we attempted to free the storage for the block of size 36 in Fig. 7.24, we could coalesce it with its two neighbors of sizes 68 and 96, getting a new large coalesced block of size 200 == (68 + 36 + 96) to return to the ring of free blocks. (To make this coalescing policy work efficiently, we need to store each free block's *size* and a mark bit designating it as *free* not only at the top of each block but also at its bottom boundary.)

We say that a storage allocation policy is operating under *equilibrium* when, over time, the average amount of space in new blocks being reserved is equal to the average amount of space in blocks being freed, and when, in addition, the distribution of block sizes in the system remains the same. We need to use a coalescing policy to combat the tendency toward storage fragmentation, since, in most cases, without using a coalescing policy, the system will not achieve equilibrium over time (because the distribution of block sizes will keep getting smaller and smaller and the risk of allocation failure will increase).

**equilibrium**

One more detail is worth mentioning in connection with the use of the first-fit and best-fit policies. This concerns the importance of using a *roving pointer*, *Avail*, to point to blocks on the ring of free blocks. In the roving pointer technique, we let *Avail* point to the successive blocks on the ring of free blocks when we search for a block *B* to satisfy a request, and after *B* has been located, we make *Avail* point to the block immediately beyond *B* on the ring. (By contrast, in a nonroving pointer tech-

**using roving pointers**

nique, we always start our search for block $B$ at a fixed initial block referenced by *Avail*.) The result of using the roving pointer technique is that *Avail* keeps circulating around and around the ring of free blocks, and immediately ahead of it, the blocks have had the longest time among any others to coalesce and form bigger new blocks due to the return of freed blocks. If we keep scanning along the ring of free blocks from a fixed initial starting point (as we do in the nonroving pointer technique), then small fragments will tend to concentrate in the initial part of the search path, increasing the time required to satisfy larger requests. This inefficiency is quite noticeable and severe in some cases.

## Compacting to Deal with Allocation Failures

When we make a request to allocate a block of size $n$, and the system finds that no block on the ring of free blocks is large enough to satisfy the request, it may still be the case that the sum of the block sizes on the ring of free blocks is larger than $n$. In this case, allocation failure could be said to have occurred because of the fragmentation of free blocks on the ring of free blocks. In particular, if we had a way of coalescing all the free blocks together into a single large block, we could proceed to satisfy the original request.

The process of moving all the reserved blocks into one end of the heap, while moving all the free blocks into the opposite end and coalescing them all into one large free block is called *compacting the heap* (or *heap compaction*). But to accomplish this, we need to make it possible not only for the reserved blocks to shift position but also for all external pointers to these blocks to be updated to point to the new addresses to which the blocks have been moved.

One technique for making this process easy is to use what are called *handles*. Handles are *double pointers*—or pointers to pointers. To create handles, we set aside a region of the heap to contain a zone of *master pointers*. These master pointers point to reserved blocks. Then we use a pointer to a block $B$'s master pointer as the *handle* to $B$. We use handles both to provide external access to blocks from outside the heap, and also to allow blocks to contain pointers to point to one another inside the heap. Figure 7.25 shows a heap divided into a normal block allocation heap zone and a master pointer zone.

If we agree always to access reserved blocks in the normal heap zone using their handles, then the stage is set to make it easy to move the blocks around in the heap. All we have to do when we move a block, $B$, is to change $B$'s master pointer to point to the new location to which $B$ has been moved. After $B$ has been moved to a new location, external access to $B$ through its handle still works. To make it easy to update $B$'s master pointer when we move $B$, we can agree to store a copy of $B$'s handle inside $B$ (along with $B$'s *size* and its *mark bit* telling whether $B$ is *free* or *reserved*).

*Compacting the heap* then consists of scanning the heap zone from bottom to top, moving each reserved block down as far as possible and updating the block's master pointer to point to its new location. Finally, the free space at the top is joined into one large free block. The heap is then said to be *compacted*. Figure 7.26 shows the result of compacting the heap illustrated in Fig. 7.25.

**compacting the heap**

**handles**

**moving blocks in the heap and updating their master pointers**

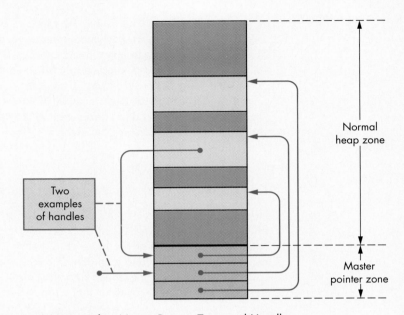

**Figure 7.25** A Heap with a Master Pointer Zone and Handles

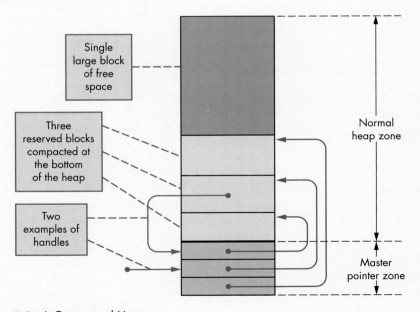

**Figure 7.26** A Compacted Heap

If the heap in an implementation of the Java Virtual Machine (JVM) were to be represented using blocks of memory for objects referenced by handles, then accessing objects from their reference values would have to be implemented by *double pointer dereferencing*. For example, to access the item field of a ListNode, L, using the expression L.item, the reference value in L would be a handle that accesses the actual block of storage for a ListNode, and implicit double dereferencing would be required to access the actual block of memory containing the item field.

*double dereferencing*

## Comparing Uses of Heaps in Applications

Comparing the use of single pointers with use of handles, we observe that it costs more both in *space* (to store two pointers instead of just one) and in *time* (to perform double dereferencing instead of single dereferencing) when we use handles instead of pointers. What we gain, however, is convenience in arranging for the underlying storage allocation scheme to be able to accommodate a range of allocation request sizes and to be able to compact memory easily so we can coalesce all fragmented blocks of free space into one large free space block.

*handles versus single pointers*

It is perhaps not surprising then that the use of heaps containing blocks referenced by handles is a popular way to organize memory in some contemporary computing systems. One vendor's operating system divides a computer memory into a *system heap* (to contain operating system data structures) and various *application heaps*, each supporting given software applications. Software vendors can write software (such as spreadsheets, word processors, painting and drawing programs, electronic mail programs, and so forth) relying on the availability of such heaps to support their applications. Application software typically uses blocks in an application heap to contain representations of data supporting menus, windows, pictures, text, file control blocks, device control blocks, buttons, scroll bars, and all manner of application support data structures.

*applications of heaps*

Some modern object-oriented programming languages allocate data structures representing *objects* in heaps and automatically assume that these objects are referenced by handles, so the programmer never needs to use double-dereferencing notation in a program to refer to objects.

## Reference Counts

There is one more concept worth mentioning before we close this section on dynamic memory allocation techniques. This is the idea of *reference counts*.

One of the troubles with the storage reclamation techniques we have discussed so far is that they cause a program to pause while they reorganize memory. The garbage collection technique uses a three pass algorithm to sweep memory setting mark bits to free, then to mark all list nodes in use, and finally to link all unused list nodes into a reconstituted available space list. The heap compaction algorithm also requires making a sweep of the heap zone during which reserved blocks get moved and their master pointers get updated. Each of these processes requires time $O(N)$, where $N$ is the size of the memory being reorganized.

*pausing for storage reclamation*

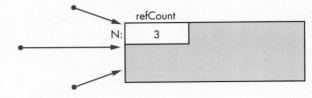

**Figure 7.27** A node, N, with a Reference Count of Three

If we have a *real-time application*, requiring a system to respond quickly—within a fraction of a second, let's say, to incoming stimulus events (as is the case in systems such as robots used in manufacturing assembly lines or in collision avoidance systems in airline aircraft)—then we have to guarantee that the system will not be taken off-line for a period of time longer than the required real-time response interval. Garbage collection and heap compaction algorithms both have two unfortunate features: (a) it is unpredictable when the moment to execute them will arise, and (b) they take a considerable amount of time to run to completion (often more than a few fractions of a second when a system has a huge list or heap memory, especially on slower computers or computers with huge random access memories). Consequently, it is important to know about alternative *storage reclamation techniques* that work *incrementally* instead of all at once. (An *incremental* technique is one that performs its work in tiny increments, doing its job bit by bit every now and then.)

The use of *reference counts* can provide an incremental storage reclamation technique under suitable circumstances. A *reference count field* in a node, N, is a data field containing a number that counts the number of pointers that reference N. Figure 7.27 illustrates a node N having three pointers that point to it and having a reference count of three in its **refCount** field.

Each time we create and use a new pointer that references N, we increase N's **refCount** by one, and each time we destroy a pointer to N, we decrease N's **refCount** by one. Whenever N's **refCount** reaches zero, we know that no more pointers in the system refer to N, so we can return the block of storage used to hold N to the available space list (or to the ring of free blocks in the heap, whichever is appropriate for the storage allocation technique we are using). This policy accomplishes something important. Namely, it automatically frees the storage for N the instant N's storage is no longer in use. Free storage in the system is therefore reclaimed incrementally (instead of all at once, as is the case for mark-and-gather garbage collection or heap compaction). If a real-time system needs to use dynamic memory allocation techniques, the reference count technique may provide a solution that helps the system meet its real-time response constraints.

*responding in real time*

*incremental storage reclamation*

## 7.6  REVIEW QUESTIONS

1. What is the difference between static and dynamic memory allocation?
2. Explain what is done in each of the three phases of garbage collection using the marking and gathering technique.

3. What is a heap? How is it used to support dynamic memory allocation?
4. What is the difference between the first-fit and best-fit policies for dynamic memory allocation?
5. What do fragmentation and coalescing refer to in the case of heaps?
6. What are handles? How are they affected by heap compaction?
7. What are reference counts? How do they provide for incremental storage reclamation?

## 7.6 EXERCISES

1. Why is it the case that, to make the free block coalescing policy work efficiently, we need to store each free block's size and a mark bit designating it as free not only at the top of each block but also at its bottom boundary?
2. Can you draw a picture of several nodes with nonzero reference counts that are linked to one another but are not referenced from the outside? What defect does this imply in the reference count method for incremental storage reclamation?

---

## ▋ Pitfalls

- *Improper initialization of your data representations*

    Did you remember to initialize all data structures properly? When creating data representations for lists, strings, or dynamic memory allocation support packages, it is easy to overlook proper initialization. Does each one-way, linked list terminate with a null link? Is each string buffer's **capacity** field initialized properly? Did you properly initialize all the links, sizes, tags, master pointers, and boundary markers in your heap?

    The use of formatted debugging aids is highly useful in detecting deficiencies in your implementations. If you can see a printed representation of each of your data structures, your errors, especially those errors related to improper initialization, will tend to leap out at you. In fact, a good policy is to implement the formatted debugging aids before implementing the algorithms for the operations. That way, you will be ready to check out the operation of each newly implemented algorithm thoroughly.

- *Unannounced overflows and allocation failures*

    When using sequential representations that can overflow some implementations do not give any overflow warnings or do not throw any Java exceptions that can be handled. In some dynamic memory allocation systems using heaps, allocation failure can happen unannounced. One policy used to signal an allocation failure in a heap is to return a null handle as the reply to an allocation request to allocate a block of size *n*. In a properly implemented Java system, the JVM will signal an **OutOfMemoryError** when you exhaust the free memory at run time.

To develop production-quality, commercial software applications, you will need to develop a style of programming that detects and overcomes overflows and allocation failures, and that anticipates running out of storage by offering the user the option to save files and data before a system crash occurs due to insufficient memory or file space.

## Tips and Techniques

- *Look at operations before choosing representations*

    It is helpful to become informed about the intended operations you need to perform on your data before choosing a low-level representation. An ideal way to proceed is as follows: First, define your intended operations abstractly (by, for instance, thoroughly specifying an ADT for your data and operations at the abstract level). Second, if possible, collect size measurements for the data structures you will need to use in your application and obtain frequency counts for the mix of operations you will need to perform on your data. Third, identify the constraints on your implementation devices and media (and determine whether space efficiency or time efficiency or both will be important to achieve). Fourth, select your data representations and algorithms to meet the implementation constraints and to optimize the performance measures (such as efficiency in time or efficiency in space) that you have selected.

    For example, in choosing a list representation to implement the List ADT operations given in Fig. 7.1, linked list representations generally will accommodate insertions and deletions more efficiently. But they will not be as efficient when accessing and updating list items randomly, starting with an item's position in the list. Storage allocation efficiency in linked lists generally will be good when the space required to hold links is small in comparison to the amount of space required to hold the rest of the information in list nodes. Sequential list representations will generally pay off when random list item access by position is frequently required, and when the risk of list overflow is absent or minimal (which can arise, for instance, if list sizes are known in advance to be bounded).

- *Supporting dynamic memory allocation*

    It is not always the case that a programmer gets to choose which dynamic memory allocation technique to use to support an application being programmed. Often the programmer is stuck with whatever methods are offered by the underlying implementation medium selected for a project. For instance, a list processing language, such as LISP, might provide dynamic memory allocation techniques supporting the construction of generalized lists using available space lists and automatic garbage collection, but it may suffer efficiency penalties for being a typeless language and for not being able efficiently to allocate and update packed sequential data structures containing items of identical type. A version of Pascal might provide fixed-length strings and methods (of unknown efficiency) for allocating blocks of memory in a heap. A vendor's operating system might provide heap operations at the microcode level, but they might have been implemented inefficiently.

It is important to measure the performance and efficiency of an externally supplied dynamic memory allocation package to make an informed decision about whether to use it or not, provided you have the choice.

If you are faced with implementing your own dynamic memory allocation support package, it would be useful to study some of the advanced techniques available in the literature (which are beyond the scope of this book), before plunging ahead and implementing a technique by trial-and-error.

## ■ References for Further Study

John McCarthy wrote a classic paper introducing list processing ideas.

*classic paper on list processing*

> McCarthy, John, "Recursive Functions of Symbolic Expressions and Their Computation by Machine, Part I," *Communications of the ACM* 3:4, pp. 184–195 (April 1960).

If you are curious to know how the performance of the *first-fit* and *best-fit* policies compare, some information is given in a more advanced book by the author.

*comparing policies*

> Standish, Thomas A., *Data Structure Techniques*. Addison-Wesley, Reading, MA (1980).

Patrick Chan and Rosanna Lee have written a complete reference on the Java class libraries including the **String** and **StringBuffer** classes.

*the Java Class Libraries*

> Chan, Patrick and Lee, Rosanna, *The Java™ Class Libraries: An Annotated Reference*. Addison-Wesley, Reading, MA (1997).

## ■ Chapter Summary

*lists*

Lists are finite, ordered sequences of items. We can represent lists by packing their items contiguously in arrays—getting the *sequential representation of lists*, or by putting the items in individual nodes and linking these nodes into chains—getting the *linked representation of lists*. The many varieties of linked list representations include one-way linked lists, circular linked lists, two-way linked lists, and linked lists having special header nodes.

*linked versus sequential representations*

Sequential list representations provide fast access to arbitrary items by position, but, in comparison to linked lists, it may be more costly to delete or insert items in the middle of sequential list representations, and they run the risk of overflowing or of wasting space not used to store items. Linked lists provide for fast insertion and deletion of items, but accessing items by position is slower than is the case for sequential lists, and linked lists can exhibit poor storage utilization efficiency.

*generalized lists*

Generalized lists are lists whose items are permitted to be sublists. As with ordinary lists, generalized lists have both sequential and linked representations. Sublists of generalized lists can either be shared, or they can exist as separate copies.

Generalized lists are used in important applications in artificial intelligence and are the main data structuring method available in various list processing languages.

Such list processing languages are often said to be *typeless*, because they allow the use of variables that can have values of any type and because items of any type can be stored in the generalized lists that these languages provide. Unfortunately, a price must be paid for the generality and flexibility that such typeless languages offer, since their generality is often purchased in the coinage of reduced efficiency.

Java Strings and
StringBuffers

Java **String** objects are read-only objects for which no methods are provided to permit alteration of the characters inside the **String**. By contrast, a Java **StringBuffer** object has methods that can be invoked to alter, rearrange, extend, or contract the characters it contains.

text files

Text files are files that contain strings representing text. In one example studied in this chapter, text files are represented on external storage media as linked blocks in which each block contains a packed array of characters holding a portion of the text. Each of these linked blocks is stamped with (a) a unique file identifier, (b) the date and time of the text file's creation, and (c) a block sequence number. In the event of a read-write failure on the storage medium, or in the event of the loss of file directory information, such a text file can be recreated using the information stamped on each block, by linking all blocks having a given unique file identifier in the order specified by their block sequence numbers.

When text files are read into main memory, the text is coalesced into a single large block, containing the sequence of characters in the text, and a separate array of *line starts* is created (which is useful for quickly displaying the text in a window on the user's workstation, and for rapidly scrolling this text up and down in the window).

static versus dynamic
storage allocation

Static storage allocation takes place before a program is executed, and it involves setting up storage areas whose size and arrangement can be calculated from declarations in the text of the program before the program is run. Dynamic storage allocation takes place during program execution. Three kinds of dynamic allocation are (1) stack-based dynamic allocation used to support method calls and returns; (2) organizing memory into an available space list to perform dynamic allocation of list nodes on demand at run-time; and (3) organizing memory into a heap that can be used to allocate blocks of different sizes on demand during program execution.

garbage collection

When an available space list containing list nodes becomes empty, storage reclamation can be attempted by an *automatic garbage collection* process. The marking and gathering method for garbage collection is a three-phase process. In the initialization phase, all list nodes are marked as *free*. In the marking phase, all list nodes in current use are marked as *reserved*. In the gathering phase, all *free* list nodes are linked into a new available space list.

heaps

A heap is a zone of memory organized to support dynamic memory allocation of blocks of storage of differing sizes. Two methods for allocating a block of size $n$ in a heap are the *first-fit* method and the *best-fit* method. The first-fit method scans a two-way linked ring of free blocks and allocates the first block big enough to satisfy the request. The best-fit policy scans the entire ring of free blocks to find the block that is the tightest possible fit satisfying the request, where the tightest possible fit is the one having the least excess size beyond the size requested.

fragmentation and
coalescing

*Fragmentation* occurs during the use of the first-fit and best-fit policies when free blocks are split into smaller blocks. *Coalescing* is a method used to counteract the tendency toward fragmentation. When a block is freed and can be returned to the ring of free blocks, it is possible to *coalesce* it with any of its neighbors that are also free, to form larger free blocks.

*Allocation failure* occurs in a heap when a request to allocate a block of size *n* cannot be accommodated either because not enough free space is left, or because all the blocks on the ring of free blocks are too small to satisfy the request. *Compacting* is a strategy that can be used for storage reclamation when allocation failure occurs in a heap. When a heap is compacted, all reserved blocks are moved to one end of the heap, allowing all free blocks to be moved to the opposite end and to be coalesced into one large free block. Handles are used to make heap compacting easy. A *handle* is a *pointer to a pointer*. Each reserved block in a heap is referenced by a *master pointer* in a special master pointer region. A handle to a block is a pointer to the block's master pointer. When a block is moved during heap compacting, its master pointer is updated to point to the block's new location. References to the block, using double dereferencing of the block's handle, are unaffected by the act of moving a block and updating its master pointer.

Garbage collection and heap compaction have the disadvantage that the system must pause to perform storage reclamation. These pauses may occur at unpredictable moments since it is difficult to forecast when allocation failures will occur. In real-time systems, which must be able to guarantee responses to external events within specified time limits, it may be unacceptable to pause for storage reclamation. An incremental technique for storage reclamation that can be used to overcome this deficiency is one based on the use of *reference counts*, in which each node contains a number equal to the number of external pointers in use to reference the node. When pointers to a node are destroyed, the node's reference count is decreased. When the node's reference count becomes zero, its storage can be returned to the pool of available space. Since this can be done incrementally, long pauses for the execution of multipass storage reclamation algorithms can be avoided.

Heaps are used in many contemporary applications to support data representations used by operating systems and by application software. Data structures supporting windows, menus, spreadsheets, pictures, drawn objects, word processor text, file and device control blocks, scroll bars, buttons, and many other sorts of objects used in programming are commonly stored in heaps, and space for them is commonly allocated using dynamic storage allocation methods, such as those explained in this chapter.

# Trees and Graphs

**Introduction and Motivation**

Trees are one of the most important data structures in computer science. They come in many forms. They provide natural representations for many kinds of data that occur in applications, and they are useful for solving a wide variety of algorithmic problems.

*trees are important and useful*

Sometimes trees are *static*, in the sense that their shape is determined before the running of an algorithm, and they do not change shape while the algorithm runs. In other cases, trees are *dynamic*, meaning that they undergo shape changes during the running of an algorithm. Tree shape can change as a result of the insertion and deletion of nodes. There are also shape-changing operations that alter the structure of a tree locally without inserting or deleting any nodes. Trees can also change shape when they are combined with one another. An example of a combining operation is the substitution of one expression tree for a node inside another expression tree (where expression trees are used to represent algebraic expressions, such as: $x^2 + 2\,x\,y + y^2$).

*static and dynamic trees*

242

Another kind of dynamic tree is one that is generated during the solution of a problem. For example, a *game tree* is a tree representing the possible moves of the players at each stage of a game. A given node in a game tree represents a specific game situation, and the branches leading from this node represent possible moves a player can make in this situation.

*game trees*

A *search tree* is a tree used to help search for prestored information that is often associated with *search keys*. Each node in the search tree may represent a test that is performed on the search key being used. The outcome of the test may determine which branch to follow in the tree to narrow the search. Search trees can be used to organize efficiently the search index to the information in a large file or database.

*search trees*

Trees can also be used to create specially efficient representations for various algorithmic tasks. For example, priority queues were defined in Chapter 5 as an ADT specifying a type of queue that holds prioritized items. Items can be put into a priority queue in any order, but they are removed in the order of highest-to-lowest priority. One of the efficient ways to represent a priority queue is to create a special kind of binary tree called a *heap*. (*Note:* This is a different use of the word "heap." In Chapter 7, another kind of heap was used to organize dynamic memory allocation strategies.)

*priority queues and heaps*

Sometimes trees can be represented efficiently using sequential representations. In other cases, linked tree representations offer advantages. Some tree representations are even implicit in the operation of an algorithm.

*sequential and linked representations*

Graphs are collections of nodes in which various pairs of nodes are connected by line segments. The nodes are usually called *vertices* and the line segments are called *edges*.

*what are graphs?*

The vertices and edges in a graph can be augmented by additional information. For example, vertices may be numbered or labeled, and edges may have numbers attached to them. Such augmented graphs are useful in a variety of contexts for modeling information encountered in computer applications. For instance, a graph in which the vertices represent cities and the edges represent the distances between those cities (or the cost of an airline ticket between those cities) can be used as a "transportation network" to study the total distances (or costs) of trips that make multiple stops at several cities. We might ask, "What is the path with one or more stops of shortest overall distance (or least overall cost) connecting a starting city and a destination city in such a transportation network?" This is an instance of a *shortest path problem* in a graph.

*graphs are useful in computer applications*

Again, we might have a graph whose edges represent a network of oil pipelines and whose vertices represent oil pumping stations. Oil might be pumped from a source through pipes in the network and might leave the network at a specific destination. If the edges in the graph are marked with the maximum oil flows that the corresponding oil pipes can carry, we might ask, "What is the maximum possible overall flow of oil from the source to the destination in such a network of oil pipes?" This is an instance of a *maximal flow problem* in a flow graph.

*flow graphs*

We might also search in a graph for a vertex having a particular property. When creating a computer program to play a board game such as chess or checkers, a game graph results when particular board configurations are represented by vertices and when edges between those vertices represent moves in the game that change one

*searching in graphs*

board configuration into another. A computer algorithm might search such a game graph to attempt to find a sequence of *forcing moves* leading to a *win*. (Here, a *forcing move* is one for which the opponent has only one legal reply, and a *win* is a board configuration, such as a checkmate in chess, in which a player is defined to have won the game according to the game's rules.)

Even though every tree is a graph (since trees are built from vertices in which pairs of vertices are joined by edges), graphs are more general than trees. For instance, paths in graphs can form *cycles* in which a path starting at a given vertex follows a sequence of successive edges that eventually return to the starting vertex (by making a "round trip" so-to-speak). Trees can never contain cycles. Also, a graph can consist of one or more *connected components*. A connected component is a portion of a graph in which there is a path connecting any two vertices in the component. If a graph has several separate connected components, there is no path from a vertex in one component to a vertex in a separate component. A tree always has exactly one connected component.

graphs are more general
than trees

There are two important consequences of the fact that graphs are more general than trees: (1) graphs are useful in a broader variety of problem representations and (2) the algorithms for processing graphs are more complex. This reveals another kind of tradeoff that we often see in computer science—the tradeoff between generality and algorithmic simplicity. The more complex and flexible that a representation becomes, the less simple are the algorithms that are used to perform fundamental operations on it (such as traversal and searching). For instance, depth-first and breadth-first searching algorithms are defined both for trees and graphs. However, these algorithms are more complicated for graphs than for trees. In the case of graphs, the algorithms must take into account the possibility that nodes being searched have already been visited before along another path in the graph, whereas, in the case of trees, a node can be reached only along one path starting at the root of the tree.

generality trades off
against simplicity

## Plan for the Chapter

Section 8.2 introduces some basic concepts and terminology pertaining to trees. The basic anatomy of trees—such as roots, leaves, and internal nodes—is discussed.

concepts and terminology

Section 8.3 begins to explore *binary trees*. These are trees that are either empty or have nodes with two children that must in turn be binary trees. Section 8.4 examines representations of binary trees. One such representation is the sequential representation, in which the nodes of a binary tree are packed next to one another in an array so that there are no gaps between the nodes. Not only does this provide quick random access to the $k^{th}$ node of the tree, it also enables us to move around the tree using efficient operations on integer array indexes. The sequential representation is much more efficient in space than the linked representation, but it does not tolerate some kinds of changes in shape very well.

binary trees

Section 8.5 presents an application of the sequential representation of binary trees to the task of representing priority queues. By arranging the values in nodes of a sequential representation of a binary tree in a special way, we obtain a *heap*. When heaps are used to represent priority queues, we can obtain good performance of the

representing priority
queues using heaps

insertion and deletion operations in the Priority Queue ADT. Section 8.5 presents algorithms for implementing the Priority Queue ADT using heaps.

*binary tree traversals*

In Section 8.6, we study some techniques for traversing binary trees. A traversal of a binary tree is a process that visits each node in the tree exactly once in some specified order. Different orders for visiting the nodes yield different traversals. One particular traversal of interest is the *postorder traversal* of an expression tree representing an algebraic expression. The postorder traversal of such an expression tree yields a postfix instruction sequence that can be used by a postfix interpreter (such as that given in Program 6.10) to calculate the value of the expression. We also present several significant techniques for traversing linked representations of binary trees using recursion, stacks, and queues.

*binary search trees*

Section 8.7 explores binary search trees. Linked binary trees were first illustrated in Fig. 3.29. The coverage in Section 8.7 shows how to insert new keys into binary search trees, how to print binary search trees, and how to search for a node in a binary search tree containing a given search key. It is known that, in the worst case, searching a binary tree of $n$ nodes can take time $O(n)$. However, in the average case, search times are known to be $O(\log n)$.

*AVL trees*

The stage is then set for the exploration of AVL trees in Section 8.8. AVL trees are binary search trees that are kept in nearly balanced—although not perfectly balanced—condition. They overcome the $O(n)$ worst case performance of unbalanced binary search trees, and they are known to have $O(\log n)$ performance for all significant operations, such as searching for a node with a given key, inserting a new node, and deleting a node. One can even give an implementation of the List ADT, using AVL trees, that overcomes the principal disadvantages of the sequential and linked representations of lists.

*2–3 trees*

Section 8.9 presents another useful kind of search tree, called a 2–3 tree. These are trees that can have nodes with either two or three children and that have all leaves on a single bottom row. These trees exhibit good performance properties similar to those of AVL trees.

*tries*

Section 8.10 introduces briefly another kind of search tree, called a *trie*, which is organized according to a "discrimination net" principle different from that used to organize binary search trees and 2–3 trees. Tries have remarkably good search tree performance, and their shape is insensitive to the order in which new keys are inserted (a property not enjoyed by binary search trees and 2–3 trees).

*Huffman codes*

In Section 8.11, we see how binary trees can be applied to the process of establishing a minimal-length encoding for messages spelled with letters in an alphabet, where the frequency of use of the letters is known. This is called a Huffman code, and the binary tree constructed to yield the code is called a Huffman coding tree.

*concepts and terminology*

Section 8.12 introduces some basic concepts and terminology pertaining to graphs. We cover the basic anatomy of graphs by describing their parts, such as vertices, edges, and components, and by introducing fundamental concepts, such as paths, cycles, and connectedness.

*graph representations*

Section 8.13 explores *graph representations*. We can represent graphs in a variety of ways using computer data structures. For example, we can use a matrix (i.e., a table) that contains ones and zeros to specify which edges connect which vertices.

We can use an array of linked lists, in which each position in the array represents a distinct vertex, and the list stored in that position gives the other vertices to which the given vertex is connected by an edge. We can also use various set representations, since a graph can be viewed as a set of pairs of vertices in which each pair of vertices corresponds to an edge.

Graph searching algorithms are explored in Section 8.14. Two well-known methods are depth-first searching and breadth-first searching. The algorithms for these two methods are similar to the corresponding depth-first and breadth-first searching algorithms for trees, in that stacks are used to implement depth-first searching and queues are used to implement breadth-first searching. The only difference is that graph algorithms must be augmented to handle situations involving several connected components as well as multiple paths that may form cycles—two situations that do not arise in trees, since trees cannot have cycles and have only one connected component. We use abstract program strategies to express these graph searching algorithms in order not to be tied down to a particular data representation. In this sense, we use the mathematical definition of graphs as an ADT, and we leave particular choices of representational details to the reader. The same policy holds true for the other graph algorithms considered in this chapter in order to maintain maximum clarity and flexibility.

*graph searching algorithms*

Section 8.15 presents a method for discovering a *topological ordering* of the vertices in a graph. Suppose that the edges in a graph define an ordering between pairs of vertices. For example, if vertices represent college courses, and vertices A and B are two such courses, then the edge from A to B might express the relationship that course A is a *prerequisite* for taking course B. In this case, a topological ordering of the courses is simply a list of the courses in which the prerequisites for every course X are listed before X itself is listed.

*topological ordering*

## 8.2   Trees—Basic Concepts and Terminology

### LEARNING OBJECTIVES

1. To learn how to refer to various parts of trees.
2. To learn about some relationships that are always true in trees.

Let's begin by reviewing some of the basic concepts and terminology related to trees, starting with "basic tree anatomy." Figure 8.1 illustrates a tree.

Tree diagrams are formed from nodes and line segments. The line segments are called either *edges* or *branches*. We draw on three sources of terminology when talking about trees: (1) *family relationships* (such as parents or children), (2) *geometric relationships* (such as left and right, or bottom and top), and (3) *biological names* for parts of trees (such as roots and leaves).

*three sources of tree terminology*

For example, in Fig. 8.1, node R is the *root* node of the tree. If we travel downward along the edges that start at R, we arrive at R's two *children*, which are the nodes S and T. Traveling upward in the tree, we say that node R is the *parent* of node S. The *descendants* of a node consist of the nodes that can be reached by traveling down-

*roots, children, and descendants*

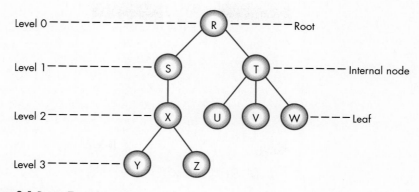

**Figure 8.1** Basic Tree Anatomy

ward along any path starting at the node. For example, the descendants of node S are the nodes X, Y, and Z.

ancestors and parents

If you start at a node in the tree and travel upward along the path toward the root, you encounter the *ancestors* of the node. For example, the ancestors of node Y are nodes X, S, and R. Of these ancestors, only X is the *parent* of node Y.

leaves

The *leaves* of the tree are the nodes that have no children. In Fig. 8.1, the leaves are the five nodes: Y, Z, U, V, and W. If a node has children, it is called an *internal node*. For example, node T is an internal node, since it has three children.

levels

The nodes of a tree can be arranged into numbered *levels*. The topmost level, which contains only the root node, is called *level 0*. *Level 1* contains all the children of the root node. *Level 2* consists of the grandchildren of the root node. In general, any node, N, can be reached by traveling downward along a path, $p$, starting at the root. If path $p$ has $n$ edges in it, then node N is said to belong to level $n$, and the *length* of path $p$ is said to be $n$. For example, in Fig. 8.1, if we start at the root, R, and travel downward to node X, we travel along a path with two edges in it (consisting of the edge from R to S and the edge from S to X). Consequently, we have traveled over a path of length 2, and node X is therefore on level 2.

In a tree, there is exactly one path from the root R to each descendant of R. (If there is *more than one path* from the root to some node N, then you do not have a tree. In particular, diagrams containing paths that are cycles are not tree diagrams, and diagrams having two paths that separate at a node and then come back together later at some other node are also not tree diagrams.)

geometric terms

We will use *geometric terms* to refer to parts of trees, also. For example, we could talk about the bottommost row of nodes in the tree in Fig. 8.1. This would refer to the leaves Y and Z at level 3 of the tree. We could also say that U is the *left child* of T, W is the *right child* of T, and V is the *middle child* of T.

Geometrically speaking, the root of a tree is its *topmost* node. It is traditional in computer science to draw diagrams of trees *upside-down*, with the root of a tree at the top and with the leaves of the tree at the bottom. Many algorithms process the nodes of a tree in an order that starts at the root and progresses to additional nodes on the lower levels. By drawing trees with their roots at the top and the descendants of the root lower down on the page, the normal order of reading of a page (from top to bottom) reflects the order in which nodes get processed in these algorithms. Consequently, the upside-down way of drawing trees makes sense in connection with the consideration of these kinds of tree-processing algorithms.

In some situations, it is convenient to define and use the *empty tree*—a tree having no nodes and no edges.

## 8.2 REVIEW QUESTIONS

1. Referring to Fig. 8.1, give a list of each of the following: (a) the ancestors of node U, (b) the children of node S, (c) the descendants of node S, (d) the parent of node V.
2. How many nodes in a tree have no ancestors?
3. What is the name for a node in a tree that has no descendants?
4. Given a particular node N in a tree, how many paths connect the root node of the tree to node N?

## 8.2 EXERCISES

1. Count the number of edges, *e*, and the number of nodes, *n*, in the tree in Fig. 8.1. Draw some other trees, and count their nodes and edges. Is there a relationship that you notice between the number of nodes and the number of edges? Can you prove that this relationship is always true for any tree, T?
2. Suppose each node in a tree T has either exactly two children or has no children. In other words, each node is either a leaf or it has exactly two *nonempty* children. We call such a tree a *full binary tree*. What is the relationship between the number of leaves and the number of internal nodes in tree T? Prove that this relationship holds true for any full binary tree.

## 8.3 Binary Trees

### LEARNING OBJECTIVES

1. To become familiar with the definition of binary trees.
2. To learn the definition of extended and complete binary trees.
3. To prepare for the discussion of binary tree representations and binary tree operations in the remainder of the chapter.

A *binary tree* is a tree in which each node has exactly two children. Either or both of these children is permitted to be *empty*. If a node has two empty chil-

3. To learn the conditions for a node being a root, a leaf, and an internal node in this representation.

Suppose we take a complete binary tree such as the one shown in Fig. 8.5 and number the nodes level-by-level. That is, we start at the topmost level and number the root node, H, as node number 1. Then we move down to the next level containing the children, D and K, of the root node, and we number these nodes from left to right, as nodes 2 and 3. On the next level, we number the nodes B, F, J, and L, from left to right as nodes 4, 5, 6, and 7. Finally, on the bottom row, we number the nodes A, C, E, G, and I as nodes 8 through 12.

*Note*: A tree need not be a binary tree to have its nodes numbered level-by-level in this fashion, since we can always number the nodes of a tree level-by-level from top to bottom, and left to right within each level. The ordering of nodes produced by this process is called the *level order* of the nodes.

Let's now create an array A[0:12] containing the information in the nodes of the binary tree of Fig. 8.5 in level order. Figure 8.6 (on p. 252) shows such an array, A, which is called the *contiguous sequential representation* of the complete binary tree of Fig. 8.5. (The word "contiguous" means "touching" and means that there are no "gaps" between the items in the sequential representation in the array A. Also A[0] remains empty.)

To travel around the binary tree in the contiguous sequential representation, we can use some arithmetic operations on the array index $i$, in A[$i$], as indicated in Table 8.7 (on p. 252). In this table we consider a more general case in which we are dealing only with array positions A[1:$n$] containing information for a complete binary tree of $n$ nodes.

Now let's apply some of the relationships in Table 8.7 to the array in Fig. 8.6 containing the sequential representation of the complete binary tree in Fig. 8.5. For example, what is the parent of node C? Since node C == A[9] in the array A of Fig. 8.6, its parent is located at A[9/2] == A[4]. Since A[4] == B, the parent of C is B. Referring to Fig. 8.5, we see that the parent of node C is also B.

Now let's calculate the right child of node F. Since F == A[5], its right child is located at A[2*5 + 1] == A[11], where A[11] contains G. We see that G is the right child of node F in the tree of Fig. 8.5 also. Similarly, the left child of F is located at A[2*5] == A[10], where A[10] contains E.

*(margin notes)*
numbering nodes level-by-level

level order

the contiguous sequential representation

locating parents

locating children

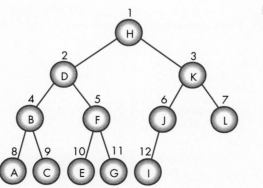

**Figure 8.5** A Complete Binary Tree with Numbered Nodes

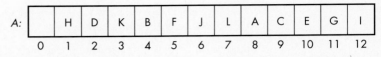

**Figure 8.6** Sequential Representation of a Complete Binary Tree (with A[0] Empty)

**Table 8.7** How to Find Nodes in a Contiguous Sequential Representation of a Complete Binary Tree, A[1:n]

| To Find: | Use: | Provided: |
|---|---|---|
| The left child of A[i] | A[2 i] | $2 i \leq n$ |
| The right child of A[i] | A[2 i + 1] | $2 i + 1 \leq n$ |
| The parent of A[i] | A[i / 2] | $i > 1$ |
| The root | A[1] | A is nonempty |
| Whether A[i] is a leaf | true | $2 i > n$ |

*the leaf test*

Let's now look at the test for whether node A[i] is a leaf. Table 8.7 asserts that A[i] is a leaf if and only if $2*i > n$. In Fig. 8.6 there are 12 nonempty nodes in the array A, so that n == 12. Consequently, A[i] is a leaf if and only if $2*i > 12$, which is the same as the condition $i > 6$. This implies that nodes A[7:12] must be leaves, and that nodes A[1:6] must be internal nodes. Checking this assertion against the tree in Fig. 8.5, we see that nodes A[7] through A[12] are the leaves.

## 8.4 REVIEW QUESTIONS

1. What is the contiguous sequential representation of a complete binary tree? How is it defined mathematically?
2. How do you find the parent of node A[i] in the contiguous sequential representation of a binary tree? What node has no parent?
3. How do you find the left child of node A[i] in the contiguous sequential representation of a binary tree? What nodes have no left children?
4. How do you find the right child of node A[i] in the contiguous sequential representation of a binary tree? What nodes have no right children?

## 8.4 EXERCISES

1. Why is it the case that A[i] is a leaf in a complete binary tree of n nodes, if and only if $2 i > n$?
2. Given that there are n nodes in a complete binary tree, T, how many levels does T have as a function of n?
3. On what level of a complete binary tree T does node A[i] reside?

## 8.5 An Application—Heaps and Priority Queues

### LEARNING OBJECTIVES

1. To learn how to represent a heap using a contiguous sequential representation.
2. To learn how heaps can serve as efficient representations for priority queues.
3. To discover some important mathematical properties of heaps that will be used later.

*a new meaning for the word "heap"*

In Chapter 7, we used the word *heap* to refer to a region of memory organized to provide dynamic memory allocation. In this section, we will discuss a separate, new meaning for the word heap, which refers to a complete binary tree with values at its nodes arranged in a certain way.

> A **heap** is a complete binary tree with values stored in its nodes such that no child has a value greater than the value of its parent.

*using heaps to represent priority queues*

Figure 8.8 shows a diagram of a heap with integer values stored in its nodes. Note that these integers decrease in value along any path, starting at the root and traveling downward. A heap provides a representation for a *priority queue*. Recall from Section 5.2 that a priority queue was defined as an ADT having the property that items are removed in the order of highest-to-lowest priority, regardless of the order in which they were inserted.

If a heap is used to represent a priority queue, it is easy to find the item of highest priority, since it sits at the root of the tree. (Exercise 8.5.1 asks you to prove this fact by considering whether values would decrease along all paths if the largest value resided in some node other than the root.) However, if we remove the value at the root, we must restructure the tree to be a heap again.

**Figure 8.8** An Example of a Heap

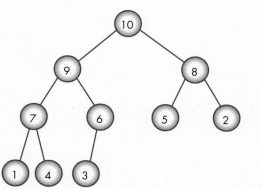

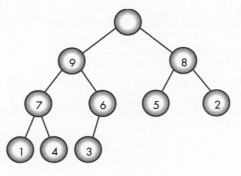

**Figure 8.9** An Arrangement of Nodes with No Root Value

deleting the last leaf in
level order

In Fig. 8.8, suppose we remove the largest value, 10, from the root node of the heap. This produces the arrangement of nodes in Fig. 8.9 that is not a heap since the root node has no value. To convert Fig. 8.9 back into a heap again, we use the following process. First, we delete the rightmost leaf on the bottom row, which is the node containing the value 3. (*Note:* The rightmost leaf on the bottom row is the *last leaf in level order*.) Then we place this deleted node's value, 3, into the root node. This gives the diagram in Fig. 8.10.

restoring the heap property

Next, we restore the heap property among the remaining nodes in Fig. 8.10 by starting at the root node and repeatedly exchanging its value with the *larger* of the values of its children, until no more exchanges are possible. Let's trace how this works.

In Fig. 8.10, starting at the root node with value 3, we see that the left and right children of the root have the values 9 and 8, respectively. We exchange the value 3 in the root node with the value 9 in the left child of the root, since 9 is the *larger* value among the two values (8 and 9) of the two children of the root. This yields the tree in Fig. 8.11, which still fails to be a heap since the node containing 3 has two children containing larger values 7 and 6. So we again exchange the value 3 with the larger of the children's values, 7, yielding the tree in Fig. 8.12.

Again, since the node containing 3 has a right child with a larger value, 4, we do not have a heap, so we make a final exchange of 3 and 4, which yields the tree in Fig. 8.13. Although the process illustrated in this example moved the value 3 from the root in Fig. 8.10 all the way down to a leaf in Fig. 8.13, it is not always the case that a

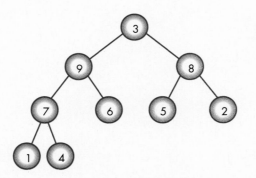

**Figure 8.10** Tree with Root Value Replaced and Last Leaf Deleted

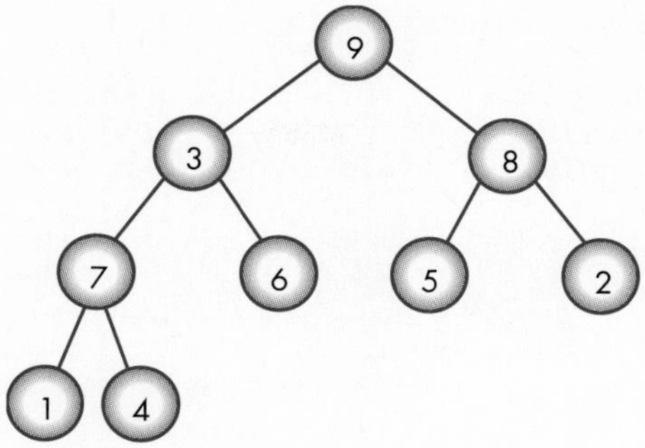

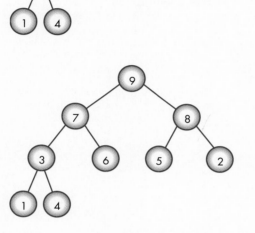

**Figure 8.11** Tree with Root Value Exchanged with Larger Child Value

**Figure 8.12** Intermediate Tree That Is Not Yet a Heap

new value in the root will move all the way into a leaf position. In general, the downward-moving value will stop at the first internal node having children with smaller values than the downward moving value.

To formulate the reheapifying process as a general procedure, suppose that $H$ is a heap, that $L$ is the last node of $H$ in level order, and that node $L$ contains the value $V$. (Again note: The last leaf in level order is the same as the rightmost leaf on the bottom row of $H$.) We must replace the value at the root of $H$ with value $V$, we must then delete node $L$, and we must finally reheapify $H$ to restore its heap property. Program Strategy 8.14 gives a sketch of the general process for doing this.

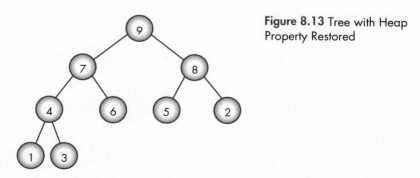

**Figure 8.13** Tree with Heap Property Restored

```
   |    ItemType remove(Heap H)  {
   |
   |          NodeType    L;               // let L be the last node of H in level order
   |          NodeType    R;               // R is used to refer to the root node of H
 5 |          ItemType    itemToRemove;        // temporarily stores item to remove
   |
   |          if  (H is not empty)  {
   |
   |                // remove the highest priority item which is stored in
10 |                // H's root node, R
   |                    itemToRemove = (the value stored in the root node, R, of H);
   |
   |                // move L's value into the root of H, and delete L
   |                    (R's value) = (the value in leaf L);
15 |                    (delete node L);
   |
   |                // reheapify the values in the remaining nodes of H starting at
   |                // the root, R, by applying the algorithm in Program Strategy 8.15
   |                // to the root node, R, in heap H
20 |                    if  (H is not empty)  {
   |                          (reheapify the heap H starting at node R);
   |                    }
   |
   |                return (itemToRemove);
25 |          }
   |    }
```

**Program Strategy 8.14** Removing an Item from a Heap

```
   |    void (reheapify the heap H starting at node N)  {
   |
   |          NodeType    N, M;
   |          ItemType    V1,V2;
 5 |
   |
   |          (let V1 refer to N's value)
   |
   |          while (node N still has children)  {
10 |
   |                (let M be the child of node N having the larger value, V2)
   |
   |                if ( V1 ≥ V2 ) {
   |                      return;
15 |                } else {
   |                      (exchange the values in nodes N and M);
   |                      (let N refer to node M and let V1 refer to N's value);
   |                }
   |
20 |          }
   |
   |    }
```

**Program Strategy 8.15** Reheapifying a Heap Starting at Node N

```
 |   void heapify(Heap H)  {
 |
 |       NodeType  N;
 |
5 |       for (N = the internal nodes of H in reverse level-order)  {
 |
 |           (reheapify the heap H starting at node N);
 |
 |       }
10 |
 |   }
```

**Program Strategy 8.16** Heapifying a Complete Binary Tree

The process for restoring the heap property by repeatedly exchanging the value at the root with the larger of its children's values, until no more exchanges are possible, is sketched in Program Strategy 8.15.

To organize the values in the nodes of an initially unorganized complete binary tree, $H$, into a heap, we can apply Program Strategy 8.15 to each of the internal nodes of $H$ in reverse level order. Program Strategy 8.16 sketches the method for doing this.

Let's now consider an example of an initial configuration of nodes and values in a complete binary tree that is not a heap. Figure 8.17 illustrates such an initial configuration.

We now illustrate how to apply the process of Program Strategy 8.16 to the configuration of nodes and values in Fig. 8.17, in order to convert it into a heap. We enumerate the internal nodes of Fig. 8.17 in reverse level order. The internal nodes in level order are the nodes containing the values 2, 4, 5, 7, and 3. Therefore, in reverse level order, the internal nodes are the nodes containing the values 3, 7, 5, 4, and 2.

Hence we start with the subtree in Fig. 8.17 rooted at the node containing 3. Since this node has a child containing a larger value 6, we exchange the 3 and the 6. performing exchanges   Let's denote this exchange by the notation $(3 \leftrightarrow 6)$. We next consider the subtree rooted at 7, and we exchange 7 with the larger of the values of its children, 9, using the exchange $(7 \leftrightarrow 9)$. We then move up to the right end of the row above to consid-

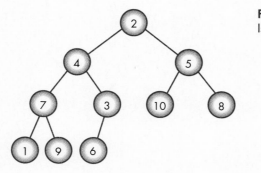

**Figure 8.17** An Initial Complete Tree That Is Not a Heap

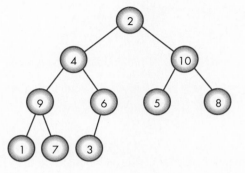

**Figure 8.18** The Configuration After Three Exchanges

er the node containing 5. We exchange 5 with the larger of its children's values, 10, using the exchange (5 ↔ 10). Figure 8.18 illustrates the composite effect of these three exchanges (3 ↔ 6), (7 ↔ 9), and (5 ↔ 10).

The next node to be considered in reverse level order contains the value 4. After exchanging 4 with the larger of its children's values, 9, using the exchange (4 ↔ 9), we must continue exchanging 4 with 7, using (4 ↔ 7) in order to reheapify the subtree rooted originally at the node containing 4. This yields the tree of Fig. 8.19.

Finally, we consider the root node, containing 2, which is the last node in reverse level order. Figure 8.19 requires only two more exchanges (2 ↔ 10) and (2 ↔ 8) to convert it to a heap. The heap that results is identical to the one we started with earlier in Fig. 8.8 (before removing the root value 10 and reheapifying).

## Converting to the Sequential Representation

In the previous discussion, we performed operations on the nodes of binary trees without committing ourselves to a particular underlying tree representation, such as a sequential representation or a linked representation. Let's now see what happens when we represent heaps by the contiguous sequential representation of complete binary trees. A useful way to illustrate this is to provide a third implementation for

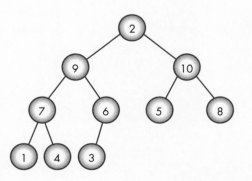

**Figure 8.19** Almost Final Tree During Conversion to a Heap

the **PriorityQueue** class that was originally introduced in Section 5.3 of Chapter 5. (Recall that two other implementations for priority queues were presented in Section 5.3. These implementations used representations based on sorted linked lists and on unordered arrays, respectively.)

Program 8.20 uses item arrays (with empty zeroth items) to implement heaps representing priority queues. In particular, Program 8.20 uses the operations and relationships given in Table 8.7 to represent heaps in item arrays. The **PriorityQueue** class defined in Program 8.20 can be substituted in a completely plug-compatible manner for the other **PriorityQueue** class implementations used in Sections 5.3 and 5.4. For example, when this substitution is performed on Program 5.3, which defined a method for sorting using priority queues, a version of *heapsort* is obtained.

*obtaining a version of heapsort*

Heapsort is a sorting method that first converts an array of items to be sorted into a heap (using the **heapify** process sketched in Program Strategy 8.16), and then, treating the heap as a priority queue, removes items from the heap one by one (using the algorithm in the **remove** method of Program 8.20) to arrange them in sorted order. While the variations of priority queue sorting studied in Section 5.3 worked in time $O(n^2)$, it can be shown that heapsort does better, by working in time $O(n \log n)$. The details of heapsort are given in Chapter 10, which covers sorting.

```
  |  class PriorityQueue {
  |
  |      private int    count;              // the number of items in the priority queue
  |      private int    capacity;           // the number of available array positions
5 |      private int    capacityIncrement;     // the amount to increase the capacity
  |                                                // during array expansion
  |      private ComparisonKey[ ] itemArray;        // the array that holds PQ items
  |
  |      // here, we need to define our own no-arg constructor
10|
  |      public PriorityQueue() {              // holds capacity–1 items because
  |          count = 0;                    // itemArray[0] is always empty and unused
  |          capacity = 16;
  |          capacityIncrement = 8;
15|          itemArray = new ComparisonKey[capacity];
  |      }
  |
  |
  |      /* the methods implementing the Priority Queue ADT are now defined */
20|
  |  /*----------------*/
  |
  |      public int size( ) {               // the size( ) method returns the number
  |          return count;                  // of items in the priority queue
25|      }
  |
  |  /*----------------*/
  |
```

**Program 8.20** The Heap Implementation of the Priority Queue Class (*continued*)

Program 8.20 The Heap Implementation of the Priority Queue Class (*continued*)

```
        public void insert(ComparisonKey newItem) {
30

            // if the itemArray does not have enough capacity,
            // expand the itemArray by the capacityIncrement

            if (count == capacity − 1) {
40              capacity += capacityIncrement;
                ComparisonKey[ ] tempArray = new ComparisonKey[capacity];
                for (int i = 1; i <= count; i++) {
                    tempArray[i] = itemArray[i];
                }
45              itemArray = tempArray;
            }


            // increase the priority queue's count by one and insert the newItem
50          // at the end of the current priority queue item sequence

            count++;
            int childLoc = count;
            int parentLoc = childLoc/2;
55
            while (parentLoc != 0) {                      // while a parent still exists

                if (newItem.compareTo(itemArray[parentLoc]) <= 0 ) {
                    itemArray[childLoc] = newItem;        // store the newItem
60                  return;                               // and return
                } else {
                    itemArray[childLoc] = itemArray[parentLoc];
                    childLoc = parentLoc;
                    parentLoc = childLoc/2;
65              }

            }

            itemArray[childLoc] = newItem;     // put newItem in final resting place
70
        }//end insert( )

        /*----------------*/

75      public ComparisonKey remove() {

            if (count == 0) {                        // if the priority queue is empty, return null
                return null;
            } else {                                 // otherwise, return the root's item and reheapify
80
                // declarations
                int currentLoc;                          // location currently being examined
                int childLoc;                            // a child of currentLoc
                ComparisonKey itemToPlace;               // an item value to relocate
85              ComparisonKey itemToReturn;              // removed item value to return
```

(*continued*)

Program 8.20 The Heap Implementation of the Priority Queue Class (*continued*)

```
                    // initializations
                        itemToReturn = itemArray[1];              // save root item to return later
                        itemToPlace = itemArray[count- -];            // last leaf's item
                        currentLoc = 1;                          // currentLoc starts at root
 90                     childLoc = 2*currentLoc;           // childLoc starts at root's left child

                        while (childLoc <= count) {                // while a child still exists

                            // set childLoc to larger child of currentLoc
 95                         if (childLoc < count) {                  // if right child exists
                                if (itemArray[childLoc+1].compareTo(itemArray[childLoc])>0)
                                    childLoc++;
                            }

100                         // if the item at childLoc is larger than itemToPlace
                            // move this larger item into currentLoc, and move
                            // currentLoc down
                            if (itemArray[childLoc].compareTo(itemToPlace) > 0 ) {
                                itemArray[currentLoc] = itemArray[childLoc];
105                             currentLoc = childLoc;
                                childLoc = 2*currentLoc;
                            } else {
                                itemArray[currentLoc] = itemToPlace;
                                return itemToReturn;
110                         }
                        }//end while

                        // final placement of itemToPlace
                        itemArray[currentLoc] = itemToPlace;
115
                        // return the item originally at the root
                        return itemToReturn;

                    }//end if
120
                }//end remove( )

                /*-----------------*/

            }// end PriorityQueue class
```

It is worth mentioning that a subtle optimization was used in implementing the **remove** method in Program 8.20—one that was not used in Program Strategy 8.14 for removing an item from a heap. You might have noticed, while studying the examples in Figs. 8.8 through 8.13, which show how to restore the heap property

**a subtle optimization**

after removing the item at the root, that the value 3 was repeatedly exchanged with the larger values 9, 7, and 4 in child nodes as the value 3 was moved downward toward its final resting place. Instead of doing pairwise exchanges of values to accomplish this motion, we could instead have moved the values 9, 7, and 4 upward, while making a hole at the bottom for the final resting place in which to store 3. The

| Priority Queue Operation | Heap Representation | Sorted List Representation | Unsorted Array Representation |
|---|---|---|---|
| Organize a priority queue | $O(n)$ | $O(n^2)$ | $O(1)$ |
| Remove highest priority item | $O(\log n)$ | $O(1)$ | $O(n)$ |
| Insert a new item | $O(\log n)$ | $O(n)$ | $O(1)$ |

**Table 8.21** Comparing Running Times of Priority Queue Operations for Three Representations

**remove** method in Program 8.20 uses this more efficient latter strategy (which amounts to a cyclical shift) instead of using less efficient pairwise exchanges. The **insert** method in Program 8.20 uses a similar strategy for the upward motion of a new item being inserted in a heap.

### Some Facts About the Performance of Heap Operations

Suppose we have a heap containing $n$ items. It is useful to know how much time it takes to establish the heap property in the sequential heap representation, starting with an initially unorganized array of $n$ items, and how much time it takes to insert and remove heap items.

It can be shown that inserting and removing items in a heap each takes $O(\log n)$ time. Also, it is known that converting an unorganized array of $n$ items into a heap (using the process given in Program Strategy 8.16) takes time $O(n)$. This is significant. It implies that we can heapify an array of values in *linear time*, using the contiguous sequential representation of complete binary trees.

Let's combine these facts with some facts that are known about the running times of priority queue operations for the other two representations we studied in Section 5.3. The results are presented as Table 8.21. We see that the heap representation for a priority queue does not have the worst running time in any row of the table. Moreover, since a heap can be initialized in linear time and subsequently can accommodate insertions and deletions in logarithmic time, it is a potentially superior representation for priority queues, possessing good performance characteristics. The facts summarized here will come in handy in Chapter 10 when we comment on how well **HeapSort** performs.

## 8.5 REVIEW QUESTIONS

1. Give the definition of a heap as it is used in this section (not as it is discussed in Chapter 7 in connection with dynamic memory allocation).
2. How can a heap be used to represent a priority queue? Discuss how to perform the operations of item insertion and removal in heaps used to represent priority queues.

3. How do you go about organizing the items in an initially unorganized complete binary tree into a heap? How long does it take to do this efficiently?
4. How long does it take to insert and remove items from a heap containing $n$ items?

## 8.5 EXERCISES

1. Prove that if $H$ is a heap, its largest value must be found at the root of $H$. [*Hint:* Consider what would happen if the largest value were in some node, $N$, other than the root. In this case $N$'s parent would have a smaller value than $N$'s value. Could the heap property then hold true for $H$?]
2. Let $H$ be a heap with $n$ nodes in it. How many of these nodes are internal nodes? How many are leaf nodes?
3. Give a Java implementation of Program Strategy 8.16 as it applies to the contiguous sequential representation of heaps. Apply the for-statement on lines 5:9 of Program Strategy 8.16 only to the internal nodes of the array containing the heap items, using a decreasing sequence of values ( for ( N = U; N >= 1; N–– ) ) whose initial value U is determined by the answer to Exercise 2.
4. Demonstrate that Program 8.20 can be used interchangeably to implement priority queues by invoking it in Program 5.3 and executing Program 5.3 to perform priority queue sorting.
5. Change the priority queue item types from integers to strings (by using Program 5.7 to define the ComparisonKey interface and Program 5.9 to define string item types implementing the ComparisonKey interface). Then use the heap representation of the PriorityQueue class in Program 8.20 to run Program 5.10 (which sorts string items using priority queues).
6. Using the heap representation of priority queues, measure the running times for item insertion and removal using arrays of different sizes, and compare these times to the corresponding running times for the use of the sorted list and unsorted array representations of priority queues. What do you conclude about the relative efficiencies of these three representations for this task?

## 8.6   Traversing Binary Trees

### LEARNING OBJECTIVES

1. To learn about four types of traversal orders commonly applied to the nodes of binary trees.
2. To understand how to write programs to perform these traversals on the linked representation of binary trees.
3. To learn how stacks and queues can be used to perform nonrecursive traversals of linked binary tree representations.

*Expression trees* are binary trees used to represent algebraic expressions formed with binary operators. For example, Fig. 8.22 gives the expression tree corresponding to the algebraic expression, $(b^2 - 4 * a * c) / (2 * a)$.

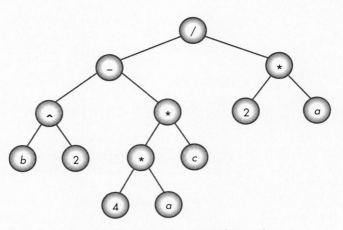

**Figure 8.22** The Expression Tree for $(b^{\wedge}2 - 4 * a * c) / (2 * a)$

In Fig. 8.22, we have used the caret operator ($\wedge$) to indicate exponentiation (meaning that $b^{\wedge}2$ stands for $b^2$), and we have assumed that the normal operator precedence rules for algebraic expressions have been used. In particular, in the absence of parentheses to indicate otherwise, we assume exponentiation ($\wedge$) is performed before multiplication and division (* and /), which are, in turn, performed before addition and subtraction (+ and −). Moreover, among operators of equal precedence, such as (+ and −) or (* and /), we assume association is to the left, so that $4 * a * c$ means $((4 * a) * c)$. Here, we performed the left multiplication $(4 * a)$ first. Similarly, had we not put parentheses around the denominator $(2 * a)$ to indicate multiplication was to be performed with 2 and $a$, and had we casually written: $(b^{\wedge}2 - 4 * a * c) / 2 * a$, it would have signified the same as $((b^{\wedge}2 - 4 * a * c) / 2) * a$, since, by the left association rule, any expression of the form $x / y * z$ signifies, $((x / y) * z)$, and not $(x / (y * z))$.

*using operator precedence rules to form expression trees*

Using various parsing algorithms, it is possible to read in an algebraic expression expressed in linear form as a string of characters, and to parse the expression to determine the boundaries of its various subexpressions according to the rules of operator precedence. An intermediate expression representation, called a parse tree, can then be constructed to represent the results of parsing the input expression. An expression tree is one of the forms that such a parse tree could take. Such expression trees can then be converted into assembly code by code generators, or they can be converted to postfix instructions for interpretation by postfix interpreters.

In this section, we explore some traversal techniques for visiting the nodes of a binary tree, which can be used, among other purposes, for conversion of expression trees into postfix or prefix operation code sequences.

A traversal of a tree is a process that visits each node in the tree exactly once in some particular order. Three popular traversal orders for binary trees are *PreOrder*, *InOrder*, and *PostOrder*. Table 8.24 defines how to traverse the nodes of a binary tree in each of these three orders. Let's assume that each node of an expression tree con-

*three traversal orders*

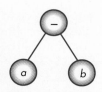

**Figure 8.23** Expression Tree for (a − b)

tains a single character, and that what it means to *visit a node* in such a tree is to print the character contained in that node.

Let's take a simple case first. Consider the expression tree in Fig. 8.23 for the expression (a − b).

If we perform the three traversals of Table 8.24 on the expression tree in Fig. 8.23, we get the following results:

| | |
|---|---|
| PreOrder: | − a b |
| InOrder: | a − b |
| PostOrder: | a b − |

If we perform the three traversals of Table 8.24 on the somewhat more complicated expression tree of Fig. 8.22, we get the following results:

| | |
|---|---|
| PreOrder: | / − ^ b 2 * * 4 a c * 2 a |
| InOrder: | b ^ 2 − 4 * a * c / 2 * a |
| PostOrder: | b 2 ^ 4 a * c * − 2 a * / |

Using the postorder traversal of an expression tree gives us the postfix string representing the original expression. If we have a postfix interpreter, such as the one given in Program 6.10 in Chapter 6, we can evaluate the postfix string to obtain its value.

A common strategy used in early language processors was to parse the input into an expression tree and then to convert the expression tree into a postfix operator expression sequence suitable for subsequent interpretation by a run-time interpreter.

## Traversals Using the Linked Representation of Binary Trees

A convenient representation of binary trees to use in connection with traversal algorithms is the *linked representation* of binary trees. An illustration of this representation was first given in Fig. 3.29 in Section 3.6 of Chapter 3.

To declare the types for tree nodes to use in linked binary tree representations of expression trees, we can provide a Java class definition such as the following:

```
class TreeNode {
    String      info
    TreeNode    llink;
    TreeNode    rlink;
}
```

| PreOrder | InOrder | PostOrder |
|---|---|---|
| Visit the root<br>Traverse left subtree in PreOrder<br>Traverse right subtree in PreOrder | Traverse left subtree in InOrder<br>Visit the root<br>Traverse right subtree in InOrder | Traverse left subtree in PostOrder<br>Traverse right subtree in PostOrder<br>Visit the root |

**Table 8.24** Traversal Orders for Binary Trees

Here, the llink and rlink fields of a **TreeNode** contain pointers to the respective left and right subtrees of a node. If a subtree is empty, its corresponding node pointer is **null**. For example, Fig. 8.25 shows both the expression tree for the expression $(x - y + z)$, and its linked representation using the **TreeNode**s defined above.

It is easy to write a general recursive procedure to perform traversals in the various traversal orders given in Table 8.24, starting with the linked representation of binary trees. We first assume that we have declared three Java **final static int** constants (PRE_ORDER = 1; IN_ORDER =2; and POST_ORDER = 3) giving names for the three traversal orders. We then use a second parameter in the general traversal procedure to specify which traversal order to use. Program 8.26 gives the general recursive procedure for visiting nodes of a linked representation of a binary tree, where the second parameter is a Java **final static int** constant specifying the particular traversal order to be followed.

Using the Stack ADT and using the linked representation of binary trees, we can write nonrecursive traversal procedures in which a stack is used to hold pointers to subtrees awaiting further traversal. For example, Program 8.27 uses a stack to perform an iterative preorder traversal of an expression tree, writing out the symbols in the nodes as it visits each node in preorder.

We can view the stack, S, in Program 8.27 as being used to hold *postponed obligations* for further processing. During the preorder traversal process, when we come to each node, N, we first print the symbol in node N. Next, we stack first the right link of N and then the left link of N. The stack now holds two postponed obligations to process first the left subtree of N and later the right subtree of node N. Since we pushed N's right link first and its left link second, the left link will be processed before the right link (since stacks always use the *last-in-first-out* order of processing).

Now suppose we change the type of container used to hold the postponed obligations for further processing, by using a queue instead of a stack. Suppose that after vis-

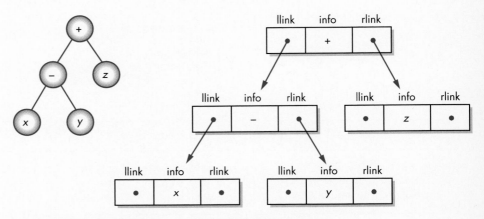

**Figure 8.25** An Expression Tree and Its Linked Representation

```
     |     void traverse(TreeNode T, int traversalOrder) {
     |
     |         /* to visit T's nodes in the order specified by the */
     |         /* traversalOrder parameter */
  5  |
     |         if (T != null) {                                    // if T == null, do nothing
     |
     |             if ( traversalOrder == PRE_ORDER ) {
     |
 10  |                 visit(T);
     |                 traverse(T.llink, PRE_ORDER);
     |                 traverse(T.rlink, PRE_ORDER);
     |
     |             } else if ( traversalOrder == IN_ORDER ) {
 15  |
     |                 traverse(T.llink, IN_ORDER);
     |                 visit(T);
     |                 traverse(T.rlink, IN_ORDER);
     |
 20  |             } else if ( traversalOrder == POST_ORDER ) {
     |
     |                 traverse(T.llink, POST_ORDER);
     |                 traverse(T.rlink, POST_ORDER);
     |                 visit(T);
 25  |             }
     |         }
     |     }
```

**Program 8.26** Generalized Recursive Traversal Method

```
     |     void preOrderTraversal(TreeNode T)  {
     |
     |         Stack  S = new Stack( );              // let S be an initially empty stack
     |         TreeNode  N;                          // N points to nodes during traversal
  5  |
     |         S.push(T);                   // push the pointer T onto the empty stack S
     |
     |         while ( !S.empty( ) ) {
     |
 10  |             N = (TreeNode)S.pop( );           // pop top pointer of S into N
     |
     |             if (N != null) {
     |                 System.out.print(N.info);            // print N's info field
     |                 S.push(N.rlink);              // push the right pointer onto S
 15  |                 S.push(N.llink);              // push the left pointer onto S
     |             }
     |
     |         }
     |     }
```

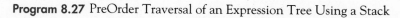

**Program 8.27** PreOrder Traversal of an Expression Tree Using a Stack

```
  |    void levelOrderTraversal(TreeNode T) {
  |
  |        Queue Q = new Queue( );            // let Q be an initially empty queue
  |        TreeNode N;                        // N points to nodes during traversal
5 |
  |        Q.insert(T);                       // insert the pointer T into queue Q
  |
  |        while ( ! Q.empty( ) ) {
  |
10|            N = (TreeNode) Q.remove( );            // remove first pointer of Q
  |                                                   // and put it into N
  |            if (N != null ) {
  |                System.out.print(N.info);              // print N's info field
  |                Q.insert(N.llink)              // insert left pointer on rear of Q
15|                Q.insert(N.rlink)             // insert right pointer on rear of Q
  |            }
  |        }
  |    }
```

**Program 8.28** LevelOrder Binary Tree Traversal Using Queues

iting a node, **N**, and printing its symbol, we insert its left and right links (in that order) into a queue, **Q**. Now **Q** holds postponed obligations to process the left and right subtrees. When we remove pointers from **Q** and process the nonnull ones, we first print the symbols in the nodes referenced by the pointers, and then we insert the left and right links of these nodes on the rear of **Q**. What happens when we do this is that we print the symbols in the nodes of the original tree in level order. Program 8.28 gives an explicit example of this process for printing the symbols in expression trees in level order. For example, the level order traversal of the linked representation of the binary expression tree given in Fig. 8.22 is: $/ - * \wedge * 2\, a\, b\, 2 * c\, 4\, a$.

## 8.6 REVIEW QUESTIONS

1. What are the names for three traversal orders of binary trees given in Table 8.24?
2. How do you define these three traversal orders?
3. Is a level order traversal of a binary tree equivalent to any of the three traversal orders given in Table 8.24? If so, which one is it? If not, why not?
4. Describe how stacks and queues can be used to define nonrecursive binary tree traversals. What different kinds of traversals can be defined naturally using stacks and queues?

## 8.6 EXERCISES

1. Give the PreOrder, InOrder, PostOrder, and LevelOrder traversals of the nodes in the tree of Fig. 8.2.
2. Construct the expression tree whose PostOrder traversal is $a\, 2 \wedge 2\, a * b * - b\, 2 \wedge +$ $a\, b - /$.

3. Write a program to construct an expression tree, given a character string specifying its preorder traversal.
4. Given an expression tree, $T$, write a program to print the infix expression corresponding to $T$ in which parentheses are printed only when required by operator precedence or right associativity among operators of equal precedence. For example, if $T$ is the expression tree corresponding to $((a * (b + c)) * d)$, your program should print: $a * (b + c) * d$. If $T$ is the expression tree corresponding to $((b \wedge 2) / (2*a))$, your program should print: $b^2 / (2*a)$.

## 8.7  Binary Search Trees

### LEARNING OBJECTIVES

1. To learn how to search for a key K in a binary search tree.
2. To learn what shapes binary search trees must take to yield the best and worst search performance.
3. To learn how binary search trees perform in the average case.

**the binary search tree property**

In Chapter 3, we briefly introduced the linked representation of binary trees (see Fig. 3.29). In a *binary search tree*, a node $N$ with key $K$ is inserted so that the keys in the left subtree of $N$ are less than $K$, and such that the keys in the right subtree of $N$ are greater than $K$. To summarize, for each node $N$ in a binary search tree:

Keys in left subtree of $N$ < Key $K$ in node $N$ < Keys in right subtree of $N$.

We assume we are using keys that implement the **ComparisonKey** interface (see Program 5.7) for which it is possible to compare any two keys $K_1$ and $K_2$ using the **compareTo( )** method to determine which one of the following three possible relations holds: $K_1 < K_2$, $K_1 == K_2$, or $K_1 > K_2$. Since numerical and alphabetical order have this property, we can use numerical keys compared in numerical order or string keys compared in alphabetical order.

**how to search for a key**

To search for a key, $K$, in a binary search tree, $T$, we compare $K$ to the key, $K_r$, in the root of $T$. If $K == K_r$, the search terminates successfully. If $K < K_r$, the search continues in the left subtree of $T$, and if $K > K_r$, the search continues in the right subtree of $T$. If $T$ is the empty tree, the search fails.

For example, to search for the key ORD in the binary search tree of Fig. 8.29, we compare the search key ORD to the key ORY in the root. Since ORD < ORY, we continue searching in the left subtree of the root. ORD is next compared to JFK. Since ORD > JFK, the search continues in the right subtree of JFK. Since ORD > MEX, the search continues in the right subtree of MEX. Finally, ORD matches the key in the root of the right subtree of MEX, so the search terminates successfully.

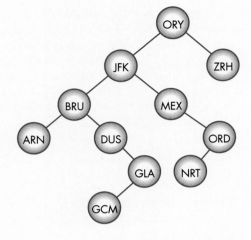

**Figure 8.29** A Binary Search Tree

If we search the tree of Fig. 8.29 for the key DCA (the airport code for Washington, D.C.'s National Airport), the search fails and we conclude DCA is not present, since the search path traced out by the comparisons DCA < ORY, DCA < JFK, DCA > BRU, and DCA < DUS leads to the empty left subtree of DUS. If we insert a new node for DCA as the left subtree of DUS, we obtain a new binary search tree of twelve nodes. In fact, the binary search tree of Fig. 8.29 was built up in this fashion by inserting the airport codes of Table 8.30 in top-to-bottom order, starting with an empty tree. Thus, ORY was considered first and was placed at the root of a new binary search tree. JFK was considered second and was inserted as the new left subtree of ORY. BRU was considered third and was inserted as the new left subtree of JFK. DUS was considered fourth and was inserted as the new right subtree of BRU. ZRH was considered fifth and was inserted as the new right subtree of the root ORY, and so on. This is called the *insertion method*.

Program 8.31 defines an applet that constructs the tree of Fig. 8.29 by inserting the string keys from Table 8.30 in the order given, and then searches first for the node containing ORD and second for a node containing DCA (that doesn't exist). A class called **StringKey** is defined to implement the **ComparisonKey** interface, and the binary search tree class is defined to work on keys belonging to any class that implements the **ComparisonKey** interface.

## Some Known Performance Advantages of Binary Search Trees

Binary search trees are interesting, in part, because they yield important performance advantages. It will turn out that searching for keys takes logarithmic time in a tree of *n* keys, provided the tree is balanced, but that it takes linear time if the tree is deep and skinny.

To get a handle on the issues, we will examine known formulas for the number of comparisons needed to locate keys in a binary search tree in the *best case*, the *worst case*, and the *average case*. We will assume that each of the keys in a binary search tree

*using failed searches to locate insertion points*

*the insertion method*

*performance advantages*

*the best, worst, and average cases*

**Table 8.30** Airport Codes Used to Construct Fig. 8.29

| 1. | ORY | Orly Field, Paris, France |
| 2. | JFK | Kennedy Airport, New York |
| 3. | BRU | Brussels, Belgium |
| 4. | DUS | Düsseldorf, Germany |
| 5. | ZRH | Zürich, Switzerland |
| 6. | MEX | Mexico City, Mexico |
| 7. | ORD | O'Hare, Chicago, Illinois |
| 8. | NRT | Narita Airport, Tokyo, Japan |
| 9. | ARN | Stockholm, Sweden |
| 10. | GLA | Glasgow, Scotland |
| 11. | GCM | Grand Cayman, Cayman Islands |

is equally likely to be chosen for use in a successful search. Furthermore, we will assume that the binary trees used to characterize the "average" binary search tree of $n$ nodes were chosen with equal likelihood from the set of all trees constructed using the insertion method, by inserting keys $K_1, K_2, \ldots , K_n$ in each of their possible different orders.

counting comparisons

Now suppose we want to count the comparisons used by a binary tree searching program. The work needed to find a particular key, $K$, in a binary search tree, $T$, could be measured by counting the number of comparisons needed to locate $K$ in $T$. If $K$ is located at level $l$ in $T$, the number of comparisons is just $C = l + 1$. (*Recall*: The level $l$ containing key $K$ is the length of the path from the root of tree $T$ to the node containing $K$. For example, the level $l$ containing the key ORD in Fig. 8.29 is $l = 3$, since the length of the path from the root node ORY to the node containing ORD is 3. Also recall that length of a path is the number of edges in it. There are three separate edges in the path from ORY to ORD in Fig. 8.29.) Accordingly, $C = 4$ comparisons are needed to find ORD in Fig. 8.29, since substituting $l = 3$ in the formula $C = l + 1$ yields $4 = 3 + 1$.

the internal path length

What these observations reveal is that the length, $l$, of the path from the root to a given node, $N$, provides a number from which we can calculate the actual number of comparisons used. If we are trying to calculate the *average* number of comparisons used to locate a key, $K$, in binary search tree $T$, (where keys are chosen with equal likelihood), it is convenient to define a quantity, $I$, called the *internal path length* of the tree $T$. The internal path length is just the sum of all of the path lengths to the individual

```
 |  import java.io.*;
 |  import java.applet.Applet;
 |
 |  public class BinaryTreeSearch extends Applet {
5 |
 |      // construct the binary search tree of Fig. 8.29, then search for ORD and DCA
```

**Program 8.31** Constructing and Searching a Binary Search Tree (*continued*)

Program 8.31  Constructing and Searching a Binary Search Tree *(continued)*

```
     |    public void init( ) {
     |
     |        // begin by constructing an empty binary search tree
  10 |            BinarySearchTree T = new BinarySearchTree( );        // T is initially empty
     |
     |        // then use the insertion method to insert the keys of Table 8.30
     |            T.insert("ORY");                    // "ORY" is the key in the root of tree T
     |            T.insert("JFK");
  15 |            T.insert("BRU");                    // insert the remaining keys into T in
     |            T.insert("DUS");                    // the order given by Table 8.30
     |            T.insert("ZRH");
     |            T.insert("MEX");
     |            T.insert("ORD");
  20 |            T.insert("NRT");
     |            T.insert("ARN");
     |            T.insert("GLA");
     |            T.insert("GCM");
     |
  25 |        // print out the tree that was constructed
     |            System.out.println("The tree of Fig. 8.29 has been constructed and is:");
     |            T.print( );
     |            System.out.println( );
     |
  30 |        // search for the node with key "ORD"
     |            System.out.println("We now search for the node with key \"ORD\"");
     |            TreeNode N = T.find("ORD");
     |            System.out.println("Key of node that was found = " + N.key);
     |            System.out.println( );
  35 |
     |        // now search for a key that is not in the tree
     |            System.out.println("We now search for the node with key \"DCA\"");
     |            TreeNode P = T.find("DCA");
     |            if (P != null) {
  40 |                System.out.println("Key of node that was found = " + P.key);
     |            } else {
     |                System.out.println("Node that was found = null");
     |            }
     |            System.out.println( );
  45 |
     |    }// end init( )
     |
     | }// end BinaryTreeSearch applet
     |
  50 | /*------------------------------------------------------------*/
     |
     |    class TreeNode {                            // define the TreeNode class
     |        ComparisonKey      key;
     |        TreeNode           llink;
  55 |        TreeNode           rlink;
     |    }
     |
     | /*------------------------------------------------------------*/
```

*(continued)*

Program 8.31  Constructing and Searching a Binary Search Tree *(continued)*

```
      class BinarySearchTree {
60
        // there is one private data field in a BinarySearchTree that holds a
        // pointer to the root node of the binary search tree (or holds null for
        // an empty tree)

65        private TreeNode rootNode;

        // the various methods of the BinarySearchTree class follow:

        /*------------*/
70
        /** this private auxiliary method is used by the insert method */

        private TreeNode insertKey(TreeNode T, ComparisonKey K) {

75          if (T == null) {
                TreeNode N = new TreeNode( );         // construct a new TreeNode
                N.key = K;                                    // set its key to K
                return N;                                     // and return it
            } else {
80              if ( K.compareTo(T.key) < 0 ) {       // if K is less than T's key then
                    T.llink = insertKey(T.llink, K);      // insert K in T's left subtree
                    return T;
                } else {
                    T.rlink = insertKey(T.rlink, K);      // otherwise, insert K in T's
85                  return T;                                  // right subtree
                }
            }

        }//end insertKey( )
90
        /*------------*/

        /** this method inserts a new node containing key K into the tree */

95      void insert(ComparisonKey K) {

            // use the recursive auxiliary method insertKey
            // to do the actual work of insertion
                rootNode = insertKey(rootNode,K);
100
        }//end insert( )

        /*------------*/

105     /** this is an overloaded version of insert( ) that takes a String argument */

        void insert(String K) {
            rootNode = insertKey(rootNode,new StringKey(K));
        }//end insert( )
```

*(continued)*

Program 8.31  Constructing and Searching a Binary Search Tree *(continued)*

```
      |    /*------------*/
      |
      |      /** the find( ) method returns a pointer to the TreeNode containing */
      |      /** key K. Otherwise, it returns null if K is not in the tree */
115   |
      |      TreeNode find(ComparisonKey K) {
      |
      |        TreeNode T = rootNode;
      |        int result;
120   |
      |        while (T != null) {
      |            if ( (result = K.compareTo(T.key)) < 0 ) {
      |                T = T.llink;
      |            } else if (result == 0) {
125   |                return T;
      |            } else {
      |                T = T.rlink;
      |            }//end if
      |        }
130   |
      |        return T;                                  // return null, if search failed
      |
      |      }//end find( )
      |
135   |
      |    /*------------*/
      |
      |      /** overloaded version of find( ) that accepts a String argument */
      |
140   |      TreeNode find(String K) {
      |        return find(new StringKey(K));
      |      }//end find( )
      |
      |
145   |    /*------------*/
      |
      |      /** the private printNode( ) method is an auxiliary */
      |      /** recursive method used by the print( ) method */
      |
150   |      private void printNode(TreeNode N) {
      |
      |        if (N != null) {                           // do nothing if the node is null
      |            System.out.print("(");
      |            printNode(N.llink);
155   |            System.out.print("  " + N.key + "  ");
      |            printNode(N.rlink);
      |            System.out.print(")");
      |        }
      |
160   |      }//end printNode
      |
      |
```

*(continued)*

Program 8.31  Constructing and Searching a Binary Search Tree *(continued)*

```
          /*------------*/

165       /** the print( ) method prints a parenthesized version */
          /** of the tree showing the subtree structure */

          void print( ) {

170         printNode(rootNode);
            System.out.println();

          }//end print( )

175     /*------------*/

        }//end class BinarySearchTree


180     /*----------------------------------------------------------*/


        interface ComparisonKey {

185         // if k1 and k2 are ComparisonKeys, k1.compareTo(k2) is
            // 0, +1, or −1 according as k1 == k2,  k1 > k2, or k1 < k2 in
            // the order defined by the compareTo method

                int compareTo(ComparisonKey value);
190

            // converts item to printable string

                String toString();
195
        }//end interface

        /*----------------------------------------------------------*/


200
        class StringKey implements ComparisonKey {

            // the key data field holds the String that is the value of the key

205         private String key;

          /*----------------*/

            // the single String-argument constructor sets the key to its argument
210
                StringKey(String value) {
                  key = value;
                }
```

Program 8.31  Constructing and Searching a Binary Search Tree (*continued*)

```
215 |      /*----------------*/
    |
    |      // the toString( ) method converts a StringKey into a string
    |
    |          public String toString( ) {
220 |              return key;
    |          }
    |
    |      /*----------------*/
    |
225 |      // the k1.compareTo(k2) method is a three-way comparison of two
    |      // keys, k1 and k2, that returns 0, 1, or –1 when k1 == k2, k1 > k2,
    |      // or k1 < k2, respectively
    |
    |          public int compareTo(ComparisonKey value) {
230 |              String a = this.key;
    |              String b = ((StringKey)value).key;
    |              return a.compareTo(b);      // uses the inherited compareTo method
    |                                          // defined already for Java Strings
    |          }
    |
235 |      /*----------------*/
    |
    |      }//end StringKey class
    |
    |
240 |      /*-----------------------------------------------------------*/
    |
```

nodes in $T$. For example, the internal path length of the tree in Fig. 8.29 is $I = 28$, since:

$$28 = (0 + 1 + 1 + 2 + 2 + 3 + 3 + 3 + 4 + 4 + 5).$$

**the average number of comparisons in a successful search**

If search for each of the keys, $K$, in a binary search tree of $n$ nodes is equally likely, and if $I$ is the internal path length of the tree, then the number of comparisons required by an average successful search is $C_n = (I + n) / n$. For example, the average number of comparisons used in a search for a key $K$ in Fig. 8.29 is $(28 + 11)/11 = 39/11 = 3.55$. Figure 8.32 is a version of Fig. 8.29 in which each node contains the number of comparisons needed to find the key in that node. There are eleven nodes in Fig. 8.32. By adding up numbers of comparisons in all of the nodes of this figure $(1 + 2 + 2 + 3 + 3 + 4 + 4 + 4 + 5 + 5 + 6 = 39)$ and dividing by 11 $(39/11 = 3.55)$, we confirm that the average number of comparisons needed in binary searching of Fig. 8.29 is 3.55.

**external path lengths**

For unsuccessful searches, it turns out to be convenient to examine properties of the extended binary trees we defined earlier (as illustrated in Fig. 8.3). The extended binary tree corresponding to the binary search tree of Fig. 8.29 is shown in Fig. 8.33. Recall that the square boxes ($\square$) explicitly indicate the empty subtrees in

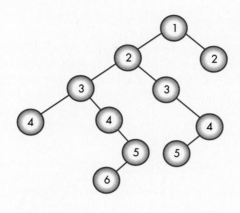

**Figure 8.32** Comparisons Needed to Locate Keys in Nodes of Fig. 8.29

an extended binary tree. We can now define the *external path length*, $E$, of an extended binary tree to be the sum of the path lengths from the root to each of the square boxes. Thus the external path length of the tree in Fig. 8.33 is $E = 50$, since

$$50 = (4 + 4 + 4 + 6 + 6 + 5 + 3 + 5 + 5 + 4 + 2 + 2).$$

average comparisons used in unsuccessful searches

If an unsuccessful search for a key $K$ occurs in an extended binary tree, $T$, then the search lands in one of the square boxes of the extended tree. Moreover, if a particular box is at level $l$ in the extended tree, it takes exactly $l$ comparisons to determine that the search is unsuccessful. If the extended tree, $T$, has $n$ internal nodes, then it has $(n + 1)$ boxes as leaves. (If you traverse the boxes and internal nodes of Fig. 8.33 in InOrder, the boxes and internal nodes alternate and there is one more box than internal nodes in this alternating sequence.) Therefore, if each of the boxes in $T$ is an equally likely target for an unsuccessful search, then the total number of comparisons required for an average unsuccessful search is $C'_n = E/(n + 1)$. For exam-

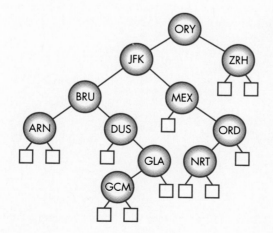

**Figure 8.33** Extended Binary Search Tree

ple, an average unsuccessful search of the tree in Fig. 8.33 requires $C_n' = 50/12 = 4.17$ comparisons.

There is an important relationship between the internal and external path lengths of a binary tree that is useful for calculating the average number of comparisons needed for searching and for deriving the equation, $C_n' = (n/(n+1))*(C_n+1)$, that gives $C_n'$ in terms of $C_n$. This is given by Eq. 8.1. Let $T$ be a binary tree with $n$ internal nodes. Then,

$$E = I + 2\,n. \tag{8.1}$$

Relationship Between Internal and External Path Lengths

Now, we are ready to ask, "What are the shapes of binary trees having minimum and maximum average search times, assuming each key in the tree is equally likely to be chosen?"

## The Best Case

It can be proven that an extended binary search tree of $n$ nodes can have a minimum internal path length only if its leaves ($\square$) are on at most two adjacent levels. Figure 8.34 illustrates some shapes of trees having minimal internal path lengths. Two of these (the first and the third) are complete binary trees, since all the leaves on the bottommost row of trees 1 and 3 are in the leftmost possible positions. However, binary tree 2 is not a complete tree, even though its leaves are on two adjacent levels. The minimal internal path lengths of trees of $n$ nodes, such as those shown in this figure, are calculated by taking the sum of the floors of the base-2 logarithms of the integers from 1 to $n$. If you assign an integer to each node giving its position in level order in such a tree, the root node is numbered 1, the nodes on the next level are numbered 2 and 3, the nodes on the next level are numbered 4, 5, 6, and 7, and so on. The path length, $l$, from the root to node $i$ in this ordering is just the floor of the base two logarithm of $i$, $l = \lfloor \lg i \rfloor$. In the latter expression, the base two logarithm $\log_2 i$ is denoted by $\lg i$, and the floor function, denoted $\lfloor x \rfloor$, gives the largest integer less than or equal to $x$. For positive real numbers $x$, the floor of $x$ is the same as the integer part of $x$, and is obtained by dropping the fractional part of $x$. For example, if $x = 2.807$, $\lfloor x \rfloor = 2$. If

*tree shapes that minimize path lengths*

*calculating minimal path lengths*

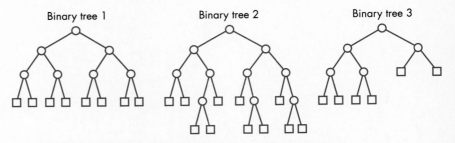

Figure 8.34 Some Tree Shapes with Minimum Internal Path Lengths

you study the numbers in Table 8.35, you can quickly see why the path lengths to each node $i$ in level order are given by $\lfloor \lg i \rfloor$.

If we could find a way to calculate the sum of the floors of the base-2 logarithms of the numbers from 1 to $n$, we would have a formula for the internal path length, $I$, that we are seeking. Unfortunately, finding such a formula requires techniques beyond the scope of this book. However, if we use the known result in the literature, which is that $I$ is approximately $n \lg n - 2n$, substitute it in the formula $C_n = (I + n)/n$, and then simplify, we get the result given in Eq. 8.2.

$$C_n = (I + n)/n \approx \lg n - 1.$$
(8.2)

approximating the best case

Hence, in the best case, the average number of comparisons needed in a successful search of a binary search tree, $T$, of $n$ nodes, is approximately $C_n \approx \lg n - 1$, for which the O-notation is $O(\log n)$.

## The Worst Case

The maximum internal path length is exhibited by trees that are as deep and skinny as possible. It can be proven that any tree with exactly one internal node on each level has a maximum possible internal path length. Figure 8.36 illustrates three trees that maximize internal path length, each having exactly one internal node on each level. The internal path length for any such tree having $n$ internal nodes takes the form $I = (0 + 1 + 2 + \ldots + (n - 1))$. This is a simple arithmetic progression having the sum $I = n(n - 1)/2$.

maximum internal path lengths

Thus, the average number of comparisons needed to locate keys successfully in binary search trees of the worst possible shape takes the form, $C_n = (n + 1)/2$, as illustrated in Eq. 8.3:

$$C_n = (I + n)/n = \left( \frac{n(n-1)/2 + n}{n} \right) = \frac{n+1}{2}.$$
(8.3)

| $i$ | $\lg i$ | $\lfloor \lg i \rfloor$ |
|---|---|---|
| 1 | 0.000 | 0 |
| 2 | 1.000 | 1 |
| 3 | 1.585 | 1 |
| 4 | 2.000 | 2 |
| 5 | 2.322 | 2 |
| 6 | 2.585 | 2 |
| 7 | 2.807 | 2 |
| 8 | 3.000 | 3 |
| 9 | 3.170 | 3 |

Table 8.35 The Relationship Between the $i^{th}$ Node in Level Order and the Length of the Path from the Root to Node $i$

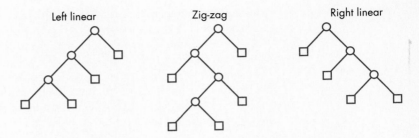

**Figure 8.36** Some Tree Shapes with Maximum Internal Path Lengths

## The Average Case

defining what
"average" means

Now what happens in the *average* case with equally likely choice of each tree in the set of binary search trees built-up using all the different possible orderings of $n$ keys, and with equally likely choice of each of the search keys in such a tree? Although the derivations are very pretty, they fall outside the scope of this book. [The interested reader can find these derivations in two other books by the author on pages 371–373 of *Data Structures, Algorithms, and Software Principles* (in Pascal), or pages 371–373 of *Data Structures, Algorithms, and Software Principles in C*. These two books are listed in the references at the end of this chapter.]

the known formula for
the approximate result

The known approximate formula for $C_n$, the average number of comparisons in a successful search in an average binary search tree, is given by Eq. 8.4

$$C_n \approx 1.386 \lg n - 1.846 .$$                                    (8.4)

**Table 8.37** The Shape That a Binary Search Tree Takes in the Best, Worst, and Average Cases

| Case | Tree Shape |
|------|-----------|
| Best case | Leaves on at most two adjacent levels |
| Worst case | Exactly one internal node on each level |
| Average case | Reasonably balanced, only occasionally deep |

**Table 8.38** Approximate Average Numbers of Comparisons for Successful Searches ($C_n$) and Unsuccessful Searches ($C_n'$) in the Best, Worst, and Average Binary Search Trees

| Case | $C_n \approx$ | $C_n' \approx$ |
|------|-----------|-----------|
| Best case | $\lg n - 1$ | $\lg n$ |
| Worst case | $(n + 1)/2$ | $(n + 3)/2$ |
| Average case | $1.38 \lg n - 1.8$ | $1.38 \lg n - 0.8$ |

### Comparison and Summary of Results

average trees are
reasonably well balanced

Now compare Eq. 8.4 for the average number of comparisons in an average tree with Eq. 8.2 giving the average number of comparisons in the best possible tree. For large enough $n$, the constants 1 and 1.846 in these formulas will be small in relation to their first terms. Consequently, we discover that, in the average case, the number of comparisons for a successful search is about 38.6 percent greater than in the best case. This implies that, on the average, deep unbalanced trees are relatively rare, and that most trees constructed by inserting keys in a random order are reasonably well balanced.

Once we know the results for the best, worst, and average cases for $C_n$, we can use the equation $C_n' = (n/(n+1))*(C_n + 1)$ to derive the results for $C_n'$. After performing this conversion, we can list our conclusions in Tables 8.37 and 8.38. In summary, the best and average cases are $O(\log n)$ and the worst case is $O(n)$.

## 8.7 REVIEW QUESTIONS

1. What is a binary search tree?
2. How do you search for a key in a binary search tree?
3. Define the external and internal path lengths of a binary search tree? How are they related?
4. Give the O-notation for the number of comparisons required in an average successful search for a key, $K$, in a binary search tree of $n$ keys, assuming each key, $K$, in the tree is equally likely to be chosen: (a) in the best case, when the tree has the shape that minimizes the average search time; (b) in the worst case, when the tree has the shape that maximizes the average search time; and (c) in the average case when trees being searched are drawn with equal likelihood from the set of trees constructed by inserting keys in the order given by each ordering of the keys in the set of all possible different orderings of keys.

## 8.7 EXERCISES

1. Leff Wright wrote the following recursive method to perform search for **ComparisonKeys** in binary search trees. He intends to replace the find() method given on lines 116:133 of Program 8.31. Is his program correct or incorrect?

```
     |   // Auxiliary method used by the find( ) method below
     |
     |   private TreeNode findNode(TreeNode T, ComparisonKey K) {
     |       if (T != null) {
  5  |           int result = K.compareTo(T.key);
     |           if (result == 0) {
     |               return T;
     |           } else if (result < 0) {
     |               return findNode(T.llink, K);
 10  |           } else {
     |               return findNode(T.rlink, K);
     |           }
     |       }
     |       return T;
 15  |   }
```

```
    |
    |     // the following find( ) method uses the auxiliary findNode( ) method
    |
    |         TreeNode find(ComparisonKey K) {
20  |             return findNode(rootNode,K);
    |         }
```

2. If you believe that Leff Wright's solution in Exercise 1 is incorrect, write your own correct version.
3. Verify that the binary search tree of Fig. 8.29 can be constructed by inserting the nodes of Table 8.30 into an initially empty binary tree. The nodes should be inserted in the order given in Table 8.30.
4. (For mathematically inclined readers only) Using induction, and starting with an empty tree ($\square$) as a base case, prove that the relationship between the internal and external path length of a binary tree with $n$ nodes is $E = I + 2\,n$.
5. Write a program to delete a node in a binary search tree having a given key K. Can you devise an algorithm that gives a result that does not have deeper leaves than the input tree?

## 8.8  AVL Trees and Their Performance

### LEARNING OBJECTIVES

1. To learn the definition of AVL trees.
2. To learn about some tree transformations that keep AVL trees balanced.
3. To understand the performance advantages of AVL trees.

From the results in Table 8.38, we see that balanced binary search trees have the best search times. If trees get out of balance or have deep search paths, their search performance deteriorates. In the worst case, instead of having $O(\log n)$ search times, the performance degrades to $O(n)$ search times.

Suppose we decide to keep a given binary search tree, $T$, as completely balanced as possible by rebalancing it each time a new key is inserted. Then it would be guaranteed that $T$ would always have $O(\log n)$ search times.

There is only one trouble with this idea. That is that the cost of rebalancing the tree can sometimes take $O(n)$ operations. To see why, consider the binary search trees in Fig. 8.39, which use integers as keys. In this figure, a new key, 1, has been inserted into the left tree to yield the middle tree, and this middle tree has been rebalanced to yield the right tree. Note that every key in the left tree was moved to a new node when the right tree was constructed by balancing the middle tree. This demonstrates that rebalancing can take time $O(n)$ in the worst case.

the trouble with complete balancing

If restoring complete balance is made a part of the key insertion operation, then even though searching will be guaranteed to take $O(\log n)$ time, the insertion operation can take time $O(n)$. We are therefore led to ask, "Is there some way of achieving $O(\log n)$ search times while also achieving $O(\log n)$ insertion times?"

It turns out that the answer is *yes*. The main idea is to define a class of binary search trees that are almost balanced, but not completely balanced. These almost-balanced trees can be shown to have O(log *n*) search times and also O(log *n*) insertion times for new keys. They were discovered by two Russian mathematicians, Adelson-Velskii and Landis, after whom they are named, and they are commonly known as AVL trees in the computer science literature.

Here is the key idea. We define the *height* of a binary tree to be the length of the longest path from the root to some leaf. (As a special case, we define the height of the empty tree to be −1.) If *N* is a node in a binary tree, *T*, we say that node *N* has the AVL *property* if the heights of the left and right subtrees of node *N* are either equal or if they differ by 1. An *AVL tree* is defined to be a binary tree in which each of its nodes has the AVL property.

It helps to look at a few examples in order to make the concept of AVL trees clear. Figure 8.40 shows some AVL trees, and Fig. 8.41 illustrates some trees that are not AVL trees.

Let's take a closer look at some of the properties of the AVL trees in Fig. 8.40. First, let's get the concept of the *height* of a tree clear in our minds. The three trees in Fig. 8.40 have heights of 2, 3, and 4 respectively, since the length of the longest paths from the root to some leaf in these trees is 2, 3, and 4. Focusing now on AVL tree 1, we see that the height of the left subtree of the root is 1, and the height of the right subtree of the root is zero (since the right subtree is a single node having no nonempty subtrees). Consequently, the heights of the left and right subtrees of the root of AVL tree 1 differ by at most 1, and therefore the root of this tree has the AVL property. All the other nodes in AVL tree 1 also have the AVL property. For example, the node that is the root of the left subtree in AVL tree 1 has an empty right subtree, whose height is −1 (by definition) and has a left subtree of height 0 (since a single leaf is a subtree of height 0). Consequently, the root of the left subtree has the AVL property.

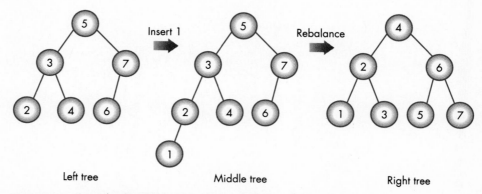

Figure 8.39 Completely Rebalancing After Inserting a New Key

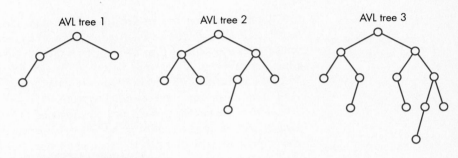

**Figure 8.40** Some AVL Trees

a quicker way to check

A quicker way to tell whether a node, $N$, in a tree has the AVL property is to compare the lengths of the longest left and right paths starting at $N$ and traveling downward. For example, the root of AVL tree 3 in Fig. 8.40 has a longest left path of 3 and a longest right path of 4. Since these left and right path lengths differ by at most one, AVL tree 3 has the AVL property at its root node. (For practice, you should verify that each node of each tree in Fig. 8.40 has the AVL property by checking that their longest left and right paths differ in length by at most one.)

Figure 8.41 illustrates some trees that are not AVL trees. The root of the first tree fails to have the AVL property since the left subtree of the root has height 1, and the right subtree of the root, being the empty tree, has height –1. These two heights (1 and –1) differ by 2, violating the AVL property. (Alternatively, since the longest left path starting at the root has length 2 and the longest right path has length 0, the root fails to have the AVL property.) In non-AVL tree 2 of Fig. 8.41, the right subtree of the root is not an AVL tree. In non-AVL tree 3, the right subtree of the root again fails to have the AVL property since the longest left path starting at its root has length 1 whereas the longest right path has length 3.

using rotation to restore the
AVL property

When we are building up a binary search tree using the insertion method, it is possible that the AVL property will be lost at some point. For example, starting with the empty tree, if we insert the three airport codes, JFK, DCA, and GCM in the order

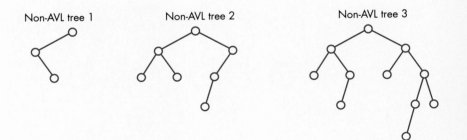

**Figure 8.41** Trees That Are Not AVL Trees

given, we get a binary search tree whose shape is that of non-AVL tree 1 in Fig. 8.41. When the AVL property is lost at a node, we can apply some shape-changing tree transformations to restore the AVL property. Only four different transformations are needed, and these are called *rotations*. Figure 8.42 illustrates the four rotations: single right, single left, double right, and double left.

There is a close analogy between the rotations depicted in Fig. 8.42 and some applications of the associative law of algebra. If we imagine that the trees in Fig. 8.42 are expression trees (such as those given earlier in Fig. 8.22) in which the nodes Ⓐ, Ⓑ, and Ⓒ play the role of operators and the subtrees $T_1$, $T_2$, $T_3$, and $T_4$ play the role of operands, then the AVL tree rotations of Fig. 8.42 can be expressed as shown in Fig. 8.43 on page 287.

relationship to the associative law of algebra

You may be wondering why the last two transformations in Fig. 8.43 are called "double" rotations. The reason is that each of the double rotations can be achieved by composing two single rotations.

For example, starting with $( (T_1 Ⓐ (T_2 Ⓑ T_3) ) Ⓒ T_4)$, a double right rotation can be accomplished first by doing a single left rotation on the left subtree of Ⓒ rooted at Ⓐ,

$$(T_1 Ⓐ (T_2 Ⓑ T_3) ) \Rightarrow ( (T_1 Ⓐ T_2) Ⓑ T_3)$$

which gives $( ( (T_1 Ⓐ T_2) Ⓑ T_3) Ⓒ T_4)$. This can be followed by a single right rotation applied to the root Ⓒ, which yields, $( (T_1 Ⓐ T_2) Ⓑ (T_3 Ⓒ T_4) )$.

The semicircular arrows in Figure 8.42 indicate the directions in which the single rotations are applied in order to yield the double rotations.

## Building an AVL Tree Using Insertions and Rotations

Let's watch what happens when we build up a binary search tree, using the keys of Table 8.30, and applying AVL rotations as necessary to maintain the AVL tree property at all times. We will use the keys in Table 8.30 in the order that they were given: ORY, JFK, BRU, DUS, ZRH, MEX, ORD, NRT, ARN, GLA, and GCM. The first node is ORY.

We can insert the next node, JFK, without destroying the AVL property:

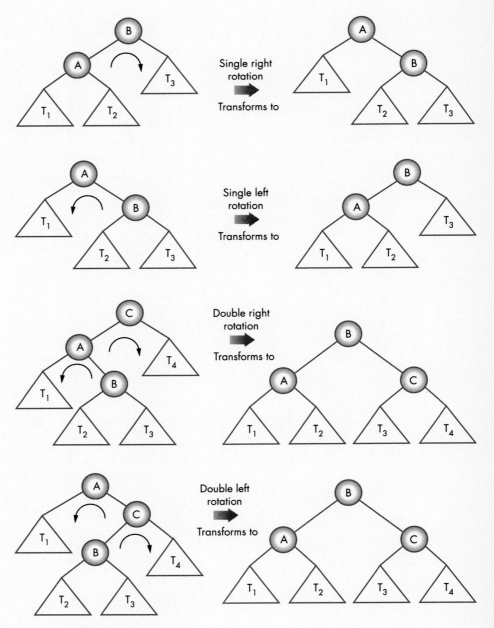

**Figure 8.42** AVL Tree Rotations

Single right rotation:

$$( (T_1 \, Ⓐ \, T_2) \, Ⓑ \, T_3) \Rightarrow (T_1 \, Ⓐ \, (T_2 \, Ⓑ \, T_3))$$

Single left rotation:

$$(T_1 \, Ⓐ \, (T_2 \, Ⓑ \, T_3)) \Rightarrow ((T_1 \, Ⓐ \, T_2) \, Ⓑ \, T_3)$$

Double right rotation:

$$( (T_1 \, Ⓐ \, (T_2 \, Ⓑ \, T_3)) \, Ⓒ \, T_4) \Rightarrow ((T_1 \, Ⓐ \, T_2) \, Ⓑ \, (T_3 \, Ⓒ \, T_4))$$

Double left rotation:

$$(T_1 \, Ⓐ \, ((T_2 \, Ⓑ \, T_3) \, Ⓒ \, T_4)) \Rightarrow ((T_1 \, Ⓐ \, T_2) \, Ⓑ \, (T_3 \, Ⓒ \, T_4))$$

**Figure 8.43** AVL Rotations Expressed Using the Associative Law

But adding the next node BRU creates an unbalanced tree that fails to have the AVL property at its root.

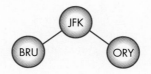

We apply a single right rotation to the root, ORY, to remove the imbalance, getting:

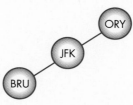

The next four airport codes can be inserted in the sequence DUS, ZRH, MEX, and ORD without requiring any rotations:

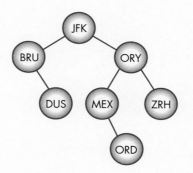

However, when we try to add NRT, the subtree rooted at MEX becomes unbalanced and requires a double left rotation to restore the AVL property:

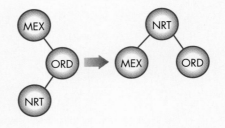

The next two airports, ARN and GLA, can be added without requiring any rotations to yield:

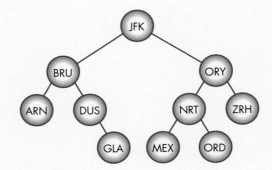

However, the attempt to insert the final airport code GCM produces an unbalanced subtree rooted at DUS. Another double left rotation is needed to remove this imbalance.

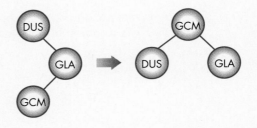

The final AVL tree is shown in Figure 8.44. Assuming that the search keys in this figure are equally likely to be used, the average successful search requires

$$C_n = \frac{(1+2+2+3+3+3+3+4+4+4+4)}{11} = \frac{33}{11} = 3.00 \text{ comparisons.}$$

This is an improvement over the binary search tree of Fig. 8.29 (using the same insertion order but no rebalancing), since the average number of comparisons required to search the tree of Fig. 8.29 was 3.55.

## Balance Factors and Comments on Rotation Algorithms

By adding a new data field to each node of an AVL tree, we can keep track of whether the left and right subtrees are of equal height, or whether one is higher than the other. Let three **final static int** constants representing *balance factors* be declared and initialized as follows:

LEFT_HEAVY = –1;  BALANCED = 0;  RIGHT_HEAVY = +1;

Then let nodes of AVL trees be specified using the following Java class definition:

```
class AVLTreeNode {
    int           balanceFactor;
    ComparisonKey key;
    AVLTreeNode   llink;
    AVLTreeNode   rlink;
}
```

An analysis of various possibilities can reveal the different cases when it is necessary to apply one of the four AVL tree rotations (of Fig. 8.42) when inserting new nodes to build up an AVL Tree.

For instance, let the symbols, $\oslash$, $\ominus$, and $\obslash$, denote the situations where subtrees of a node make the node left heavy, balanced, or right heavy, respectively. (The symbols $\oslash$, $\ominus$, and $\obslash$ are simply visible representations of the balance factors of the nodes.)

Now suppose that subtrees $T_1$, $T_2$, and $T_3$ each have height $h$. Suppose that a new node is inserted that makes $T_1$ into a new AVL subtree $T_1'$ of height $h + 1$. Then if the balance factors before changing $T_1$ into $T_1'$ are indicated by

$$( (T_1 \ominus T_2) \oslash T_3 )$$

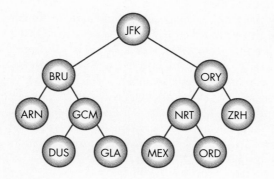

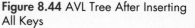

**Figure 8.44** AVL Tree After Inserting All Keys

then after changing $T_1$ into $T_1'$, the tree loses the AVL property at the root. But applying a single right rotation to the root restores the AVL property, by producing the new tree

$$(T_1' \ominus (T_2 \ominus T_3)).$$

Note that, beforehand, if the height of a subtree $((T_1 \ominus T_2) \oslash T_3)$ is $h + 2$, then after changing $T_1$ into $T_1'$ and rotating, the height of $(T_1' \ominus (T_2 \ominus T_3))$ is also $h + 2$. Consequently, none of the balance factors need to be changed in the entire tree above the subtree where the insertion and rotation took place. In other words, the single local rotation was sufficient to restore the AVL property to the entire tree.

In the case of double rotations, similar considerations apply. For instance, if subtrees $T_1$ and $T_4$ have height $h$, subtrees $T_2$ and $T_3$ have height $h - 1$, and these subtrees are arranged into a larger tree of the form

$$(T_1 \oslash ((T_2 \ominus T_3) \ominus T_4)),$$

then any insertion that unbalances the tree by increasing the height of either $T_2$ or $T_3$ by one (creating, say, $T_2'$ or $T_3'$ in the process) can have this imbalance removed by applying a double left rotation to create a tree of the form

$$((T_1 \ominus T_2') \ominus (T_3' \ominus T_4)).$$

Again, if the height of

$$(T_1 \oslash ((T_2 \ominus T_3) \ominus T_4))$$

before insertion was $h + 2$, then after insertion of the new node to create $T_2'$ or $T_3'$ followed by double rotation to restore the AVL property, the subtree

$$((T_1 \ominus T_2') \ominus (T_3' \ominus T_4))$$

also has height $h + 2$. Thus none of the nodes above this subtree needs to have its balance factor changed, and one double rotation suffices to restore the AVL property everywhere in the tree.

By analyzing all the possible combinations of subtree heights and balance factors, such as those illustrated in the two cases considered above, it is possible to write an algorithm that searches for a node $N$ in an AVL tree $T$ having a search key $K$, and if the search is unsuccessful, inserts a new node with key $K$, adjusts balance factors and applies a rotation to remove imbalances if necessary.

You are invited to work out the details in Exercise 8.8.3. This is a challenging set of algorithms to devise successfully—perhaps the most challenging in this entire book. Almost every upper-division data structures book covers the solution of this problem in detail. Therefore if you get stuck, a variety of published solutions will be readily available.

## Known Performance Results for AVL Trees

It is informative to ask how many comparisons are needed to locate a search key $K$ in an AVL tree $T$ having $n$ nodes.

The best case AVL tree has the same shape as the best case binary search tree—namely, a tree with leaves on at most two levels. In such a best case AVL tree of $n$ nodes, the height $h$ (i.e., the length of the longest path from the root to a leaf) is no shorter than $\lceil \lg(n+1) \rceil$. That is, $h \geq \lceil \lg(n+1) \rceil$. (Here, the notation $\lceil x \rceil$ is called the ceiling of $x$, which is defined to be the smallest integer greater than or equal to $x$. For example $\lceil 2.301 \rceil = 3$. If a positive real number $x$ has a nonzero fractional part, you get its ceiling $\lceil x \rceil$ by rounding $x$ up to the next integer that is greater than $x$.) Thus, the largest number of comparisons, $C$, needed to locate a key in the best case AVL tree of $n$ nodes is no smaller than $\lceil \lg(n+1) \rceil + 1$ (using $C = h + 1$, and recalling that the number of compaisons $C$ is one greater than the path length $h$). Thus, we have,

*a lower bound for the maximum number of comparisons*

$$C > \lceil \lg(n+1) \rceil + 1.$$

It can also be shown that, in the worst case, the height of the deepest AVL tree of $n$ nodes is bounded above by $h < 1.44042 \lg(n+2) - 1.327724$. Again applying $C = h+1$, we have,

*the worst case*

$$C < 1.4404 \lg(n+2) - 0.328.$$

*AVL trees are no more than 44 percent worse than optimal trees*

Comparing this result with the previous result, that the smallest $C$ can get in a deepest search of the best case AVL tree is $C > \lceil \lg(n+1) \rceil + 1$, we can conclude that, in the worst case, AVL tree searches can require no more than about 44 percent more comparisons than required in the most costly search of an optimum shaped AVL tree.

By conducting empirical tests, it has been shown that the average search in an AVL tree takes about $\lg n + c$ comparisons for some small constant $c$ (where $c \approx 0.25$ for large $n$). So the worst case AVL tree search is no more than about 44 percent more expensive than the average search.

Since path lengths in AVL trees of $n$ nodes are bounded above by $1.44 \lg(n+2)$, it can be shown that searches, insertions, and deletions are each $O(\log n)$ in the worst possible cases. (Essentially, the amount of work involved can be no more than proportional to the work needed for processing each of the nodes in the search path from the root to the node containing the search key, or to the node where insertion or deletion will take place, plus a small constant additional amount of work.)

As Exercise 8.8.1 shows, by adding a field to each node in an AVL tree that contains one more than the number of nodes in the node's left subtree, the time needed to find the $k^{\text{th}}$ item given $k$, becomes $O(\log n)$. Thus using AVL trees to represent a List ADT can have several advantages—namely, one can perform rapid insertion (overcoming the drawback of using sequentially allocated linear list representations), and one can perform rapid random access (overcoming the drawback of using one-way, linked list representations).

## 8.8 REVIEW QUESTIONS

1. Define the *height* of a binary tree.
2. What does it mean for a node N in a binary search tree T to have the AVL property? Then define what it means for tree T to be an AVL tree.
3. Draw diagrams illustrating four types of rotations that can be used to restore the AVL property in a binary search tree.
4. What is the O-notation for the worst case search time for a key K in an AVL tree of n nodes?

## 8.8 EXERCISES

1. (Using AVL trees to represent a List ADT) Show that AVL trees can be used to provide a representation for the List ADT defined in Fig. 7.1 so that each list operation takes no more than O(log n) time for a list representation containing n items. [*Hint:* Add to each node of an AVL tree a field containing 1 + the number of nodes in the left subtree of the node. Use this field to compute the list length and to find the $k^{th}$ item in O(log n) time.]
2. (TreeSort) It is possible to sort n keys by inserting them one-by-one into a binary search tree and then reading them off using an **InOrder** traversal. Implement a **TreeSort** algorithm. Does it help to use AVL trees? How?
3. (AVL rotation algorithms) Implement the AVL tree rotation programs using the sketch given in the text as a hint.
4. Implement an algorithm to delete a node containing a given key K in an AVL tree T.
5. (Efficient dynamic memory allocation) Chapter 7 described two algorithms, **FirstFit** and **BestFit**, which are commonly used to allocate blocks of storage in dynamic memory allocation schemes. These two methods are linear time algorithms in the worst case. (Since they must search the entire list of n free blocks, they can each take time at most O(n).) Can AVL trees be used to organize the free blocks in a dynamic memory allocation scheme so that block allocation takes O(log n) time instead of time O(n)? [*Hint:* Take all free blocks of a given size, S, and link them into a two-way ring. This partitions free memory into a collection of rings, where each ring contains blocks of the same size. Now take one block on each ring and treat it as the *representative* of that ring. Organize these representatives into an AVL tree using block sizes as search keys. To locate a best-fit block in this AVL tree, given a request size, N, search the AVL tree for a block of size N. Either an exact-fit block of size N is found, or the last node from which a left descent was made along the search path will give the best fit for N.]

## 8.9    Two–Three Trees

## LEARNING OBJECTIVES

1. To learn another effective method for implementing dynamic search trees.
2. To understand how to insert new nodes and to search for keys.
3. To understand the performance characteristics of these trees.

As we noted in the previous discussion, maintaining perfect balance in binary trees yields shortest average search paths, but the attempt to maintain perfect balance when we insert or delete nodes can incur costly rebalancing in which every node of the tree has to be rearranged. AVL trees presented a method in which we agreed to abandon the goal of trying to maintain perfect balance and to adopt the goal of keeping the subtrees of nodes "almost balanced." We discovered that we could get good performance in searches, insertions, and deletions by adopting this slight compromise from the maintenance of perfect balance.

the idea behind 2–3 trees

Another way to compromise on the goal of maintaining perfect balance is to arrange for all subtrees to be perfectly balanced with respect to their heights, but to permit the number of search keys stored in nodes to vary. This is the main idea behind 2–3 trees. Each node in a 2–3 tree is permitted to contain either one or two search keys, and to have either two or three descendants. All leaves of the tree are empty trees that lie on exactly one bottom level.

Figure 8.45 illustrates a 2–3 tree in which we have used letters of the alphabet as search keys. Note that all leaves of the tree, denoted by small square boxes ( □ ), lie on the bottommost level.

how to search for a key

To search for the key L, for example, we start at the root and note that L > H, so we follow the pointer to the right subtree of the root node. Now we note that the key L lies *between* the keys J and N in alphabetical order, since J < L and L < N, so we follow the *middle* pointer between J and N to the node containing the keys K and L where the search terminates successfully by locating the key L.

Now let's look at the process of inserting new keys. In the simplest case, we will attempt to add a new key to a node containing only one key already and which has room to expand in order to contain two keys. For instance, suppose we want to insert the new key B into the tree of Fig. 8.45. Since B < H, we follow the left pointer from the root node to the node containing D in the second row. Again, we follow the left pointer of D's node to the node containing A. The node containing A has room for one more key, so we plant B in this node. The leftmost node on the bottom row of internal nodes in Fig. 8.46 shows the result of this insertion, starting with the tree of Fig. 8.45.

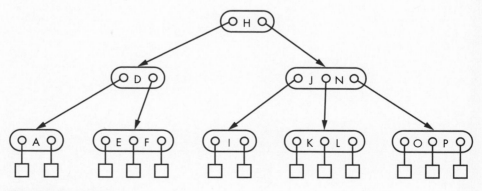

**Figure 8.45** A 2–3 Tree

A more challenging case occurs when we try to insert a new key into a node that already contains two keys. In this case, the node would overflow (by containing three keys), so we need a policy for insertion that maintains the 2–3 tree property. The method is this: "*Split the overflowed node into two nodes and pass the middle key up to the parent.*" This could cause a sequence of further splits, leading possibly to splitting the root, adding a new root, and deepening the 2–3 tree by one more level.

To see how this works, let's consider inserting more keys into the 2–3 tree of Fig. 8.45. First, let's insert the key M. This leads to the attempt to add M to the node ⊙ K ⊙ L ⊙.

However, if we did this, we would get an overflowed node of the form ⊙ K ⊙ L ⊙ M ⊙ having four children and three keys, in violation of the 2–3 tree property. Hence, we split ⊙ K ⊙ L ⊙ M ⊙ into two new nodes ⊙ K ⊙ and ⊙ M ⊙, and we pass the middle key L up to the parent node ⊙ J ⊙ N ⊙. The attempt to add L to this parent node yields another overflowed node in which the key L lies between the keys J and N, ⊙ J ⊙ L ⊙ N ⊙.

So we split this parent into two new nodes ⊙ J ⊙ and ⊙ N ⊙, and we pass the middle key L up to the root. The root has room for L, so we change it from ⊙ H ⊙ to ⊙ H ⊙ L ⊙. These changes are illustrated in Fig. 8.46.

If we were to attempt to add the new keys Q, R, and S to the tree of Fig. 8.46, the root of the tree ⊙ H ⊙ L ⊙ would split when P was passed up from below, and we would pass L up to form a new root with two children. This would deepen the tree by one more level.

You might think that the number of node splits on insertion could become excessive and could hinder the performance of 2–3 trees. However, since each split produces exactly one new node, the total number of splits to create a tree is just one less than the number of nodes in the tree. Moreover, if a split starts at level $k$, it could progress upward toward the root and could split the root, so, in the worst case, $(k + 1)$-splits are needed when we insert a new key at level $k$. But a 2–3 tree containing $n$ keys with the maximum number of levels takes the form of a binary tree in which each internal node has one key and two children. In such a tree $n = 2^{k+1} - 1$, where $k$ is the number of the

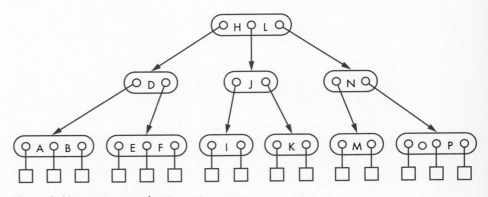

**Figure 8.46** A 2–3 Tree After Some Insertions

lowest level. This implies that $(k + 1) = \lg (n + 1)$, from which we see that the number of splits per insertion is at worst $O(\log n)$. Similar considerations yield the result that searches and deletions are also $O(\log n)$ in the worst cases.

In summary, 2–3 trees have $O(\log n)$ search, insertion, and deletion times, and can be recommended for reasons similar to those connected with the advantages of using AVL trees.

## B–Trees—A Generalization of 2–3 Trees

The basic principle of operation of 2–3 trees is used extensively in practical circumstances to handle indexes to large files containing many records. A generalized version of 2–3 trees, called B–trees, is used for this purpose.

If we increase the number of children allowed in a nonroot node of a 2–3 tree to be some number in the range, say, from 128 to 256, then we have a B–tree of order 256. In general, in a B–tree of order $m$, each internal node except the root and the leaves must have between $\lceil m/2 \rceil$ and $m$ children. The root can either be a leaf or it can contain from two to $m$ children. All leaves lie on the same bottommost level and are empty.

*increasing the number of children*

Roughly speaking, a B–tree of order $m$ has nodes that have some number of children between half of $m$ and $m$. When we insert a new key, $K$, into a node, and the node overflows by containing $m$ keys, and requiring it to have $m + 1$ children, we split the node. To do this, we line the keys up in increasing order, pass the middle key up to the parent, and form two new nodes containing the remaining bottom and top halves of the ordered key sequence in the overflowed node.

Suppose we have a B–tree, $T$, of order $m$ in which each internal node is as full as possible and has $m$ children. The number $m$ is called the *branching factor* of the tree. If $T$ contains $n$ keys and $p$ nodes, then $p = n/(m - 1)$, since each node of $T$ contains $m - 1$ keys. We can now ask how many levels tree $T$ has. In general, there is one node (the root) on level 0, and there are $m$ nodes on level 1, $m^2$ nodes on level 2, ... , and $m^k$ nodes on level $k$. The total number of nodes, $p$, is therefore just the sum of a geometric progression $p = 1 + m + m^2 + ... + m^k$. Hence, $p = (m^{k+1} - 1)/(m - 1)$.

*branching factors*

We can combine the result that $p = n/(m - 1)$, with the last result to eliminate $p$ and solve for $k$ in terms of $n$. This yields,

$$k = \log_m (n + 1) - 1.$$

For example, if $m = 256$ and $n = 16,777,215$, $k = \log_{256} (16777216) - 1 = 3 - 1 = 2$. Consequently, a full B–tree of order 256 can store 16 million records in just three levels (numbered level 0, level 1, and level 2), and it requires accessing just three nodes to find a given search key.

By contrast, if we store the same 16,777,215 keys in a completely balanced binary tree, the bottom level is given by $k = \log_2 (16777216) - 1 = 23$, so it could take up to 24 accesses of nodes on different levels to find a key. In general, the larger the branching factor $m$, the smaller the number of levels needed to store a given fixed number $n$ of keys in a completely balanced tree. (Another way of saying this is that a balanced tree of $n$ nodes has $\log_m(n+1)$ rows, and the larger we make the base of the logarithm, the smaller the logarithm will be.)

The use of trees with high branching factors makes sense when we store the tree nodes on external memory devices with slow access times, such as disks or drums. Storing 16 million records on an external disk as a binary tree could require up to 24 separate disk accesses, whereas storing it as a B–tree of order 256 could require at most 5 accesses to separate nodes. Consequently, binary trees may be efficient when used in fast internal primary memory, but trees with higher branching factors are substantially more efficient when storing and accessing tree nodes on slow, rotating external memory. (*Note*: For efficiency, we usually read the entire ordered key sequence in a B–tree node into internal memory all at once. Then we use fast binary searching in internal memory to search for a key in this ordered sequence.)

## 8.9 REVIEW QUESTIONS

1. Define what it means for a tree $T$ to be a 2–3 tree.
2. What is the advantage of using 2–3 trees rather than trees that are completely balanced?
3. What is the branching factor of a tree?
4. When is it advantageous to use trees with high branching factors?

## 8.9 EXERCISES

1. Draw the 2–3 tree that results from inserting the keys Q, R, and S into the 2–3 tree of Fig. 8.46. Perform node splits as necessary to maintain the 2–3 tree property at all times.
2. Derive a formula giving the height $k$ of the tallest B–tree, $T$, of order $m$, such that $T$ contains $n$ keys.

## 8.10 Tries

### LEARNING OBJECTIVES

1. Learning another efficient storage and retrieval method based on trees.
2. Learning how to construct and use Tries.

A *Trie* is a special kind of information access tree whose name comes from the word Re*trie*val. It is a common convention to pronounce the word "*trie*" as if it rhymed with "*try*" or "*pie*," to distinguish it from the word "*tree*" when spoken.

In constructing a *trie* from a collection of search keys, we use the initial alphabetic prefixes of the keys to construct a *discrimination net* such as the one shown in Fig. 8.47. In this figure a trie is constructed from the airport code search keys given in Table 8.30. These keys, in alphabetic order are ARN, BRU, DUS, GCM, GLA, JFK, MEX, NRT, ORD, ORY, and ZRH.

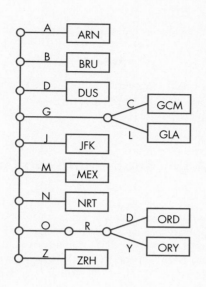

**Figure 8.47** A Trie Using Airport Codes

how to search in a trie

At the root of the tree, we use the first letter of each airport code to distinguish which branch to pursue further. In many cases, the first letter alone is sufficient to distinguish a given airport code from all others in the tree. For example, in Figure 8.47, ARN and BRU are the only airport codes beginning with A and B, respectively. Therefore a test on the first letter of ARN and BRU is sufficient to lead to two separate branches of the tree having ARN and BRU as the only leaves. No further analysis needs to be performed to find ARN or BRU.

By contrast, GCM and GLA share the same first letter, G. Analyzing the first letter, and following the "G" branch of the trie leads to a second node at which a second discrimination is made on the second letter of GCM and GLA. Here, the second letters "C" and "L" are sufficient to differentiate between GCM and GLA, and so a test on the second letter leads to the separate leaves containing GCM and GLA respectively. In the final case of interest, both ORD and ORY begin with the same two letters "OR." Consequently, we have to use their third letters, "D" and "Y" to distinguish them. Hence, the trie in Fig. 8.47 does not discriminate between ORD and ORY until testing their third letters.

Tries have surprisingly good search times. If we use "random" keys, $K$ (such as base $m$ fractional numbers evenly distributed in the interval $0 \leq K \leq 1$), then the number of characters examined during a random average search (with each of the keys considered equally likely to be used) is approximately $\log_m N$, for nodes with $m$ links and for N random keys stored in the trie.

Tries are insensitive to the order of insertion of the keys, but they are sensitive to clustering in the spelling of prefixes of the keys.

## 8.10 REVIEW QUESTIONS

1. How do you pronounce the word "*trie*"?
2. Explain how a trie works.

3. What are the advantages and disadvantages of tries when used for searching?

## 8.10 EXERCISES

1. Discuss how you could represent a trie efficiently when search keys are (a) three letter airport codes, and (b) words in a dictionary containing 65,000 words with a longest word length of 33.

## 8.11  An Application—Huffman Codes

### LEARNING OBJECTIVES

1. Learning how to employ binary trees to construct minimal length encodings of strings based on known letter frequencies.
2. Learning how to construct and use Huffman trees.
3. Understanding why Huffman trees minimize the weighted path lengths of coding trees.

Binary trees can be used in an interesting way to construct minimal length encodings for messages when the frequency of letters used in the messages is known. A special kind of binary tree, called a *Huffman coding tree*, is used to accomplish this.

For example, we might take some samples of free-running English text, such as that which might be found in a newspaper, and we might try to count the frequencies of the letters of the alphabet used in these text samples. After analyzing several samples of such text, we might discover that the numbers of times each letter was used have the same relative proportions as the numbers given in Table 8.48.

The numbers in Table 8.48 are called *frequencies*, since each number gives the frequency of occurrence of its corresponding letter in the samples analyzed. If the frequencies in the sample are representative of the frequencies that will be encountered in future samples of text, we can use such frequencies to construct an encoding of the letters that will minimize the length of the encodings. The idea is to use bit-sequences of differing lengths to encode the various letters, with short bit-sequences being used to represent the frequent letters, and longer bit-sequences to represent less frequently used letters. But how can we proceed so as to achieve the minimum possible length encodings?

*using shorter codes to represent more frequent letters*

| | | |
|---|---|---|
| E — 1231 | L — 403 | B — 162 |
| T — 959 | D — 365 | G — 161 |
| A — 805 | C — 320 | V — 93 |
| O — 794 | U — 310 | K — 52 |
| N — 719 | P — 229 | Q — 20 |
| I — 718 | F — 228 | X — 20 |
| S — 659 | M — 225 | J — 10 |
| R — 603 | W — 203 | Z — 9 |
| H — 514 | Y — 188 | |

**Table 8.48** Some Frequencies of Letters Typical for English Text

| E — 29 |
|---|
| T — 10 |
| N — 9 |
| I — 5 |
| S — 4 |

**Table 8.49** Five Letters and Their Frequencies

Let's consider a small example to illustrate the process of building and using a Huffman coding tree. Suppose we are given only the five letters and five corresponding frequencies shown in Table 8.49.

We start with the frequency values and sort them into increasing order, getting (4, 5, 9, 10, 29). Then we choose the two smallest values 4 and 5, and we construct a binary tree with labeled edges using these two smallest values,

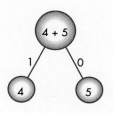

Here, 4 and 5 are placed inside the leaves, and the root contains the sum of the values in the leaves, 4 + 5. The left branch is labeled "1" and the right branch is labeled "0."

Next we return to the sequence of values (4, 5, 9, 10, 29) and we replace the two smallest values 4 and 5 with their sum 9, getting a new sequence (9, 9, 10, 29), which we must rearrange to be in increasing order (if it is not that way already). We again take the two new smallest values, 9 and 9, in this sequence, and we construct a labeled binary tree:

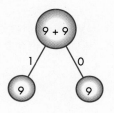

The root again contains the sum of the values of the leaves. Now, we substitute the first tree above into the second tree to get a composed tree:

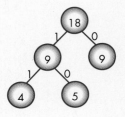

Continuing in this fashion, we return to the sequence (9, 9, 10, 29). We replace the first two frequencies, 9 and 9, with their sum 18, to get (18, 10, 29) and we rearrange the new sequence into ascending order, (10, 18, 29). We again build a tree from the two lowest frequencies:

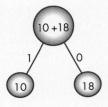

and we again compose the second to last tree above with the last tree above so as to substitute the root 18 for a leaf having the matching value 18, getting:

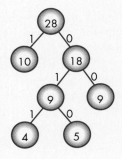

The final step is to replace the two smallest terms in (10, 18, 29) with their sum, getting the sequence (28, 29) and to build the tree:

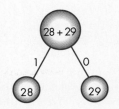

This tree can be composed with the next to last tree by substituting the root with value 28 for the leaf with value 28, getting the final composed tree:

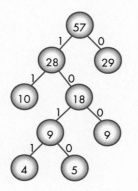

We now convert the final composed tree into a Huffman coding tree by making a one-for-one replacement of the frequencies of the leaves with letters from Table 8.49 having those frequencies. This gives the tree in Fig. 8.50, which is used to encode and decode strings in the alphabet A = (E, T, N, I, S). The code assigned to each letter is found by following the path from the root of the coding tree to the leaf containing the letter and by reading the labels on the edges in the path in succession. This results in the assignment of the codes given in Table 8.51. Note that the most frequent letters in this table have the shortest codes assigned and that the least frequent letters have the longest codes assigned.

To encode a string, we replace each letter with its corresponding bit code, using the correspondence in Table 8.51. Some examples are:

| String | Encoded String |
|--------|----------------|
| SENT   | 1011010011     |
| TENNIS | 11010010010101011 |
| NEST   | 1000101111     |
| SIT    | 1011101011     |

To decode a bit-string S, we use the successive bits of S to find a path through the coding tree of Fig. 8.50, starting at the root. A "1" means descend to the left, and a

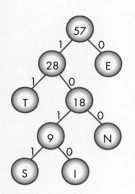

**Figure 8.50** Huffman Coding Tree for Letters in Table 8.49

| Letter | Bit code | Frequency |
|--------|----------|-----------|
| E      | 0        | 29        |
| T      | 11       | 10        |
| N      | 100      | 9         |
| I      | 1010     | 5         |
| S      | 1011     | 4         |

**Table 8.51** Huffman Codes Assigned to Letters of Table 8.49

"0" means descend to the right. Each time we reach a leaf in the coding tree, we emit the letter that the leaf contains, and we return to the root of the coding tree to start a fresh path using the next bit of the encoded sequence. For example, the encoded string,

$$1\ 1\ 0\ 1\ 0\ 0\ 1\ 1\ 1\ 0\ 1\ 1,$$

decodes as "**TENTS**" because the initial **1  1** leads to a **T**, the next **0** leads to an **E**, the succeeding **1  0  0** leads to an **N**, the following **1  1** leads to a **T**, and the final **1  0  1  1** leads to an **S**.

It is actually possible to prove that a Huffman code minimizes the length assigned to coded messages that use letters with the same frequency as the frequency in the sample from which the Huffman code was constructed.

**the weighted path length**

The critical measure to minimize is a quantity called the *weighted path length* of the Huffman tree. Looking at Table 8.51, for the alphabet A = (**E, T, N, I, S**), if we multiply each number in the Frequency column, $f_i$, by the length, $l_i$, of the corresponding Huffman code in the Bit code column, we would get the total number of bits needed to represent $f_i$ of the letters in the Letter column. By adding all the products of frequencies and bit code lengths, $\sum_{(1 \leq i \leq n)} f_i * l_i$, for all $n$ letters in the alphabet, we get the length of the bit code for an encoded message that uses each letter in the alphabet exactly as many times as its frequency specifies. This sum, $W = \sum_{(1 \leq i \leq n)} f_i * l_i$, is called the weighted path length because it represents the sum of the path lengths in Fig. 8.50 weighted by their frequencies, in the following sense: (a) multiply the length, $l_i$, of the path from the root to a leaf by the frequency, $f_i$, of the letter, $L_i$, at that leaf, and (b) add up all such individual path lengths in the tree weighted by their frequencies to obtain the weighted path length, $W = \sum_{(1 \leq i \leq n)} f_i * l_i$. The average number of bits per letter needed to encode a message is then given by, Average = $W / \sum_{(1 \leq i \leq n)} f_i$, since the average consists of the total number of bits used to encode all letters in the sample divided by the total number of letters in the sample. It is possible to prove that $W$ is minimized among all possible coding trees by a Huffman coding tree.

## 8.11 REVIEW QUESTIONS

1. What is a Huffman code?
2. What is a Huffman coding tree and how do you use it to encode and decode strings?
3. Why is a Huffman code advantageous in comparison to codes that assign fixed-length bit codes to the characters in an alphabet?

## 8.11 EXERCISES

1. Using the Huffman coding tree in Fig. 8.50, encode the strings **STINT** and **SINE**.
2. Using the Huffman coding tree in Fig. 8.50, decode the bit strings **100101010001011** and **101010011010011**.
3. Write a program to build a Huffman coding tree, starting with a set of letters and their corresponding frequencies. Build the Huffman coding tree using the letters and frequencies given in Table 8.48.

## 8.12 Graphs—Basic Concepts and Terminology

### LEARNING OBJECTIVES

1. To establish a basic vocabulary of graph concepts.
2. To introduce concepts such as paths, components, and connectedness that are essential for understanding graph algorithms.

*an informal description*

Let's start with an informal description. A *graph* is a collection of points in which some pairs of points are connected by line segments. If the line segments have arrowheads on them, which indicate a direction of travel, we have a *directed graph* (which is sometimes called a *digraph*, for short). In an *undirected graph*, the line segments have no arrowheads on them. In both kinds of graphs, the points are usually referred to as *vertices*, and the line segments or arrows connecting pairs of vertices are usually referred to as *edges*. Figure 8.52 shows examples of both directed and undirected graphs.

*paths, cycles, and adjacency*

Two different vertices, *x* and *y*, in a graph are said to be *adjacent* if an edge connects *x* to *y*. A *path* is a sequence of vertices in which each vertex is adjacent to the next one. The *length* of a path is the number of edges in it. A *cycle* is a path of length greater than one that begins and ends at the same vertex. In an undirected graph, a *simple cycle* is a cycle formed from three or more distinct vertices in which no vertex is visited more than once along the simple cycle's path (except for the starting and ending vertex, which must be identical in order for the cycle to close and form a loop as it is supposed to do.)

*connectivity and components*

In an undirected graph, two distinct vertices, *x* and *y*, are *connected*, if there is a path between them. Also, a subset of the vertices, *S*, is said to be *connected* if there is a path from each vertex *x* of *S* to any other distinct vertex *y* of *S*. An undirected graph can always be divided into separate *connected components*. Each connected component consists of a subset of vertices that are all connected to each other (in the sense that any two distinct vertices are connected by some path lying inside the component). However, if an undirected graph consists of one or more separate components, there is

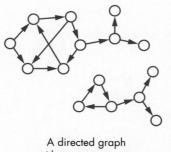

A directed graph
with two components

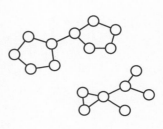

An undirected graph
with two components

**Figure 8.52** Directed and Undirected Graphs

never a path from a vertex in one component to some vertex in another separate component.

free trees A *free tree* is a special kind of undirected graph consisting of exactly one connected component having no simple cycles.

Let's now give some slightly more formal definitions of these informal concepts in order to establish a notation useful for developing the graph algorithms studied later in the chapter.

## Some Formal Definitions

Formally speaking, a *graph* $G = (V, E)$, consists of a set of vertices, $V$, together with a set of edges, $E$, where the edges in $E$ are formed from pairs of distinct vertices in $V$. In an *undirected graph*, each edge $e = \{v_1, v_2\}$ is an *unordered pair* of distinct vertices, which connects the two vertices $v_1$ and $v_2$, without prescribing a direction from $v_1$ to $v_2$ or from $v_2$ to $v_1$. By contrast, in a *directed graph* (or *digraph*, for short), each edge $e = (v_1, v_2)$ is an *ordered pair* of vertices, which connects the pair of vertices $v_1$ and $v_2$, in the direction *from $v_1$ to $v_2$*. In this case, we say $v_1$ is the *origin* of the edge $e = (v_1, v_2)$ and $v_2$ is the *terminus* of the edge $e$.

*Note:* When we use the word *graph* without a modifier, we shall usually mean an *undirected graph*, and we shall reserve the terms *digraph* and *directed graph* for graphs whose edges are directed.

## Paths, Cycles, and Adjacency

Two vertices $v_i$ and $v_j$ in a graph $G = (V, E)$ are *adjacent* if there exists an edge $e \in E$ such that $e = (v_i, v_j)$. A *path* $p$ in a graph $G = (V, E)$ is a sequence of vertices of $V$ of the form, $p = v_1 v_2 \ldots v_n$, $(n \geq 2)$, in which each vertex $v_i$ is adjacent to the next one, $v_{i+1}$ (for $1 \leq i \leq n - 1$). A *cycle* is a path $p = v_1 v_2 \ldots v_n$, such that $v_1 = v_n$ (so that $p$ starts and ends at the same vertex and forms a loop). Figure 8.53 illustrates paths and cycles in a graph.

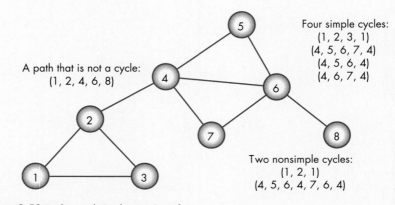

**Figure 8.53** Paths and Cycles in Graphs

In an undirected graph, a simple cycle is a path that travels through three or more distinct vertices and connects them into a loop. Formally speaking, this means that if $p$ is a path of the form, $p = v_1 \, v_2 \ldots v_n$, then $p$ is a *simple cycle* if and only if $(n > 3)$, $v_1 = v_n$, and $v_i \neq v_j$ for distinct $i$ and $j$ in the range $(1 \leq i, j \leq n - 1)$. Put differently, when you travel around the loop in a simple cycle, you must visit at least three different vertices, and you cannot travel through any vertex more than once.

## Connectivity and Components

connectivity

Two vertices in a graph $G = (V, E)$ are said to be *connected* if there is a path from the first to the second in G. Formally, this means that if $x \in V$ and $y \in V$, where $x \neq y$, then $x$ and $y$ are *connected* if there exists a path, $p = v_1 \, v_2 \ldots v_n$, in G, such that $x = v_1$ and $y = v_n$.

connected components

In the graph $G = (V, E)$, a *connected component* is a subset, $S$, of the vertices $V$ that are all connected to one another. Formally, $S$ is a *connected component* of G if, for any two distinct vertices, $x \in S$ and $y \in S$, $x$ is connected to $y$. A connected component $S$ of G is a *maximal connected component* provided there is no bigger subset, $T$, of vertices in $V$, such that $T$ properly contains the vertices of $S$ (i.e., $T \supset S$), and such that $T$ itself is a connected component of G. Informally, this means that $S$ is a maximal connected component of G if you cannot enlarge $S$ by adding new vertices not already in $S$ that are connected to other vertices in $S$. An undirected graph G can always be separated into distinct maximal connected components, $S_1, S_2, \ldots, S_k$, such that $S_i \cap S_j = \varnothing$ whenever $i \neq j$. The considerations for directed graphs are slightly different.

In a directed graph, suppose there is a path from vertex $v_1$ to vertex $v_2$, but that there is no path from $v_2$ back to $v_1$. Then, according to the definition of connectivity given previously, $v_1$ is connected to $v_2$, but $v_2$ is not connected to $v_1$. This implies that we need to define a slightly different version of connectivity for components in directed graphs than we did for those in undirected graphs. We say that a subset $S$ of vertices in a directed graph G is *strongly connected* if for each pair of distinct vertices $(v_i, v_j)$ in $S$, $v_i$ is connected to $v_j$ and $v_j$ is connected to $v_i$. By contrast, we say that a subset $S$ of vertices in a directed graph G is *weakly connected* if for each pair of distinct vertices $(v_i, v_j)$ in $S$, *either* $v_i$ is connected to $v_j$ or $v_j$ is connected to $v_i$. Figure 8.54 gives two examples of directed graphs, one of which is strongly connected and one of which is weakly connected.

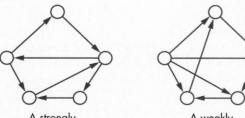

A strongly connected digraph    A weakly connected digraph

**Figure 8.54** Strongly and Weakly Connected Digraphs

## Adjacency Sets and Degrees

adjacency sets

Another way to define a graph $G = (V, E)$ that is equivalent to the definition using G's vertex set $V$ and its edge set $E$, is to specify *adjacency sets* for each vertex in $V$. Let $V_x$ stand for the set of all vertices adjacent to $x$ in the graph G. Formally, we define $V_x$ to be the set of all vertices $y$ such that $(x,y)$ is an edge in $E$. $V_x = \{\, y \mid (x,y) \in E \,\}$ in symbols. If we give both the vertex set $V$ and the collection $A = \{\, V_x \mid x \in V \,\}$ of adjacency sets for each vertex in $V$, we have given enough information to specify the graph G. In an undirected graph G, the *degree* of a vertex $x$ is the number of edges $e$ in which $x$ is one of the endpoints of edge $e$.

in-degrees and out-degrees

If $x$ is a vertex in a directed graph $G = (V, E)$, we can speak of the *predecessors* of $x$ and the *successors* of $x$. The predecessors of $x$, denoted Pred($x$), is the set of vertices $y \in V$ such that $(y,x)$ is an edge in $E$. The successors of $x$, denoted Succ($x$), is the set of vertices $y \in V$ such that $(x,y)$ is an edge in $E$. The *in-degree* of a vertex $x$ is the number of predecessors of $x$, and the out-degree of $x$ is the number of successors of $x$.

Some of the data representations for graphs that we shall discuss in the next section directly use representations of the adjacency sets for each vertex in the graph.

## 8.12 REVIEW QUESTIONS

1. Give the formal definition of a *directed graph* and of an *undirected graph*.
2. How do directed and undirected graphs differ?
3. What is a *path* in a graph? What is a *cycle* in a graph?
4. Define the concept of a *simple cycle*.
5. When are two vertices in a graph connected?
6. What is a connected component of a graph?
7. What is an *adjacency set* for a vertex $x$ in a graph G?
8. Define the *in-degree* and the *out-degree* of a vertex in a directed graph G.

## 8.12 EXERCISES

1. List the vertices of degree 3 in the graph of Fig. 8.53.
2. List the adjacency sets for each vertex in the graph of Fig. 8.53.
3. You are given an undirected graph G consisting of the vertices $V$ = {a, b, c, d, e, f, g, h, i} and having the following adjacency sets $V_a$ = {b,c}, $V_b$ = {a,c}, $V_c$ = {a,b,d}, $V_d$ = {c,e,f}, $V_e$ = {d}, $V_f$ = {d}, $V_g$ = {h,i}, $V_h$ = {g,i} and $V_i$ = {g,h}. Draw a diagram of the graph G. How many separate connected components does G have? Give the vertices in each of the two simple cycles of G.

## 8.13 Graph Representations

### LEARNING OBJECTIVES

1. To learn about adjacency matrices and edge lists.
2. To understand how to use both sequential and linked allocation techniques to represent graphs.
3. To understand several possible data representations for graphs.

Let $G = (V, E)$ be a graph. Suppose we number the vertices in $V$, as $v_1, v_2, \ldots, v_n$ (for some integer $n$). Now let's make a table $T[i,j]$ having $n$ rows and $n$ columns, such that row $i$ corresponds to $v_i$ and column $j$ corresponds to $v_j$, $(1 \le i, j \le n)$. We will fill table $T$ with ones and zeros by putting a 1 in row $i$ and column $j$ exactly when there is an **adjacency matrices** edge $e = (v_i, v_j)$ in $E$, and by putting a zero in $T[i,j]$ otherwise. Formally, $T[i,j] = 1$ iff[1] there exists $e \in E$, such that $e = (v_i, v_j)$ and $T[i,j] = 0$ iff there *does not* exist an edge $e \in E$, such that $e = (v_i, v_j)$. Such a table, $T$, is called an *edge matrix*, or an *adjacency matrix* for the graph G. Figure 8.55 shows a graph and its corresponding *adjacency matrix*.

Let's focus for a moment on a row $R_i$ corresponding to a vertex $v_i$ in the adjacency matrix, $T$, for a graph G. Row $R_i$ has a one in each column $j$ for which an edge $e = (v_i, v_j)$ exists in the edge set $E$ of graph G. We could represent the information in row $R_i$ using a bit vector. A bit vector representing row $R_i$ would consist of a sequence of $n$ bits packed together, $R_i = b_1 b_2 \ldots b_n$, such that bit $b_j = T[i,j]$. We can use the **BitSet** class from the **java.util** package in the Java class library to support this representation directly. Each object that is an instance of the **BitSet** class contains a bit array for which each element in the bit array is a bit that is either *set* (to **1**) or *cleared* (to **0**). You can create a bit array with an initial size having all bits cleared (to **0**). For example,

    BitSet B = new BitSet(64);

creates a **BitSet** whose bit array has 64 bits that are initially cleared (to **0**). You can then set bits in **B**. For example, executing **B.set(23)**, sets bit **23** (to **1**). The method

---

[1] The symbol "iff" means "if and only if."

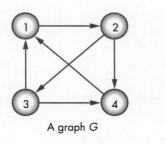

A graph G

| | 1 | 2 | 3 | 4 |
|---|---|---|---|---|
| 1 | 0 | 1 | 0 | 0 |
| 2 | 0 | 0 | 1 | 1 |
| 3 | 1 | 0 | 0 | 1 |
| 4 | 1 | 0 | 0 | 0 |

An adjacency matrix
$T[i,j]$ for G

**Figure 8.55** A Graph G and Its Adjacency Matrix

call B.get(i), returns the boolean value true if bit i is set to 1, and returns the boolean value false if bit i is cleared (or if the index i falls beyond the end of B's bit array). Given two bit sets, $B_1$ and $B_2$, you can take their bitwise logical and (using $B_1$.and($B_2$)) or their bitwise logical or (using $B_1$.or($B_2$)). Moreover, you can copy them, test two of them for bitwise equality, and generate the string representation of their bit arrays (using B.toString( )) in order to print their representations. (In this section, we informally refer to Java BitSets as *bit vectors* because they are ordered sequences of bits indexed by integers rather than being unordered "sets" of elements, and because this terminology is used sufficiently often that it is worth mentioning.)

using Java bit vectors to
represent edge sets

Thus, row $R_i$ of adjacency matrix $T$ can be represented by a Java bit vector specifying which vertices belong to row $R_i$ and which do not belong, where vertex $v_j$ at the top of column $j$ is defined to belong to row $R_i$ iff $T[i,j] = 1$. You can see that this bit vector representation for $R_i$ is identical to the adjacency set for vertex $v_i$, because the vertices $v_j$ that belong to it are exactly those that are adjacent to vertex $v_i$.

Another family of representations for a graph uses list representations of the adjacency sets $V_x$ for the vertices $x$ in the graph. For instance, we could replace each row $R_i$ of the adjacency matrix $T$ with a list of the numbers $j$ of the vertices $v_j$ corresponding to the 1's in row $R_i$. Such adjacency lists are just another representation for the adjacency sets mentioned above, and these adjacency lists could be represented either with sequential or linked representations as shown in Fig. 8.56. Here, the length of each sequentially represented adjacency list is given in the *degree* column. Recall that, in an undirected graph the *degree* of a vertex $v$ is the number of edges that touch $v$, whereas, in a directed graph each vertex has two kinds of degrees. The *in-degree* of $v$ is the number of arrows that terminate on $v$. The *out-degree* of $v$ is the number of arrows that start at vertex $v$. Consequently, the *degree* column in the sequentially represented adjacency list table actually gives the out-degree of each vertex in Fig. 8.56.

You can see that the adjacency matrix $T$ corresponding to an *undirected graph* is a *symmetric matrix*. In particular, $T[i,j] = T[j,i]$ for all $i$ and $j$ in the range ($1 \le i, j \le n$). This means that the top half of the matrix $T$ above the diagonal $d$ (which runs from the top-left corner to the bottom-right corner of $T$) is a mirror image of the bottom half of

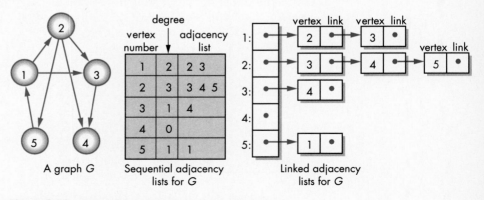

A graph G        Sequential adjacency        Linked adjacency
                 lists for G                  lists for G

**Figure 8.56** Sequential and Linked Adjacency Lists

matrix $T$ that lies below the diagonal $d$. Also, the diagonal entries of $d$ are themselves zero—i.e., $T[i,i] = 0$ for $i$ in $(1 \leq i \leq n)$, since graphs as we have defined them are not permitted to have looping self-referential edges that connect a vertex to itself.

The adjacency matrix $T$ for a directed graph need not be a symmetric matrix, since it is permissible for a directed edge to go from $v_i$ to $v_j$ without there being an edge from $v_j$ to $v_i$ traveling in the reverse direction. In such a case we would have $T[i,j] = 1$ and $T[j,i] = 0$. The adjacency matrix in Fig. 8.55 is an example of such an unsymmetric matrix.

In considering search or traversal algorithms for graphs, in which we would like to visit the vertices of a graph $G$ in some systematic order, it is useful to distinguish two separate cases. If $G$ is an undirected graph consisting of a single big connected component, or $G$ is a directed graph consisting of a single strongly connected component, then we can start at any arbitrary vertex of $G$ and we can reach all the other vertices of $G$ by following various paths in $G$. That is, all vertices of $G$ are accessible, starting from any arbitrary vertex in $G$.

On the other hand, if $G$ is a directed graph with a single weakly connected component, or if it is either an undirected or a directed graph with several separate components, then we cannot start at any arbitrary vertex $v$ of $G$ and expect to reach all the other vertices of $G$ by following paths starting at $v$. In the search algorithms explored in the next section, the algorithms we study will take into account this more difficult situation where we may possibly start at a vertex $v$ in $G$ from which it is not possible to access all vertices of $G$.

*accessing all vertices from a starting vertex*

## **8.13** REVIEW QUESTIONS

1. What is the adjacency matrix for a graph G? How do the adjacency matrices for directed and undirected graphs differ?
2. Describe how to use Java **BitSet**s to represent a graph, G.
3. What do adjacency sets represent in a graph representation that uses them?
4. What is the difference between the in-degree and the out-degree of a vertex in a directed graph?

## **8.13** EXERCISES

1. In Fig. 8.56, the adjacency lists actually list the vertices in the successor vertex sets, Succ(x) for each vertex x in the graph G. Describe how to compute lists of the predecessor vertices, Pred(x) for each x in the graph G, starting with an adjacency matrix, T[i,j] for G.
2. Give an algorithm for converting a representation of a directed graph G, given as an array of linked lists of successor vertices, into a representation of G that uses Java **BitSet**s to represent the adjacency sets.

## 8.14　Graph Searching

### LEARNING OBJECTIVES

1. To learn about abstract algorithms for depth-first and breadth-first searching in graphs.
2. To learn about the roles stacks and queues can play in organizing searches in graphs.

*the basic idea*

Let's start with some preliminaries. To search a graph G, we need to visit all of G's vertices in some systematic order. To do this, we usually proceed by identifying some vertex $v$ in G as a starting point. We then systematically enumerate all the other vertices accessible from $v$ along paths in G. Program Strategy 8.57 presents this basic idea.

*visiting accessible vertices*

We next develop some ideas for enumerating and visiting all vertices $w$ in V that are accessible from an initial starting vertex $v$ in V. First, because the graph we are searching may contain cycles, we need some way for marking a vertex as having been visited so that we do not travel around cycles in an endless loop visiting vertices we have already seen before.

Let's assume that each vertex $v$ is a Java object having a **boolean**-valued data field **v.visited**, which is initially set to **false** for all vertices in G (which are all initially unvisited) and which later gets set to **true**, immediately after we have visited $v$.

Now we need a way to enumerate the vertices accessible from some vertex $x$. To do this, we can assume we have an adjacency list $V_x$ (or an equivalent representation for $x$'s adjacency set chosen from the possibilities we discussed in the last section). If vertex $x$ has not been visited before, we mark it as having been visited, by setting **x.visited = true;**. Then we access the adjacency list $V_x$ and we enter all the unvisited vertices on the list $V_x$ into some sort of storage container, C, which holds unvisited vertices we need to visit in the future.

*continuing the search*

To continue the search process, provided that container C is not empty, we remove a new vertex $x$ from C, mark $x$ as having been visited, and then enter all the unvisited vertices on $V_x$ into C. This process is repeated until C becomes empty.

*two kinds of containers*

Let's now write this as Program Strategy 8.58, which is a refinement of Program Strategy 8.57, and see what happens in two separate cases: (1) when the container C is a *stack*, and (2) when the container C is a *queue*.

```
|    void graphSearch(G,v) {              // search graph G starting at vertex v
|
|        (let G = (V,E) and let v ∈ V be a vertex of G.)
|
5 |      for (each vertex w ∈ V that is accessible from v) {
|            visit(w);
|        }
|    }
```

**Program Strategy 8.57** Preliminary Graph Searching Strategy

```
 |    void graphSearch(G,v) {                        // search graph G beginning at vertex v
 |
 |        (let G = (V,E) be a graph.)
 |        (let C be an empty container.)
5 |
 |            for (each vertex x ∈ V) {
 |                x.visited = false;        // mark each vertex x ∈ V as being unvisited
 |            }
 |
10 |        // use vertex v ∈ V as a starting point, and put v in container C
 |
 |            (put v into C);
 |
 |            while (C is non-empty) {
15 |
 |                (remove a vertex x from container C);
 |
 |                if ( !(x.visited) ) {              // if vertex hasn't been visited already
 |                    visit(x);                                      // visit x, and then
20 |                    x.visited = true;            // mark x as having been visited.
 |                    for (each vertex w ∈ Vₓ) {      // enter all unvisited vertices
 |                        if ( !(w.visited) )  (put w into C);       // of Vₓ into C
 |                    }
 |                }
25 |            }
 |
 |    }
```

**Program Strategy 8.58** First Refinement

the stack

When C is a stack, let's suppose that the meaning of the operation **(put v into C)** means "push the vertex *v* onto the top of stack C." Let's also suppose that the operation **(remove a vertex x from container C)** means "pop the topmost vertex from C and put it in *x*."

Let's now try executing this stack-container version of Program Strategy 8.58 on the tree in Fig. 8.59, using vertex 1 at the root of the tree as a starting point.

First, we push vertex 1 onto the top of an initially empty stack C, getting C = (1). Then we repeatedly pop vertices from C, mark them visited, and push their unvisited neighbors on C, until C becomes empty. Let's trace this through.

**Figure 8.59** A Tree to Search

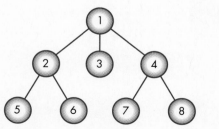

First C = (1). Then we pop 1 from C and put it in $x$, after which C = () and $x$ = 1. We then visit $x$, and mark it as visited, denoting this, say, by changing $x$ = 1 into $x$ = $\underline{1}$. Following this, we push the unvisited vertices on $V_1$ = (2,3,4) onto C, which gives C = (2,3,4). (Here, we suppose that we push the vertices onto C in the order 4, 3, 2.)

Since C is not empty, we perform the statements in the while-loop on lines 14:25 of Program Strategy 8.58. First, we pop C into $x$, giving C = (3,4) and $x$ = 2. We mark $x$ visited, giving $x$ = $\underline{2}$, and we push the unmarked vertices on $V_2$ = (5,6) onto C, again in the order: 6, 5. This gives C = (5,6,3,4).

Since C is again nonempty, we pop 5 from C, mark it as $\underline{5}$, and push its unmarked neighbors (of which there are none) onto C. This makes C = (6,3,4). Similarly, 6 and 3 are popped from C and are marked as $\underline{6}$ and $\underline{3}$. Since neither $\underline{6}$ nor $\underline{3}$ have any unmarked neighbors, C now becomes C = (4). After removing 4 from C and marking it as $\underline{4}$, we push $\underline{4}$'s unmarked neighbors (7,8) onto C. These are in turn popped from C, and marked as $\underline{7}$ and $\underline{8}$. But since neither 7 nor 8 had any unmarked neighbors, C became empty and remained empty after the removal of $\underline{7}$ and $\underline{8}$. Consequently, the while-loop on lines 14:25 terminates the next time the while-condition on line 14 is tested, immediately after the iteration on which 8 got marked as $\underline{8}$.

You can see that the order in which the nodes of Fig. 8.59 got visited was 1, 2, 5, 6, 3, 4, 7, and 8. This is called a *depth-first order* since any unvisited descendants of a given node $x$ were always visited before any unvisited right brothers or sisters in the tree. In short in any tree, given a choice, depth-first searching always goes *down* (by visiting unvisited children) before going *across* (by visiting unvisited brothers and sisters of a previous parent vertex). If you go down before going across, you are performing depth-first search.

In generalized graphs, however, the directions *down* and *across* lose their meanings. Instead, what happens when depth-first searching is used is that immediate unvisited neighbors of a given vertex $v$ are always visited before any unvisited neighbors of the vertex $w$, which was visited immediately before $v$. If you look at the (di)graph of Fig. 8.60, which turns the graph of Fig. 8.59 on its side and adds directed edges to it, you'll see that depth-first search of Fig. 8.60, beginning at vertex 1, still visits the same numbered vertices in the same order.

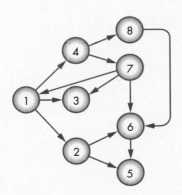

**Figure 8.60** Another Graph to Search

using a queue as a
container

Now let's change the container C used in Program Strategy 8.58 from a stack into a queue. Given that C is a queue, let's suppose that the meaning of the operation (put v into C) means "insert the vertex $v$ onto the rear of queue C," and let's also suppose that the operation (remove a vertex x from container C) means "remove the first vertex from the front of queue C and put it in $x$."

Let's again trace the execution of Program Strategy 8.58 on the tree of Fig. 8.59 under these new conditions using a queue C. Suppose that we again start with C = (1).

tracing the search process
using a queue

We first remove the vertex 1 from the front of queue C and put it in $x$, giving C = () and $x$ = 1. After marking $x$ = $\underline{1}$ as visited, we enter the unvisited neighbors of vertex $\underline{1}$ onto the rear of queue C, giving C = (2,3,4). (However, this time, we enter the vertices 2, 3, and 4 in left-to-right order: 2, 3, 4.) We again remove the first vertex 2 from the *front* of queue C and mark it as $\underline{2}$, after which we insert its unmarked neighbors (5,6) onto the *rear* of queue C, giving C = (3,4,5,6). Removing and marking 3 from C leaves C = (4,5,6). Since $\underline{3}$ had no unvisited neighbors, C's rear did not grow as a result of processing $\underline{3}$. After removing 4 and processing it, $\underline{4}$'s unvisited neighbors (7,8) are added to the rear of C, which yields C = (5,6,7,8). These final vertices in C are removed and processed in order, after which C becomes empty and the process terminates.

The order in which the vertices of Fig. 8.59 were visited in this version of graph searching was 1, 2, 3, 4, 5, 6, 7, and 8. You can see that the vertices of the tree in Fig. 8.59 have been visited in level order. We call this process *breadth-first searching*,

breadth-first searching

since we process all unvisited immediate neighbors of a given vertex $x$ *before* processing any neighbors of $x$'s neighbors—meaning that we go *broad* in the search before we go *deep*. Again, if you perform breadth-first search on the graph of Fig. 8.60, you visit the nodes in the order 1:8, even though there are additional directed edges in the graph when it is compared to the simple tree of Fig. 8.59.

making sure we visit
all vertices

Either the stack version or the queue version of Program Strategy 8.58 will visit every vertex in a graph G provided G is a directed graph with a single strongly connected component or an undirected graph with a single connected component. However, under other circumstances in which some vertices of G are not accessible via paths starting at the initially chosen vertex $v$ in the search, Program Strategy 8.58 will not visit all vertices of G. In such cases, we can embed Program Strategy 8.58 inside an enumeration of vertices of G to ensure all vertices of G will eventually be visited, as shown in Program Strategy 8.61.

```
    |   void exhaustiveGraphSearch(G) {
    |
    |       (let G = (V,E) be a graph.)
    |
 5  |       for (each vertex v ∈ V) {              // perform Program Strategy 8.58
    |           graphSearch(G,v);                  // for each v ∈ V
    |       }
    |
    |   }
```

**Program Strategy 8.61** Exhaustive Version of Graph Searching

If you know whether or not every vertex in G is accessible from any arbitrary starting vertex $v$ in G, you'll have the information you need to choose whether to use the simpler Program Strategy 8.58 or the stronger version given in Program Strategy 8.61.

## 8.14 REVIEW QUESTIONS

1. Describe the difference between depth-first searching and breadth-first searching in a tree, then describe the difference between depth-first and breadth-first searching in a general graph.
2. What are the differences between using stacks and using queues to hold unvisited vertices that need to be visited in the future during graph searching?
3. How can we ensure that a graph searching process will visit all possible vertices, even though the graph being searched is not a single connected component?

## 8.14 EXERCISES

1. Trace the operation of Program Strategy 8.58, using a queue as the container C, on the graph of Fig. 8.60, and show both the order in which the vertices are visited and the contents of the queue C at each stage.
2. Implement a refinement of Program Strategy 8.58 in which adjacency sets $V_x$ are represented using linked lists.
3. Implement a new version of Program Strategy 8.58 that performs depth-first searching using recursion instead of using a stack container C.
4. Implement new versions of Program Strategies 8.58 and 8.61 that are guaranteed to visit each vertex of a graph once and only once.

## 8.15 Topological Ordering

### LEARNING OBJECTIVES

1. To understand the concept of a topological order.
2. To learn an algorithm for producing a topological order.

topological order

Suppose we have a directed graph G that contains no cycles. For example, G might be a graph in which the vertices represent college courses to take and in which an edge is directed from the vertex for course A to the vertex for course B if course A is a prerequisite for course B. A *topological ordering* for the vertices in graph G is a sequential list L of G's vertices such that if there is a directed path from vertex A to vertex B in G, then A comes before B in the list L. In the case of the prerequisite graph G for college courses, L would list courses in an order such that all prerequisites of each course C are listed before C itself occurs in the list L.

Figure 8.62 shows a directed graph G containing no cycles and gives a topological order for the vertices in G. (If a graph G contains no cycles, it is said to be an *acyclic graph*. The abbreviation *DAG* is sometimes used for a *directed acyclic graph*.)

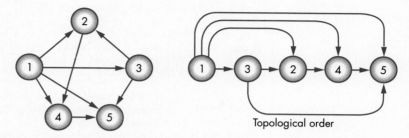

**Figure 8.62** A Directed Acyclic Graph and Its Vertices in Topological Order

Let G be a DAG. Let's see if we can think through a rough general strategy for discovering a topological order for the vertices of G. We know that we cannot place a particular vertex $v$ in G on the list $L$ until all of $v$'s predecessors have been listed in $L$. Suppose we have an array $D[v]$ that gives the in-degree of each vertex $v$ in G. The vertices $v$ in G that have no predecessors in G are the ones in array $D$ having zero for in-degrees. That is, if $D[v] == 0$, it means $v$ has no predecessors, since the in-degree counts the number of predecessors. So to start the list $L$, we could initially list all vertices $v$ of G that have no predecessors, which consists of those vertices $v$ such that $D[v] == 0$. A step of an abstract program strategy to accomplish this might read

*initializing the list L*

(initially let $L$ be the list of all vertices $v$, such that $D[v] == 0$).

Now, suppose we decide to make the array entry $D[v]$ keep track of the number of remaining predecessors of $v$ that have not already been listed in $L$. That is, we decide to change the meaning of $D[v]$ from

$$D[v] == \text{(the number of predecessors of vertex } v \text{ in graph G)}$$

to become

$$D[v] == \text{(the number of predecessors } p \text{ of vertex } v \text{ in graph G, such that } p \notin L).$$

To update the array $D$ to keep track only of the number of predecessors that have *not been listed* in list $L$, we need to change the counts in $D$ at the moment we add a new vertex $v$ to the end of list $L$. To do this, we can enumerate the successors of $v$ and decrease each of their remaining in-degree counts by 1. Some steps of a program strategy to do this would be

*updating the remaining in-degree counts*

```
// add vertex v to the end of list L
    for (each successor w ∈ Succ(v) in the graph G) {
        D[w] − −;
    }
```

*adding new vertices to the list L*

When the successors $w \in Succ(v)$ have their in-degree counts decreased, as a result of putting $v$ on the end of list $L$, some of them may reach a condition in which their in-

```
   |    List topologicalOrder(Graph G) {
   |
   |        (let G = (V,E) be a graph.)
   |        (let L be a list of vertices.)                      // see Figure 6.4
  5|        (let Q be a queue of vertices.)                     // for queue operations
   |        (let D[V] be an array of integers indexed by vertices in V.)
   |
   |        // compute the in-degrees D[x] of the vertices x in G
   |            for (each vertex x ∈ V) D[x] = 0;               // initialize D[x] to zero
 10|            for (each vertex x ∈ V) {
   |                for (each successor w ∈ Succ(x)) D[w]++;
   |            }
   |
   |        // initialize the queue Q to contain all vertices having zero in-degrees
 15|            Q = new Queue( );              // initialize Q to be the empty queue
   |            for (each vertex x ∈ V) {                       // insert x on the
   |                if (D[x] == 0) Q.insert(x);           // rear of Q if D[x] == 0
   |            }
   |
 20|        // initialize the list L to be the empty list
   |            L = new List( );
   |
   |        // process vertices in the queue Q until the queue becomes empty
   |            while ( !Q.empty( ) ) {
 25|                x = Q.remove( );             // remove vertex x from the front of Q
   |                L.append(x);                      // insert x on the rear of list L
   |                for (each successor w ∈ Succ(x)) {
   |                    D[w] – –;                    // decrease predecessor count of w
   |                    if (D[w] == 0) Q.insert(w);        // insert w on the rear of Q
 30|                }
   |            }
   |
   |        // the list L now contains the vertices of G in topological order.
   |            return L;
   |    }
```

**Program Strategy 8.63** Topological Ordering

degrees have diminished to zero, $D[w] == 0$. This signifies that all of their predecessors have already been listed in $L$. Consequently, there is an opportunity to put $w$ on the end of list $L$, since it now has no predecessors that have not been listed already. If we maintain a queue of vertices with in-degree 0 to be added to the end of list $L$, we can place $w$ on this queue immediately after its in-degree decreases to zero. Let $Q$ be a queue of vertices with in-degree 0 awaiting processing. We can then rewrite the above program fragment as

```
// add vertex v to the end of list L
    for (each successor w ∈ Succ(v) in the graph G) {
        D[w] – –;
        if ( D[w] == 0 ) (insert w in queue Q);
    }
```

We can agree to let the role of the queue, $Q$, be the same as that for the queue used in breadth-first searching of a graph G. Namely, $Q$ can contain vertices that remain to be visited in breadth-first order. Essentially, we can modify the algorithm for performing a breadth-first search, using the queue $Q$, so that it repeatedly removes a new vertex $v$ from the front of queue $Q$, puts $v$ on the end of list $L$, decreases the in-degrees of the successors of $v$, and inserts on the end of $Q$ any such successors of $v$ whose in-degrees have decreased to zero. By this means, a queue-driven, breadth-first searching process enumerates vertices in topological order and adds them to the end of the list $L$.

A complete strategy for accomplishing this is presented as Program Strategy 8.63. Exercise 8.15.1 asks you to implement this program strategy in Java using an array of references to linked representations of adjacency lists as the representation for the directed graph G.

## 8.15 REVIEW QUESTIONS

1. What is a DAG (i.e., a directed acyclic graph)?
2. Define the concept of a topological order for the vertices of a DAG.
3. Sketch a process for finding a topological order for the vertices of a DAG.

## 8.15 EXERCISES

1. Implement Program Strategy 8.63 in Java using an array of references to linked representations of adjacency lists as the representation for the directed acyclic graph G.
2. How could you augment Program Strategy 8.63 to detect illegal cycles in the graph G?
3. Can you give a second abstract strategy for producing a topological ordering of the vertices in a directed, acyclic graph using a modification of the recursive strategy for performing a depth-first search of G?
4. Analyze the running time of your implementation of Program Strategy 8.63. Can you show that it is $O(e + n)$, where $n$ is the number of vertices in G and $e$ is the number of edges in G?

---

## ▮ Pitfalls

- *Not treating empty trees carefully during tree traversals*

   When designing tree traversals both recursive and nonrecursive techniques come readily to mind. The nonrecursive techniques can often profit from the systematic use of stacks and queues. One pitfall that seems to be encountered frequently is failure to consider the case of empty trees properly. If tests for empty trees are absent in key places, it can cause nonrecursive traversal algorithms to attempt to dereference the null pointer, and recursive traversal algorithms can fail to terminate with the proper base cases. As an illustration, determine what is wrong with the following version of Program 8.26.

```
       |    void traverse(TreeNode N, int traversalOrder) {
       |
       |        if ( traversalOrder == PRE_ORDER ) {
       |
    5  |            visit(N);                        // if N == null, visit(N) does nothing
       |            traverse(N.llink, PRE_ORDER);
       |            traverse(N.rlink, PRE_ORDER);
       |
       |        } else if ( traversalOrder == IN_ORDER ) {
   10  |
       |            traverse(N.llink, IN_ORDER);
       |            visit(N);
       |            traverse(N.rlink, IN_ORDER);
       |
   15  |        } else if ( traversalOrder == POST_ORDER) {
       |
       |            traverse(N.llink, POST_ORDER);
       |            traverse(N.rlink, POST_ORDER);
       |            visit(N);
   20  |        }
       |    }
```

- *The hidden expense of dynamic memory allocation*

   When implementing certain kinds of search trees, such as 2–3 trees, one often uses an underlying dynamic memory allocation scheme of unknown expense to allocate nodes of different sizes (such as nodes having either two or three children). Not all underlying dynamic memory allocation schemes operate with peak efficiency. Some use costly linear search algorithms to find new free blocks to allocate. If performance is critical, it might be best to apply the philosophy of *measurement and tuning* by measuring the performance of the underlying dynamic memory system, and comparing it, if necessary, to one that you implement from scratch using arrays of node types of identical size having available space lists of free nodes under your own direct control.

## ■ Tips and Techniques

- *Be prepared to use binary search tree representations to achieve performance*

   Binary search trees can often supply representations that yield substantial performance advantages when representing List ADTs or tables. If the mix of operations involves insertions and deletions, as well as searches, then AVL trees can provide substantial performance advantages over linked list or sequential list representations. The trick of adding an extra field, **F**, to each node, **N**, of an AVL tree, such that **F** contains one plus the number of nodes in **N**'s left subtree, can be used as a basis for algorithms giving rapid random access to the $k^{\text{th}}$ node, given $k$, and for calculating the total number of nodes in the tree to represent the length function of a List ADT). Look-up tables that associate records with search keys can also profit from the use of binary search tree representations when the table is expected to undergo changes resulting from insertions and deletions of new rows.

- *Know when to use AVL trees instead of ordinary binary search trees*

    The use of AVL trees incurs a substantial programming expense, so it may not be appropriate to use them when it suffices to use ordinary binary search trees. If keys arrive for insertion in an ordinary binary search tree in fairly random order, then it may not be necessary to implement AVL trees to maintain reasonable balance. However, if keys tend to arrive in sorted order, or in runs or bursts of a given order (such as descending or ascending order), then trees constructed from them will tend to become deep and skinny (these being the binary search trees with poor performance). Under such circumstances, it may pay to convert to the use of AVL trees.

- *Use heaps to implement priority queues when appropriate*

    If you have an application that needs to use priority queues, using the heap representation for priority queues could yield important payoffs. Priority queues can occur in many contexts. Some examples are (a) event-driven simulation systems (in which events are time-stamped and the next event to simulate is the one closest in time to the current time); (b) searches in game-trees in which the next move to explore is the one starting from the node in the game-tree having the highest strategic score; (c) priority scheduling algorithms in operating systems, in which the task to schedule for execution next is the one having highest priority; and (d) various "best-first" algorithms, where the next step in the algorithm involves choosing the best candidate among the available candidates at the moment.

## ■ References for Further Study

*a thorough reference*

Donald E. Knuth has written a classical, thorough reference that develops the performance characteristics of many kinds of trees.

> Knuth, D. E., *The Art of Computer Programming, Searching and Sorting*, vol. 3, 2nd ed. Addison-Wesley, Reading, MA (1973).

*a useful survey*

Jurg Nievergelt has written a survey article that explores balanced binary trees a bit further than the discussion in this book.

> Nievergelt, J., "Binary Search Trees and File Organization," *Computing Surveys* 6: 3 (September 1974), pp. 195–207.

*where to find those missing derivations*

The missing mathematical derivations of the results cited but not derived in this book are found in two other books by the author.

> Standish, T. A. , *Data Structures, Algorithms, and Software Principles* (in Pascal) and *Data Structures, Algorithms, and Software Principles in C*. Addison-Wesley, Reading, MA (1994 and 1995, respectively).

some references
on graph theory

Claude Berge has written a classical reference on the mathematical theory of graphs.

> Berge, C., *The Theory of Graphs and Its Applications*. John Wiley,
> New York, NY (1968).

and graph algorithms

A good book on graph algorithms has been written by Shimon Even.

> Shimon Even, *Graph Algorithms*. Computer Science Press, Rockville, MD (1979).

## ■ Chapter Summary

In computer science, it is traditional to draw diagrams of trees *upside-down* with the *root* at the top and the *leaves* at the bottom. The *leaves* of a tree are the nodes having no *descendants*, and the *root* is the node having no *parent*. There is always exactly one path from the root of a tree to a given node. Nodes that are not leaves are called *internal nodes*.

basic tree anatomy

A *binary tree* is either the empty tree or a node having left and right subtrees that are binary trees.

binary trees

A *complete binary tree* is one having leaves either on a single level or on two adjacent levels, such that the leaves on the bottommost level are in the leftmost positions and such that all levels, except possibly the last, have nodes in all possible positions. A complete binary tree of $n$ nodes has an efficient contiguous sequential representation in which the nodes are placed in level order into an array $A[1{:}n]$. In this representation, $A[1]$ contains the root, and the children of $A[i]$, if they exist, are in $A[2{*}i]$ and $A[2{*}i + 1]$. A node $A[i]$ is a leaf just when $2{*}i > n$ (since, to the contrary, if $A[i]$ were not a leaf, it would then have a left child at position $2{*}i$, which would have to be less than or equal to the position, $n$, of the last node $A[n]$).

complete binary trees

*Heaps* are complete binary trees having values at the nodes such that the values are arranged in descending order along any path from the root toward the leaves. In a heap, the highest value always sits at the root. Heaps provide efficient representations for *priority queues*. A complete tree of $n$ items can be arranged into a heap in time $O(n)$ and items can be removed and inserted into heaps in time $O(\log n)$. Consequently, heaps provide a more efficient representation for priority queues than alternatives such as linked lists, or arrays of items kept in sorted or random order.

heaps

A *traversal* of a binary tree is a process that systematically visits each node in the tree exactly once. Three common traversal orders for binary trees are *PreOrder*, *InOrder*, and *PostOrder*. If a binary tree for an algebraic expression is traversed in postorder and the symbols at its nodes are emitted when the nodes are visited, a postfix instruction string results. The value of this postfix string can be calculated by a postfix interpreter, using a stack to hold intermediate values of subexpressions. This idea served as the basis for many early programming language processors, which translated source programs into postfix, and used stack-based, run-time interpreters to execute the postfix instructions.

tree traversals

Traversals of linked representations of binary trees can be accomplished easily using recursive methods. Traversals can also be accomplished by nonrecursive methods that use stacks or queues to hold pointers to subtrees awaiting further traversal. When a stack is used, if, after visiting node $N$, the pointers to the right and left subtrees of $N$ are pushed onto the stack, a preorder traversal occurs by processing subtrees in the order that results from popping subtree pointers from the stack. Using a queue, and inserting subtree pointers on the rear of the queue, while removing subtree pointers from the front of the queue, yields a *level order* tree traversal.

**binary search trees**

*Binary search trees* are binary trees with keys stored in the nodes, such that, for each node, $N$, the keys in the left subtree of $N$ are less than the key in node $N$, and the keys in the right subtree of $N$ are greater than the key in node $N$. If you traverse a binary search tree using InOrder, the keys in the nodes are visited in ascending order. A sorting method called **TreeSort** consists of inserting keys into a binary search tree in the order originally given, and then in reading off the keys in the resulting binary search tree using an InOrder traversal.

In a binary search tree, the *level* of a node, $N$, is the length of the path from the root to node $N$ (where the *length* of a path is the number of edges in it). The *height* of a binary search tree is the length of the longest path from its root to some leaf (where the *height* of an *empty tree* is defined to be −1 as a special case).

**the performance of binary search trees**

Among binary search trees built up by inserting keys into an initially empty tree in random order, the worst case search times occur in trees that are deep and skinny—those having only one internal node on each level. In this worst case, with keys in a tree of $n$ nodes chosen with equal likelihood for use in the search, the average search time is $O(n)$. The best case search times occur in trees that are as balanced as possible—those having leaves on one level or on two adjacent levels. In this case, average search times are $O(\log n)$, where, again, each key in such a tree is equally likely to be chosen for use in the search. If trees are randomly constructed, using with equal likelihood any of the possible orderings of keys for building up the tree by the insertion method, then deep skinny trees are relatively rare and reasonably balanced trees are fairly common. In such trees, on the average, a search for a randomly chosen key takes only 38.6 percent more time than it does in the best case, using balanced trees with leaves on at most two levels.

**AVL trees**

An *AVL tree* is a binary search tree in which each node, $N$, has the property that the height of $N$'s left and right subtrees differ by at most one. If insertion of a new node should cause an AVL tree to lose the AVL property at a given node, four shape-changing tree transformations, called *rotations*, can be applied to a local portion of the tree to restore the AVL property. AVL trees have good performance, in that searches, insertions, and deletions require at most $O(\log n)$ time. This overcomes the worst case $O(n)$ performance possible with randomly constructed binary search trees.

Theoretically, the worst case performance of an AVL tree can be at most 44 percent worse than that of the best case binary search tree (with leaves on at most two levels). Moreover, empirical studies indicate that the *average* performance of AVL trees is remarkably close to that of the best case binary search trees. AVL trees can therefore be warmly recommended for use any time a binary search tree representation is advantageous. For example, using AVL trees to represent a List ADT provides $O(\log n)$ performance, overcoming the disadvantage of linked list representations (which require time $O(n)$ to locate the $k^{\text{th}}$ item, given $k$) and overcoming the disadvantage of contiguous sequential representations (which require time $O(n)$ to perform insertions).

2–3 trees are an alternative data structure useful for providing representations of search trees. In a 2–3 tree, nodes other than the leaves have either two or three children, and all leaves are on the same bottom level. Each node in a 2–3 tree contains either one or two keys. To insert a new key in a 2–3 tree, if adding a key to a node causes the node to overflow, the overflowed node is split into two new nodes, each containing a single key, and the middle key (among the three that caused the overflow) is passed up to be inserted into the parent node. 2–3 trees enjoy O(log n) performance properties similar to those exhibited by AVL trees.

**2–3 trees**

A *trie* is another kind of search tree based on the idea of a *discrimination net*. At the root of a trie, the initial letter of a search key is used to determine which subtree to use for further search. If the initial letter in a key distinguishes the key from all others in the trie, no further discrimination is needed, and the key resides in a leaf that is a subtree of the root accessed by a branch labeled with the key's first letter. If two or more keys share a common prefix, *p* (i.e., if the first few initial letters, *p*, of a group of keys is identical), then a search path starting at the root and labeled with the successive letters of *p* leads to a node at which a discrimination is made, using the different letters following the prefix *p* in the various keys. Unlike AVL trees and 2–3 trees, the shape of a trie is insensitive to the order in which the trie was built up, using insertions of keys. However, a trie's shape is sensitive to bunching in the prefixes of keys. Tries have remarkably good logarithmic search times.

**Tries**

Binary trees can be applied to determine minimal length encodings for messages whose letters occur with known frequency. To achieve this result, a *Huffman coding tree* is constructed. This tree assigns bit codes of differing lengths to the various letters. In general, Huffman coding trees assign shorter length bit codes to more frequent letters, and longer length bit codes to less frequent letters in a fashion that minimizes the total expected length of encoded messages.

**Huffman coding trees**

A *graph* is a collection of *vertices* in which some or all of the pairs of vertices are connected by line segments called *edges*. If directions are prescribed on the edges, we have a *directed graph*. If no directions are prescribed on the edges, we have an *undirected graph*. A *path* in a graph is a sequence of vertices in which each vertex in the sequence, except the last, is connected to its successor in the sequence by an edge in the graph. If the starting and ending vertices in a path are the same, the path forms a *cycle*.

**basic anatomy of graphs**

Undirected graphs can be divided into connected components. A *connected component* is a maximal subset of the vertices in which any two vertices are connected by a path. Any two separate components are disconnected in the sense that there is no path joining a vertex in one to a vertex in the other.

**connected components**

A *free tree* is an undirected graph that is connected but has no cycles. A *directed acyclic graph* (DAG) is a directed graph having no cycles.

**free trees**

There are many ways to represent graphs using computer data structures. For example, an adjacency matrix, $T$, with rows and columns representing the vertices, can have entries, $T[i,j]$, which are either 0 or 1. If $T[i,j] = 1$, then the edge from vertex $v_i$ to vertex $v_j$ is in the graph, whereas if $T[i,j] = 0$, then the edge from vertex $v_i$ to vertex $v_j$ is not in the graph. Rows of the adjacency matrix, $T$, can be represented compactly, using bit vectors. One can also give an array, A, of adjacency lists, where the array entry A[i] corresponds to the $i^{th}$ vertex, $v_i$, and provides a list of the other

**data representations for graphs**

vertices to which $v_i$ is connected by an edge in the graph. Such adjacency lists can be represented in either sequential or linked form. Another possibility is to use set representations of various kinds. For instance, a graph can be represented by a set of the pairs of vertices that form edges of the graph. Also, the rows of the adjacency matrix, $T$, can be represented by sets of vertices.

Graphs can be searched to find vertices having particular properties. Two methods are *depth-first search* and *breadth-first search*. When a vertex is enumerated in a search, it is marked as having been *visited*. This way, if the vertex is encountered a second or succeeding time during the search and is marked already visited, it need not be visited again. Multiple encounters of a given vertex in a graph search are possible if **graph searching** the vertex is accessible by more than one path from the starting point in the search. In graphs this can happen when paths form cycles or provide alternative routes from the starting vertex to a given destination vertex. In depth-first searching, when we arrive at a vertex $v$ along an edge from a predecessor vertex $w$, we search the unvisited successors of $v$ before searching the unvisited successors of $w$. By contrast in breadth-first searching, we search the unvisited successors of $w$ before searching the unvisited successors of $v$.

If G is a DAG, then it is possible to provide a sequential list, $L$, of the vertices of G in which each vertex $v$ of G appears on the list $L$ before any of its successors appear **topological orders** on $L$. Such an order is called a *topological order*. For example, if G gives the prerequisite relations among college courses, then a topological ordering in $L$ lists all prerequisites of each course before listing the course itself. Topological orderings for a given graph G are not unique and there are several algorithms for producing them.

# Hashing and the Table ADT

**Introduction and Motivation**

In this chapter, we can think of a *table* as an abstract storage device that contains *table entries*. Moreover, we'll agree that each table entry contains a unique key, $K$. That is, we agree that different table entries always have different keys. This implies that the key in a given table entry uniquely identifies that entry and distinguishes it from all other separate table entries. A table entry may also contain some information, $I$, associated with its key. Abstractly, then, we can think of a table entry as an ordered pair $(K,I)$, consisting of a unique key, $K$, and its associated information, $I$.

what are tables?

Given a table, $T$, *table searching* is an activity in which, given a search key, $K$, we attempt to find the table entry $(K,I)$ in $T$ containing the key $K$. Once we have found such an entry, we may wish to *retrieve* or *update* its information, $I$, or we may wish to *delete* the entire table entry $(K,I)$, by removing it from the table. If no entry with key $K$ exists in table $T$, we may wish to *insert* a new table entry having $K$ as its key. Occasionally, we may wish to *enumerate* all entries in table $T$—for example, to print a report of the contents of the table. If an ordering is defined on the keys, we may wish

some table operations

324

to perform this enumeration in, say, ascending order of the keys in the table entries. (This would be useful, for instance, if we wanted to print a report listing all table entries in the alphabetical or numerical order defined by their keys.)

By now, you can easily imagine that there are numerous ways to represent an abstract table, $T$, and to implement abstract table operations such as *retrieve*, *update*, *delete*, *insert*, or *enumerate*. For example, you could represent a table entry by a Java object having various data fields in which to store its key and its information items. Then you could use an array of such objects, stored sequentially in ascending order of their keys, to represent table $T$. On the other hand, you could add additional data fields to the objects for the table entries to contain links and balance factors, and you could link them into an AVL tree.

*some table representations*

In this chapter, we will investigate another class of representations for abstract tables relying on a technique called *hashing*. If you have never been introduced to the concepts underlying hashing before, this chapter should have great value for you, because it will expand your repertoire of useful techniques quite significantly. That is because hashing is an extraordinary discovery in computer science that provides methods yielding truly amazing performance advantages.

*hashing, an amazing discovery*

In some cases, in which there are only a small number of possible keys, $K$, that can be used in table entries, it is possible to reserve one table entry in advance for each possible key. For example, suppose we have a card game in which there are 52 cards being used. Suppose, further, that we wish to keep some information associated with each possible card, such as whether or not it has been seen in play during the game so far. Under these circumstances, it would be possible to keep a table, $T$, of 52 entries, and to reserve one entry for each possible card. We would then need a mapping to send a key, $K$, identifying a particular card (such as the 7 of spades: 7 ♠) onto one of the table addresses. These table addresses might be the integers in the range, 0:51, for example.

In other cases, although we might have a very large number of possible keys, $K$, only a fraction of all of these possible keys would be used in an actual table. For example, suppose we want to keep a table of employee records for a firm that employs 5000 people. If the firm is located in the United States, we might decide to use nine-digit social security numbers to identify each employee record. Or we might decide to issue our own employee-identification numbers chosen so as to encode information about the corporate division and department in which the employee works. For instance, on my campus of the University of California (UC), employee numbers are nine-digit numbers in which the first two digits provide a code specifying one of the nine UC campuses where the employee works. Since there are one billion ($10^9$) different nine-digit numbers, if we have 5000 employees in a given firm, only five ten-thousandths of one percent (0.0005%) of all possible keys are needed to provide a set of unique keys such that each employee record in the table is guaranteed to have a unique key.

*of the many possible keys, only a few are used*

Now let's consider the problem of how to retrieve employee records efficiently in this context. Given a search key, $K$, consisting of a particular employee number, and given a table, $T$, consisting of 5000 employee records, how shall we organize table $T$ so that retrieval of the employee record containing key $K$ is as efficient as

*retrieving records in this situation*

possible? One technique we could use is to place the records into an array in ascending (numerical) order of the keys and to use binary search to locate the record. Binary search is known to take approximately ($\log_2 5001 - 1$) comparisons (or $\approx 11.3$ comparisons), on the average, if each key is equally likely to be used. Another possibility is to arrange the employee records into an AVL tree, according to the (numerical) order of the employee numbers used as keys. In this case, on the average, searching in an AVL tree takes ($\log_2 5000 + 0.25$) comparisons (or $\approx 12.5$ comparisons).

On the other hand, we might use a technique called *double hashing*, which we will introduce later in this chapter. If we were to store the 5000 employee records in a table $T$ that had space for 6000 records, we could reduce the average number of comparisons needed to locate an employee record to fewer than 2.15 comparisons! In other words, using hashing techniques in this case enables us to perform retrieval more than four times more efficiently.

why hashing wins

Now let's consider, for a moment, how we map keys into table addresses. A *hash function* is a mapping, $h(K)$, that sends a key $K$ onto the address of a table entry in table $T$. Ordinarily, we try to store the table entry $(K,I)$ containing the key $K$ at the table address given by $h(K)$, but it may not always be possible to do so because of *collisions*. Almost always, we use hashing techniques in cases in which there are many more distinct keys $K$ than there are table addresses, and so we can encounter a situation in which two distinct keys, $K_1 \neq K_2$, map to the same table address (meaning that $h(K_1) = h(K_2)$). In this case, we cannot store both table entries $(K_1,I_1)$ and $(K_2,I_2)$ at the same table address, since there is not room for both of them, and we have what is called a *collision*. Under these circumstances, we need to invoke and use some sort of *collision resolution policy* to find additional storage in which to store one of the two table entries that cannot be stored directly at the table address given by the hash address of its key.

collision resolution policies

Three such collision resolution policies that we will mention in this chapter are collision resolution by: (1) *chaining*, (2) *open addressing*, and (3) *buckets*. We will study the first two of these policies in this chapter, and we will mention the third policy briefly. In the case of open addressing, we will find that some collision resolution methods that are initially appealing, because they are so simple to understand and implement, in fact have some performance drawbacks. However, we will discover that some alternative techniques exist, such as double hashing, that have extraordinarily good performance, and which, nonetheless, are not too difficult to understand and implement.

We will also study a couple of different ways to compute hash functions, $h(K)$, given some set of keys, $K$, that we wish to hash into table addresses. One of these methods relies simply on *division* of one integer by another.

comparing representations of abstract tables

Finally, we will compare three ways to represent abstract tables using (1) arrays of records kept in ascending sequential order of their keys, (2) AVL trees, and (3) hash tables using double hashing. Of special significance is the comparison between the efficiencies of the table operations for searching and enumeration using these three separate representations. This comparison will reveal the advantages and drawbacks of hashing in relation to the other representations.

## Plan for the Chapter

Section 9.2 introduces the concept of the Table ADT, which provides an abstract model of a table as a storage device. Table ADTs can be represented by various actual data representations, three of which are (a) hash tables, (b) AVL trees, and (c) arrays of table entries sorted in the ascending order of their keys. The Table ADT supports abstract table operations such as retrieving, updating, inserting, and deleting table entries, as well as enumeration of all entries in the table in increasing order of their keys. In Section 9.7, the performance of these three Table ADT representations is compared.

Section 9.3 introduces hashing concepts by means of a series of simple examples. The goal is to provide a clear notion of how hashing works, while introducing concepts such as collisions and probe sequences.

Section 9.4 defines the concepts of collisions, load factors and clustering more formally, and develops their properties. It is known that even in sparsely occupied hash tables, collisions are relatively frequent. Primary clustering is defined, and data are presented to show that the use of linear probing leads to the formation of primary clusters, whereas the use of double hashing does not lead to primary clustering.

Section 9.5 introduces algorithms for hashing by open addressing. It then presents two examples that use hash insertion algorithms to illustrate the formation of primary clusters when linear probing is used, but which avoid primary clustering when double hashing is used. Also, Section 9.5 shows how to choose probe sequences used by the hashing algorithms so that they completely cover all table addresses during search and insertion. Near the end of Section 9.5, performance formulas are presented that cover the average number of probes used in hashing. Finally, theoretical results from the performance formulas are compared with actual measured results from hashing experiments in order to help develop insight into when hashing methods perform well and when they do not.

Section 9.6 investigates how to choose hashing functions so that they work well, and how to avoid several pitfalls that are known to produce hashing functions that do not work well.

## 9.2 The Table ADT

### LEARNING OBJECTIVES

1. To introduce a model for a table, seen as an abstract storage device with several useful table operations.
2. To lay the groundwork for a later comparison of three actual data representations of the Table ADT in Section 9.7.
3. To present an abstraction of a table useful in modular programming using clean interfaces and deferred choice of the actual data representation to be used.

A *table*, *T*, is an abstract storage device that contains *table entries* that are either *empty* or are pairs of the form $(K,I)$, where $K$ is a key and $I$ is some information associated

1. *Construct* an initially empty table, *T*. The *empty table* is filled with *empty table entries*, $(K_0, I_0)$, where $K_0$ is a special *empty key*, distinct from all other non-empty keys.
2. Determine whether or not the table, *T*, is *empty*.
3. *Insert* a new table entry $(K, I)$, having key, *K*, and information, *I*, into the table, *T*, provided *T* is not already full.
4. *Delete* the table entry $(K, I)$ from table *T*.
5. Given a search key, *K*, *retrieve* the information, *I*, from the table entry $(K, I)$ in table, *T*.
6. *Update* the table entry $(K, I)$ in table, *T*, by replacing it with a new table entry $(K, I')$, which associates new information, *I'*, with key *K* in table *T*.
7. *Enumerate* the table entries $(K, I)$ in table, *T*, in increasing order of their keys, *K*.

**Figure 9.1** Table Operations Defining a Table ADT

with key *K*. Distinct table entries have distinct keys. Figure 9.1 presents the operations defining a Table ADT.

As an example of an abstract table ADT, consider Table 9.2, which has three-letter airport identifier codes as keys and has, as information items, the names of the associated cities where the airports are located. Each row represents a table entry, $(K, I)$, which contains a key, *K*, and some associated information, *I*, where the key, *K*, is a three-letter airport code, and the associated information, *I*, is the name of the city where the corresponding airport, designated by key *K*, is located.

In this chapter, we will explore some new ways of representing the Table ADT based on hashing. But from your knowledge of previous chapters, you can already imagine how to represent a Table ADT using techniques such as binary search trees (including AVL trees), arrays of records stored in ascending order of their keys, linked lists of records containing keys, and so forth.

**Table 9.2** Airport Codes and Names

| Key<br>K = Airport Code | Associated Information<br>I = City |
|---|---|
| AKL | Auckland, New Zealand |
| DCA | Washington, D.C. |
| FRA | Frankfurt, Germany |
| GCM | Grand Cayman, Cayman Islands |
| GLA | Glasgow, Scotland |
| HKG | Hong Kong, China |
| LAX | Los Angeles, California |
| ORY | Paris, France |
| PHL | Philadelphia, Pennsylvania |

## **9.2** REVIEW QUESTIONS

1. What is a Table ADT?
2. What operations are defined on a Table ADT?
3. Name some possible data representations for a Table ADT.

## **9.2** EXERCISES

1. Sketch how you would implement the Table ADT operations if the Table ADT were represented using arrays of table entry objects, sorted in the ascending order of their keys.
2. Sketch how you would implement the Table ADT operations if the Table ADT were represented using AVL trees of table entry objects.

## **9.3**   **Introduction to Hashing by Simple Examples**

### LEARNING OBJECTIVES

1. To gain an intuitive understanding of hashing concepts using simple examples.
2. To become familiar with hash functions, collisions, collision resolution policies, open addressing, probe sequences, chaining, and buckets.
3. To lay the groundwork for understanding the performance of hashing algorithms.

*some simple examples*

A good way to introduce basic concepts of hashing is to consider some simple examples. Once these are fresh in our minds, it will be easy to understand the more general principles of hashing.

*keys with subscripts*

In these simple examples, we will use, as keys, letters of the alphabet having subscripts, such as $A_1$, $B_2$, $C_3$, $R_{18}$ and $Z_{26}$. Each letter's subscript is an integer giving the letter's position in alphabetical order. For instance, since the letter "A" is the first letter in the alphabet, its subscript is "1," yielding $A_1$ as a key. Similarly, since Z is the last of the 26 letters in the alphabet, its key is $Z_{26}$. Again, from the key, $R_{18}$, we can verify that the letter "R" is the 18th letter in the alphabet.

The table, $T$, that we will use is deliberately chosen to be very small. In fact, table $T$ contains space for only seven entries, numbered from 0 to 6.

Figure 9.3 shows an example of table $T$, with the keys $J_{10}$, $B_2$, and $S_{19}$ inserted. (For simplicity, no associated information has been shown along with the keys in table $T$. In other words, we are considering only where to store the keys in $T$, and we are ignoring the associated information, for the sake of simplicity.)

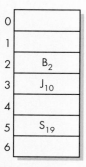

The locations in table $T$ used for storing the keys $J_{10}$, $B_2$, and $S_{19}$, were computed by dividing 7 into the value of the key's subscript and determining the *remainder* after division by 7. For example, to find where to try to insert the key $J_{10}$ into an initially empty table $T$ we divide the subscript 10 by 7, getting a quotient of 1 and a remainder of 3. So we try to insert $J_{10}$ into location 3 in table T.

**Figure 9.3** Table T

Likewise, to insert $B_2$ into table $T$, we divide the subscript 2 by 7, getting a quotient of 0 and a remainder of 2. So we try to insert $B_2$ into location 2 in table $T$. Finally, to place the key $S_{19}$ into table $T$, we divide the subscript 19 by 7, getting a quotient of 2 and a remainder of 5. So we try to insert $S_{19}$ into location 5 in table $T$.

In general, to find where in table $T$ to try initially to place a key, $L_n$, consisting of the letter "L" and the subscript "$n$," we take the remainder of $n$ after division by 7 (which is computed by evaluating $n \% 7$ in Java). The function, $h(L_n)$ which computes this location is given in symbols by

the definition of $h(L_n)$

$$h(L_n) = n \% 7. \tag{9.1}$$

We refer to $h(L_n)$ as a *hash function* of the key, $L_n$. A good hash function, $h(L_n)$, will map keys, $L_n$, uniformly and randomly onto the full range of possible locations (0:6) in table $T$.

Now let's try inserting the new keys $N_{14}$, $X_{24}$, and $W_{23}$ into the table $T$ shown in Fig. 9.3. If we try placing the key $N_{14}$ into the table location, $h(N_{14}) = 0$, we are lucky to find an empty slot. So $N_{14}$ can be inserted directly into position 0 in table $T$. This gives the configuration of table $T$ shown in Fig. 9.4. However, when we try to place key $X_{24}$ into position $h(X_{24}) = 3$, we are not so lucky, since position 3 of table $T$ already contains the key $J_{10}$. This is called a *collision*, because the keys $X_{24}$ and $J_{10}$ collide at the same *hash address*, $3 = h(J_{10}) = h(X_{24})$, when we try to insert them both into table $T$. Now we need a policy for resolving the collision.

The simple collision resolution policy we shall use for our first example is to look in table $T$ to find the first empty entry at a lower location than the location of the collision and to insert the colliding key into that empty location. (If all the lower numbered locations below the collision location are already filled, we "wrap around" and start searching for empty locations at the highest numbered location in the table.)

For example, since $h(X_{24}) = 3$, and location 3 in table $T$ in Fig. 9.4 is already occupied by the key $J_{10}$ we look at the next lower table location, location 2, to see if it is empty. Since location 2 is occupied by the key $B_2$, we look next at location 1 and we find that location 1 is empty. Therefore we place the key $X_{24}$ in location 1. This gives the configuration of table $T$ shown in Fig. 9.5.

| 0 | $N_{14}$ |
|---|---|
| 1 | |
| 2 | $B_2$ |
| 3 | $J_{10}$ |
| 4 | |
| 5 | $S_{19}$ |
| 6 | |

**Figure 9.4** Table $T$

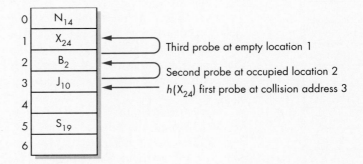

**Figure 9.5** Table $T$

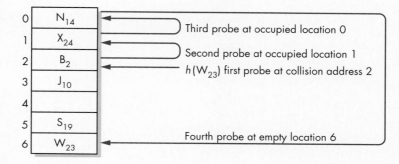

**Figure 9.6** Table T

Finally, let's try to insert the new key, $W_{23}$. When we first try to insert $W_{23}$ at its hash address, $h(W_{23}) = 2$, we find location 2 is already occupied by the key $B_2$. Consequently, we search consecutive lower numbered locations 1 and 0 to try to find an empty location. Since locations 1 and 0 are already occupied, we *wrap around* and start searching at the highest numbered location in $T$, which is location 6. Because location 6 is empty, we insert $W_{23}$ in location 6. This yields the configuration of table $T$ shown in Fig. 9.6.

**wrapping around during search**

The locations that we examine when we attempt to insert a new key, $L_n$, into table $T$ are called a *probe sequence*, since we "probe" each location in the probe sequence to see if we can find an empty location in which to insert the new key. The first location in the probe sequence is the hash address, $h(L_n)$. The second and succeeding locations in the probe sequence are determined by the *collision resolution policy*. In the case of Fig. 9.6, the probe sequence for the key $W_{23}$ starts at location 2, since $h(W_{23}) = 2$, and it continues with locations 1, 0, 6, 5, 4, and 3. The probe sequence is arranged so that it examines every different location in table $T$ exactly once.

**probe sequences**

To guarantee that we will always find an empty location in every probe sequence, we define a "full" table, $T$, to be a table having exactly one empty table entry. This way, when we search for an empty entry along the route given by the probe sequence, we need not count the number of locations visited to see if the total count equals the table size in order to determine when to stop searching. Instead, we can always expect to find an empty location somewhere along the probe sequence path, in order to stop the search.

**full tables**

In the example just given, the probe sequence for a key, $L_n$, is determined by a simple downward count, starting at the hash address, $h(L_n)$, counting downward in decrements of 1, and wrapping around to the top of table $T$ when we "fall off" the bottom. In this case, we say the *probe decrement* is 1, since 1 is used to decrease the current probe location each time we need to find the next probe location in the probe sequence. We also refer to such a probing process as *linear probing*, because the sequence of table locations that are consecutively probed forms a straight line.

**linear probing**

Also, the method of inserting keys into empty locations in table $T$ is called *open addressing*. A bit later, we will discover that the method of *open addressing with linear probing,* which we have illustrated in Figs. 9.3 to 9.6, has some serious performance drawbacks, especially when the table becomes nearly full.

In fact, there are other open addressing methods that perform much better than open addressing with linear probing. One of these methods, called *double hashing,* uses nonlinear probing by computing different probe decrements for different keys. Let's now give a second simple example by showing how double hashing works for the same empty table, $T$, and for the same keys we inserted in $T$ previously.

**double hashing**

First, however, we need to define the probe decrement function, $p(L_n)$, which computes the *probe decrement* for the key $L_n$. For our simple illustration, we let the value of $p(L_n)$ be the quotient of $n$ after division by 7, except that if the quotient is zero, we define the value to be 1 instead (since using a probe decrement of 0 would not accomplish the goal of ensuring that the probe sequence probes all of the table locations). The way we can express this idea mathematically is to say that $p(L_n)$ is defined to be the maximum value of the pair of quantities $(1, n / 7)$, since if $n / 7$ has the value 0, the maximum of $(1,0)$ is equal to 1, whereas if $n / 7$ has a value of 1 or greater, the maximum value of $(1, n / 7)$ is the same as $n / 7$. Equation 9.2 defines the probe decrement function.

**using quotients for the probe decrements**

$$p(L_n) = \max(1, n / 7). \tag{9.2}$$

For example, $p(W_{23}) = 3$, since the quotient of 23 divided by 7 equals 3 (with the remainder of 2 discarded).

Here, when we divide 23 by 7, we use the remainder 2 as the value of the hash function $h(W_{23})$, and we use the quotient 3 as the value of the probe decrement function $p(W_{23})$.

As another example, $p(B_2) = 1$, because, even though 2 divided by 7 has a quotient of 0, (i.e., $2 / 7 = 0$), we choose the maximum of $(1,0)$ to obtain the value 1 for $p(B_2)$.

Table 9.7 summarizes the values of $h(L_n)$ and $p(L_n)$ for each of the keys to be inserted into table $T$. Now, let's start by inserting the first four keys, $J_{10}$, $B_2$, $S_{19}$, and $N_{14}$ into the empty table $T$. Again, we use the value of the hash function, $h(L_n)$, to determine the hash location where we first try to insert these keys. Since there are no

| Key = $L_n$ | $h(L_n)$ | $p(L_n)$ |
|---|---|---|
| $J_{10}$ | 3 | 1 |
| $B_2$ | 2 | 1 |
| $S_{19}$ | 5 | 2 |
| $N_{14}$ | 0 | 2 |
| $X_{24}$ | 3 | 3 |
| $W_{23}$ | 2 | 3 |

**Table 9.7** Values of $h(L_n)$ and $p(L_n)$

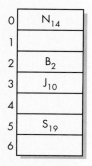

**Figure 9.8** Table T

inserting the last key

collisions when we try to insert these keys at their hash addresses in $T$, we obtain the configuration of table $T$ shown in Fig. 9.8.

Up until this moment, the key insertions are identical to those for open addressing with linear probing illustrated before, since only the probe sequences used for collision resolution differ between the linear probing and double hashing methods.

Next, we try to insert the key $X_{24}$ at location $3 = h(X_{24})$ in the table shown in Fig. 9.8. This produces a collision at location 3, which is already occupied by the key $J_{10}$. This time, however, we use a probe decrement of $3 = p(X_{24})$ to determine the probe sequence to be used to resolve the collision. Consequently, the next table location to be probed is 0, which is determined by subtracting the probe decrement of 3 from the starting hash address 3. Since location 0 is occupied by the key $N_{14}$, we need to determine the next location in the probe sequence. This requires us to "wrap around" from the other end of table $T$ (by counting 6, 5, 4) to arrive at the location 3 less than location 0 after wrapping around. Consequently, we probe location 4, and, after finding it empty, we insert $X_{24}$ there. This yields the configuration of table $T$ shown in Fig. 9.9.

Finally, we attempt to insert the key $W_{23}$ into table $T$. We start by trying to insert $W_{23}$ at its hash address, $2 = h(W_{23})$. But this yields a collision with the key $B_2$, already occupying location 2. So, using the probe decrement $3 = p(W_{23})$, we try to find the next empty location in the probe sequence for $W_{23}$. Starting at location 2 and counting down 3 takes us past the lowest location in table $T$, and causes us to wrap around, starting at the highest numbered location in $T$, which is 6. Since location 6 is empty, we can place $W_{23}$ in location 6 in $T$. This yields the final configuration for table $T$, as shown in Fig. 9.10.

In double hashing, when two keys collide at the same initial hash address, they usually follow different probe sequences when a search is made for the first available empty table location. For instance, the keys $J_{10}$ and $X_{24}$ both collide at hash address 3 in table $T$. But, since $p(J_{10}) = 1$ and $p(X_{24}) = 3$, we see that the two colliding keys have different probe decrements, even though they have identical hash addresses (which caused the initial collision). When colliding keys trace out *different* search paths by following their probe sequences after a collision, they will tend to find empty locations more quickly than in the case when all keys colliding at a given initial hash

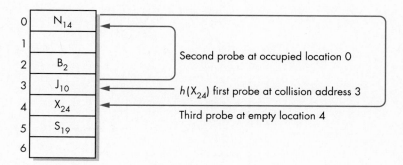

Second probe at occupied location 0

$h(X_{24})$ first probe at collision address 3

Third probe at empty location 4

**Figure 9.9** Table T

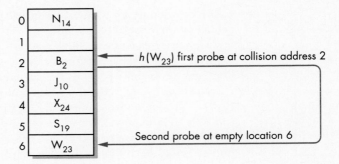

**Figure 9.10** Table T

address follow *identical* search paths. In open addressing with linear probing, all keys colliding at a given address follow the same probe sequence. But in open addressing with double hashing, colliding keys tend to follow different probe sequences. Consequently, double hashing tends to perform better than linear probing. Later we will give the performance formulas that characterize just how much better double hashing is than linear probing.

*separate chaining*

Let's now give another in our series of simple examples by showing a third method for resolving collisions in a hash table, $T$: *collision resolution by separate chaining*. The idea is simply to place all keys that collide at a single hash address on a linked list starting at that address.

For instance, if we had entered the keys $J_{10}$, $B_2$, $S_{19}$, $N_{14}$, $X_{24}$, and $W_{23}$ into an initially empty table T, using collision resolution by chaining (and using hash addresses given by $h(L_n) = n \% 7$, the same as those shown in Table 9.7), then the resulting table configuration would be that shown in Fig. 9.11.

*hashing with buckets*

To complete our series of examples, we will mention briefly one additional hashing method called *hashing with buckets*, which will not be explored further in this book. Suppose we had a big hash table, $T$, with, say, 20,000 empty entries. We could divide this big table into 200 smaller subtables each containing 100 empty entries, and we could call each such small subtable a "bucket." We could agree to store keys in each bucket sequentially in increasing order of their keys. Initially, we would hash a key, $K$, into one of the 200 different buckets. That is, $h(K)$ would be an integer in the

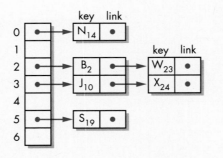

**Figure 9.11** Table T

range 0:199, specifying one of the 200 smaller subtables (each of size 100). Then we could use binary search to locate key $K$ in the ordered sequence of entries in the bucket designated by the hash address $h(K)$. While this technique does not give superior performance if table $T$ is stored in primary memory, it turns out to give quite good performance when $T$ is stored on relatively slow rotating external memory (such as disks). For this reason, hashing with buckets can often be used to advantage on large collections of data stored on relatively slow external memory.

## 9.3 REVIEW QUESTIONS

1. Explain how linear probing differs from double hashing.
2. Explain how collision resolution with separate chaining works.
3. Describe the method of hashing with buckets.

## 9.3 EXERCISES

1. Give the final configuration of table, $T$, that results from inserting the keys in Table 9.7 into an initially empty table $T$, using linear probing, if the order of insertion of the keys is $X_{24}$, $W_{23}$, $J_{10}$, $B_2$, $N_{14}$, and $S_{19}$.
2. Repeat Exercise 1, with double hashing used in place of linear probing. What is the final configuration of table $T$?
3. Implement algorithms to insert and search for table entries using the method of separate chaining, as illustrated in Fig. 9.11.
4. How could you redesign the hash search algorithm in order to reduce the time for unsuccessful searching using the method of separate chaining, given an implementation of chaining that initially keeps keys on each chain in the order they were inserted?

## 9.4 Collisions, Load Factors, and Clusters

## LEARNING OBJECTIVES

1. To be able to define collisions, load factors, and clustering.
2. To discover that collisions are frequent, even in sparsely occupied tables.
3. To discover how primary clusters form when using linear probing, and how they do not form when using double hashing.

To extend our understanding of hashing ideas a bit further we need to introduce and define a few terms, and we need to characterize the performance properties of the hashing methods introduced in the previous section.

First, let's talk a bit about hashing functions themselves. Suppose $T$ is a hash

*uniform random hashing*

table having M table entries whose addresses lie in the range 0:M – 1. (You might think of this as a one-dimensional Java array of the form $T[0:M – 1]$.) An ideal hashing function, $h(K)$, maps keys, $K$, onto table addresses in the range 0:M − 1 in a *uniform and random* fashion. The words "uniform and random" mean that for any arbitrarily chosen key $K$, any of the possible table addresses in the range 0:M − 1 is *equally likely* to be chosen (at random) by the function, $h$, which sends key $K$ onto its hash address $h(K)$.

It is actually a bit tricky to select good hashing functions. We will have more to say on this subject later in Section 9.6, which deals with choosing hashing functions. For now, simply think of a hashing function as something akin to tossing numbered balls into a row of numbered slots. Each numbered slot corresponds to a table location in table $T$, and each numbered ball corresponds to a key, $K$. If the person or device that tosses the balls into the slots randomly selects the target slot from the table with each slot having equal probability to be selected, it models the characteristic of a good hashing function that we will assume in the following discussion.

## Collisions

Let's now discuss the phenomenon of collisions. A collision happens when two separate keys, $K$ and $K'$, map onto the same hash address in table $T$.

> A **collision** between two keys, $K$ and $K'$, occurs if, when we try to store both keys in a hash table, $T$, both keys have the same hash address, $h(K) = h(K')$.

A *collision resolution policy* is a method for finding an empty table entry in which to store a key, $K'$, if, after trying to store key $K'$ in a hash table, $T$, we find the table location given by the hash address $h(K')$ already occupied by another key, $K$, which has been entered into table $T$ previously.

collision resolution policies

One of the remarkable facts about collisions that is contrary to most peoples' intuition is that collisions are relatively frequent, even in sparsely occupied hash tables. There is a famous "paradox," called the *von Mises Birthday Paradox*, that helps us to understand the issue. According to this paradox, if there are 23 or more people in a room, the chance is greater than 50 percent that two or more of them will have the same birthday. (Another variant of this says that if there are 88 or more people in a room, the chance that three or more will have the same birthday is greater than 50 percent.)

collisions are likely, even in sparsely occupied tables

When you think about the von Mises paradox in terms of the model we just described, in which we toss balls into numbered slots, it seems, at first, to be unlikely to be true. In terms of the ball-tossing model, the von Mises paradox says that, given a table $T$ with 365 numbered slots (where each slot corresponds to a different day of the year on which a person could have a birthday—ignoring leap years, for the moment), if we toss 23 balls at random into these 365 slots (with each toss selecting a slot independently and randomly among the 365 possible slots), the chance is greater than 50 percent that we will toss two or more balls into the same slot. Most people initially have the opinion that this result is inaccurate, since when 23 balls are placed in a table with 365 positions, the table is only 6.3 percent full (since 23/365 = 0.063), and we are asserting that there is better than a 50–50 chance of a collision when the table is only 6.3 percent occupied. How can that be? The answer comes from an argument in probability theory, which we discuss next, and which nonmathematically oriented readers may wish to skip.

## The von Mises Probability Argument

We can compute the probability of one or more collisions when we randomly toss 23 balls into 365 slots as follows. Let $Q(n)$ be the probability that when we randomly toss $n$ balls into a table, $T$, with 365 slots, then none of the $n$ balls collide, and let $P(n)$ be the probability that there is at least one collision when we randomly toss $n$ balls into a table with 365 slots. We see that $P(n)$ and $Q(n)$ are related by the formula

$$P(n) = 1 - Q(n),$$

since 1 minus the probability of no collisions equals the probability of one or more collisions.

Now, it is easy to compute $Q(n)$ by the following argument. $Q(1) = 1$, since whenever we toss one ball into an empty table, the probability is 1 (i.e., it is totally certain) that there will be no collisions. When we toss the second ball into the table, the chance of hitting an unoccupied slot is now 364 out of 365, since there are only 364 unoccupied slots left in a table having one ball already occupying one slot. So $Q(2) = Q(1) * (^{364}/_{365})$. When we toss the third ball into the table, the chance of hitting an unoccupied slot now drops to 363 out of 365, since we have to miss the two slots occupied by the two balls already in the table. This means that $Q(3) = Q(2) * (^{363}/_{365}) = Q(1) * (^{364}/_{365}) * (^{363}/_{365})$.

computing the probability<br>of no collisions

Continuing in this fashion, we get two recurrence relations:

$$Q(1) = 1 \text{ and}$$
$$Q(n) = Q(n-1) * (365 - n + 1)/365 \qquad (9.3)$$

**Recurrence Relations**

Using $Q(1) = 1 = (^{365}/_{365})$ and substituting repeatedly with these recurrence relations, we get

$$Q(n) = \frac{365 * 364 * \ldots * (365 - n + 1)}{365^n}.$$

The last equation can be rewritten in terms of factorials, as follows:

$$Q(n) = \frac{365!}{365^n(365-n)!}.$$

Substituting this for $Q(n)$ in the equation $P(n) = 1 - Q(n)$ gives

von Mises birthday paradox
collision probability

$$P(n) = 1 - \frac{365!}{365^n(365-n)!}. \tag{9.4}$$

Exercise 9.4.1 challenges you to write a Java program to compute values of $P(n)$ for various $n$. Table 9.12 gives some of these values. Figure 9.13 plots $P(n)$ on the $y$-axis versus $n$ on the $x$-axis. As you can see, the von Mises probability (i.e., the probability of two or more people in a room having the same birthday) rises rapidly and passes 50 percent when 23 or more people are in the room. Moreover, as soon as 47 or more people are in the room, the chances are better than 19 out of 20 that two or more people will have the same birthday. In terms of a hash table with 365 entries, this means that as soon as the table is 12.9 percent full, there is greater than a 95 percent chance that at least two keys will have collided. This investigation con-

**Table 9.12** Values of P(n) for Various n

| n | P(n) |
|-----|------------|
| 5 | 0.02713557 |
| 10 | 0.11694818 |
| 15 | 0.25290132 |
| 20 | 0.41143838 |
| 22 | 0.47569531 |
| 23 | 0.50729723 |
| 25 | 0.56869970 |
| 30 | 0.70631624 |
| 35 | 0.81438324 |
| 40 | 0.89123181 |
| 45 | 0.94097590 |
| 50 | 0.97037358 |
| 55 | 0.98626229 |
| 60 | 0.99412266 |
| 65 | 0.99768311 |
| 70 | 0.99915958 |
| 75 | 0.99971988 |
| 80 | 0.99991433 |
| 85 | 0.99997600 |
| 90 | 0.99999385 |
| 95 | 0.99999856 |
| 100 | 0.99999969 |

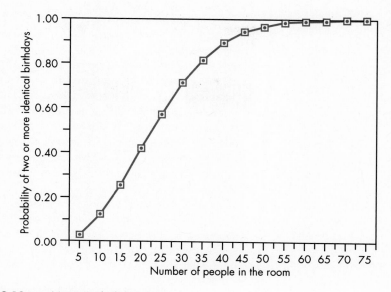

**Figure 9.13** von Mises Probability Curve

firms the statement that, "Even in sparsely occupied hash tables, collisions are relatively common."

Actually, the word "paradox" is misapplied in the strict sense of mathematical logic, when referring to the von Mises paradox. In mathematics, the word "paradox" refers to a statement that is self-contradictory. In the von Mises paradox, the word "paradox" refers to a situation that is contrary to common sense, or "counter-intuitive." It is not actually a self-contradiction in the mathematical sense. (See Exercise 9.4.2 for an example of a paradox in the sense of mathematical logic.)

## Load Factors and Clustering

In this subsection, let's focus our attention only on open addressing methods (and let's put aside, for the moment, considerations of hashing using separate chaining and buckets).

the load factor

In this context, a useful term to define is the *load factor* of a hash table $T$. Suppose that table $T$ is of size M, meaning that it has space for M table entries, and suppose that N of these M entries are *occupied* (whereas M – N entries are *empty*). We define the load factor, $\lambda$, of table $T$ to be the ratio of N to M.

> The **load factor**, $\lambda$, of a hash table of size M with N occupied entries is defined by
>
> $$\lambda = \frac{N}{M}.$$

For example, if a hash table $T$ of size 100 has 75 occupied entries and 25 empty entries, then $T$'s load factor is 0.75. The load factor, $\lambda$, is always a fraction lying between zero and one, $0 \leq \lambda < 1$. (The reason that the load factor can never be exactly equal to 1 is because, in open addressing, we define a *full* table to be a table with exactly one empty entry. Later, we will see that it is important to guarantee that there is at least one empty entry so that the algorithms for searching for a key and for inserting a new key in a table will terminate efficiently.)

You can also think of the load factor as being related to the percentage of entries in table $T$ that are occupied. For instance, a table with a load factor of 0.25 is 25 percent full, and a table that is 50 percent full has a load factor of 0.50. We will see later that the load factor determines how efficient searching and insertion are in open addressing hash tables.

Let's now turn to the subject of clustering. A *cluster* is a sequence of adjacent occupied entries in a hash table. Clusters have no empty keys in them, and consist of contiguous runs of occupied entries. It turns out that the method of linear probing is subject to something called *primary clustering*. We can see that, when a number of keys collide at a given location, and when we use linear probing to resolve the collisions, the colliding keys are inserted into empty locations immediately below the collision location (because linear probing looks for empty table locations at the immediately lower addresses starting at the collision location). This can cause a small puddle of keys to form at the collision location.

Roughly speaking, what happens in primary clustering is as follows. The small puddles of keys grow larger, and the larger they get the faster they grow, since they are wider targets for new keys that are being inserted. Whenever we try to insert a new key into the middle of a puddle, linear probing always makes us look to the bottom edge of the puddle to find the first empty location in which to insert the new key. Consequently, bigger puddles collect more "hits" of new keys being inserted, and they grow rapidly at their lower edges (where "lower" refers to the direction of low table addresses, and "higher" refers to the direction of high table addresses). Moreover, during growth, small puddles join together to form bigger puddles, and the bigger puddles formed by such mergers grow even faster. This phenomenon of puddle formation, puddle growth, and puddle mergers is called primary clustering.

By contrast, when we perform collision resolution by *double hashing*, instead of by linear probing, there is no primary clustering. It will turn out that double hashing performs much better than linear probing because of the absence of clustering in double hashing.

You can get a slight appreciation of the phenomenon of primary clustering by examining and comparing Figs. 9.14 and 9.15, although you have to be a keen observer to see what is going on.

Figure 9.14 illustrates a hash table being filled by open addressing with linear probing at increments of 10 percent full. The black bands in this figure represent clusters (or "puddles" of adjacent keys, as we described them metaphorically in the informal description just given). Figure 9.15 illustrates the same table being filled by double hashing in increments of 10 percent full.

You can see that primary clustering has taken place in Fig. 9.14 by the fact that the clusters are larger on the average and that there are fewer of them than is the case

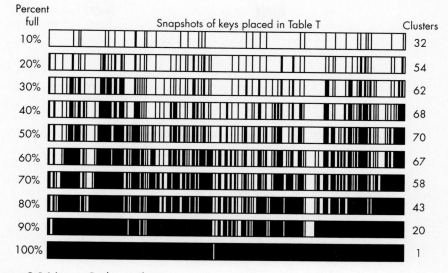

**Figure 9.14** Linear Probing Clusters

in Fig. 9.15, which has no primary clustering. (The clusters in Fig. 9.15 occur because of random placement of keys into adjacent table locations, illustrating that random placement generates a certain amount of natural clustering. As an aside, the author wrote this in California at a time when the state had just experienced several earthquakes above magnitude 6.0 in a period of a few days. There was a debate between

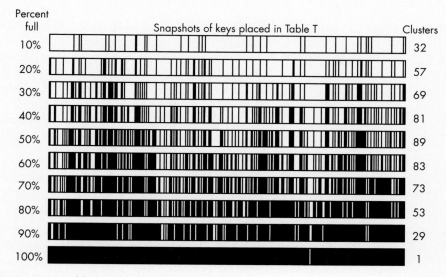

**Figure 9.15** Double Hashing Clusters

seismologists in the local newspaper. One seismologist argued that the cluster of earthquakes in northern and southern California were possibly related and were possibly symptoms of a period of increased seismic activity, while another argued that such clusters were most likely to be purely random since it is the nature of collections of random occurrences to have clustering—otherwise, the occurrences are not random. Who was right? In retrospect, the cluster turned out to be purely random.)

In the rightmost column of Figs. 9.14 and 9.15 the number of clusters in each row has been indicated (assuming that, because of "wrap around," the clusters at the opposite ends of the table are part of the same cluster and do not count as two separate clusters).

Examining the rows of each figure corresponding to 70 percent full, we see that linear probing has generated 58 clusters, whereas double hashing has generated 73 clusters. In other words, there are 26 percent more clusters (which are, on the average, smaller) when using double hashing at 70 percent full than there are when using linear probing. This is because of primary clustering.

Again, if you look at Fig. 9.14 starting, say, in the row corresponding to 60 percent full, and you scan downward from the biggest clusters in the 60 percent full row, you will see primary clusters growing at their left ends (or low table address ends), and you will see clusters join to form bigger clusters that grow even faster, as you move downward from row to row.

When you try to find this phenomenon in Fig. 9.15, you discover that it does not work the same way. Clusters do not tend to grow fastest only at their left edges, nor do nearby clusters tend to join together so readily. This is symptomatic of the absence of primary clustering.

comparing cluster counts

## 9.4 REVIEW QUESTIONS

1. Define what it means for two keys to collide in a hash table.
2. What is a collision resolution policy?
3. Under what conditions will the chances be greater than 50 percent that a collision will happen in a hash table with room for 365 table entries, assuming the hash function $h(K)$ is uniform and random?
4. Define the load factor of a hash table, $T$, having room for M table entries of which N entries are occupied and (M − N) entries are empty.
5. What is primary clustering? How and when does it occur?

## 9.4 EXERCISES

1. Write a Java program to compute values of $P(n)$, as given in Eq. 9.4 for various values of $n$. Determine the value of $n$ for which $P(n) \geq 0.5$ and for which $P(n-1) < 0.5$.
2. (The Barber of Seville paradox) There is a barber in Seville, Spain, who shaves those and only those who don't shave themselves. Can he shave himself? (This is

called a paradox of self-reference.) Investigate the logical consequences of two initial assumptions: (a) the Barber of Seville shaves himself, (b) the Barber of Seville does not shave himself.

## 9.5 Algorithms for Hashing by Open Addressing

### LEARNING OBJECTIVES

1. To learn how the actual algorithms work for hashing with open addressing.
2. To illustrate how the use of these algorithms leads to the formation of primary clusters for linear probing but not for double hashing.
3. To learn the conditions under which probe sequences in these algorithms are guaranteed to inspect all possible hash table locations.
4. To learn about some of the performance formulas characterizing how well hashing works.
5. To compare the theoretical and actual measured experimental performance of hashing techniques and to develop intuition for when they work well and when they don't.

To develop some algorithms for hashing with open addressing, let's assume we have an array of hash table entries $T$ of size M, and let's assume we are using integers as keys with the understanding that there exists a special **emptyKey** having a value of 0. (It is easy to generalize the algorithms so that the keys are not integers, such as those used in subsequent examples, where we use strings representing three-letter airport codes as keys.)

As a context for the presentation of the principal algorithms, we define some preliminary classes and constants. We start by defining classes for hash table entry objects and for the information contained in table entries, as follows:

```
class TableEntry {
    int        key;          // for the initial examples, the keys are integers
    InfoType   info;         // the info field's object is associated with the key
}

class InfoType {                 // the information associated with a key is an
    Object   dataField1;         // object having various data fields.
    Object   dataField2;         // . . . and so forth
}
```

Next, we define the HashTable class. It declares a **public final static** integer constant **emptyKey == 0**, and later uses this **emptyKey** constant to initialize empty entries and to test keys in various table entries during search and insertion to see if they are empty. Furthermore, it declares a data field **M** that holds an integer giving the table size. The *capacity* of the hash table (i.e., the maximum number of nonempty entries that the table can hold) will always be, **M − 1**, which is one less than the table size, because the algorithms defined next depend on there being at least one empty entry to stop the table searches that occur during insertion and retrieval. The HashTable class also declares a count field that holds the current number of nonempty table entries. Finally, the data field T holds the hash table's array of table entries.

```
class HashTable {

    public final static int emptyKey = 0;              // the integer empty key is 0

    int          M;              // the table size M, where capacity = M − 1
    int          count;          // the current number of entries in the hash table
    TableEntry[ ] T;                   // T is the hash table's array of table entries

    // insert here the constructor below for HashTable(int tableSize)

    // insert here the hash table insertion and search methods
    // from Programs 9.16 and 9.17 given below
}
```

Specifically, we intend for table entry array T to have M entries, numbered starting at 0 and ending at M − 1, where M − 1 is the maximum table address. We then search for the table entry in table T containing the search key K. If we find key K in the table entry T[i], we will return the location i as the result of a successful search. However, if the search is unsuccessful, we will agree to return the special value, −1, to denote that the search was unsuccessful. The only other preparatory action we need to take is to define a single-argument constructor that constructs a HashTable object having a table entry array of a specified size. This is done as follows:

```
HashTable(int tableSize) {        // tableSize gives the size of the table
    M = tableSize;                                // to be constructed
    count = 0;                              // the table is empty initially
    T = new TableEntry[M]          // the array, T, contains table entries

    for (int i = 0; i < M; i++) {             // initialize all entries of the
        T[i] = new TableEntry();              // entry array T to be
        T[i].key = emptyKey;                      // empty entries
    }

}
```

In the methods that follow, we will speak informally of the array T holding the table entries as if T were the hash table itself (rather than being an array in a data field of a HashTable object). Also, we use a general type, KeyType, to declare the keys used.

Now, suppose we want to insert a key, $K$, and some associated information, $I$, into table $T$. Let's assume that we have defined a hash function $h(K)$ and a probe decrement function $p(K)$. How could we proceed? Program 9.16 gives a hash insertion algorithm. Next, we need to specify the algorithm for searching for the table entry $T[i]$ containing a given search key, $K$. This is performed by Program 9.17. You can see that if the probe decrement function $p(K) = 1$, then Program 9.16 performs *linear probing*, whereas if $p(K)$ is a secondary hash function that computes different probe decrements for different keys $K$, then Program 9.16 performs *double hashing*.

```
    |    void hashInsert(KeyType K, InfoType I) {
    |
    |        int   i;
    |        int   probeDecrement;
 5  |
    |        i = h(K);                              // let i be the first hash location
    |        probeDecrement = p(K);                 // compute the probe decrement
    |
    |        while (T[i].key != emptyKey) {
10  |            i -= probeDecrement;               // compute next probe location
    |            if (i < 0) {
    |                i += M;                        // wrap around if needed
    |            }
    |        }
15  |
    |        T[i].key = K;                          // insert new key K in table T, and then
    |        T[i].info = I;                         // insert new info I in table T
    |        count++;                               // increment current entry count
    |    }
```

**Program 9.16** Inserting a New Table Entry into a Hash Table

```
    |    int hashSearch(KeyType K) {
    |
    |        int          i;
    |        int          probeDecrement;
 5  |        KeyType      probeKey;
    |
    |
    |        // initializations
    |        i = h(K);                              // let i be the first hash location
10  |        probeDecrement = p(K);                 // compute probe decrement
    |        probeKey = T[i].key;                   // extract first probe key from table
    |
    |
    |        // search loop
15  |        while ( ( K != probeKey) && (probeKey != emptyKey) ) {
    |            i -= probeDecrement;               // compute next probe location
    |            if (i < 0) {
    |                i += M;                        // wrap around if needed
    |            }
20  |            probeKey = T[i].key;               // extract next probe key
    |        }
    |
    |        // determine success or failure
    |        if (probeKey == emptyKey) {
25  |            return -1;                         // return -1 to signify that K was not found
    |        } else {
    |            return  i;                         // return location, i, of key K in table T
    |        }
    |    }
```

**Program 9.17** Searching for a Table Entry with Search Key K

**Table 9.18** Hash Function and Probe Decrement Values

| Key<br>K = Airport Code | Hash Function<br>h(K) | p(K) for<br>Double Hashing | p(K) for<br>Linear Probing |
|:---:|:---:|:---:|:---:|
| PHL | 4 | 4 | 1 |
| ORY | 8 | 1 | 1 |
| GCM | 6 | 1 | 1 |
| HKG | 4 | 3 | 1 |
| GLA | 8 | 9 | 1 |
| AKL | 7 | 2 | 1 |
| FRA | 5 | 6 | 1 |
| LAX | 1 | 7 | 1 |
| DCA | 1 | 2 | 1 |

## Two Examples of Primary Clustering and Its Absence

We now study two small examples that have been carefully chosen to illustrate how primary clusters form when we use linear probing, and how such clusters do not form when we use double hashing. Since the table size used is so small, the examples have been chosen to play the role of caricatures of what happens in larger tables.

To do this, we will execute Programs 9.16 and 9.17 on a hash table, $T$, of size M = 11, with entries numbered 0:10, and will use three-letter airport codes as search keys. Table 9.18 gives the values of the hash function, $h(K)$, and gives two separate probe decrement functions $p(K)$, one of which will be used for linear probing and the other of which will be used for double hashing.

The hash function $h(K)$, used in Table 9.18, was computed by considering the keys to represent base-26 integer values and by reducing these integer values modulo the table size, 11. When we let a three-letter airport code, $X_2X_1X_0$, represent a base-26 integer, we let the letter "A" represent the digit-value 0, the letter "B" represent the digit-value 1, the letter "C" represent the digit-value 2, the letter "D" represent the digit-value 3, and so on, up until the letter "Z," which represents the digit-value 25.

Then the three-letter airport code, $K = X_2X_1X_0$, can be converted from a base-26 number into a decimal integer, using the formula

$$Base26ValueOf(K) = X_2*26^2 + X_1*26^1 + X_0*26^0.$$

For example, if $K$ = "DCA," then, since the digit values of "D," "C," and "A" are 3, 2, and 0, respectively, we have

$$Base26ValueOf(\text{"DCA"}) = 3*26^2 + 2*26^1 + 0*26^0$$
$$= 3*676 + 2*26 + 0*1$$
$$= 2028 + 52$$
$$= 2080.$$

We then define the value of the hash function $h(K)$ to be the remainder of *Base26ValueOf(K)* after division by 11, which is computed by

$$h(K) = Base26ValueOf(K) \% 11. \tag{9.5}$$

For example, $h(\text{"DCA"}) = 2080 \% 11 = 1$, since $2080 = 11*189 + 1$. The hash function values in the second column of Table 9.18 are each computed using Eq. 9.5.

The values of the double hashing probe decrement function, $p(K)$, used in the third column of Table 9.18 are computed using the formula

$$p(K) = max(1, (Base26ValueOf(K) / 11) \% 11)). \tag{9.6}$$

In other words, to compute the probe decrement $p(K)$ to use for double hashing, you take the quotient of *Base26ValueOf(K)* after division by 11, and you reduce that quotient to a number in the range 0:10, by taking its remainder modulo 11. Then if the result turns out to be 0, you use 1 instead, to ensure that the probe decrement will always have a value of 1 or greater. Equation 9.6 is used to determine the values in the third column of Table 9.18.

Finally, the probe decrement function $p(K)$ used for linear probing is defined by the formula $p(K) = 1$, since linear probing always decrements the current probe location by 1 in order to get the next probe location. This fact is reflected in the fourth column of Table 9.18, which gives probe decrements of 1 for every possible key.

Now that we have determined values of $h(K)$ and $p(K)$, we are ready to insert some airport code keys into an initially empty table, $T$. Let's use the method of open addressing with linear probing first. This means, we will use $p(K) = 1$ for all keys $K$. We proceed to insert keys in the order given by the first column of Table 9.18, using the hash insertion algorithm Program 9.16 for hash insertion. After inserting the first three keys, PHL, ORY, and GCM, we get the table configuration shown in the left-most (or first) column of Fig. 9.19.

*computing probe decrements*

*linear probing is tried first*

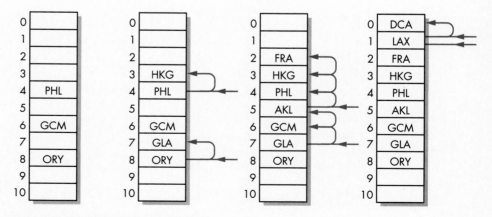

**Figure 9.19** Table T with Linear Probing

primary clusters begin
to form

After inserting the next two keys, HKG and GLA, we get the configuration shown in column two of Fig. 9.19. When we try to insert the key HKG, we find that it collides at location 4 with the key PHL already in the table, and we probe downward in increments of one location to try to find an empty table location. The first empty table location below 4 is location 3, so we insert HKG into location 3. The arrows to the right of column two illustrate the probe sequence followed during insertion. Similarly, when we try to insert GLA, it collides with the key ORY already in location 8, and we search downward to find the first empty location, which is location 7. So we place GLA in location 7. Note that the two colliding keys PHL and HKG have formed a small, two-key primary cluster at the point of collision. Note also that inserting GLA has caused a three-key cluster to form by joining two nearby one-key clusters. Primary clusters have already begun to form, even in this simple example.

When we next insert the keys AKL and FRA, we get the configuration shown in the third column of Fig. 9.19. First, AKL collides with the key GLA already in location 7. Downward searching in probe decrements of 1 locates the first empty table entry at location 5. So AKL is placed in location 5. This joins the previous two primary clusters together into one big primary cluster. Next, when we try to insert the key FRA at location 5, we find it is occupied, and, after probing downward, we find the first empty table entry at location 2. So we insert FRA in location 2.

When we try to insert the last two keys, LAX and DCA, we find LAX goes into an empty entry at location 1 on the first probe. DCA then collides with LAX and is inserted below location 1 at location 0.

If we try to search for the key AKL, using Program 9.17, we see that we first attempt to find AKL at its hash location $h(AKL) = 7$, and, not finding it there, we trace along the probe sequence in decrements of 1, until finding AKL at location 5. Similarly, if we search for a key, such as MIA, which is not in table $T$, where $h(MIA) = 4$, we first probe at location 4, and trace out the probe sequence 4, 3, 2, 1, 0, 10, looking for a table entry containing MIA or for the first empty table entry. Since we

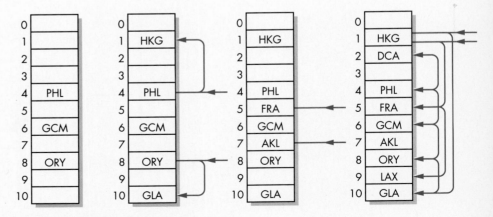

**Figure 9.20** Table T with Double Hashing

encounter an empty entry at location 10 before finding an entry containing MIA, we conclude that MIA is not in table $T$, and we return the special table address, −1, to signal that MIA is not in table $T$.

Let's now switch from linear probing to double hashing and let's see what happens when we fill table $T$ with the keys in Table 9.18 in the same order as before. This time we will use values of $p(K)$ from column three of Table 9.18. Figure 9.20 gives four snapshots of the insertion process.

now we try double hashing

In the first column of Fig. 9.20, we have inserted the keys PHL, ORY, and GCM. We are again inserting keys in the order given by Table 9.18. Since there are no collisions, these first three keys are inserted in their first hash locations. Consequently, the first column of Fig. 9.20 looks exactly like the first column of Fig. 9.19. However, when we insert the next two keys, HKG and GLA, to produce the configuration shown in the second column of Fig. 9.20, we begin to see how collision resolution by double hashing differs from collision resolution by linear probing.

how double hashing differs from linear probing

First, we attempt to insert HKG at its hash location, 4, but we find location 4 is already occupied by the key PHL. To resolve this collision, we look up the probe decrement, $p(\text{HKG})$, in Table 9.18, and we find $p(\text{HKG}) = 3$. So we subtract 3 from the initial probe location 4 to find the next probe location in the probe sequence for HKG, which is location 1. Here we find an empty location, so we insert HKG in location 1. In the second column of Fig. 9.20, the straight arrow pointing at location 4 shows the first probe at the hash address, $h(\text{HKG}) = 4$, and the curved arrow starting at location 4 and ending at location 1 shows the second probe in the probe sequence. By a similar process, the key GLA collides with ORY at table location 8, and lands in location 10. Comparing the second columns of Figs. 9.19 and 9.20, we see that double hashing has avoided creating the primary clusters associated with linear probing.

Next we insert the keys AKL and FRA to get the configuration of table $T$ shown in the third column of Fig. 9.20. Here we are lucky, because both AKL and FRA go directly into empty locations at their hash addresses without encountering any collisions, as is shown by the straight arrows to the right of column three.

Finally, we attempt to insert the last two keys, LAX and DCA. When we attempt to insert LAX at the location $h(\text{LAX}) = 1$, we encounter a collision with HKG. So we compute the probe decrement $p(\text{LAX}) = 7$, and we start counting down seven locations from location 1 to find the next location in the probe sequence. After counting down one location out of the seven we have to travel, we fall off the bottom of the table, so we wrap around to the top, and continue counting down six more locations from location 10, the topmost location. This brings us to location 5, which is already occupied by the key, FRA. Consequently, we need to count down seven more locations, starting at location 5, to find the next location in the probe sequence. Again we fall off the bottom of the table and wrap around to location 9. Since location 9 is empty, we insert LAX in location 9.

Finally, we attempt to insert the key DCA. DCA's initial hash address is also location 1, which is occupied by HKG. So we use $p(\text{DCA}) = 2$, as the probe decrement to compute locations in DCA's probe sequence. After wrap around, this leads us to examine locations 10, 8, 6, 4, and 2, in sequence. We find that location 2 is the first empty table entry in this probe sequence, so we can place DCA in location 2.

Note here that even though the two keys LAX and DCA collide initially at the same occupied hash address, 1, they trace out separate probe sequences after their first point of collision. Thus double hashing often leads initially colliding keys to search for empty locations along *separate* probe sequence paths. This is more efficient than linear probing, which causes all keys colliding at the same initial location to trace out identical search paths when looking for an empty table entry. Because colliding keys (usually) trace out separate probe sequences in the double-hashing method, there is no primary clustering in double hashing.

Now let's look at what happens when we try to search for the key, MIA, which is not in the table given in the fourth column of Fig. 9.20. The key MIA has an initial hash location of $h(MIA) = 4$ and has a probe decrement of $p(MIA) = 8$. Program 9.17 directs us to look first at location 4, where we have a collision with the key, PHL. We then trace out locations on the probe sequence starting at location 4 and decrementing by 8 locations each time. (It turns out that decrementing by 8 and wrapping around from bottom-to-top is identical to incrementing by 3 and wrapping around from top-to-bottom.) So we investigate locations 4, 7, 10, 2, 5, 8, and 0. We find that location 0 is empty, so we conclude that MIA is not in table $T$, and we return the special table address, –1, to signal that MIA is not in table $T$.

## Ensuring That Probe Sequences Cover the Table

In order for the open addressing hash insertion and hash searching algorithms to work properly, we have to guarantee that every probe sequence used can probe all locations in the hash table. Otherwise, the hash insertion algorithm would not be guaranteed to find a new empty table entry in which to insert a new key, and the hash search algorithm would not be guaranteed to find an empty entry to signal it to stop, when searching for a key that is not in the table.

It is rather obvious that the linear probing method generates a probe sequence that covers all possible table locations, since, starting at the initial collision location, linear probing moves downward, systematically enumerating a contiguous linear sequence of table addresses, until it falls off the bottom of the table and then wraps around to the top to continue its downward march—returning eventually to the original collision location in an unbroken wrap-around cycle.

It is not so obvious that the differing probe decrements, $p(K)$, used for double hashing will always cover all table locations in some order in the probe sequences they generate. Let's start with an example. Choose any key from Table 9.18 and retrieve its hash address, $h(K)$ and its probe decrement (for double hashing), $p(K)$. For instance, choosing the key, HKG, we have $h(HKG) = 4$, and $p(HKG) = 3$. This means we initially probe at the hash address 4. Then we probe in decrements of 3, at location 1, and, after a first wrap-around, at locations 9, 6, 3, 0. After a second wrap-around, we continue probing at locations 8, 5, and 2. After a third wrap-around, we probe at locations 10 and 7, before returning to the original hash location, 4. You can see that all 11 table locations were covered exactly once in the probe sequence

$$4, 1, 9, 6, 3, 0, 8, 5, 2, 10, 7.$$

Moreover, no table location was enumerated twice before all original locations were covered once.

If you try the same experiment for any other key in Table 9.18, you will discover that the probe sequence for double hashing covers all table locations exactly once, no matter what the initial hash address is, and no matter what the probe decrement is. Evidently, there is some sort of clever design principle lurking beneath the example we have been using that guarantees this aspect of double hashing's performance. It's now time to mention what this design principle is. Simply put, whenever the table size M and the probe decrement $p(K)$ are *relatively prime*, it is guaranteed that the probe sequence will cover the entire table. (Whenever two integers $a$ and $b$ are relatively prime, it means they have no common divisors other than 1. This concept is probably familiar to you because when you reduce a fraction to least common terms so that the numerator and denominator have no common divisors, the numerator and denominator are relatively prime. For example, after reducing the fraction 36/45 to least common terms, 4/5, the numerator 4 and the denominator 5 are relatively prime because they have no common divisors other than 1.)

*a clever design principle*

It so happens that the table sizes, 7 and 11, for both examples we have used so far in this chapter have been prime numbers. Our first example in Section 9.3 used a table size of M = 7 locations with keys of the form $L_n$, where L was a letter of the alphabet, and $n$ was its ordinal position in the alphabet. Our second example used a table size of M = 11 locations and used three-letter airport codes as keys. The values of the probe decrements, $p(K)$, were chosen to be positive integers in the range $1 \le p(K) < M$. Consequently, the probe decrement $p(K)$ and the table size were relatively prime and thus the probe sequences were guaranteed to cover the entire table. Whenever you choose a table size that is a prime number, you can use any probe decrement size that is one or greater, and you will be guaranteed that the probe sequences will cover the entire table.

Another idea is to choose the table size, M, to be a power of two, and to choose $p(K)$ to be any odd number. Then it is still guaranteed that the probe sequences cover the entire range of table addresses.

For example, suppose $M = 2^3 = 8$, and we choose $p(K) \in \{1, 3, 5, 7\}$. Then, starting at any initial hash address, $h(K)$, in the range of table addresses, 0:7, and using any odd probe decrement, the probe sequence covers all addresses in 0:7 exactly once before repeating. For example, if $h(K) = 5$ and $p(K) = 3$, the probe sequence is: 5, 2, 7, 4, 1, 6, 3, 0.

In summary, two popular and effective ways to set up double hashing tables are (a) to choose a prime number, such as 997, as the table size M, and to choose as probe decrements, any integer in the range, 1:M − 1, and (b) to choose a power of two, such as $2^{10} = 1024$, as the table size M, and to choose as probe decrements, any odd integer in the range, 1:M − 1.

## Performance Formulas

Now let's turn to the subject of characterizing the efficiency of performance of open addressing methods using both linear probing and double hashing.

You can imagine that, as the load factor $\lambda$ of a hash table $T$ increases, the efficiency of inserting new keys $K$, decreases. This is because, as table $T$ gets more and more full, when we attempt to insert a new key $K$, there is less and less chance that we will accidentally hit an empty location on the first hash, and in the event of a collision, it will take more and more time to enumerate the sequence of table locations in the probe sequence before finding the first empty table location in which to insert the new key, $K$.

If we search for a key $K$ already known to be in table $T$, the number of probes required to locate it will be exactly the same as the number of probes required when it was inserted in the first place. This is because the exact same probe sequence is followed both during a successful search and when it was inserted originally. Recall that when we inserted key $K$ originally, we were either lucky and found an empty table location at its hash address $h(K)$ where we inserted it with just one probe, or we used a collision resolution policy by following successive locations in the probe sequence until finding the first empty location in the probe sequence. We then inserted key $K$ at this first empty location. So when we search for $K$, we again follow the identical probe sequence used when inserting it, and we locate it at the former empty location at the last address visited in the same probe sequence used for inserting it.

Suppose hash table $T$ of size M has exactly N occupied entries, so that its load factor, $\lambda$, is N/M. Let's now define two quantities, $C_N$ and $C_N'$, where $C_N$ is the average number of probe addresses examined during a successful search, and where $C_N'$ is the average number of probe addresses examined during an unsuccessful search (or, what is identical, during the insertion of a new key, $K$).

For open addressing with linear probing, we have the two performance formulas:

$$C_N \approx \frac{1}{2}\left(1 + \frac{1}{1-\lambda}\right) \qquad \text{for successful search}$$

efficiency of linear probing

$$C_N' \approx \frac{1}{2}\left(1 + \left(\frac{1}{1-\lambda}\right)^2\right) \qquad \text{for unsuccessful search}$$

(9.7)

These formulas are known to apply when table $T$ is up to 70 percent full (i.e., when the load factor, $\lambda$, obeys the inequality, $\lambda \le 0.7$).

For open addressing with *double hashing*, the two corresponding performance formulas are

$$C_N \approx \frac{1}{\lambda}\ln\left(\frac{1}{1-\lambda}\right) \qquad \text{for successful search}$$

efficiency of double hashing

$$C_N' \approx \left(\frac{1}{1-\lambda}\right) \qquad \text{for unsuccessful search}$$

(9.8)

Finally, for collision resolution by *separate chaining* (in which you keep all keys colliding at a given hash location on a linked list starting at that location, as in Fig. 9.11), the two corresponding performance formulas are

efficiency of
separate chaining

$$C_N \approx 1 + \frac{1}{2}\lambda \qquad \text{for successful search}$$

$$C'_N \approx \lambda \qquad \text{for unsuccessful search} \tag{9.9}$$

## Comparing Theoretical and Empirical Results

It is now of critical importance to build some intuition for what these theoretical results mean, and to compare both theoretical results and actual measurements from experiments for a range of load factors.

Table 9.21 gives the theoretical results for several load factors. Table 9.22 (on p. 354) gives some actual measured results for hash tables of size 997. The experimental results in Table 9.22 come from averaging the number of probes in the two open addressing methods over 50 trials, and the results for chaining come from averaging the number of key comparisons over three trials. Comparing the two open addressing methods, note how primary clustering damages the actual measured performance of linear probing as compared to that of double hashing for load factors of 0.75 or greater.

Also observe that the performance of these hashing techniques is not dependent on the total number of keys stored in a hash table. Instead, the performance is dependent on how full the hash table is. For example, if 897 keys are stored in a hash table with

| Load Factors | | | | | | |
|---|---|---|---|---|---|---|
| | 0.10 | 0.25 | 0.50 | 0.75 | 0.90 | 0.99 |
| Successful Search | | | | | | |
| Separate chaining | 1.05 | 1.12 | 1.25 | 1.37 | 1.45 | 1.49 |
| Open/linear probing | 1.06 | 1.17 | 1.50 | 2.50 | 5.50 | 50.5 |
| Open/double hashing | 1.05 | 1.15 | 1.39 | 1.85 | 2.56 | 4.65 |
| Unsuccessful Search | | | | | | |
| Separate chaining | 0.10 | 0.25 | 0.50 | 0.75 | 0.90 | 0.99 |
| Open/linear probing | 1.12 | 1.39 | 2.50 | 8.50 | 50.5 | 5000 |
| Open/double hashing | 1.11 | 1.33 | 2.00 | 4.00 | 10.0 | 100.0 |

**Table 9.21** Theoretical Results for Number of Probes

| Load Factors | | | | | | |
|---|---|---|---|---|---|---|
| | 0.10 | 0.25 | 0.50 | 0.75 | 0.90 | 0.99 |
| Successful Search | | | | | | |
| Separate chaining | 1.04 | 1.12 | 1.25 | 1.36 | 1.44 | 1.49 |
| Open/linear probing | 1.05 | 1.16 | 1.46 | 2.42 | 4.94 | 16.4 |
| Open/double hashing | 1.05 | 1.15 | 1.37 | 1.85 | 2.63 | 4.79 |
| Unsuccessful Search | | | | | | |
| Separate chaining | 0.10 | 0.21 | 0.47 | 0.80 | 0.93 | 0.97 |
| Open/linear probing | 1.11 | 1.37 | 2.38 | 8.36 | 39.1 | 360.9 |
| Open/double hashing | 1.11 | 1.33 | 2.00 | 4.10 | 10.9 | 98.5 |

**Table 9.22** Measured Experimental Results for Number of Probes

997 locations (so that $\lambda \approx 0.9$), double hashing was measured to take 2.63 probes for an average successful search and 10.9 probes for an average unsuccessful search. But if those same 897 keys are stored in a table roughly twice as big with 1801 hash table locations (so that $\lambda \approx 0.5$), measurements (averaged over 50 trials) show that an average successful search took 1.37 probes, and an average unsuccessful search took 2.01 probes.

## 9.5 REVIEW QUESTIONS

1. Sketch the method by which Program 9.16 inserts a new table entry with key $K$ into a hash table using open addressing with double hashing.
2. What happens when Program 9.17 searches for a key $K$ in a table $T$, which has no table entry containing key $K$, using open addressing with linear probing?
3. What is a probe sequence? How do the probe sequences used in linear probing and in double hashing differ?
4. Name some conditions under which it can be guaranteed that the probe sequences used in double hashing will enumerate all of the table locations exactly once without duplications.
5. Which of the following methods theoretically takes the least average number of probes (or key comparisons) to locate a key successfully in a hash table with a load factor of 0.9: (a) separate chaining, (b) open addressing with linear probing, or (c) open addressing with double hashing?

## **9.5** EXERCISES

1. If you have access to a computer graphics device such as a plotter or a color pixel-mapped display screen, set up and run some experiments that use Program 9.16 to insert keys into a hash table using open addressing with linear probing and double hashing. Generate experimentally produced diagrams, such as those given in Figs. 9.14 and 9.15 that illustrate primary clustering and its absence when linear probing and double hashing are used.

2. Set up and run experiments that measure the number of probes (or key comparisons) used for open addressing with linear probing and double hashing, and for separate chaining. Do your experimental results confirm or reject the theoretical results given in Table 9.21?

3. (Triangle Number Hashing) Another class of open addressing methods explored in the computer science literature is the class of methods that use what is called *quadratic probing*. One such quadratic probing method is called triangle number hashing. In this method the probe decrements used for collision resolution are chosen to be the sequence of decrements 0, 1, 3, 6, 10, and so on, where the probe decrement 0 is considered to have been used up when the hash address $h(K)$ is first probed. The numbers in this probe decrement sequence are called triangle numbers since they give the number of dots in triangles of the form:

$$
\begin{array}{ccccc}
0 & 1 & 3 & 6 & 10
\end{array}
$$

↑ the hollow dot (∘) signifies the empty triangle

Since all keys colliding at a given initial hash location, $h(K)$, trace out the same probe sequence, quadratic hashing methods are said to be affected by *secondary clustering* (even though they are not affected by the primary clustering evident in linear probing).

For hashing methods affected by secondary clustering, the theoretical performance formulas for a hash table with load factor $\lambda$ are

$$C_N \approx 1 - \ln(1 - \lambda) - \frac{\lambda}{2}$$
for successful search

$$C_N' \approx \left(\frac{1}{1-\lambda}\right) - \lambda - \ln(1-\lambda)$$
for unsuccessful search

Implement the following algorithms for triangle number hashing and measure their performance on tables having a table size that is a power of two (e.g., $M = 2^{10} = 1024$). Show that the probe sequence covers the table. Compare the theoretical and actual measured experimental results. Do they agree reasonably well, averaged over a suitable number of trials? Is quadratic hashing superior in performance to either linear probing or double hashing?

```
/*--------------------------------------------------------------------------*/

     void hashInsert(KeyType K, InfoType I) {

             int          i, j;
             KeyType      probeKey;
5

             // initializations
             i = h(K);                                        // first hash
             j = 0;                    // initialize counter for triangle number hashing
10           probeKey = T[i].key;

             // find first empty slot
             while (probeKey !=  emptyKey) {
                 j++;                    // increment triangle number hashing counter
15               i -= j;                          // compute next probe location
                 if (i < 0) {
                     i += M;                            // wrap around if needed
                 }
                 probeKey = T[i].key;
20           }

             // insert new key K and info I into table T
             T[i].key = K;
             T[i].info = I;
25           count++;
     }

/*--------------------------------------------------------------------------*/




/*--------------------------------------------------------------------------*/

     int hashSearch(KeyType K)  {

             int          i, j;
             KeyType      probeKey;
5
             // initializations
             i = h(K);                                        // first hash
             j = 0;                    // initialize counter for triangle number hashing
             probeKey = T[i].key;
10
             // find either an entry with key, K, or the first empty entry
             while ( ( K != probeKey) && (probeKey != emptyKey) ) {
                 j++;                    // increment triangle number hashing counter
                 i -= j;                      // decrement probe location by the amount j
15               if (i < 0) i += M;                        // wrap around if needed
                 probeKey = T[i].key
             }
```

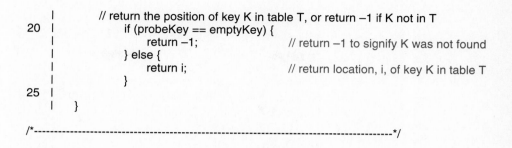

```
20 |      // return the position of key K in table T, or return −1 if K not in T
   |          if (probeKey == emptyKey) {
   |              return −1;                    // return −1 to signify K was not found
   |          } else {
   |              return i;                     // return location, i, of key K in table T
   |          }
25 |
   |      }

/*--------------------------------------------------------------------------------------*/
```

## 9.6 Choosing a Hash Function

### LEARNING OBJECTIVES

1. To learn how an ideal hash function is supposed to perform.
2. To learn about the division method for choosing a hash function and about how to avoid pitfalls in its design.
3. To learn about other methods for designing a good hash function.

*ideal hash functions are uniform and random*

In order for the hashing methods analyzed in the preceding sections to work well, the hash function $h(K)$, which maps keys $K$ into hash table locations, must be chosen properly. Ideally, $h(K)$ will map keys uniformly and randomly onto the entire range of hash table locations with each location being equally likely to be the target of $h(K)$ for a randomly chosen key, $K$. A poorly chosen hash function might map keys nonuniformly into table locations, or might map contiguous clusters of keys into clusters of hash table locations.

As an example of a pitfall in the design of hash functions, suppose we are using the method of open addressing with double hashing, and suppose we select a table size that is a power of two, such as $M = 2^8 = 256$. We decide to define our hash function by the equation, $h(K) = K \% 256$, where the keys $K$ are variables up to three characters long in a particular assembly language using 8-bit ASCII characters. Thus, we can represent each key $K$, by a 24-bit integer that is divided into three equal 8-bit sections, each representing a single ASCII character.

The trouble with this policy is that it has the effect of selecting the low-order character of the three-character key, $K$, as the value of $h(K)$. (This is because the three-character key, $C_3C_2C_1$, when considered as a 24-bit integer, has the numerical value, $C_3*256^2 + C_2*256^1 + C_1*256^0$, and when this is reduced $\% 256$, it has the value $C_1$.)

Now consider what happens when we hash the six keys, X1, X2, X3, and Y1, Y2, Y3, using $h(K)$. Since only the last character is selected by $h(K)$, we have

$$h(X1) = h(Y1) = \text{'1'}$$
$$h(X2) = h(Y2) = \text{'2'}$$
$$h(X3) = h(Y3) = \text{'3'}$$

(In fact, the integer values of the ASCII codes for '1', '2', and '3' will be the actual values of the table locations selected by $h(K)$. These values are 50, 51, and 52 respectively.) Consequently, the six original keys will be mapped into a common cluster of three contiguous table addresses. Moreover, contiguous runs of keys in the key space will map into contiguous runs of table locations, so it could be said that $h(K)$ preserves clusters, which is poor. A well-designed $h(K)$ will *spread* clusters of keys instead of preserving them or clustering them even more tightly.

## The Division Method

One method for choosing a hash function $h(K)$ that can be made to work well for double hashing applications is to choose a prime number as the table size M, and, interpreting the keys, $K$, as integers, to divide $K$ by M getting a quotient Q and a remainder R. The remainder R is used as the value of $h(K)$, and the quotient Q can be used as the value of the probe decrement for double hashing (except that if Q = 0, then 1 must be used instead, since all probe decrements must be nonzero). In symbols, we take

double hashing by the<br>division method

$$h(K) = K \% M, \quad \text{and}$$
$$p(K) = \max(1, K / M). \tag{9.10}$$

In practice, it is useful to reduce $p(K)$ to a number in the range 1:M − 1, by replacing $p(K) \geq M$ with $\max(1, p(K) \% M)$, if necessary.

However, we need to take some precautions in choosing the prime number, M, to use in conjunction with the division method. In particular, if $r$ is the radix of the character set for the keys, $K$, and $k$ and $a$ are small integers, then we should not choose a prime of the form $M = r^k \pm a$.

For example, suppose we again consider three character keys, $C_3C_2C_1$, in 8-bit ASCII, where the radix of the character set is again, $r = 256$. Suppose we then choose a table size M = 65537, which is known to be a number called a Fermat prime, with the value $2^{16} + 1$. If we then compute $h(C_3C_2C_1)$, we get the result

$$h(C_3C_2C_1) = (C_2C_1 - C_3)_{256}.$$

Thus, as a base-256 number, the value of $h(C_3C_2C_1)$ is simply a difference of products of the characters. Generally, if M is of the form, $r^k \pm a$, the value of $h(K)$ will tend to be simple sums and differences of products of the characters $C_i$. Such a hash function will not spread clusters of keys, nor will it map keys uniformly and randomly onto the space of hash table locations.

## Other Hash Function Methods

Three other methods of choosing a hash function are: *folding*, *middle-squaring*, and *truncation*.

In *folding*, the key is divided into sections, and the sections are added together. For example, if we had 9-digit keys, such as the key $K = 013402122$, we could divide

$K$ into three sections: 013, 402, and 122, and we could add them together getting 537 for the value of $h(K)$. (We could also use multiplication, subtraction, and addition in some fashion to combine the sections into the final value.)

In *middle-squaring*, if we again had the 9-digit key, $K = 013402122$, we could take the middle digits, 402, and square them, getting $h(K) = 402^2 = 161604$. If 161604 exceeded the table size, M, we could choose, say, the middle four digits of the result, getting $h(K) = 6160$.

In *truncation*, we simply delete part of the key and use the remaining digits (or bits or characters). For example, if $K = 013402122$, we could ignore all but the last three digits, getting $h(K) = 122$. While truncation takes hardly any time to compute, it tends not to spread the keys randomly and uniformly into the space of hash table locations. For this reason, it is often used in conjunction with the other methods mentioned, but it is seldom used alone.

## **9.6** REVIEW QUESTIONS

1. When can we say that a hash function $h(K)$ performs well, and when can we say that it performs poorly?
2. What is the division method of hashing in reference to open addressing with collision resolution by double hashing? What does the term "double hashing" refer to?
3. Give an example of a pitfall when choosing a hash function.

## **9.6** EXERCISES

1. Mr. Alf Witt decides to use $h(K) = (K \% M)$ for his hash function. He selects M = 4096 as a table size, and uses keys that are 24-bit integers representing three character keys in an assembly language that represents characters in 8-bit ASCII. Did Witt choose a good hash function?
2. (Multiplicative Hash Functions) Suppose we choose a hash table size M = $2^n$, which is a power of two (such as M = $2^{12}$ = 4096). Suppose we are using keys, $K$, which are 16-bit integers in the range 0:32767. Let $w = 32768$, let $\theta = 0.6125423371$, and choose an integer A such that $\theta \approx A/w$. Now compute $h(K)$ by taking the leftmost $n$ bits of $((A*K) \% w)$. Run an experiment to show how $h(K)$ maps the keys $K = 1, 2, 3, 4$, etc. into a table, $T$, whose size M is a power of 2 (such as M = $2^{12}$). Does $h(K)$ disperse the keys reasonably uniformly and randomly? In this exercise, $h(K)$ is called a multiplicative hashing function.
3. (Perfect Hash Functions) A *perfect hash function* is one that maps a finite set of $n$ distinct keys onto a finite hash table of size M = $n$, such that $h(K)$ is a 1–1, onto function. Can you find a perfect hash function for the set of 47 Java reserved words: {abstract, boolean, break, byte, case, catch, char, class, const, continue, default, do, double, else, extends, final, finally, float, for, goto, if, implements, import, instanceof, int, interface, long, native, new, package, private, protected, public, return, short, static, super, switch, synchronized, this, throw, throws, transient, try, void, volatile, while}?

## 9.7 Comparison of Searching Methods Using the Table ADT

### LEARNING OBJECTIVES

1. To compare the performance of three actual data representations that can be used to represent Table ADTs.
2. To understand which of these three representations performs the best.

Consider the Table ADT introduced earlier in Section 9.2. Recall that an abstract table, $T$, was defined to be a collection of pairs of the form $(K,I)$, where $K$ was an identifying key, and $I$ was some information associated with key $K$, such that no two distinct pairs in the collection had identical keys, and such that seven operations were defined to *construct* an empty table $T$, to determine if $T$ is *empty*, to *enumerate* the entries in $T$, and to *insert*, *delete*, *retrieve*, and *update* table entries.

*recalling the features of the Table ADT*

It is clear that we can choose a variety of different underlying data representations for the Table ADT. Figure 9.23 presents three interesting possible representations to compare. Let's analyze the relative efficiencies of these three representations. Suppose there are $n$ table entries in table $T$.

*using sorted arrays of table entries*

Consider first representation 1—using a *sorted array* of table entries. We can search for an entry containing a given key, $K$, in time $O(\log n)$, using binary search. We can enumerate the entries of $T$ in time $O(n)$, since they are already in the proper order for enumeration (i.e., the ascending order of their keys, $K$). Inserting and deleting entries can be done in time $O(n)$, since, on the average, we need to move half of the table entries when we insert or delete a new entry. Retrieving and updating take the same time as searching, $O(\log n)$.

*using AVL trees*

Now consider representation 2—using *AVL trees* of table entries. We can search for an entry containing a given key, $K$, in time $O(\log n)$, using AVL tree search. We can enumerate the entries of $T$ in time $O(n)$ by using an InOrder traversal of the nodes of the AVL tree. Inserting and deleting nodes in AVL trees can be done in time $O(\log n)$, and retrieving and updating take the same time as searching, $O(\log n)$.

*using hash tables*

Finally, consider representation 3—using *hash tables*. In a hash table, we can search for an entry containing a given key, $K$, in time $O(1)$. It may seem strange to characterize hash table search as occurring in time $O(1)$, so consider why we might make this claim. Suppose we agree to use a hash table that is never more than half-full. (If the table ever gets more than half-full, we can expand the table by choosing a new table twice as big, and by rehashing the entries of the original table so they reside in the new, larger table.) In summary, suppose we are guaranteed that the load factor of our table obeys the constraint, $\lambda \leq 0.50$. Suppose, also, that we elect to use double hashing as our hashing method (similar arguments can be made for the other hashing methods).

1. Representing $T$ by an *array of entries* sorted in increasing order of their keys, $K$.
2. Representing $T$ by a *hash table*.
3. Representing $T$ by an *AVL-tree* organized using keys, $K$, from the table entries.

**Figure 9.23** Three Table ADT Representations

Then, from Tables 9.21 and 9.22, or, equally, from Eqs. 9.8, we know that the average number of key comparisons used in a successful search will be at most 1.39 and that the average number of key comparisons used in an unsuccessful search will be at most 2.00, regardless of the size, $n$, of the table. Consequently, the number of comparisons is independent of the table size and independent of the number of keys stored in the table. As long as we agree to use hash tables that are no more than half full, the average number of key comparisons is bounded above by 2. Speaking more generally, if we agree to obey some predetermined limit on the percentage of the hash table that contains occupied table entries, we can be guaranteed that the average number of comparisons will not exceed some given, fixed, predetermined constant number. So, being a constant independent of both the table size and the number of keys, hash table search is $O(1)$.

To enumerate the entries of a hash table, $T$, we must first sort the entries into ascending order of their keys. This requires time $O(n \log n)$, if we use a suitably efficient comparison-based sorting technique. Hence, the table enumeration operation is $O(n \log n)$. Because insertion of a new table entry in a hash table takes the same number of key comparisons as unsuccessful search, insertion takes time $O(1)$. Finally, retrieving and updating in a hash table take the same time as searching, $O(1)$.

Deletion in some hash table representations is easy, but in the open addressing methods, deletion poses troublesome problems. For instance, if we are using the chaining method, deletion of a table entry containing a given key requires only that we delete a node from a linked list, which is straightforward. However, if we try physically to delete a particular table entry, $E$, from a hash table using open addressing, leaving a table entry with an empty key in place of $E$, we destroy the validity of the searching operations for subsequent keys. The reason is that search always terminates when it finds an empty table entry in the probe sequence being examined. If we artificially introduce an empty entry, it could interrupt the original probe sequence starting at the initial hash address, $h(K)$, and ending at the location where another key $K$ is to be found.

*deletion can be troublesome*

Consequently, in open addressing techniques, when we need to delete a given table entry, what is normally done is to mark the entry as deleted with a special bit, while leaving it physically present in the table. The searching algorithms then probe past entries marked as deleted, treating them as if they had not been deleted. But the insertion algorithms can insert new entries in place of any entry that is marked as deleted. In short, insertion algorithms treat deleted entries as if they were empty entries, and search algorithms treat deleted entries as if they were nonempty entries. Unfortunately, under this policy, a hash table can fill up and can become clogged with entries marked as deleted. If this happens, it is possible to rehash the table entries so that only the ones not marked as deleted are retained, and actually to delete the ones marked as deleted. In any event, the time required to delete a table entry with a given search key, $K$, is still $O(1)$, no matter which of the hash table methods we are using.

We now put these results together into Table 9.24 so we can make some comparisons. Some observers express the opinion that such comparisons lead them often to

| Operations ⇒ Representations ⇓ | Initialize | Determine if full | Search Retrieve Update | Insert | Delete | Enumerate |
|---|---|---|---|---|---|---|
| Sorted array of entries | O(n) | O(1) | O(log n) | O(n) | O(n) | O(n) |
| AVL tree of entries | O(1) | O(1) | O(log n) | O(log n) | O(log n) | O(n) |
| Hash table | O(n) | O(1) | O(1) | O(1) | O(1) | O(n log n) |

**Table 9.24** Comparative Performance of Table ADT Representations

recommend AVL trees as a good representation, since the operation times for AVL trees are uniformly not the worst in any column of the table.

Other observers sometimes express the opinion that which representation best suits a given application depends on the frequency of the different operations to be performed. For instance, suppose we have both an AVL tree and a double-hashing table, each containing $2^{12} = 4096$ entries. Suppose the load factor of the hash table is $\lambda = 1/2$, because we are using a hash table with 8192 table entries.

Then an average successful search takes 1.39 key comparisons in the hash table, but takes 12.25 key comparisons in the AVL tree (using the formula, lg $n$ + 0.25). If searches are much more frequent than, say, deletions or enumerations, the hash table representation offers an enormous efficiency advantage.

## 9.7 REVIEW QUESTIONS

1. Name three possible data representations for a Table ADT.
2. Sketch how the Table ADT operations would be implemented in the case of a hash table representation.

## 9.7 EXERCISES

1. Under what circumstances will a hash table representation of a Table ADT be superior?
2. Under what circumstances will an AVL tree representation of a Table ADT be superior?
3. (Interpolation Search) This exercise asks you to do a mini research project on a new kind of searching called *interpolation search*. Suppose you are given a Table ADT representation using an array of M table entries sorted in ascending order of their keys. Interpolation searching is a search technique that finds a table entry containing the search key $K$ in time O(log log M). Roughly speaking it works by predicting where to locate a key $K$ in table $T$ by predicting where to look for $K$ in its current search interval using a calculated *interpolation point*. By analogy with telephone-book searching, suppose you are looking for the name "Adams." You

might start searching for this name right near the beginning of the phone book. But if you were searching for "Williams," you would look near the end, and for "Miller" near the middle. In general, if the search key K is a name that is, say, X percent of the way through the alphabet in alphabetical order, you would start searching for K at a point X percent through the phone book. Interpolation searching works similar to binary searching in selecting a sequence of increasingly smaller search intervals in which to search for a key, K. But it computes the endpoints of those search intervals using interpolated estimates, instead of using the half-way division points that binary searching uses. Given this hint, can you implement your own version of interpolation searching? After trying to do it yourself, go search the literature for an explanation of how it works and for the algorithm analysis showing that it runs in time $O(\log \log M)$. Then compare the theoretical and actual search times of your algorithm with hashing techniques. Which ones perform better on tables of various sizes?

## Pitfalls

- *Choosing a poor hash function*

    If you are careless, it is easy to choose a hash function, $h(K)$, that does not work very well. A common mistake is to choose a table size, M, as a power of 2, say $2^n$, and to choose $h(K) = K \% M$, which has the effect of truncating the key by selecting its last $n$ bits. Since this is equivalent to the truncation method, it suffers the same disadvantages. A more subtle pitfall is to choose to use the division method with the table size chosen to be a prime number M of the form $r^k \pm a$, where $r$ is the radix of the character set used for forming keys, and where $k$ and $a$ are small integers. In this case, the hash function tends to superimpose sums and differences of products of the characters used in the keys, which is not very effective.

- *Choosing a probe decrement that fails to enumerate all table locations*

    In double hashing, it is easy to make a mistake by choosing a probe decrement function, $p(K)$ that fails to enumerate all table locations. An easy, but frequently made mistake, is to forget that $p(K)$ must always be defined to have a value of 1 or greater. If $p(K)$ is defined to be zero for some key K, then Programs 9.16 and 9.17 will get into endless loops. Another precaution to observe is to ensure that $p(K)$ is relatively prime to the hash table size, M. For example, if M is a prime, then any $p(K) \geq 1$ is suitable. But if M is a power of 2, such as $M = 2^{14}$, then $p(K)$ must be chosen to be an odd integer for double hashing to work properly.

## ▪ Tips and Techniques

- *Postpone selection of your table data representations*

    A good programming technique is to design your program to use an abstract table and to employ the Table ADT operations in a Java class interface to be used by the rest of your program. Later, you can chose a good representation for your Table ADT when you develop information about the frequency of operations to be performed on your table, and when you know if any of the operations must be performed efficiently enough to meet real-time or total-processing-time constraints.

    Hash tables are enthusiastically to be recommended if you need to perform numerous table searches with the highest possible efficiency. AVL trees can be recommended if table deletions, insertions, and enumerations must be performed relatively often, and if the efficiency of searching is not at a premium.

- *Always check the performance of your hashing method*

    A careful programmer will always do some experiments and performance measurements to check that an implementation of a particular hashing method is working properly. The use of formatted debugging aids to picture what is going on is strongly encouraged, since any anomalies or misperformances of hashing implementations tend to leap out when presented visually. For example, a poorly designed hash function, which preserves clustering of the keys or which does not cover the table address space evenly will be quickly revealed when visual data on its performance for a set of typical keys is examined. Also, if probe sequences fail to cover all table addresses, visual inspection can frequently reveal the presence of the problem.

- *Use Java's built-in Hashtable class when it is advantageous to do so*

    The **java.util** package contains a **Hashtable** class that implements the Table ADT discussed in this chapter. You can construct a **Hashtable** object to have a given initial capacity that you specify, and you can set it up so that if its load factor exceeds a threshold that you specify, the table will expand automatically to twice its size and will move all the current table entries to new rehashed positions in the expanded table, which will then have half the former load factor in order to provide improved performance. Hash table entries are **(Key, Element)** pairs, in which the **Keys** can be any object. The **hashCode( )** method of an object returns a hash code that can be used to store objects as keys in **Hashtables**. (The **hashCode( )** method is defined for every Java object and has a default implementation that uses the object's reference. On the other hand, many objects, such as **Doubles**, **Longs**, **Integers**, **Floats**, and **Strings**, define their own versions of the **hashCode( )** method to override the default implementation and to be a function of that object's numerical or string value.)

## ▪ References for Further Study

Almost every data structure and algorithms book covers hashing. In this chapter, we have been able to cover only a few of the rudiments of hashing techniques. You may wish to pursue additional topics such as multiplicative hashing functions (which was only sketched in Exercise 9.6.2), extendible hashing (which can be used to expand hash tables that are too full for good performance), and ordered hashing (which gives an efficiency improvement for unsuccessful search, by ordering the keys along a probe sequence).

recent developments

Horowitz and Sahni's book covers some of the more recent developments in hashing discovered during the last decade.

> Horowitz, E. and Sahni, S., *Fundamentals of Data Structures in Pascal.* Computer Science Press, New York, NY (1990).

more on hashing

The classical reference by Donald E. Knuth covers multiplicative hashing and ordered hashing.

> Knuth, D. E., *The Art of Computer Programming,* vol. 3: *Searching and Sorting.* Addison-Wesley, Reading, MA (1973), pp. 506–549.

where to find missing proofs and derivations

For the curious, pages 476-478 of another book by the author provide a proof that if the table size and probe decrement are relatively prime, the probe sequence covers all the hash table addresses. Also covered in Chapter 11 are derivations of some of the hashing algorithm performance formulas.

> Standish, T. A., *Data Structures, Algorithms, and Software Principles in* C. Addison-Wesley, Reading, MA (1995).

## ■ Chapter Summary

Hashing is a method for storing and retrieving information in tables. Individual items of information, $I$, are stored in table entries of the form $(K, I)$, identified by unique keys, $K$. Given a key, $K$, to find the table entry, $(K, I)$, containing $K$, a hash function, $h(K)$, is computed. The value of $h(K)$ is a table location where we can start searching

the basic idea of hashing

for the table entry $(K, I)$. If we do not find the table entry $(K, I)$ immediately at the location given by $h(K)$, we invoke a collision resolution policy that enables us to search systematically through the remaining locations in the table to find $(K, I)$, if it exists, or to conclude that there is no table entry having the key $K$.

A *Table ADT* is an abstract storage device that models the storage and retrieval properties of tables. We can think of a Table ADT, $T$, as a collection of table entries, $(K,I)$, where $K$ is a key, and $I$ is some information associated with $K$, such that no two distinct table entries have the same key. The operations we can perform on table $T$

the Table ADT

include constructing the empty table $T$, determining whether or not $T$ is empty, enumerating the table entries in $T$ in increasing order of their keys, and retrieving, updating, inserting, and deleting table entries in $T$. Table ADTs can be represented by hash tables, AVL trees, and sorted arrays of records. Java provides a useful predefined Hashtable class in the java.util package that implements the Table ADT.

collisions and collision resolution policies

When we attempt to store two distinct keys, $K_1 \neq K_2$, with the same hash address, $h(K_1) = h(K_2)$, in a given hash table, $T$, a *collision* is said to occur. When this happens, a *collision resolution policy* is needed to resolve the collision. Three different collision resolution methods are (a) the separate chaining method, (b) hash bucket methods, and (c) open addressing methods. Even though, at first, you might think that collisions would be relatively rare, in fact, collisions are relatively frequent, even in sparsely occupied tables. For example, in a table of 365 locations, the chance of having a collision is greater than fifty-fifty as soon as the table is more than 6.3 percent full (i.e., as soon as there are 23 or more table entries). So it is important to have effective methods for resolving collisions.

In the method of *separate chaining*, when keys collide at a given hash address, the table entries containing them are placed on a linked list (or chain) starting at the collision address.

In *hash bucket* methods, a big hash table is divided into a number of smaller subtables called buckets. The hash function $h(K)$, maps a key $K$ into one of the buckets where it is stored sequentially. These bucket methods work comparatively well with large tables stored on external memory devices. Java's built-in **Hashtable** class uses the method of hashing with buckets to implement extensible (i.e., expandable) hash tables.

In *open addressing methods*, table entries containing the keys are placed in open (or empty) locations in the hash table. When a collision occurs, a systematic search is conducted among the other table locations to identify another open address (or empty entry) in which to place a new table entry containing the colliding key. Two noteworthy collision resolution policies for use with open addressing methods are (a) *linear probing*, in which you scan sequentially among the hash table locations, starting at the collision location, to find the first available empty entry, and (b) *double hashing*, in which, when a key, $K$, collides at a given location, you compute a second hash function, $p(K)$, to determine a *probe decrement*.

The probe decrement is used to determine a probe sequence by starting at the collision location and probing for empty entries at intervals equal to the probe decrement in the direction of decreasing table locations. Whenever you fall off the bottom of the table during this process, you "wrap around" and start examining locations starting at the top of the table. In double hashing, different probe decrements, $p(K)$, are computed for different keys, $K$, so even though two keys collide at the same initial hash location, they tend to trace out *different* probe sequences when searching for the first available empty table location.

When using open addressing with linear probing, colliding keys tend to occupy contiguous sequential runs of table entries called *clusters*. Linear probing is subject to a phenomenon called *primary clustering* in which, roughly speaking, colliding keys begin to form clusters, which tend to join with other clusters to make even bigger clusters. The bigger the clusters get, the wider they are as targets for collecting collisions by new keys that are being inserted. Thus, the bigger they become, the faster they grow.

By contrast, when using double hashing, primary clusters do not form since colliding keys tend to follow separate probe sequences that bounce around among the table locations when looking for an available empty entry, and which do not cause colliding keys to be inserted in clusters containing the original collision locations.

The *load factor* of a hash table is the ratio of the number of table entries to the total number of table entries. The higher the load factor of a hash table, the worse the

*separate chaining*

*hash bucket methods*

*open addressing methods*

*clustering*

*load factors*

performance of a hashing method becomes. However, some methods are worse than others at high load factors. For example, when a hash table is three-quarters full, it takes on the average of 8.5 probes to locate an empty table entry in which to insert a new key when *linear probing* is used, but it takes only 4 probes when *double hashing* is used. At higher load factors, the performance advantage of double hashing over linear probing is even more pronounced. Double hashing works better than linear probing at high load factors because double hashing does not produce any primary clustering. At low load factors (for example, when a hash table is at most 25 percent full), linear probing and double hashing perform about the same.

*ensuring complete table search*

In the open addressing methods, it is important to ensure that probe sequences used in linear probing and double hashing cover all the possible table locations, so that searches for available empty entries will be complete. This can be guaranteed for double hashing methods whenever the value of the second hash function, $p(K)$, used to compute the probe decrement, is *relatively prime* to the hash table size.

*comparative performance of hashing methods*

Even though clustering hinders the performance of open addressing hash methods, still, the performance of hashing methods, in general, can be quite superior to competing techniques, such as the use of AVL trees or the use of sorted arrays of table entries. For example, considering only the operation of *searching* in a table, $T$, for a table entry $(K,I)$, given a search key, $K$, suppose table $T$ has 4096 entries. Then searching in an AVL tree representation of table $T$ takes on the average of 12.25 key comparisons; searching in a sorted-array representation of $T$, using binary search, takes 11 key comparisons; and searching in a hash table that is 50 percent full or less, using either linear probing or double hashing, takes at most 1.5 key comparisons.

*choosing hash functions carefully*

It is important to choose hash functions, $h(K)$, carefully so that they map keys, $K$, uniformly and randomly onto table locations in the hash table. In the division method, a key $K$ is imagined to represent a number, and it is divided by the size, M, of a hash table, $T$, to produce a quotient, Q, and a remainder, R. The remainder (reduced modulo M to fit in the range of table addresses, 0:M – 1), can be used for the value of the hash function, $h(K)$, and the quotient, Q, can be used to derive the value of the probe decrement, $p(K)$, to be used for double hashing. Other techniques for choosing hash functions are (a) *folding*, in which a key, $K$, is divided into sections that are added, subtracted, or multiplied together; (b) *middle-squaring*, in which a middle section of $K$, treated as a number, is squared; and (c) *truncation*, in which all but the low-order portion of key $K$ is deleted.

*finding the best Table ADT representations*

Suppose $T$ is an abstract Table ADT. Then $T$ could be represented by a variety of data representation techniques, including hashing, AVL trees, and arrays of table entries sorted in ascending order of their keys. Which of these three representations is advantageous to use in a given application depends on the mix of operations being performed on the table $T$. If search and retrieval are the only operations to be performed and if speed is at a premium, then hash table techniques are the best performers. However, if searches are intermingled with frequent insertions, deletions, and ordered enumerations of the table entries in $T$, then AVL trees might offer the best overall performance.

# Sorting

**Introduction and Motivation**

The problem of sorting an initially unordered collection of keys to produce an ordered collection is one of the richest in computer science. The richness derives, in part, from the fact that the number of different ways of solving the sorting problem is plentiful. Because the sorting problem has fascinated theoretical computer scientists, much is known about the efficiency of various solutions, and about limitations on the best possible solutions. Consequently, an investigation of various sorting algorithms makes an excellent case study for acquainting you with the kind of progress in our understanding of computer science that has been made during the last half-century.

*the richness of the sorting problem*

For instance, if an algorithm uses comparisons between keys as its means for deciding how to arrange the keys in sorted order, then it cannot sort a sequence of $n$ keys in an average amount of time less than proportional to $n \log n$. This $n \log n$ *lower bound* for comparison-based sorting does not imply that there do not exist even faster sorting methods that do not use key comparisons. In fact, there exist $O(n)$ sorting algorithms relying on what are called address-calculation techniques. For some strange

*the $n \log n$ barrier for comparison-based methods*

368

reason, most algorithm and data structures books cover only the $O(n \log n)$ comparison-based methods, and rarely, if ever, comment on the existence of the faster $O(n)$ address-calculation techniques.

Sometimes a sorting technique that works well in primary memory does not work at all well for sorting large files contained on external memory media, such as disks or tapes. Also, among the $O(n \log n)$ techniques, even though a fast technique, such as **QuickSort**, can sort $n$ keys twice as fast on the average as a competing $O(n \log n)$ technique, such as **HeapSort**, the worst case time for **QuickSort** is $O(n^2)$, whereas the worst case time for **HeapSort** is $O(n \log n)$.

worst case times are occasionally important

The fact that **HeapSort** has a much better worst case behavior than **QuickSort** could turn out to be important, even though **HeapSort** is twice as slow as **QuickSort** on the average. For instance, if you are applying a sorting technique to meet a time constraint under which you need to guarantee that $n$ keys will be sorted within a specified time limit, you might choose to use **HeapSort** over **QuickSort** because **HeapSort** will always finish in time $O(n \log n)$.

learning how to choose the best method

Familiarity with the performance characteristics of different sorting methods could be of significant value in helping you select a sorting technique that is well-matched to the characteristics of a particular problem you need to solve. If your goal is to become a proficient software engineer, then it is essential to know how to choose the best available methods for solving important often-encountered software problems.

goal: basic knowledge + comparative performance

Although the kind of comparative study offered in this chapter is not as highly detailed as those that you might encounter in graduate or professional software engineering courses, or in advanced undergraduate courses on algorithms, it nonetheless provides you with a good start on the subject of sorting. The goal is to give you an intuitive grasp of how the various sorting methods work, how they are related to one another as common instances of unifying abstract themes (such as *divide-and-conquer* or *priority queue sorting*), and some of what is known about their comparative performance.

## Plan for the Chapter

sorting themes

Sorting methods can be grouped in various clusters that share common themes. One way to organize them (although not the only possible way) is suggested by the diagram in Fig. 10.1 (on page 370). In fact, we have chosen to organize the sections in this chapter to discuss each of the different sorting themes shown in this figure.

Before discussing specific sorting techniques, however, Section 10.2 lays some theoretical groundwork by discussing the fact that $n \log n$ is a lower bound for the average time that comparison-based methods must take to sort $n$ keys.

priority queue methods

Section 10.3 investigates two priority queue sorting methods: **SelectionSort** and **HeapSort**. Recall that a priority queue is a collection of items in which items can be inserted in any order, but in which only the item of top-priority can be removed. Suppose that $PQ$ is a priority queue, and that when we remove items from $PQ$ one after another, they are removed in largest to smallest order. If, when we remove items from $PQ$, we then place them on the rear of an ordinary queue, $Q$, their order of arrival on the rear of $Q$ is in sorted order from largest to smallest. In both **SelectionSort** and **HeapSort**, we treat the remaining items to be sorted as a priority

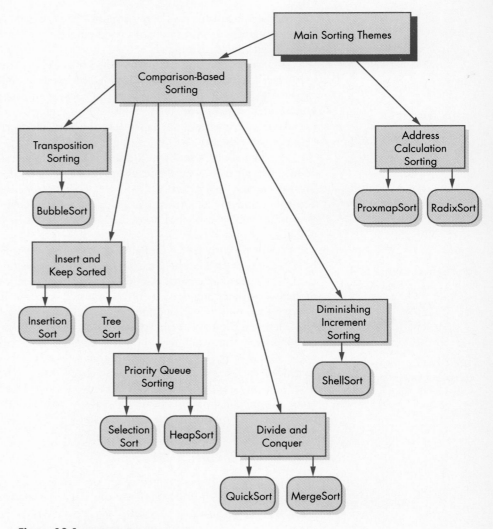

**Figure 10.1** Sorting Themes

queue. In the case of **HeapSort**, these remaining unsorted items are organized into a heap, and we remove the largest item from this heap at each stage. In the case of **SelectionSort**, the remaining unsorted items are treated as an unordered sequence, and we scan the entire sequence each time we remove an item in order first to locate the position of the largest item to remove. Thus **SelectionSort** can be viewed as using the unordered-array-representation for a priority queue, whereas **HeapSort** can be viewed as using the heap representation of a priority queue.

     Section 10.4 studies two *divide-and-conquer* methods: **MergeSort** and **QuickSort**. A divide-and-conquer sorting method is one that first *divides* a sequence of *n* keys into

*divide-and-conquer methods*

two subsequences, such as a *left subsequence* and a *right subsequence*. It then sorts these two subsequences. Finally, it combines the two sorted subsequences into a single sorted result.

Section 10.5 studies two sorting methods that use insertion: **InsertionSort** and **TreeSort**. Such methods start with an empty storage container, C, and insert new keys into the container one after another. The inserted keys are always maintained in sorted order inside C.

Section 10.6 investigates two methods, **ProxmapSort** and **RadixSort**, that use address-calculation techniques and that run in average time $O(n)$. It is of some interest that *RadixSort* was one of the methods used by early electromechanical, punched-card sorting machines that were employed in business data processing before the advent of electronic-digital computers.

Section 10.7 investigates two additional methods: **ShellSort** and **BubbleSort**. **ShellSort** is called a diminishing-increment sorting technique. **BubbleSort** makes repeated passes through an unsorted sequence of keys, and transposes any adjacent pair of keys that is not in sorted order. **BubbleSort**'s performance is particularly poor unless the sequence of keys it is given to sort is nearly sorted already.

Section 10.8 provides a discussion that attempts to compare the various methods and put them in perspective. It also covers some additional special cases not previously mentioned, such as the case in which the keys are a permutation of the integers from 0 to $n - 1$ and can be used directly as table addresses for final placement of the keys.

insertion-based methods

address-calculation methods

comparing the methods

## 10.2 Laying Some Groundwork

### LEARNING OBJECTIVES

1. To learn how comparison trees are defined.
2. To see how to use comparison trees to conclude that comparison-based sorting methods must use at least $n \log n$ comparisons on the average.
3. To understand that this $n \log n$ lower bound applies only to comparison-based methods and not to all possible sorting methods.

Many sorting methods decide how to rearrange keys into sorted order by first comparing the values of the keys. These methods are called comparison-based methods.

It turns out that, on the average, any comparison-based method must make a certain minimum number of comparisons between pairs of keys to gather enough information to decide how to rearrange them into sorted order. The argument that demonstrates why this must be the case depends on defining what are called *comparison trees*. A comparison tree is a binary tree in which, at each internal node, a comparison is made between two keys, and in which each external (or leaf) node contains a sorted arrangement of keys. The left descendant of each decision node represents a *yes* decision, and the right descendant represents a *no* decision. The decisions made on a path from the root to a given leaf node are sufficient to determine that the keys must be arranged in the order specified by the ordered sequence of keys given in that leaf node.

In the following examples and arguments, we assume we are dealing with distinct keys and that the decisions comparing two keys, *a* and *b*, can have only two outcomes: *a* < *b* and *a* > *b*. Treating the more complicated case, in which two keys, *a* and *b*, could be equal (as in *a* = *b*), would add more case analysis and complexity to the argument but would not reduce the minimum average number of comparisons needed to decide how to sort distinct keys. Consequently, to establish the minimum average number of comparisons, we need consider only the simpler case in which all keys are distinct from one another.

**dealing only with distinct keys**

Let's now consider a simple example of a comparison tree. Suppose we are trying to sort an array A[0:2] containing three distinct keys, *a*, *b* and *c*:

| A[0] | A[1] | A[2] |
|------|------|------|
| *a*  | *b*  | *c*  |

Figure 10.2 illustrates a comparison tree in which we compare various pairs of keys and, based on the (*yes* or *no*) outcome of each comparison, follow a path downward through the tree that performs additional comparisons until enough information is gathered to decide upon a final sorted order for the keys.

**comparison trees**

For example, in Fig. 10.2, if the result of comparing *a* < *b* is *yes*, we then descend from the root downward to the left, and compare *b* and *c*. If the result of comparing *b* < *c* is *no*, we descend further to the right and compare *a* and *c*. Finally, if the result of comparing *a* < *c* is *yes*, we know that the ascending sorted order for the keys must be (*a*, *c*, *b*). Therefore the ordered sequence of keys in the box that is the left descendant of the node containing the comparison *a* < *c* is the sequence (*a*, *c*, *b*).

In general, a given comparison-based sorting algorithm, *S*, will compare pairs of keys in some order. Comparisons of pairs of keys will usually be interleaved with rearrangements of the order of various pairs of keys, as algorithm *S* progressively moves the keys into final sorted order. The particular comparisons that *S* performs at a given stage in its execution will, in general, depend on the outcomes of previous comparisons and previous rearrangements of the keys that *S* has already performed. In any event, each comparison-based sorting algorithm, *S*, must perform comparisons be-

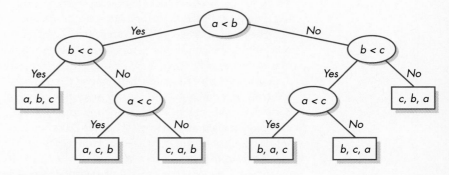

**Figure 10.2** A Comparison Tree

tween designated pairs of keys in *some* order, until it eventually terminates after having arranged the keys in sorted order. Let's now reason about the minimum possible number of comparisons $S$ could use, on the average, to sort a collection of distinct keys successfully.

The comparison tree in Fig. 10.2 sorts only three keys. Let's now suppose that we have $n$ distinct keys, instead of just three keys, and let's ask, "How many distinct sorted orders could result from sorting $n$ distinct keys?"

We see that, for three keys, $a$, $b$ and $c$, any one of the three could be the smallest and could appear first in sorted order. So there are three distinct ways in which a sorted sequence of three distinct keys could begin. Then, having chosen one of the three keys as the smallest, two possibilities remain for choosing the next smallest key. Finally, after the second smallest is chosen, by a process of elimination, only one key is left to be the largest. If we choose the first key any one of three ways, and then choose the second key any one of two ways, we get six total possible ways of choosing an order for the three distinct keys. These six distinct possible orderings are shown in the boxes that are the leaves of the comparison tree in Fig. 10.2.

In the special case of three distinct keys, the total number of distinct orders (6) is equal to the factorial of the number of keys (3!), since $6 = 3! = 3 * 2 * 1$. The same holds true for $n$ distinct keys—namely, that the total number of distinct orderings of $n$ keys is given by $n$ factorial ($n!$). The reason is that any of the $n$ keys could be the smallest and could appear first in sorted order. So an ordered arrangement of keys could start any one of $n$ distinct ways. Second, any of the remaining $(n-1)$ keys could occur next in sorted order. Third, any of the remaining $(n-2)$ keys could occur in third place in sorted order, and so on until, by a process of elimination, only one key remains to place last in sorted order. The product $n * (n-1) * (n-2) * \ldots * 2 * 1$, which is the same as $n!$, then gives the total number of distinct sorted orders that are possible outcomes for sorting $n$ distinct keys. (In mathematics, each such distinct order is called a *permutation* of the $n$ keys, and it is known that $n!$ gives the total number of permutations of the keys.)

Now that we know that there are $n!$ distinct orders for $n$ keys, we can reason about the minimum average number of comparisons needed to sort $n$ keys. Consider all possible comparison trees that correspond to algorithms that sort $n$ keys. The boxes at the leaves of such comparison trees each contain one of the $n!$ distinct permutations of the $n$ keys, and there must be at least $n!$ such leaves (or external nodes) in any valid comparison tree that can sort $n$ keys. (Otherwise, if there were fewer than $n!$ external nodes, one or more of the possible sorted orders could not be achieved, and the algorithm would fail to sort properly in such cases.)

If we travel down a path in a comparison tree, the number of comparisons encountered on the path from the root down to an external node (or leaf node) is identical to the number of comparisons needed to decide how to sort the original $n$ keys into the particular order given in the box at the external node. Moreover, the number of comparisons is identical to the path length from the root to the external node (since there is exactly one edge in the path below each internal comparison node on the path). Therefore the average number of comparisons needed to sort $n$ keys, according to the comparison tree, can be obtained by dividing the *external path length* of

six possible orders for three distinct keys

$n!$ orders for $n$ distinct keys

the minimum average
number of comparisons

the tree by the number of external nodes. (Recall, from Chapter 8, that the *external path length* is the sum of the lengths of the paths from the root to each external node.)

Consequently, the average number of comparisons will be at a minimum just when the external path length of the comparison tree is at a minimum. Again recalling the discussion of binary trees in Chapter 8, we know that among all possible binary trees, the binary trees having minimal external path lengths are those with leaves either on one level or on two adjacent levels.

If a comparison tree has $k$ external nodes and has minimal external path length, then the length, $p$, of the shortest path from the root to a leaf must be constrained by the inequality, $p \geq \lfloor \lg k \rfloor$. (Here, the notation $\lfloor x \rfloor$ stands for the *floor of x*, in which, if $x$ is a positive real number, $\lfloor x \rfloor$ is just the integer part of $x$ with the fractional part of $x$ thrown away. Also, the notation $\lg k$ stands for the base-2 logarithm of $k$, $\log_2 k$.) You can reason that $p \geq \lfloor \lg k \rfloor$, since if $r$ is the level number of any leaf at least distance from the root in a binary tree with leaves on at most two adjacent levels, and the number of leaves, $k$, lies in the range $2^r : (2^{(r+1)} - 1)$, then $r = \lfloor \lg k \rfloor$, and a path from the root to any leaf must contain at least $r$ edges.

The minimum average number of comparisons required for comparison-based sorting of $n$ keys can now be obtained by using a comparison tree of minimum external path length having $k = n!$ external nodes. In such a tree, the minimum average path length $p$ must obey the inequality, $p \geq \lfloor \lg (n!) \rfloor$. Consequently, if we could obtain a good estimate for the expression $\lg (n!)$, we would have a good lower bound for the minimum average number comparisons required to sort $n$ keys using comparison-based methods.

By using a famous approximation for $n!$, called Stirling's Approximation, and by doing some manipulation involving logarithms, it can be shown that

$$\lg(n!) > \tfrac{1}{2}\, n \lg n\,.$$

In this latter result, the constant of proportionality ($\tfrac{1}{2}$) can be eliminated by changing the base of the logarithm on the right side, giving

$$\lg n! > n \log_4 n\,.$$

Because any such constant of proportionality can be converted to the constant 1 by an appropriate choice of a logarithm base, the $n \log n$ barrier for comparison-based sorting is often expressed without writing an explicit logarithm base. (This same convention is followed when writing the O-notation for $O(n \log n)$ without a logarithm base. For more on this subject, please see Section B.4 of Appendix B.) Figure 10.3 states the overall conclusion, which is known as the *$n \log n$ barrier* for comparison-

> The minimum average number of comparisons required to sort $n$ keys using a comparison-based sorting method is proportional to $n \log n$.

**Figure 10.3** The $n \log n$ Barrier for Comparison-Based Sorting

based sorting. (For the missing details of the mathematical derivation used to reach the conclusion stated in Fig. 10.3, you can refer to Section 13.2 of another book by the author, *Data Structures, Algorithms, and Software Principles in C*. The full reference is listed in the references section at the end of this chapter. The missing details of the remaining derivations in this chapter establishing the O-notation for various sorting methods can also be found there.)

Many of the sorting techniques we shall investigate in the remaining sections of this chapter are comparison-based methods. For example, SelectionSort, InsertionSort, MergeSort, QuickSort, HeapSort, BubbleSort, ShellSort and TreeSort, are all comparison-based methods. In view of Fig. 10.3, you should be prepared to confirm that all of these can sort $n$ keys in an average amount of time no faster than that given by the complexity class $O(n \log n)$.

## 10.2 REVIEW QUESTIONS

1. What is a comparison-based sorting method?
2. What is a comparison tree?
3. What is a lower bound for the minimum average time required to sort $n$ keys using any comparison-based method?
4. If a *full binary tree* is defined as a binary tree in which each internal node has exactly two nonempty children, what is the shape of a full binary tree having minimum external path length?
5. Why is a comparison tree with minimum external path length also a tree that represents the minimum average number of comparisons to sort $n$ keys?

## 10.2 EXERCISE

1. If $r$ is the level number of any leaf at least distance from the root in a full binary tree with leaves on at most two adjacent levels, and the number of leaves, $k$, lies in the range $2^r \leq k \leq 2^{(r+1)} - 1$, why is it the case that $r = \lfloor \lg k \rfloor$ and why must a path from the root to any leaf contain at least $r$ edges?

## 10.3 Priority Queue Sorting Methods

### LEARNING OBJECTIVES

1. To learn about abstract priority queue sorting.
2. To learn how SelectionSort and HeapSort are each refinements of abstract priority queue sorting.
3. To see how SelectionSort represents its priority queue of yet-to-be-sorted keys as an unsorted subarray.
4. To see how HeapSort represents its collection of yet-to-be-sorted keys as a heap.
5. To learn the O-notation for the sorting times for SelectionSort and HeapSort.

Before we begin discussion of the priority queue sorting techniques covered in this section, we need to introduce some preliminary assumptions that will hold throughout the discussion of most of the sorting techniques in the remainder of the chapter.

## Some Preliminary Assumptions

In what follows, we will be sorting arrays of keys. The keys can be of any type whatsoever. For instance, the keys could be integers, or strings, or floating point numbers. The important thing about keys is that any two given keys, $K_1$ and $K_2$, can be *compared*, as a result of which, one and only one of the following relationships will be true: $K_1 < K_2$, $K_1 = K_2$, or $K_1 > K_2$. Consequently, by rearranging the order of the keys in an array, A, the keys can be put into *ascending order* (where, specifically, ascending order means *nondecreasing order* such that $A[i] \leq A[i + 1]$ for all $i$ in the range $0 \leq i < n - 1$).

In the algorithms that follow, we shall assume that we always start with an unsorted array, A, of $n$ keys of type **KeyType**, and that the objective is to arrange the keys in A into ascending order. The array indices for A are assumed to start at 0 and to end at some largest index, $n - 1$, which is one less than the size of the array, A. The class **KeyType** is assumed to be any Java class that implements the **ComparisonKey** interface defined in Program 5.7 of Section 4 in Chapter 5. This simply means that any two keys k1 and k2 that are of type **KeyType** always have a **compareTo** method defined for them such that the result of invoking the method call k1.compareTo(k2) is −1, 0, or +1 according to whether k1 < k2, k1 == k2, or k1 > k2 respectively. In other words, any two keys of type **KeyType** can always be compared using a three-way comparison operation. Figure 10.4 expresses these assumptions in Java.

## Priority Queue Sorting

Section 5.2 introduced the Priority Queue ADT, and Section 8.5 introduced heaps as a representation for priority queues. Then, in Table 8.21, we compared running time efficiencies of operations on three priority queue representations: (a) heaps, (b) sorted lists, and (c) unsorted arrays.

```
// defined constant

    final int n = anyArbitrarySize;              // n gives the number of items
                                                 // in the array to be sorted
// assumed class definition

    class KeyType implements ComparisonKey {
        // gives a definition of the method k1.compareTo(k2)
    }

// assumed array declaration

    KeyType[ ]  A;                               // A[0:n – 1] is an array of keys to be sorted
```

**Figure 10.4** Java Definitions Assumed for Sorting Algorithms

sorting based on
priority queues

We can imagine a family of sorting algorithms based on the use of priority queues, as follows. First, given the initial unsorted array, A, we can imagine that we organize the keys in A into a priority queue representation, PQ. Then, we imagine that we have an output queue, Q, which is initially empty and which will accumulate new keys in arrival order as they are inserted on Q's rear end.

We then remove keys from PQ, one at a time, and insert them on the rear of Q. We repeat this process until PQ is empty. Since the keys removed from PQ were removed in largest to smallest order, and were inserted into Q in arrival order, Q will contain keys in decreasing order at the end of the process.

two refinements of abstract
priority queue sorting

Let's first look at Program Strategy 10.5, which expresses this process of abstract priority queue sorting. Then we will give two specific representations of priority queue sorting. The first will represent the priority queue, PQ, as an unsorted subarray of the array A. The second will use a heap to represent the priority queue PQ. In both cases, the output queue, Q, will be represented by a subarray of array, A, lying at the highest index positions of array A, and PQ will be represented by a subarray lying at the lowest index positions of array A. In the first case, we will discover that we have implemented a variant of **SelectionSort**. In the second case, we will have implemented an algorithm called **HeapSort**.

Programs 5.3 and 5.10 gave implementations of abstract priority queue sorting using various substitutable Java priority queue classes (each having identical interfaces but having different underlying data representations). Recall that these examples were given to illustrate the *substitutability* of data representations in modular programming. We shall now give two specific refinements of abstract priority queue sorting that use two separate subarrays of array A to hold the priority queue PQ and the output queue Q, and which therefore actually accomplish sorting by rearranging the order of the keys in A.

```
    | void priorityQueueSort(KeyType[ ] A) {
    |
    |     (let Q be an initially empty output queue)
    |     (let PQ be a priority queue)
    |     KeyType  k;
  5 |
    |
    |     (organize the keys in A into a priority queue, PQ)
    |
    |     while (PQ is not empty) {
 10 |
    |         (remove the largest key, k, from PQ)
    |         (insert key, k, on the rear of output queue, Q)
    |
    |     }
 15 |
    |     (move the keys in Q into the array A in ascending sorted order)
    |
    | }
```

**Program Strategy 10.5** Abstract Priority Queue Sorting

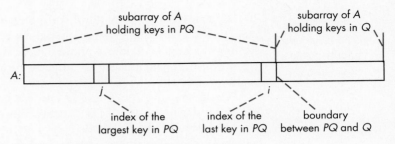

**Figure 10.6** General Situation in Priority Queue Sorting

Figure 10.6 gives a diagram of the general situation we expect during the priority queue sorting process. Here, the sorting array, A, is divided into two subarrays, with the subarray holding the keys in PQ on the left, and the subarray holding the keys in Q on the right.

Let's imagine that we have been engaged in priority queue sorting for a while, and that the first few of the largest keys have already been placed in the subarray Q of array A, holding output keys in their final ascending order.

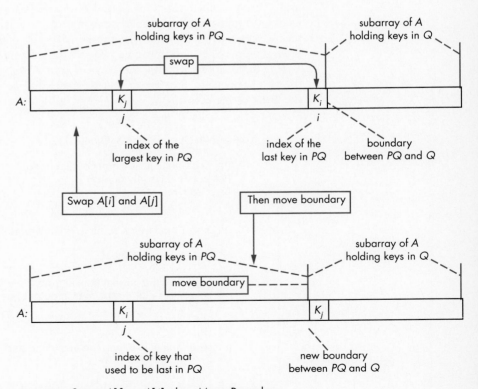

**Figure 10.7** Swap $A[i] \leftrightarrow A[j]$, then Move Boundary

Now, let's focus on how we remove the next key from $PQ$, and place it on the rear of $Q$. We first identify the index position of the largest key in subarray $PQ$. Suppose this occurs at index position, $j$. Suppose also that index, $i$, points to the last position in the subarray $PQ$. We then exchange the keys in $A[i]$ and $A[j]$, and we move the boundary between $PQ$ and $Q$ one position to the left. This action is shown in Fig. 10.7.

The net effect of the actions illustrated in Fig. 10.7 is to remove the largest key in $PQ$ and insert it on the rear of the output queue, $Q$. If this action is performed repeatedly until $PQ$ becomes empty, then $Q$ will expand to become the entire array $A$, and it will contain keys in ascending order.

## SelectionSort

If we now refine abstract priority queue sort by using an unsorted subarray of keys as the representation for the priority queue, $PQ$, we get the **SelectionSort** algorithm. At each stage, to identify the position of the largest key, $j$, in the subarray $PQ$, we scan all

```
     |    void SelectionSort(KeyType[ ] A) {
     |
     |          int          i, j, k;
     |          KeyType      temp;
  5  |
     |          // initially, Q is empty, and PQ contains all keys in A, so the index, i,
     |          // of the last key in PQ is set to n – 1, the index of the last key in A.
     |
     |          i = n – 1;
 10  |
     |          // while PQ contains more than one key,
     |          // identify and move the largest key in PQ into Q
     |
     |          while ( i > 0) {
 15  |
     |                // let j initially point to the last key in PQ
     |                j = i;
     |
     |                // scan remaining positions in 0:i – 1 to find largest key, A[j]
 20  |                for (k = 0; k < i; k++) {
     |                     if ( A[k].compareTo(A[j]) > 0 ) j = k ;
     |                }
     |
     |                // exchange the largest key, A[j], and the last key, A[i]
 25  |                temp = A[i]; A[i] = A[j]; A[j] = temp;
     |
     |                // move boundary between PQ and Q downward one position
     |                i – –;
     |          }
 30  |    }
```

**Program 10.8 SelectionSort** as a Refinement of Priority Queue Sort

the keys in $PQ$, remembering the position, $j$, of the current maximum as we go. Then we swap $A[j]$, the largest key in $PQ$, with $A[i]$, the last key in $PQ$, and decrease $i$ by 1 to move the boundary between $PQ$ and $Q$. Program 10.8 gives the details.

In constructing Program 10.8 as a refinement of abstract priority queue sorting, as given in Program Strategy 10.5, some optimizations have been subtly introduced. First, no work is involved in organizing the keys in the unsorted array, $A$, into a priority queue, $PQ$, since $A$ is being used directly as the representation of $PQ$. Second, no effort is required to move the keys from the final output queue, $Q$, into array $A$ in ascending order, since $Q$ has grown from an empty subarray of $A$ into the entire array, $A$, by the time the algorithm finishes. Third, and finally, the while-loop, which extracts keys from $PQ$ and puts them into $Q$, terminates when $PQ$ contains one key, instead of terminating when $PQ$ is empty, as shown in Program Strategy 10.5. It is possible to stop when $PQ$ contains only one key, since that key must be the smallest key in $A$, by a process of elimination, and since that smallest key is already in its final position in $A$.

some program optimizations

## Known Performance of SelectionSort

SelectionSort runs in time O(n²)

**SelectionSort** is known to run in time $O(n^2)$. Roughly speaking, here is why this is so. Since Program 10.8 exchanges $A[j]$ with $A[i]$ for each $i$ starting at $n - 1$ and counting down to 1, **SelectionSort** performs $(n - 1)$ exchanges. Also, the number of key comparisons performed on line 21 of Program 10.8 is a sum of the form: $(n - 1) + (n - 2) + \ldots + 2 + 1$, which is known to have the value $(n*(n - 1))/2$, (using the formula for the sum of an arithmetic progression). Therefore, since **SelectionSort** does $O(n^2)$ comparisons and $O(n)$ exchanges, it is an $O(n^2)$ sorting algorithm.

## HeapSort

Let's reconsider the abstract priority queue sorting algorithm given in Program Strategy 10.5. We will construct a new refinement by representing the priority queue, $PQ$, as a heap, using the sequential representation of the heap as a subarray $A[1:n]$ of an extended sorting array declared in Java by: **KeyType[ ] A = new KeyType A[n+1];**

We first consider $PQ$ to be the entire subarray $A[1:n]$, and we organize its keys into a heap by applying the heapifying process sketched in Program Strategy 8.16 in Section 8.5. At the conclusion of this heapifying process, the largest element in the heap sits in position, $A[1]$. We can now swap the first and last keys in $PQ$ by performing the exchange, $A[1] \leftrightarrow A[n]$, after which we can move the boundary between $PQ$ and $Q$, so that $Q$ now contains one key that is the former largest key in $PQ$, and so that $PQ$ has been shortened to contain one fewer key.

representing the priority queue by a heap

We then have to reheapify $PQ$ because the new key at its root may have made it lose the heap property, after which the largest among the remaining keys in $PQ$ will have been moved into position $A[1]$. We then repeatedly swap the first and last keys in the subarray $PQ$, move the boundary between $PQ$ and $Q$, and reheapify $PQ$ until only one key remains in $PQ$.

At the conclusion of this process, $PQ$ contains the smallest of the original keys in $A$, $Q$ contains the remaining keys of $A$ in ascending order, and $A$, which consists

```
    |   void HeapSort(KeyType[ ] A)  {
    |
    |           int             i;
    |           KeyType     temp;
 5  |
    |           // heapify all subtrees except the subtree containing the root
    |
    |           for ( i = n / 2;  i > 1;  i − −) {
    |               siftUp(A,i,n);
10  |           }
    |
    |           // reheapify starting at the root, remove the root's key, put it
    |           // on the output queue, and replace the root's key with the key
    |           // in the last leaf in level order, until the heap contains one key
15  |
    |           for (i = n; i > 1; i − − ) {
    |               siftUp(A,1,i);
    |               temp = A[1]; A[1] = A[i]; A[i] = temp;          // swap A[1] and A[i]
    |           }
    |   }
```

```
/* ------------------------------------------------------------------------------------------------ */
```

```
    |   void siftUp(KeyType[ ] A, int i, int n)  {
    |
    |           // let i point to the root and let n point to the last leaf in level order
    |
 5  |               int j;
    |               KeyType  rootKey;
    |               boolean  notFinished;
    |
    |           // let rootKey be the key at the root
10  |               rootKey = A[i];
    |
    |           // let j point to the left child of i
    |               j = 2*i;
    |               notFinished = (j <= n);       // siftUp is not finished if j exists in the tree
15  |
    |           // move any larger child that is bigger than the root key upward one
    |           // level in the tree
    |               while (notFinished) {
    |
20  |                   if (j < n) {                      // if a right child of i also exists in the tree
    |                       if (A[j+1].compareTo(A[j]) > 0)  j++;              // set j to point
    |                   }                                                       // to the larger child
    |
    |                   if (A[j].compareTo(rootKey) <= 0) {          // if the larger child is
25  |                       notFinished = false;              // not bigger than the root key,
    |                                                           // no more keys sift up
```

**Program 10.9** HeapSort *(continued)*

Program 10.9 **HeapSort** (*continued*)

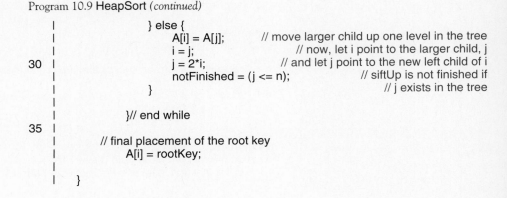

of the subarray *PQ* followed by the subarray *Q*, now contains the original keys of *A* in ascending order. Hence nothing needs to be done to extract the keys in *Q* and rearrange them in *A*, since *A* is already sorted.

Program 10.9 gives an optimized refinement of priority queue sorting, using the sequential representation of heaps.

When **HeapSort** begins, it is assumed that all keys in the subarray $A[1:n]$ are to be organized into a heap, *PQ*, representing a priority queue. Observe that during the initial heapification of these keys, on lines 8:10 of **HeapSort**, the subtrees of *PQ* are heapified in reverse level order. Moreover, only the nontrivial subtrees of *PQ* are heapified (meaning only those that are not single leaf nodes), and the subtree consisting of the entire tree is not heapified, since that action is deferred until executing line 17 during the first cycle through the for-loop on lines 16:19.

The procedure, **siftUp(A,i,n)**, is an auxiliary routine that converts a tree that is almost a heap into a heap, by using a cyclical shift of keys, starting at the root node and moving downward on a path along which the largest of the keys larger than the original root key are moved upward to create a hole for final placement of the root key, which in turn is moved downward. **siftUp(A,i,n)**, is applied only to trees that depart from satisfying the heap property at their roots, if at all. Because **siftUp** uses a cyclical shift of keys, it is more efficient than the reheapifying process illustrated in Program Strategy 8.15, which uses repeated pairwise exchanges of keys instead. (Recall that Program 8.20 also uses the efficient cyclic shift method when removing an item from a priority queue.)

## Known Performance of HeapSort

Let's use the mathematical facts about heaps that we mentioned in Section 8.5 to reason about the running time of **HeapSort**. First, it was stated that the process of converting the unorganized keys in array *A* into a heap takes time $O(n)$. Moreover, the process of removing the root of the heap, replacing it with its last leaf in level order, and reheapifying the resulting tree containing *i* keys, is known to take at most $\lfloor \lg i \rfloor$

**HeapSort runs in time $O(n \log n)$**

pairwise exchanges of keys (and in the similar case of siftUp, takes $\lfloor \lg i \rfloor + 2$ shifts of keys from one node or temporary variable to another, forming a cyclic shift). Consequently, the total effort to remove all keys, except the last, from $PQ$ and to move them to the rear of $Q$, takes at most an amount of effort proportional to the sum of the floors of the logarithms from 2 to $n$, $\Sigma_{(2 \le i \le n)}$ ($\lfloor \lg i \rfloor + 2$). The total number of key comparisons is a like sum, bounded above by $\Sigma$ ($2\lfloor \lg i \rfloor + 1$). The sum of the logarithms of the integers from 1 to $n$, and also the sum of the floors of the base-2 logarithms of the integers from 1 to $n$, can both be shown to be $O(n \log n)$. Since this is the dominant time, HeapSort runs in time $O(n \log n)$.

## 10.3 REVIEW QUESTIONS

1. Explain how abstract priority queue sorting works.
2. Describe the representation of priority queues used in SelectionSort.
3. What is the O-notation for the running time of SelectionSort?
4. Describe the representation of priority queues used in HeapSort.
5. Why does HeapSort use an array $A[1:n]$ indexed by the integers $i$ in the range $1 \le i \le n$, instead of using a normal array of the form, $A[0:n-1]$?
6. What is the O-notation for the running time of HeapSort?
7. Why is HeapSort more efficient than SelectionSort?

## 10.3 EXERCISE

1. Why is siftUp(A,i,n) applied only to the subtrees rooted at i in the range 2:n/2, and why are these roots, i, considered in decreasing order?

## 10.4  Divide-and-Conquer Methods

## LEARNING OBJECTIVES

1. To understand the divide-and-conquer theme, as applied to sorting methods.
2. To learn that MergeSort is an $O(n \log n)$ sorting method.
3. To learn how QuickSort works.
4. To learn that QuickSort runs in average time $O(n \log n)$ and worst case time $O(n^2)$.

*the main idea*

In this section, we consider two *divide-and-conquer* sorting methods, MergeSort and QuickSort. The theme behind these sorting methods is a three-step process: (1) divide the initially given unsorted array into two subarrays, (2) sort the two subarrays, and (3) combine the two sorted subarrays into the overall solution.

The abstract program strategy for divide-and-conquer sorting is given in Program Strategy 10.10 (on page 384). It is expressed in a form that allows it to be applied recursively to subarrays of array A.

```
 |   void Sort(KeyType[ ] A, int m, int n)  {          // to sort the subarray A[m:n] of
 |                                                     // array A into ascending order
 |
 |      if (there is more than one item to sort in A[m:n]) {
5|          (divide A[m:n] into two subarrays A[m:i] and A[j:n])
 |          (sort the subarray A[m:i])
 |          (sort the subarray A[j:n])
 |          (combine the two sorted subarrays to yield the sorted original array)
 |      }
10|
 |   }
```

**Program Strategy 10.10** Divide-and-Conquer Sorting Strategy

## MergeSort

the basic idea for merge sorting

The basic idea for merge sorting a list, such as (5, 3, 8, 6, 7, 2, 4, 1), is a three-step process: (1) *divide* the list in two halves, L = (5, 3, 8, 6) and R = (7, 2, 4, 1); (2) *sort* the two half-lists, getting L = (3, 5, 6, 8) and R = (1, 2, 4, 7); and (3) *merge* the two half-lists into the final sorted list, Merge(L, R) = (1, 2, 3, 4, 5, 6, 7, 8). The abstract program strategy for doing this is given as Program Strategy 10.11. Suppose that the original list has $n$ items in it. Then L and R each have $n/2$ items in them. (For simplicity, let's imagine that $n$ is divisible evenly by 2, so that $n/2$ is an integer.)

how to merge two lists

If we think for a moment about how to merge two sorted half-lists, L and R, into a single sorted result list, SL, we can imagine that we start with an empty list, SL, and we repeatedly remove the smaller first item from the beginning of L or R and put it at the end of SL. When both L and R are empty, SL will be a merged list sorted in ascending order. This merging process involves moving all $n$ items into SL, and may involve comparing as few as $n/2$ of them or as many as $(n–1)$ of them. Thus merging is a linear time process known to require $O(n)$ running time.

## Known Performance of MergeSort

MergeSort runs in time $O(n \log n)$

It can be shown that **MergeSort** runs in time $O(n \log n)$. The details of the derivation are given on pages 236–240 in Section 6.5 of another book by the author, *Data Structures, Algorithms, and Software Principles in C*, (*cf.* references at end of chapter).

```
 |   void MergeSort(KeyType[ ] A, int m, int n) {       // to sort the subarray A[m:n] of
 |                                                      // array A into ascending order
 |
 |      if (there is more than one item to sort in A[m:n]) {
5|          (divide A[m:n] into two halves, leftArray and rightArray)
 |          (MergeSort the leftArray A[m:middle])
 |          (MergeSort the rightArray A[middle+1:n])
 |          (merge the leftArray and the rightArray to obtain the result)
 |      }
10|
 |   }
```

**Program Strategy 10.11** Strategy for MergeSort

```
    |   void QuickSort(KeyType[ ] A, int m, int n)  {    // to sort the subarray A[m:n] of
    |                                                     // array A into ascending order
    |
    |        if (there is more than one key to sort in A[m:n]) {
  5 |             (Partition A[m:n] into a leftPartition and a rightPartition)
    |             (using one of the keys in A[m:n] as a pivot key.)
    |             (QuickSort the leftPartition)
    |             (QuickSort the rightPartition)
    |        }
 10 |
    |   }
```

**Program Strategy 10.12** Strategy for QuickSort

## QuickSort

QuickSort is another divide-and-conquer sorting method that runs in average time $O(n \log n)$.

The main theme behind QuickSort is as follows. You first choose some key in the array $A$ as a *pivot key*. This pivot key is used to separate the keys in $A$ into two partitions: (1) A *left partition* containing keys less than the pivot key, and (2) a *right partition* containing keys greater than or equal to the pivot key. QuickSort is then applied recursively to sort the left and right partitions. After this has been done, no further rearrangement is needed, since the original array, $A$, containing the two sorted left and right partitions, is now in ascending order. The main theme behind QuickSort is given in the abstract strategy shown in Program Strategy 10.12.

*the main theme used in QuickSort*

A Java version of QuickSort is given as Program 10.13. As you can see, the actual procedure, QuickSort, is an executive routine that calls a subprogram, partition(A,i,j), to create the left and right partitions, after which QuickSort calls itself recursively to sort the left and right partitions.

The partition algorithm is given as Program 10.14. Its goal is to partition the subarray $A[i:j]$ into a left and right partition, using the key in the middle of the subarray as a pivot key. After partitioning has taken place, the pivot key sits at location $A[p]$ which lies between, and therefore separates, the left and right partitions. The heart of the QuickSort algorithm, then, is the partitioning method, given by the Program 10.14, partition(A,i,j). Let's examine five stages of the partitioning process.

```
    |   void QuickSort(KeyType[ ] A, int m, int n)  {    // to sort the subarray A[m:n] of
    |                                                     // array A into ascending order
    |        if (m < n) {
    |             int p = partition(A,m,n);               // p gives the position of the pivot
  5 |             QuickSort(A,m,p–1);                      // after partitioning takes place
    |             QuickSort(A,p+1,n);
    |        }
    |
    |   }
```

**Program 10.13** QuickSort

```
     | int partition(KeyType[ ] A, int i, int j)  {
     |
     |      KeyType  pivot, temp;
     |      int  k, middle, p;
  5  |
     |      middle = ( i + j ) / 2 ;                      // choose the middle key as the pivot
     |
     |      pivot = A[middle]; A[middle] = A[i]; A[i] = pivot;      // place pivot in A[i]
     |      p = i;                                         // and let p point to the pivot
 10  |
     |      for (k = i+1; k <= j; k++) {                   // scan the rest of the keys in A[i+1:j]
     |           if (A[k].compareTo(pivot) < 0) {          // any key A[k] less than the pivot
     |                temp = A[++p]; A[p] = A[k]; A[k] = temp;      // moves to A[++p]
     |           }
 15  |      }
     |
     |      temp = A[i]; A[i] = A[p]; A[p] = temp;         // then place the pivot in A[p]
     |
     |      return p;                                      // return the position of the pivot as the result
 20  |
     | }
```

**Program 10.14** QuickSort's Partition Algorithm

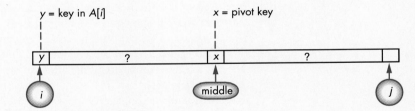

**Figure 10.15** At the Start of the Partitioning Process

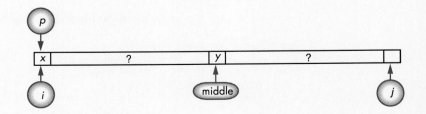

**Figure 10.16** After Exchanging A[i] and A[middle]

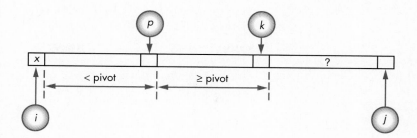

**Figure 10.17** Maintaining the Invariant ( (A[i+1:p] < pivot) and (A[p+1:k] ≥ pivot) )

At the beginning of the partitioning process, we compute the index of the middle key in the subarray A[i:j] using the assignment middle = (i + j) / 2; given on line 6 of Program 10.14. Figure 10.15 illustrates this situation. The key x in A[middle] will be used as the pivot key, and will soon become the value of the variable, pivot.

Figure 10.16 portrays the situation after lines 8:9 of Program 10.14 have been executed. At this moment, the pivot key x in A[middle] has been exchanged with the leftmost key y in A[i], so that A[i] now contains the pivot key and A[middle] now contains the key y that occupied A[i] before. Also, an integer pointer variable p is set to point to A[i].

The next phase of the partitioning process is performed by the for-statement on lines 11:15 of Program 10.14. The idea is to examine all keys A[k] in the subarray A[i+1:j] and to move keys with values less than that of the pivot into a subarray A[i+1:p] while maintaining a subarray A[p+1:k] of keys with values greater than or equal to that of the pivot key. Figure 10.17 shows the general situation inside the for-statement after the execution of the if-statement on lines 12:14.

The index variable k, used in the for-statement, is initialized to k = i+1, and increases in steps of one until reaching j as its final value. Each time k is increased by one, a new key A[k] is considered. If A[k] < pivot, the pointer p is increased by one to point to a key previously known to be greater than or equal to the pivot key, and A[k] and A[p] are exchanged. Thus, the truth of the relationship ((A[i+1:p] < pivot) and (A[p+1:k] ≥ pivot)) is maintained. On the other hand, if it is not the case that A[k] < pivot, then it must be true that A[k] ≥ pivot, and, because p is then left unchanged, the truth of the relationship ((A[i+1:p] < pivot) and (A[p+1:k] ≥ pivot)) is still maintained.

In either case, after k has been incremented and when control reaches the end of the body of the for-statement on lines 11:15, the relationship ((A[i+1:p] < pivot) and (A[p+1:k] ≥ pivot)) remains true. [Note: Here the notation A[r:s] < v means that every key in the subarray A[r:s] is less than v, and A[r:s] ≥ v means that every key in the subarray A[r:s] is greater than or equal to v. Also, a relationship in a for-statement that remains true on every repetition is called a *loop invariant*.]

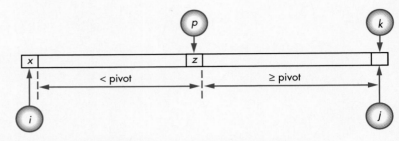

**Figure 10.18** After Completing the Placement of All Keys in $A[i+1:j]$

Eventually, the value of the index variable $k$ in the for-statement on lines 11:15 becomes equal to its final value, $j$, and the for-statement terminates after its last repetition. At this moment, not only is the loop invariant still true, but also we can substitute the final value $k = j$ for $k$ to obtain a description of what is true after the for-statement terminates. This reveals that the relationship $((A[i+1:p] < \text{pivot})$ and $(A[p+1:j] \geq \text{pivot}))$ must be true, as is shown in Fig. 10.18, which illustrates the situation immediately prior to executing lines 17:19 of Program 10.14.

Finally, on line 17, the keys in $A[i]$ and $A[p]$ are exchanged, which moves the pivot key, previously held in $A[i]$, into $A[p]$, and moves a key whose value is known to be less than the pivot into $A[i]$. At this moment, we know that $A[i:p-1] < \text{pivot}$, $A[p] = \text{pivot}$, and $A[p+1:j] \geq \text{pivot}$. Figure 10.19 depicts this situation. The partition function then terminates on line 19 by returning the position $p$ of the pivot key.

## Known Performance of QuickSort

**QuickSort** is known to run in time $O(n \log n)$ on the average. However, in the worst possible case, it is known that **QuickSort** could require time $O(n^2)$ to run to completion. (For a derivation of this fact, see pages 544–547 of the book, *Data Structures, Algorithms, and Software Principles in C*, by the author.)

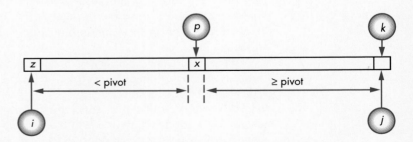

**Figure 10.19** Final Configuration Upon Completion of the Partition

## **10.4** REVIEW QUESTIONS

1. What does it mean to sort using a divide-and-conquer method?
2. How does the MergeSort method work?
3. Why is QuickSort an instance of a divide-and-conquer sorting method?
4. Explain what QuickSort's partition method does?
5. In QuickSort's partition method, what is the pivot element, and what role does it play in constructing the partition?

## **10.4** EXERCISES

1. Given an array $A$, assume that the two subarrays $A[m:middle]$ and $A[middle+1:n]$ have already been sorted, where $middle = (m + n) / 2$. Using an auxiliary array, $S$, into which you first copy the items of $A[m:n]$, write a method to merge the two sorted subarrays $S[m:middle]$ and $S[middle+1:n]$ into a single sorted subarray $A[m:n]$.
2. Assuming that the merging method you defined in your answer to Exercise 1 is called with the method call merge(A, m, middle, n), define a refinement of Program Strategy 10.11, having the method call MergeSort(A, m, n) that merge sorts the subarray $A[m:n]$.
3. Give an example of an array, $A$, that causes QuickSort to realize its worst case running time of $O(n^2)$.
4. One method of choosing the pivot key is to choose the median of the first, last, and middle keys in the array, $A$. (The median of three values is the middle value—for example, median(1,7,3) = 3, median(4,9,1) = 4, and median(1,3,3) = 3.) Under what conditions would it be advantageous to choose the pivot key using the "median of three" method?

## 10.5 **Methods That Insert Keys and Keep Them Sorted**

### LEARNING OBJECTIVES

1. To learn two sorting methods, InsertionSort and TreeSort, which insert unsorted keys into an initially empty container, C, and keep them sorted at all times inside C.
2. To learn about the efficiency of InsertionSort and TreeSort.

*the basic idea*

Some sorting methods are based on the idea of dividing the keys to be sorted into two collections: (a) a collection, $U$, of unsorted keys, yet to be sorted, and (b) a collection, $S$, of keys that have already been sorted and are to be maintained in sorted order. Initially, $U$ is the entire set of unsorted keys, and $S$ is empty. The idea is to remove keys, one-at-a-time, from $U$ and to insert them in $S$, while maintaining the sorted order of keys in $S$. When the last key is removed from $U$ and inserted into $S$, the process terminates.

The InsertionSort method uses subarrays of an array $A$ to hold the sets of keys, $S$ and $U$. The TreeSort method takes keys from $U$ and inserts them one-at-a-time into a binary search tree, $S$. When $U$ becomes empty, an InOrder traversal of tree $S$ is performed to enumerate the keys in ascending order.

## InsertionSort

The InsertionSort method uses the original array, $A$, to contain subarrays $S$ and $U$, which sit side-by-side in $A$. In particular, $S$ is a subarray at the left end of $A$, containing keys always arranged in ascending sorted order, and $U$ is a subarray at the right end of $A$, containing keys yet to be sorted.

how InsertionSort works
At each stage of the InsertionSort process, a new key to insert, $K$, is detached from the left end of $U$, and is inserted into $S$. The way this new key is inserted is illustrated in Fig. 10.20. First, the insertion key, $K$, is removed from the left end of

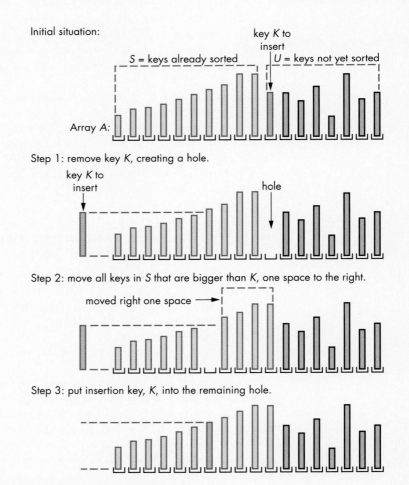

**Figure 10.20** Inserting a Key During InsertionSort

```
|        void InsertionSort(KeyType[ ] A) {
|
|                int            i,j;
|                KeyType        K;
5|               boolean        notFinished;
|
|
|                // for each i in the range 1:n − 1, let key K be the key, A[i].
|                // insert K into the subarray A[0:i − 1] in ascending order
10|
|                for (i = 1;  i < n;  i++)  {
|
|                        // move each key bigger than K in A[0:i − 1]
|                        // one space to the right
15|                          K = A[i];
|                          j = i;
|                          notFinished = (A[j − 1].compareTo(K) > 0);
|
|                        while (notFinished) {
20|                            A[j] = A[j − 1];          // move A[j −1] one space to the right
|                              j − −;
|                              if (j > 0) {
|                                    notFinished = (A[j − 1].compareTo(K) > 0);
|                              } else {
25|                                  notFinished = false;
|                              }
|                        }
|
|                        // move the key K into the hole opened up by moving
30|                       // the previous keys to the right
|                          A[j] = K;
|                }
|
|        }
```

**Program 10.21** The InsertionSort Algorithm

$U$, creating a hole. Second, all keys in $S$ bigger than $K$ are moved right one space. Third, and finally, $K$ is inserted into the remaining hole in $S$. This process is repeated until all keys in $U$ are inserted in $S$, at which point $S$ occupies the entire array $A$.

Program 10.21 gives the algorithm for InsertionSort.

### Known Performance of InsertionSort

It is known that InsertionSort runs in time $O(n^2)$. Roughly speaking, here is why this is so. For each key $K == A[i]$, where $i = 1, 2, \ldots, n − 1$, Program 10.21 inserts $K$ into the subarray $A[0:i − 1]$. The lengths of the respective subarrays, $S$, in which each $K$ gets inserted are therefore $1, 2, \ldots, (n − 1)$. On the average, half of the keys in a given subarray, $S$, will be bigger than $K$, and half will be smaller than $K$. The bigger keys will have been moved to the right to allow $K$ to be inserted, and during this process $K$ will have been compared to each of the bigger ones, plus one additional

InsertionSort runs in time $O(n^2)$

key in $S$ that is less than or equal to $K$, to stop the search for bigger ones to move rightward. This implies that, if there are $j$ keys in $S$, then the number of comparisons, $C(j)$, will be $j/2 + 1$.

Therefore to compute the average total number of comparisons used during the entire insertion sorting process to sort an array, $A[0:n-1]$, we need to evaluate the sum, $\sum_{(1 \le j \le (n-1))} C(j) = \sum_{(1 \le j \le (n-1))} (j/2 + 1) = (1/2) \sum_{(1 \le j \le (n-1))} j + (n-1) = (1/4)n^2 + (3/4)n - 1$. Consequently, InsertionSort runs in time $O(n^2)$.

## TreeSort

In TreeSort, you take the unsorted keys in the original array, $A[0:n-1]$, and insert them into an initially empty binary search tree, $S$, one at a time. After all keys in $A$ have been inserted into $S$, you perform an InOrder traversal of $S$, reading $S$'s keys off in ascending order during the traversal, and you move them back into $A$ in ascending order.

### Known Performance of TreeSort

TreeSort is known to run in time $O(n \log n)$. Roughly speaking, the reasoning showing why this is so is as follows. From Table 8.38, if $S$ is a binary search tree containing $i$ keys, it takes approximately $1.38 \lg i - 0.8$ comparisons to insert a new key, $K$, into $S$, since the number of comparisons required for insertion is identical to the number of comparisons required for an unsuccessful search.

Consequently, to compute the average total number of comparisons, $C(n)$, used to insert all keys originally in $A$ into $S$, when $S$ has sizes, 0, 1, 2, ..., $(n-1)$, we have to compute $\sum_{(1 \le i \le (n-1))} (1.38 \lg i - 0.8)$. This is the same as

$$1.38 \sum_{(1 \le i \le (n-1))} \lg i - 0.8(n-1).$$

An approximation for the sum of the logarithms $\lg n! = \sum \lg i$ can be obtained by taking logarithms of both sides of Stirling's Approximation and converting from natural logarithms to base-2 logarithms. Thus, from the following facts

$$\ln n! \approx n \ln n + O(n), \text{ and}$$
$$\lg n! = (\ln n! / \ln 2),$$

it can be shown that $C(n)$ is $O(n \log n)$.

> TreeSort runs in time
> $O(n \log n)$

## 10.5 REVIEW QUESTIONS

1. Give a rough description of how InsertionSort works.
2. How does TreeSort work?
3. Give the O-notations for the average running times of InsertionSort and TreeSort.

## 10.5 EXERCISES

1. Can you find and fix the bug in the following incorrect version of InsertionSort? [*Hint:* Will this program throw an ArrayIndexOutOfBoundsException under some circumstances?]

```
     |    void InsertionSort(KeyType[ ] A, int m, int n) {
     |
     |        int i; KeyType C;
     |
  5  |        if (n > m) {
     |
     |            // insertion sort the subarray A[m:n – 1].
     |            InsertionSort(A,m,n – 1);
     |
 10  |            // move each key bigger than A[n] in A[m:n – 1]
     |            // one space to the right
     |            C = A[n];
     |            i = n;
     |            while ( (A[i – 1].compareTo(C) > 0) && (i > m) ) {
 15  |                A[i] = A[i – 1];
     |                i – –;
     |            }
     |
     |            // move A[n] into the hole opened by moving previous keys
 20  |            A[i] = C;
     |
     |        }
     |
     |    }
```

2. Characterize how many keys get moved on the average in InsertionSort. Is this number greater than or less than the corresponding number of times that keys are moved on the average in SelectionSort?

## 10.6 *O(n) Methods—Address Calculation Sorting*

### LEARNING OBJECTIVES

1. To learn that despite the *n* log *n* barrier on comparison-based sorting methods, there exist still faster O(*n*) sorting methods, not based on the use of comparisons.
2. To explore two O(*n*) methods, ProxmapSort and RadixSort.

the basic idea

In sorting by address calculation, you define a mapping on the keys to be sorted, which sends them into a location in the output array that is expected to be close to what the final sorted position will be. Some local rearrangement in the vicinity of the final location of each key may be necessary to move keys into their actual final locations.

Since you are using a mapping on keys, instead of comparisons of keys with one another, to send keys into locations close to their final sorted locations, the techniques are not "comparison-based." Hence, the $n \log n$ barrier for comparison-based methods may not apply.

## ProxmapSort

In proxmap sorting, you compute a "proximity map," or *proxmap* for short, which indicates, for each key, $K$, the beginning of a subarray of the array $A$ in which $K$ will reside in final sorted order. You then enumerate the keys in $A$ and insertion sort them into their final subarrays. We proceed by example in order to help reveal the main ideas.

Let's suppose we have an array $A$ of 13 keys to sort, as shown in Fig. 10.22. You can see that the keys used in $A$ are decimal numbers ranging in value from a low of 0.4 to a high of 11.5. When we map a key, $K$, to an array index, $i$, we will use the simple mapping of rounding $K$ down to the next lower integer by taking the floor of $K$. That is, **MapKey**$(K) == \lfloor K \rfloor$. For example, **MapKey**$(3.7) == 3$, **MapKey**$(1.2) == 1$, and **MapKey**$(0.4) == 0$. (Although designed to be easy to use and easy to follow for the purposes of our simple example, this mapping is not a good one, in general. We will discuss how to design effective **MapKey** functions for actual examples later on in this section.)

If we were to use $i ==$ **MapKey**$(K)$ to send $K$ into a location, $A[i]$, in array $A$ where we kept a linked list of keys, sorted in ascending order, we could scan through the original unsorted array, $A$, and send its keys into a collection of sorted linked lists, as shown in Fig. 10.23.

For example, starting with the first key, $A[0] == 6.7$, of Fig. 10.22, we map the key, 6.7, into position 6, (using **MapKey**$(6.7) == 6$), and we insert 6.7 on an empty list in position 6. Sometime later, we encounter key, $A[11] == 6.1$, and map it also into position 6, (using **MapKey**$(6.1) == 6$). Here, we insert it into the linked list that already contains the key 6.7. Since each linked list is to be kept in sorted order, we insert 6.1 before 6.7 on this linked list in position 6. You can see that the remaining linked lists in Fig. 10.23 were formed by inserting each key, $A[i]$, for $i$ in 0:12, into the linked list in position, **MapKey**$(A[i])$, and keeping the keys in each linked list in ascending order. If we now make a pass in left-to-right order along the diagram of Fig. 10.23 and enumerate the keys in each linked list in the order given by each list, we would enumerate the keys of the original array $A$ in ascending sorted order.

Now, **ProxmapSort** does not use linked lists such as those in Fig. 10.23. Instead, it reserves, in advance, subarrays of the array $A$ for the keys in each of the linked lists, and it insertion-sorts these keys into the reserved subarrays. For example, the keys in the linked list containing (1.1, 1.2, 1.8) of Fig. 10.23 would eventually be inserted

*inserting keys into sorted linked lists*

*insertion locations*

| $i =$ | 0 | 1 | 2 | 3 | 4 | 5 | 6 | 7 | 8 | 9 | 10 | 11 | 12 |
|-------|---|---|---|---|---|---|---|---|---|---|----|----|----|
| $A[i] =$ [6.7, | 5.9, | 8.4, | 1.2, | 7.3, | 3.7, | 11.5, | 1.1, | 4.8, | 0.4, | 10.5, | 6.1, | 1.8] |

**Figure 10.22** Initial Unsorted Array, $A$, for Use in ProxmapSort

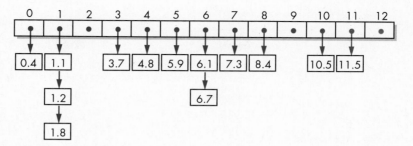

**Figure 10.23** Sorted Linked Lists of Keys

in the subarray $A[1:3]$ of $A$, and this subarray of $A$ is reserved for each of the keys, 1.1, 1.2, and 1.8, using location $A[1]$ as the future *insertion location* for each key in (1.1, 1.2, 1.8). Similarly, the list of keys, (6.1, 6.7), will map into the future reserved subarray, $A[7:8]$, using $A[7]$ as the future insertion location for keys 6.1 and 6.7.

The actual *proxmap* (which is short for "proximity map") is a mapping that can be used to send each key $K$ into the beginning location of the reserved subarray of $A$ where it will be inserted in ascending order. When all keys have been mapped into their respective reserved subarrays and have been inserted in ascending order, the array $A$ contains the final sorted arrangement of the original keys. The **proxmap** is computed in advance of moving any keys and is based on *hit counts* derived from mapping keys, $K$, in $A$, using **MapKey**$(K)$, during a preliminary pass through $A$.

Let's now proceed, step-by-step, with our example to see how we compute (a) *hit counts*, (b) the *proxmap*, and (c) the future *insertion locations* for each key, $K$, in the original array, $A$. After computing the future insertion locations, we then begin to move keys to their reserved, final subarrays, where we insertion-sort them to complete the final phase of the **ProxmapSort** process. In short, in **ProxmapSort**, we first compute in advance where the reserved subarrays containing each final sorted key will lie. Then we move each key into its final reserved subarray where it is inserted in ascending order (using some local insertion sorting inside the reserved subarray).

hit counts      First, we compute the hit counts. Suppose $H$ is an array of 13 positions, $H[0:12]$, each of which initially contains zero ($H[i] == 0$ for $i$ in 0:12). If we execute the for-statement

```
// compute hit counts, H[i], for each position, i, in A
    for (i = 0; i < 13; i++) {
        j = MapKey(A[i]);
        H[j] ++;
    }
```

then each location $H[i]$ will contain the number of keys in $A$ that map into location $i$. Figure 10.24 (on page 396) shows the hit counts corresponding to the keys in Fig. 10.22. You can see that the hit count in each location, $H[i]$, is identical to the number of keys on the linked list in position $i$ of the diagram in Fig. 10.23.

| $i =$ | 0 | 1 | 2 | 3 | 4 | 5 | 6 | 7 | 8 | 9 | 10 | 11 | 12 |
|---|---|---|---|---|---|---|---|---|---|---|---|---|---|
| $A[i] =$ [6.7, | 5.9, | 8.4, | 1.2, | 7.3, | 3.7, | 11.5, | 1.1, | 4.8, | 0.4, | 10.5, | 6.1, | 1.8] |
| $H[i] =$ [ 1 | 3 | 0 | 1 | 1 | 1 | 2 | 1 | 1 | 0 | 1 | 1 | 0 ] |

**Figure 10.24** Hit Counts for the Array A

**computing the proxmap**

From the hit counts, $H[i]$, we compute a proxmap, $P[i]$, where each entry $P[i]$ gives the location of the beginning of the future reserved subarray of A that will contain keys, $K$, mapping to location, $i$, under the mapping MapKey($K$) == $i$. The proxmap, $P[i]$, is shown in Fig. 10.25.

For instance, all keys, such as (6.7, 6.1), which map to $P[6]$ find that $P[6]$ == 7, meaning that 7 is the location of the beginning of the reserved subarray where (6.7, 6.1) will both be inserted in the future. A for-statement that computes the proxmap, $P[i]$, starting with the hit counts, $H[i]$, and using a running total is as follows:

```
// convert hit counts to a proxmap
    runningTotal = 0;                          // initialize a running total to 0
    for (i = 0; i < 13; i++)  {
        if (H[i] > 0) {
            P[i] = runningTotal;
            runningTotal += H[i];
        }
    }
```

You can see how executing this for-statement on the hit counts, $H[i]$, in Fig. 10.25 produces the values of the proxmap, $P[i]$, (assuming the values of $P[i]$ were initially 0).

The final step is to compute future insertion locations, $L[i]$, for the key, $K$, in each position, $A[i]$, of the original unsorted array, A. A for-statement that does this is

```
// compute insertion locations, L[i], for each key, K == A[i], in array A
    for (i = 0; i < 13; i++)  {
        L[i] = P[ MapKey(A[i]) ];
    }
```

Figure 10.26 gives the future insertion locations, $L[i]$, that were computed using this process. (In the ProxmapSort algorithm given later, we will actually save the locations MapKey($A[i]$) when they are first computed, so we do not have to compute them twice in case the MapKey function turns out to be expensive to compute. Thus this for-statement is a bit oversimplified and is intended only to help convey the general flavor of what needs to be accomplished.)

| $i =$ | 0 | 1 | 2 | 3 | 4 | 5 | 6 | 7 | 8 | 9 | 10 | 11 | 12 |
|---|---|---|---|---|---|---|---|---|---|---|---|---|---|
| $A[i] =$ [6.7, | 5.9, | 8.4, | 1.2, | 7.3, | 3.7, | 11.5, | 1.1, | 4.8, | 0.4, | 10.5, | 6.1, | 1.8] |
| $H[i] =$ [ 1 | 3 | 0 | 1 | 1 | 1 | 2 | 1 | 1 | 0 | 1 | 1 | 0 ] |
| $P[i] =$ [ 0 | 1 | 0 | 4 | 5 | 6 | 7 | 9 | 10 | 0 | 11 | 12 | 0 ] |

**Figure 10.25** Proxmap for Array A

| $i =$ | 0 | 1 | 2 | 3 | 4 | 5 | 6 | 7 | 8 | 9 | 10 | 11 | 12 |
|---|---|---|---|---|---|---|---|---|---|---|---|---|---|
| $A[i] =$ [ | 6.7, | 5.9, | 8.4, | 1.2, | 7.3, | 3.7, | 11.5, | 1.1, | 4.8, | 0.4, | 10.5, | 6.1, | 1.8] |
| $P[i] =$ [ | 0 | 1 | 0 | 4 | 5 | 6 | 7 | 9 | 10 | 0 | 11 | 12 | 0 ] |
| $L[i] =$ [ | 7 | 6 | 10 | 1 | 9 | 4 | 12 | 1 | 5 | 0 | 11 | 7 | 1 ] |

**Figure 10.26** Future Insertion Locations, $L[i]$, for each Key, $A[i]$

For example, the keys 6.7 and 6.1 in positions $A[0]$ and $A[11]$ each have future insertion locations $L[0] == 7$ and $L[11] == 7$, since they will both be moved into the reserved subarray $A[7:8]$ for insertion into final placement in sorted order. Similarly, the
keys 1.2, 1.1, and 1.8, in positions $A[3]$, $A[7]$, and $A[12]$, each have future insertion
locations of 1 (i.e., $L[3] == L[7] == L[12] == 1$), since they will each be mapped into
the beginning location $A[1]$ of the reserved subarray, $A[1:3]$, for future insertion into
final sorted order.

The final phase of ProxmapSort consists in moving each key, $A[i]$, in the original
unsorted array $A$ into the location $L[i]$ at the beginning of its reserved future subarray,
and in inserting it in ascending order into the sequence of keys already occupying its
reserved subarray. If we had two copies of $A$, say $A_1$ and $A_2$, where $A_1$ was the original
unsorted array, and $A_2$ was an initially empty copy of $A$ designed to accumulate the
keys of $A$ in final sorted order as they were being inserted, then we could map each
key, $A_1[i]$, into its insertion location, $L[i]$, in $A_2$, and insert it in ascending order into
the sequence of keys beginning at $L[i]$ in $A_2$. For example, Fig. 10.27 shows $A_1$ and $A_2$
before the process of moving keys begins. Figure 10.28 shows $A_1$ and $A_2$ after the first
7 keys have been moved, and Fig. 10.29 shows $A_1$ and $A_2$ after the first 11 keys have
been moved.

To obtain Fig. 10.28, starting with the situation shown in Fig. 10.27, we move
key $A_1[0] == 6.7$ into location $L[0] == 7$ in $A_2$, we move 5.9 into location 6 of $A_2$,
and so forth, until moving key $A_1[6] == 11.5$ into location 12 of $A_2$.

The next key to be moved is key $A_1[7] == 1.1$, which is supposed to go into location $L[7] == 1$ of array $A_2$. This is an interesting situation, since location $A_2[1]$ already contains the key 1.2, from a previous insertion. What happens is that the key
1.1 is insertion-sorted into the reserved subarray, $A_2[1:3]$ beginning at location $A_2[1]$.
Recall that the subarray $A_2[1:3]$ has been reserved by the proxmap computation to
handle the keys, 1.2, 1.1, and 1.8. At this particular moment, the second of the three
final keys that will occupy $A_2[1:3]$ is being inserted. When 1.1 is inserted into the sequence of keys in ascending order beginning at $A_2[1]$, the situation that results is

*final phase: moving the keys*

*inserting keys into a common reserved subarray*

| $i =$ | 0 | 1 | 2 | 3 | 4 | 5 | 6 | 7 | 8 | 9 | 10 | 11 | 12 |
|---|---|---|---|---|---|---|---|---|---|---|---|---|---|
| $A_1[i] =$ [ | 6.7, | 5.9, | 8.4, | 1.2, | 7.3, | 3.7, | 11.5, | 1.1, | 4.8, | 0.4, | 10.5, | 6.1, | 1.8 ] |
| $L[i] =$ [ | 7 | 6 | 10 | 1 | 9 | 4 | 12 | 1 | 5 | 0 | 11 | 7 | 1 ] |
| $A_2[i] =$ [ | –.–, | –.–, | –.–, | –.–, | –.–, | –.–, | –.–, | –.–, | –.–, | –.–, | –.–, | –.–, | –.– ] |

**Figure 10.27** Before Moving any Keys into Their Reserved Subarrays

$i$ = 0    1    2    3    4    5    6    7    8    9   10   11   12

| $i$ = | 0 | 1 | 2 | 3 | 4 | 5 | 6 | 7 | 8 | 9 | 10 | 11 | 12 |
|---|---|---|---|---|---|---|---|---|---|---|---|---|---|
| $A_1[i]$ = [ | 6.7, | 5.9, | 8.4, | 1.2, | 7.3, | 3.7, | 11.5, | 1.1, | 4.8, | 0.4, | 10.5, | 6.1, | 1.8 ] |
| $L[i]$ = [ | 7 | 6 | 10 | 1 | 9 | 4 | 12 | 1 | 5 | 0 | 11 | 7 | 1 ] |
| $A_2[i]$ = [ | –.–, | 1.2, | –.–, | –.–, | 3.7, | –.–, | 5.9, | 6.7, | –.–, | 7.3, | 8.4, | –.–, | 11.5] |

**Figure 10.28** After Moving 7 Keys into Their Reserved Subarrays

| $i$ = | 0 | 1 | 2 | 3 | 4 | 5 | 6 | 7 | 8 | 9 | 10 | 11 | 12 |
|---|---|---|---|---|---|---|---|---|---|---|---|---|---|
| $A_1[i]$ = [ | 6.7, | 5.9, | 8.4, | 1.2, | 7.3, | 3.7, | 11.5, | 1.1, | 4.8, | 0.4, | 10.5, | 6.1, | 1.8 ] |
| $L[i]$ = [ | 7 | 6 | 10 | 1 | 9 | 4 | 12 | 1 | 5 | 0 | 11 | 7 | 1 ] |
| $A_2[i]$ = [ | 0.4, | 1.1, | 1.2, | –.–, | 3.7, | 4.8, | 5.9, | 6.7, | –.–, | 7.3, | 8.4, | 10.5, | 11.5] |

**Figure 10.29** After Moving 11 Keys into Their Reserved Subarrays

shown in subarray $A_2[1:2]$ of Fig. 10.29. Note that the key 1.2 has been moved one space to the right to accommodate the newly inserted key 1.1.

When the final two keys $A_1[11]$ == 6.1, and $A_1[12]$ == 1.8 are inserted into $A_2$, at insertion locations 7 and 1 respectively, the insertion-sorting process causes 6.1 to be inserted into location $A_2[7]$ after displacing 6.7 one space to the right into $A_2[8]$ and causes 1.8 to be inserted into location $A_2[3]$. The array $A_2$ is now in final sorted order, as shown in Fig. 10.30.

Now, actually, the version of **ProxmapSort** given in Program 10.32 (on pages 401–402) does not use two copies of the array A, as illustrated in Figs. 10.27 through 10.30. Instead, **ProxmapSort** rearranges the keys of A in place. This is called an *in situ* rearrangement (from the Latin words *in situ*, which mean "in place").

Some slight trickery is needed to accomplish this, which involves marking each entry in A with a *status code* indicating whether it is *empty*, *not-yet-moved*, or already *moved*, and then playing a game resembling "musical chairs," in which when a key, $K_1$, is inserted into its future reserved subarray and displaces another key, $K_2$, which has not yet been moved, then $K_2$ is the very next key to be moved. If, however, $K_1$ lands in an empty slot that has been vacated by removing a key previously moved, $K_1$ is placed in the empty slot, and a left-to-right scan is undertaken to find some new key that has not yet been moved.

Figure 10.31 shows the placement of successive keys in A using this *in situ* rearrangement game of "musical chairs."

| $i$ = | 0 | 1 | 2 | 3 | 4 | 5 | 6 | 7 | 8 | 9 | 10 | 11 | 12 |
|---|---|---|---|---|---|---|---|---|---|---|---|---|---|
| $A_1[i]$ = [ | 6.7, | 5.9, | 8.4, | 1.2, | 7.3, | 3.7, | 11.5, | 1.1, | 4.8, | 0.4, | 10.5, | 6.1, | 1.8 ] |
| $L[i]$ = [ | 7 | 6 | 10 | 1 | 9 | 4 | 12 | 1 | 5 | 0 | 11 | 7 | 1 ] |
| $A_2[i]$ = [ | 0.4, | 1.1, | 1.2, | 1.8, | 3.7, | 4.8, | 5.9, | 6.1, | 6.7, | 7.3, | 8.4, | 10.5, | 11.5] |

**Figure 10.30** After Moving All Keys into Their Reserved Subarrays

Original Unsorted Array A

```
[ 6.7 , 5.9 , 8.4 , 1.2 , 7.3 , 3.7 , 11.5, 1.1 , 4.8 , 0.4 , 10.5, 6.1 , 1.8 ]
   0     1     2     3     4     5     6     7     8     9    10    11    12
```

Hit Counts

```
   1     3     0     1     1     1     2     1     1     0     1     1     0
```

Proxmap

```
   0     1     0     4     5     6     7     9    10     0    11    12     0
```

Insertion Locations

```
   7     6    10     1     9     4    12     1     5     0    11     7     1
```

Successive Stages of Insertion at One Key per Stage

```
   0     1     2     3     4     5     6     7     8     9    10    11    12
[ --- , --- , --- , --- , --- , --- , --- , --- , --- , --- , --- , --- , --- ]
[ --- , --- , --- , --- , --- , --- , --- , 6.7 , --- , --- , --- , --- , --- ]
[ --- , 1.1 , --- , --- , --- , --- , --- , 6.7 , --- , --- , --- , --- , --- ]
[ --- , 1.1 , --- , --- , --- , --- , 5.9 , 6.7 , --- , --- , --- , --- , --- ]
[ --- , 1.1 , --- , --- , --- , --- , 5.9 , 6.7 , --- , --- , --- , --- , 11.5]
[ --- , 1.1 , 1.8 , --- , --- , --- , 5.9 , 6.7 , --- , --- , --- , --- , 11.5]
[ --- , 1.1 , 1.8 , --- , --- , --- , 5.9 , 6.7 , --- , --- , 8.4 , --- , 11.5]
[ --- , 1.1 , 1.8 , --- , --- , --- , 5.9 , 6.7 , --- , --- , 8.4 , 10.5, 11.5]
[ --- , 1.1 , 1.8 , --- , --- , --- , 5.9 , 6.1 , 6.7 , --- , 8.4 , 10.5, 11.5]
[ --- , 1.1 , 1.8 , --- , --- , 4.8 , 5.9 , 6.1 , 6.7 , --- , 8.4 , 10.5, 11.5]
[ --- , 1.1 , 1.8 , --- , 3.7 , 4.8 , 5.9 , 6.1 , 6.7 , --- , 8.4 , 10.5, 11.5]
[ --- , 1.1 , 1.8 , --- , 3.7 , 4.8 , 5.9 , 6.1 , 6.7 , 7.3 , 8.4 , 10.5, 11.5]
[ 0.4 , 1.1 , 1.8 , --- , 3.7 , 4.8 , 5.9 , 6.1 , 6.7 , 7.3 , 8.4 , 10.5, 11.5]
[ 0.4 , 1.1 , 1.2 , --- , 3.7 , 4.8 , 5.9 , 6.1 , 6.7 , 7.3 , 8.4 , 10.5, 11.5]
[ 0.4 , 1.1 , 1.2 , 1.8 , 3.7 , 4.8 , 5.9 , 6.1 , 6.7 , 7.3 , 8.4 , 10.5, 11.5]
```

Final Sorted Array A

```
   0     1     2     3     4     5     6     7     8     9    10    11    12
[ 0.4 , 1.1 , 1.2 , 1.8 , 3.7 , 4.8 , 5.9 , 6.1 , 6.7 , 7.3 , 8.4 , 10.5, 11.5]
```

**Figure 10.31** *In Situ* Rearrangement of Keys in *A*

inserting keys by the
musical chairs process

Note, for example, what happens on the first few rearrangements, in Fig. 10.31. Assume that the proxmap and the future insertion locations have been computed, and that the algorithm has reached the stage where it is ready to move keys in A by the musical chairs rearrangement process. The first key to be considered is the not-yet-moved key, A[0] == 6.7. This is moved into location 7 (using the future insertion location L[0] == 7). However, when 6.7 is placed into location A[7], it displaces the not-yet-moved key, 1.1. Thus the displaced key 1.1 is the next key to be moved (as if it had been bumped out of its seat in a musical chairs game). When 1.1 is inserted into its future location, A[1], it bumps the key 5.9, which was previously located in A[1]. So key 5.9 is the next key to be moved, and so on.

The details of this process, which are somewhat subtle, are given in Program 10.32. Before looking at this program, however, we have to redesign the items in array A, to hold new information in addition to the keys to be sorted, such as the status flags, the future insertion locations, and the values of the proxmap. We do this by defining a **ProxmapKeySlot** to replace the simple **KeyType** used in the earlier comparison-based sorting methods. Then, a **ProxmapKeySlot** array is an array of *n slots*, where each slot is a **ProxmapKeySlot** object having a **status** field, two **proxmap** and **insertionLoc** fields containing integers, and a **key** field, containing the key to be sorted. The following definitions specify these new objects for use in **ProxmapSort**:

```
// symbolic constant and class definitions used in ProxmapSort

final int n = anyArbitrarySize;

final static int EMPTY = 0;
final static int NOT_YET_MOVED = 1;
final static int MOVED = 2;

class ProxmapKeySlot {
        int             status;
        int             proxmap;
        int             insertionLoc;
        KeyType         key;
}
```

saving time and storage

In Program 10.32, we have economized on the use of time and storage a bit by (a) using the **proxmap** field of each slot to store the *hit counts* before they are converted to a proxmap, instead of defining and using a separate hit count field in each slot, and (b) saving the values of **MapKey(A[i].key)** in the **insertionLoc** fields of each slot, so they need not be recomputed (at possibly considerable expense) during the later computation of the insertion locations. This allows us to compute **MapKey(A[i].key)** only once for each key during the execution of the program.

## Designing the MapKey Function

The function **MapKey**($K$) should be designed to map keys, $K$, chosen from the full range of possible keys, onto the entire set of array indexes for array A. Let's look at two cases to see how **MapKey**($K$) can be designed properly.

```
void ProxmapSort(ProxmapKeySlot[ ] A)  {

    int          i, j, runningTotal, tempInt;
    KeyType      keyToInsert, tempKey;
    boolean      notInserted;

    // initialize status and proxmap
        for (i = 0; i < n; i++)  {
            A[i].proxmap = 0;                    // initialize all proxmap entries to zero
            A[i].status = NOT_YET_MOVED;         // initialize status of each slot
        }

    // count hits when keys are mapped into MapKey locations
        for (i = 0; i < n; i++)  {
            j = MapKey(A[i].key);
            A[i].insertionLoc = j;               // save value of MapKey for later use
            A[j].proxmap++;                      // store hit counts in proxmap field
        }

    // convert hit counts to a proxmap
        runningTotal = 0;
        for (i = 0; i < n; i++)  {
            if (A[i].proxmap > 0) {              // any nonzero hit count is
                tempInt = A[i].proxmap;          // converted to a proxmap entry
                A[i].proxmap = runningTotal;     // by substituting the
                runningTotal += tempInt;         // running total
            }
        }

    // compute insertion locations
        for (i = 0; i < n; i++)  {
            A[i].insertionLoc = A[A[i].insertionLoc].proxmap;
        }

    // now, A[i].insertionLoc gives the insertion location for A[i].key
    // and A[i].status is NOT_YET_MOVED for all i in 0:n − 1

    // rearrange A[i] in situ in A into ascending sorted order
        for (i = 0; i < n; i++)  {

            // find next key in ascending order of i that is NOT_YET_MOVED
                if (A[i].status == NOT_YET_MOVED) {
                    j = A[i].insertionLoc;
                    keyToInsert = A[i].key;              // pick up A[i]'s key as keyToInsert
                    A[i].status = EMPTY;                 // and plan to insert it in A[j], where j is
                    notInserted = true;                 // its insertion location
```

**Program 10.32** ProxmapSort *(continued)*

Program 10.32 **ProxmapSort** (*continued*)

```
                              while (notInserted) {
                                  if (A[j].status == NOT_YET_MOVED)  {
50
                                      tempKey = A[j].key;                    // swap keyToInsert
                                      A[j].key = keyToInsert;                // with A[j]'s key.
                                      keyToInsert = tempKey;      // mark A[j] as moved, and
                                      A[j].status = MOVED;   // plan to insert the keyToInsert
55                                    j = A[j].insertionLoc;            // in its insertion location, j

                                  } else if (A[j].status == MOVED) {        // insertion sort the
                                                                   // keyToInsert in the subarray
                                      if (keyToInsert.compareTo(A[j].key) < 0) {      // of A
60                                                                // beginning at j. If
                                          tempKey = A[j].key;        // keyToInsert < A[j].key
                                          A[j].key = keyToInsert;        // swap keyToInsert
                                          keyToInsert = tempKey;         // with A[j]'s key
                                      }
65
                                      j ++;                        // and move to next key at A[j+1]

                                  } else {                              // A[j].status == EMPTY
                                      A[j].key = keyToInsert;            // insert keyToInsert
70                                    A[j].status = MOVED;               // in the empty entry
                                      notInserted = false;
                                  }
                              }
                          }
75              }
          }
```

First, suppose the keys, $K$, are floating point numbers in the range $0 \le K < 1$, and suppose that the index range of array $A[0:n-1]$ is $0 \le i < n$. Then, a good definition for **MapKey**($K$) in Java is

**MapKey = (int)Math.floor(n * K);**                    // where Math.floor(x) == $\lfloor x \rfloor$

This mapping will send the key $K == 0.0$ onto 0, and will send the key $K == 0.99999$ onto $n - 1$ (provided $n \le 100{,}000$). A key value of 0.50 will tend to map close to 50 percent of the way between 0 and $n - 1$, and a key value of 0.75 will tend to map close to 75 percent of the way between 0 and $n - 1$.

Now let's suppose that our keys are three-letter airport codes, such as ACK (for Nantucket, Massachusetts), MEX (for Mexico City, Mexico), or ZRH (for Zürich, Switzerland). We could consider the three-letter airport codes to be base-26 numbers, chosen from a range of keys having a maximum value of $ZZZ_{26} == 17575$ and a minimum value of $AAA_{26} == 0$. The value of the key, $K$, as a base-26 number is given by Program 10.33, where it is assumed that each airport code key is just a three-character Java **String** object.

```
    |    int value(char L) {
    |
    |        return (int)(L) − (int)('A');        // returns value of the letter 'L', base 26
    |    }
  5 |
    |    int base26Value(String K) {
    |
    |        return value(K.charAt(0))*26*26 +  value(K.charAt(1))*26
    |               + value(K.charAt(2));
    |    }
```

**Program 10.33** Base-26 Value of an Airport Code Key $K$

Using Program 10.33, we get the following values:

$$
\begin{aligned}
\text{base26Value("AAA")} &= 0 \\
\text{base26Value("ZZZ")} &= 17575 \\
\text{base26Value("ACK")} &= 62 \\
\text{base26Value("MEX")} &= 8239 \\
\text{base26Value("ZRH")} &= 17349
\end{aligned}
$$

We can map an airport code, $K$, into a real number, $r(K)$, in the range $0 \le r(K) < 1$, by dividing $K$'s base-26 value by one plus the base-26 value of "ZZZ" according to the formula

$$r(K) = \text{(double)}\,\text{base26Value}(K)\, /\, \text{(double)}(1 + \text{base26Value("ZZZ")}).$$

In other words, we could convert the base-26 values of ACK, MEX, and ZRH into floating point numbers in the range $0 \le r(K) < 1$ by dividing their base-26 values by 17576 (which equals $26^3$). This yields $r(\text{ACK}) == 0.00353$, $r(\text{MEX}) == 0.46876$, and $r(\text{ZRH}) == 0.98708$.

Suppose, now, that the array, A[0:14], had $n == 15$ positions in it, and that we wanted to map ACK, MEX, and ZRH into locations in A, using a suitable **MapKey** function. We could then use the assignment statement

$$\text{MapKey} = \text{(int) Math.floor(n * r(K))};\qquad\text{// where Math.floor(x)} == \lfloor x \rfloor$$

to accomplish this. In this case, **MapKey**(ACK) $== 0$, **MapKey**(MEX) $== 7$, and **MapKey**(ZRH) $== 14$. This seems acceptable, since (a) we wanted ACK to map into a location near the beginning of A (because ACK is near the beginning of its key space in key order), (b) we wanted MEX to map somewhere near the middle of A (since MEX is near the middle of its key space in key order), and (c) we wanted ZRH to map to a location near the end of A (since ZRH is near the end of its key space in key order).

However, in the interest of efficiency, a better idea for computing **MapKey**($K$), for an airport code key, $K$, is to compute a *scale factor*, $s$, consisting of the size, $n$, of the index range of array A, divided by $26^3$, the number of possible keys in the key space. That is, $s == n/26^3$. After the scale factor, $s$, is precomputed, **MapKey**($K$) can be computed simply by using the assignment statement

*using a single scale factor*

$$\text{MapKey} = \text{(int)Math.floor( s * base26Value}(K)\text{)};\qquad\text{// where s is a scale factor}$$

In the case of the array $A[0:14]$ with $n == 15$ positions and three-letter airport codes, $K$, taken as base-26 numbers, the scale factor is $s = 0.000853437$.

It is important that **MapKey**$(K)$ be computed efficiently (in relation to the cost of comparing keys) to make **ProxmapSort** competitive in running time with the best comparison-based sorting methods.

## Known Performance of ProxmapSort

In the worst case, **ProxmapSort** can take time $O(n^2)$. This occurs, for example, when all keys in $A$ have an equal value, forcing **MapKey** to map them into the same location in $A$. In this case, the future subarray reserved for inserting all of these equal-valued keys becomes the entire array, and all keys are insertion-sorted into $A$, which takes time $O(n^2)$.

a nonrigorous argument

Even though a rigorous mathematical argument for why **ProxmapSort** runs on the average in time $O(n)$ is beyond the scope of this book, a rough, partial, and intuitive argument as to why this is so can be offered.

Suppose that the array $A$ contains keys, $K$, drawn randomly and uniformly from the space of all possible keys, and suppose that **MapKey**$(K)$ is defined to map keys onto the full range, $0:n - 1$, of index locations of array, $A$. If we are extremely lucky, all unsorted keys in the original unsorted array $A$ will map onto separate locations in the final sorted array, $A$. In this case, the insertion locations for rearrangement of the unsorted keys in $A$ will all be separate, and four linear passes through $A$ (to compute hit counts, to compute the proxmap, to compute insertion locations, and finally, to relocate keys) will suffice to sort $A$.

However, we are rarely so lucky as to have hit counts that are all 1. Instead, some hit counts will be zero, and others will be greater than 1. In the case of hit counts greater than one, such as $c > 1$, the proxmap will reserve a subarray of $c$ locations in $A$ where $c$ keys will eventually be insertion-sorted, at a cost of $O(c^2)$.

In the case of an array $A$ with $n$ keys chosen randomly and uniformly, we can choose a value of $c$, such that it almost never occurs that some subset of $c$ keys will collide at the same **MapKey** location to create a hit count of $c$. For example, if we have $n = 1000$ keys in $A$, then it is of very small probability that a hit count will ever be greater than $c = 50$. So suppose that we divide the $n = 1000$ locations into $n/c = 20$ separate reserved subarrays, and that we insertion-sort each of the $n/c = 20$ subarrays. This would cost $(n/c)\, O(c^2)$, since each such reserved subarray takes time $O(c^2)$ to sort, using insertion sorting. Supposing that the $O(c^2)$ function actually required is of the form: $O(c^2) = a\, c^2 + b\, c + f$, then $(n/c)\, O(c^2) = (n/c)\, (a\, c^2 + b\, c + f) = (n\, a\, c + n\, b + n\, f\, /\, c)$, which is $O(n)$.

In the average case, where the proxmap for the array $A$ normally divides $A$ up into reserved subarrays smaller than subarrays of size $c$, each such smaller reserved subarray, of size $d < c$, will be insertion-sorted in time $a\, d^2 + b\, d + f$, which will be less than $a\, c^2 + b\, c + f$. Moreover, the total time to sort an array $A$ composed of smaller reserved subarrays will always be less than the time to sort an array $A$ composed of larger reserved subarrays.

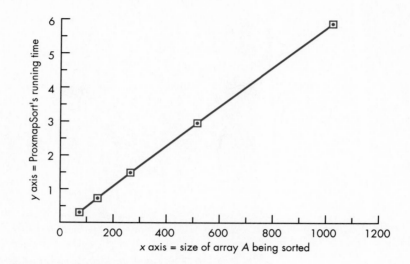

**Figure 10.34** Graph of ProxmapSort's Running Times

Since, in the improbable case of $n/c$ subarrays of size $c$, we can sort A in total time $O(n)$, it follows that we can sort any collection of smaller subarrays also in time at most $O(n)$. In conclusion, in the average case, **Proxmap** must run in time $O(n)$—because only an unusual nonaverage case could be worse than the case of sorting $n/c$ subarrays of size $c$, in order to exceed the $O(n)$ barrier established for sorting $n/c$ subarrays of size $c$.

If you graph the actual measured sorting times for **ProxmapSort**, given later in Table 10.47 in Section 10.8, and reproduced here,

| n = | 64 | 128 | 256 | 512 | 1024 |
|---|---|---|---|---|---|
| ProxmapSort | 0.38 | 0.75 | 1.51 | 3.00 | 5.99 |

you will find that they actually lie very close to the straight line shown in Fig. 10.34. This suggests that the $O(n)$ characterization of **ProxmapSort**'s sorting time can indeed be verified experimentally. For example, graphing these actual measured times results in the graph shown in Fig. 10.34.

## RadixSort

Radix sorting is a process that was used on electromechanical, punched-card sorting equipment of an earlier generation. To get a rough idea of how it works, let's consider an example. Suppose we have a set of 3-digit numerical keys, where each 3-digit key is punched on a separate card in a deck of cards. The deck of cards to be sorted is placed in a hopper on the card-sorter machine, and cards to be sorted are fed, one at a time, from the bottom of the deck. A crank on the sorting machine can

how the card sorter works

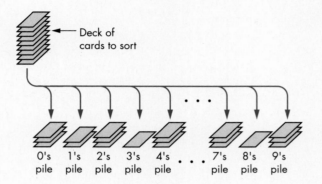

**Figure 10.35** Card Sorter

be set to sort either the first digit, the middle digit, or the last digit, of the 3-digit key. Suppose C is the card on the bottom of the deck that is currently being read by the sorting machine. If the digit currently selected in C is a 0, then C is fed mechanically to a bin where it drops down on top of the pile of cards containing 0's digits. This is called the *0's pile* in Fig. 10.35. Similarly, if C's currently selected digit, *d*, is 1 through 9, it is fed to the respective bin numbered *d*, where it drops on top of the respective *digit-d-pile*.

When the entire deck is processed, the piles of cards in the digit bins are stacked to reconstitute a new deck, with the 9's pile on the bottom, the 8's pile next to the bottom, and so on, until the 0's pile is placed on top of the deck. This deck is fed through the sorting machine another time, with a different digit selected for sorting. By a process that we will illustrate in a moment, the entire original unsorted deck can be sorted in three passes.

how RadixSort works

Now, let's study an example in which we have used columns of 3-digit numbers to represent the keys on the cards in the decks. Figure 10.36 shows the various stages

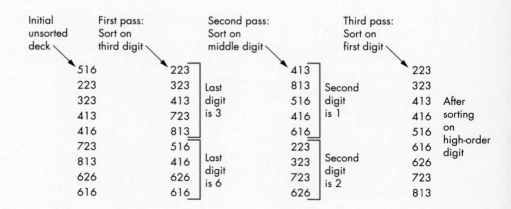

**Figure 10.36** Stages of the RadixSorting Process

of the **RadixSort** process. An unsorted deck of keys is shown as the leftmost column of 3-digit numbers. On the first pass through the deck, the third (or least significant) digit is selected for sorting. Taking keys one at a time from the bottom of the deck and passing them through the sorting machine of Fig. 10.35, you can see that the keys will end up either in the 6's pile or the 3's pile, since the keys end either in 3 or in 6. After the entire deck has been processed in bottom-to-top order, the keys in the 3's pile are placed on top of the keys in the 6's pile, to give the new deck shown in column 2 of Fig. 10.36.

On the second pass, the middle digit is selected, and the keys are sorted so that the keys with a middle 1's digit are on top of those with a middle 2's digit in the deck that results (shown as the third column in Fig. 10.36). On the third and final pass, the first digit is selected for sorting, and the keys are sorted in the order of their first digits. The keys in the fourth column of Fig. 10.36 result from this last pass, after the separate digit piles are reassembled into the final sorted deck.

In the numbers in the fourth (and last) column of Fig. 10.36, you can see that competitions between the third digit (such as between the third digit of keys 413 and 416) have been resolved correctly, as have competitions between values of the second digit (such as between the second digit of keys 616 and 626).

### Known Performance of RadixSort

**RadixSort** is an O($n$) sorting process because it makes exactly $k$ linear passes through the deck of $n$ keys when the keys have $k$ digits.

## **10.6** REVIEW QUESTIONS

1. Describe roughly how **ProxmapSort** works.
2. What are the *hit counts* in **ProxmapSort**? How are they defined?
3. How is the *proxmap* defined in **ProxmapSort**? How do you convert the hit counts into a proxmap?
4. What are the *insertion locations* in **ProxmapSort**? How are they determined?
5. During **ProxmapSort**, what process is used to insert keys into reserved subarrays of the form A[m:n], starting at the insertion location $m$?
6. Describe roughly how **RadixSort** works and why it runs in time O($n$).

## **10.6** EXERCISES

1. From the rough outline of **RadixSort** explained in the last subsection, implement a version of **RadixSort** on three-letter airport code keys, using 26 separate "bins," each of which is a doubly linked list containing nodes with airport code keys and links to the next and previous nodes.
2. Compute the hit counts, the proxmap, and the insertion locations for an unsorted array of 13 keys, A, using the method illustrated in the example in the text, when A is the array:

$$A = [\, 3.5, 12.3, 4.2, 1.5, 5.7, 12.6, 4.7, 7.2, 12.1, 2.9, 0.7, 8.1, 9.3 \,]$$

## 10.7   Other Methods

LEARNING OBJECTIVES

1. To explore ShellSort, which is called a "diminishing increment sorting method," and BubbleSort, which is called a "transposition sorting method."
2. To learn why to avoid using BubbleSort.

The two methods considered in this section do not fit neatly into any of the other main categories shown in Fig. 10.1. Nonetheless, they are important and interesting. **ShellSort**'s performance can be competitive with some of the $O(n \log n)$ methods, and **BubbleSort**'s performance can be disastrously bad, even though it is simple to program.

### ShellSort

A good way to introduce **ShellSort** is to consider an example. For instance, suppose we are attempting to sort an array, A, containing 14 integer keys, such as the one shown in Fig. 10.37.

We are going to use a sequence of increments: 5, 3, and 1. The current increment that we will use at a given moment will be given by the value of the variable, **delta**. Thus we begin by setting the value of the variable **delta** to five, **delta = 5**.

The current increment, **delta**, is used to partition the keys in $A[0:n - 1]$ into several subsequences of keys. Then each subsequence is sorted using an insertion-sort process. Each subsequence consists of keys in A that are an equal distance, **delta**, apart from their left and right neighbors. Using **delta == 5**, the subsequences of keys in array, A, five spaces apart from each other are shown in Fig. 10.38.

| $i$ | 0 | 1 | 2 | 3 | 4 | 5 | 6 | 7 | 8 | 9 | 10 | 11 | 12 | 13 |
|-----|---|---|---|---|---|---|---|---|---|---|----|----|----|----|
| $A[i] =$ | 13 | 3 | 4 | 12 | 14 | 10 | 5 | 1 | 8 | 2 | 7 | 9 | 11 | 6 |

**Figure 10.37** An Initially Unsorted Array, A[0:13]

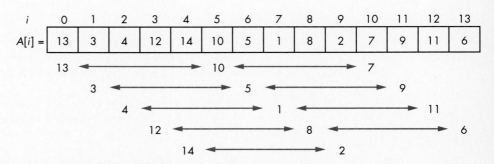

**Figure 10.38** Five Unsorted Delta-5 Subsequences

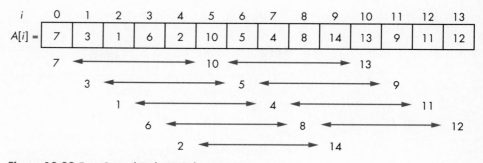

**Figure 10.39** Five Sorted Delta-5 Subsequences

For example, the delta-5 subsequence of A beginning at A[0] consists of the subsequence of keys 13, 10, and 7, which are contained in the array locations A[0], A[5], and A[10], respectively. These array locations are five spaces apart.

After each of these five unsorted delta-5 subsequences is sorted separately, using an insertion-sorting process, the array A is converted to the configuration shown in Fig. 10.39. Note how each delta-5 subsequence in this figure is the sorted version of the corresponding subsequence in Fig. 10.38.

Next, the value of delta is changed from its previous value of 5 to a new smaller value of 3: **delta = 3**. Then, the unsorted delta-3 subsequences of A, as shown in Fig. 10.40 are considered. These unsorted delta-3 subsequences are individually sorted separately from one another, using an insertion-sorting process, yielding the configuration shown in Fig. 10.41.

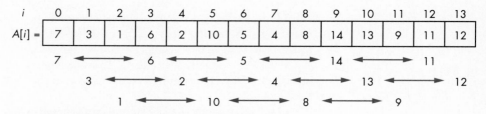

**Figure 10.40** Three Unsorted Delta-3 Subsequences

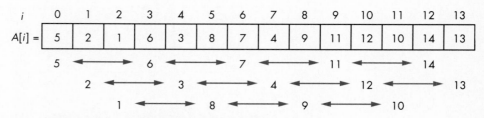

**Figure 10.41** Three Sorted Delta-3 Subsequences

| $i$ | 0 | 1 | 2 | 3 | 4 | 5 | 6 | 7 | 8 | 9 | 10 | 11 | 12 | 13 |
|-----|---|---|---|---|---|---|---|---|---|---|----|----|----|----|
| $A[i]=$ | 5 | 2 | 1 | 6 | 3 | 8 | 7 | 4 | 9 | 11 | 12 | 10 | 14 | 13 |
| $A[i]=$ | 1 | 2 | 3 | 4 | 5 | 6 | 7 | 8 | 9 | 10 | 11 | 12 | 13 | 14 |

**Figure 10.42** Unsorted and Sorted Delta-1 Array, A

Finally, the value of delta is changed from 3 to 1, using **delta = 1**. There is only one subsequence of the array A consisting of keys spaced a distance of one apart from their left and right neighbors, and this consists of the entire array A itself. Thus, in the final stage of the process, the entire array is insertion-sorted. The final transformation is shown in Fig. 10.42.

You might wonder how a sorting process that repeatedly applies an insertion sorting technique could possibly be efficient, given that insertion sorting is known to take time $O(n^2)$ on the average. Part of the answer is that, initially, when delta has a fairly large value, insertion sorting takes place on subsequences containing few keys, and it tends to move keys large distances in the array A so that they land near to their eventual final sorted positions, whereas when **delta**'s value is small, the insertion-sort process tends to move keys locally over short distances, which does not require very many key comparisons and key movements.

*how can ShellSort do better than $O(n^2)$?*

Figure 10.43 presents four views of the array A above when it is unsorted, delta-5 sorted, delta-3 sorted, and delta-1 sorted. If $A[i]$ contains the key $K$, then $K$ is shown as a small solid square at a height of $K$ on the y-axis and at position $i$ on the x-axis. Consequently, the completely sorted array, which is the same as the delta-1 sorted array shown in the rightmost diagram in Fig. 10.43, is simply a diagonal arrangement of solid squares (with key $A[0] == 1$ shown as the solid square at coordinates $(1,1)$, key $A[1] == 2$, shown as the solid square at coordinates $(2,2)$, and, in general, key $A[i-1] == i$ shown as the solid square at coordinates $(i,i)$). You can see how the values in A get closer and closer to their final positions (which lie on the diagonal of the square) each time a new smaller delta increment is used.

**ShellSort** is sometimes called a *diminishing increment sort*, since the values of the increment, **delta**, diminish in a sequence toward the final value, 1, starting from some initial value.

One way to compute the diminishing increments assigned to be the successive values of the variable **delta**, is to start with a value of **delta** close to one-third of the

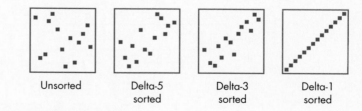

Unsorted     Delta-5
              sorted     Delta-3
                          sorted     Delta-1
                                      sorted

**Figure 10.43** Snapshots of ShellSort

```
  |    void ShellSort(KeyType[ ] A) {
  |
  |        int   i, delta;
  |
5 |        delta = n;
  |
  |        do {
  |            delta = 1 + delta / 3;
  |
10 |            for (i = 0; i < delta; i++) {
  |                deltaInsertionSort(A,i,delta);
  |            }
  |
  |        } while (delta > 1);
  |    }
```

**Program 10.44** Main Procedure for ShellSort

number of keys in the array $A$, delta $\approx n/3$, and then to replace delta with one-third of its former value each time its value is diminished. An assignment statement that performs this is

    delta = 1 + delta / 3;

This assignment statement is used on line 8 of Program 10.44 to compute a value for delta before the insertion sorting process is applied to the $i$th delta subsequence in $A$ using the subroutine call deltaInsertionSort(A,i,delta). All of the separate delta subsequences in $A$ are insertion-sorted using the for-statement on lines 10:12.

The subroutine that insertion-sorts the $i$th delta subsequences in $A$ is given in Program 10.45 (on page 412). The strategy for the insertion sorting used in this program is identical to that of the insertion-sorting algorithm given in Program 10.21, except that the distance between keys being insertion-sorted is delta in Program 10.45 and 1 in Program 10.21.

## Known Performance of ShellSort

ShellSort's performance has been hard to characterize analytically. Nevertheless, experimental measurements suggest that, on the average, ShellSort runs in time $O(n^{1.25})$.

## BubbleSort

*the main idea*

Given that the array $A[0:n-1]$ initially contains unsorted keys, suppose we make repeated passes through $A$, starting at $A[0]$ and moving toward $A[n-1]$, each time exchanging any adjacent pair of keys, $(A[i], A[i+1])$, that are not in sorted order. If we make enough passes, eventually the keys in $A$ will be rearranged in ascending order. This is the idea behind BubbleSort.

```
     | void deltaInsertionSort(KeyType[ ] A, int i, int delta)  {
     |
     |         int          j, k;
     |         KeyType      keyToInsert;
 5   |         boolean      notDone;
     |
     |         j = i + delta;
     |
     |         while (j < n) {
10   |
     |                 // obtain a new keyToInsert
     |                     keyToInsert = A[j];
     |
     |                 // move each key > keyToInsert rightward by delta spaces
15   |                 // to open up a hole in which to place the keyToInsert
     |                     k = j;
     |                     notDone = true;
     |                     do {
     |                         if (A[k – delta].compareTo(keyToInsert) <= 0 ) {
20   |                             notDone = false;
     |                         } else {
     |                             A[k] = A[k – delta];
     |                             k –= delta;
     |                             if (k == i)  notDone = false;
25   |                         }
     |                     } while (notDone);
     |
     |                 // put keyToInsert in hole A[k] opened by moving
     |                 // keys > keyToInsert rightward
30   |                     A[k] = keyToInsert;
     |
     |                 // consider next keyToInsert at an increment of delta to the right
     |                     j += delta;
     |
35   |         }
     |
     | }
```

**Program 10.45** Subroutine to **InsertionSort** $i$th Delta Subsequence in $A$

Program 10.46 gives the algorithm for **BubbleSort**. On line 6, the Boolean flag, **notDone**, is set to *false*. On any given pass through the array A, if an out-of-order pair of keys, (A[i], A[i + 1]), is encountered, the Boolean flag, **notDone**, is set to *true*, to indicate that at least one unordered pair was swapped and that another pass will be needed. If a complete pass is made without finding and exchanging any unordered pair of keys, then **notDone** will remain *false*, and the do-while loop, on lines 5:15 of Program 10.46 will terminate. This is the proper moment for termination since no pair of keys was found to be out of sorted order on the last pass through the array A.

```
 |     void BubbleSort(KeyType[ ] A)  {
 |
 |         int  i;   KeyType  temp;   boolean notDone;
 |
5 |         do {
 |             notDone = false;                      // initially, assume notDone is false
 |             for (i = 0;  i < n − 1;  i++) {
 |                 if (A[i].compareTo(A[i+1]) >0) {    // if (A[i], A[i + 1]) is out of order
 |                     // exchange A[i] and A[i + 1] to put them in sorted order
10|                     temp = A[i]; A[i] = A[i + 1]; A[i + 1] =temp;
 |                     // if you swapped you need another pass
 |                         notDone = true;
 |                 }
 |             }
15|         } while (notDone);            // notDone == false if no pair of keys was
 |     }                                  // swapped on the last pass
```

**Program 10.46** BubbleSort

### Known Performance of BubbleSort

Unfortunately, **BubbleSort** is renowned to be one of the most inefficient sorting algorithms known unless it is applied to an array, $A$, that is only slightly out of order.

An O-notation analysis of **BubbleSort** is fairly simple. On each pass, **BubbleSort** is guaranteed to move at least one key into its final position in sorted order, and not to move that key on subsequent passes. Therefore, after at most $n$ passes, all $n$ keys will be in their final sorted order. On each pass, **BubbleSort** performs $(n - 1)$ comparisons of keys. Therefore the total number of comparisons performed is at most $n*(n - 1)$, which is $O(n^2)$.

*BubbleSort runs in time $O(n^2)$*

The actual performance of **BubbleSort** will be compared to that of the other $O(n^2)$ sorting algorithms, and indeed to other sorting algorithms that run in times $O(n \log n)$, $O(n^{1.25})$, and $O(n)$, in Section 10.8. There, data will show that in the average case, **BubbleSort** is by far the worst among the $O(n^2)$ sorting algorithms, and, in fact, is the worst sorting algorithm overall.

## 10.7 REVIEW QUESTIONS

1. Describe how **ShellSort** works. Why is it called a "diminishing increment sorting method"?
2. Describe how **BubbleSort** works. Why is it called a "transposition sorting method"?
3. What is the O-notation for **BubbleSort**'s running time?

## 10.7 EXERCISES

1. Can you improve **BubbleSort** to run twice as fast by scanning from $0:i − 1$ on each pass, instead of from $0:n − 1$? Write an improved version of **BubbleSort** using this hint, and compare its performance to the original, given in Program 10.46.

2. Cocktail Shaker Sort is a variation of transposition sorting in which passes are alternately made in ascending order and then in descending order of the array indexes of array A, transposing out-of-order pairs of keys on each pass. Write a program for Cocktail Shaker Sort, and compare its performance to that of the improved BubbleSort you implemented as your answer to Exercise 1.

## 10.8 Comparison and Perspective

### LEARNING OBJECTIVES

1. To compare some experimental data that measure the performance of several of the sorting methods introduced in this chapter.
2. To learn from the comparisons when to use and when not to use various sorting methods.

Table 10.47 shows the results of running an experiment that measured sorting times for several of the sorting algorithms described in this chapter.

Five different sizes were used for the array, A, to be sorted: 64, 128, 256, 512, and 1024. On each trial, A was filled with floating point numbers chosen uniformly and randomly in the interval $0 \leq r < 1$. The running times given in Table 10.47 are measured in ticks (where a tick is a 60th of a second) and constitute averages taken over 100 different runs of each algorithm.

To get the numbers in Table 10.47, floating point compare operations and floating point multiply operations were compiled to run on a 68881 floating point chip. The relative times for three operations on keys used in sorting were also measured under these conditions. They are shown in Table 10.48.

As you can see from Table 10.47, even with the cost of a MapKey operation being about three and a third times greater than the cost of comparing two keys, ProxmapSort beats its nearest competitor, QuickSort, by a factor of 1.8 for an average array of 1024 keys. ShellSort and HeapSort are also good sorting techniques to use under these conditions.

and the winner is...

**Table 10.47** Measured Sorting Times for Various Array Sizes

| Array Size n = | 64 | 128 | 256 | 512 | 1024 |
|---|---|---|---|---|---|
| QuickSort | 0.40 | 0.98 | 2.22 | 4.94 | 10.86 |
| HeapSort | 0.61 | 1.43 | 3.28 | 7.43 | 16.57 |
| ProxmapSort | 0.38 | 0.75 | 1.51 | 3.00 | 5.99 |
| ShellSort | 0.42 | 1.04 | 2.37 | 5.44 | 11.97 |
| BubbleSort | 2.76 | 11.36 | 46.42 | 189.35 | 766.22 |
| InsertionSort | 1.12 | 4.47 | 17.58 | 69.89 | 280.27 |
| SelectionSort | 1.40 | 5.56 | 22.18 | 88.66 | 354.48 |
| MergeSort | 0.99 | 2.28 | 5.13 | 11.45 | 25.11 |

| Average move | 0.26 milliticks |
|---|---|
| Average compare | 0.56 milliticks |
| Average MapKey | 1.85 milliticks |

**Table 10.48** Cost of Floating Point Operations Used in Sorting Floats (a millitick = a 60,000th of a second)

The $O(n^2)$ techniques are clearly the worst among the methods compared in Table 10.47, with **InsertionSort** beating **SelectionSort** by a factor of 1.26 and beating **BubbleSort** by a factor of 2.73 on arrays of size 1024.

Among the comparison-based methods, the best method, **QuickSort**, beats the worst method, **BubbleSort**, by a factor of over 70 on arrays of size 1024.

Although the data in Table 10.47 do not show it, nor does the discussion in this chapter cover it, one fact worth mentioning is that even though **HeapSort**'s average running time is about twice that of **QuickSort**, **HeapSort** has both an $O(n \log n)$ worst case running time and a tighter spread between its various running times than does **QuickSort**, whose worst case time is $O(n^2)$. This means that if you want to use a sorting technique that is guaranteed to run in time $O(n \log n)$, and whose overall average running time is not too shabby, then **HeapSort** is a good choice. For example, **HeapSort** would be a safe technique to use if you were trying to guarantee that your software could meet a real-time schedule deadline in, say, a real-time radar air traffic control system.

*when it makes sense to use HeapSort*

Although **ProxmapSort** is the fastest technique, under the circumstances in the experiments used to derive the measurements in Table 10.47, there are some circumstances in which it is not the best. One of these is if the keys in the array $A$ to be sorted are bunched together in one portion of the key space (as in sorting all names in the phone book beginning with the letter M), or consist of several bunches that are each tightly clustered in the key space. Another circumstance is when the cost of computing the **MapKey** function is high in relation to the cost of comparing and moving keys. For example, suppose that integer keys are used on a small personal computer on which floating point operations are simulated in software, rather than being performed by special floating point hardware. Under these circumstances, the floating point multiply operation used to multiply the scale factor, $s$, by the integer key, $K$, in **MapKey**$(K)$, can take over 50 times longer than simple comparison of two integer keys (such as comparing $K_1 > K_2$). Table 10.49 gives one set of experimentally measured circumstances in which this is the case.

*when ProxmapSort is not good to use*

In the case of Table 10.49 the **MapKey** function costs over 185 times more than a comparison between two keys. Under these circumstances, the measured average sorting time for **QuickSort** and **ProxmapSort** turned out as shown in Table 10.50. Here,

| Average move | 0.26 milliticks |
|---|---|
| Average compare | 0.17 milliticks |
| Average MapKey | 31.47 milliticks |

**Table 10.49** Cost of Operations Used in Sorting Integers—Second Case

**Table 10.50** Measured Sorting Times for Integer Keys Using Simulated Floating Point Operations

| Array Size $n$ = | 64 | 128 | 256 | 512 | 1024 |
|---|---|---|---|---|---|
| QuickSort | 0.48 | 1.09 | 2.40 | 5.23 | 11.32 |
| ProxmapSort | 2.25 | 4.50 | 9.01 | 17.99 | 36.00 |

since QuickSort uses only relatively cheap key comparison and movement operations, it beats ProxmapSort by a factor of about 3.2 for arrays of size 1024.

*ProxmapSort wins when floating point operations are simulated*

On the other hand, for floating point keys (such as single-precision floats), if both key comparisons and floating point multiplies are simulated in software, the advantage of ProxmapSort over QuickSort can become even more pronounced. For example, Table 10.51 gives the relative cost of operations for single-precision floating point numbers, when both floating point compares and floating point multiplies are simulated in software. The MapKey function now costs only 3.5 times more than a comparison between two keys. Under these circumstances, the measured average sorting time for QuickSort and ProxmapSort turned out as shown in Table 10.52.

Under these conditions, the advantage of ProxmapSort over QuickSort is compelling. QuickSort takes over 2.88 times longer to finish than ProxmapSort on an average array, A, containing 1024 keys. Circumstances comparable to those shown in Table 10.51 might be typical of some sorting problems that use keys, such as long strings of characters requiring the use of software-based key comparisons and software-based MapKey functions, each of which will take much longer than the time required to move simple single-precision real keys or short integer keys.

*space disadvantage of ProxmapSort*

One disadvantage of ProxmapSort is that, in addition to the space required to store keys, it requires space for two extra integer fields and for an extra two-bit status field in every entry in the array, A, to be sorted. If this extra space is not available, some of the efficient $O(n \log n)$ techniques might be preferable to use. (It is possible, however, to write a version of ProxmapSort that allocates local temporary arrays for this extra space only during the time that ProxmapSort is being executed.)

*if space is scarce, use HeapSort*

If space is at a premium, then even QuickSort may not be the best $O(n \log n)$ technique to use, since it implicitly eats up stack space when it calls itself recursively. Instead, HeapSort may be the best bet, since it runs in bounded workspace.

If the array A is only slightly out of order, then BubbleSort and InsertionSort will often quickly eliminate any minor disorders in which keys are only a few transpositions away from their final sorted order, and both algorithms will terminate quickly. However, one rule of thumb used by some good programmers is: "Never use BubbleSort." These programmers maintain that when they are tempted to use BubbleSort to restore order in a slightly disordered array, they have found it safer, in the long run, to use InsertionSort instead.

| Average move | 0.22 milliticks |
|---|---|
| Average compare | 10.80 milliticks |
| Average MapKey | 37.32 milliticks |

**Table 10.51** Cost of Operations Used in Sorting Floats—Third Case

**Table 10.52** Measured Sorting Times for Float Keys Using Simulated Floating Point Operations

| Array Size $n =$ | 64 | 128 | 256 | 512 | 1024 |
|---|---|---|---|---|---|
| QuickSort | 5.73 | 13.63 | 31.38 | 70.84 | 155.98 |
| ProxmapSort | 3.39 | 6.76 | 13.51 | 27.07 | 54.12 |

### Some Simple Wisdom

Finally, when you are faced with a new sorting problem, sometimes it pays to examine the situation carefully to see if some special, simple solution might apply.

For example, suppose you have an array A containing 100 keys, K, which are guaranteed to be distinct small integers in the range: $101 \leq K \leq 200$. Then it is a simple matter to map each key to its final sorted position in A[0:99], using a mapping that sends key K into location A[K – 101].

looking for special cases with simple solutions

Similarly, suppose you have keys representing cards in a deck of cards, where each key is a pair (S, V) consisting of a card's suit, $S \in \{\clubsuit, \diamondsuit, \heartsuit, \spadesuit\}$, and its face value, $V \in \{A, 2, 3, 4, 5, 6, 7, 8, 9, 10, J, Q, K\}$. Then, to sort a deck of 52 cards, each card with key (S, V) can be mapped onto its final sorted position in A[0:51] by devising a mapping which sends (S, V) into A[13*s + v], where the suit S and face value V have been represented by small integers s in the range $0 \leq s \leq 3$ and v in the range $0 \leq v \leq 12$.

Under most circumstances, it may not be crucial which sorting algorithm you choose, assuming that you use reasonable wisdom to avoid the pitifully inefficient methods. For an overall conclusion, however, the two morals of the story are: (a) "If you absolutely need to select the best sorting algorithm, use measurement and tuning to discover it," and (b) "Under differing circumstances, different sorting algorithms will be the best. There is no single best sorting algorithm that beats all the others all of the time."

## 10.8 REVIEW QUESTIONS

1. Which is the best among the $O(n^2)$ sorting techniques, according to the data in Table 10.47?
2. Which is the best among the $O(n \log n)$ sorting techniques, according to the data in Table 10.47?
3. Describe some special conditions under which it is not advantageous to use any of the sorting techniques mentioned in Table 10.47.

## 10.8 EXERCISES

1. Run some experiments in which you compare the running times of **BubbleSort** and **InsertionSort** when sorting arrays that are only "slightly" out of order. Which ones perform the best under which circumstances? How did you define what it means for an array of keys to be "slightly" out of order?

2. Which of the sorting methods of Table 10.47 would run fastest on an array, A, that is already sorted?

3. Are there hybrid techniques that will run faster than the single techniques shown in Table 10.47? For example, can you improve **QuickSort** by making a hybrid of **QuickSort** and **InsertionSort** in which **InsertionSort** is used to sort all subarrays of three or fewer keys, whereas ordinary **QuickSort** is used to sort subarrays containing four or more keys?

 **Pitfalls**

- *Using* **BubbleSort**

    You might be tempted to use **BubbleSort** if the keys to be sorted are only slightly out of order. Don't do it. Instead, use **InsertionSort**, and if the keys are randomly arranged, then use one of the better $O(n)$ or $O(n \log n)$ sorting methods.

## Tips and Techniques

- *Take advantage of special circumstances for a quick solution if they exist*

    Sometimes the keys used in a sorting problem are a simple permutation of the integer indexes of the sorting array, A, or they can be mapped into A's index range by a simple 1–1, onto function. Under these circumstances, it pays to use a mapping that sends each key onto its final position in A, instead of using one of the more elaborate and costly sorting methods studied in this chapter.

- *If you absolutely have to use the fastest possible technique…*

    And if the circumstances are favorable for applying the **ProxmapSort** method, then the guaranteed $O(n)$ behavior of **ProxmapSort**, plus its superior observed experimental running times, may suggest using it as the best possible solution. But remember, **ProxmapSort** will not perform well unless (a) the keys to be sorted in array A are reasonably close to a distribution chosen uniformly and randomly from the entire key space, (b) the **MapKey** function sends keys $K$ onto the entire index range of array A and does so uniformly with respect to keys in the key space, and (c) the cost of the **MapKey** operation is not vastly more expensive than the cost of the key comparison operation that could be used to implement competing comparison-based sorting methods.

- *If you absolutely have to use the fastest possible technique…*

    Use measurement and tuning to measure and tune several candidate solutions before concluding that you know for certain that you have selected the best method.

- *If you absolutely have to use the fastest possible technique...*

   Be careful about what happens in the worst cases when you use some of the fastest techniques. For example, QuickSort and ProxmapSort each have worst case running times of $O(n^2)$, even though they are the fastest techniques to use under average circumstances. HeapSort, though a tad slower than QuickSort, has much better worst case times than QuickSort, and so it can be relied upon under widely ranging conditions to perform within a comparatively narrow range of overall sorting times.

## ▊ References for Further Study

the classical reference on sorting

Donald E. Knuth has written the classical reference on sorting.

Knuth, D. E., *The Art of Computer Programming*, vol. 3: *Searching and Sorting.* Addison-Wesley, Reading, MA (1973).

where to find those missing derivations

Another book by the author gives derivations of results mentioned in this chapter.

Standish, T. A., *Data Structures, Algorithms, and Software Principles in C.* Addison-Wesley, Reading, MA (1995).

## ▊ Chapter Summary

The problem of sorting an initially unsorted collection of keys into sorted order is a rich one that has fascinated serious computer scientists for many decades. Decades of intensive investigation have yielded crucial insights and illustrate the kind of progress computer science has made in the last half-century on an important central topic.

why the sorting problem is important

If a sorting method, M, sorts an array, A, of n keys, relying only on comparisons between pairs of keys and on moving keys to new positions in A, then method M's average running time can be no faster than proportional to n log n. This crucial fact can be proven using *comparison trees*. However, the fact that comparison-based methods can sort in average time no faster than n log n does not mean that there do not exist other methods that can break the n log n barrier. In fact, there are known methods, such as ProxmapSort and RadixSort, based on address calculations, that can sort in average time $O(n)$. At least one of the address-calculation methods, ProxmapSort, is competitive with the fastest $O(n \log n)$ method, QuickSort, under certain circumstances.

the n log n barrier

One way to organize sorting methods for study and presentation is to classify them into categories such as (a) priority queue methods, (b) divide-and-conquer methods, (c) methods that insert keys and keep them sorted, (d) address-calculation methods, (e) diminishing increment methods, and (f) transposition sorting methods.

different categories of sorting methods

Two priority queue sorting methods are SelectionSort and HeapSort. Each method divides an array, A, into a subarray, PQ, representing a priority queue, and a subarray, Q, representing an ordinary output queue. The idea is to find the largest key among the yet-to-be-sorted keys in PQ, and to move it to the end of the output queue, Q. When keys are removed from PQ in decreasing order and are inserted at the end of Q in arrival order, they form a sorted arrangement of keys in Q.

SelectionSort

In **SelectionSort**, the subarray *PQ* represents a priority queue by using the unsorted array representation of *PQ*, in which, to identify the largest key in *PQ* to remove, we scan all keys in *PQ* to locate the position of the largest key. Because of this representation, **SelectionSort** runs in time $O(n^2)$.

HeapSort

**HeapSort** uses the sequential array representation of a heap to represent the priority queue, *PQ*. Because of this, the initial unsorted array *A* can be organized into a heap in time $O(n)$, and the largest key can be removed from a heap of *k* keys in time $O(\log k)$. Since the times required to remove keys from successively smaller and smaller heaps of sizes *n*, $(n - 1)$, $(n - 2)$, ... , 2, is no larger than a sum of numbers of the form: $a * \Sigma_{(1 < i \leq n)} \lg i$, (for some constant of proportionality *a*), **HeapSort**'s dominant running time component is determined by the sum of the logarithms of the numbers from 2 to *n*, which can be shown to be of the form $O(n \log n)$. Moreover, **HeapSort**'s running times are clustered narrowly in a band around $O(n \log n)$, and are not dispersed as widely as, for instance, the running times for **QuickSort**, which can even deteriorate to times that are $O(n^2)$ in **QuickSort**'s worst case. **HeapSort** is therefore a good technique to use when an $O(n \log n)$ worst case running time is desirable.

divide-and-conquer
methods

The divide-and-conquer sorting methods work by dividing the original unsorted array, *A*, into two smaller subarrays, *L* and *R*, sorting these two smaller subarrays using recursive calls, and then combining the sorted subarrays, *L* and *R* to yield the final sorted result, *A*.

MergeSort

**MergeSort** divides the array *A* into two half-arrays, *L* = A[0:*middle*] and *R* = A[*middle* + 1:*n* − 1], and combines the sorted versions of *L* and *R* by merging them together into a single sorted result, *A*. It runs in time $O(n \log n)$.

QuickSort

At the outset, **QuickSort** chooses a key in *A*, called the *pivot*, to use in separating *A* into two subarrays, *L* and *R*, where *L* contains keys < *pivot*, and *R* contains keys ≥ *pivot*. A partitioning process is used to accomplish this separation of *A* into subarrays *L* and *R*. Once *L* and *R* are sorted (by recursively applying **QuickSort** to them), no further actions are needed to produce a sorted final array, *A*, since *L* and *R* already occupy their final positions as subarrays of *A* the moment they are formed by the partitioning process.

**QuickSort** is the fastest known comparison-based sorting method, on the average, under favorable circumstances, and it is known to run in average time $O(n \log n)$, even though its worst case running time is $O(n^2)$.

**InsertionSort** and **TreeSort** are two sorting methods that work by inserting keys of the initial unsorted array, *A*, into an initially empty container, *C*, and by always maintaining the keys in *C* in sorted order. When all keys of *A* have been inserted into *C*, the keys can be read out of *C* in sorted order.

TreeSort

In **TreeSort**, the keys in *A* are inserted into an initially empty binary search tree, *C*. As new keys are inserted into *C* they are placed into the binary search tree in binary-search-tree order. When *C* is full, its keys can be read out in sorted order by performing an InOrder traversal of *C*. **TreeSort** is an $O(n \log n)$ method, in the average case.

InsertionSort

**InsertionSort** works by letting *C* be a subarray of the array *A*. Initially, *C*, consists of just one key. As each of the remaining $(n - 1)$ keys, *K*, of *A* is inserted into *C*, *K* is placed into *C* so as to maintain all keys inside *C* in sorted order. This can be accomplished by moving all keys in *C* greater than *K* one space to the right, opening up a hole in C in which to insert K. Eventually, when all unsorted keys of A have been inserted into C, the subarray C occupies the entire array A, so that A is then completely sorted. InsertionSort runs in time $O(n^2)$ on the average, although it will terminate fairly quickly when applied to an array A that is only slightly out-of-order initially.

address-calculation methods

Two sorting methods that run in average time $O(n)$, breaking the $n \log n$ barrier for comparison-based methods, are ProxmapSort and RadixSort. These methods work using techniques of address calculation.

ProxmapSort

In ProxmapSort, a proxmap is computed that calculates and reserves subarrays of the final sorted array A in which to move each key, K, of the original unsorted array, A. The word *proxmap* is short for "proximity map" because it is used to determine, for each key, K, a location in A, called the *insertion location*, at the beginning of a reserved subarray of A, in which to insert key K, which is in *proximity* to the final position of K in the sorted array A.

When keys K are inserted into their reserved subarrays of A, starting at their insertion locations, they are insertion-sorted so that each reserved subarray always contains keys in ascending sorted order. ProxmapSort can be shown to run in time $O(n)$ in the average case, even though its worst case takes running time $O(n^2)$. Under certain circumstances, ProxmapSort runs considerably faster than QuickSort. However, during the time it runs, ProxmapSort requires more space than QuickSort in the form of some extra data fields to hold the proxmap and the insertion locations for each key. These extra data fields can be allocated in auxiliary arrays declared locally within the ProxmapSort method such that when the ProxmapSort method terminates, the auxiliary arrays vanish.

RadixSort

RadixSort is an older technique used with electromechanical punched-card sorting machines. If a key has $d$-digits, RadixSort makes $d$ linear passes through the keys to be sorted. On the $i$th pass, it separates them into piles containing common values of the $i$th digit among the $d$-digit keys. These piles are reassembled into a "deck" with the high-digit piles on the bottom and the low-digit piles on the top, in preparation for the next pass. During each pass, keys are removed from the "bottom" of the deck and are placed on the "top" of the appropriate separate piles for the different digits. RadixSort runs in time $O(n)$ since it makes $d$ linear passes, each requiring an amount of time proportional to the $n$ keys to be sorted.

ShellSort

The last two sorting methods presented in this chapter are ShellSort and BubbleSort. ShellSort is sometimes called a *diminishing increment sort*, since it uses a sequence of diminishing increments (such as delta == 14, 5, 2, 1) on successive passes through the array, A. Using the current value of the increment, delta, it considers delta different subsequences of the array, A, each of which contains keys separated by a distance of delta from its left and right neighbors in the subsequence. It uses insertion-sorting to sort each such subsequence of keys, spaced delta keys apart from one another. On each subsequent pass, a smaller value for delta is used. Eventually, the increment delta == 1, is used, in which case, ShellSort performs ordinary insertion-sorting, and rearranges A into its final sorted order. ShellSort has been hard to analyze, but empirical data suggest that it runs in time $O(n^{1.25})$. In actual experimental measurements, ShellSort is competitive with the better $O(n \log n)$ sorting techniques under favorable circumstances.

BubbleSort

BubbleSort is the final sorting method considered. It is sometimes called a *transposition sorting method*, since it works by making repeated passes through the array, A, *transposing* (i.e., swapping) any pair of adjacent keys, (A[i], A[i + 1]), that are not in sorted order. Eventually, it makes a pass in which it finds no pair is out of order, at which point, it terminates. BubbleSort runs in time $O(n^2)$ in the average case. Unfortunately, it is renowned to be one of the worst sorting methods ever discovered. Although it can be efficient when applied to an array that is only slightly out of order, many programmers recommend that it never be used.

looking for direct, simple
sorting solutions

Under some circumstances, direct methods can be applied to rearrange an array into sorted order. For instance, if an array, A[0:n − 1], contains n keys that are a permutation of the set of integers: 0:n − 1, each key, K, can be sent directly to location A[K]. In other similar circumstances, a simple 1–1, onto mapping can be used to send keys onto final sorted array locations in A. You should always be ready to seize upon the opportunity to use such a direct method, if the circumstances warrant, since such direct methods are vastly simpler and more efficient than the general-purpose sorting methods.

conclusion

In the end, to choose a good sorting method, you might need to rely on measurement and tuning. No single sorting method performs best under all circumstances. Instead, differing circumstances favor the use of one method over the others, and different methods perform best under different conditions.

# A Review of Some Java™ Basics

## A.1 Getting Oriented Toward Java™

Java™ is a new programming language oriented toward writing programs that migrate over computer networks and execute on remote computers. These migrating programs are called *applets*. (Java can also be used to write ordinary stand-alone applications that execute on a given computer in the usual fashion.) But Java has several important features not found in ordinary programming languages that support smooth, secure execution of applets on remote network computers.

To support network security, Java permits only carefully authenticated file access on the remote computer on which the applet executes, and Java provides no pointer data types that enable an applet to read or write the contents of an arbitrary memory address specified by a pointer.

A Java applet can be executed on an Internet web page provided the *Hypertext Mark Up Language* (HTML) description of the web page refers to the Java applet code. The applet code is given in the form of *Java bytecodes*, which are instructions for an imaginary computer, called the *Java Virtual Machine* (JVM). In order for a given computer to be able to execute Java applets, it must supply an interpreter for Java bytecode instructions. This interpreter can be a software program that imitates the actions of the Java Virtual Machine. Another possibility is to have a hardware computer chip that can execute Java bytecodes directly, as is the case with several new *Network Computers* (or NCs) that have appeared recently.

Java aware web browsers

Some network browser programs (such as Netscape® and Microsoft's Explorer®) are *Java aware*, meaning that they incorporate interpreters capable of executing the bytecode instructions of the Java Virtual Machine, allowing them to execute the Java applets contained in web pages. By this means, Java applets can bring life to the activity of web browsing by allowing web pages to display animations and to become highly interactive with users through enhanced *Graphical User Interfaces* (GUIs).

just-in-time Java compilers

Because the Java Virtual Machine can be implemented either in software (as a JVM interpreter) or in hardware (as a JVM chip), Java programs can be made highly *portable* (where the word "portable" means they can be executed on many different kinds of computers). Another development that enhances efficient cross-platform portability is the recent appearance of fast Java compilers, called *just-in-time* (JIT) compilers. A fast just-in-time compiler is capable of rapidly compiling a Java bytecode program into native instructions for a target computer. This enables Java applets to be shipped across computer networks in bytecode form and to be JIT-compiled in order to execute rapidly on the target computer without significantly increased delay (when compared to the applet bytecode's normal network transmission time).

Java provides concurrent execution threads

Java provides for concurrent execution of multiple processes by providing separate *threads* of control. More than one stream of instructions can be executing at the same time in Java by creating and running separate Java threads. The capacity for such concurrent execution is vital to being able to provide for satisfactory user interaction over networks, as for instance happens when a user must wait for a large picture or file to download across the network into a web browser page. If there is only a single execution thread, meaning that a program can do only one thing at a time, the user must sit frozen at the screen, waiting for the picture or file to finish downloading. On the other hand, if multiple threads are implemented, the picture or file can download in a background thread, and a foreground thread can support continued user interaction with the user interface. Java also provides ways of synchronizing the activities of concurrently executing threads so that they can coordinate their actions and their timing, or so that they can avoid getting into deadlocks and race-conditions.

exception handling

Java also has a carefully designed mechanism for *exception handling*. Exceptions occur in Java when unusual conditions arise in the execution of programs. For example, if you divide an integer by zero, or attempt to access a position in an array beyond the array's index bounds, Java will *throw* an exception. To handle the exception, you *catch* it after it is thrown. You can *try* executing a block of code that may *throw* an exception, and you can attempt to *catch* any thrown exceptions in a section of code immediately after the section that might have thrown the exception.

object-oriented programming

Finally, and most important of all for the purposes of a data structures course, Java supports *object-oriented programming* (OOP). Chapter 2 of this book introduces object-oriented programming in Java and provides insight into why OOP has become popular and important in contemporary programming practice. Two of the most important implications of OOP are: (1) OOP provides an effective way for building collections of reusable software components—a study of software economics shows that building systems from reusable components is cheaper and more reliable than building everything from scratch, starting with a clean sheet of paper; and (2) OOP provides an effective means to support modularity and information hiding, making it is possible to build software components presenting simple user-interfaces whose internal details are hidden from outside view and are thus made tamper-proof.

Java comes with an extensive library of software components, called the Java *Application Programming Interface* (API). In addition to the usual components we expect to find in a program library associated with a typical programming language (such as math routines), the Java API contains a package of components called the *Abstract Window Toolkit* (AWT). The AWT provides Java with a library of GUI components, such as windows, buttons, checkboxes, sliders, menus, scrollbars, and graphics drawing primitives, essential for user interface programming. A component in the Java AWT, such as a window or a menu, is a machine-independent abstraction that actually gets implemented by *peers* on a given local platform (or computer). For example, on an IBM PC or compatible, the peer for an abstract Java window might look and behave exactly like a window in Windows 95, whereas on a Macintosh, the peer might look and behave exactly like a MacOS window. Thus, the peers that implement the abstract Java GUI components have different appearances on different brands of computers to achieve consistency with their local operating system features. Nonetheless, their abstract behaviors implement the requirements of the abstract Java components in the Java AWT.

*Java's software component library*

While an operating systems course might delve deeply into concurrent programming in Java, and a computer graphics course might delve deeply into how to write graphical user interfaces using the Java AWT, the basic mission of a data structures course is to convey the important ideas about data structures and algorithms that every literate computer scientist should know about. To a large extent, these key ideas can be conveyed using any contemporary programming language as a vehicle. The situation is analogous to using various brands of trucks to deliver vegetables. The nutrition is in the vegetables regardless of whether a Ford or GM truck was used to deliver the vegetables. Similarly, the basic algorithm and data structure ideas are conceptually independent of the particular programming language used to illustrate them.

*the basic data structure concepts are programming language independent*

For example, take the concept of linked data representations. Even though Java does not have explicit pointer data types, it always uses implicit references (i.e., hidden pointers that can't be manipulated or printed) to provide access to objects and arrays. By storing such implicit references in fields of other objects and arrays, linked data representations can be composed, much as they can in programming languages that provide explicit pointer data types. Chapter 3 of this book is devoted entirely to explaining how linked data representations can be built and manipulated in Java, providing you with the skills you'll need to master the fundamental concepts involved in linked-data-representation programming. For example, a visual notation for pointer diagrams is introduced and used to help you reason about linked representations. Once you learn this visual pointer diagram notation and once you understand how to use it to develop linked-data-representation algorithms in Java, you'll be prepared to

*linked data representations*

learn rapidly how to do linked-data-representation programming in other programming languages such as C++, Ada, and Object Pascal, that use explicit pointer data types to represent linked data structures.

For reasons such as these this book focuses on explaining concepts at a level of understanding that will transfer in the future to other new circumstances you are likely to face in your career, such as adapting to the requirement to learn and use a new programming language. (It appears that the popularity of a given programming language does not last forever. Over the time span of a career, the author and many others have had to learn to use many new programming languages, text editors, computers, user interfaces, operating systems, word processors, spreadsheets, artwork drawing programs, network browsers, email systems, and more. Both hardware and software have been constantly changing. So you can appreciate why computer scientists try to identify ways of thinking about the core data structure and algorithm concepts that are likely to outlast the ever-shifting flux of the marketplace of artifacts. If computer science courses are to provide you with intellectual tools serviceable for a lifetime, they have to focus on fundamental ideas that will survive the kaleidoscopic shifts in unimportant detail. To do this properly, computer scientists have to rely on extensive experience, looking backward to cull from the ever-shifting flux, those central concepts that have shown long-lasting value. The concept of linked data representations is an example of such a central idea with long-lasting value, even though the particular details of how linked data representations are expressed will tend to vary slightly using some particular popular programming language of the moment.)

*focusing on concepts having lasting value*

## Plan for the Appendix

Because our aim is to convey long-lasting, valuable concepts of data structures and algorithms, independent of the programming language vehicle used to convey them, we shall confine ourselves in this book to write Java programs using Java features that are either common to many programming languages or that have reasonable equivalents in other languages. For example, we use Java *classes* to build composite data structures having named data components of different types. The same sort of data structure is built using *struct* data types in C or using *record* data types in Pascal. But since Java has no *struct* or *record* data types, Java *classes* provide the closest available mechanism to express the key concept we need, namely, a way to bundle nonalike named data components into a composite data structure that can be treated as a single value, and whose data components (or members) can be separately accessed and changed.

*the features of Java we will use*

We will not spend much time on Java AWT components (although the case study of a shape drawing applet in Chapter 2 will give some of the flavor of what is involved). Instead, the focus will be on the following: (1) Java's ordinary data types—both the primitive data types (such as integers, characters, floating point numbers, and boolean values) and the reference data types (arrays and objects); (2) Java's ordinary expressions consisting of operators applied to operands; (3) Java's ordinary statement types, such as assignments, conditionals, switch statements, while-loops, for-loops, do-while-loops, and return statements; and (4) Java class definitions, method definitions, and method calls.

Chapter 2 introduces the object-oriented features of Java: class declarations, constructors, storage allocation, method declarations, method calls, subclassing, inheritance, and overriding. This appendix reviews the other basic features of Java that we shall need.

## A.2 Identifiers, Reserved Words, Names, and Variables

*Java identifiers*

In Java, identifiers must begin with a letter and may contain additional letters and digits. (Actually, in place of a letter, you can use a dollar sign ($), an underscore character (_), or letters from other alphabets, such as the Greek, Japanese, Arabic, Cyrillic, and Devanagari alphabets that are part of the Unicode character set.) Java identifiers are case sensitive, meaning that upper- and lowercase characters are treated as distinct characters. Thus, the identifier rectangle and the identifier Rectangle are treated as two distinct nonidentical identifiers in Java, whereas these two identifiers would be identical in a case-insensitive language like Pascal.

*reserved words*

In Java, identifiers are used as names of declared entities such as variables, constants, classes, and methods. Some Java identifiers are set aside as reserved words of the Java language. These reserved words cannot be used as names of declared entities. Table A.1 lists the Java reserved words.

In addition, the boolean truth values true and false may not be used as names of declared entities.

In Java, as in other programming languages, you can declare variables and use them to hold values that can change during program execution. A declaration of a variable always gives both the *type* of the variable and its *name*. The variable name must be a valid Java identifier, meaning that it must obey the spelling rules for Java identifiers we just described, that it cannot be a Java reserved word or the boolean truth values true and false, and that it cannot use the same name as another variable that is declared in the same scope.

**Table A.1** Java Reserved Words

| | | | |
|---|---|---|---|
| abstract | double | int | super |
| boolean | else | interface | switch |
| break | extends | long | synchronized |
| byte | final | native | this |
| case | finally | new | throw |
| catch | float | package | throws |
| char | for | private | transient |
| class | goto | protected | try |
| const | if | public | void |
| continue | implements | return | volatile |
| default | import | short | while |
| do | instanceof | static | |

**declarations and scopes**

In most other programming languages, the declaration of a variable must be given at the beginning of the code for a procedure, function, or block. In Java, however, it is possible to declare variables anywhere within the code for a class, a method, or a block (where a "block" consists of a sequence of statements enclosed in curly braces '{' and '}'). The scope of a variable is the region of the code where the variable is visible and can be accessed or changed. When a variable is declared in the middle of a block, its scope extends from the place it is declared until the end of the block. As an example, consider the method, sumSquares(n), given in Program A.2 that computes the sum of the squares of the integers from 1 to n.

On line 3 of Program A.2, the declaration int partialSum; declares the variable partialSum to be an integer variable having the *type* int and the *name* "partialSum." On line 5, this variable is assigned the initial value 0, using the assignment statement partialSum = 0;. On line 7, an integer counting variable i is declared and is immediately initialized to have the initial value 1, using the initializing declaration int i = 1;. The scope of the variable i extends from line 7 up to and including line 16. In other words, the place where the value of i can be accessed or changed extends from the place it is declared on line 7 up to the end of the block in which it is declared. This implies that i is not visible on lines 2 through 6 in the same block. An attempt to print the value of i on lines 2 through 6 would result in a compile-time error with an error message such as, "Error: Undefined variable: i."

In a short while, we will explain the meaning of the while-loop on lines 9:12, the special assignment statement partialSum += i*i; on line 10, and the incrementing statement i++; on line 11 (but for those who already know C or C++, the meaning in Java is identical to that in C and C++).

```
     |   int sumSquares(int n) {              // find the sum of 1² + 2² + . . . + n²
     |
     |       int partialSum;                  // let partialSum contain a running total
     |                                        //     of the squares 1² + 2² + . . . + i².
  5  |       partialSum = 0;                  // initially, let partialSum be zero
     |
     |       int i = 1;                       // let i be a counting variable initialized to 1
     |
     |       while (i <= n) {                 // for each value of i from 1 to n
 10  |           partialSum += i*i;           //     add i² to the running total in
     |           i++;                         //     the variable partialSum
     |       }
     |
     |       return partialSum;               // return the total of 1² + 2² + . . . + n²
 15  |                                        //     as the value of the method sumSquares
     |   }
```

**Program A.2** The Sum of the Squares

## A.2 REVIEW QUESTIONS

1. How is a valid Java identifier composed?
2. Describe some uses for identifiers in Java.
3. Can you use a Java reserved word, such as **double**, as the name of a variable?
4. In Java, are the identifiers **myVariable** and **MyVariable** considered to be the same or different?

## A.2 EXERCISES

1. Which of the following are valid Java identifiers and which are not?
   $20,    myRectangle,    MAX_VALUE,    _1_2_3_,    long,    longints
2. In Program A.2, give the ranges of line numbers that are the respective scopes of the variables i and partialSum. What is the scope of the formal parameter n?

## A.3 Data Types in Java

*primitive data and reference data*

In Java, there are two broad classes of data: *primitive data* and *reference data*. Primitive data types support integer, floating-point, boolean, and character values. Java is pre-programmed to deal with the primitive data types, whereas it is not preprogrammed to deal with classes and objects defined by programmers. The reference data types are comprised of references to instances of objects and arrays. You can think of a class definition as a template that is used to create instances of objects. You use the Java keyword **new** in an expression to create an instance of an object. A reference to the instance may be assigned as the value of an object variable. Similarly, you can create and assign references to instances of arrays.

Table A.3 lists the primitive data keywords you use in Java declarations to declare variables that hold primitive data types.

*literals*

Each of these primitive data types has literals. In Java, a literal prescribes the way unnamed constant data values are written. Some nonprimitive data types in Java also have literals. For example, a string literal, such as **"abc"** is an expression whose value is a reference to an instance of Java's (read-only) **String** class. Table A.4 gives examples of some Java literals.

**Table A.3** Java Primitive Data Types

| | |
|---|---|
| int | 32-bit signed integer |
| long | 64-bit signed integer |
| byte | 8-bit signed integer |
| short | 16-bit signed integer |
| float | 32-bit (IEEE 754-1985) floating point number |
| double | 64-bit (IEEE 754-1985) floating point number |
| boolean | true or false |
| char | 16-bit Unicode 1.1 character |

**Table A.4** Examples of Java
Literals

| | |
|---|---|
| 27 | an integer |
| 033 | an octal (base 8) integer |
| 0x1B | a hexadecimal (base 16) integer |
| 1.6e1 | a double-precision (64-bit) floating point number |
| 16.0f | a single-precision (32-bit) floating point number |
| 16.0d | a double-precision (64-bit) floating point number |
| false | a boolean value |
| 'c' | a 16-bit Unicode 1.1 character |
| "abc" | a String literal |

In Table A.4, the first three lines give examples of ways to write the integer **27** in base 10, base 8, and base 16. If an integer begins with a leading zero (**0**), it is given in octal (base 8). Thus, the octal number **033** signifies an integer whose value is $3 \times 8^1 + 3 \times 8^0 = 24 + 3 = 27$. If an integer begins with **0x** or **0X** it signifies a hexadecimal (base 16) integer. Thus, the hexadecimal number **0x1B** signifies an integer whose value is $1 \times 16^1 + B \times 16^0 = 16 + 11 = 27$. The precision of an integer literal is assumed to be 32-bits (i.e., type **int**) unless the suffix **L** is added, as in **27L**, which specifies an integer of type **long** (64-bit precision). To create integer values of type **byte** or type **short**, you can assign an integer literal to be the value of a variable declared to be of type **byte** or type **short** (provided the integer value being assigned is within the range of permissible values of type **byte** or type **short**).

*floating point literals*

The literals having floating point values can be designated several ways in Java. First, if you write a number containing a decimal point (such as **16.0**, or **16.** or **.16**) you get a double-precision (64-bit) floating point number. You can also specify exponents and/or you can append the letter **F** or the letter **D** to denote single-precision (32-bit) or double-precision (64-bit) floating point numbers. For example, **0.16e2**, **1.6E1**, and **16.** all denote a double-precision floating point number having the value sixteen. Whereas the trailing **F** in **16.0F** denotes a number of type **float**, the trailing **D** in **16.0D** denotes a **double**.

*boolean literals*

The Java keywords **true** and **false** denote the two **boolean** values. Expressions with boolean values are used as conditions in if-statements, while-statements, and do-while-statements to determine whether or not other groups of statements contained within these if-statements or repetition statements will be executed.

*character literals*

Character data can be specified in Java by enclosing a single character within apostrophes. Thus **'c'** signifies the lowercase character **c**, **'C'** signifies the uppercase character **C**, and **'%'** signifies the percent character. To specify certain nonprinting characters such as tabs, backspaces, and quote marks, you can use Java escape sequences beginning with the backslash character **'\'**. For example, **\n** denotes a newline, **\t** denotes a tab, **\b** denotes a backspace, **\\** denotes the backslash itself, **\'** denotes an apostrophe, and **\"** denotes a double quote. You can also use a backslash followed by a three digit octal value (such as **\273**) or a backslash followed by a **u** and four hexadecimal digits (such as **\u00b6**) to specify a character designated by that octal or hexadecimal value.

*integer literals*

string literals

A sequence of characters enclosed in double quotes (such as "abc123") specifies an instance of a Java **String** class. In Java, such strings are read-only entities whose characters may be accessed but not changed. (Java provides another type of object called a **StringBuffer** to enable you to manipulate the characters inside a string, as is explained in Chapter 7.)

## Reference Data Types in Java

We have just seen that the primitive data in Java (such as integers, floating point numbers, booleans, and characters) are each single values not having named or numbered components. By contrast, it is possible to have composite data in Java consisting of values that have several separate numbered components, or that have several separate named components.

arrays

Arrays are used in Java to hold data with distinct numbered components. The numbering of the components always begins at position **0**, and ends at a position whose number is one less than the number of components. For example, to designate an array, **A**, of five integers, you could give the following declaration:

```
int [ ] A = {11, 22, 33, 44, 55};        // let A be an integer array with 5 items
```

array initializers

The quantity {11, 22, 33, 44, 55} is called an array initializer, and can be used to initialize the array's components. After this declaration has been given, **A**'s array component values are in the positions **A[0]**, **A[1]**, **A[2]**, **A[3]**, and **A[4]**. If you attempt to access an array position that is not defined, such as **A[5]**, you will cause Java to throw an **IndexOutOfBoundsException**. An alternative way to create and initialize the array **A** having the initial values given previously is as follows:

```
int [ ] A = new int[5];        // declare A to be an array holding 5 integer items
A[0] = 11;                     // initialize A[0] to 11
A[1] = 22;                     // initialize A[1] to 22
A[2] = 33;                     // initialize A[2] to 33
A[3] = 44;                     // initialize A[3] to 44
A[4] = 55;                     // initialize A[4] to 55
```

The expression **new int[5]** allocates space for a new integer array holding five integer items indexed by the integers in the range **0:4**. A reference to this newly allocated integer array is assigned to be the value of the variable **A**.

To create arrays of two or more dimensions in Java, you can use declarations such as:

```
int [ ] [ ] M = new float [4] [7];        // creates a four by seven array M
```

multidimension arrays

In this case, **M** is a floating point array whose individual array components can be accessed by expressions of the form **M[i][j]**, where i is in the range **0:3** and j is in the range **0:6**. For example, the assignment M[3][2] = M[1][4] + 5.0; adds 5.0 to the value of the array item in row **1** and column **4** of M and stores it in the array item in row **3** and column **2** of M.

**Table A.5** Some Data on
Various Cities

| Name | Population | Country |
|------|-----------|---------|
| Reykjavik | 83,376 | Iceland |
| Bangalore | 1,540,741 | India |
| San Cristóbal | 151,717 | Venezuela |
| Pointe-à-Pitre | 23,899 | Guadeloupe |
| Dundee | 191,517 | Scotland |

You can also use nested array initializers to initialize arrays of two or more dimensions, as in the following example declaring a four by four identity matrix:

```
double [ ] [ ]  identityMatrix = {
                  { 1.0, 0.0, 0.0, 0.0 },
                  { 0.0, 1.0, 0.0, 0.0 },
                  { 0.0, 0.0, 1.0, 0.0 },
                  { 0.0, 0.0, 0.0, 1.0 },
                };
```

Perhaps you are familiar with *record* data types in Pascal or with *structs* in C or C++. These data types allow you to represent composite data values having named components of possibly differing types. For instance, we might want to represent some data about various cities, giving for each city its *name*, its *population*, and the *country* in which it is located. Table A.5 gives an example of such data.

composite data values with named components

Thus, various programming languages allow you to declare a composite data type to represent a **City** containing, say, strings to represent the city's name and country, and containing an integer to represent the city's population. In Java, classes are used to represent composite data types. For instance, we could declare a **City** class as follows:

```
class City {
    String    name;
    int       population;
    String    country;
}
```

To create a composite data value for a city, such as Dundee, Scotland, we could write the following Java declaration and initialization code:

```
City d1 = new City( );           // construct a new City object, d1

d1.name = "Dundee";              // initialize d1's name to Dundee
d1.population = 191517;          // initialize d1's population to 191517
d1.country = "Scotland";         // initialize d1's country to Scotland
```

*using dot notation to access or change data fields*

This declares the variable **d1** to be a variable holding a reference to an object that is an instance of the **City** class, and then initializes this **City** object's **name** field to contain the **String** value **"Dundee"**, its **population** field to contain the **int** value **191517**, and its **country** field to contain the **String** value **"Scotland"**. In general, we can use dot-notation to access and assign the fields of the object **d1**. For example, if we want to change the **population** of the city **d1** to reflect some new census figures, later, we might write:

    d1.population = 197214;            // change population to new census results

Or, to increase a running total by half of Dundee's population, we might write:

    runningTotal += d1.population/2;

Likewise, whenever we please, we can access or change Dundee's city name using **d1.name** and we can access or change Dundee's country designation using **d1.country**.

In Chapter 2, we cover the fact that, in addition to containing *named data fields*, Java classes can contain *methods*, which are procedures that operate on such data fields. For now, however, it suffices to note that, on occasion, we use Java classes having data fields but having no methods, to bundle some data components into an aggregate data value that contains named data components of possibly differing types.

*automatic default initializations in Java*

If you declare a variable **v** in Java without giving an explicit initialization for it, Java automatically initializes **v** to a *default value*. These default initializations are as follows: Integer variables are initialized to **0**; floating point variables are initialized to **0.0**; character variables are initialized to **\u0000**; and all reference variables are initialized to **null**.

## **A.3** REVIEW QUESTIONS

1. What are Java's primitive data types?
2. What are Java's reference data types?
3. What is the reserved word **new** used for in Java?
4. Suppose a class definition **class Point{ int x; int y;}** is given, and suppose a variable **P** is declared using the declaration, **Point P;**. After a point object is allocated and assigned to be the value of **P**, what expression designates the **y**-coordinate of **P**? What assignment statement changes the **x**-coordinate of **P** to the value **3**?

## **A.3** EXERCISES

1. Give a Java declaration for a **5** by **5** array, **A**, of **String**s.
2. Give a Java **String** literal whose value contains the characters in the string,
    "She said, "Please, don't eat the daisies.""

## A.4  Java Operators and Expressions

In Java, operators apply operations to one or more operands and return values as a result. A *unary operator* applies an operation to one operand, a *binary operator* applies an operation to two operands, and a *trinary operator* applies an operation to three operands.

Some unary operators are applied to operands in prefix form in which the operator **op** comes *before* the operand. The format is **op operand**, as in:

```
– N        // unary negation operator (–) applied to numerical operand N
! B        // unary complement operator (!) applied to boolean operand B
~ N        // unary bitwise complement operator (~) applied to operand N
```

Yet other unary operators are applied to operands in postfix form in which the operator **op** comes *after* the operand. The format is **operand op**, as in:

```
N++        // unary postincrement operator (++) applied to integer operand N
N––        // unary postdecrement operator (––) applied to integer operand N
```

In the case of binary operators, the operator **op** is placed *between* the two operands. The format is **operand op operand**, as in:

```
s1+s2      // the binary plus operator (+) concatenates String s1 and String s2
n1+n2      // the binary plus operator (+) also adds numbers n1 and n2
N<<3       // the binary left shift operator (<<) shifts N's bits 3 places to the left
```

*the conditional operator*

Java also has a trinary conditional operator ( ? : ) that is applied to its three operands in the form **b?c:d**. This could be pronounced "if **b** then **c** else **d**." Given that **b** is a boolean expression, the value of **b?c:d** is determined the following way. First evaluate the boolean expression **b**. If the result is **true**, then the value of **b?c:d** is the value of **c**, and if **b**'s value is **false**, then the value of **b?c:d** is the value of **d**.

*forming expressions*

In Java, expressions are built up from subexpressions by applying several composition techniques, such as:

- Forming a single expression from a single variable or literal
  for example: "Scotland", 1.6e7, runningTotal, 'c', true
- Applying operators to other expressions as operands
  for example: runningTotal++, (length–2)*(width–1),
  where subexpressions can be enclosed in parentheses
- Following a method name by a list of argument expressions that are enclosed in parentheses and separated by commas
  for example: rotateClockwise(60, rectangle2), createEmptyRow( )
- Following an array valued expression by a sequence of subscript expressions enclosed in square brackets
  for example: A[row++] [2 * (column – 6)]
- Using dot notation to select a data field of an object or to invoke an object's method
  for example: d1.population, myOval.drawOval(blueBorder)

- Applying the **new** operator or a **(typecast)** operator to an expression
    for example: **new City()** to create a new **City** object, or
    **(float)d1.population** to convert city **d1**'s integer population value
    into a floating point number for that population

## Operator Precedence and Associativity in Java

*Java's operator*<br>*precedence rules*

The various operations used to form expressions are applied in an order specified by Java's operator precedence rules. Generally speaking, operations inside parentheses are always performed before operations outside parentheses, but in the absence of parentheses, an operation with higher precedence is performed before an operation with lower precedence whenever two such operations compete to apply to a common operand.

Consider the following two examples:

- **3 * (7 − 2)** has the value **15**,
    because operations inside parentheses are performed before operations outside parentheses. In this case, the binary minus operator (**−**), indicating the subtraction operation, is performed on its operands 7 and 2, yielding 5, before the binary multiplication operator (**\***) is applied to its operands 3 and 5, yielding 15.
- **3 * 7 − 2** has the value **19**,
    because the binary multiplication operator (**\***) has a higher operator precedence than the binary subtraction operator (**−**). In this case, the **\*** and **−** operators compete for a common operand **7**, since **7** is the right operand of **\*** while, at the same time, **7** is also the left operand of **−**. Here, one of the two operations **\*** and **−** must be applied to **7** first, and the remaining operation must be applied second. When multiplication is performed first, **3 * 7** yields **21**, after which **21 − 2** yields **19**.

*associativity rules*

The associativity of operators comes into play when two operators of equal precedence compete for the same operand. For example, consider the expression **7 − 3 − 2**. The two instances of the minus operator (**−**) compete to apply to the operand **3**. Two orders of application of the operators to the operands are possible: (1) the left subtraction is performed first, followed by the right subtraction, as in the parenthesized expression **(7 − 3) − 2**, or (2) the right subtraction is performed first, followed by the left subtraction, as in the parenthesized expression **7 − (3 − 2)**. If the left subtraction is performed first, we say subtraction is *left associative*, and if the right subtraction is performed first, we say subtraction is *right associative*. In Java, left association applies to all binary operators except assignment operators (for which association is to the right). Thus, in our example,

- **7 − 3 − 2** has the value **2**,
    because if operators of equal precedence compete to apply to a common operand, the Java associativity rules apply to determine the outcome, and, in the case of the binary minus operator (**−**), association is to the left. This means that **7 − 3 − 2** is evaluated as if it were parenthesized to the left, as in **(7 − 3) − 2**, giving the result **(7 − 3) − 2 = 4 − 2 = 2**.

**Table A.6** Operator
Precedence in Java

| | |
|---|---|
| postfix operators | . [ ] (arglist) exp++ exp−− |
| unary prefix operators | ++exp −−exp +exp −exp !exp ~exp |
| creation and typecast | new exp (type)exp |
| multiplicative operators | * / % |
| additive operators | + − |
| shifting operators | << >> >>> |
| relational operators | < > >= <= instanceof |
| equality operators | == != |
| bitwise and operator | & |
| bitwise exclusive XOR | ^ |
| bitwise inclusive OR | \| |
| logical AND | && |
| logical OR | \|\| |
| conditional operator | ? : |
| assignment operators | = += −= *= /= %= ^= |
| | &= \|= <<= >>= >>>= |

Table A.6 specifies the operator precedence for Java operators. In addition, you need to recall that Java binary operators associate to the left, except assignment operators, which associate to the right. In Table A.6, the operators having highest precedence are at the top, and those with lowest precedence are at the bottom. If the row for operator $\alpha$ is above the row for operator $\beta$, then operator $\alpha$ has higher precedence than operator $\beta$. Operands are signified by **exp**, and a (possibly empty) list of arguments separated by commas is signified by **arglist**.

*the Java operator precedence table*

For your convenience, Tables A.7 through A.12 give various groups of Java operators. Brief discussions of some of these tables are given to review some notable features of the operators mentioned. In these tables, the symbols **op**, **op1**, **op2**, and **op3** signify operands of the operators. We start with the ordinary arithmetic operators given in Table A.7.

*integer division*

When **op1** and **op2** are integer operands in **op1/op2**, the result is the integer quotient of **op1** divided by **op2** with the remainder thrown away. For example, 9/2 is the integer 4, not the floating point number 4.5. In the case of negative integers truncation is toward zero. For example, −9/2 is −4.

*incrementing and decrementing operators*

In Java, there are special unary operators (++ and −−) for incrementing and decrementing the contents of a variable by one (see Table A.8). These incrementing and decrementing operators can be applied either in postfix form (**x++**, **x−−**) or in prefix form (**++x**, **−−x**). In the postfix form, they are called postincrementing and

**Table A.7** Arithmetic Operators

| | |
|---|---|
| op1 + op2 | Adds op1 and op2 |
| op1 − op2 | Subtracts op2 from op1 |
| op1 * op2 | Multiplies op1 by op2 |
| op1 / op2 | Divides op1 by op2 |
| op1 % op2 | Computes the remainder of dividing op1 by op2 |
| − op | Arithmetically negates op |

**Table A.8** Incrementing and Decrementing Operators

| postincrement | op++ | Expression value is the value of op before op is incremented |
| postincrement | ++op | Expression value is the value of op after op has been incremented |
| preincrement | op-- | Expression value is the value of op before op is decremented |
| predecrement | --op | Expression value is the value of op after op has been decremented |

postdecrementing operators because they perform their incrementing or decrementing operation on the variable **x** after **x**'s value has been obtained to be used as the value of the expression **x++** or **x--**. In other words, to get the value of the expression **x++** (or **x--**) you first take the value of **x** to be used as the value of the expression, and then you increment (decrement) **x**'s contents by 1. In the prefix form **++x** (**--x**), you first increment (decrement) **x** before taking the newly incremented (decremented) value of **x** as the value of the expression **++x** (**--x**).

Java provides a handy abbreviation for various assignment operators. The basic assignment operator is **op1 = op2**, which replaces the current value of **op1** with the value of **op2**. Also, the value of the assignment expression **op1 = op2** is the value of **op2**. Recall that the assignment operator is right associative, so that the compound assignment expression **op1 = op2 = op3** means the same as **op1 = (op2 = op3)** in which the value of **op3** is first assigned to become the value of **op2**, and, after **op3**'s value becomes the value of the subexpression **(op2 = op3)**, the value of **op3** is also assigned to become the new value of **op1**. The net effect is that **op1 = op2 = op3** assigns **op3**'s value to become the new values of **op1** and **op2** and **op3**'s value becomes the value of the entire compound assignment expression **op1 = op2 = op3**.

*abbreviated assignment operators*

Now let β be one of the binary operators in the set {+, −, *, /, %, &, |, ^, <<, >>, >>>}. If we write the assignment **op1 β= op2** in Java, it is an abbreviation for **op1 = op1 β op2**. Table A.9 spells this out in detail by listing each specific case.

**Table A.9** Assignment Operators

| The assignment expression | Means the same as |
| --- | --- |
| op1 += op2 | op1 = op1 + op2 |
| op1 -= op2 | op1 = op1 − op2 |
| op1 *= op2 | op1 = op1 * op2 |
| op1 /= op2 | op1 = op1 / op2 |
| op1 %= op2 | op1 = op1 % op2 |
| op1 &= op2 | op1 = op1 & op2 |
| op1 \|= op2 | op1 = op1 \| op2 |
| op1 ^= op2 | op1 = op1 ^ op2 |
| op1 <<= op2 | op1 = op1 << op2 |
| op1 >>= op2 | op1 = op1 >> op2 |
| op1 >>>= op2 | op1 = op1 >>> op2 |

**Table A.10** Relational
Operators

| Expression | Meaning |
|---|---|
| op1 == op2 | op1 is equal to op2 |
| op1 != op2 | op1 is not equal to op2 |
| op1 > op2 | op1 is greater than op2 |
| op1 >= op2 | op1 is greater than or equal to op2 |
| op1 < op2 | op1 is less than op2 |
| op1 <= op2 | op1 is less than or equal to op2 |
| op1 instanceof op2 | object op1 is an instance of class op2 |

*relational operators*

The relational operators test for equality and inequality among two quantities or they test for class membership of an object. They always yield a boolean result (**true** or **false**). Expressions with boolean results can be used in if-statements and while-statements to determine the flow of control. Table A.10 gives Java's relational operators.

In the first three rows of Table A.11, **op1** and **op2** are boolean expressions used as operands. The short circuit *and* operator in **op1 && op2** yields the value **true** if both boolean subexpressions **op1** and **op2** have the value **true**, otherwise it yields the value **false**. However, in contrast to the normal Java policy for evaluation of the operands of an operator (in which both operands of a binary operator are evaluated in left-to-right order before the operator is applied to the values of the operands), Java uses "short circuit evaluation" to find the value of **op1 && op2**. In particular, if **op1** has the value **true**, then the value of **op1 && op2** is determined by finding the value of **op2**, but if **op1** has the value **false**, then the value of **op1 && op2** is **false**, and **op2** is not evaluated. This policy is useful in expressions such as:

*short circuit*
*logical operators*

```
if ( (denominator != 0) && (A[numerator/denominator] >1) ) {
        g.fillOval(Color.green);
}
```

Here, we want to avoid attempting to evaluate a fraction in which the denominator is zero (in order not to throw an **ArithmeticException**). Thus, we need first to verify that the denominator is nonzero, and only afterward do we want to evaluate the fraction using this nonzero denominator. In the boolean short circuit *and* expression

```
(denominator != 0) && (A[numerator/denominator] >1)
```

we first evaluate the left operand (**denominator != 0**), and if its value is **false** (meaning

**Table A.11** Logical
Operators

| Expression | Meaning |
|---|---|
| op1 && op2 | short circuit boolean AND |
| op1 \|\| op2 | short circuit boolean OR |
| ! op1 | boolean NOT |
| op1 ? op2 : op3 | if op1 is true then op2, otherwise op3 |

**Table A.12** Bitwise Operators

| Expression | Function |
|---|---|
| op1 & op2 | bitwise and |
| op1 \| op2 | bitwise or |
| op1 ^ op2 | bitwise xor (exclusive or) |
| ~ op | bitwise complement |
| op1 >> op2 | shift bits of op1 right op2 bit-positions and fill with sign bits on left side |
| op1 << op2 | shift bits of op1 left op2 bit-positions |
| op1 >>> op2 | shift bits of op1 right op2 bit-positions and fill with zero bits on left side |

the denominator is zero), the value of the entire expression becomes **false** without evaluating the right operand of the **&&** operator. Thus, the division by zero in the right operand of **&&** is avoided. However, if (**denominator != 0**) has the value **true**, the value of the entire expression is determined by evaluating the right operand (**A[numerator/denominator] >1**) in which it has already been ascertained that the denominator is nonzero (and thus will not cause an arithmetic zero-division exception to be thrown).

the short circuit OR operator

The evaluation of **op1 || op2** is similar in that if the value of **op1** is **true**, then the value of the entire expression is taken to be **true** without evaluating the right operand **op2**. However, if the value of **op1** is **false**, then the value of the entire expression **op1 || op2** is determined by taking the value of **op2**. This means the value of **op1 || op2** is **true** if either **op1** or **op2** or both are **true**, but in the case **op1** is **true**, **op2** is never evaluated.

In the case of the trinary conditional operator expression **op1 ? op2 : op3**, the boolean expression **op1** is first evaluated, and if its value is **true**, then **op2** is evaluated and its value becomes the value of the entire expression. However, if **op1**'s value is **false**, then **op3** is evaluated and its value becomes the value of the entire expression.

bit-shift operators

Java also has efficient bitwise operators that can be used to shift bits left or right and to perform bitwise logical operations on a sequence of bits. These are summarized in Table A.12.

## A.4 REVIEW QUESTIONS

1. What is the difference between **++x** and **x++** for an **int** variable **x**?
2. What does it mean to say that a binary operator is left associative?
3. In Java, which binary operators are left associative and which are right associative?
4. How can you use parentheses to show the order in which operators are applied to operands in a Java expression that contains no parentheses initially?
5. What kind of values are returned by relational expressions of the form **op1 β op2**, where β is a relational operator?
6. Define the meaning of the short circuit operators in the expressions **op1 && op2** and **op1 || op2**.

## A.4 EXERCISES

1. Place parentheses in the following expression to indicate the order in which operators are applied to operands:

    x = y = z += k[3]++ >= 4 | | a − b − c <= 17 ? (int)−m(h[i].top++) : −−k[3];

2. Is the expression a/b*c equivalent to (a*c)/b or a/(b*c)? Why?

## A.5 Control Flow in Java

**blocks and flow of control**

In Java, *blocks* consist of a sequence of (zero or more) statements grouped within curly braces { and }. Statements within a block are executed one-after-another in sequence, unless the "flow of control" is changed by a "flow of control" statement. This section considers several kinds of Java statements used for flow of control.

**some notation**

Let the notation {s1; s2; . . . sn;} denote a block in Java (i.e., a sequence of statements each terminated by a semicolon and enclosed in curly braces). We will also use the notation **statements;** to denote a sequence of such statements s1; s2; . . . sn; not enclosed in curly braces, and we will let the word **condition** denote a boolean expression (i.e., an expression whose value is one of the two boolean values **true** or **false**).

An example of a basic block, not containing any special control flow statements is

```
{
    int i = 1;                    // declare an integer variable i and initialize it to 1
    int j;                                        // declare an integer variable j

    i = 3*i + 7;                          // an assignment statement that sets i to 10
    i++;                              // an incrementing statement that increments i by 1

    j = (2*i)/4;                           // another assignment that sets j to the value 5

    System.out.println("the value of j = " + j);                          // a statement
                                                           // consisting of a method call
}
```

The statements and declarations in such a basic Java block are executed one after another in top-to-bottom order.

Java control flow statements can be used to alter the normal sequential flow of control in basic blocks.

### Selection Statements

*If-statements* and *switch-statements* are used in Java to select other groups of statements to execute. The most basic form of an if-statement is:

```
if (condition) {
    statements;
}
```

In this if-statement, the condition is first evaluated, and if its value is true, then the statements enclosed in curly braces are executed next. If the value of the condition is false, the statements in braces are not executed. An example of an if-statement is:

```
if (L[i] instanceof ShapeList) {
    L[i].drawList( );
    g.updateWindow( );
    i++;
}
```

compound if-statements

Sometimes it is useful to test a variety of conditions and to execute various subgroups of statements under conditions that apply to them. For this purpose, the previous basic if-statement can be extended by adding else-if and else parts, as shown in the following example:

```
if (gender == male && maritalStatus == married && age >25) {
    insuranceRate = maxDiscountRate;
} else if (gender == female && maritalStatus == married) {
    insuranceRate = middleDiscountRate;
} else if (gender == male && age >25) {
    insuranceRate = lowDiscountRate;
} else if (gender == male && maritalStatus == unmarried && age <=25) {
    insuranceRate = uninsurable;
} else {
    insuranceRate = normalRate;
}
```

The statements following the else-part are executed when all the conditions in the previous if-part and else-if-parts are all false. The statements following an else-if-part are executed when the corresponding condition in the else-if part is true and none of the preceding conditions in the if-part or else-if-parts were true.

Another mechanism for selecting subgroups of statements to execute in various differing cases is the switch-statement. For example, consider:

```
switch (weekday) {
case 1:  System.out.println("Sunday");
         break;
case 2:  System.out.println("Monday");
         break;
case 3:  System.out.println("Tuesday");
         break;
// and so forth
case 7:  System.out.println("Saturday");
         break;
default:
         System.out.println("invalid day number");
}
```

Here, weekday is an integer-valued expression, and the cases numbered 1 through 7 are executed just when the value of weekday matches the integer specified in the case. The default case is executed when the value of weekday does not match any of the specific previous cases. The break statements send control past the end of the right curly brace } at the end of the block, and are required whenever you want to prevent control from flowing to the next case in sequence after the code for a given case has been executed.

## Repetition-Statements

*Repetition-statements* cause a group of enclosed statements (called the *body* of the repetition-statement) to be executed repeatedly if certain conditions are met.

The simplest form of repetition-statement in Java is the *while-statement*, which is of the form:

```
while (condition) {
    statements;
}
```

Here, the condition is evaluated and if the value is true, the statements in the body (inside the curly braces) are executed, following which, control returns to the beginning of the while-statement again. This results in repeatedly testing the condition and executing the statements in the body so long as the condition evaluates to true. The first time the condition evaluates to false, the statements in the body are not executed and control passes to the statement following the closing right curly brace }. For example,

*while-statements*

```
int sum = 0;                           // initialize an integer sum to zero

int i = 1;                             // initialize a counting variable i to 1

while (i <= 10) {                      // for each value of i between 1 and 10
    sum += i*i;                        // add the square of i to the sum
    i++;                               // increment the value of i by 1
}

// finally, print the value of the sum
System.out.println("the sum of the squares from 1 to 10 = " + sum);
```

*for-statements*

A *for-statement* can be used to abbreviate the action of a while-statement, such as the one just given, in which a counting variable, such as i, is first initialized to an initial value and then counts up or down to some final value, and in which the enclosed statements in the body are executed for each distinct value of i that is enumerated. The for-statement equivalent to the preceding while-statement is:

```
for (i = 1; i <= 10; i++) {
    sum += i*i;
}
```

⇓     // is equivalent to

```
i = 1;

while (i <= 10) {
    sum += i*i;
    i++;
}
```

The general format of a for-statement is:

```
for(initialization; test; increment) {
     statements;
}
```

This is equivalent to:

```
initialization;                                          // first perform the initialization

while (test) {                                                     // if the test is true
     statements;                                          // execute the statements
     increment;                                           // perform the increment
}                                                                    // and repeat
```

Another type of repetition statement in Java is the *do-while-statement*. It takes the general form:

```
do {
     statements;
} while (condition);
```

**do-while-statements**

In this case, the boolean **condition** is evaluated after the **statements** have been performed. If the **condition** evaluates to **true**, control returns to the beginning at the line containing "**do {**" and the action repeats. If the **condition** evaluates to **false**, control passes to the next statement after the do-while-statement and does not return to the beginning for another repetition. The statements enclosed in a do-while-statement are always executed at least once, whereas, by contrast, the statements enclosed in a while-statement are never executed whenever the while condition is initially false upon being first evaluated.

## Break-, Continue-, and Return-Statements

**break-statements**

Sometimes it is convenient to be able to terminate the execution of a repetition-statement before all of its expected repetitions have been performed. For example, if you are using a repetition-statement to search through an array to find the first item having a specific property, you might want to exit from the body as soon as you find what you are looking for without wasting the effort to enumerate all the remaining possibilities. You can use a *break-statement* in Java to exit from the middle of any for-, while-, do-while- or switch-statement. For example, you might write:

```
for ( i = 0; i < n; i++ ) {                               // search the array A[0:n−1]
     if (A[i].matchesColor(myColor)) {                    // if A[i]'s color matches, then
          break;                                          // jump out of the for-loop
     }                                                              // because
}                                                         // we found what we are looking for
```

A break-statement exits the innermost for-, while-, do-while-, or switch-statement. If you want to exit a nest of one or more nested for-, while-, do-while-, or switch-statements, you can use a *labeled break-statement.* You label the outermost such statement you wish to exit by preceding it with a label followed by a colon, such as "outerLoop:". Then you use a labeled break-statement, such as "break outerLoop;" to exit the entire nest of statements. An example of a labeled break-statement is given in the following code:

```
boolean notFound = true;

outerLoop:
    for (i = 0; i < Table.height; i++) {
        for (j = 0; j < Table.width; j++) {
            if (Table.itemArray[i][j] == searchItem) {
                notFound = false;
                break outerLoop;
            }
        }
    }

if (notFound) {
    throw new UnsuccessfulSearchException( );
}
```

When encountered in the middle of a loop's body, a *continue-statement* causes control to skip past the remaining statements in the loop and to evaluate the loop's boolean loop test condition. This implies that a continue-statement causes control to return to the beginning of a for-loop or a while-loop without executing the remaining statements inside the loop. This is often convenient when you are treating cases inside a loop and a particular case encountered does not need to be processed by the remainder of the loop's contents. For example, you might write:

**continue-statements**

```
while ( ! atEndOfList( ) ) {
    item = myList.getNextItem( );
    if (item.isSkippable( ) ) {
        continue;                          // go get the next item to process
    }
    // ... code to process cases for non-skippable items
}
```

**return-statements**

When you are writing methods in Java, the computation for the method may terminate in the middle of the method's statement block, and you may want to return control to the method's caller (perhaps at the same time giving the value to be returned by the method, in case the method is required to return a value). The Java *return-statement* is used for this purpose. For example, you might write:

```
     boolean isPrime(int n) {                  // suppose that n is a positive integer
         if (n < 3) {
             return true;                       // 1 and 2 are considered to be primes
         } else if (n%2 == 0) {                          // otherwise, if n is even
5            return false;                                        // it is not prime
         }


                               // in all other cases, try dividing by divisors that are odd numbers
                                                // between 3 and the square root of n
10
         int s = (int)Math.floor(Math.sqrt(n));
         int i;

         for (i = 3; i <= s; i += 2) {          // try odd divisors between 3 and sqrt(n)
15           if ( n%i == 0 ) {                           // if n is evenly divisible by any
                 return false;                          // such odd divisor, n is not prime
             }                                                  // so return false as the
         }                                          // value of the isPrime method

20       return true;                  // if no such odd divisor divided into n evenly
                                                  // then n was a prime, so return true
     }
```

In this method, the statement **return false;** on line 16 exits from the method and returns the boolean value **false** immediately after a divisor i has been found that divides into n evenly, because n cannot be a prime number if it has a divisor (which is neither itself nor 1) that divides into it evenly.

**compatible return types required**

To return a value from a method that is required to return a value of type T, you must always use a statement of the form **return expr;** where **expr** is an expression having a value of type T. The Java compiler checks the compatibility of the return type of **expr** with the type required to be returned by the method, and refuses to compile methods where inconsistent return types have been given.

## A.5 REVIEW QUESTIONS

1. What is a repetition-statement in Java? Name three kinds of repetition-statements that use three distinct kinds of Java reserved words.
2. If you are inside the body of a while-statement and you want to exit the body and afterward execute the next statement in sequence following the while-statement's body, what Java statement could you use to accomplish this?
3. How is the Java word **default** used in the body of a Java switch-statement?
4. In Java, how could you exit from the body of a while-statement that is inside the body of a for-statement, returning to the outer for-statement to continue executing it with the next for-variable value in its sequence?

## A.5  EXERCISES

1. Give a while-statement that is equivalent to the following for-statement:

```
int i;
for (i = 3; i < n; i += 5) {
    System.out.println(i);
}
```

2. Rewrite the following statements using a do-while-statement instead of a while-statement to eliminate the double method invocation of theObject.firstMethod();.

```
theObject.firstMethod();
while (theObject.xCoordinate < maxValue) {
    theObject.firstMethod();
}
```

## A.6  Classes, Methods, and Objects in Java

Java is a language suited for *object-oriented programming* (OOP). Roughly speaking, an *object* is an entity that is created during the running of a program. Each object is created as an *instance* of a template specified by its *class*. The class definition, giving the template for building object instances, can bundle together some data components that describe an object's local state together with some behavioral components, called *methods*, that operate on the local data to give the object its characteristic behaviors. Thus objects are instances of classes, which, in turn, are templates specifying the data state and behaviors common to all of the instances of the class.

classes, objects, and methods

It is possible to define a new class S to be a *subclass* of a given class P, in which case P is said to be the *parent* of subclass S. Such classes and subclasses can participate in a *class hierarchy* (that works like a family tree) in which they *inherit* data components and methods from their immediate parents (and also from remote ancestors one or more generations removed). Even though a given subclass inherits a named method, such as a draw( ) method, from an ancestor class, it can replace the inherited meaning of this method with its own local variation by *overriding* the inherited method. By overriding inherited methods, individual subclasses provide customized behaviors giving the descendants of a common ancestor class some local variations in behavior that can be useful for organizing the behaviors of related sets of entities in a clean, careful fashion. Chapter 2 develops these concepts gradually, using the specific example of a Java applet that draws various shapes such as ovals, rectangles, and rounded rectangles, which are all descendants of a common abstract ancestor shape class.

class hierarchies, inheritance, and overriding

Classes and objects are also useful for providing the mechanisms needed to implement information hiding, modularity, and interfaces. Various access modifiers can be specified in a class definition that make the entities internal to the class invisible to outside users, or that make them selectively visible or invisible to descendant classes in the class hierarchy. One reason for wanting to hide the internal details of a class from outside view is to ensure that objects that are instances of the class are tamperproof, in the sense that outside users cannot interfere with the operation of their internal mechanisms—this being called *information hiding*.

information hiding, modularity, and interfaces

In addition, when objects allow external users to interact with them only in certain carefully managed ways through their external *interfaces*, while hiding their internal representations from external view, it makes it possible to program applications in a clean, modular fashion that allows for later replacement of the internal data representations, when required for purposes of efficiency improvement, without having to change code in the external users of the class. This way of organizing a large software system, called modular programming, or, sometimes, data encapsulation, enhances the ease of maintaining the software. (It is known that software maintenance is a major expense item in the lifecycle of large software systems.) Chapter 5 develops the ideas of modularity and data abstraction more thoroughly and elaborates on the concepts touched on only briefly in this section.

This section has given only a brief general overview of classes, objects, and interfaces. Chapters 2 and 5 introduce these concepts and the related Java notations in a more thorough fashion.

## A.6 REVIEW QUESTIONS

1. What is the difference between a Java class and an object that is an instance of that class?
2. What does it mean to say that a given class is a subclass of another in Java?
3. What does it mean to say that a set of Java classes form a class hierarchy?
4. What is the meaning of inheritance in a Java class hierarchy?
5. What does it mean to say that a method defined in a particular Java class overrides an identically named method in an ancestor class?
6. What is information-hiding?

## A.6 EXERCISE

1. List some benefits of organizing a large software system into modules that have well-defined interfaces accessible to outside users, and that have their internal details of operation hidden.

## A.7　Importing Packages in Java

In Java, a *package* is a named collection of class definitions. To use the predefined classes in the packages in Java's class library, you must first *import* the class or package you need to use. The *import statements* must appear first in your program before any class definitions you give.

*importing math functions*　For example, to use mathematical functions such as the square root method (sqrt(x)) or the floor method (floor(x)), you need to access the Math class that is defined in the java.lang package. To do this, you can write:

```
import java.lang.Math;                          // import mathematical functions
```

at the beginning of your program.

using wild-card characters

As another example, to be able to write lines of text to the default output window, using the print( ) or println( ) methods, you must first import input/output classes specified in the package java.io. You can use the star (*) character as a "wild card" character to import all classes in the java.io package by writing the following import statement:

    import java.io.*;                                    // import input/output operations

As a final example, to be able to create a new Java applet class as a subclass of the predefined Applet class, you must first import the Java Applet class, using the following import statement:

    import java.applet.Applet;

Here, java.applet is a package that contains a specific class named Applet. You would ordinarily begin a Java program specifying an applet, such as MyApplet, which subsequently uses java.io and Math capabilities, in the following way:

```
    |    import java.applet.Applet;
    |    import java.io.*;
    |    import java.lang.Math;
    |
 5  |    public class MyApplet extends Applet {
    |
    |                                      // here define the data fields for your applet
    |
    |                                      // next define the methods for your applet
10  |
    |    }
```

This is the fundamental template for writing a Java applet that is used throughout the book.

## A.7 REVIEW QUESTIONS

1. What is a package in Java?
2. How do you get access to the classes in Java's library of predefined classes?
3. What does it mean to place the statement import java.lang.Math; as the first statement in a Java program?
4. What is a wild-card character? Give an example of how to use one.

## A.7 EXERCISE

1. Give a template for defining a new applet called SimpleApplet that uses some Java Math methods, such as sqrt(x), and that uses some Java input-output methods, such as System.out.print("this message");.

### A.8 Comments in Java

Throughout this book we use three styles of Java comments: (1) single-line comments, (2) multiline comments, and (3) Javadoc comments.

Single-line comments begin with two consecutive slashes and extend up to the end of the line. Such comments are terminated automatically at the end of the line. For example

```
j += i*i;                              // a comment that ends at the end of this line
```

We use right justified, single-line comments in color in the programs in this book to explain *what* the Java code to the left does or *how* the Java code to the left works. We use single-line comments in black that precede a section of code to state the *goal* or *purpose* to be achieved by that code. For example, in the code:

```
// compute the center of the rectangle, myRect
center.x = myRect.x + myRect.width/2;     // compute center's x coordinate
center.y = myRect.y + myRect.height/2;    // compute center's y coordinate
```

"*// compute the center of the rectangle, myRect*" is a goal comment, and the other comments explain *what* the code to their left does. Goal comments function like topics in an outline of a story that are elaborated into the actual text of the story.

multiline comments

Multiline comments begin with /* and end with */. Sometimes, such multiline comments surround a section of explanatory or descriptive text that is not appropriate to write in actual Java program syntax. An example of a multiline comment is:

```
/*
 *    The following applet draws shapes when the mouse is dragged.
 *    The shapes include ovals, rectangles, and rounded rectangles.
 *    Shapes can be filled with the colors blue, yellow and red, or they
 *    can be hollow shapes that are drawn as "wire frame" shapes.
 */
```

Javadoc comments

Finally, a comment that begins with /** and ends with */ surrounds a *Javadoc comment*. Such comments are placed immediately before declarations in a Java program. A tool called **Javadoc** extracts them and automatically creates some **HTML** documentation for the program.

### A.8 REVIEW QUESTIONS

1. What is a Javadoc comment? Give an example.
2. What characters indicate that a comment begins at a given place and extends to the end of the line, but not beyond?
3. How can you make a region of text that extends over several lines into a comment?
4. What form do goal comments take in this book?

## A.8 EXERCISE

1. Suppose you have a table of values that are not given in Java syntax and you would like to include this table in a Java comment at the beginning of an applet. What Java comment type might you use to accompish this?

## References for Further Study

A good book for gaining a quick but thorough understanding of the Java programming language is:

basics of Java

> Arnold, Ken and Gosling, James, *The Java™ Programming Language*. Addison-Wesley, Reading, MA (1996).

Some references on the Java class libraries are:

> Chan, Patrick, and Lee, Rosanna, *The Java™ Class Libraries: An Annotated Reference*. Addison-Wesley, Reading, MA (1997).

Java Class Libraries

> Gosling, James, Yellin, Frank, et al, *The Java™ Application Programming Interface, Vol. 1: Core Packages, and Vol. 2: Window Toolkit and Applets*. Addison-Wesley, Reading, MA (1996).

A good tutorial on object-oriented programming in Java is:

a good tutorial

> Campione, Mary, and Walrath, Kathy, *The Java™ Tutorial: Object-Oriented Programming for the Internet*. Addison-Wesley, Reading, MA (1996).

# The Language of Efficiency

## B.1   Introduction and Motivation

*the use of mathematics in the exact sciences*

In the exact sciences, precise scientific laws are discovered and are expressed in the language of mathematics. In physics, for example, Newton's second law, $F = ma$, states that if you apply a force, $F$, to an object of mass, $m$, in a frictionless medium (such as outer space), it will respond to the force by accelerating at rate, $a$, in the direction that the force is applied.

Some areas of computer science constitute an exact mathematical science. In particular, some parts of its subject matter—within the subfield of algorithms and data structures—have been found to obey certain precisely stated mathematical laws. These laws have been formulated using techniques of mathematical analysis.

*the importance of knowing about precise laws of computer science*

It is important for you to know some of the major results that have been discovered by computer scientists who have analyzed algorithms and data structures over the years. In this way you will be equipped with a knowledge of the most efficient ways to solve certain widely encountered algorithmic problems and you can make use of the

451

quantitative laws that characterize the known efficiencies. Also, knowledge of quantitative laws will help you perform tradeoff analyses, in the event that you have to choose among several solutions to a problem.

Eventually, at some future time in your computer science career, it is important for you to learn how to perform at least elementary and simple analyses of algorithms on your own. In developing software systems, many of the algorithms and data structures used have simple forms that are susceptible to straightforward analysis. If you can analyze the performance of even the simplest algorithms you will have gained a widely useful skill that can significantly improve your ability to develop high-quality software solutions.

*developing your own ability to analyze algorithms*

## Plan for the Appendix

We begin by asking, "What do we use for a yardstick?" That is, exactly how can we characterize and measure the performance of a given algorithm, A, when this algorithm could be expressed in many different programming languages and could be executed on many different kinds of computers—some fast and some slow? Measuring the wall clock time taken by algorithm A when it executes on a given computer might not be a very meaningful way to characterize A's essential performance characteristics. So what can we do to devise a way of characterizing A's essential performance properties when hard performance measures, such as wall clock time, will vary significantly when we use different computers, compilers, and programming languages for expressing and running A?

This leads to an introduction to O-notation, pronounced "Oh-notation" (or sometimes, "big-Oh-notation," since there is also something called "little-Oh-notation"). O-notation gives us a language for talking about the comparative efficiency of algorithms. A key goal for the appendix is to help you develop an intuition for the meaning of this language, which is commonly used by computer scientists. The objective is to master the intuition behind O-notation sufficiently so that you can understand what computer scientists mean when they say things like, "Since this search algorithm runs in time $O(\log n)$, it is better than that other one which is only an $O(n)$ algorithm." We will also learn about various common categories of possible algorithm efficiencies characterized by their O-notations.

*using O-notation to compare efficiencies of algorithms*

By the end of the appendix, you should be able to understand and appreciate the intuitive meaning of O-notation sufficiently well that you can use it to help you identify which algorithms are of high-quality and which are of poor-quality in relation to the solution of given programming problems. We will also cover some skills for manipulating O-notation that are helpful to master so that you will know how to use easy short cuts to help you know the simplest O-notation that is commonly used.

We close our discussion by addressing the topic, "What O-notation doesn't tell you." We learn that for small problem sizes, the conclusions based on analyses of O-notation don't hold, and we investigate what other considerations apply in such cases.

*some limitations*

## B.2 What Do We Use for a Yardstick?

### LEARNING OBJECTIVES

1. To learn why data giving raw measurements of algorithm performance cannot be used to compare algorithms.
2. To understand how equations describing the resource consumption patterns of algorithms stay in the same family, even though computers, compilers, and languages may change.
3. To see how the dominant term of the running time equation accounts for most of an algorithm's running time for large problem sizes.

*the problem of measurement*

We start by posing the question, "What do we use for a yardstick?"—meaning how can we measure and compare algorithms meaningfully when the same algorithm will run at different speeds and will require different amounts of space when run on different computers or when implemented in different programming languages?

*looking at selection sorting*

It helps to reason with a specific example. Consider the selection sorting algorithm given in Program B.1. Table B.2 presents some running times that might typically be used by this algorithm to sort an array of 2000 integers on different computers. As expected, the selection sorting algorithm runs faster on more powerful computers.

*benchmarks*

In fact, running the same algorithm on different computers is sometimes used as a way of comparing the computers' relative speeds. A program used for this purpose is called a *benchmark*. Computer magazines such as *Byte* frequently run batteries of benchmark programs on new models of computers to help their readers understand the

```
    |    void SelectionSort( int[ ] A) {              // sorts an array of integers, A,
    |                                                  // into increasing order
    |        int   maxPosition, temp, i, j;
    |
 5  |        for (i = A.length − 1; i > 0; i−− ) {     // for each i in 1:A.length − 1
    |                                                  // in decreasing order of i
    |            maxPosition = i;
    |
    |            for( j = 0;  j  <  i;  j++) {
10  |
    |                if (A[j] > A[maxPosition]) {      // find the position, maxPosition, of
    |                    maxPosition = j;              // the largest integer in A[0:i]
    |                }                                 // then exchange
    |                                                  // A[i] and A[maxPosition]
15  |            }
    |
    |            // exchange A[i] and A[maxPosition]
    |            temp = A[i]; A[i] = A[maxPosition]; A[maxPosition] = temp;
    |
20  |        }
    |    }
```

**Program B.1** Selection Sorting Algorithm for Sorting an Integer Array **A**

| Type of Computer | Time |
|---|---|
| Home computer | 51.915 |
| Desktop computer | 11.508 |
| Minicomputer | 2.382 |
| Mainframe computer | 0.431 |
| Supercomputer | 0.087 |

**Table B.2** Running Times in Seconds to Sort an Array of 2000 Integers

computers' performance. For example, a frequently used benchmark program is the *Sieve of Eratosthenes*, which is a program that computes prime numbers.

In addition to changing according to which computer is used, running times are also affected by the programming language used to express the algorithm. Even if a single programming language such as Java is used, different Java compilers implemented by different vendors might compile the same Java program into different sequences of Java bytecodes or native machine instructions, some of which might execute faster than others.

*the effect of using different compilers*

With all of these sources of possible variation—different computers, different programming languages, and different compilers—how can we use any of the performance numbers we measure to decide which algorithms are the best? Answer: We can't. We are forced to do something else instead.

*resource consumption patterns*

What we can observe is that algorithms usually consume resources (such as time and space) in some fashion that depends on the size of the problem they solve. Usually, though not always, the bigger the size of the problem that an algorithm solves, the more resources it consumes.

In what follows, let's agree to use the integer variable, $n$, to stand for the size of a problem. For instance, $n$ could be the length of a list that an algorithm searches, or the number of nodes in a tree that an algorithm prints, or the number of items in an array that an algorithm sorts into descending order.

When we run a particular algorithm, A, such as **SelectionSort**, written in a particular programming language, such as Java, on a particular computer using a particular compiler—and we measure the time it takes to run algorithm A on problems of various sizes, $n$, we usually get a set of timing measures that lie on a curve, and we can usually find an equation that fits the curve.

| Array Size $n$ | Home Computer | Desktop Computer |
|---|---|---|
| 125 | 12.5 | 2.8 |
| 250 | 49.3 | 11.0 |
| 500 | 195.8 | 43.4 |
| 1000 | 780.3 | 172.9 |
| 2000 | 3114.9 | 690.5 |

**Table B.3** SelectionSort Running Times in Milliseconds on Two Types of Computers

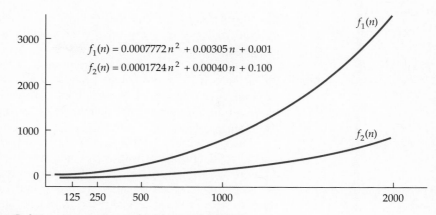

**Figure B.4** Two Curves Fitting the Data in Table B.3

For example, the **SelectionSort** algorithm, given in Program B.1, has two sequences of running times when it is run on two different computers—a home computer and a desktop computer, as shown in Table B.3. If we plot these numbers on a graph and try to fit curves to them, we find that they lie on two curves, each of which has the form $f(n) = an^2 + bn + c$. The difference between the two curves is that they have different constants ($a$, $b$, and $c$). Figure B.4 plots these two curves. The equations for these two curves are given in Eqs. B.1, where $f_1(n)$ fits the home computer data in Table B.3 and $f_2(n)$ fits the desktop computer data.

*fitting curves to the data*

$$f_1(n) = 0.0007772\ n^2 + 0.00305\ n + 0.001$$
$$f_2(n) = 0.0001724\ n^2 + 0.00040\ n + 0.100$$

(B.1)

A function of the form, $f(n) = an^2 + bn + c$, is called a *quadratic function of n* (because the highest power of $n$ in it is $n^2$). What we have discovered so far is that when we run the **SelectionSort** algorithm (given in Program B.1) on two different computers, the time taken in both cases is a quadratic function of the size, $n$, of the array A[0:n−1] to be sorted.

*quadratic functions*

It turns out that we have taken the first steps toward discovering something fundamental. If we were to continue to implement selection sorting algorithms and to measure their performance using different computers, languages, and compilers, we would discover that no matter what computer we ran the selection sorting algorithm on—whether it is a blazing fast supercomputer or a pokey home computer—the amount of time it consumed would be a quadratic function of the size of the array that is sorted.

*a common pattern of resource consumption*

Another way of saying this is that when you run the same selection sorting algorithm on a variety of different computers of differing speeds, or you express the algorithm in different programming languages, or you compile the program for the algorithm with different compilers—you get a family of identically shaped quadratic curves of the form, $f(n) = an^2 + bn + c$, which fit the data for the measured running times as a function of the problem size, $n$. Each distinct curve in this family of quadratic curves has its own special coefficients ($a$, $b$, $c$) associated with a particular computer, language, and compiler used.

So even though the particular running time measurements for selection sort vary under changing circumstances, what stays the same is the *shape of the curve* that expresses the running time as a function of the problem size. That is, all of the curves plotting running time versus problem size share the shape of the quadratic function, $f(n) = an^2 + bn + c$.

The generalization we are heading toward is this: When we analyze the running time of an algorithm, we will try to come up with the general shape of the curve that characterizes its running time as a function of the problem size. We won't care what the constants of proportionality are (i.e., what the coefficients such as $a$, $b$, $c$ are), since these can change depending on the particular details of the computer, language, or compiler used. But we will care a great deal about general shape of the curve that relates the resources consumed (such as running time or running space needed) to the size of the problem solved.

It turns out that running times for different algorithms fall into different *complexity classes*. Each complexity class is characterized by a different family of curves. All of the curves in a given complexity class share the same basic shape. This shared shape is characterized by an equation that gives running times as a function of problem size. Different curves in the family are special cases of this equation for the given complexity class in which only the constants (or coefficients) are different. You could say, then, that the *complexity class* for the running time of the selection sorting algorithm is *quadratic*, since the function, $f(n) = an^2 + bn + c$, that gives the running time $f(n)$ as a function of the problem size, $n$, is a quadratic function.

In what follows, we will introduce O-notation. This notation is used by computer scientists for talking about the complexity classes of algorithms. In giving the O-notation for the quadratic function, $f(n) = an^2 + bn + c$, we will say that $f(n)$ is $O(n^2)$—pronounced "$f$ of $n$ is Oh of $n$ squared." In arriving at the O-notation for $an^2 + bn + c$, we first focus on the dominant term, $an^2$, and ignore the lesser terms, $bn + c$. (The dominant term is the one that grows the fastest when $n$ grows.) Then we ignore the coefficient (or constant of proportionality), $a$. Thus $O(an^2 + bn + c)$ simplifies first to $O(an^2)$—by throwing away all but the dominant term, $an^2$—and $O(an^2)$ then simplifies to $O(n^2)$—by throwing away the coefficient (or constant of proportionality) $a$. Thus $O(n^2)$ stands for the class of functions, $f(n)$, whose dominant terms are quadratic (of the form $an^2$). When we say that the running time of an algorithm is $O(n^2)$, it simply means that the dominant term in its running time equation is of the form $an^2$. (It may have lesser terms that grow more slowly than the quadratic term, but for large problem sizes, the running times are dominated by the effect of the quadratic term, so these lesser terms are of lesser significance, and they can be ignored for simplicity.)

Let's explore, for a moment, why it might make sense to focus on the dominant term in $an^2 + bn + c$, and to ignore the lesser terms. Study the numbers in Table B.5. You can see that, for problem sizes of $n = 250$ or greater, over 98 percent of the value of $f(n)$ comes from the dominant term $an^2$. The lesser terms, $bn + c$, contribute very little, even though the coefficient $c$ is 250 times bigger than the coefficient $b$, and

*complexity classes*

*introducing the language of O-notation*

*dominant terms*

**Table B.5** Percentage Contribution of $n^2$ Term to the Total

| $f(n) = an^2 + bn + c$ where $a = 0.0001724$, $b = 0.0004$ and $c = 0.1$ | | | |
|---|---|---|---|
| $n$ | $f(n)$ | $an^2$ | $n^2$-term as % of total |
| 125 | 2.8 | 2.7 | 94.7 |
| 250 | 11.0 | 10.8 | 98.2 |
| 500 | 43.4 | 43.1 | 99.3 |
| 1000 | 172.9 | 172.4 | 99.7 |
| 2000 | 690.5 | 689.6 | 99.9 |

even though $b$ is more than twice the coefficient $a$. The rationale for focusing on the dominant term, then, is that since, for big problems, the dominant term in $f(n)$ usually accounts for most of $f(n)$'s value, we can simplify our considerations without losing too much accuracy by ignoring the contribution of the lower terms.

In O-notation, we also ignore the constant of proportionality, $a$, on the dominant term, $an^2$, since our aim is to discover the general family of growth curves characterizing a given algorithm's resource consumption. We know that the exact resource consumption curves fitting data measured on different computers will have differing constants of proportionality, $a$, associated with their dominant terms, but we are trying to ignore differences in speeds of the different computers, and to identify the common resource consumption growth pattern associated with the algorithm itself. To do this, we have to ignore the constant of proportionality, $a$.

*ignoring the constant of proportionality*

You will see in Section B.4 how the formal definition of O-notation is constructed so as to achieve three important properties: (1) focusing on the dominant term for large problem sizes, (2) ignoring the lesser terms and ignoring what happens on small problems, and (3) ignoring the constant of proportionality.

*a road map*

Now let's step back for a moment and see where we are going. We are going to introduce O-notation as the solution to the problem of finding a suitable yardstick to use to compare the efficiency of algorithms. In the next section, before defining O-notation formally, we are going to try to gain an intuitive insight into it—so you will get the "feeling" for it, so-to-speak, before you are introduced to its formal definition. Then in Section B.4, we will present the formal definition of O-notation. We will also introduce a few rules for manipulating it, and we will give you some practice using them.

## B.2 REVIEW QUESTIONS

1. What is meant by the question, "What do we use for a yardstick?"
2. When an algorithm is written in different programming languages and is executed on different computers, what measures of the algorithm's performance can be expected to change? What facts or relations about the algorithm's performance remain unchanged?
3. What is the dominant term in the running time equation for an algorithm?

4. Why might we be justified in focusing on the behavior of the dominant term in a running time equation and in ignoring the contributions of the lesser terms?

## B.2 EXERCISE

1. Two other algorithms for **SelectionSort** are given in Appendix C as Programs C.29 and C.35. One is recursive and the other is iterative. They both differ from the version of **SelectionSort** given as Program B.1. Table C.36 gives their running times. Do you suppose that these other versions of **SelectionSort** have quadratic running times characterized by the equation, $f(n) = an^2 + bn + c$, (for suitable constants $a$, $b$, and $c$)? Try to fit curves to the data in Table C.36 by choosing values for the constants $a$, $b$, and $c$. Can you get a clean fit (say to within a tenth of a millisecond)? Compare your results with Eqs. B.1. What does this tell you about the basic resource consumption laws governing selection sorting algorithms? Is it important whether they are expressed iteratively or recursively, or with or without the use of for-statements, while-statements, or do-while–statements in Java?

### B.3   The Intuition Behind O-Notation

## LEARNING OBJECTIVES

1. To develop intuition for the meaning of O-notation by exploring patterns in some data.
2. To learn how O-notation is used by computer scientists to refer to the performance properties of algorithms.

*learning a new temperature scale*

Learning about O-notation is a bit like learning about a new temperature scale. For example, if you were brought up using Fahrenheit temperatures, have you ever tried to learn the Celsius temperature scale (or vice versa)? It doesn't do to memorize temperature conversion formulas between Celsius degrees (C°) and Fahrenheit degrees (F°) such as those given in Eqs. B.2:

$$C° = \frac{5}{9}\left(F° - 32\right) \quad \text{or} \quad F° = \frac{9}{5}C° + 32 \tag{B.2}$$

Knowing the conversion formula isn't the same as knowing the intuition behind the temperature scale. Instead, to develop intuition, you have to acquaint yourself with the temperatures on the new scale you are learning for lots of familiar situations. For example, consider the temperature situations given in Table B.6. If you spend time studying a table such as this, and you practice using it to describe temperatures on the new scale you are trying to learn, you will gradually develop confidence that you "have a feeling" for the new scale.

**Table B.6** Approximately Equal Temperature Situations in C° and F°

| Common Temperature Situations | Celsius | Fahrenheit |
|---|---|---|
| Boiling water | 100° | 212° |
| Seriously high fever | 40° | 104° |
| Mild fever | 37.3° | 99.2° |
| Normal body temperature | 37° | 98.6° |
| Extremely hot summer day | 35° | 95° |
| Warm summer day | 30° | 86° |
| Pleasant spring day | 24° | 75° |
| Normal room temperature | 22° | 72° |
| Slightly cool room temperature | 20° | 68° |
| Cold rainy day in fall | 7° | 45° |
| Freezing (rain just turns to snow) | 0° | 32° |
| Severe cold | −18° | 0° |
| Frostbite temperature | −28° | −18° |

developing intuition for Celsius temperatures

Let's assume you are trying to learn the Celsius scale. If you go into a room that seems a little warm and stuffy, you might try to guess the Celsius temperature by saying to yourself, "Let's see, this room temperature is about 24° C." If everybody in the room is breaking out in sweat, you might guess something like, "It's hot enough in here to be about 27° C." If you have a way of confirming your guesses and correcting them, and you practice until you can make reasonably close guesses, you will begin to feel that you have developed an intuition for Celsius temperatures.

developing intuition for O-notation

Now let's try to learn the intuition behind a few of the common complexity classes used in analysis of algorithms. We'll also try to learn the language commonly heard among computer scientists when they use O-notation to describe algorithmic complexity. The goal, by the end of this section, is for you to begin to be confident that you have the "feeling" for what O-notation means.

As a starting point, let's look at Table B.7, which gives some adjective names and the corresponding O-notation for seven common complexity classes. In a moment, we will study data aimed at helping you develop a feeling for what these different com-

**Table B.7** Some Common Complexity Classes

| Adjective Name | O-Notation |
|---|---|
| Constant | $O(1)$ |
| Logarithmic | $O(\log n)$ |
| Linear | $O(n)$ |
| $n \log n$ | $O(n \log n)$ |
| Quadratic | $O(n^2)$ |
| Cubic | $O(n^3)$ |
| Exponential | $O(2^n)$ |
| Exponential | $O(10^n)$ |

plexity classes imply. But before doing that, let's look at one example of the way computer scientists commonly talk about these complexity classes in everyday speech.

some eavesdropping

Dropping in on a conversation, we might overhear one computer scientist say to another, "Well, since **SelectionSort** runs in quadratic time, it ought to be fast enough for this sorting application." Suppose a second computer scientist replies, "Yes, you are probably correct, but why not be safe and use an $O(n \log n)$ sorting algorithm such as **HeapSort**? That way, your system might be free from the risk of sluggish response times, if the problem sizes get too big."

what does $O(n^2)$ mean?

Instead of using the phrase, "**SelectionSort** runs in quadratic time," the first computer scientist could equally well have said, "**SelectionSort** runs in time $O(n^2)$." (When spoken, $O(n^2)$ sounds like "Oh of en squared.") What is meant by this? The answer is that the first scientist is claiming that **SelectionSort** runs in an amount of time no greater than $n^2$ times some constant of proportionality, provided the problem sizes are big enough.

what does $O(n \log n)$ mean?

When the second scientist said, "Why not be safe and use an $O(n \log n)$ sorting algorithm such as **HeapSort**?" (where $O(n \log n)$ is spoken as, "Oh of en log en"), the second scientist was asserting that, for suitably large problems, the **HeapSort** algorithm runs in an amount of time bounded above by a constant times $n \log n$. We'll see in a moment why $O(n \log n)$ algorithms can be preferable to $O(n^2)$ algorithms.

Now let's look at some data derived from a hypothetical situation. Suppose we have an algorithm called algorithm A, which is being executed on a computer that can perform one step of this algorithm each microsecond. (In effect, we can imagine that this computer operates at a speed of one MIP, where a MIP = a million instructions per second, and where each instruction performs one step of algorithm A.) Suppose that the number of steps required by algorithm A to solve a problem of size $n$ is given by $f(n)$. We might be interested in the number of microseconds it takes for algorithm A to compute its solution for various values of the problem size $n$ and various $f(n)$. Table B.8 gives examples of such values.

an imaginary computer

translating these results into familiar time units

We need to translate the microsecond values in Table B.8 into familiar time units to get a feeling for what the data are telling us. For instance, given that there are $3.15 \times 10^{13}$ microseconds in a year, if algorithm A takes $2^n$ steps to solve a prob-

| Algorithm A stops in $f(n)$ microseconds | | | | |
|---|---|---|---|---|
| $f(n)$ | $n = 2$ | $n = 16$ | $n = 256$ | $n = 1024$ | $n = 1048576$ |
| 1 | 1 | 1 | 1 | $1.00 \times 10^0$ | $1.00 \times 10^0$ |
| $\log_2 n$ | 1 | 4 | 8 | $1.00 \times 10^1$ | $2.00 \times 10^1$ |
| $n$ | 2 | $1.6 \times 10^1$ | $2.56 \times 10^2$ | $1.02 \times 10^3$ | $1.05 \times 10^6$ |
| $n \log_2 n$ | 2 | $6.4 \times 10^1$ | $2.05 \times 10^3$ | $1.02 \times 10^4$ | $2.10 \times 10^7$ |
| $n^2$ | 4 | $2.56 \times 10^2$ | $6.55 \times 10^4$ | $1.05 \times 10^6$ | $1.10 \times 10^{12}$ |
| $n^3$ | 8 | $4.10 \times 10^3$ | $1.68 \times 10^7$ | $1.07 \times 10^9$ | $1.15 \times 10^{18}$ |
| $2^n$ | 4 | $6.55 \times 10^4$ | $1.16 \times 10^{77}$ | $1.80 \times 10^{308}$ | $6.74 \times 10^{315652}$ |

**Table B.8** Running Times for Different Complexity Classes

lem of size $n = 256$, then it takes $2^{256} = 1.16 \times 10^{77}$ microseconds, which translates into $3.7 \times 10^{63}$ years. By the way, that's a lot of years. It is estimated that the sun will burn out in five billion years (i.e., $5 \times 10^9$ years) after it exhausts its fuel. Thus, if you start a computation to compute the answer to a problem of size $n = 256$, which is going to take $2^n$ steps at one microsecond per step, the sun will burn out long before your computation finishes. (Exercise B.3.1 asks you to find the largest size problem that could be solved before the sun burns out if the problem requires $2^n$ microseconds to find its solution.)

In Table B.9, where it was meaningful to do so, we have translated the microsecond values given in Table B.8 into time units that are easier to interpret. Let's draw a few conclusions from the data. First, we can conclude that if the problem size is small, say $n \leq 16$, then the complexity class of $f(n)$ might not matter very much, since algorithm A finishes in under a tenth of a second for all the different $f(n)$. However, as soon as the problem size gets medium large, say $n = 1024$, then algorithms that are no more complex than $n^2$ finish in a second or less and could still be considered useful. But algorithms as complex as $n^3$ begin to take inconveniently long, and algorithms as complex as $2^n$ take way too long to be of any practical use. For problems of large size, such as $n = 1,048,576$, the difference between $n \log_2 n$ algorithms, which take 21 seconds, and $n^2$ algorithms, which take 1.8 weeks is astonishing. (See Exercise B.3.2 for a practical situation in which this difference is highly significant.) Another conclusion you can draw from studying Table B.9 is that exponential algorithms, such as those that take $2^n$ steps, tend to take a disastrously long time for all but small problems.

*drawing a few conclusions*

Let's continue to build intuition by taking another point of view. (Changing points of view, or looking at something "from another angle" so-to-speak, is often a good way to build more intuition and understanding.) Let's do this by asking an inverse question. Suppose again that $n$ is the problem size and that algorithm A takes exactly $f(n)$ steps, at one microsecond per step, to finish its task, where $f(n)$ is one of the functions in Table B.8. Now we can ask: How big can $n$ be if we expect the computation for algorithm A to terminate before a year (a week, or a day) has expired?

*changing points of view*

| $f(n)$ | $n = 2$ | $n = 16$ | $n = 256$ | $n = 1024$ | $n = 1048576$ |
|---|---|---|---|---|---|
| 1 | 1 µsec* | 1 µsec | 1 µsec | 1 µsec | 1 µsec |
| $\log_2 n$ | 1 µsec | 4 µsecs | 8 µsecs | 10 µsecs | 20 µsecs |
| $n$ | 2 µsecs | 16 µsecs | 256 µsecs | 1.02 msecs | 1.05 secs |
| $n \log_2 n$ | 2 µsecs | 64 µsecs | 2.05 msecs | 10.2 msecs | 21 secs |
| $n^2$ | 4 µsecs | 25.6 µsecs | 65.5 msecs | 1.05 secs | 1.8 wks |
| $n^3$ | 8 µsecs | 4.1 msecs | 16.8 secs | 17.9 mins | 36,559 yrs |
| $2^n$ | 4 µsecs | 65.5 msecs | $3.7 \times 10^{63}$ yrs | $5.7 \times 10^{294}$ yrs | $2.1 \times 10^{315639}$ yrs |

* 1 µsec = one microsecond = one millionth of a second; 1 msec = one millisecond = one thousandth of a second; sec = one second; min = one minute; wk = one week; and yr = one year.

**Table B.9** Running Times for Algorithm A in Different Time Units

| Number of steps is | T = 1 min | T = 1 hr | T = 1 day | T = 1 wk | T = 1 yr |
|---|---|---|---|---|---|
| $n$ | $6 \times 10^7$ | $3.6 \times 10^9$ | $8.64 \times 10^{10}$ | $6.05 \times 10^{11}$ | $3.15 \times 10^{13}$ |
| $n \log_2 n$ | $2.8 \times 10^6$ | $1.3 \times 10^8$ | $2.75 \times 10^9$ | $1.77 \times 10^{10}$ | $7.97 \times 10^{11}$ |
| $n^2$ | $7.75 \times 10^3$ | $6.0 \times 10^4$ | $2.94 \times 10^5$ | $7.78 \times 10^5$ | $5.62 \times 10^6$ |
| $n^3$ | $3.91 \times 10^2$ | $1.53 \times 10^3$ | $4.42 \times 10^3$ | $8.46 \times 10^3$ | $3.16 \times 10^4$ |
| $2^n$ | 25 | 31 | 36 | 39 | 44 |
| $10^n$ | 7 | 9 | 10 | 11 | 13 |

**Table B.10** Size of Largest Problem That Algorithm $A$ Can Solve if Solution Is Computed in Time $\leq T$ at 1 Microsecond per Step

The number of seconds in a year is $60 \times 60 \times 24 \times 365 = 31{,}536{,}000$, so the number of microseconds in a year is $3.15 \times 10^{13}$. Thus, the answer to our question is determined by finding the largest $n$ such that $f(n) \leq 3.15 \times 10^{13}$. If $f(n) = 2^n$, then $n$ can be at most 44 if algorithm $A$ is to finish in less than a year. In other words, if algorithm $A$ takes exactly $2^n$ steps of a microsecond each, then the largest problem that we can handle with a year's worth of computing effort is a problem of size $n = 44$. If $f(n) = 10^n$, matters are even worse—we can solve only a problem of size $n = 13$ in a year. If a year seems impossibly long to wait for our answer, or the solution seems impractical because contemporary computers cannot usually operate reliably for that long, we might see what size problem we could solve in an hour, a day, or a week. If $f(n) = 10^n$, we are still in deep trouble—the biggest $n$ can be if the computation is to terminate in less than an hour is $n = 9$, and if we are allocated a week, the biggest $n$ can be is $n = 11$. Thus, if the running time of our algorithm is characterized by an exponential function, we usually cannot expect to solve practical problems of very large size. Table B.10 gives more results along these lines for functions $f(n)$ of linear or greater complexity.

*how big can n get in order to finish within a time limit?*

Thus, we see that, given an hour, we can solve a problem of size 3.6 billion if algorithm $A$ takes $n$ steps, but only size 60,000 if $A$ takes $n^2$ steps, size 1,532 if $A$ takes $n^3$ steps, and size 31 if $A$ takes $2^n$ steps.

*some dramatic shifts*

These dramatic shifts in the sizes of problems we can handle as we ascend the scale of complexity are equally dramatically reversed as we descend the scale. Thus, if we can replace a linear algorithm $A$ that takes $n$ steps by a logarithmic algorithm $B$ that takes only $\log_2 n$ steps of equal duration, then a problem that is solved by algorithm $A$ in one hour, would be solved by algorithm $B$ in just 31.75 microseconds!

## A Word of Caution

Our intuition-building discussion has been oversimplified a bit. Although the basic theme has been correct, some of the nuances and subtleties remain to be covered. For instance, a given algorithm, such as **QuickSort**, does not always take the same time to run on problems of a given size, regardless of its input data. Some kinds of arrays of items we may wish to sort may take much longer for QuickSort to sort than certain other kinds of arrays (depending on various ways the original array is out of order to begin with). Consequently, it will turn out that QuickSort has an *average* running time, a *worst case* running time, and a *best case* running time. It turns out that even though the average running time for QuickSort is $O(n \log n)$, QuickSort's worst case running time is $O(n^2)$.

## What Is Covered Elsewhere

Now let's take a quick peek at some of the algorithmic complexity results mentioned elsewhere in the book. This is the final intuition-building step before we study O-notation formally.

First, consider different methods of searching. One method is *sequential searching*. Under usual conditions, this is an $O(n)$ algorithm (i.e., an algorithm that runs in *linear* time). In sequential searching of a list or an array, you look at items one after another in sequential order until you find the one you are looking for. By contrast, *binary searching* in an ordered array of items runs in *logarithmic* time (i.e., it can be performed in time $O(\log n)$), provided the array is sorted beforehand. For searching in large tables, lists, or arrays, binary searching is incredibly more efficient than sequential searching.

*sequential searching versus binary searching*

Yet more efficient are techniques for searching using *hashing*. The time that hash searching takes depends on how full the hash table is. If a hash table is not filled completely with items but is instead kept no more than say 80 percent full, the average search times take no more than a *constant* amount of time, $O(1)$. (In Section B.4, we will give the reason why $O(1)$ is the O-notation for a constant amount of time.) The term *constant time* means that the time required is fixed and doesn't vary when the problem size changes.

*using hashing to perform searching*

We can also use trees in searching algorithms. For instance, we can put items into binary search trees, and use binary tree searching for looking up items in the trees. If we maintain these search trees in approximately balanced condition (meaning that the left subtree of each node is made to contain about as many nodes as the right subtree does), then we can guarantee logarithmic search times, $O(\log n)$, on the average. Even though binary searching in ordered arrays also runs in average time $O(\log n)$, we can insert new items in binary search trees more efficiently than we can in ordered sequential arrays. Binary search trees therefore have some advantages (which are discussed in Chapter 8).

*using trees to perform searching*

Now, let's turn to sorting. For large problem sizes, the sorting method you choose can make a big difference (see, for example, Exercise B.3.2). In sorting methods that compare the relative sizes of items and move them about (which are called comparison-based sorting methods), you can prove that you can't sort any faster in the average case than proportional to $n \log n$. Table B.11 lists the complexity classes for the average sorting times of several methods. There are even some fast sorting methods that work in *linear* time, $O(n)$. These methods work using address-calculation techniques. Some of these are explored in Chapter 10 on sorting.

*sorting methods*

**Table B.11** Sorting
Methods of Various
Complexities

| Complexity | Method Names |
|---|---|
| $O(n^2)$ | SelectionSort, InsertionSort |
| $O(n \log n)$ | QuickSort, HeapSort, MergeSort |
| $O(n)$ | Address Calculation Sorting (ProxmapSort, RadixSort) |

We have already sensed that exponential running-time algorithms are not very practical to use for any but small problems. Unfortunately, there are some kinds of algorithmic problems for which the very best solutions known to date take exponential running time. For instance, the best known algorithm for solving what is called the *traveling salesperson problem* takes exponential time. In this problem you have a map that gives cities the salesperson is supposed to visit. The map also gives the costs of traveling between various pairs of cities (for which transportation is possible). The problem is to find the route of least cost that allows the salesperson to visit each of the cities exactly once. Certain algorithms for computing moves in game-playing situations also take exponential time. These are exhaustive algorithms that explore the game-tree for the game in order to compare all possible moves and to select the best one.

At the opposite end of the spectrum from exponential algorithms are algorithms that run in constant time, $O(1)$. $O(1)$ algorithms are those that take no more than a fixed amount of time to run no matter how big the problem size is. An example of a

constant time algorithms

constant-time algorithm is one that chooses and prints a single random array item $A[i]$ in an array, $A[0:n-1]$. It takes a fixed amount of time to compute a random number, $i$, lying in the index range, $0:n-1$, of the array. It takes an additional fixed amount of time to access $A[i]$ and print it. No matter how big the problem size, $n$, gets, it still takes the same amount of time to select and print a random array item, $A[i]$ (assuming we stay within the limits of a given computer).

If we are careful enough, many important problems can be solved with algorithms that run in linear time, $O(n)$. For instance, the parsing algorithm in your Java compil-

linear time algorithms

er is usually a linear algorithm that runs in time proportional to the length of your Java program (measured in characters). Also, string pattern matching algorithms (such as the algorithm that searches for occurrences of a given word in your word processor) can be made to run in linear time, relying on clever tricks (see Exercises B.3.3 and B.3.4).

Occasionally, we encounter $O(n^3)$ algorithms. An example of an $O(n^3)$ algo-

cubic time algorithms

rithm is the straightforward algorithm for multiplying two square $n \times n$ matrices. Matrices are two-dimensional tables of numbers that can be multiplied with other mathematical entities and with each other. They can be used to represent many interesting systems. For instance, if you have a computer graphics program with a three-dimensional model in it, and you want to draw a two-dimensional perspective image of what an observer would see when looking through a window at three-dimensional objects in the distance, you could use a model based on three-dimensional coordinate geometry. If you then wanted to simulate what the observer would see when moving through the model (as in making a landing on an aircraft carrier, for instance), you could use matrices to multiply the coordinates defining the lines, points, and surfaces in the model so that they would turn, expand, and shrink appropriately to compute the perspective view that the observer would see when moving.

## B.3 REVIEW QUESTIONS

1. Give the O-notation corresponding to the following adjective names for various complexity classes: constant, logarithmic, linear, $n \log n$, quadratic, cubic, and exponential.
2. If you have problems of small size, does the complexity class of the algorithm make a big difference in the algorithm's running time?
3. Under what circumstances would it make a difference whether you use an $O(n^2)$ sorting algorithm or an $O(n \log n)$ sorting algorithm? Name some $O(n^2)$ sorting algorithms. Name some $O(n \log n)$ sorting algorithms.
4. Is there any restriction on the use of exponential algorithms for practical purposes?

## B.3 EXERCISES

1. What is the largest problem size, $n$, that could be solved before the sun burns out, if the computation requires $2^n$ steps at one microsecond per step? Assume the sun will burn out after $1.5768 \times 10^{23}$ microseconds (which equals 5 billion years).
2. Suppose you are working for a catalog company that prints various kinds of catalogs for use by targeted industries. Your boss wants you to take a tape containing 262,144 records for the entries in the telephone book for your city, and sort it in the order of increasing telephone numbers, so your company can print a "reverse telephone book" to sell to real estate brokers (who, for business reasons, like to be able to look up the name and address of the person having a given telephone number, starting with the telephone number). For simplicity, you can think of your task as sorting 262,144 telephone numbers into increasing order. Your boss has decided to rent time on a local mainframe at $100 per minute. There are two sorting algorithms you can run on this mainframe. SelectionSort runs in exactly $n^2$ microseconds, and QuickSort runs in exactly $n \log_2 n$ microseconds, where $n$ is the number of items to be sorted. How much time will SelectionSort and QuickSort take to sort the 262,144 numbers? How much will each method cost, at $100 per minute? Which method is preferable on the basis of cost?
3. If you have an option for doing "syntax checking only" on your Java compiler, try timing how long it takes for your Java compiler to parse programs of various lengths. Plot the parsing times (measured with a stopwatch or a wall clock) versus the program lengths (in characters) on a graph. What is the relationship? Do you conjecture that your Java parsing algorithm runs in time $O(n)$?
4. Try searching for words in your word processor on documents of various lengths (measured in bytes or word counts). Plot search times versus document lengths on a graph. Do you conjecture that the search algorithm is an $O(n)$ algorithm?

## B.4    O-Notation—Definition and Manipulation

### LEARNING OBJECTIVES

1. To learn the formal definition of O-notation.
2. To learn how to prove formally that a given function $f(n)$ is $O(g(n))$.
3. To learn some useful shortcuts for manipulating O-notation.

what O-notation means

Throughout the discussion in several chapters of this book we use the language of O-notation in the form $O(g(n))$ to help characterize the time or space requirements of various algorithms. If $n$ is a parameter that characterizes the size of the input to a given algorithm, and if we say the algorithm runs to completion in $O(g(n))$ steps, we mean that the actual number of steps executed is no more than a constant times $g(n)$, provided we deal with sufficiently large problems.

the formal definition

The preceding sections in this appendix were intended to help you develop intuition for O-notation in advance of encountering its formal definition. But now the moment has arrived to give the precise, formal definition.

> **Definition of O-Notation:** We say that $f(n)$ is $O(g(n))$ if there exist two positive constants $K$ and $n_0$ such that $|f(n)| \leq K|g(n)|$ for all $n \geq n_0$.

It helps to shift our point of view by trying to interpret what this definition is trying to say in graphical terms. Figure B.12 shows graphically the meaning of the definition of O-notation.

the graphical meaning
of O-notation

Assume for the moment that we are dealing with positive functions, meaning that when we plot $f(n)$ and $g(n)$, their curves both lie above the horizontal axis. Basically, Figure B.12 says that a given function $f(n)$ can be shown to be $O(g(n))$ provided the curve, $K \times g(n)$, for some constant multiple of $g(n)$, can be made to lie above the curve for $f(n)$ whenever we are to the right of some big enough value $n_0$. A second way of saying this is that there is some way to choose a constant of proportionality $K$ so that the curve for $f(n)$ is bounded above by the curve for $K \times g(n)$, whenever $n$ is big enough (i.e., whenever $n \geq n_0$). A third way of saying this is that for all but finitely many small values of $n$, the curve for $f(n)$ lies below the curve for some suitably large constant multiple of $g(n)$.

### An Example of a Formal Proof of O-Notation

a formal reasoning process

Suppose algorithm A sorts a sequence of $n$ numbers in an array into ascending order, and suppose it can be shown that the exact number of steps algorithm A executes is $f(n) = 3 + 6 + 9 + \ldots + 3n$ steps. Then it can be asserted that the algorithm runs in $O(n^2)$ steps by the following formal reasoning process.

First, we attempt to find what is called a closed-form expression for the sum $f(n) = 3 + 6 + 9 + \ldots + 3n$, meaning a formula for $f(n)$ in terms of $n$ that does not use

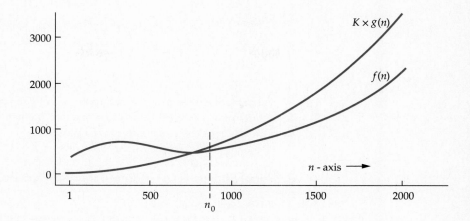

**Figure B.12** Graphical Meaning of O-Notation

the three dots (. . .) in it. To do this, we could note that $f(n) = 3 (1+ 2 + \ldots + n)$, and we could use the formula for the sum of the first $n$ integers (which you might have learned when you studied *arithmetic progressions* in high school), which tells us that $S = 1 + 2 + \ldots + n = n(n+1)/2$. This allows us to write:

$$f(n) = \frac{3n(n+1)}{2}.$$

**the key to the formal proof**

Then, choosing $K = 3$, $n_0 = 1$, and $g(n) = n^2$, and substituting in the formal definition for O-notation, we can demonstrate that $|f(n)| \leq K |g(n)|$ for all $n \geq n_0$, provided we can demonstrate that the following inequality holds true for all $n \geq 1$:

$$\frac{3n(n+1)}{2} \leq 3n^2.$$

Multiplying both sides by 2/3 and multiplying out the left side yields:

$$n^2 + n \leq 2n^2.$$

Subtracting $n^2$ from both sides gives:

$$n \leq n^2.$$

Dividing the latter inequality by $n$ gives, $1 \leq n$, which clearly holds for all $n \geq 1$.

$$O(1) < O(\log n) < O(n) < O(n \log n) < O(n^2) < O(n^3) < O(2^n) < O(10^n).$$

**Figure B.13** Scale of Strength for O-Notation

Thus we have formally proven that $f(n)$ is $O(n^2)$ by showing that $f(n)$ satisfies the formal definition of $O(n^2)$. In actual practice, we can use some shortcuts to make the determination of the O-notation much simpler.

## Practical Shortcuts for Manipulating O-Notation

*making it easy to determine O-notation*

To prove rigorously that $f(n)$ is $O(g(n))$, we have to provide a formal proof such as the one given in the previous paragraphs. However, computer scientists have learned to apply some shortcuts that make it much easier to determine a suitable O-notation for $f(n)$, once a closed form for $f(n)$ has been obtained.

Basically, this involves separating the expression for $f(n)$ into a dominant term and lesser terms and throwing away the lesser terms. In symbols, if

$$f(n) = (\text{dominant term}) \pm (\text{lesser terms})$$

then

$$O(f(n)) = O(\text{dominant term} \pm \text{lesser terms}) = O(\text{dominant term}).$$

*using a scale to identify dominant terms*

We can rank the functions given in Table B.7 on a scale of strength such as the one given in Fig. B.13. Then we can use this scale to determine which among a number of terms is dominant and which are the lesser terms. Given two terms $A$ and $B$ on the scale in Fig. B.13, we say $A$ is a dominant term and $B$ is a lesser term, if $O(B) < O(A)$ on the scale. For example, $O(n^3)$ dominates $O(n \log n)$ on the scale. This means that we could write $O(n^3 + n \log n) = O(n^3 + n \log n) = O(n^3)$.

If coefficients (or constants of proportionality) are involved, we can ignore them when determining dominant and lesser terms, and then simply cross them out in the final step. For instance, we could write:

$$O(6n^3 - 15n^2 + 3 n \log n) = O(6n^3 - 15n^2 + 3 n \log n) \quad \text{drop lesser terms}$$
$$= O(6n^3) \quad \text{drop coefficient 6}$$
$$= O(n^3). \quad \text{final result is } n^3$$

*ignoring bases of logarithms*

You may have noticed that, when writing O-notation, we never used the bases of the logarithms involved, as in writing $O(\log n)$ or $O(n \log n)$. Why didn't we write logarithms with specific bases, as in writing $O(n \log_2 n)$? The answer is related to the fact that changing the bases of logarithms involves multiplying by a suitable constant. For instance, to change a base-2 logarithm into a base-10 logarithm, we can use the conversion formula:

$$\log_{10} n = \frac{\log_2 n}{\log_2 10}$$

but since

$$\frac{1}{\log_2 10}$$

is a specific constant of proportionality with the value, 0.3010, we could have written this conversion formula as:

$$\log_{10} n = 0.3010 \times \log_2 n.$$

So since changing logarithm bases only involves multiplying by new constants of proportionality, and since O-notation ignores constants of proportionality, we ignore logarithm bases inside O-notation.

A similar consideration holds for the reason we always write O(1) to denote the O-notation for constants. Suppose we could prove that algorithm $A$ runs in a number **why we write O(1)** of steps $f(n)$ that are always less than $K$ steps, no matter what the problem size $n$ is. Then we would have proven that $f(n) \le K$ for all $n \ge 1$. But this is the same as proving that $f(n) \le K \times 1$ for all $n \ge 1$, which, in turn proves $f(n)$ is O(1), or that $f(n)$ is $O(g(n))$ where $g(n) = 1$, according to the formal definition of O-notation.

To achieve mathematical rigor, we would actually have to prove that the kinds of manipulations we used above are permissible. For instance, suppose we are trying to justify $O(6\,n^2 + \text{5 n log n}) = O(\text{6}\,n^2) = O(n^2)$. We could start with a known inequality, such as $\log_2 n < n$, for all $n \ge 1$. Multiplying both sides of the inequality by $5n$ gives: $5\,n \log_2 n < 5n^2$, for all $n \ge 1$. Then, by adding $6\,n^2$ to both sides, we could use this last **why our shortcuts** inequality to show that $6\,n^2 + 5\,n \log_2 n < 6\,n^2 + 5n^2$ for all $n \ge 1$. Now, if we take **are justified** $f(n) = 6\,n^2 + 5\,n \log_2 n$ and $g(n) = n^2$, what we have shown is that $f(n) < 11 \times g(n)$, for all $n \ge 1$. But this is just a formal proof that the function $f(n) = 6\,n^2 + 5\,n \log_2 n$ is $O(n^2)$. We have succeeded in justifying our actions of cancelling lesser terms and throwing away constants of proportionality, in this one case. (Other cases are similar, and involve starting with inequalities that establish $f(n) \le g(n)$ for $n \ge n_0$ on the scale of Fig. B.13. Such inequalities are then multiplied by other inequalities or equalities and are added together to establish the proof of the cancellations being investigated.)

In actual practice, when O-notation is used by computer scientists, there are two more implicit assumptions:

1. The bound is as tight as the speaker can make it, even though the definition of O-notation does not require a tight bound. For example, if we say that an algorithm is $O(n^2)$, then so far as we know, the algorithm is neither $O(n \log n)$, nor $O(n)$, nor in any of the classes weaker than $O(n^2)$ in Fig. B.13. Note that, according to the formal definition of O-notation, if a function $f(n)$ is $O(n)$, then it is also $O(n^2)$, $O(n^3)$, ... , but we speak only of the tightest upper bound we know of.

2. When we speak of a function being $O(g(n))$, we make $g(n)$ as simple as possible. In particular, we make $g(n)$ a single term with a coefficient of one. For example, we would choose to say that $f(n)$ is $O(n^2)$ rather than saying that $f(n)$ is $O(3n^2 + n \log n)$, even though both statements are correct.

## B.4  REVIEW QUESTIONS

1. Give the formal definition of O-notation from memory. Compare your result with the definition given in this section to make sure you have given it correctly.
2. In your own words, describe what it means to say that $f(n)$ is $O(g(n))$.
3. In your own words, describe what you need to do to provide a formal proof that $f(n)$ is $O(g(n))$.
4. In your own words, describe some shortcuts that could allow you to conclude quickly that the O-notation for $O(18\, n \log_2 n + 19\, n + 3)$ is $O(n \log n)$.
5. Why is there no base in the logarithm notation used in the O-notation, $O(n \log n)$?
6. Why is the O-notation for a constant running time always given as $O(1)$?

## B.4  EXERCISES

1. What is the simplest and best O-notation for $f(n) = 2\, n \log_2 n + 4n + 17 \log_2 n$ ?
2. What is the simplest and best O-notation for $f(n) = 5n^3 + 3n^2 + 4n + 8$ ?
3. Give a formal proof that $f(n) = 5n^3 + 3n^2 + 4n + 8$ is $O(n^3)$.
4. Give a formal proof that $f(n) = 7*2^n + 9*n^3$ is $O(2^n)$.
5. Give a formal proof that $\log (n + 1)$ is $O(\log n)$.

## B.5  What O-Notation Doesn't Tell You

### LEARNING OBJECTIVES

1. To learn about circumstances in which O-notation analysis does not apply.
2. To learn what to do to find optimal algorithms under these circumstances.

*O-notation may give invalid results for small size problems*

We have seen that the definition of O-notation applies only to problem sizes that are sufficiently large for the O-notation condition to hold. For small problem sizes, the constants in the running time equations that fit the actual running time data may dominate the running times observed. Consequently, the conclusions that hold for large problem sizes, based on O-notation, may not hold at all for small problem sizes.

For example, we have to be quite careful in using O-notation comparisons between functions in the classes $O(\log \log n)$, $O(\log n)$, and $O(n)$, because the constants used in the running time equations for different algorithms often differ, sometimes by large multiples. (We haven't mentioned the complexity class $O(\log \log n)$ before in this appendix, but there is such a class, which we now introduce for the first time.)

To pursue this example a bit further, it can be shown that if we use straightforward *sequential search* to try to find an item in an ordered list, we must inspect $(n+1)/2$ (or $O(n)$) items on the average, assuming each item searched for is equally likely to be chosen. It can also be shown that if we use *binary search*, the number of comparisons needed to locate the item searched for is $O(\log n)$. A third kind of search, not studied in this book, is called *interpolation search*. It works by estimating where a search key $K$ is likely to be located in a range of keys, much like the way you would search for a name beginning with "V" starting in the back of a phone book, whereas you would search for a name beginning with "B" starting near the front, and a name beginning with "L" starting near the middle. If we use *interpolation search*, then, under proper conditions, we need make only $O(\log \log n)$ comparisons, on the average.

*comparing three methods for searching*

As you might imagine, $O(\log \log n)$ beats $O(\log n)$ handsomely for large $n$. For example, if $n = 2^{64} = 1.84 \times 10^{19}$, then $\log_2 n = 64$, and $\log_2 \log_2(n) = 6$. However, we cannot conclude too hastily that interpolation search is superior to the other methods. In fact, it is more costly to execute a step of a program for interpolation search than it is to execute the corresponding steps in binary search and sequential search. This is because the calculation of the "interpolation point" used in deciding where to search is more costly than calculating the midpoint used in binary searching, or in calculating how to move to the next item in sequential searching.

Thus one set of empirical data comparing the measured performances of these three searching methods showed that interpolation search was faster for searching tables of more than 500 items, whereas binary search was faster for searching tables of between 20 and 500 items, and sequential search was fastest for tables of up to 20 items. Another set of empirical data showed interpolation search was faster only for tables of more than 5000 items. (These boundaries are rough, of course, and depend on details of the implementations.)

*the $O(n)$ method is fastest for very small problem sizes*

If you are trying to write an extremely efficient searching algorithm to use on problems of very small size, say less than 20 items, it might be best to write a very tight sequential searching loop (possibly even writing it in assembly language so that it counts down toward zero and takes advantage of a test for zero in the machine instruction set, thus avoiding a memory access to retrieve the lower bound used in the test for loop termination).

The method of *measurement and tuning* might be the best way to optimize the performance of algorithms for small problem sizes, given that the conclusions based on O-notation cannot be trusted to apply to small problems. In the method of measurement and tuning, you repeatedly measure where an algorithm is spending its time and then you attempt to tune it to improve those parts of the algorithm that the measurements have revealed to be the most significant sources of inefficiency.

## **B.5** REVIEW QUESTIONS

1. When is it inappropriate to apply the conclusions normally derived from O-notation analysis to an algorithm's running time equation?
2. What is the method of measurement and tuning?

3. What can you do to find optimal algorithms to run on small-sized problems?

4. Give an example of three algorithms that perform a common task (such as sorting or searching) whose O-notation does not reveal their comparative efficiencies for small problem sizes.

## B.5 EXERCISES

1. Measure the difference in average running times for sequential searching and binary searching in an ordered array of integers, $A[0:n-1]$, for a range of small problem sizes $1 \leq n \leq 100$. Take care to use the most efficient form of sequential searching you can devise. (Programs C.41 and C.42 in Appendix C give algorithms for binary searching. Program C.41 is an iterative binary search algorithm and Program C.42 is a recursive binary search algorithm.) Do your data show that binary searching is always more efficient than sequential searching, no matter what size problem is being considered? Did the $O(n)$ running time for sequential searching and the $O(\log n)$ running time for binary searching tell you which algorithm was the fastest for the smallest of the problem sizes that you investigated?

2. Measure the comparative efficiencies on small problems (say, for $n \leq 16$) of the following sorting algorithms from Chapter 10: **QuickSort**, **InsertionSort**, **HeapSort**, and **SelectionSort**. Which algorithms are the fastest? Does the O-notation for these algorithms given in Table B.11 tell you which algorithm is the fastest for these problems of small size?

## ■ References for Further Study

Two books that cover more about O-notation and algorithm analysis are:

Alfred V. Aho, John E. Hopcroft, and Jeffrey D. Ullman, *The Design and Analysis of Computer Algorithms*. Addison-Wesley, Reading, MA (1974).

Sara Baase, *Computer Algorithms—Introduction to Design and Analysis*. Addison-Wesley, Reading, MA (1988).

## ■ Appendix Summary

*precise analysis of algorithms is possible*

Computer algorithms are precise mathematical objects that are susceptible to precise analysis using techniques of mathematical investigation. Quantitative analysis of many algorithms has resulted in the development of an extensive body of results that tell us a great deal about how well or how poorly various algorithms perform. At the present time, substantial progress has been made by computer scientists in determining the comparative efficiencies of algorithms that solve important, commonly-occurring problems, especially when this progress is compared to the state of knowledge about such matters in the early days of computing.

*comparing performance using shapes of resource consumption curves*

Initially, it might seem like an impossible chore to compare the performance of various algorithms when the performance data we can measure are so hard to untangle from the distorting influence of different computers, programming languages, and compilers used to implement and run the algorithms. However, it has been discovered that we can often associate with each algorithm a family of similarly shaped curves that characterize their resource consumption pattern (by giving the time or space they consume) as a function of the problem size. These resource consumption curves can be put into different complexity classes, provided (1) we ignore what happens for small problem sizes, and (2) we ignore constants of proportionality. Computer scientists commonly use O-notation to refer to the different complexity classes. O-notation is defined to work only for suitably large problem sizes, and only as an upper bound. But in giving the O-notation for $O(f(n))$, it is common practice to choose $f(n)$ to be as simple as possible and as tight an upper bound as possible.

It is important to develop an intuition for the language of O-notation—especially for what it means and for how computer scientists commonly use it. Developing such intuition is a bit like learning an unfamiliar temperature scale. It pays to learn the O-notation names of several specific complexity classes and to develop an appreciation for the properties of each such complexity class.

For instance, the *exponential* complexity class, associated with O-notation of the form $O(c^n)$, for some constant $c$, describes algorithms that cannot be used practically for any but fairly small-sized problems. You can develop the intuition for why this is true by studying examples that show that an $O(2^n)$ algorithm cannot solve problems of size $n > 77$ before the sun burns out, even when the algorithm is executed on a fast computer at speeds of up to a million steps per second. The same intuition-building process might lead you to learn that, all other things being equal, $O(\log n)$ algorithms execute much faster on large-sized problems than $O(n)$ algorithms. For instance, on large problems, binary searching, which is an $O(\log n)$ algorithm, handsomely beats sequential searching, which is an $O(n)$ algorithm. There are significant performance differences between various sorting algorithms, too. $O(n \log n)$ sorting algorithms have very significant performance advantages over $O(n^2)$ sorting techniques for large problem sizes.

developing intuition for the various complexity classes

Having decided that O-notation is a good language to use for characterizing the comparative performance of algorithms (independently of varying characteristics of computers, compilers, and languages), and having developed an intuition for what O-notation means, the next step is to learn a bit about how to define and manipulate O-notation formally. The formal definition of the O-notation for a function, $f(n)$, says that $f(n)$ is $O(g(n))$ provided the curve for $f(n)$ is bounded above by some constant multiple of $g(n)$ for sufficiently large problem sizes, $n$. To manipulate O-notation, using shortcuts, the first step is to establish a scale of increasing complexity classes, such as $O(1) < O(\log n) < O(n) < O(n \log n) < O(n^2) < O(n^3) < O(2^n) < O(10^n)$. The shortcut for determining the O-notation for a sum or difference of multiples of functions on this scale involves first identifying the dominant term $D$ and the lesser terms $L$, according to this scale, then dropping the lesser terms, $L$, and finally dropping the constant of proportionality on the dominant term. For example, $O(3n^2 + 2 n \log n + 5n + 3) = O(3n^2 + \cancel{2 n \log n + 5n + 3}) = O(\cancel{3} n^2 ) = O(n^2)$.

learning how to define and manipulate O-notation

The algorithms covered in this book include algorithms in several of the principal complexity classes. For instance, sequential searching has an $O(n)$ running time. Selection sorting runs in time $O(n^2)$. Quicksort, however, can be shown to run in time $O(n \log n)$. And binary searching in ordered arrays has an $O(\log n)$ running time.

examples of algorithms in different complexity classes

Finally, it is important to know that O-notation should not be used to draw general conclusions for problems of small size, in which the constants in the actual running time equations may, and usually do, dominate the observed running times. Consequently, it is important to use the method of measurement and tuning to identify optimal algorithms for solving small-sized problems.

when O-notation can't
be trusted

# APPENDIX C

# Software Engineering Concepts

## C.1 Introduction and Motivation

As mentioned in Chapter 1, the term *programming-in-the-small* refers to the activities that center on the creation of small programs—those consisting of a few lines or a few pages, and the term *programming-in-the-large* refers to the activities that center on the creation and modification of large software systems—those that are hundreds of thousands of lines long or longer. Programming-in-the-large involves organizing and coordinating the activities of large software development teams using substantial resources. It involves considerations of software lifecycle processes and methods. These tend to be somewhat different in flavor and content from the issues that arise in programming-in-the-small. This appendix covers software engineering concepts useful for developing small programs.

*small-scale versus large-scale programming*

Although many small programs are easy to write, occasionally some small programs are quite difficult to write. The creation of such difficult small programs can then involve great subtlety of thought and can require great precision and ingenuity. To deal successfully with such situations, it is important for you to learn to be able to reason about small programs with clarity and mental precision.

*small programs can be subtle*

475

One important form of reasoning about small programs involves what are called *correctness proofs*. It is sometimes possible to prove that programs accomplish stated objectives called the *program specifications*, which can often be described in a precise, logical language. When a mathematical proof shows that a program, when executed, achieves the outcomes described by its specifications, it is said to be a correctness proof.

correctness proofs

Of course, such correctness proofs are not infallible—logical arguments that are intended to be proofs can contain mistakes. There can also be doubt that the program specifications correctly describe and capture the true goals of a program. This brings us to the subject of testing. Although testing is helpful for detecting bugs in programs, it also has limitations. A famous adage in computer science says, "Testing can reveal the presence of bugs, but it can never prove their absence."

testing

So neither testing nor attempting to give correctness proofs are completely infallible methods for raising our confidence that programs do exactly what they are supposed to do.

*Object-oriented design* (OOD) consists of designing a software system using a collection of interacting objects. The goal is to have the objects interact in clean, simple ways using concise interfaces, and to hide the internal details of how objects work by means of encapsulation. A helpful technique is to employ objects that embody abstract data types—using external operations whose implementations are not yet known but whose expected behaviors have been precisely specified. This promotes clarity of thinking at the top level of the design, since we can write concise, lucid programs that are not contaminated with low-level details. In the later stages of implementation, we select data representations and algorithms (in parallel) to implement the top-level abstractions. This makes the whole system of parts work together cooperatively, while preserving clarity of structure in the top-level design. Such clarity of structure is important for making the program easy to understand, easy to prove correct, and easier to modify later (if the need arises).

object-oriented design

One of the helpful methods for developing small programs is called *top-down programming by stepwise refinement*. In this method, we start with a top-level goal for what the program is supposed to accomplish, and we sketch a rough program strategy for how the program might go about attaining its objectives. Then, in a series of stepwise modifications, we refine the program strategy by progressively supplying more and more detail, until precise low-level details are completely filled in.

top-down programming by stepwise refinement

## Plan for the Appendix

The appendix begins by presenting a couple of examples of object-oriented design using top-down programming with stepwise refinement. Actually, we have already been using object-oriented design and top-down programming in the earlier parts of this book. Each time we designed an ADT or designed a Java class to solve a problem, we used object-oriented design, and each time we refined "program strategies" into actual "programs" we used top-down programming. Given this preparation, the essential concepts should come naturally to you.

examples of OOD and top-down programming

We then study "reasoning about programs" and tackle the problem of finding the position of the largest element in an array, proving that the program that does it is

reasoning about programs

correct. We introduce the idea of *assertions*—including the special kinds of assertions known as *preconditions*, *postconditions*, and *loop invariants*—and then we give a correctness proof. Following this, we show how to use the correctness proof for finding the biggest element as a step inside the proof of correctness of a selection sorting program. We then study a bit of formal logic to introduce a formal language in which we can state assertions and which we can use to reason about them precisely.

**transforming and optimizing programs**

Next, we study ideas that are useful for transforming and optimizing programs to make them more efficient. We illustrate recursion removal by transforming the version of **selectionSort** with a tail recursion (that we used in the correctness proof) into a corresponding iterative program. Then we perform a further optimization by replacing a subroutine call with its body. We compare the performance of the original and optimized versions to see how much gain in efficiency has been achieved.

**program testing**

Our next topic is program testing. We introduce the concepts of unit testing, integration testing, regression testing, and acceptance testing. We also introduce the concepts of stubs and drivers, and we illustrate them with examples.

**measurement and tuning**

We then investigate the philosophy of measurement and tuning. Oftentimes, it is surprising where the inefficiencies in programs occur, and it is hard to know in advance where programs spend their time. Frequently, over 80 percent of the execution time is spent in less than 10 percent of the code. If we can identify where the inefficiencies occur, we can often rewrite the inefficient sections to make them much more efficient. We'll compare several versions of iterative and recursive binary searching to illustrate the concepts involved.

**reusable software components**

Next we turn to the topic of reusable software components. We investigate economic arguments that tell us why taking advantage of reusable components is such a good idea. In this connection, we briefly discuss the advantages of bottom-up programming.

**structured programming**

Finally, we discuss some concepts that help us give programs good structure so that they are easy to understand, and we discuss some related concepts of what makes good program documentation.

## C.2 · Object-Oriented Design and Top-Down Programming

### LEARNING OBJECTIVES

1. To learn how to design programs using object-oriented design (OOD).
2. To learn the difference between top-down and bottom-up programming.
3. To understand the process of stepwise refinement.
4. To learn how to postpone the choice of a data representation by employing abstraction appropriately.
5. To examine how to refine choices of data structures and algorithms in parallel.

### Do You Have a Winning Ticket?

**winning in the lottery**

In some state lotteries, you can buy a $1 ticket with an opaque coating to scratch off (see Fig. C.1). Once you remove the coating, six numbers representing dollar amounts

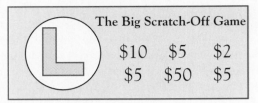

**Figure C.1** An Example of a Scratch-Off Lottery Ticket

become visible, and you can hand in the ticket and receive the largest dollar amount repeated three or more times. If no amount is repeated three or more times, you don't win anything. Suppose your task is to write a Java applet that inputs the six dollar amounts from one of these scratch-off lottery tickets and displays the winning amount if there is one. If there is no winning amount $0 should be displayed. Figure C.2 shows the graphical user interface (GUI) of a Java applet that accepts six dollar amounts in its input text box and then displays the dollar amount won in its output box (after the user presses the Enter key).

The topmost level of the object-oriented design for our lottery winner detector applet consists of three interacting Java objects, each of which encapsulates its own hidden, private data fields. These objects interact only by making method calls on each other's "services" (where the "services" are the publicly available methods in each object's interface). There are no global variables that hold shared values or data structures on which different objects operate. Consequently, the design is an example of pure modular programming in which the modules (i.e., the Java objects) interact only in clean simple ways through their interfaces with their internal mechanisms hidden from view.

To keep the exposition from being too lengthy and to practice the virtues of software reuse that are later preached in Section C.7, we reuse the object-oriented designs of two of the three objects that comprise the lottery winner detector, and we focus on two alternatives for the object-oriented design of the third object—the one that actually computes the solution to the problem.

*pure modular programming based on object-oriented design*

*practicing the virtues of software reuse*

---

| ☐ ▬▬▬ Applet Viewer:WinnerDetector.class ▬▬▬ |
|---|
| Type six dollar amounts separated by spaces, and press the Enter key. |
| input:   10   5   2   5   50   5 |
| output:   You just won $ 5 |
| Applet started |

**Figure C.2** User Interface for Lottery Winner Detector

In particular, we reuse the graphical user interface of the postfix interpreter applet, shown earlier in Fig. 6.9, that provided an interactive window having text input and output boxes, and having instructions for the user. (We modify the instruction string slightly to ask the user to give six dollar amounts as inputs, as shown in Fig. C.2, instead of asking the user to give a postfix string as the input.) Also, we reuse the translator code from the postfix interpreter that converted the user's input string into individual postfix tokens so that, in the case of the lottery winner detector, it converts the user's input string giving six dollar amounts into an integer array, A, containing six integer dollar amounts. The actual problem solving for detecting the winning amount can then be accomplished by a separate module, called the **Table** object, that accepts the integer array, A, as its input, and computes the integer dollar amount that was won (or returns $0, if no amount was won). This winning integer amount returned by the **Table** object is then translated to a string and is displayed in the output text box of the GUI window by the translator object.

**reusing the GUI and the string translator**

There are several benefits to this act of software reuse, aside from avoiding an inappropriately long exposition in this section. One is that the applet's GUI is an *event-driven interface* in which the text-input event (generated by the user's typing in six dollar amounts into the input box and pressing the Enter key) must be handled by event-handler code. The applet and GUI must be set up to handle text-input events so as to trigger method calls on the problem-solving objects, to receive the computed solutions they return, and to display the results (in string form) in the output box. The second is that the translator code that translates from input strings into integer arrays is not completely trivial. The event-handling and string conversion mechanisms that lie at the heart of these two reused objects are just intricate enough that our act of reuse saves us from the effort of having to reinvent (and debug) them. By this means we can achieve important enhancements to software productivity—the quantitative nature of which is explored further in Section C.7.

**productivity benefits of software reuse**

The programs for the **WinnerDetector** applet and for the **Translator** object are given as Programs C.3 and C.4 (on pp. 480–482), respectively. Because their principles of operation have been studied before in Chapter 6, we do not explain them again here. Instead, we focus, in detail, on the object-oriented design of the **Table** object that actually computes the winning solution to the problem. This **Table** object encapsulates its internal mechanisms, using private data fields and methods, and presents in its interface only three public methods available to its external users: (1) its constructor, **Table T = new Table( )**, (2) the method **T.getInput(A)**, used to obtain its integer input array, A, and (3) **T.findWinningAmount( )**, used to return the winning amount found. We explore two alternative solutions to the design of this **Table** object, and, in the process, we illustrate how to develop the solutions using the method of top-down programming.

**focusing on designing the Table object**

In *top-down programming by stepwise refinement*, we begin at the topmost conceptual level, by imagining a general, abstract solution. This can be expressed by sketching a program strategy in outline form before choosing any particular low-level data representations or algorithms. Then, step-by-step in progressive refinements, we make choices to fill in the details—much like the process of writing a story starting with an outline of the story's plot. Generally speaking, we choose

**top-down programming by stepwise refinement**

```
 1  import java.applet.*;
 2  import java.util.StringTokenizer;
 3  import java.awt.*;
 4
 5
 6  public class WinnerDetector extends Applet implements ActionListener {
 7
 8      // declare the applet's data fields as follows:
 9
10      Label
11          instructionLabel,              // gives the instructions for user input
12          inputLabel,                    // labels the input text box
13          outputLabel;                   // labels the output text box
14
15      TextField
16          inputField,                    // the input text box
17          outputField;                   // the output text box
18
19      Translator   Trans;        // the object that translates inputs and solutions
20
21      // now give the Applet's methods
22
23      /*-----------*/
24
25      /** the init( ) method constructs the GUI and the Translator object, Trans */
26
27      public void init( ) {
28
29          constructGUI( );           // construct the applet's user interface
30
31          Trans = new Translator( );       // create a new Translator object
32
33      } // end init
34
35      /*-----------*/
36
37      /** the actionPerformed( ) method handles user input text */
38      /** events by sending  the user's input string containing six */
39      /** substrings for the six dollar amounts to the Translator object, */
40      /** Trans, and by getting the output string back from Trans to */
41      /** display in the output box */
42
43      public void actionPerformed(ActionEvent e)  {
44
45          Trans.setInput(e.getActionCommand());         // send input string to
46                                                         // Translator object
47          outputField.setText(Trans.getOutput( ));      // put result in output box
48
49      } // end actionPerformed
50
51      /*-----------*/
52
```

**Program C.3** The Winner Detector Applet *(continued)*

Program C.3 The Winner Detector Applet *(continued)*

```
55          private void constructGUI( ) {

                // place user instructions in the GUI
                    instructionLabel = new Label(
                        "Type six dollar amounts separated by spaces, and press Enter.",
                        Label.CENTER
60                  );
                    add(instructionLabel);   // add instruction label to top of applet layout

                // install an input text field in the GUI
                    inputLabel = new Label("  input:");                // add an input label
65                  add(inputLabel);
                    inputField = new TextField(45);        // create a 45-column input field
                    add(inputField);                       // and add it to the layout in the applet.
                    inputField.addActionListener(this);    // then attach an event handler

70              // install an output text field in the GUI
                    outputLabel = new Label("output:");                // add an output label
                    add(outputLabel);
                    outputField = new TextField(45);   // create a 45-column output field
                    add(outputField);                  // and add it to the layout in the applet
75
                // focus GUI attention on the input text field
                    inputField.requestFocus( );        // put blinking text cursor in inputField

                }// end constructGUI
80
            /*-----------*/

            } // end applet
85
        /*-------------------------------------------------------*/

        /* ---< insert here the text of Programs C.4 and one of C.15 or C.17 >--- */




        /** the Translator object has two public methods that the event handler */
        /** of the WinnerDetector applet calls. After the Translator object, Trans, */
        /** is constructed by calling "new Translator( );" the WinnerDetector applet */
        /** passes the user's input string to it by calling "setInput( )," after which */
5       /** the Winner Detector causes Trans to compute and return the result  */
        /** string,using the method call, "Trans.getOutput( )"  */

        class Translator {

10          private String inputString, outputString;

            private int[ ] inputArray = {0, 0, 0, 0, 0, 0};            // holds six inputs in
                                                                       // the inputArray[0:5]
```

**Program C.4** The Translator Class *(continued)*

Program C.4 The Translator Class (*continued*)

```
15      /*-----------*/

            public void setInput(String input) {

                inputString = input;   // store the user's input string in inputString field
20
            } // end setInput

        /*-----------*/

25          public String getOutput( )  {

                // convert input text string to an integer array
                    convertInputTextToArray( );

30              // construct a Table object
                    Table T = new Table( );

                // pass input array to Table object
                    T.getInput(inputArray);
35
                // have the Table object find the winning amount and return it
                    return "You just won $" + T.findWinningAmount( );

            } // end getOutput
40
        /*-----------*/

            private void convertInputTextToArray() {

45              int i = 0;                          // index for the inputArray's items
                String token;                       // contains the string for the next
                                                    // input token from the parser
                StringTokenizer parser = new StringTokenizer(inputString," ",true) ;

50              while (parser.hasMoreTokens()) {
                    token = parser.nextToken();
                    if ( (token.length() == 1) && (token.charAt(0) == ' ') ) {
                                                    // if token was a space
                        /* do nothing */;                           // ignore it
55                  } else {            // otherwise, place input amount into inputArray[i]
                        if (i < 6) {
                            inputArray[i++] = Integer.parseInt(token);
                        }
                    }
60              } // end while

            } // end convertInputTextToArray( )

        /*-----------*/
65
        } // end class Translator
```

algorithms and data structures in parallel to implement the parts of the solution sketched previously in higher-level descriptions. Eventually, we arrive at an executable Java program.

We now focus on the problem of designing a Java **Table** class that accepts an input array consisting of an array of six integer amounts, and both finds and returns the largest integer amount repeated three or more times in this input array.

There are usually many ways to solve a problem. It's a good idea not to stop searching for solutions once a single initial solution has been sketched. Instead, it might be worthwhile to try to imagine, say, three or more solutions, and then to compare their advantages and disadvantages in order to do a thorough job of searching for a good solution.

The problem we have selected to illustrate this process is deliberately not too challenging, so that solutions will easily come to mind. Moreover, we use only one layer of refinements instead of going through several layers. Solutions to more complex problems might typically involve multiple layers of data representations and many iterations of the stepwise refinement process. By studying an easy problem with several simple, short solutions, we can compare the properties of different solutions and we can bring out some key concepts in a simple form.

At this moment, the reader might take pleasure in trying to devise a solution to the problem, before reading further.

One possible solution follows the theme, "make a table and search it to find the solution." This is shown in Fig. C.5. Another possible solution follows the theme, "sort the inputs into descending order and find the first run of three repeated amounts." This is shown in Fig. C.6.

Let's illustrate the process of top-down programming with stepwise refinement by going through the refinement steps for the solution shown in Fig. C.5. We can start by making a Java program strategy giving a template for the top-level structure of the **Table** class whose goals are those of Fig. C.5. This is given as Program Strategy C.7.

*investigating several solutions*

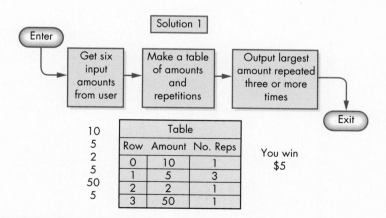

**Figure C.5** Make a Table and Search It

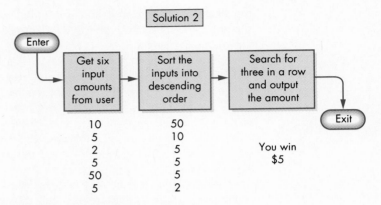

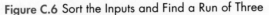

**Figure C.6** Sort the Inputs and Find a Run of Three

The **Translator** class, shown in Program C.4, translates the input string (typed by the user in the GUI input text box) into an integer input array after which it constructs a table object, **T**, using the method call **Table T = new Table( )**; given on line 31 of Program C.4. It then passes the integer input array to **T**, using the method call **T.getInput(inputArray)**; given on line 34 of Program C.4. If we implement **Table T**'s getInput method by simply writing,

```
public void getInput(int[ ] A) {
    inputArray = A;
}
```

we can be assured that **Table T** will have an array of six integer inputs stored as the value of its private data field **inputArray** (declared on line 4 of Program Strategy C.7).

```
     |    class Table {
     |
     |        // declare private data fields hidden inside the Table class
     |            private int [ ] inputArray;   // saves a sharable copy of the input array
  5  |            // plus, various private fields to store the table's contents
     |
     |        // define publicly accessible interface methods for a Table object T
     |            public void    T.getInput(int[ ] A) { ... }
     |            public int      T.findWinningAmount( ) { ... }
 10  |
     |        // define private methods used to implement the public methods
     |            private void   makeTable( )  { ... }
     |            private void   insertAmount(int amt)  { ... }
     |            private int     winningAmount( )  { ... }
 15  |
     |    } // end class Table
```

**Program Strategy C.7** Template for theTable Class

For example, if the user had typed: 10 5 2 5 50 5 in the GUI input text box and had pressed the Enter key, the text input event would have been handled, the input string would have been translated into an integer array, and that integer array would have been transmitted to be the value of the private data field variable inputArray in the Table object, T, as follows:

| | | | |
|---|---|---|---|
| inputArray[0] = | 10 | inputArray[3] = | 5 |
| inputArray[1] = | 5 | inputArray[4] = | 50 |
| inputArray[2] = | 2 | inputArray[5] = | 5 |

The Translator object, Trans, next makes a call on Table T's method for finding the winning amount, using the method call T.findWinningAmount( ), given on line 37 of Program C.4. When this winning amount is computed and then returned by the Table object T, the integer result is converted to a string that is transmitted back to the WinnerDetector applet for display in the GUI output text box.

Having decided what the public interface methods of the Table class must do, we now turn to the implementation of the Table method findWinningAmount( ) as the only remaining unsolved part of our object-oriented design for the Table class. We use top-down programming to accomplish this.

Thus, to do a stepwise refinement of the method findWinningAmount( ), whose method prototype is given on line 9 of Program Strategy C.7, we can simply write:

```
   |    public int findWinningAmount( ) {
   |
   |        // make a table of amounts and repetitions from the input array
   |            makeTable( );
 5 |
   |        // find the winning amount in the table and return it as an integer amount
   |            return winningAmount( );
   |    }
```

Here, the method makeTable( ) builds a table of amounts and repetitions, as suggested by the middle box in Fig. C.5, and the method winningAmount( ) searches this table to find and return the largest integer amount repeated three or more times. Thus, our refinement of the top-level method, findWinningAmount( ), has led to the creation of two new, as-yet-unwritten methods, makeTable( ) and winningAmount( ). In the top-down programming technique, the refinement of each method can lead to the generation of new unwritten methods such as these. If we keep putting the unwritten methods on a list, and refining them, one-by-one, we eventually encounter a condition in which all methods have been written and the program is completed. Thus, we turn next to the task of refining the method, makeTable( ).

We might try to choose the data structure for the table before designing the strategy for the algorithm, or, alternatively, we might try to design the algorithm before choosing the details of the data structure. The second alternative is called *postponing the choice of data representations*. Let's try this second idea—designing the algorithm before choosing the data structure. To do this, we have to use abstract table operations that make no commitments to the representation. We can accomplish this by using abstract method calls that do not reveal any underlying representational choices.

```
    |    private void makeTable( ) {                              // make a table of amounts
    |                                                             // and their repetitions
    |
    |            (initialize the table to be empty)
    |
 5  |            (insert each of the six input amounts into the table)
    |                for (i = 0; i < 6; ++i) {
    |
    |                        (insert the amount inputArray[i] into the table)
    |                        insertAmount(inputArray[i]);
10  |
    |                }
    |    }
```

**Program Strategy C.8** Making the Table

Program Strategy C.8 presents a way to make a table that contains integer amounts and their repetition counts. On line 9, it makes a call on another abstract unwritten method, insertAmount(inputArray[i]). Program Strategy C.9 gives a refinement of the method insertAmount( ). When we call methods that we have not yet written, we can put their names on a list of remaining methods to write. When we have written all the methods on this list, we have completed one level of the stepwise refinement process. This technique proceeds *top-down*, because the activity of creating program strategies at the top level leads to the creation of methods calls, whose lower-level method definitions have not yet been written. Thus we find ourselves filling in the levels and details of the overall program strategy in a top-to-bottom order—proceeding layer by layer, starting with the topmost (or most abstract) layer, and progressively defining lower (or more detailed) layers.

*using a list of unwritten methods*

```
    |    private void insertAmount(int amountToInsert) {          // insert an amount
    |                                                             // into the table
    |
    |            (if one of the rows in the table already contains the amount to insert,)
 5  |            (increase the number of repetitions in the row and exit the method)
    |
    |                for (each row in the table) {
    |                    if ( (the row's amount) == amountToInsert )  {
    |                        (increase the row's repetition count by one)
10  |                        (and return from the method)
    |                    }
    |                }
    |
    |            (if no row's amount matched the amount to insert, then add a new row to)
15  |            (the table containing the amount to insert and a repetition count of one)
    |
    |    }
```

**Program Strategy C.9** Inserting an Amount into the Table

**bottom-up programming**

The opposite strategy is called a *bottom-up method*. In a bottom-up method, we first write the definitions of methods before using calls on them inside other higher-level methods. This causes us to give the details of the bottom layers of the overall program before filling in the higher levels that use the methods we have already written at the lower levels. Thus, in bottom-up programming, we *define methods before using them*— whereas in top-down programming, we *use methods before defining them*.

Let's now provide the abstract program strategy for searching the table to determine and return the winning amount, which is the largest amount repeated three or more times. This is given as Program Strategy C.10.

Note that we have given program strategies that refine all of the methods in the top-level, object-oriented design for the **Table** class (Program Strategy C.7), but we have not yet chosen a data representation for the table to be used to store amounts and repetitions. At this point, we know all of the abstract operations on the table that will be needed to solve the problem. There are two such table operations: *inserting* an amount and *searching* the table to find the largest amount repeated three or more times. Once we know the nature of the insertion and searching operations to be used, we are in a good position to judge what kinds of representations and algorithms will work well.

## Choosing a Data Representation for the Table

**the advantage of postponing the choice of data representations**

Note that we have given Program Strategies C.8–C.10 for making a table, inserting new amounts into the table, and searching the table to find the largest amount won, *without having chosen the data representation for the table yet*. This means we have used

```
     |    private int winningAmount( )  {          // search the table for a row having the
     |                                              // largest amount repeated three
     |        int amountWon;                        // or more times and return it
     |
  5  |        (initially establish the amountWon to be zero.)
     |        (it will remain 0 unless a higher amount is discovered during the search.)
     |
     |        (search the table to find the largest amount won among the rows)
     |        (having three or more repetitions)
 10  |
     |            for (each row in the table) {
     |                if ( (the row's number of repetitions ≥ 3) &&
     |                        (the row's amount  > amountWon)  ) {
     |                    amountWon = (the row's amount);
 15  |                }
     |            }
     |
     |        return amountWon;
     |
     |    }
```

**Program Strategy C.10** Returning the Winning Amount

```
class Row {

  // each Row object has two data fields
    int   amount;
    int   repetitions;

  // there is one Row constructor defined
    Row(int amt, int reps) {
        amount = amt;
        repetitions = reps;
    }

}
```

**Program C.11** The Row Class

abstraction to postpone the commitment to the choice of data representation for the table. Consequently, we are free to consider different table representations (such as arrays of objects representing the rows, or two-dimensional integer arrays, or linked lists of nodes representing the rows, or various binary tree representations that are considered in Chapter 9 that studies the Table ADT). And we are free to choose a representation for which there exist algorithms that efficiently implement the (insertion and searching) table operations we need to perform.

We will not get involved in the comparative advantages and disadvantages of the many possible representational choices for tables here, since we study alternative table representations in Chapters 8, 9, and 10. However, we emphasize that this is the golden moment for selecting an advantageous data representation. The choice would be especially significant if we needed to use huge tables having efficient insertion and search times for many items. (This would be important, for instance, if we were given the problem of finding the largest amount repeated 50 or more times among 20,000 amounts.) In the present case, however, the problem is so small that almost any reasonable representational choice we make for the table will be sufficient. So let's proceed to choose an array of simple **Row** objects for our table representation. Program C.11 gives the Java class definition for these **Row** objects.

Let's now make the agreement to store an array of up to six **Rows** in an array, **rowArray**, kept as a private data field in the **Table** class, using the following data field declarations, to be inserted on line 5 of Program Strategy C.7.

```
private Row[ ]    rowArray;
private int       numberOfRows;
```

We further agree that the private integer data field **numberOfRows** will keep the number of occupied rows in the **rowArray**.

Once we have made the decision to use this representation for the table, the details of the final stepwise refinements of Program Strategies C.8–C.10 are fairly easy to fill in. For instance, let's now refine Program Strategy C.8 for making the table into a detailed, executable Java method. This yields Program C.12.

```
     |      private void makeTable( ) {                      // create a table of amounts
     |                                                         // and their repetitions
     |            // initialize the table to be empty
     |                 rowArray = new Row[6];
  5  |                 numberOfRows = 0;        // initially there are no rows in the rowArray
     |
     |            // insert each of the six input amounts into the table
     |                 for (int i = 0; i < 6; i++) {
     |                      insertAmount(inputArray[i]);
 10  |                 }
     |      }
```

**Program C.12** Making the Table

We see that line 9 of Program C.12 contains a call on the method, **insertAmount**, which we have not written yet. Proceeding top-down, we are supposed to define the details of methods that have been called but have not yet been written. So, it is time to define the details of the method, **insertAmount**. Program C.13 provides these details (which refine Program Strategy C.9).

Knowing the details of the data representation for the table also enables us to fill in the details of the table searching process. To do this, we follow the outline supplied in Program Strategy C.10, and we provide specific steps in Java to accomplish its goals. The results are given as Program C.14 for the **winningAmount( )** method.

Now that all the detailed, low-level methods and data representations have been completed, we can assemble them into Program C.15, giving a finished program for the **Table** class. When this assembled version of the **Table** class is, in turn, inserted into the program for the **WinnerDetector** applet (on line 87 of Program C.3) a complete executable version of the **WinnerDetector** applet is obtained.

```
     |      private void insertAmount(int amountToInsert) {        // insert an amount
     |                                                              // into the table
     |            // if one of the rows in the table already contains the amountToInsert
     |            // increase the number of repetitions in that row and exit the method
  5  |                 for (int j = 0; j < numberOfRows; j++) {
     |                      if (rowArray[j].amount == amountToInsert) {
     |                           rowArray[j].repetitions++;     // increase repetition count
     |                           return;                           // and exit
     |                      }
 10  |                 }
     |
     |            // otherwise, if no row's amount matched the amountToInsert,
     |            // then add a new row to the table containing the amountToInsert
     |            // and a repetition count of one; then increase the numberOfRows
 15  |            // by one.
     |                 rowArray[numberOfRows] = new Row(amountToInsert, 1);
     |                 numberOfRows++;
     |      }
```

**Program C.13** Inserting an Amount into the Table

```
 1 | private int winningAmount( ) {          // search the table for a row having the
   |                                         // largest amount repreated three
   |     int amountWon;                      // or more times and return it
   |
 5 |     // initially establish the amountWon to be zero.
   |     // it will remain 0 unless a higher amount is
   |     // discovered during the search.
   |         amountWon = 0;
   |
10 |     // search the table to find the largest amount won among rows
   |     // having three or more repetitions
   |
   |         for (int i = 0; i < numberOfRows; i++) {
   |             if ( (rowArray[i].repetitions >= 3) &&
15 |                         (rowArray[i].amount > amountWon) ) {
   |                 amountWon = rowArray[i].amount;
   |             }
   |         }
   |
20 |     // finally, return the integer for the amount won
   |         return amountWon;
   | }
```

**Program C.14** Finding and Returning the Winning Amount

```
 1 | class Table {
   |
   |     // declare three private data fields hidden inside the Table class
   |         private int [ ] inputArray;          // holds the array of input amounts
 5 |         private Row[ ] rowArray;             // gives the rows of the table
   |         private int numberOfRows;            // the number of rows in the table
   |
   |     // define publicly accessible interface methods for a Table object
   |
10 |         public void getInput(int[ ] A) {
   |             inputArray = A;
   |         }
   |
   |         public int findWinningAmount( ) {
15 |             makeTable( );                    // make table of amounts and repetitions
   |             return winningAmount( );         // find winning amount and return it
   |         }
   |
   |     // define private methods used to implement the public methods
20 |         private void   makeTable( ) { ... }           // insert Program C.12
   |         private void   insertAmount(int amt) { ... }  // insert Program C.13
   |         private int    winningAmount( ) { ... }       // insert Program C.14
   |
   | } // end class Table
25 |
   | /* ---<insert here the definition of the Row class from Program C.11 >--- */
```

**Program C.15** Final Assembly of Components into the Table Class

## A Second Refinement

Another way to find a lottery winner is to refine the second top-level strategy given in Fig. C.6, which proposes to solve the problem by sorting the inputs in descending order followed by finding the first run of three adjacent identical amounts, if there is one. (In part, we perform this second refinement to set up an example to use in the next section on proofs of program correctness.) In creating this second refinement, we need only refine the **Table** class in a second new way, while leaving the **WinnerDetector** applet and the **Translator** class untouched. In fact, in the **Table** class shown in Program C.15, all we need do to accomplish this second refinement is: (1) to delete the private data field declarations given on lines 5:6 (for the **rowArray** and the **numberOfRows**), (2) to replace the method for findWinningAmount( ) on lines 14:17 with the following new refinement:

```
public int findWinningAmount( ) {
    selectionSort(inputArray,0,5);      // sort inputArray into descending order
    return winningAmount( );            // find winning amount and return it
}
```

and, (3) to give new refinements for the **selectionSort** and **winningAmount** methods.

As you know, there are many ways to sort an array of numbers, **inputArray**, into descending order. (Several of the most important sorting algorithms are compared in Chapter 10.) For the purpose of performing the sorting process specified in this replacement for the findWinningAmount( ) method, we use a selection sorting method. We assume that the method call, **selectionSort(inputArray,0,5)**, can be used to sort the numbers in the input array, **inputArray[0:5]**, into descending order. We will define the actual details of this selection sorting algorithm last in this section, after developing the rest of the program, so that it will be fresh on our minds when we use it as the focus for our proof of program correctness in the next section. (In other words, we assume that we can solve the sorting problem at this point in our program development, which allows us to move on to the next unsolved refinement step.)

*using the selection sorting method*

Let's now solve the problem of refining the **winningAmount( )** method on the next line of the previous replacement—namely, searching for three identical numbers next to one another in an array already sorted into descending order, and printing the thrice-repeated amount, if it exists. Program C.16 finds and prints the first amount repeated three times in succession in an array, **inputArray**, assumed to contain numbers sorted in descending order.

The **Table** class can now be refined in our second new way by inserting the method calls that accomplish (or have been assumed to accomplish) its top-level goals. Here we include references to the selection sort method developed later in Program C.19, and to its subroutine, **findMax**, given in Program C.20. This yields Program C.17 as our final working program for the **Table** class, which can now be substituted on line 87 of Program C.3 to give a second complete executable version of the **WinnerDetector** applet.

```
 1  |   private int winningAmount( )  {
    |
    |       int   amountWon;              // amountWon is the winning amount, if any
    |       int   i;                      // i is an index for the inputArray
 5  |
    |       // initially establish the amountWon to be zero
    |       amountWon = 0;
    |
    |       // for each possible starting position i = 0,1,2, and 3, where a run
10  |       // of three identical values could start in the sorted inputArray,
    |       // check to see if a run of three exists, and exit if it does.
    |       for (i = 0; i < 4; i++)  {
    |           if ( (inputArray[i] == inputArray[i+1])
    |               && (inputArray[i+1] == inputArray[i+2]) ) {
15  |                   amountWon = inputArray[i];  // a winning amount was found
    |                   break;            // exit for-statement after winning amount found
    |           }
    |       }
    |
20  |       // return the integer amount won
    |       return amountWon;
    |   }
```

**Program C.16** Finding and Returning the Winning Amount

```
 1  |   class Table {
    |
    |       // declare the inputArray as a hidden data field of the Table class
    |       private int [ ] inputArray;          // holds the array of input amounts
 5  |
    |       // define publicly accessible interface methods for a Table object
    |
    |           public void getInput(int[ ] A) {
    |               inputArray = A;
10  |           }
    |
    |           public int findWinningAmount( ) {
    |               selectionSort(inputArray,0,5);   // sort the inputArray amounts
    |                                                // into descending order
15  |               return winningAmount( );     // find winning amount and return it
    |           }
    |
    |       // define private methods used to implement the public methods
    |           private int    winningAmount( ) { ... }      // insert Program C.16
20  |           private void   selectionSort( )  { ... }     // insert Program C.19
    |           private int    findMax( )  { ... }           // insert Program C.20
    |
    |   } // end class Table
```

**Program C.17** Second Final Assembly of Components into the Table Class

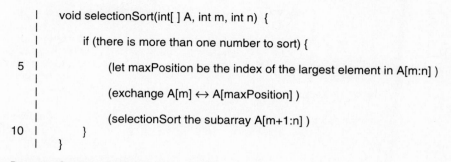

```
 |      void selectionSort(int[ ] A, int m, int n)  {
 |
 |          if (there is more than one number to sort) {
 |
5|              (let maxPosition be the index of the largest element in A[m:n] )
 |
 |              (exchange A[m] ↔ A[maxPosition] )
 |
 |              (selectionSort the subarray A[m+1:n] )
10|          }
 |      }
```

**Program Strategy C.18** Selection Sorting

We have deliberately deferred until last, the task of writing the sorting algorithm, selectionSort(A,m,n), which sorts the subarray A[m:n] into descending order, using the method of *selection sorting*.

The idea behind selection sorting is first to *select* the largest number among the numbers in positions A[m], A[m + 1], ... , A[n], then to exchange this largest number with whatever number is in the first position A[m] (after which, A[m] contains the largest number in the subarray A[m:n]), and finally to selection sort the remaining numbers in the subarray A[m+1:n]. The top-level strategy for doing this is expressed in Program Strategy C.18. If we assume we have a function, findMax(A,m,n), that returns the position of the largest number in the subarray A[m:n], then we can use it to refine Program Strategy C.18 into the recursive selection sorting algorithm given in Program C.19.

the key idea behind
selection sorting

```
 |      void selectionSort(int[ ]A, int m, int n)  {
 |
 |          int   maxPosition;          // maxPosition is the index of A's biggest item
 |          int   temp;                 // temp is used to exchange items in A
5|
 |          if (m < n) {                // if there is more than one number to sort
 |
 |              // let maxPosition be the index of the largest number in A[m:n]
 |                  maxPosition = findMax(A,m,n);
10|
 |              // exchange A[m] ↔ A[maxPosition]
 |                  temp = A[m];
 |                  A[m] = A[maxPosition];
 |                  A[maxPosition] = temp;
15|
 |              // selectionSort the subarray A[m+1:n]
 |                  selectionSort(A, m+1, n);
 |          }
 |
 |      }
```

**Program C.19** Selection Sorting

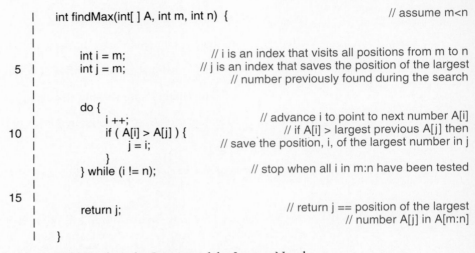

```
  |    int findMax(int[ ] A, int m, int n)  {                           // assume m<n
  |
  |
  |        int i = m;                          // i is an index that visits all positions from m to n
5 |        int j = m;                          // j is an index that saves the position of the largest
  |                                            // number previously found during the search
  |
  |        do {
  |            i ++;                            // advance i to point to next number A[i]
10|            if ( A[i] > A[j] ) {             // if A[i] > largest previous A[j] then
  |                j = i;                       // save the position, i, of the largest number in j
  |            }
  |        } while (i != n);                    // stop when all i in m:n have been tested
  |
15|
  |        return j;                            // return j == position of the largest
  |                                             // number A[j] in A[m:n]
  |
  |    }
```

**Program C.20** Finding the Position of the Largest Number

finding the position of
the largest

The only remaining missing piece of our overall program that needs to be completed is to write the function, findMax(A,m,n), which finds the position of the largest integer in the subarray A[m:n]. This is an easy program to write, of the kind usually covered in a first programming course in Java. Program C.20 gives one solution (among many that are possible).

In Section C.3, we will investigate how to prove that this program does what it is supposed to do. For now, we note that it is the last of the unwritten programs that needs to be defined in order to complete all the pieces needed to get Program C.17 for the **Table** class to work properly. Before moving on to the next section, let's pause to make two brief observations:

1. We didn't need to define another data structure while doing the second refinement, since the input array was sufficient.
2. We used *searching* in the first solution and *sorting* in the second solution. Searching and sorting are general purpose building blocks useful for solving many kinds of problems. This is why attention is given to them in computer science, in general, and in Chapter 10, in particular.

## C.2 REVIEW QUESTIONS

1. What is object-oriented design?
2. What is the difference between top-down and bottom-up programming?
3. What does it mean to postpone the choice of data representations and algorithms?
4. What is stepwise refinement? What gets refined? What are the steps in stepwise refinement?

## C.2 EXERCISES

1. Create a different stepwise refinement of Programs C.11 to C.15, using a linked list of **Row** nodes to represent the table. Each **Row** node in the linked list should represent a row of the table, and should contain: (a) a dollar amount, (b) the number of times that dollar amount is repeated in the input array, **A**, and (c) a link to the next **Row** node in the linked list representing the table. These items are given in the three data fields shown in the class definition for a **Row** node that follows:

```
class Row {

    // the data fields are as follows:
        int      amount;            // the dollar amount
        int      repetitions;       // how many times it is repeated
        Row      link;              // pointer to next Row node

    Row(int amt, int reps) {        // a constructor that constructs
        amount = amt;               // a Row node with an amount
        repetitions = reps;         // and initial repetitions, and
        link = null;                // that has a null link
    }

}
```

2. A powerful programming idea is to create new programs from reusable software components. (We will explore this important idea later in Section C.7.) Suppose you had access to a Java priority queue class, whose interface is given in Program 5.3, and suppose you are given the following method:

```
  |    boolean threeOrMore(int amt) {          // returns true if and only if
  |        int k = 0;                          // the inputArray contains
  |        for (int j = 0; j < 6; j++) {       // the amount, amt, repeated
  |            if (inputArray[j] == amt) k++;  // three or more times
5 |        }
  |        return (k >= 3);
  |    }
```

Can you make use of these reusable components to refine the following program strategy into another short solution to the **winningAmount( )** method in the **Table** class? (Two other solutions were given as Programs C.14 and C.16.)

```
   |    private int winningAmount( ) {
   |
   |        (assume the inputArray holds the six input amounts.)
   |        (initialize the priority queue, PQ, to make it empty.)
 5 |
   |        for (int i = 0; i < 6; i++) {
   |            if ( threeOrMore(inputArray[i]) ) PQ.insert(inputArray[i]);
   |        }
   |
10 |        return ( PQ.empty( ) ? 0 : PQ.remove( ) );
   |    }
```

3. Show that Program C.16 can be made more efficient by replacing lines 13:14 with the replacement line: if ( inputArray[i] == inputArray[i+2] ) { . Give a reason why this optimization does not cause Program C.16 to compute incorrect results.

## C.3 Proving Programs Correct

### LEARNING OBJECTIVES

1. To understand how to annotate a program with assertions.
2. To learn about preconditions, postconditions, and loop invariants.
3. To understand the process of proving programs correct by studying some preliminary examples.
4. To learn a bit about formal logic.

the importance of<br>reasoning about programs

Reasoning about programs is an important ability for computer scientists to master. This skill comes into play at many crucial times, such as: (a) when creating algorithms initially, (b) when debugging them, (c) when figuring out how to improve their performance, and (d) when verifying that procedures and functions inside a larger program work correctly.

In this section, we are going to walk step-by-step through an example of how to prove that a program does what it is intended to do. This process is called *program verification*.

The first problem you face in trying to prove that a program, P, does what it is *intended to do* is to come up with a precise statement of what P is intended to do. A helpful way to do this is to provide *assertions* that express the conditions both *before* and *after* P is executed. You might think of assertions as statements that can be either *true* or *false*, and that are expressed in a *precise logical language*.

assertions

The first assertion, called the *precondition*, describes the conditions that hold true *before* P is executed. The second assertion, called the *postcondition*, describes the conditions that hold true *after* P has been executed (assuming that the precondition was true beforehand). The general pattern is:

preconditions and<br>postconditions

```
{precondition}          // logical conditions that are true before P is executed
    P                   // a program to execute
{postcondition}         // logical conditions that are true after P is executed
```

For example, suppose we consider the function selectionSort(A,m,n), which is supposed to sort the items in the subarray, A[m:n], into descending order. To fill in this pattern in the case of selectionSort, we might write:

```
{m ≤ n}                        // asserts A must have at least one item to sort
    selectionSort(A,m,n);       // the sorting program to execute
{A[m] ≥ A[m+1] ≥ ... ≥ A[n]}   // asserts A's items are in descending order
```

To prove that selectionSort(A,m,n) sorts A[m:n] into descending order, we need to construct a proof that: if the precondition holds true and selectionSort(A,m,n) is executed, then afterwards the postcondition will be true—namely, the items in A[m:n] will be rearranged into descending order: $A[m] \geq A[m+1] \geq ... \geq A[n]$.

In the process of trying to prove this final result, we may do two things: (a) place additional assertions inside the text of the selectionSort program to describe intermediate conditions that arise during different phases of the computation, and (b) construct proofs of correctness of the subroutines used by selectionSort, so we can use the results of the subroutines' proofs to complete the main proof.

In fact, we will start with step (b)—proving that the method, findMax, used by selectionSort, succeeds in finding the position of the largest item in the subarray A[m:n]. Then we will use the results of this first proof inside the main proof that selectionSort works properly.

The pre- and postconditions for findMax(A,m,n) are as follows:

```
{m < n}                              // asserts A[m:n] must have more than one item
    j = findMax(A,m,n);                       // the program to execute
{A[j] ≥ A[m:n]}                  // asserts A[j] is the largest item in A[m:n]
```

Here, we use the notation, A[j] ≥ A[m:n], as a synonym for asserting the truth of each of the individual assertions: A[j] ≥ A[m], A[j] ≥ A[m+1], ... , and A[j] ≥ A[n].

Let's now look at Program C.21, which is a version of findMax in which we have added some extra intermediate assertions. These intermediate assertions are given

```
     |   int findMax(int[ ] A, int m, int n)  {
     |
     |
     |       // precondition: m < n
  5  |       // postcondition: returns position of largest item in subarray A[m:n]
     |
     |       int i;
     |       int j;
     |
 10  |       i = m;
     |       j = m;
     |
     |           {♦ ( i == m) ∧ (j == m) ∧ (m < n) ♦}
     |
 15  |       do {
     |
     |           i++ ;
     |
     |           if ( A[i] > A[j] )  j = i;
 20  |
     |                {♦ loop invariant: A[j] ≥ A[m:i] ∧ (i ≤ n) ♦}
     |
     |       } while ( i != n );
     |
 25  |           {♦ final assertion: A[j] ≥ A[m:n] ♦}
     |
     |       return j;              // return j as position of largest item in A[m:n]
     |
     |   }
```

**Program C.21** Finding the Position of the Largest Item

inside curly braces specially marked with beginning and ending diamonds, of the general form: {♦ assertion ♦}. (In several of these assertions, the symbol, ∧, from formal logic, is used to denote the logical *and* operator.)

We will next go through a step-by-step reasoning process to show how we can reason forward from the precondition to the postcondition. Along the way, we will use the intermediate assertions together with some reasoning about the actions performed by the program's statements.

When we start to execute the program, findMax, we can assume that the precondition (given on line 4 of Program C.21) is true. Hence, the assertion, m < n, holds true at the moment execution begins. The first two statements to be executed are: i = m; and j = m; given on lines 10:11. After executing these two statements, the variables i and j both have the value m. Consequently, on line 13, we know that the assertion {♦ (i == m) ∧ (j == m) ∧ (m < n) ♦}, must hold true.

Now we come to the challenging part, which is the do-while loop, given on lines 15:23. There is only one assertion inside this loop, the loop invariant on line 21. A loop-invariant assertion is an assertion with the special property that it is always true, no matter how many times you have executed the loop.

We are going to try to prove that the loop invariant always holds true using a process that resembles a proof by mathematical induction. First, we prove it holds true on the first trip through the loop. Then, assuming it holds true on the $i^{th}$ trip through the loop, we prove that it must hold true on the $(i+1)^{st}$ trip through the loop.

Before we enter the do-while loop for the first time, the assertion on line 13 holds true. This implies that the variable, i, has the value i == m, when the loop is entered for the first time. Executing the statement, i++; on line 17, changes the value of i to be i == m + 1. On line 19, the statement, if (A[i] > A[j]) j = i; is executed under conditions in which (j == m) and (i == m + 1). This means that in case A[m+1] is bigger than A[m], j is set equal to (m+1). Otherwise, if A[m+1] ≤ A[m], then j retains its former value, (j == m). In either case, j's value is set to the position of the larger item among the two items: A[m] and A[m+1]. This means that: A[j] ≥ A[m:m+1]. But since i == (m+1), we can rewrite this as asserting that: A[j] ≥ A[m:i], which is the first part of the loop invariant on line 21. The second part of the loop-invariant assertion, namely (i ≤ n), follows from the fact that, for any three integers, i, m, and n, if (m < n) and (i == m + 1), then (i ≤ n). (*Reason:* (m < n) means the integer m is at least 1 less than n, so adding 1 to m can make it equal to n, but can't make it greater than n.)

Let's now tackle the hard part—reasoning inductively about what happens on the $(i+1)^{st}$ trip through the loop, assuming the loop-invariant assertion is true on the $i^{th}$ trip through the loop. Suppose we know that: A[j] ≥ A[m:i] ∧ (i ≤ n) is true just before we test the while-condition, while (i != n); at the end of the $i^{th}$ pass through the do-while loop. Suppose the while-condition (i != n) is still true, meaning we get sent around the loop one more time for the $(i+1)^{st}$ pass. Then, we need to combine two facts:

(i ≠ n)                              // from the while-condition (i != n) which was true,
A[j] ≥ A[m:i] ∧ (i ≤ n)                     // and the loop-invariant which was true

to get:

$$A[j] \geq A[m:i] \wedge (i < n)$$

// the condition that holds at the beginning
// of the (i+1)$^{st}$ trip around the loop

We get this because (i $\neq$ n) and (i $\leq$ n) combine to yield (i < n). (*Reason*: (i $\leq$ n) means i was either equal to n or less than n. But i couldn't have been equal to n if (i $\neq$ n) was also true. Consequently, the only remaining possibility was that i had to be strictly less than n, each time we were sent back around the loop.)

On the (i+1)$^{st}$ trip around the loop, on line 17, we first increase i by 1, knowing beforehand that: A[j] $\geq$ A[m:i] $\wedge$ (i < n). This means that after increasing i by 1, another assertion: A[j] $\geq$ A[m:i $-$ 1] $\wedge$ (i $\leq$ n) must hold. Now, on line 19, the statement, if (A[i] > A[j]) j = i; is executed. What this does is to compare A[j], which we know to be the largest item in A[m:i $-$ 1], with A[i]. If A[i] is bigger, j is set to i's value, so j then points to the largest item in A[m:i], whereas if A[i] is not bigger, then even though j's value is not changed, nonetheless, j still points to the largest item in A[m:i]. In either case, after line 19 is executed, we conclude that A[j] $\geq$ A[m:i] must be true. Combining this with (i $\leq$ n), (which remained true since i's value was not changed on line 19), we conclude that after line 19 has been executed on the (i+1)$^{st}$ trip through the loop, the loop-invariant assertion A[j] $\geq$ A[m:i] $\wedge$ (i $\leq$ n) still holds true. Thus we can establish that the loop-invariant assertion holds true on every trip through the loop, using an induction proof of the following form: We know the loop-invariant is true on the first trip through the loop. We also know that if it is true on any given trip, it will remain true on the next trip. Consequently, it is true on every trip through the loop.

We can finish our proof by reasoning about what happens when we exit the do-while loop on lines 15:23. Knowing the loop invariant on line 21 is true, suppose we test the while-condition in while (i != n); on line 23, and find that it is false. This causes us to exit the do-while loop. Upon exit, we can combine the knowledge that (i == n) with the conditions in the loop invariant: A[j] $\geq$ A[m:i] $\wedge$ (i $\leq$ n). To do this, we note that (i $\leq$ n) simplifies to (i == n), since the alternative (i < n) couldn't have been true after we exited the loop. Moreover, we can substitute (i == n) in the first part of the condition, A[j] $\geq$ A[m:i], getting the result: A[j] $\geq$ A[m:n]. But this was the postcondition result we were hoping to establish. It asserts that A[j] is the largest item in the entire subarray A[m:n], as is stated in the final assertion, on line 25: {$\blacklozenge$ **final assertion**: A[j] $\geq$ A[m:n] $\blacklozenge$}. Finally, when we return j's value as the value of the method on line 27, we can be confident j gives the position of the largest item.

We're now ready to go back and prove that **selectionSort(A,m,n)** sorts A[m:n], using the fact we just established that j = findMax(A,m,n); sets j to the position of the largest item in A[m:n]. To see how to do this, we examine Program C.22, which is a version of the **selectionSort** program annotated with some new intermediate assertions.

The statement, **maxPosition = findMax(A,m,n)**, on line 12 of Program C.22 can be executed only when the if-condition (m < n), on line 10, is true beforehand. This means that when the function findMax(A,m,n) is called on line 12, its precondition (m < n) is satisfied. We have just proven that, under these conditions, findMax(A,m,n) returns the position of the largest item in A[m:n]. Consequently the variable, **maxPosition**, is set to this position, and on line 14, we can assert:

*finishing the proof*

```
 |     void selectionSort(int[ ] A, int m, int n)  {
 |
 |
 |         // precondition: m ≤ n
5|         // postcondition: A[m:n] is sorted such that: A[m] ≥ A[m+1] ≥ ... ≥ A[n]
 |
 |         int maxPosition;
 |         int temp;
 |
10|        if (m < n) {                                    // if there is more than one item to sort
 |
 |             maxPosition = findMax(A,m,n);
 |
 |                 {♦ A[maxPosition] ≥ A[m:n] ♦}
15|
 |             // exchange A[m] ↔ A[maxPosition]
 |             temp = A[m]; A[m] = A[maxPosition]; A[maxPosition] = temp;
 |
 |                 {♦ A[m] ≥ A[m:n] ♦}
20|
 |             selectionSort(A, m+1, n);   {♦ yields: A[m+1] ≥ A[m+2] ≥ ... ≥ A[n] ♦}
 |
 |                 {♦ A[m] ≥ A[m+1] ≥ ... ≥ A[n] ♦}
 |
25|        }
 |
 |                 {♦ final assertion: A[m] ≥ A[m+1] ≥ ... ≥ A[n] ♦}
 |
 |     }
```

**Program C.22** Selection Sorting

{♦ A[maxPosition] ≥ A[m:n] ♦}, meaning A[maxPosition] is the largest item in the subarray A[m:n].

On line 17, we exchange the subarray's first item, A[m], with the subarray's largest item, A[maxPosition]. After doing this, we assert (on line 19) that the first item, A[m], is now the largest item in A[m:n], by writing: {♦ A[m] ≥ A[m:n] ♦}.

Our final step is to sort the remaining items, A[m+1:n], into decreasing order, using the recursive call, selectionSort(A, m+1, n), given on line 21. The effect of making this recursive call is to rearrange the items in A[m+1:n] into decreasing order, as indicated by the assertion {♦ A[m+1] ≥ A[m+2] ≥ ... ≥ A[n] ♦} on the right side of line 21. But since A[m] was not moved by the rearrangements made during the recursive call and was the largest item in the array before the recursive call was made (according to the assertion on line 19), we know that A[m] ≥ A[m+1] must also hold true after returning from the recursive call. Putting the fact, A[m] ≥ A[m+1], together with the fact, A[m+1] ≥ ... ≥ A[n], yields the final assertion: A[m] ≥ A[m+1] ≥ ... ≥ A[n], given on line 27, but only in the case that the if-statement on lines 10:25 was executed.

In the remaining case that the if-condition (m < n), on line 10, was false, combining the falsehood of (m < n) with the precondition (m ≤ n), on line 4, implies (m == n)

*our final step*

must have been true. In this case, A[m:n] degenerates to the subarray, A[m:m] with just one item in it, so there are no items to sort. In this case, the final assertion can be viewed as being what mathematicians call "vacuously true." Loosely translated, we could say this means that subarrays containing just one item can always be considered to be sorted in decreasing order.

Alert readers might have noticed that we used a second form of induction in constructing the proof of **selectionSort**. This is sometimes called *recursion induction*. This method is applied by assuming that recursive calls on smaller-sized problems within the text of the main outer recursive function, correctly solve the smaller subproblems. Then the truth of the postcondition for the subproblem can be assumed inside the proof of correctness of the main recursive function. It is also necessary to prove that the postcondition holds for the base cases of the recursion.

recursion induction

(*Note:* It is furthermore necessary to prove that base cases are always encountered in a finite number of steps so that the recursion is guaranteed to stop eventually. Otherwise, an infinite regress may exist. In the case of the **selectionSort** method, since the size of the subproblems encountered in the recursive calls goes down by one each time, and since the base case occurs when the subarray has one item in it, the **selectionSort** function is guaranteed to terminate.)

This completes our proof that **selectionSort** correctly rearranges the items in A[m:n] into descending order: $A[m] \geq A[m+1] \geq ... \geq A[n]$.

## A Subtle Bug

Alert readers may have noticed a loophole in what we did. Our final postcondition, $A[m] \geq A[m+1] \geq ... \geq A[n]$, required only that the values in A[m:n] be in decreasing order at the conclusion of the sorting process. What if some (impish) programmer had written Program C.23 for **selectionSort**?

This program just replaces all the items in A[m:n] with a copy of the first item A[m]. Is this program a correct sorting algorithm?

```
    void impishSelectionSort(int[ ] A, int m, int n) {


        // precondition: m ≤ n
5       // postcondition: A[m:n] is sorted such that: A[m] ≥ A[m+1] ≥ ... ≥ A[n]

        int i;

        for ( i = m; i <= n; i++ ) {
10          A[i] = A[m];
        }
            {♦ final assertion: A[m] ≥ A[m+1] ≥ ... ≥ A[n] ♦}

    }
```

**Program C.23** Impish Selection Sorting

According to the criteria we have been discussing, it is a correct sorting algorithm, since whenever the precondition ($m \leq n$) is true, it carries out an action that makes the postcondition true. (Note that the postcondition, $A[m] \geq A[m+1] \geq \ldots \geq A[n]$, is true when all the items in $A[m:n]$ are equal to $A[m]$.)

the problem of
incomplete assertions

The problem here is that the postcondition, as we have stated it, is *incomplete*. What we really intended to say was that sorting the items in $A[m:n]$ meant rearranging them into decreasing order, without deleting or duplicating any items, or introducing any new ones. It turns out that our original selection sorting algorithm did, in fact, rearrange items without destroying any of them or adding any new ones. That this is so follows from the fact that the action of repeatedly exchanging different pairs of items (on line 17 of Program C.22) always preserves the original items as it rearranges their order.

a deep flaw in the method

The flaw that we have exposed is philosophically a very deep one in software engineering. How do we know that the formal logical assertions in the preconditions and postconditions correctly and completely express the true statement of what the program is supposed to do? The answer is that we don't. We can never prove that the pre- and postconditions really capture the intentions of the program. All that a correctness proof accomplishes is to prove the correspondence between statements expressed in a language of logical assertion and the net effect of executing actions defined by the statements in the program. It can tell us that the net effect of executing those statements is to create the situation described by the postconditions, provided the preconditions held true beforehand. It cannot tell us that the formal description given by the pre- and postconditions completely captures the true meaning that the people who wrote them should have had in mind. That is, a proof of correctness won't reveal to us the fallacies that might exist when the pre- and postconditions fail to state something important that should have been captured and expressed, but was in fact left out.

This is one of the reasons why software engineers use extensive program testing in addition to techniques such as correctness proofs. Doing correctness proofs helps raise our confidence that the program will do what it is supposed to do. But testing helps raise this confidence further. In fact, thorough testing may help reveal cases where the program didn't work as intended—cases that were missed because the pre- and postconditions didn't completely capture all the possible situations in which the program was meant to work.

## A Bit of Formal Logic

Reasoning about programs benefits from the use of precise thinking. Sloppy, error-prone reasoning is seldom helpful. A good way to attain precision in logical reasoning is through the correct use of formal logic.

using formal logic

propositional logic,
predicate logic, and
quantifiers

In fact, if you have already taken a first course in Java programming, you already know a lot of useful things about formal logical reasoning. Specifically, the Java programming language contains logical expressions formed from things like: (1) variables, (2) relational operators (such as '>' in $x > 3$), and (3) logical operators (such as &&, | |, and ! ). Each logical expression has a **boolean** value that is either **true** or **false**.

Logical expressions used in programming correspond to a class of propositional expressions used in what is called *propositional logic*, and the propositional expressions used in propositional logic are, in turn, a subset of an even larger set of expressions used in what is called *predicate logic*. Roughly speaking, you can think of propositional logic as using a slightly extended class of Java's logical expressions, and you can think of predicate logic as adding *quantifiers* to propositional logic. Quantifiers express ideas such as, "For all x, P(x) is true," symbolized as $\forall x P(x)$, or "There exists an x, such that P(x) is true," symbolized as $\exists x P(x)$. (This treatment is oversimplified slightly. In particular, Java's "short-circuit" operators **&&** and **||** do not correspond exactly to the logical *and* ($\wedge$) and *or* ($\vee$) operators of logic.)

For example, let's consider how to express the idea that "the array element A[j] is the largest element among the elements in the subarray, A[m:n]." The subarray, A[m:n], consists of the individual array elements: A[m], A[m + 1], ... , A[n]. To say that A[j] is the largest among these is the same as saying that $A[j] \geq A[m]$, $A[j] \geq A[m + 1]$, ... , and $A[j] \geq A[n]$. By using the quantifier, "for all," we can say this in another way, in English, as: "For all integers, i, if i lies in the range ($m \leq i \leq n$), then it is true that $A[j] \geq A[i]$." Using symbols in predicate logic, this could be written as, "$\forall i [ (m \leq i \leq n) \supset (A[j] \geq A[i]) ]$." (Here, the horseshoe symbol in $A \supset B$, is a logical connective that is pronounced "A implies B," which means, "*if* A is true, *then* B must be true.")

In the correctness proof given previously, we avoided using logical quantifiers ($\forall$ and $\exists$), by using two special notations. First, we used the expression, "$A[j] \geq A[m:n]$," to mean that A[j] was greater than or equal to each of the elements in the subarray A[m:n]. Second, we used the ellipsis (three dots in a row "..."). The occurrence of an ellipsis in the expression A ... B signifies that all the missing elements in the sequence between A and B are filled in. For example, to indicate that the elements in A[m:n] were arranged in decreasing order, we wrote: "$A[m] \geq A[m + 1] \geq ... \geq A[n]$." To state that A[m:n] is sorted in decreasing order without using the ellipsis (...), we could write: $\forall i [(m \leq i < n) \supset (A[i] \geq A[i+1])]$. In English, this is pronounced as follows: "For all i, if i is greater than or equal to m and is strictly less than n, then A[i] is greater than or equal to A[i+1]." The only logical connective we used in our proof was the "and" operator ($\wedge$). But in addition to this "and" operator, there are a few other logical operators that are worth considering. Table C.24 presents five logical connectives commonly used in propositional calculus and the quantifiers used in first-order predicate calculus.

If you have not already done so, an investment you can make that will have significant payoff later is to build up some skills for manipulating and stating formal logical expressions.

There are many laws of logical equivalence that can be used to manipulate formal logic expressions. You probably know some of them already from your earlier study of Java. For instance, some introductory Java courses cover deMorgan's laws: $\sim(A \wedge B) \equiv ((\sim A) \vee (\sim B))$ and $\sim(A \vee B) \equiv ((\sim A) \wedge (\sim B))$.

DeMorgan's laws can be extended to cover existential quantifiers ($\exists x P(x)$) and universal quantifiers ($\forall x P(x)$), as follows: $\sim(\forall x P(x)) \equiv (\exists x [\sim P(x)])$ and $\sim(\exists x P(x)) \equiv (\forall x [\sim P(x)])$.

using quantifiers

| Expression | Pronunciation | The expression is *true:* |
|---|---|---|
| ~A | not A | when A is *false* |
| A ∧ B | A and B | when both A and B are *true* |
| A ∨ B | A or B | if either A or B is *true* |
| A ⊃ B | A implies B | if A is *true*, then B is *true* also |
| A ≡ B | A is equivalent to B | only if A and B are both *true* or A and B are both *false* |
| ∀ x P(x) | for all x, P(x) | if P(x) is *true* for all possible x |
| ∃ x P(x) | there exists an x, such that P(x) | if there exists an x, such that P(x) is *true* |

**Table C.24** Logical Symbols and Their Meanings

There are also many logical laws that allow us to replace a subexpression inside a bigger logical expression with something that is equivalent, or to deduce that an expression Q must be true if P is true beforehand and we also know that $P \supset Q$ holds true. A few of these laws are shown in Table C.25.

Let's study just two examples of the uses of these laws to illustrate how they can be applied to the process of logical manipulation of assertions.

First, suppose you wanted to show that if the subarray A[m:n] is not sorted in decreasing order, then there exists an adjacent pair of items, A[i] and A[i+1], such that A[i] < A[i+1]. Could we possibly show this by formal logical manipulations? The answer is, yes. Here's how. We start with the logical expression, E, that defines when A[m:n] is sorted in decreasing order. Then to assert that A[m:n] is not sorted, we could assert ~E.

$$E \equiv \forall i\,[(m \leq i < n) \supset (A[i] \geq A[i+1])]$$
$$\sim E \equiv \sim (\forall i\,[(m \leq i < n) \supset (A[i] \geq A[i+1])])$$

Now, we manipulate the right side of the last line by applying several exchange laws in sequence, as shown in Table C.26.

| | | | |
|---|---|---|---|
| A ⊃ B | ≡ | (~A) ∨ B | The definition of *implication* |
| A ≡ B | ≡ | (A ⊃ B) ∧ (B ⊃ A) | "≡" is sometimes called *coimplies* |
| A ∧ (A ⊃ B) | ⊃ | B | This law is called *modus ponens* |
| (A ∨ B) ∧ (~B) | ⊃ | A | The *modus tollendo ponens* law |
| ~(~A) | ≡ | A | The double negation law |

**Table C.25** Some Logical Laws

| | |
|---|---|
| $\sim (\forall\ i\ [(m \leq i < n) \supset (A[i] \geq A[i+1])])$ | The expression to manipulate |
| $\sim (\forall\ i\ [(\sim(m \leq i < n)) \vee (A[i] \geq A[i+1])])$ | Using $[A \supset B] \equiv [\ (\sim A)\ \vee B]$ |
| $\exists\ i \sim [(\sim(m \leq i < n)) \vee (A[i] \geq A[i+1])]$ | DeMorgan's law for $\sim(\forall\ x\ P(x))$ |
| $\exists\ i\ [(\sim(\sim(m \leq i < n))) \wedge \sim(A[i] \geq A[i+1])]$ | DeMorgan's law for $\sim(A \vee B)$ |
| $\exists\ i\ [(m \leq i < n) \wedge \sim(A[i] \geq A[i+1])]$ | Double negation law $\sim\sim A \equiv A$ |
| $\exists\ i\ [(m \leq i < n) \wedge (A[i] < A[i+1])]$ | Since $\sim(x \geq y) \equiv (x < y)$ |

Table C.26 Some Formal Logic Manipulations

*translating back into English*

Now we translate the last line back into English. It says, "There exists an i such that i lies in the range ($m \leq i < n$) and ($A[i] < A[i+1]$)." You can see that this is the same as saying that there exists an adjacent pair of array items $A[i]$ and $A[i+1]$ inside the subarray $A[m:n]$, such that $A[i] < A[i+1]$, which is exactly what we wanted to show.

Now you might say, "Why do we need to do all this strenuous formal manipulation, when it is intuitively obvious that if a subarray $A[m:n]$ is not sorted in decreasing order, then there *has to be* some pair of elements that are not in decreasing order?" One possible answer to this question is that the formal manipulation can help us check our intuitive, informal reasoning when doubts arise concerning whether we are absolutely certain that we have reasoned correctly.

Our second example comes from the correctness proof of the **findMax** function given in Program C.21. When we were trying to prove by induction that the loop invariant on line 21, {♦ $A[j] \geq A[m:i] \wedge (i \leq n)$ ♦}, was true each time through the do-while loop, we assumed by induction that it was true on the $i^{th}$ trip, and then tried to prove it true on the $(i+1)^{st}$ trip. As part of this process, we used the fact that if we evaluated the while-condition, on line 23, and found that ( i != n ), then we would repeat the loop again. We then combined the fact that ( i != n ) with the assertion that ( i ≤ n ), given inside the loop invariant, and we concluded that ( i < n ) had to hold true. Table C.27 illustrates how we can justify using this formal logic.

*formal logic helps when complexity clouds our reasoning*

Few people would have any doubt about the validity of the following story. "The clay tablets were either in the King's chamber or they were on the Scribe's writing table. The Scribe determined that they weren't on his writing table. Therefore, they had to be in the King's chamber." This is a straightforward application of the law of

| | |
|---|---|
| $(\ i \leq n\ ) \wedge (\ i\ != n\ )$ | To start with |
| $((\ i < n\ ) \vee (\ i == n\ )) \wedge (\ i\ != n\ )$ | Expanding $(\ i \leq n\ )$ |
| $((\ i < n\ ) \vee (\ i == n\ )) \wedge \sim (\ i == n\ )$ | Replacing $(\ i\ != n\ )$ with $\sim (\ i == n\ )$ |
| $(\ i < n\ )$ | Applying the *modus tollendo ponens* law from Table C.25 |

Table C.27 Another Formal Logic Manipulation

*modus tollendo ponens*, at the level of common sense. But when we are reasoning about programs, intuition can sometimes become clouded by complexity. Under these circumstances, the ability to do a little formal logical expression manipulation can help raise our confidence that our reasoning is correct.

Unfortunately, space does not permit us to go much beyond this brief and sketchy introduction to the subject of formal logic. However, the experience of many computer scientists suggests that time invested in acquiring some skills in formal logic and formal reasoning pays dividends later. One immediate benefit to the practical programmer is an improved ability to reason about and simplify complex logical conditions in if-statements, while-loops, and do-while-loops in Java.

## **C.3** REVIEW QUESTIONS

1. What is an assertion inside a program?
2. What is a precondition?
3. What is a postcondition?
4. What is a correctness proof for a program?
5. What is a loop invariant?
6. What role do loop invariants play in correctness proofs?
7. Mention a deep flaw in the idea that providing correctness proofs infallibly establishes that programs are free of errors.

## **C.3** EXERCISES

1. Translate the following expression from logic into English:

$$\exists K \, [\, \exists n_0 \, [((K > 0) \wedge (n_0 > 0)) \supset \forall n \, [(n > n_0) \supset (\, |g(n)| < K |f(n)|)]\,]\,]$$

2. Translate the following expression from logic into English:

$$\exists k \, [(1 \leq k) \wedge (k \leq n) \wedge \forall i \, [((1 \leq i) \wedge (i \leq n)) \supset (A[k] \geq A[i])]\,]$$

3. Translate the following expression from English to formal logic: "For any $\varepsilon > 0$, there exists a $\delta > 0$, such that if $|x - c| < \delta$, then $|f(x) - f(c)| < \varepsilon$."
4. Translate the following expression from English to formal logic: "There exists a $k$ in the range $(1 \leq k \leq n)$ such that $A[k] \leq A[i]$ for all $i$ in $(1 \leq i \leq n)$."
5. The logical denial of an assertion A is ~A, which is obtained by applying the logical negation operator to A. Take the logical denial of the assertion in Exercise 1 and then simplify it by applying DeMorgan's laws and other transformations from Tables C.25 and C.26.
6. What is the loop invariant inside the while-loop in the following program? After annotating the program with appropriate assertions, prove that it correctly computes the sum of the integers in the array A[0:n−1].

```
int sum(int [ ] A, int n)  {                          // assume n > 0

        int i = 0;
        int s = 0;
5
        while ( i < n ) {
            s += A[i];
            i++;
        }
10      return  s;
    }
```

7. Let $n!$ denote the product of the integers in the range $1{:}n$. Given the assertions annotating the following factorial program, prove that it correctly computes $n!$.

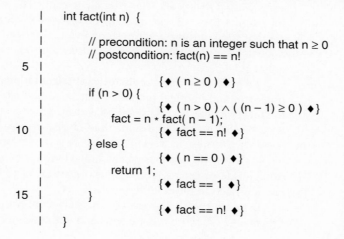

```
int fact(int n)  {

        // precondition: n is an integer such that n ≥ 0
        // postcondition: fact(n) == n!
5
                            {♦ ( n ≥ 0 ) ♦}
        if (n > 0) {
                            {♦ ( n > 0 ) ∧ ( (n − 1) ≥ 0 ) ♦}
            fact = n * fact( n − 1);
10                          {♦ fact == n! ♦}
        } else {
                            {♦ ( n == 0 ) ♦}
            return 1;
                            {♦ fact == 1 ♦}
15      }
                            {♦ fact == n! ♦}
    }
```

## Transforming and Optimizing Programs

### LEARNING OBJECTIVES

1. To understand program transformations.
2. To understand an example of tail recursion elimination.
3. To appreciate how applying transformations can improve program efficiency.

In this section, we are going to transform the **selectionSort** program of the previous section, in order to improve it. Making a method call incurs a certain *overhead* consisting of extra program execution time spent: to transfer the parameters, to make the call, and to return from the call. If we can eliminate calls from a program, we can sometimes get the program to run faster.

*recursion elimination*     In the case of a recursive program, we can sometimes eliminate the recursive calls inside the program, by converting it to an equivalent iterative program. This is called *recursion elimination*. Usually, the equivalent iterative program is more efficient, since it avoids the overhead of making repeated recursive calls. Another way to eliminate calls that can be used sometimes is to substitute directly the body of a method in place of the method call.

Generally speaking, we can manipulate programs using what are called *program transformations*. Program transformations can be thought of as exchange laws that permit us to replace one form of a program with an equivalent form—or perhaps a subexpression inside a program with an equivalent subexpression.

Program transformations include familiar laws of algebraic manipulation and logical expression manipulation. For instance, Program Transformation C.28 illustrates how to perform a series of replacements inside an if-statement in a program.

It is clear why the if-condition (i < n) is simpler to compute than the original if-condition (i <= n) && (i != n) that it replaced. Also, comparing the polynomial ((x + 3)*x + 5)*x + 2 with the polynomial x*x*x + 3*x*x + 5*x + 2 that it replaced, we see that it takes three additions and five multiplications to evaluate the original polynomial, but only three additions and two multiplications to evaluate the replacement polynomial.

To generalize then, ordinary algebraic and logical manipulations can be used to transform and improve programs. But we shouldn't stop there. It might be profitable to view programs themselves (and parts of programs such as compound statements) as an extended set of expressions that can be manipulated using appropriate exchange laws. By this means, we might open up a wider range of possible program improvements than if we limited ourselves merely to rearranging logical and algebraic expressions inside programs. Some transformations of the **selectionSort** program from the previous section illustrate these ideas.

Let's start with the text of the **selectionSort** program, which is reproduced as Program C.29, without comments and with fewer blank spaces (to shorten the size of the program to be transformed).

```
if ( (i <= n) && (i != n) ) {                          // original if-statement
      y = x*x*x + 3*x*x + 5*x + 2;
}

                    ⇓                                   // ⇓ means "transforms to"

if (i < n) {                                            // first, replace condition in if-statement,
      y = x*x*x + 3*x*x + 5*x + 2;                      // using results from Table C.27
}

                    ⇓

if (i < n) {                                            // second, replace the polynomial on the
      y = ((x + 3)*x + 5)*x + 2;                        // right side of the assignment
}
```

**Program Transformation C.28** Improving Expressions in an If-Statement

```
   |    void selectionSort(int[ ] A, int m, int n)  {
   |
   |        int maxPosition, temp;
   |
   |        if ( m < n ) {
 5 |            maxPosition = findMax(A,m,n);
   |            temp = A[m]; A[m] = A[maxPosition]; A[maxPosition] = temp;
   |            selectionSort(A, m+1, n);
   |        }
   |    }
```

**Program C.29** Recursive Selection Sorting without Comments

The recursive call **selectionSort(A, m + 1, n)**, on line 7 of Program C.29, is called a *tail recursion*, since it is a recursive call that occurs at the tail end of the program. Program Transformation C.30 enables us to eliminate tail recursions that are given inside if-statements. Line 5 of the top program in this program transformation contains the tail-recursion call **p(e1, e2, e3)**, where **e1**, **e2**, and **e3** represent actual parameter expressions used in the method call. The formal parameters of method **p** are represented by **a**, **b**, and **c**, on line 1.

The tail-recursion elimination transformation converts the if-statement into a while-loop and replaces the tail-recursion call with assignment statements that assign the actual parameter expressions to be values of the formal parameters of the method.

Applying Program Transformation C.30 to Program C.29 yields Program C.31. This function is not quite in final form, since two of the three assignments created

```
   |    void p(a,b,c)  {
   |
   |        if (condition C1) {
   |            (statements S1)
 5 |            p(e1, e2, e3);              // this line contains the tail recursion
   |        }
   |    }

                 ⇓

   |    void p(a,b,c)   {
   |
   |        while (condition C1)  {
   |            (statements S1)
 5 |            a = e1; b = e2; c = e3;
   |        }
   |    }
```

**Program Transformation C.30** Tail-Recursion Elimination[1]

---

[1] In general, for this transformation to work, statements **S1** cannot contain recursive calls.

```
    |    void selectionSort(int [ ] A, int m, int n)  {
    |
    |        int maxPosition, temp;
    |
5   |        while ( m < n ) {
    |            maxPosition = findMax(A,m,n);
    |            temp = A[m]; A[m] = A[maxPosition]; A[maxPosition] = temp;
    |            A = A; m = m+1; n = n;
    |        }
    |    }
```

**Program C.31** Selection Sorting after Tail-Recursion Elimination

```
    |    void selectionSort(int [ ] A, int m, int n)  {
    |
    |        int maxPosition, temp;
    |
5   |        while ( m < n ) {
    |            maxPosition = findMax(A,m,n);
    |            temp = A[m]; A[m] = A[maxPosition]; A[maxPosition] = temp;
    |            m++;
    |        }
    |    }
```

**Program C.32** Selection Sorting after Useless Assignment Elimination

by literal application of the tail-recursion elimination transformation are useless. Specifically, on line 8 of Program C.31, we can eliminate the useless assignments: A = A; and n = n; and we can replace m = m+1; with m++; this yields Program C.32.

Next, we will transform Program C.32 by replacing the method call findMax(A,m,n) with the body of the method given in Program C.20. It is reproduced without comments and with fewer blank spaces as Program C.33. To replace the method call findMax(A,m,n) in the assignment statement maxPosition = findMax(A,m,n); on line 6 of Program C.32, with the text of Program C.33, we first have to substitute the assignment

```
    |    int findMax(int[ ] A, int m, int n)  {              // assume m<n
    |
    |        int i, j;
    |
5   |        i = m; j = m;
    |        do {
    |            i++;
    |            if ( A[i] > A[j] )  j = i;
    |        } while (i != n );
10  |        return j;
    |    }
```

**Program C.33** Finding the Position of the Largest Number

```
     |    selectionSort(int[ ] A, int m, int n)  {
     |
     |        int maxPosition, temp, i, j ;
     |
 5   |        while ( m < n ) {
     |
     |            i = m; j = m;
     |            do {
     |                i++;
10   |                if ( A[i] > A[j] ) j = i;
     |            } while ( i != n );
     |            maxPosition = j;
     |
     |            temp = A[m]; A[m] = A[maxPosition]; A[maxPosition] = temp;
15   |
     |            m++;
     |        }
     |
     |    }
```

**Program C.34** Almost Final Iterative Selection Sorting

maxPosition = j; for the statement **return** j; on line 10, inside the body of Program C.33, and we also have to add the declarations of the variables i and j to the declaration section of the resulting transformed version of Program C.32. This transformation yields Program C.34.

It is even possible to eliminate the variable j from lines 7:12 of Program C.34, since j plays exactly the same role as the variable, maxPosition. This yields Program C.35.

```
     |    void selectionSort(int[ ] A, int m, int n)  {
     |
     |        int maxPosition, temp, i;
     |
 5   |        while ( m < n ) {
     |
     |            i = m;
     |            maxPosition = m;
     |
10   |            do {
     |                i++;
     |                if ( A[i] > A[maxPosition] ) maxPosition = i;
     |            } while (i != n);
     |
15   |            temp = A[m]; A[m] = A[maxPosition]; A[maxPosition] = temp;
     |
     |            m++;
     |        }
     |
     |    }
```

**Program C.35** Iterative Selection Sorting from Transformations

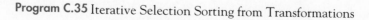

| Array size n | Iterative selectionSort | Recursive selectionSort |
|---|---|---|
| 125 | 3.5 | 3.9 |
| 250 | 13.9 | 15.4 |
| 500 | 55.4 | 61.1 |
| 1000 | 221.1 | 242.8 |
| 2000 | 884.4 | 968.6 |

**Table C.36** Iterative versus Recursive selectionSort Running Times (in milliseconds)

Let's now compare the efficiency of the original unoptimized recursive version of selectionSort, given in Program C.29, with that of the optimized iterative version, given in Program C.35. Table C.36 compares the running times in milliseconds for these two programs on arrays of various sizes. You can see from the data in that table that recursive selectionSort, as given in Program C.29, has running times that are between 9.5 percent and 11.4 percent longer than those for the iterative selectionSort, given in Program C.35. This tells us that our program transformations bought us about a 10 percent improvement in running time. These improvements in performance resulted mostly from the elimination of the overhead involved in calling methods both nonrecursively (as in the case of findMax) and recursively (as in the case of the recursive calls on selectionSort inside itself).

*what improvements did we achieve*

It turns out that iterative selectionSort takes less space during execution than recursive selectionSort does. This is because "call-frames" for the recursive calls need to be allocated in Java's run-time memory management system. For an array of size n, there are (n − 1) of these recursion call-frames. By contrast, the iterative version of selectionSort uses only one call-frame for its (single) call. So the iterative version is more efficient both in *time* and in *space*. (The manner in which Java allocates space for call-frames is studied in Chapter 6 in the section on stacks.)

However, it seems more complicated to devise a correctness proof for Program C.35 than for recursive selectionSort. The subroutine and recursive structure of the original recursive design for selectionSort helped to break the overall correctness proof into simple steps. We were able to use the correctness proof of findMax as a building block in the construction of the correctness proof of recursive selectionSort.

*the method of transformational implementation*

Suppose we had a way of knowing that the program transformations we used preserved program correctness. Then the following philosophy of correct program development might be open to us. First, we might be able to write very concise, lucid top-level programs. Because these top-level programs would be short, simple, and clear, we might find it easy to prove them correct. Then we might be able to apply program transformations to them to optimize them and make them more efficient, perhaps at the expense of making them more detailed and less easily understood. Some of these transformations might even accomplish stepwise refinements of the original top-level programs—by selecting data representations and algorithms to refine top-level abstractions, for instance. These ideas lie at the heart of a philosophy of software development called transformational programming, which has been explored by software engineering researchers.

## C.4 REVIEW QUESTIONS

1. What is a program transformation?
2. Can we use exchange laws from algebra and logic to transform programs?
3. Mention two program transformations that are not simply instances of either algebraic or logical equivalence laws.

## C.4 EXERCISE

1. Eliminate the tail recursion from the following program, which reverses an array of integers by swapping the integers at its "edges":

```
   |    void reverseArray(int[ ] A, int m, int n) {      // to reverse the integers
   |                                                      // A[m:n] in array A
   |        int i;
   |
 5 |        if ( m < n ) {
   |            i = A[m]; A[m] = A[n]; A[n] = i;          // first, swap the edges
   |            reverseArray(A, m+1, n – 1);              // then reverse the center
   |        }
   |    }
```

Run a timing experiment to compare the running times of the recursive and iterative versions of **reverseArray**. How much does the elimination of the tail recursion reduce the running time performance of **reverseArray**?

## C.5   Testing Programs

### LEARNING OBJECTIVES

1. To learn about unit, integration, regression, and acceptance testing.
2. To learn how to use test drivers and stubs.
3. To understand the separate roles of testing and verification.
4. To understand the difference between top-down and bottom-up testing.
5. To appreciate the value of formatted debugging aids.
6. To understand what a test plan is.

If you want to produce quality software, one of the most important skills you can learn is how to perform thorough and systematic program testing.

Suppose you have created a detailed design for a software system, perhaps in the form of a document that gives English descriptions of the data structures and variables you'll need, plus some explicit program strategies for each of the system's methods (using, say, Java containing English comments, to express your detailed design plans). You have refined your detailed design into actual Java code, and now you are ready to test your overall program piece-by-piece. How should you proceed?

*how do you go about testing?*

## Bottom-Up Testing

Even though you may have used *object-oriented design* and *top-down design with stepwise refinement* as a strategy for arriving at your detailed design and refining it into actual Java code, it may make sense to proceed in the *opposite* order when testing. That is, it may make sense to proceed *bottom-up*. What does this mean? Suppose you first try to identify pieces of your program that are at the bottom level of your code—a set of methods or classes, $S_1$, that do not use any of the other methods or classes. These are the bottommost components in your system (since they don't call on any lower-level ones). You begin testing these bottom-level components thoroughly, to make sure they are working properly, before doing anything else. Now you have confidence that the components in $S_1$ are working components, suitable for use in subsequent activities.

Next you identify another layer of classes, $S_2$, which uses the classes or methods in $S_1$, but which do not use any others. You then test the components in $S_2$. Following this, you identify the next layer of components, $S_3$, which use components already tested in $S_1$ or $S_2$, and you test the functions in $S_3$.

Proceeding in this fashion, at each stage you identify a new layer of components, $S_n$, which use those you have already tested, and you expand the collection of tested parts of your overall system by testing the components in $S_n$. Eventually, you get to the final, topmost layer of the program—the "main program" or "main applet" part of your system's design—and you test that.

Figure C.37 illustrates a possible arrangement of layers of classes that are parts of a larger software system. The downward pointing arrows represent "uses" relationships. For example, the node labeled A represents a main applet that uses classes B, C, and D. Class B, in turn, uses classes E, F, I, and J.

*layers of classes*

The layer $S_1$, consisting of classes I, J, K, and L, is the bottommost layer, since it consists of classes that are used by higher-level classes but do not use any lower-level classes. You would test the classes in layer $S_1$ first.

Layer $S_2$ is the second-to-bottom layer. In bottom-up testing, after testing the classes in layer $S_1$, you would test the classes in layer $S_2$. The tests of classes in layer $S_2$ could make calls on already tested methods in layer $S_1$. Likewise, the tests of methods in classes in layer $S_3$ could make calls on already tested methods in layers $S_1$ and $S_2$.

In bottom-up testing, sometimes the order of testing among methods is influenced by the manner in which the methods manipulate data, as well as by the order

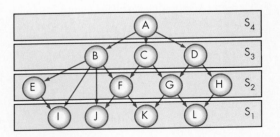

**Figure C.37** Layers of Classes in a Software System

in which they make calls on one another. For instance, you would test an initialization method that sets up the initial values in a table or a list before testing any function that operates on the table or list, assuming it had already been initialized.

**mutually recursive methods**

In some cases, methods are mutually recursive. For instance, given three methods X, Y, and Z, it may happen that X calls Y, Y calls Z, and Z calls X. In such cases, you have to test all three methods at the same time, in a "cluster" so-to-speak.

There is just one key idea that defines the bottom-up order of testing.

> **Bottom-Up Testing Order Principle:** Whenever possible, before testing a given method, X, test all methods that X calls or that prepare data that X uses.

## Unit Testing, Formatted Debugging Aids, and Test Drivers

Suppose now that you have identified a bottom-up testing order for the classes and methods in your software system. It's time now to answer a key question: "How are you supposed to test a given method or class?"

Testing a given method or class is called *unit testing*. (Note: The term unit testing originated with and is often used in industrial software engineering practice.)

**testing boundary cases**

It's important to use tests that thoroughly cover all the possible behaviors of a method, if feasible. All the different execution paths through the code in the method should be exercised, if possible. It is especially important to test "boundary cases." For example, what happens when a table or list is empty, or when a table is full? Does the method correctly handle these cases? What happens in a loop, when no iterations occur, as in the case of the following for-loop, when n == 5?

```
|    for (i = 10; i <= n; ++i) {
|        (some statements)
|    }
```

Or what happens when a sorting method is given an array that is already in sorted order? It is important to build up your skill for imagining all the possible special cases that can occur—especially the unusual ones. Sometimes this is quite hard to do, as in the case of trying to test a user interface to see that it doesn't break when used by naive users who can do the strangest things when they don't understand how to use the system. In such cases, it might be advisable to find some actual naive users and get them to bang away at the interface to elicit the kinds of unusual behavior that system designers find hard to imagine (since the system designers' thinking is usually strongly influenced by expectations for how the system is supposed to behave).

**checking initializations**

It's also important to check that data structures are initialized properly, and that all data structures created by a method are left in well-formed condition. For example, in creating a linked list, it is important to make sure that the last node has a null link in it.

```
| // display picture of D before executing R
|      R;                // then call method R
| // and display picture of D after executing R
```

**Figure C.38** Before-After Testing with Formatted Debugging Aid

formatted debugging aids

About 30 years ago, in the dawn of the evolution of software engineering practice, it was discovered that formatted debugging aids were of special importance. A formatted debugging aid is simply a method that prints (or draws a graphical display of) a data structure. It was discovered that debugging times for a software project could often be cut in half if formatted debugging aids were implemented *first*, before implementing and testing the rest of the system.

before-after pictures

If you want to follow this philosophy, you should first implement and test a set of methods that can display every possible data structure your software system uses. Then you can build up test methods that use these display methods to display the *before* and *after pictures* of each data structure that a given method changes. A test case for a method R that alters some data structures D might then assume the form shown in Fig. C.38.

test drivers

Another important idea is to implement what are called *test drivers*. A test driver, T, for a method, S, is a method that enumerates test cases for S, calls S for each test case, and checks the outputs afterward to see that they are correct.

## Integration Testing

In the philosophy of bottom-up testing, unit testing is performed first to check the behavior of each class or method in the system. Following this, *integration testing* is performed. In integration testing, you check that combinations of the classes or methods work together properly.

checking that things work together

Even though you have ascertained that each of the unit classes or methods in a system works correctly, there is still room for error. Perhaps, in your system design, you overlooked some possible conditions that arise when one method, S, creates inputs for another method, T, that method T was not designed to handle. Perhaps T's test driver has already tested T and found that it meets its specifications. But T's unit specifications may have been wrong and may not have taken into account the inputs S could create for T.

When a system grows in size and complexity, things naturally get confusing. Mismatches can occur between the inputs a method or class is designed to handle and the inputs actually given to it by its users. Integration testing is designed to check that the interactions between the parts of the system occur as expected, and that the parts do, in fact, cooperate successfully to achieve correct overall system behavior.

## Acceptance Testing and Regression Testing

Using test drivers, a battery of tests can then be put together to exercise each of the components in a system and to test them thoroughly. Moreover, integration tests, which exercise combinations of the parts working together, can be used to furnish additional batteries of tests. In some cases, these batteries of tests can be made to run automatically, without human intervention, and they can deliver printed test results for later inspection.

Assuming you have created a *test suite* consisting of batteries of thorough unit and integration tests that run automatically, you are in a position to accomplish two more important testing activities: *acceptance* and *regression testing*.

*Acceptance tests* are tests that are run before a system is released into active service. Sometimes, there is a formal development contract between the client who is acquiring the system and the system builder. Such a contract may specify that the system is not legally considered to have been "delivered" until it passes an acceptance test. The contract may even specify what the acceptance test is, or that another independent contractor will be hired to devise and conduct the acceptance test.

**acceptance testing**

Once the system is released into service it enters what is called the *maintenance phase* of its software lifecycle. During maintenance, software errors are discovered and fixed, and, almost inevitably, the system gets upgraded to perform new functions that are needed to ensure that it remains useful to its users under changing conditions of use. After a bug is fixed or the system is upgraded to do something new, it is of course important to test that the bug was actually removed or that the new feature actually works. Moreover, it is important to check that everything that used to work still continues to work properly. *Regression testing* thus means checking that everything that used to work before a change was made still continues to work after the change is installed.

**regression testing**

A discipline is usually followed when applying test suites during regression testing. It has four steps: (1) find a bug; (2) fix the bug; (3) add a test case to the test suite that tests whether or not the bug was fixed; and (4) run the test suite.

*A word to the wise*: You'd be surprised how often the elimination of a bug or the introduction of a new feature causes something else in the system to "break." Regression testing is designed to catch such problems before a new system is released into use. This practice enables software maintainers to avoid the unhappy situation in which users become predictably irate when they discover that what used to work last week in the old system release no longer works this week in the new release.

## Top-Down Testing and Stubs

Bottom-up testing makes sense, since it means you always check out the behavior of the parts before testing the behavior of anything else that uses them. Nevertheless, there are circumstances in which you may want to do the reverse by testing the top levels of a system *before* testing the components that it uses. The latter order of testing is called top-down testing.

Referring again to Figure C.37, a top-down testing order would mean testing class A before testing classes B, C, and D. In general you would test layer $S_{i+1}$ before testing layer $S_i$, in top-down testing order.

Why would anyone want to do this? Wouldn't it complicate matters immensely to test class A before knowing that B, C, and D worked properly? Wouldn't it be difficult to find the cause of any misbehavior the test revealed, since any of A, B, C, and D could have caused it? By contrast, with bottom-up testing, if you are confident that B, C, and D are working properly, then when you test A, it is highly likely that any

```
|    double compound(double A, double r, int n)  {
|
|         return ( A * power(1 + r/100, n) );
|    }
```

**Program C.39** Investment Growth under Compound Interest

misbehavior that results is A's fault. You can see that the advantage of bottom-up testing is that it enables you to assign blame for misbehavior to different small regions of the program text when troubles arise, and to ascertain that each component in your system works, one step at a time, in a logical progression.

In top-down testing, if the first thing you do is to fire up and test the topmost method in the system, which can potentially call any other method in the system, then you may not be able easily to localize the cause if the test reveals faulty behavior.

This is where the concept of *stubs* comes in. A stub is a method that stands in place of another method (that will be written later), and can *fake* its output on certain test cases. For example, suppose you decide to do top-down testing of the following method to compute the growth in an invested amount of money A, which accumulates compound interest at an interest rate of r percent over a period of n years. This is illustrated in Program C.39.

*stubs*

This calls on the function, **power(1 + r/100, n)**, where **power(x,n)** is supposed to compute the exponential quantity, $x^n$. Your test driver will test the function **compound(A,r,n)**, by making three test calls:

|                         |                                  |
|-------------------------|----------------------------------|
| compound(100,6.0,5);    | // $100 invested at 6% for 5 years |
| compound(100,6.0,0);    | // $100 invested at 6% for 0 years |
| compound(100,0.0,5);    | // $100 invested at 0% for 5 years |

These three test cases will make three respective calls on **power(x,n)**, which are: **power(1.06,5)**, **power(1.06,0)**, and **power(1.00,5)**.

Suppose now that the function **power(x,n)** is not yet available for use in your top-down testing activities. In the absence of the real thing, you could write a stub that fakes the behavior of **power(x,n)** in exactly the three test cases you are going to use, as shown in Program C.40.

Now you can use your stub to fake the expected outputs for **power(x,n)** in top-down tests of **compound(A,r,n)** provided you stick to your intention to use only the three test cases specified previously.

```
|    double power(double x, int n)  {
|
|         if ( (x == 1.00) || (n == 0) ) {
|              return 1.00;              // since 1ⁿ == 1 and x⁰ == 1 for any x and n
5 |         } else if ( (x == 1.06) && (n == 5) ) {
|              return 1.3382256;                    // since 1.06⁵ == 1.3382256
|         }
|    }
```

**Program C.40** Stub for **power(x,n)**

Now let's consider some circumstances in which you might want to perform top-down testing. Suppose you are working on a software project with five teammates. You have completed the design of your system and you have divided the work into five subprojects in which four of you will implement separate modules providing services for (a) the data calculations required, (b) the user interface, (c) printing reports, and (d) saving and restoring files of data. A fifth teammate has the job of writing the main part of the system that uses these four modules to (1) accept and interpret user commands and (2) execute commands to open or close files, perform computations, and print reports. Your team is on a tight schedule and each of you would like to test your section of the code before you can expect to call on tested, working software components supplied by your other teammates. By using stubs to fake the actions you expect the missing components eventually will perform, you can test your piece of the system in parallel with the development of the other pieces of the system by your teammates, or in advance of their efforts so that they can use your finished pieces in bottom-up testing of their work. You can see that top-down testing can be used to accelerate an implementation schedule that might otherwise have to be stretched out to accommodate serial dependencies.

*when to use top-down testing*

Another case in which top-down testing is useful is when the modules or components comprising a system are mutually dependent—meaning that each one uses the services of the others. In this case, using stubs to fake the expected actions of the other pieces enables the pieces to be tested independently before trying to test them together.

*testing mutually dependent components*

## Test Plans

When software projects advance from small-scale projects to medium or large-scale ones, a helpful practice is to write a *test plan* document. A test plan enumerates the test cases, including inputs and the corresponding expected outputs, the purposes of the tests, and the exact conditions under which it can be claimed that tests succeed or fail. Test plans can be subjected to analysis for thoroughness of coverage and for whether or not they ensure that the system design specifications have been achieved.

*test plan documents*

## Comparing the Roles of Testing and Verification

Testing and verification are each different activities that can help to raise our confidence that a given module works as intended. However, each activity has its weaknesses.

Testing can reveal the presence of bugs, but it can never prove their absence (in all but the simplest of cases where every possible behavior can be checked). On the other hand, verification can check only the correspondence between a statement of what a program is supposed to do (expressed by some assertions in the formal language of logic) and the actions performed by the program. However, verification cannot prove that these formal logical assertions correctly and completely capture the true program intentions.

*testing and verification complement one another*

Recall, for a moment, the example stating that a program that is supposed to sort the array A[m:n] into descending order is supposed to satisfy the ordering assertion

$A[m] \geq A[m+1] \geq \ldots \geq A[n]$. And recall that this assertion was incomplete because it failed to mention that sorting was supposed to be accomplished only by rearranging the order of the original items in $A[m:n]$ without deleting any. In the absence of the complete assertion, $A[m:n]$ could have been sorted by a nonsensical program such as for ( i = m; i <= n; i++ ) A[i] = A[m];. This revealed the problem of the possible incompleteness or inaccuracy of the assertions used in verification.

Consequently, the benefits of both testing and verification complement one another. Each helps to raise our confidence that a program does what it is supposed to do, but neither alone is completely sufficient to accomplish this task.

## C.5 REVIEW QUESTIONS

1. What is the difference between unit testing and integration testing?
2. Explain the concepts of regression testing and acceptance testing.
3. What is the difference between bottom-up testing and top-down testing?
4. What are stubs and test drivers?
5. Why is it wise to implement formatted debugging aids before implementing a system?

## C.5 EXERCISES

1. Draw the calling relationships for all the methods used in Program 2.16. Draw dotted lines around the layers and label the bottommost layer $S_1$, the second-to-bottom layer $S_2$, and so on. Finally, give an ordered list of method names in bottom-up testing order.
2. Do the same for the methods in the priority queue sorting Programs 5.3 and 5.5.

## C.6　The Philosophy of Measurement and Tuning

### LEARNING OBJECTIVES

1. To understand the philosophy of measurement and tuning.
2. To learn how measurement and tuning techniques can help make a program run more efficiently.

The *philosophy of measurement and tuning* is a method for improving the efficiency of actual running programs. Experienced programmers have frequently found two things to be true about programs: (1) Oftentimes a disproportionate amount of the running time (say 80 to 90 percent) is spent in a small portion of the code (say 7 to 10 percent), and (2) Oftentimes the places where a program is inefficient are surprising and difficult to predict.

Since it is hard to predict where the inefficiencies will occur, it makes sense *first* to measure the running program and find out, and *second* to do something about it.

Once you have identified the region(s) where the program is spending most of its time, you then know the place(s) where it pays off to try to improve the program's efficiency. You then concentrate on trying to replace inefficient code with better code in these critical regions. Next, you measure the results to see how much improvement has been achieved. You might need to iterate the process of introducing trial improvements and measuring their effects. This latter process is called *tuning*.

Some modern programming environments provide tools for measuring where a program is spending its time. One type of tool for doing this is called an *execution-time profiler*. You turn on the profiler and conduct a trial run of the program you are measuring. The profiler then gives you a breakdown of what percentage of the total time was spent in different places in the code for the program. Some versions provide a pictorial histogram. Others create a file associating the names of methods with the percentage of time spent in them during the test run.

**execution-time profiles**

If you don't have access to a profiler, perhaps your system has access to a real-time clock. In this case, you can still gain useful information by measuring the time spent by a method, M, that is repeatedly executed inside a test driver. You can arrange to have your test driver print the difference between the starting time and stopping time of the real-time clock, divided by the total number of times method M was executed. This yields the approximate average running time for method M. (If you find that the measured average time was distorted by the fact that some overhead time, consumed by the test driver, was included in the measurement, you can often arrange to measure the time consumed by the test driver running an empty test. The test driver time can then be subtracted out to get an undistorted measure of the correct test time.)

In this section, we will provide a dramatic illustration of the point we are trying to make by comparing the running times for several versions of iterative and recursive binary searching.

## Comparing Some Methods for Binary Searching

Since most introductory computer science courses and textbooks cover the process of binary searching, we will assume you know a little bit about it from your past experience. We will review the subject here, and we will compare some solutions.

The problem to be addressed in binary searching is to find the position of a search key, K, in an ordered array A[0:n−1] of distinct keys, (arranged, say, in ascending order: A[0] < A[1] < ... < A[n−1]).

The method is to choose the key in the middle of A[0:n−1], which is located at A[middle], where middle = (0 + (n−1)) / 2, and to compare the search key K and A[middle]. If K == A[middle], the search terminates successfully, since K has been found at the middle position of A[0:n−1]. On the other hand, if K < A[middle] then further search is conducted among the keys to the left of A[middle] (since all of the keys to the right of A[middle] are greater than K). But if K > A[middle], then further search is conducted among the keys to the right of A[middle] (since all the keys to the left of A[middle] are less than K).

**a sketch of the method**

In short, either we are *lucky* by finding K == A[middle] on the first try, so that we can stop immediately, or we are *fortunate*, because we can continue searching in either

**we are either lucky or fortunate**

the left half array or the right half array, confining our search to a problem only half as big as the original one. By repeatedly halving the size of the search interval where we look for K, we rapidly converge on the solution in $O(\log n)$ steps.

Actually, binary searching is one of those algorithms having a simple general plan, for which it turns out to be tricky to work out the details. In one study, more than 80 percent of a group of programmers with more than a year's programming experience got their first versions of binary search wrong when asked to write one. There are many ways to write the conventional iterative binary searching algorithm. The version given in Program C.41 is fairly straightforward.

*but it's tricky to do it right*

```
     |   int binarySearch(int K) {          // to find the position of the integer search
     |                                       // key K in the ordered array A[0:n−1]
     |
     |       int L;                          // L == left boundary of search interval
  5  |       int midpoint;                   // midpoint == midpoint of search interval
     |       int R;                          // R == right boundary of search interval
     |
     |       // initializations
     |           L = 0;                      // initially, L is the leftmost index,  0, and
 10  |           R = n − 1;                  // R is the rightmost index, n − 1
     |
     |
     |       // while the interval L:R is non-empty test K against the middle key
     |
 15  |       while ( L <= R ) {              // while the interval is nonempty
     |
     |           midpoint = (L+R) / 2;       // compute midpoint of interval L:R
     |
     |           if ( K == A[midpoint] ) {   // if key K was found at the midpoint,
     |                                       // return from the function
 20  |               return midpoint;        // with midpoint as the result
     |
     |           } else if ( K > A[midpoint] ) {   // otherwise, if K is to the
     |                                             // right of the midpoint, search
     |               L = midpoint + 1;             // next in the interval midpoint+1:R
 25  |
     |           } else {                    // whereas if K is to the
     |                                       // left of the midpoint, search
     |               R = midpoint − 1;       // next in the interval L:midpoint−1
 30  |           }
     |
     |       }
     |
     |       // if the search interval became empty, key K was not found
 35  |
     |       return − 1;                     // −1 means K was not in A[0:n−1]
     |   }
```

**Program C.41** Iterative Binary Search

This version of binary searching divides A[0:n−1] into a middle item, A[middle], a left subarray A[0 : middle − 1], and a right subarray A[middle + 1 : n−1]. If we don't find that K == A[middle] then we search further in the left or right subarrays, depending on whether K > A[middle] or not.

Because it is so difficult to write a binary search program that works properly, it is helpful to illustrate briefly a technique for applying a small, thorough set of test cases. First, we initialize an array, A[10], to contain squares: 1, 4, 9, ... , 100, with the code:

```
int i, A[10];                                  // declare A[0:9] to be an array of integers
for ( i = 0; i < 10; i++ )  A[i] = (i + 1)*(i + 1);        // let A[i] == the square of (i+1)
```

Not only do we test *successful searching* for each of the keys, $i^2$, in the array A, we also test all the cases for *unsuccessful searching* by looking for keys of the form, $i^2$−1 and $i^2$+1. In particular, when testing unsuccessful searching, we test all possible "gaps" between keys in A (including before A[0] and after A[9]).

```
for ( i = 1; i <= 10; i++ ) {                       // test all keys and gaps in A[0:9]
    if (binarySearch(i*i) != (i−1) ) {
        System.out.println("key " + (i*i) + "not found in A[" + (i − 1) + "]" );
    }
    if (binarySearch(i*i + 1) != − 1 ) {
        System.out.println("result for key  " + (i*i + 1) +" != −1");
    }
    if (binarySearch(i*i − 1) != − 1 ) {
        System.out.println("result for key  " + (i*i − 1) +" != −1");
    }
}
```

expressing binary search recursively

The solution to the binary searching problem can also be expressed naturally as a recursive algorithm because binary searching breaks down the overall searching problem into a combination of base cases and subproblems that are half as big and that can be solved by applying the same search method recursively. (It is instructive for you to try writing a recursive binary search program before looking at the solution.) Program C.42 presents a recursive binary searching algorithm.

It is interesting to compare the efficiency of the recursive and iterative versions. Let's find out what happens when we measure actual running times. Table C.43 presents some experimentally measured running times for the iterative and recursive versions of the binary search Programs C.41 and C.42. The numbers give *average running times* measured in microseconds. By average running times, we mean running times averaged over searches of all of the n keys in an ordered array of keys, A[0:n−1], where each of the n keys is equally likely to be used in the search. The data in this table tell us that for small numbers of keys, such as n == 10, the recursive version is 23 percent more expensive, and for larger numbers of keys, such as n == 800, the recursive version is 35 percent more expensive.

comparing the programs to see why

If you study the differences between the iterative Program C.41 and the recursive Program C.42, you'll conclude that the recursive program makes a recursive call each time it tries to solve a subproblem (consisting of searching in a nonempty interval of keys half as big as the original interval), whereas the iterative version simply performs one assignment (to adjust one of the endpoints of the search interval to confine it to

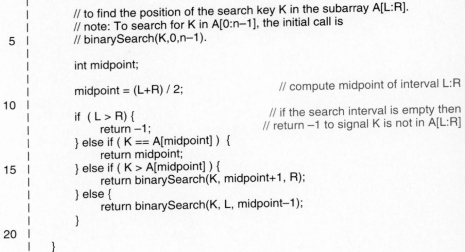

```
     int binarySearch(int K, int L, int R) {

         // to find the position of the search key K in the subarray A[L:R].
         // note: To search for K in A[0:n−1], the initial call is
5        // binarySearch(K,0,n−1).

         int midpoint;

         midpoint = (L+R) / 2;                      // compute midpoint of interval L:R

10       if  ( L > R ) {                            // if the search interval is empty then
             return −1;                             // return −1 to signal K is not in A[L:R]
         } else if ( K == A[midpoint] ) {
             return midpoint;
15       } else if ( K > A[midpoint] ) {
             return binarySearch(K, midpoint+1, R);
         } else {
             return binarySearch(K, L, midpoint−1);
         }

20   }
```

**Program C.42** Recursive Binary Search

a new search interval half as big) and then returns to perform another iteration of its main loop. The difference in running times could then be explained by the hypothesis that the time required to make recursive calls is significantly greater than that required to perform a simple assignment to adjust the search interval size.

So far, what we have discovered isn't too surprising. We already know that, when both underlying algorithms are in the same complexity class, recursion is likely to be a little less efficient than iteration due to the fact that method calls take an amount of overhead time that is almost always greater than the times required to make simple adjustments and return to the beginning of a loop.

But now it is time for some surprises associated with the fact that small changes in the algorithms being measured may cause surprisingly large changes in their running times. Sometimes, what may at first seem to be a relatively trivial change, may actually cause an increase in the running time so large that it dwarfs the difference in running times between iteration and recursion. To bring this issue into sharper focus, let's look at the data in Table C.44.

*but, beware! often things aren't so simple*

**Table C.43** Iterative Versus Recursive Binary Search Running Times (in microseconds)

| Array Size | Iterative Version | Recursive Version |
|------------|-------------------|-------------------|
| 10         | 3.5               | 4.3               |
| 50         | 5.1               | 6.7               |
| 100        | 5.9               | 7.9               |
| 200        | 6.8               | 9.1               |
| 400        | 7.6               | 10.3              |
| 800        | 8.5               | 11.5              |

| Array Size n | Iterative Version A | Iterative Version B | Iterative Version C | Recursive Version |
|---|---|---|---|---|
| 10 | 3.5 | 11.8 | 110.0 | 4.3 |
| 50 | 5.1 | 19.2 | 185.6 | 6.7 |
| 100 | 5.9 | 22.7 | 221.0 | 7.9 |
| 200 | 6.8 | 26.3 | 257.4 | 9.1 |
| 400 | 7.6 | 30.0 | 294.6 | 10.3 |
| 800 | 8.5 | 33.7 | 332.0 | 11.5 |

Table C.44 shows running times for three versions of iterative binary searching labeled as versions A, B, and C. Version A is the same as that given in Program C.41. Version B is the same as version A, but with the variables L, R, and midpoint declared to be double precision integers (longs) instead of single precision integers (on lines 4:6 of Program C.41). Version C is the same as version A, but with the computation of the midpoint, given as midpoint = (L+R) / 2; on line 17 of Program C.41, replaced with midpoint = (long) Math.floor((L+R) / 2.0);. That is, version C replaces the integer division of (L+R) by 2 of version A with floating point division, which returns a floating point result, and then takes the floor of this floating point result by discarding its fractional part, after which it converts the result to a long integer. Version C was compiled with a compiler that did not produce code to utilize the floating point operations of the underlying computer, but instead called on floating point simulation routines. Typically, to simulate floating point operations requires from 30 to 50 non–floating-point instructions.

The recursive version in the last column of Table C.44 is the same as Program C.42. Iterative version A and the recursive version in Table C.44 are identical to the iterative and recursive versions compared in Table C.43.

a not so innocent change

The apparently innocent change of declaring the three integer variables L, R, and midpoint to be double precision long integers has caused roughly a fourfold increase in running time between iterative version A and iterative version B. The new version B now takes up to three times longer to run than the recursive version, whereas iterative version A was more efficient than the recursive version. All the advantage of using iteration over recursion has been lost three times over by this one supposedly innocent change. Matters get far worse with iterative version C, which runs up to 30 times slower than the recursive version.

*Moral: Things are not what they seem to be.* Seemingly innocent differences in the details of an algorithm may make more of a difference in their running times than can be saved by replacing the known inefficiency of recursion by the somewhat greater efficiency of iteration.

repeatability of experiments

Repeating these experiments and measurements might well yield quite different results when performed with different Java compilers and different computers (e.g., Java bytecode compilers or Java JIT compilers that compile to native code for chips with or without floating point instructions). We live in a world where the details can make significant differences. Using different computers or compilers could well yield substantially different running time results. For instance, on the same computer as used previously, a Java JIT compiler that compiles native code to take advantage of floating point instructions might well yield substantially reduced running times for iterative version C. And on a supercomputer that efficiently processes double precision integers, there may be no running time differences between iterative versions A and B.

That such differences could occur only emphasizes the importance of using the philosophy of measurement and tuning if you are trying to improve the efficiency of your programs.

## C.6 REVIEW QUESTIONS

1. Explain the philosophy of measurement and tuning.
2. What is an execution-time profile tool (or a profiler, for short)?
3. Does experience show that most programs consume running time approximately uniformly throughout their code, or is the distribution of time consumed often more uneven?
4. What do you do when tuning a program to make it more efficient?
5. Give some examples of cases in which small changes in a program can cause surprising differences in efficiency.

## C.6 EXERCISES

1. Find the inefficiency in the following program, and then tune it to improve its running time.

```
     int findMin(int[ ] A, int m, int n)  {        // to find the minimum integer
                                                    // in the subarray A[m:n]
          int leftMin, rightMin, middle;            // where m ≤ n

  5       if ( m == n ) {
              return A[m];
          } else {
              middle = (int) Math.floor( ( m + n ) / 2.0 );
              leftMin = findMin(A,m,middle);
 10           rightMin = findMin(A,middle+1, n);
              if ( leftMin < rightMin ) {
                  return leftMin;
              } else {
                  return rightMin;
 15           }
          }
     }
```

2. Compile the four versions of iterative and recursive binary searching used in Table C.44, and measure their running times on your computer. If possible, compare Java bytecode compilers with Java JIT compilers that compile native code. Do your results agree or disagree with those in Table C.44? What do your results tell you about the value of the philosophy of measurement and tuning?

3. Can you rewrite Program C.41 so that it uses only one comparison of key **K** with A[midpoint], instead of two, in the while-loop on lines 15:32? If so, how much does this improve its efficiency? Measure your results by conducting timing experiments.

## C.7    Software Reuse and Bottom-Up Programming

### LEARNING OBJECTIVES

1. To learn about software reuse and programming with reusable software components.
2. To understand the rudiments of software productivity and how productivity can be increased by employing reusable components.

Suppose you want to build a radio. You wouldn't begin by wrapping your own capacitors starting with tin foil and wax, nor would you smelt your own iron ore to make magnets for the speakers. Instead, you might start with antennas, speakers, dials, and power supplies as ready-made components, and you might then try to put them together.

Now let's consider what you do when you build software. First, an inescapable truth is that you have to start with components at some level any time you build software— even the lowest possible level components that are individual keystrokes at your keyboard. However, if you can use higher-level components, you can build higher-level systems more easily, quickly, and reliably than if you "roll your own," starting from scratch. In many cases—for example, if you are using operating system services for file system calls, printer calls, and so on—you have no choice because you are forced to use the level of components supplied by the system with which you must interface. But at other levels of system design, such as computer graphics functions, you often have a choice. For instance, you can either "roll your own" or acquire and use functions from a library.

*you must always use components at some level*

Oddly enough, to gain the understanding necessary for making sense in our later discussion of software reuse, we need to digress for a moment to consider the subject of software economics. In software economics we try to understand what determines the cost of performing various software activities in software system development. Costs can be measured in terms of resources required to accomplish a given task. For example, the costs associated with building a given software system might include (a) the number of person-months of effort needed and (b) the amount of computer resources needed (computer time, disk storage, etc.). Ultimately, the various kinds of resources used may be priced in dollars, yielding an overall dollar cost figure.

*some software economics*

One important equation predicting the effort required to build the most familiar class of software system comes from Barry W. Boehm's COCOMO model (the word COCOMO is an acronym for "COnstructive COst Model"[2]). This equation gives the

---

[2] See Boehm's book, *Software Engineering Economics*, Prentice-Hall, Englewood Cliffs, N.J. (1981). Two other classes of software projects have COCOMO equations with different constants.

number of person-months (PM) required to build a system in terms of the size of the system, as follows:

$$PM = 2.4*(KDSI)^{1.05} \qquad\qquad (C.1)$$

Effort Required to Build a Software System

The quantity KDSI refers to the *Kilo-Delivered Source Instructions* in the system. For example, if a documented, delivered software system had 37,600 lines of source code, it would have 37.6 KDSI (i.e., 37.6 thousand lines of source code). Boehm's equation predicts that 108.2 person-months would be required to build this system. (108.2 PMs are approximately nine person-years of effort.)

Actually, Equation C.1 gives a *baseline* estimate, which is used only as a first approximation. To arrive at a refined estimate, this first approximation has to be adjusted, using some multipliers that depend on various characteristics of the software project. For instance, experienced software teams are much more productive than inexperienced teams, so a multiplier of 0.55 might be used to adjust the initial estimate to predict the effort required by an experienced software team. (Here, 108.2 PMs multiplied by 0.55 equals 59.5 PMs, which means that the experienced team might take only 59.5 person-months to complete the same project that an average team would take.) There are other multipliers in Boehm's model based on things like the adequacy of the computer resources available and the severity of the constraints the system being built has to meet.

However, a key fact implied by Equation C.1 is that the effort required to build a software system is an *exponential function* of its size. This implies that size is the biggest *cost-driver* of the cost of building a software system. Consequently, all other things being equal, if you can reduce the size of the software you are required to build, you can accomplish the greatest possible reduction in the effort needed to build it.

This is where the notion of building software from reusable software components comes in. If you can acquire a set of useful software components and if you can figure out how to use them to build your system (in a fashion that meets the system requirements), then you may be able to reduce dramatically the effort required to build it, compared to writing it from scratch, starting with a blank page. The reason why is because Equation C.1 tells you that your cost of construction is the cost of implementing the "glue" to compose the software components, rather than the cost of implementing the components themselves. The number of KDSI required to implement "glue" almost always is dramatically less than the number of instructions required to implement the components.

For example, suppose a company called Contemporary Software, Inc., is under contract to build a word processor system, called WP-2000. It can either start from scratch, or it can buy both a *system shell* and a *library of word processing routines* from two separate commercial sources. It compares two ways of building WP-2000: (1) start from scratch, using 68,546 as the estimate of the number of lines of source code required to build WP-2000, or (2) buy the system shell and library for $50,000 each and implement 34,273 additional lines of source code (consisting of glue code plus original lines of code needed to implement functions not provided in the library and

*adjusting the initial estimate*

*software size is the biggest cost driver*

*estimating software project costs*

the shell). *Question:* Which alternative is cheaper, if a fully burdened person-year of programmer effort costs $100,000? (The term "fully burdened" means that the cost of a person-year includes computer time, worker benefits, and company overhead costs.) Assume that Equation C.1 has been determined to be an accurate predictor of effort under the conditions existing in the WP-2000 project at Contemporary Software.

In the case of alternative (1), we can use Equation C.1 to predict the number of person-months needed to build WP-2000. By plugging 68.546 into Equation C.1 we determine that 203.2 PMs are required. This translates into 16.94 person-years, which costs $1,694,000 at $100K per person-year.

programming with reusable components wins

In the case of alternative (2), it costs $100,000 to buy both the system shell and library, and it requires 98.15 PMs to implement the remaining 34,273 lines of code. But 98.15 PMs equals 8.18 person-years (PYs), which costs $818,000 at $100K per PY. Thus the total cost of alternative (2) is $918,000, which is only 54 percent of the cost of writing the system from scratch. If the project leaders at Contemporary Software can trust their estimating equations, these results indicate that working with reusable software components is clearly preferable to writing WP-2000 from scratch.

Although the WP-2000 project is an example of medium-scale programming, lying somewhere between programming-in-the-small and programming-in-the-large, the ideas about software reuse and software economics that it illustrates are applicable to programming on any small or large scale.

Even before you graduate from college, you may be faced with a situation in which you alone, or you and some teammates, are assigned to build a small, yet substantial, piece of software. If you are faced with such a task, you might want to remember to consider using software component libraries, or prefabricated system shells, if any are available. The use of such components and shells can substantially cut the amount of work you need to do and can make much brighter the prospects for finishing on time (or within the amount of effort you can afford to devote). The use of table-driven software component generators is also worth considering by the same reasoning.

avoiding debugging costs

Remember, too, that debugging times are included in the estimates given by Equation C.1. When you use components from a well-tested software component library, you are starting with reliable, proven components. If you implement your own from scratch, the debugging times needed to develop the components into reliable trustworthy condition may be quite considerable, especially if you don't entirely understand the task at the outset (and who does?). Using library components could then represent a very intelligent cost-avoidance strategy on your part.

This brings us once again to the subject of bottom-up programming. In bottom-up programming the strategy is to implement general purpose software components first, and then to assemble them together into higher-level systems. Under some economic conditions—associated with developing proprietary reusable software component libraries—bottom-up programming may be preferable to top-down programming.

when is bottom-up programming an advantage?

gaining competitive advantage

Even though it is nearly twice as expensive for Contemporary Software to implement WP-2000 starting from scratch as it is to purchase and use software components, the company may nevertheless decide to start from scratch, reasoning as follows: "If we start from scratch and implement our own set of proprietary word processor components and our own proprietary system shell, then we will finish the job of writing WP-2000 with some very important extra corporate assets. Namely, we will own proprietary reusable components (and we'll have the in-house expertise that comes from having built them). If we take care to implement our word processor components in a popular language that compiles on almost all types of computers, we will then be in a position to rehost WP-2000 on other platforms (i.e., on other kinds of computers). This will put us in a highly competitive posture in the future."

**winning market share**

There is much more to gaining a foothold in the commercial software market than the short glimpse of considerations mentioned here. (For example, to win market share, you may need to analyze the competition, analyze the available market niches, estimate the cost of advertising needed to capture your projected market share, and determine whether you have the capital to accomplish your objectives.) You can see how software economics begins to interact with the skills required of business executives, and how business expertise in marketing, financing, advertising, and project management all enter into the picture.

Another important consideration in developing reusable software components is to build the components so they can serve many general purposes, if possible. As we have seen in Chapters 2 and 5, object-oriented programming (OOP) techniques can help meet this goal.

Whether you contemplate small, medium, or large scale programming, the wisdom you can glean from thinking about the issues in this section might consist of an expanded awareness, based on two important facts:

1. The effort required to build software is an exponential function of its size.
2. Making use of reusable components can reduce the size of software you need to build.

## C.7 REVIEW QUESTIONS

1. Why does making use of reusable software components reduce the effort required to build a given software system?
2. What is Boehm's COCOMO equation relating the size of a software system to the person-months required to build it?
3. What is bottom-up programming? When might it be useful to plan to implement a software system using bottom-up programming?

## C.7 EXERCISE

1. A software system, called *VisiPhysics*, to be used for visualizing physics data, is estimated to require 56,000 lines of source code to implement starting from scratch, but it is estimated to require only 32,000 lines of extra source code to be implemented starting with two numerical and graphics subroutine libraries. If programmer time costs $100,000 per PY and the two libraries cost $150,000 each to purchase, is it cheaper to implement *VisiPhysics* by starting from scratch, or by

buying and using the two libraries? (Assume that Equation C.1 accurately predicts the effort needed on the *VisiPhysics* project.)

## C.8   Program Structuring and Documentation

### LEARNING OBJECTIVES

1. To review a few concepts for good program structuring.
2. To discuss some ideas that help produce good documentation.

Most beginning Java courses cover elementary concepts of good program structuring. In this section, we will review a few of these structuring concepts and we will consider the characteristics of effective program documentation. We can highlight only a few of the structuring concepts here, since program structuring has been the subject of many entire books.

*some general software requirements*

Our starting point is to consider the properties good programs should have. Generally, software engineers try to build software to satisfy *requirements* that state what characteristics the software is supposed to have to meet the needs of its users. Certain requirements are common to most software: (1) it should work properly and be free of errors; (2) it should be as efficient as it needs to be; (3) it should be completed on time and within budget; and (4) it should be modifiable in the future in response to needs to upgrade it.

*programming proverbs*

Oftentimes advice on helpful practices is given in the form of a set of proverbs or aphorisms about programming. Table C.45 gives a small list of some of the most common ones.

*using meaningful variable names*

Let's consider proverb (a) in Table C.45. You can perform your own experiments to convince yourself that programs are hard to understand in the absence of well-chosen, meaningful variable names. To do this, take some common algorithms from one of your early programming classes, and replace the meaningful identifier names with neutral meaningless names (such as x, y, and z for variables, or F and G for method names). Then ask friends who took the class with you to figure out what the changed program does. Do they have trouble? If they do, does this suggest to you that human memory for what programs do might function so as to associate meaning with well-chosen names, as opposed to structural program features?

As an example, try to figure out what Program C.46 does. When you succeed, go back over your solution method. Was it obvious at first what it did because you

**Table C.45** Some Programming Proverbs

| |
| --- |
| (a)  Use meaningful names for your variables. |
| (b)  Define named constants once at the beginning of your program. |
| (c)  Avoid using goto's and never write spaghetti code. |
| (d)  Write short methods that do just one thing and do it well. |
| (e)  Modularize your programs so the parts interact cleanly and simply. |

```
 1  | float g(float x, int n)  {
    |
    |     float p;
    |
 5  |     if ( n == 0 ) {
    |
    |          return 1.0;
    |
    |     } else {
10  |
    |          p = g(x, n / 2);
    |
    |          if ( n%2 == 0 ) {
    |             return p * p;
15  |          } else {
    |             return x * p * p;
    |          }
    |
    |     }
20  |
    | }
```

**Program C.46** Mystery Program—What Does This Do?

instantly recognized its structural features as being familiar to you? Or were you puzzled at first? Did you then attempt to try it out on various data values and make a table of inputs and outputs to see if you could find a pattern of some sort?

Now let's discuss the significance of proverb (b) in Table C.45. Suppose you are writing a computer program that computes various geometric figures to display in a computer-graphic user interface. You discover you need to use the constant, $\pi$, in several formulas, such as the formulas for the area and circumference of a circle ($A = \pi r^2$ and $C = 2 \pi r$). Knowing the value $\pi = 3.14159$ and lamenting the lack of Greek letters on your computer, you decide to write 3.14159 everywhere that $\pi$ is needed.

*defining named constants*

Suppose that, at some later time, your program has gotten quite big—say 9,000 lines distributed across seven separate Java packages. You discover a bug that indicates the value for $\pi$ you had been using didn't have quite enough numerical precision, and that you should have used the value 3.141592654 instead. If you had used defined constants at the beginning of your modules, you could have changed the definition:

```
public static final double PI  =  3.14159                // 6 digit value for PI
```

into:

```
public static final double PI  =  3.141592654            // 10 digit value for PI
```

But, alas, now you will have to search for each occurrence of 3.14159 in your 9,000 lines of code and replace it with the new value. And what if you made a typographical error, typing one of the values of $\pi$ that was accidentally typed incorrectly as 3.14195? Your text search procedure may be too literal-minded to locate such erroneous values.

In fact, maybe the accuracy problems you discovered resulted from improperly typed values for $\pi$ in just a few places. How can you know for sure? (In fact, Java has a pre-defined double precision floating point constant for PI defined in its Math package, named Math.PI, that you can use without defining it yourself.)

concentrating your definitions in one place

If you learn to concentrate your definitions in one place (such as at the beginning of your class definitions or in special Java packages), you can always be confident that any changes you decide to make need to be made in only one place. If you concentrate these in one place, rather than spreading them all over your program and duplicating them, your program is likely (a) to be easier to modify, (b) to contain fewer errors, and (c) to be easier for a reader to understand. You can see how following this proverb could enhance the dimensions of desirable software quality such as modifiability, correctness, and ease of comprehension.

Let's skip over proverb (c) in Table C.45 concerning the avoidance of goto's and spaghetti code, since Java has no goto's and since the principles behind it are usually covered in first courses in computer science. (The key idea is simple—write programs using structured features of the programming language at hand that make the structure of the text mirror the structure of the control in the program.) We also will not cover proverb (e), which was covered extensively in Chapter 5.

keep it simple

Let's look only at proverb (d), which states, *Write short methods that do just one thing and do it well.* What could possibly be behind this prescription? Why not attempt to write methods packed with functionality, so that they do as much as possible in the shortest amount of code? Wouldn't the latter policy tend to produce highly efficient programs? Wouldn't legibility and correctness be easy to guarantee, using good documentation and program verification practices?

since programming is complex and error-prone

The wisdom behind proverb (d) expresses a problem-solving strategy that says the following, in essence: "Programming is known to be a complex, error-prone cognitive activity. When human beings try to consider too many things at once, they have trouble keeping all the details straight. Consequently, to control cognitive complexity and to keep it manageable, it makes sense to try to break down complex problems into simple subproblems."

Let's take a look at a problem that has, by now, become a classic in the literature on the psychology of programming—the problem of finding the average rainfall in New Haven. The problem is to write a program that will ask the user to input values for daily rainfalls in New Haven and that will print the average rainfall at the end. The user signals the end of the data by inputting a special *sentinel* value, 99999. Negative rainfalls are illegal. The program should give an error message upon encountering a negative rainfall value, and it should not count such a negative rainfall value as being valid for purposes of counting the number of observations used to compute the average.

Program C.47 gives a solution in Java to the rainfall problem, translated from a Pascal solution given in an article by Elliot Soloway[3] in which he explained how novice programmers tend to get confused and to make mistakes when they try to merge program plans to achieve several goals all at once in a given section of code.

---

[3] "Learning to Program = Learning to Construct Mechanisms + Explanations," *Communications of the ACM* (September 1986), p. 853.

```
 |      /*      Program to compute the average rainfall in New Haven    */
 |
 |              // a translation into Java from Soloway, CACM 9-86, p. 853
 |
5 |
 |      void computeAverageRainfall ( ) {
 |
 |          float     sum, rainfall, average;
 |          int       count;
10 |
 |          sum    =    0.0;
 |          count  =    0;
 |
 |          GUI.promptUser("Please input a rainfall: ");
15 |         rainfall = GUI.getFloatInputFromUser( );
 |
 |          while ( rainfall != 99999.0 ) {
 |
 |              while ( rainfall < 0.0 ) {
20 |                 GUI.promptUser("Rainfall cannot be <0. Input again: ");
 |                  rainfall = GUI.getFloatInputFromUser( );
 |              }
 |
 |              sum += rainfall;
25 |             count++;
 |              GUI.promptUser("input a rainfall: ");
 |              rainfall = GUI.getFloatInputFromUser( );
 |          }
 |
30 |         if ( count > 0 ) {
 |              average = sum/count;
 |              GUI.displayOutput("Average rainfall = " + average);
 |          } else {
35 |             GUI.displayOutput("No valid inputs. No average calculated.");
 |          }
 |
 |      }
```

**Program C.47** Average Rainfall with Bug (translated into Java with permission of the Association for Computing Machinery, copyright © 1986)

See if you can spot the bug in Program C.47. If you found the bug, one thing you might conclude is that the author of Program C.47 might have been trying to solve too many problems at once and didn't manage to cope with all of them successfully.

For instance, look at the while-loop on lines 19:22 of the program. This is clearly intended to screen for a legal rainfall input and to prompt the user to give another rainfall value if an illegal negative one was given. It exits only with nonnegative input values on line 22.

finding the bug        According to the program, the new rainfall values are input within a while-loop (on lines 17:28) whose while-condition screens out rainfall values that are not equal to the sentinel, 99999. The assumption appears to be made that inside this while-loop (on lines 17:28), the value of the rainfall is not equal to the sentinel, so that it can be counted and added into the running rainfall total in the variable **sum**. But this assumption can be violated by a fickle user who first gives a negative rainfall (such as −3), forcing the program to ask for a legal rainfall, using the message: "Rainfall cannot be < 0. Input again," after which the user has a sudden change of mind, and decides to give the sentinel, 99999, to quit. Now the sentinel becomes a legal value for the variable, **rainfall**, causing the sentinel value to be added into the running total in **sum**, on line 24, and causing the **count** to be increased on line 25. Using the sentinel value in place of a valid rainfall was not supposed to happen—and yet it did. Moreover, we see that the program fails to stop when the user inputs the sentinel, and it prints an incorrect average when it terminates.

Now you might think that mature computer scientists don't make this kind of silly error. But the interesting thing is, the original Pascal version of Program C.47 was labeled as a correct solution to the rainfall problem, and neither the authors of the paper, nor the referees and editors who read it, noticed and corrected the bug before publication. This is not meant to be critical of these authors, referees, and editors. Rather, it is meant to remind all of us that programming is a demonstrably difficult, error-prone process, even in apparently simple circumstances. Moreover, it highlights the wisdom of proverb (d) in Table C.45, which urges us to break things into simple components that are easy to understand and with which we can reason cleanly.

**using a subroutine that does just one task**

For example, the version of the rainfall program given in Program C.48 creates a method to get a valid rainfall value or sentinel from the user. This subroutine has just one simple objective—to obtain one input from the user that is guaranteed not to be an illegal rainfall value. The method, declared on lines 9:22, repeatedly prompts the user and gets input values from the user until a nonnegative value is obtained. This value must be either a legal rainfall value or the sentinel.

This method is used on lines 29 and 34 each time the main program needs to get a valid rainfall value (or sentinel). The while-loop on lines 31:35 can now assume a simple function of summing and counting valid rainfall values until a sentinel value causes it to skip to the final phase of the program, which prints the average rainfall value (on lines 37:41). Actually, there are studies of the psychology of programming that show that Pascal's looping control structures, such as while-loops and repeat-until loops, are not as good as they should be for solving some kinds of programming problems. (See the article by Soloway, Bonar, and Erlich, mentioned at the end of this chapter in References for Further Study.)

**using loops that exit in the middle**

In this paper, Soloway and his colleagues have shown that if you add to Pascal a looping control structure that permits an exit from its middle, then programmers find it more convenient to use this for solving problems such as the rainfall problem. For example, using a loop-exit control structure similar to the one in the programming language, Ada, Soloway *et al.* showed that programmers find it more natural to express the code on lines 29:35 of Program C.48 as shown in Program C.49 (on page 537).

In essence, this says, "Get an input from the user that is either a valid rainfall value or the sentinel. If it is the sentinel, exit from the loop and proceed to the next section of the program (to compute and print the average). Otherwise, you have a

```
/* Program to compute the average rainfall in New Haven with bug fixed */

class NewHavenRainfall {

    private final static float SENTINEL = 99999.0;
    private float        sum, rainfall;
    private int          count;

    float getValidInputFromUser( ) {            // a valid input is either
                                                // a nonnegative rainfall observation
        float rainfall;                         // or the sentinel

        GUI.promptUser("Please input a rainfall or 99999 to stop: ");
        rainfall = GUI.getFloatInputFromUser( );

        while ( rainfall < 0.0) {
            GUI.promptUser("Rainfall cannot be < 0. Input again: ");
            rainfall = GUI.getFloatInputFromUser( );
        }

        return rainfall;
    }

    void computeAverageRainfall( )  {

        sum    =    0.0;
        count  =    0;

        rainfall = getValidInputFromUser( );

        while ( rainfall != SENTINEL ) {
            sum += rainfall;
            count++;
            rainfall = getValidInputFromUser( );
        }

        if ( count > 0 ) {
            GUI.displayOutput("Average rainfall = " + (sum/count) );
        } else {
            GUI.displayOutput("No valid inputs. No average calculated.");
        }
    }

} // end class NewHavenRainfall
```

**Program C.48** Average Rainfall with Bug Fixed

valid rainfall input that is not the sentinel and that needs to be counted and added to
the running rainfall total in the variable **sum**. Now loop back and do this process over
and over until the user directs you to terminate it by giving the sentinel."

Soloway *et al.* discovered evidence that programmers naturally think of the main
repetitive action needed to solve the rainfall problem in terms that closely mirror the

advantages of using
natural control structures

```
    |   loop
    |       rainfall := GetValidInputFromUser;
    |       exit when (rainfall = sentinel);
    |       sum := sum + rainfall;
35  |       count := count + 1;
    |   end loop;
```

**Program C.49** Loop-Exit Control Structure

loop-exit control structure given in Program C.49. Comparing the use of the while-loop on lines 29:35 of Program C.48 to the loop-exit structure in Program C.49, we see that the use of the while-loop forces the assignment rainfall = GetValidInputFromUser( ); to be repeated twice. In addition to being wastefully repetitive, it is unnatural, since it doesn't correspond to the way problem-solvers think about the solution, as Soloway *et al.* have shown.

Fortunately, Java has powerful control structures that allow it to express the loop-exit control structure of Program C.49 using a while-loop containing a **break** statement, as shown in Program C.50. The **break** statement on line 33 of Program C.50 exits the while-loop if the rainfall variable contains the sentinel value in exactly the same fashion as the exit statement on line 33 of the loop-exit structure of Program C.49. (The "industrial-strength" versions of Pascal used in the contemporary software industry have been extended to include **leave** and **cycle** statements that have the same effect as Java's **break** and **continue** statements.)

A useful observation to make is that the programming language you are using might not have convenient control structures to mirror the way you naturally think about expressing your solution. Under these circumstances, you may have to use awkward circumlocutions to express what you need to say. When you are forced to express your solution indirectly, and perhaps awkwardly, cognitive complexity can creep in. Thus it is best to be alert to the danger of making a conceptual mistake.

## Programming Style Disciplines

If you are working on a software project (or if you are taking a computer science course), the project leader (or instructor) may require that you write programs following certain well-defined rules of programming style.

```
    |   while ( true ) {
    |       rainfall = getValidInputFromUser( );
    |       if ( rainfall == SENTINEL ) break;
    |       sum += rainfall;
35  |       count++;
    |   }
```

**Program C.50** A Solution in Java Using a While-Loop with a Break

advantages of following
style disciplines

In large programming projects, following such style conventions can help make programs more comprehensible to all members of the software team than would be the case if each programmer were allowed to freelance in his or her own individual style. When the team adheres to common conventions, it helps train the eye to read programs written by others more easily and accurately. What matters is not so much what the style rules are (provided they are at least minimally sensible) but that everybody adheres to them.

## Documentation

a problem-ridden subject

Documentation is a problem-ridden topic. Have you ever tried to read a moderately intricate program that you wrote several months ago for which you didn't have time to write good descriptive comments properly? Did you find it hard to remember what you were thinking about when you wrote it, and was it difficult to figure out how it worked? Then you might well imagine the difficulty somebody other than the original author might have trying to read a poorly documented program.

Documentation is, of course, a form of writing, and good writing should always be performed to meet the needs of the intended audience. The trouble is, programs may have many audiences, each having different needs. One case where it is clearly recognized that documentation needs to be written for different audiences is in writing user's manuals versus system documentation. These days, commercial firms have gotten quite good at writing user's manuals for popular mass-distributed software. User's manuals are often accompanied by guided tours that use animation and on-line interactive tutorials to illustrate how the system works and to teach novices how to use it.

the problem of multiple
audiences

A difficult type of documentation to create, however, is the documentation that explains how a large software system works. Here, the problem of multiple audiences still intrudes. When you are in the thick of writing a program, and all the details are in your mind or at your fingertips, you may find that certain kinds of comments are not only obvious but are even bothersome clutter. After you have laid the program aside for a year and you are no longer current on its details, or if you are looking at somebody else's program, you constitute quite a different audience. It is thus difficult, if not impossible, to meet the needs of all possible audiences in a single set of program comments. Project managers are yet another kind of audience who require good, clear, top-level descriptions, but who don't need to make use of low-level details very often.

paper may not be a good
container for
documentation

In fact, paper may not be a very good medium in which to write program documentation. Ideally, a form of electronic paper with, say, electronic stick-on memos suited to different audiences might be much better. We might imagine two kinds of stick-on memos—yellow ones for programming experts who have all the details fresh in their minds and blue ones for novices or project leaders, who are not up on all of the subtleties and who need to gain general understanding first. Using a computer screen, such memos might be made selectively visible or invisible in response to a user's command. This way, different readers of a document could adjust the details to suit their needs of the moment (needs that may change over time as the novice grows to be an expert then perhaps reverts to being a novice again after losing familiarity over time).

In fact, hypermedia systems have recently become available. These let you attach buttons to words in a text or to places on a page. Several kinds of actions can be attached to the buttons, so that when they are pressed (a) you can navigate to another place in the document; (b) you can show or hide a window of new explanatory text or diagrams; (c) you can play a sound (such as a spoken explanation); (d) you can initiate an animation sequence illustrating a particular point visually; or (e) you can display a video film-clip in a window on the screen. Perhaps such hypermedia systems will eventually serve as the carriers of good system documentation in the future.

*using hypermedia systems*

In the meantime, however, there is at least one thing you can do to write good documentation. If you follow the method of top-down programming by stepwise refinement, you will likely first create program strategies expressing your detailed design. Let's think of these as Java programs with comments giving the goals to be achieved by various sections of each method (and giving the expected behavioral characteristics of abstract data types that will eventually have to be implemented). When you refine a program strategy into an actual program, you can leave the goal comments in place, and write the actual Java refinement code underneath. (Sometimes, it is convenient to place the goal comments in the right margin when refining goals in the program strategy.)

In this way, you will develop commented Java programs as you write them. It may also be necessary to add additional technical comments that explain how subtle mechanisms in your refinement code work, or that describe the agreements and conventions you have used in setting up your low-level data and methods. As an example of this method, study how Program C.19 for selection sorting was derived from Program Strategy C.18.

*developing commented programs as you write them*

Two final tips for generating good documentation: (1) Remember to document your data structures and class interfaces as carefully as you document your methods, and (2) remember to put an initial comment at the beginning of each method describing the expected characteristics of the inputs and outputs (or formally giving the preconditions and postconditions of the method, if you prefer).

## C.8 REVIEW QUESTIONS

1. What is the common sense behind the programming proverb that advocates minimizing the use of global variables in a program to help communicate inputs and outputs between methods?
2. Why is it sensible to use named symbolic constants in a Java program?
3. Why is it best not to complain if a software project leader imposes a sensible but unfamiliar programming style on the project teammates and instructs everyone to use it consistently?
4. Why is it impossible to write program documentation that is bound to please everybody?

## C.8 EXERCISES

1. Figure out what the following program does, then document it by adding informative comments and by changing its variables to have meaningful variable names.

```
      |    int f(int m, int n) {
      |
      |        if ( n == 0 ) {
      |            return m;
    5 |        } else {
      |            return f(n, m % n);
      |        }
      |    }
```

2. Figure out what the method p(n) does in the following program, then document it by adding informative comments and by changing its variables to have meaningful variable names.

```
      |    void q(int d) {
      |
      |        System.out.print( (char) ( (int)'0' + d) );
      |    }
    5 |
      |
      |    void p(int n) {                              // assume n is a nonnegative integer
      |
      |        if ( n < 10 ) {
   10 |            q(n);
      |        } else {
      |            p(n / 10 );
      |            q(n % 10);
      |        }
      |    }
```

3. Give a test case that reveals the bug in Program C.47.

4. Develop a program transformation that will help eliminate wasteful duplication from the following program fragment.

```
      |    playersMove = getMoveFromUser( );
      |
      |    while ( playersMove != QUITSIGNAL ) {
      |        displayPlayersMoveOnTheBoard( );
    5 |        makeMachinesMove( );
      |        playersMove = getMoveFromUser( );
      |    }
```

[Hint: In solving this problem, it may help to recall that a break-statement can be used to exit from a while-loop in Java.]

## ◼ Pitfalls

- *Failure to implement formatted debugging aids*

  Some of the earliest studies in software engineering revealed that debugging times for software projects were cut in half by making sure to implement and use formatted debugging aids. The evidence indicates that if you fail to implement formatted debugging aids, debugging will be much tougher and will take much longer than expected. If you are interested in formulating a good software project plan, you should plan to implement and test formatted debugging aids for every data structure in your detailed system design *before* you code and test the other parts of your system. Once you can take pictures of your data structures, you can see what they look like in various stages of construction and transformation. The advantage of seeing over being blind is amazing. Errors you never dreamed could happen typically leap out at you once you begin to examine pictures of each data structure. If you don't bother to look routinely at pictures of the data your system's methods create and modify, errors will tend to propagate undetected and will usually cause symptoms to appear far from their source, making error diagnosis and debugging extremely difficult.

- *Failure to document a software system*

  Some spectacular software has been implemented by small teams, consisting of a few brilliant, talented, software geniuses. Often, though, in the passion of creation, such geniuses believe their time is better spent finishing their creations than documenting how their code works. Often after such a system is in widespread use, the original creators tire of upgrading it, and the job of maintenance is passed on to successors who must then begin to understand how the code works.

  Alas, it is rarely possible to discipline the geniuses to create documentation during their moments of spectacular creativity. So the appearance of poorly documented, yet successful software systems is likely to recur in the future. But what do you do if you are the hapless successor who is assigned the job of maintaining such a system? One intriguing answer is to persuade the original creators to sit in front of a video camera for an hour and just talk about how they designed the original system. Recent experience shows this to be a relatively painless way to get some high-quality information.

- *Failure to test user documentation*

  Remember to test the user's manuals and operator procedure manuals for your system on actual users and operators to make sure that all instructions are clear and effective. The user documentation should be considered as much a part of the overall system software as the computer code, and it should be granted the same project privileges as code with regard to design, testing, and debugging.

**Tips and Techniques**

- *Use measurement and tuning to improve program efficiency*

  Those who are experienced in software optimization and performance enhancement advocate *measurement and tuning* as a method for improving the efficiency of actual running programs. Sometimes programming environments provide execution-time profile tools to help measure where programs are spending their time. Experience suggests (1) that oftentimes a disproportionate amount of the running time (say 80 to 90 percent) is spent in a small portion of the code (say 7 to 10 percent), and (2) that oftentimes the places where a program is inefficient are surprisingly difficult to anticipate. The philosophy of measurement and tuning holds that you should use *measurement* to find out where the program is inefficient, and then concentrate on improving the inefficient places by *tuning*—judiciously replacing possible inefficient program parts with trial versions of new parts, followed by more measurement to see if the new parts, in fact, improve the efficiency.

- *Develop documentation while refining program strategies into detailed programs*

  A good moment to develop documentation for your detailed code is during the stepwise refinement process when you are translating your top-level designs, expressed, say, in the form of program strategies, into detailed code in a particular programming language, such as Java. You can often retain the goal comments in the program strategies as headers for sections of actual code that achieve those goals. Then the retained goal comments serve to announce the purpose of the code that follows. It is also good practice to place comments off to the side, explaining any intricate or unusual parts of the detailed Java code. Moreover, it is good practice to place a header comment at the beginning of each method explaining its purpose, its inputs, its outputs, and any restrictions or assumptions under which it is supposed to operate. It is of especially vital importance to document clearly the public entities in interfaces of Java classes and packages. Finally, it is good practice to explain the purpose and layout of the data structures, types, constants, and variables in the declaration section of your code.

- *Adhere to programming style guidelines*

  Experience shows that having your software team agree on a programming style (and then following it rigorously) helps improve efficiency and accuracy. If everybody writes in a common style, project personnel have a much easier time reading each other's code. If everybody freelances and writes code using widely different personal styles, it makes it hard on others to read code accurately and easily.

- *Use both testing and verification*

  Testing and verification should play mutually supporting roles in the quality assurance phase of your software development. Neither testing, nor verification, alone is as effective as using both together. The weakness of testing is that it can reveal the presence of bugs, but it can never prove their absence. The weakness of verification is that it is hard to know when formal logical assertions have correctly and completely captured the true intentions of the system requirements. Moreover, many programmers have found that it is often difficult to devise formal verification proofs for many of the algorithms they develop for use in practical systems.

## References for Further Study

Barry Boehm wrote the classical reference on software economics:

*software economics*

Boehm, Barry W., *Software Engineering Economics*. Prentice-Hall, Englewood-Cliffs, NJ (1981).

An influential book on structured programming is:

*structured programming*

Dahl, O. J., Dijkstra, E. W., and Hoare, C. A. R., *Structured Programming*. Academic Press, NY (1982).

Tony Hoare wrote an influential paper on program verification:

*key paper on verification*

C. A. R. Hoare, "Axiomatic Semantics for Computer Programming." *IEEE Transactions on Software Engineering* SE-5(2), pp. 128–138, (1979).

Some aspects of the relation between programming and cognition are covered in the following two papers:

*programming and cognition*

Soloway, Elliot, "Learning to Program = Learning to Construct Mechanisms + Explanations." CACM  29: 9 (September 1986).

Soloway, E., Bonar, J., and Erlich, K., "Cognitive Strategies and Looping Constructs: An Empirical Study." CACM 26: 11 (November 1983).

Niklaus Wirth wrote the classical paper on programming by stepwise refinement:

*original paper on stepwise refinement*

Wirth, Niklaus, "Program Development by Stepwise Refinement." CACM 14: 4, pp. 221–227 (April 1971).

## Appendix Summary

This appendix explores some aspects of software engineering applied to small programs. Among the topics covered are: object-oriented design, programming by stepwise refinement, program verification, transforming and optimizing small programs, program testing, improving program performance using measurement and tuning, programming with reusable software components, and program structuring and documentation principles.

*object-oriented design*

The goal of object-oriented design (OOD) is to divide a program into a collection of carefully designed objects that interact in simple ways through clean, concise interfaces, while hiding their internal details of operation. Such designs reap the benefits of good modular programming practice.

*top-down programming by stepwise refinement*

Usually a detailed design for a program is created before undertaking the final step of producing a running implementation in a specific programming language. In this book, we have been using sketches of our programs, called *program strategies*, to serve the role of detailed designs. A program strategy describes the goals a program is supposed to achieve without prescribing the exact mechanisms or representations to be used.

When a program strategy is implemented, the goals in the program strategy can be achieved by filling in more specific details progressively through *stepwise refinement*. The method of starting with a top-level design and expanding its details until an actual program is developed is called *top-down programming*.

Program strategies can function as abstract program designs, and their careful use can permit the postponement of decisions regarding the selection of data structures and algorithms to use, until an advantageous moment arises.

Sometimes the creation of small programs involves great subtlety of thought and requires great precision and ingenuity. It is important to be able to reason about small programs with clarity and mental precision. Techniques from mathematical logic can sometimes be used to verify that programs are correct.

reasoning about programs

To prove that a program *P* is correct, you must first supply assertions called *preconditions* and *postconditions*. The goal is to show that if the situation described by the preconditions holds true and the program is then executed, it follows logically that the situation described by the postconditions must be true.

proving programs correct

Proving programs correct is called *program verification*. Two weaknesses in program verification are: (1) It is often difficult to be sure that the preconditions and postconditions correctly and completely capture the true intentions of the program; and (2) It is sometimes difficult to establish a proof of correctness when programs are either complex or subtle.

program verification

It is sometimes possible to change the way a program is expressed without changing the result it computes. This can be done by applying exchange laws that replace parts of programs with different parts that are guaranteed to preserve program equivalence. *Program transformations* are the exchange laws or modification processes that accomplish such changes. Sometimes program transformations can be applied to a program to make it run faster or use less space. This is called optimizing program performance using program transformations.

transforming and optimizing programs

An example of a recursive program that can sometimes be optimized in this fashion is one having a *tail recursion*, which is a recursive call that occurs last in the text of a recursive method, usually inside an if-statement. Another optimizing program transformation is one that substitutes a method body in place of its call.

Programs should be tested systematically before being released into service. *Unit testing* consists of testing individual methods in isolation to see if they work on all expected classes of inputs. *Integration testing* checks the coordinated execution of methods and classes, acting together in the context of expected conditions of actual operation. *Acceptance testing* is a practice, sometimes specified in software acquisition contracts, in which a completed software system must pass a specified test in order to be accepted for delivery by the client. *Regression testing* makes sure that everything that used to work still works in any new version of a system.

program testing

A *test plan* is a document that specifies a systematic schedule of testing activities in a software project and gives the inputs and expected correct outputs for each part of the system.

**measurement and tuning**

It is frequently hard to anticipate where the inefficiencies in a program lie. Often over 80 to 90 percent of the execution time is spent in 7 to 10 percent of the code. It thus pays to spend your time improving code that accounts for most of the execution time. It is important first to *measure* where a system is spending its time, and then to concentrate on *tuning* the parts that account for most of the execution time. Measurement can sometimes be performed with an *execution profile tool. Tuning* is a repetitive process of attempting to improve a program and then measuring it to see if the expected improvements were achieved.

**reusable software components and software reuse**

The case for advocating the use of reusable software components is based on economic arguments. The cost of building software is an exponential function of its size. Since software size is the biggest cost driver in a software project, if you can reduce the size of what you have to build you can best reduce the cost.

**bottom-up programming**

A software project that first attempts to build general purpose, reusable software components, and that later uses these components in system construction employs a *bottom-up* software implementation process. This contrasts with a top-down process that specifies the top-level design of a system before implementing the lower-level details.

**program structuring**

Experience in software development has shown that clarity and simplicity of program structure and ease of comprehension are to be prized. *Structured programming* is the name given to a set of software structuring principles that help achieve these software properties.

**documentation**

Program documentation is of vital importance to anyone who needs to understand how a program works. Even the programmer who wrote the original program may be in need of such documentation after a long period of time has elapsed.

# Index